BUSINESS COMMUNICATION

Third Edition

BUSINESS COMMUNICATION

JULES HARCOURT
Murray State University

A. C. "BUDDY" KRIZAN
Murray State University

PATRICIA MERRIER
University of Minnesota, Duluth

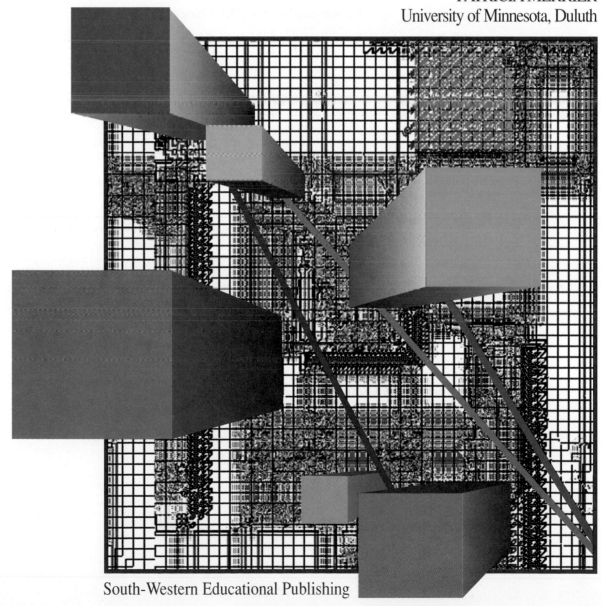

South-Western Educational Publishing

I(T)P

International Thomson Publishing

South-Western Educational Publishing is a division of International Thomson Publishing Inc. The ITP trademark is used under license.

Library of Congress Cataloging-in-Publication Data

Harcourt, Jules.
    Business communication / Jules Harcourt, A.C. "Buddy" Krizan,
Patricia Merrier. -- 3rd ed.
        p.   cm.
    Includes bibliograpical references and index.
    ISBN 0-538-71170-1
    1. Business communication.   I. Krizan, A.C.   II. Merrier,
Patricia.   III. Title.
HF5718.H288   1996   94-35088
808'.06665--dc20   CIP

Acquisitions Editor: *Karen Schneiter*
Developmental Editor: *Penny Shank*
Production Manager: *Anne Noschang*
Sr. Production Editor: *Alan Biondi*
Design: *Elaine St. John-Lagenaur and Peter St. John*
Photo Editor/Stylist: *Kathy Russell/Pix Inc.*
Marketing Manager: *Carolyn Love*

1 2 3 4 5 6 7 8 VH 02 01 00 99 98 97 96 95

Printed in the United States of America

CONTENTS

Chapter 4

Communication Technologies and Techniques 100

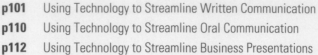

Chapter 5

International and Cross-Cultural Business Communication 125

PART 2

Business English

Chapter 6

Parts of Speech 156

Chapter 7

Sentence Structure 179

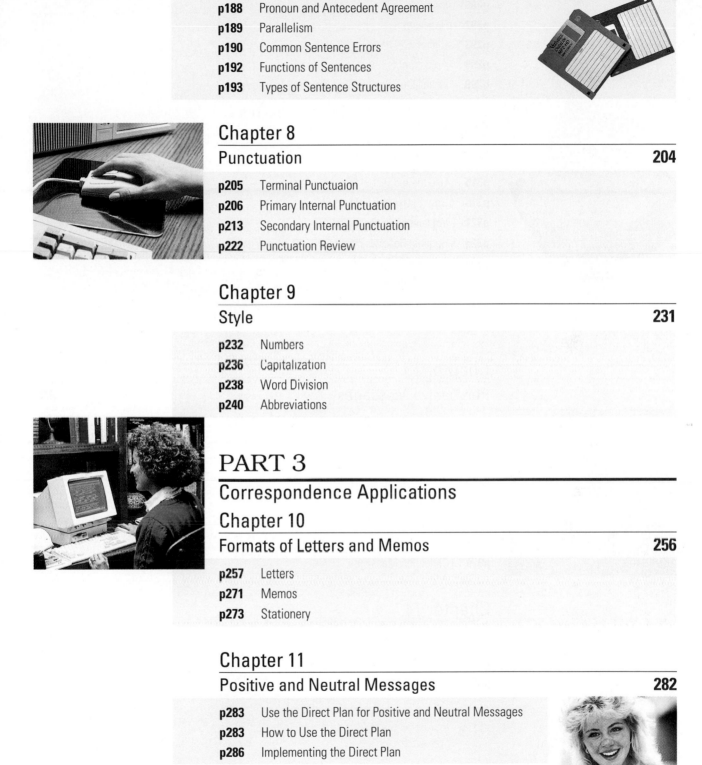

Chapter 12
Negative Messages   **314**

Chapter 13
Persuasive Messages   **356**

Chapter 14
Goodwill Messages   **390**

PART 4
Written Report Applications
Chapter 15

Business Studies and Proposals | **408**

Chapter 16

Report Preparation | **443**

Chapter 17

Graphic Aids | **493**

PART 5
Oral and Nonverbal Communication Applications
Chapter 18

Listening and Nonverbal Messages | **524**

Chapter 19

Oral Communication Essentials   538

Chapter 20

Oral Communication Applications   558

PART 6

Employment Communication

Chapter 21

The Job Search and Resume   588

Chapter 22

Employment Communication and Interviewing   616

APPENDICES

MEMO

TO: The Student

FROM: Jules Harcourt, Buddy Krizan, and Pat Merrier

DATE: February 1, 1995

SUBJECT: *Business Communication,* 3d Edition

Your ability to communicate can be improved by reading and studying *Business Communication.* This textbook will be beneficial to you immediately in your business communication and other business courses. Also, it will benefit you greatly when you become employed in your chosen profession.

You will find this textbook most useful in your business communication course when you do the following:

- Read carefully the **Learning Objectives** at the beginning of each chapter. These objectives emphasize the important concepts to be covered in the chapter.

- Study the special **terms in boldface** type. Definitions are presented the first time a new term is used in the text.

- Review the **marginal notes** after reading the text material. Marginal notes summarize the text material.

- Take time out of your chapter study to read the numerous thought-provoking **short quotations** that appear throughout the text.

- Study the **Communication News, Notes, and Quotes.**

- Compare the examples of **good** and **poor** messages. Determine why the good message is more effective in communicating the message.

- Check your understanding of a chapter by completing the **End-of-Chapter Activities** that include discussion questions, application exercises, case problems, and message analysis exercises.

- Refer to the **Appendices** when appropriate. The appendices serve as reference guides.

The Student
February 1, 1995
Page 2

For your convenience in identifying special activities, icons are used throughout the end-of-chapter activities. These symbols specify the following:

 Collaborative Writing Exercise

 Ethical/Legal Content

 International/Cross-Cultural Content

 Form Message

 Template Application

You will benefit more from this textbook and your business communication course when you attempt to understand the general concepts being discussed rather than memorizing specific message examples. A broader understanding of the concepts and how to apply them will help you advance in your profession.

Many students have found their study of business communication extremely helpful. We hope this will be true for you, too. Best wishes for personal growth and valuable learning in your business communication course!

MEMO

TO: The Instructor

FROM: Jules Harcourt, Buddy Krizan, and Pat Merrier

DATE: February 1, 1995

SUBJECT: *Business Communication,* 3d Edition

Business Communication, 3d Edition, is a comprehensive full-color textbook that guides your students from the basic business communication fundamentals through practical applications. It goes beyond theory to demonstrate what does and does not work in the real business world.

All topics are presented from a practical business point of view. Current communication topics are discussed in depth, including new, updated, and expanded material on ethics, international and cross-cultural communication, legal aspects, technology, correspondence preparation, collaborative writing, proposal and report writing, oral and nonverbal communication, and employment communication. In addition, frequent references to ethical, legal, international, and cross-cultural concerns occur throughout the text and are included in many of the extensive end-of-chapter discussion questions, application exercises, case problems, and messages for analysis.

This textbook looks at how students should develop effective letters, memos, proposals, reports, resumes, application letters, goodwill messages, minutes, policy statements, and more. Students learn simple direct and indirect plans for writing powerful positive, neutral, negative, persuasive, and goodwill messages.

The first two editions of this text were flexible so that instructors could design courses specifically for their students. This edition maintains that flexibility while adding these new features:

- **Real-world orientation** presented in summaries of news articles on part openers; brief notes from current books, periodicals, and newspapers; chapter material; and quotations from successful businesspersons

- **Communication News**—news summaries for each of six part openers

The Instructor
February 1, 1995
Page 2

- **Communication Notes**—twenty boxes of interesting information related to individual chapter topics throughout the text

- **Communication Quotes**—twelve quotations and photographs of successful businesspersons in selected chapters

- **Short quotations** from well-known and not-so-well-known individuals throughout the text

- **Collaborative writing** techniques and end-of-chapter exercises

- **Icons** beside end-of-chapter activities to identify those in which ethical and legal content, international/cross-cultural content, collaborative writing aspects, form messages, and the applications template are used

- **Message Analysis** added to end-of-chapter activities

- **Template** containing application exercises for each chapter

- **Full color** throughout the text with all new photos

While adding new features and making major improvements to many portions of the text, *Business Communication*, 3d Edition, has retained the following important features:

- Basic **communication concepts** that are straightforward and understandable

- **Marginal notes** that summarize important points

The Instructor
February 1, 1995
Page 3

- Extensive **end-of-chapter activities** that provide many practical applications

- Business English chapters that provide **grammar reviews** for students who need reinforcement

- Appendices that serve as **reference guides**

- Outstanding **instructor resource package** that includes 110 two-color acetate transparencies, printed and computerized test bank, business English microcomputer software, application templates, and student study supplement

We appreciate the support of the following individuals who have reviewed the manuscript and offered suggestions for improving *Business Communication,* 3d Edition.

Janet G. Adams
Mankato State University

Charles Beem
Bucks County Community College

Amanda Blanton
Phillips Junior College

Sandy Braathen
University of North Dakota

Roosevelt Butler
Trenton State College

LaVerne McKay Christoph
Clemson University

Jonathan Dewberry
Interboro Institute

Debbie D. DuFrene
Stephen F. Austin State University

Mildred Francheschi
Valencia Community College

Mary Giachino
Professional Career Institute

Gwen Hester
Richland College

Carol Larson Jones
California State Polytechnic University

Carol Lind
Mankato State University

Glynna Morse
Georgia College

Ross Miller
Milwaukee Area Technical
College

Ellen Trufant
The Berkeley School,
Bergen Campus

We extend a special thank you to Dr. Phillip Niffenegger, Murray State University (Murray, Kentucky) for providing a written report that was used as the basis for the example formal report in Chapter 16, Report Preparation.

Business Communication, 3d Edition, is designed to strengthen and support your business communication instruction. Previous editions of this textbook have been found effective and practical by many instructors in their business communication courses. *Business Communication* in its 3d edition has undergone a major revision in which the best of previous editions has been retained and strengthened with the addition of colorful updated instructional material.

We are pleased to have the opportunity to share with you the challenge of providing effective instruction. Best wishes for excellent business communication education in your classes!

PART **1**

Communication Fundamentals

Electronic Media Technology: A Blessing or a Curse?

Until 1993, it was customary for advance copies of bills to be presented to Congress to be distributed to members of the press in paper form. That year, however, the White House got the final version of President Clinton's health-care bill to the Government Printing Office too late on October 26 to have copies ready for the press the morning of October 27.

Rather than delay distribution of the plan and face the ire of the media, the White House turned to technology. In a matter of hours, 1,000 sets of two 3½ - inch computer disks were ready for media representatives. The disks contained not only the 1,336-page legislation and a 132-page document called The President's Report to the American People, *but also a copy of President Clinton's September 22 speech to Congress about health care.*

Although the advantages of issuing documents electronically were numerous, problems arose.

In addition to the speed achieved by turning to technology, the White House also achieved some cost savings. Each disk cost only $1; the Government Printing Office sold full copies of the health-care bill for $45 and copies of the President's report for $5.

Although the advantages of issuing documents electronically were numerous, problems arose. Within 24 hours after routing the disks to the press, one news service reported receiving disks that had been infected with a virus. A spokesperson for the company that duplicated the disks maintained that they were clean when they left her office, and the White House director of media affairs said that no other organization had reported any problem with the disks.

It's Your Turn

How could this incident have been avoided? What could have been done to help rectify the problems of electronic media distribution?

CHAPTER 1

Business Communication Foundations

Learning Objectives

Your learning objectives for this chapter include the following:

- To define business communication and describe its importance, goals, and patterns
- To explain the communication process and your role in successfully using it
- To recognize communication barriers and describe how to remove them

The ability to communicate effectively is the most important skill you can develop. How well you inform, influence, and persuade others determines the progress you make in your career and the quality of your personal relationships. Fortunately, you can make significant improvements in your ability to communicate. You can make these improvements by studying the successful methods and techniques contained in this book.

Included in this book are sections on communication fundamentals, business English, correspondence, written reports, oral communication, and employment communication. All of the information is presented in a way that will be of immediate, practical value to you.

Communication Quotes

Don't ever use the word charisma, because I don't know what that means. If it means you communicate better than other people, that's what everybody should try to do. You must, no matter what you are running, communicate effectively with your constituencies.
Lee Iacocca, former Chief Executive Officer of the Chrysler Corporation

DEFINITION AND IMPORTANCE OF BUSINESS COMMUNICATION

Your study of business communication will begin with a discussion of its definition and importance.

DEFINITION OF BUSINESS COMMUNICATION

Business communication is defined as the transmission of information within the business environment. The information may be transmitted—sent and received—between two individuals or among several individuals. Methods of communicating are speaking, gesturing, listening, writing, drawing, and reading.

At times you will be the sender of messages—the speaker or the writer. At other times you will be the receiver—the listener or the reader. In the back-and-forth transmission of information, you will be both a sender and a receiver. You must do both jobs well. When you learn how to be a capable, successful sender of messages, you will better understand how to be an effective receiver of messages.

The word *communication* comes from the Latin word *communis,* which means common. Individuals strive to transmit information to each other that will establish a commonness of understanding between or among them.

Business communication includes all contacts among individuals both inside and outside organizations—formal as well as informal. These

A sender successfully transmits business information to receivers.

contacts can consist of face-to-face conversations, letters, memos, telephone conversations, E-mail, fax messages, reports, speeches, and so on.

IMPORTANCE OF BUSINESS COMMUNICATION TO INDIVIDUALS

Individuals spend most of their time communicating.

Research shows that the average person spends about 70 percent of his or her waking hours in some form of communication. This communication ranges from conferences and memo writing at work to personal conversations and newspaper reading at home. Figure 1•1 lists the key ways that communication is important to you.

The higher the responsibility level to which individuals progress in an organization, the more time they spend communicating. Upper-level executives in many businesses or nonprofit organizations will spend up to 95 percent of their working time communicating—speaking, listening, writing, and reading. While some persons may spend as little as 10 percent of their work time communicating, it is estimated that an average of 60 percent of employee time is spent in some form of communication.

Promotions, salary increases, and productivity relate directly to communication competence.

Research on the opinions of executives and college graduates reveals that the ability to communicate effectively in business is ranked at the top of the skills necessary for job success. In addition, many studies show that an individual's communication skill level relates directly to his or her receiving promotions and salary increases. A satisfactory level of technical skill and knowledge in your field is expected of you. How effectively you communicate that technical expertise, however, determines how successful you will be on your job.

Figure 1·1 Key Ways in Which Communicating Effectively Is Important to You

- GETTING JOBS YOU WANT - The ability to communicate effectively will make it possible for you to compose a powerful resume, interview with poise and confidence, and get the jobs you want.
- GAINING PROMOTIONS THAT MOVE YOU AHEAD - Moving ahead in your career depends on being able to communicate your technical competence to others and maintaining effective relationships with them.
- PROVIDING LEADERSHIP TO OTHERS - Your ability to motivate and help subordinates achieve rests on an understanding of human nature and a mastery of communication skills.
- BEING PRODUCTIVE ON THE JOB - Your productivity and efficiency on the job are enhanced by the ability to listen effectively, to speak clearly, and to write competently.
- RELATING POSITIVELY TO OTHERS - Your success in both personal and business relationships depends on people trusting and liking you; communicating ethically, with concern and compassion, is essential.
- ASSURING THE SUCCESS OF YOUR ORGANIZATION - Your organization will succeed only if it has the support of its constituencies—support which comes from successfully communicating with customers or clients about the organization's products or services.

> *A man who has knowledge but lacks the power to express it is no better off than if he never had any ideas.*
>
> **Pericles, Greek statesman, fifth century, B.C.**

IMPORTANCE OF BUSINESS COMMUNICATION TO ORGANIZATIONS

Businesses have internal and external communication about short-range and long-range matters. The quality of this communication directly influences the success of the business.

The day-to-day operation of a business depends on the exchange of information among its employees. Information about objectives, job instructions, customer orders, production, problems, corrections, and employee recognition are examples of vital information exchanged daily in the course of business. Long-range planning and decision making are based on research, reports, proposals, conferences, evaluations, and projections—all forms of communication within business organizations.

Businesses depend on communication.

Businesses communicate:

- Internally

Equally important to a business is communication with those outside the organization. A business has frequent contact with customers, community members, government officials, and the general public.

Examples of day-to-day external communications are sales calls, product advertisements, news releases, employment notices, bank transactions, and periodic reports to governmental agencies. External communications that have a long-range impact include new product announcements, plant expansion plans, contributions to community activities, and annual reports. Effective communication with those outside the company brings in orders, builds goodwill, and ensures the continued existence and growth of the business.

Business communication is vital to both individuals and organizations. Improving your communication skills will be beneficial to both you and your employer.

GOALS OF BUSINESS COMMUNICATION

Effective business communication achieves goals for the sender and the receiver. The four basic **goals of business communication** are:

1. The receiver understands the message as the sender intended.
2. The receiver provides the necessary response to the sender.
3. The sender and the receiver maintain a favorable relationship.
4. The sender's organization gains goodwill.

The sender has the responsibility for the achievement of the four business communication goals. When you are the sender—when you are initiating messages or responding to messages—you should keep the four goals in mind and assume the responsibility for their accomplishment.

RECEIVER UNDERSTANDING

The first and *most important* goal of business communication is **receiver understanding.** The sender must transmit the message so clearly that the receiver's interpretation of it will be the same meaning that the sender intended. For example:

> If you want a friend to know that you definitely cannot go to a movie Tuesday night even though you would like to do so, you do not want to say, "I probably won't be able to go to the movie Tuesday; I might have to work or something." The meaning you may transmit to your receiver is that you could go to the movie Tuesday, but you do not want to go with him or her. It would be better for clarity and understanding to say, "Thanks for asking, but I can't go Tuesday; maybe we can go to a movie some other time."

It is a challenge for the sender to achieve the goal of receiver understanding. The sender may need to plan, research, draft, edit, and revise before the message can be understood clearly by the receiver. To develop a clear message the sender must consider the following four issues, which are discussed in more detail later in this chapter:

- the nature of the receiver
- the best form and content of the message
- the provision for feedback from the receiver
- the removal of communication barriers

RECEIVER RESPONSE

Second goal: Receiver provides necessary response.

The second goal of business communication—**receiver response**—is that the receiver provides the response the sender wants. For example, the response of the receiver could be the simple understanding and acceptance of a message announcing a meeting time to employees. Another example of receiver response could be the placement of a large order for merchandise by a customer after a salesperson's presentation.

The sender should encourage and assist receiver response.

The sender should assist the receiver in responding. The wording of the message should encourage response. In a face-to-face conversation, the sender (speaker) can ask the receiver (listener) if he or she understands the message. Furthermore, the sender can ask directly for the response needed.

In situations where the message is written, the sender can encourage a response by asking questions, providing a return envelope and order form, requesting that the receiver telephone the sender, or any one of many other possibilities for securing the desired response from the receiver. For example, suppose your music store has received a mail order for an album, but the customer did not specify whether a record, cassette, or compact disc was wanted. To get the response needed, you should write a letter requesting the information and enclose a postage-paid, addressed reply card on which the customer can simply check the choice desired.

FAVORABLE RELATIONSHIP

Third goal: Sender and receiver maintain a favorable relationship.

The third goal of business communication is that the sender and the receiver maintain a **favorable relationship.** In order to continue doing business together, the sender and the receiver must be able to relate to each other in three important ways: positively, personally, and professionally.

Both the sender and the receiver will receive benefits from maintaining a favorable relationship. If the sender is a seller, a favorable relationship will probably mean more sales and more profits; if the sender is a customer, a favorable relationship will mean a continued source of supply and possibly better prices.

The sender should maintain a favorable relationship.

The sender has the primary responsibility for maintaining a favorable relationship. Some of the ways the sender can do this include:

- using positive wording
- stressing the receiver's interests and benefits
- doing more than is expected

For example, suppose you have to refuse overtime work. If you take the initiative in finding another employee willing to work overtime in your place, you will be doing more than your receiver expected you to do.

ORGANIZATIONAL GOODWILL

Fourth goal: Sender's organization gains goodwill.

The fourth goal of business communication is to gain goodwill for the organization. The goodwill of customers or clients is essential to any business or organization. If a company has the **goodwill** of its customers, it has their confidence and their continuing willingness to buy its products or services. The more goodwill a company has, the more successful it can be.

The sender is responsible for goodwill.

Senders of messages have the responsibility to try to increase goodwill for their company whenever they communicate. They do this in much the same way that they maintain favorable individual relationships. The emphasis, however, includes message content and actions that reflect favorably on the quality and dependability of the company's products and services.

An example of how an employee can build goodwill for his or her company is found in the handling of returned merchandise. If it is company policy to accept the return of defective merchandise with few or no questions, the employee should do just that. The returned merchandise should be accepted not grudgingly, but cheerfully. The employee could say with a smile:

> It's Big M Discount Hardware's policy to offer a replacement item or a refund. Which would you prefer?" [Customer answers.] "Okay, we'll take care of that right away!"

If the communication situation is handled this way, Big M Discount Hardware will gain goodwill and the fourth goal of business communication will have been achieved.

PATTERNS OF BUSINESS COMMUNICATION

Communication patterns vary widely.

As communicators attempt to achieve the four goals of business communication, they send and receive messages that are both internal and external to their companies. Some of these messages are formal and some are informal; some are work related and others are personal. The wide variations among these patterns of business communication are discussed next.

INTERNAL COMMUNICATION PATTERNS

Within a business organization, communication flows upward, downward, and horizontally. In the organization chart for a business shown in Figure

Within a business, communication flows upward, downward, and horizontal.

1•2, the lines connecting the employees show these three **communication patterns.** Messages can flow **upward** from the workers through the supervisor to the manager. Through the same connecting lines, messages can flow **downward.** Also, messages can flow **horizontally** among the A employees and among the B employees—employees who are in the same organizational unit. Finally, messages can flow between Unit A and Unit B.

Figure 1•2 Patterns of Business Communication

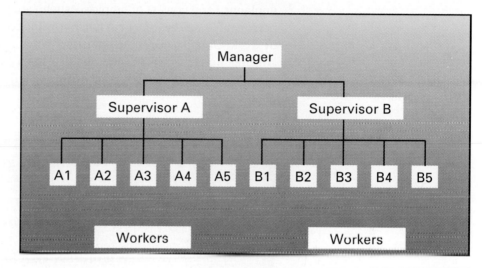

Communication also flows diagonally.

In addition, many messages flow **diagonally** in organizations. The diagonal flow of information is often referred to as *networking*. A **network** is comprised of a group of individuals who have some common bond. Figure 1•3 shows the flow of information among employees from different units and different levels of the organization.

Figure 1•3 A Network

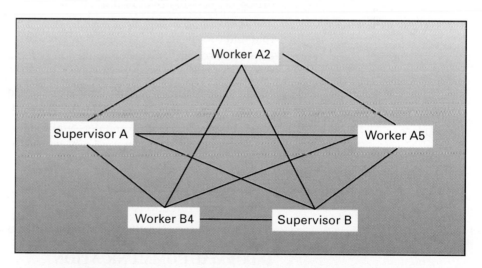

As shown by the lines connecting each employee with all the other employees in the group, communication flows directly among them regardless of their unit or their organizational level. In most network communication all participants are generally considered equal in status. However, as indicated in the "Analysis of the Receiver for the You–Viewpoint" section later in this chapter, many factors—including position, authority, and personality—influence the way network members actually communicate with each other.

A network may be a planned part of the business operation. An example of a planned network of employees is a project team that has been formed to develop and market a new product. In other cases the networks may be unplanned and consist of employees who are attracted to each other on a personal basis. They may eat lunch together or have social contacts outside of work. Organization-based personal networks can be powerful. They can consider organizational issues and decisions outside the formal communication structure and then combine efforts to influence the direction of the company.

> *People very rarely think in groups; they talk together, they exchange information, they adjudicate, they make compromises. But they do not think; they do not create.*
>
> **William H. Whyte, Jr.**

Networking extends beyond an organization and its employees into individuals' personal lives. For example, you currently participate in many different, possibly overlapping, networks. These networks consist of friends and relatives, students and faculty, current and former employers, and current and former fellow employees. Networks are valuable to you. They are important sources of professional and personal support.

FORMAL COMMUNICATION

Formal communication is business related.

In the various directional patterns of information flow, both formal and informal communication take place. **Formal communication** is business related—possibly with some personal touches—and consists predominantly of memos, written reports, and oral communication. Formal communication:

- is planned by the organization
- flows in all directions
- is essential for effective operation of the business

INFORMAL COMMUNICATION

Informal communication can be business related or personal.

Informal communication—sometimes referred to as the *grapevine*—consists of both business related and personal information. It flows in all directions. In fact, informal communication generally has extremely erratic patterns. It includes information ranging from rumors about who the new president of the company will be to a discussion of yesterday's baseball scores. Informal communication:

- is not planned by the organization
- flows in all directions
- is essential for developing and maintaining human relationships

SERIAL COMMUNICATION

A great deal of the information flowing within an organization is transmitted through three or more individuals. Employee A will send a message to Employee B, who, in turn, will send that same basic message to Employee C. The transmission chain may be longer and include more employees or groups of employees. This type of chain communication pattern is called **serial communication.**

Serial communication is common in downward and upward flows of information. For example, job instructions are developed by managers and transmitted to the supervisors who report to them. The supervisors, in turn, transmit the instructions to the employees under their supervision. Serial communication is usually oral, but it may be written, too. In serial communication:

- messages are usually changed, possibly dramatically, as they are passed from one member of the chain to another
- details are omitted, modified, or added

Special precautions are necessary to ensure accuracy and understanding in serial communication. Four techniques will assist in assuring that the same meaning is transmitted throughout the serial communication. Communicators involved in communication chains should:

- take notes
- repeat the message
- keep the message simple
- request feedback

EXTERNAL COMMUNICATION PATTERNS

External communication flows between a business organization and society and is usually formal. Companies have many external contacts such as customers, suppliers, competitors, the media, governmental agencies, and the general public. The information that flows between a business and the public consists primarily of letters, advertisements, orders, shipping and invoicing data, oral communications, and reports.

One example of an external communication pattern begins with a sales letter and an advertisement sent to prospective customers. An interested customer returns an inquiry card requesting that a salesperson call and provide more information about a particular product. The salesperson calls — on the telephone or in person — and makes an oral presentation about the

Serial communication is chain transmission of information.

In serial communication messages are usually changed.

There are techniques for improving serial communication.

Businesses communicate with many external publics.

Multiple messages are connected with one sale.

product to the customer. The customer orders the product. When the order form reaches the originating business, a series of internal communications begins. Appropriate instructions are sent to the sales, production, shipping, and accounting departments. Files are created, reports are issued, and the product is shipped to the customer. Many additional communications may follow this sale. Invoices, payments, reorders, claims, adjustments, service calls, and follow-up visits by a salesperson are some of the possibilities.

A business' success depends on the quality of its external communication. While the products or services of a business firm may be excellent, it is effective communication by salespersons and other personnel that assures the continued existence and growth of the business.

Literally thousands of formal and informal communications take place every day. The success of each individual and the success of a business organization rest on the effectiveness of these messages and the achievement of the four goals of business communication. In the next section the transmission of messages is analyzed in more detail to assist you in further strengthening your communication ability.

The success of a business depends on effective communication.

THE COMMUNICATION PROCESS

One way to improve your ability to communicate is to study the process involved in the act of communicating. The components of the communication process model and the ways to implement each component successfully are discussed in the following sections.

Understanding the communication process improves your ability to communicate.

A COMMUNICATION PROCESS MODEL

The best way to study the communication process is to analyze a model of it. An understanding of the communication process model shown in Figure 1•4 will strengthen your performance as a communicator.

Figure 1•4 A Communication Process Model

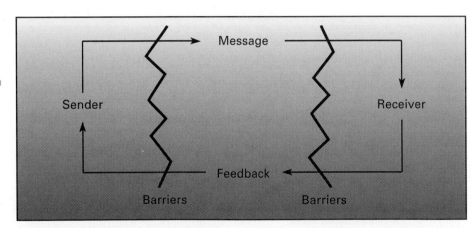

The communication process includes the sender, the message, the receiver, feedback, and barriers.

The communication process model is an open environment that includes the sender, the message, the receiver, feedback, and communication barriers. The **communication environment** includes all things perceived by the participants in that environment; namely, all things perceived by the senses — seeing, hearing, touching, smelling, and tasting. The communication

The communication environment includes all things perceived.

The communication environment is complex and distracting.

Each organization has its own culture that affects the communication environment.

environment is complex and distracting. Overcoming the distractions is necessary if the goals of business communication are to be met.

In addition, each organization has its own culture, or personality, that affects the communication environment and the way the communication process is implemented. Leaders (past and present), traditions, attitudes, methods of operating, and philosophies determine each organization's culture. An organization may be formal, as indicated by the conservative clothing worn, by the limited accessibility of leaders, and by a preference for written rather than oral communication. On the other hand, an organization may be informal—casual clothes are worn, leaders have open-door policies, and most communication is oral. Other factors influencing the culture are the organization's values relating to diversity, seniority, friendliness, teamwork, individuality, and ethics. Effective business communicators adapt to and positively influence the development of their organizations' cultures.

SENDER'S AND RECEIVER'S ROLES

The sender and the receiver have important responsibilities in the communication process. If both fulfill their roles, the communication will be successful.

SENDER'S ROLE

The sender has important tasks to perform.

In the communication process the sender initiates the message. The sender may send the message in written, oral, or nonverbal form, or some combination of these forms. The sender, therefore, may be a writer, a speaker, or one who simply gestures. The **sender's role** in the communication process includes (1) the selection of the type of message, (2) the analysis of the receiver, (3) the use of the you–viewpoint in composing and sending the message, (4) the provision for feedback, and (5) the removal of communication barriers.

RECEIVER'S ROLE

The receiver also has important tasks.

The receiver will be the listener, reader, or observer in the communication process. When you are the receiver, you will want—for your own benefit—to be a good communicator. The **receiver's role** in the communication process includes (1) listening or reading carefully, (2) being open to different types of senders and new ideas, (3) making notes when necessary, (4) providing appropriate feedback to sender, and (5) asking questions for clarification as necessary.

The sender has the responsibility for the success of the communication.

Remember, the sender has the responsibility for the success of the communication. How you, as the sender, can successfully fulfill your role in the communication process will be discussed in detail in the following sections.

TYPES OF MESSAGES

The sender chooses the type of message most appropriate for the communication situation.

WRITTEN MESSAGES

Message may be:

• Written

Written messages can be memos, letters, notes, reports, telegrams, E-mail, fax messages, newsletters, news releases, diagrams, drawings, charts, tables, and so on. Written messages are used when it is desirable to have a record of the communication or when the message is complex.

ORAL MESSAGES

Oral messages take many forms including face-to-face conversations, telephone conversations, voice-mail, in-person conferences, televideo conferences, and speeches. Oral messages provide greater opportunity for immediate feedback and confirmation of understanding. In addition, greater speed of transmission of the message is generally possible in oral communication.

NONVERBAL MESSAGES

Nonverbal messages can include a nod of the head, a raised eyebrow, a smile, a frown, an extended hand, a pointing finger, and many other gestures and facial expressions. Nonverbal communication usually is used as a supplement to oral communication. Sometimes, it can be more powerful than oral communication. When there is a conflict between the oral and nonverbal messages from a sender, the nonverbal message is believed by the receiver.

COMMUNICATION CHANNELS

The type of message—written, oral, or nonverbal— influences the channel through which the sender chooses to send the message. The channel also is determined by who the receiver is. For memos to employees, the channel usually is the interoffice mail system. For letters sent outside the business to customers and others, private or public mail systems are used. Other channels—personal visit, telephone, telegraph, television, computer, and so forth—are chosen for other types of messages.

ANALYSIS OF THE RECEIVER FOR THE YOU–VIEWPOINT

The sender's most important task in the communication process is to analyze the receiver for the you–viewpoint. The **you–viewpoint** means that the sender gives primary consideration to the receiver's point of view when composing and sending messages. This is the most powerful concept in business communication. This concept is discussed in detail later in this chapter. To use the you–viewpoint, you must first analyze your receiver.

ANALYZING THE RECEIVER

Analysis of the receiver is necessary in order to be certain that the receiver understands the message, gives the response needed, and feels favorably toward you and your organization. No two receivers are alike. You must know or learn as much as possible about how your particular receiver thinks and feels. If you have multiple receivers for the same message, such as readers of a form letter or listeners to a speech, you must analyze all members of the group.

It is helpful to analyze your receiver in four areas—knowledge, interests, opinions, and emotional state. Each of these areas is discussed next.

Knowledge. The analysis should first include a review of the receiver's education and experience. Attention should be given to the receiver's vocabulary, general knowledge, and specific knowledge on the subject of

- Oral

- Nonverbal

The type of message and its receiver influence the choice of communication channel.

The sender must analyze the receiver for the you–viewpoint.

Each receiver is unique.

Analyze the receiver's knowledge—education, experience, and vocabulary.

the message. What is the capability of the receiver to understand in a given communication situation?

For example, let's analyze the receiver in the following communication situation: Assume that you are a public accountant writing a letter to Wilson Brooks, a contractor who builds homes. Mr. Brooks prepares his own tax returns with occasional assistance from your firm. He has had last year's return audited by the Internal Revenue Service (IRS). The IRS did not allow some of the deductions Mr. Brooks listed and indicates that he owes $3,750 in additional taxes. Mr. Brooks has sent you a copy of the IRS audit report. He asks you to review the report and to give him advice in writing on what he should do.

Your analysis of Mr. Brooks's knowledge in this communication situation might reveal the following:

Education: General—high school graduate; vocabulary approximately tenth to twelfth grade reading level. About taxes—limited; no formal education on tax return preparation.

Experience: Has prepared his own tax returns with occasional professional assistance for each of the past ten years. Has had a good working relationship with you.

Based on this analysis, you will decide (1) to write to Mr. Brooks at a level a high school graduate would understand, (2) to avoid using technical tax terms where possible, and (3) to define any technical tax terms that must be used. For any message to be understood, it must be composed at the proper level and be expressed in words that mean the same thing in both the mind of the receiver and the mind of the sender. (Determining the vocabulary level of a message is discussed further in Chapter 3.)

Interests. Second, the receiver's interests should be analyzed. What concerns, needs, and motivations will the receiver have in a given situation? If you are attempting, for example, to show a receiver how your bad news message—a message in which you must give unfavorable news—is of benefit to him or her, you can do this based on an understanding of the receiver's interests and by emphasizing those interests in your message.

As another example, when communicating with managers many employees misjudge their managers' interests. Differing positions and levels of authority influence interests. For example, an employee responsible for production will have a detailed interest in any problem that stops production. In communicating to a manager about such a problem, that employee may give the manager too many technical details—details in which the manager has no interest and possibly does not even understand. The manager's only interests may be: Yes or no? Can the problem be solved? Will production resume before profits are seriously reduced? A careful analysis of your receivers will help you avoid this and similar kinds of communication errors.

Practice analysis with a specific communication situation.

Analyze the receiver's interests—concerns, needs, and motivations.

Position and level of authority affect interests.

In the communication situation described above, you, a public accountant, are writing to Wilson Brooks, a contractor, about an IRS audit. What are his interests in this situation? Your analysis of him as a receiver shows the following:

Interests: He does not want to be in violation of the tax laws; he wants to pay only those taxes actually due.

This information about his interests will be helpful to you. You will want to emphasize in your letter the benefits he can receive by following your advice. These benefits include removing the potential tax law violation and paying only the amount he actually owes.

Opinions. Third, the opinions of the receiver should be examined. What values, attitudes, biases, and viewpoints does the receiver have? What words or symbols will make a positive impression on the receiver? a negative impression? What ideas can be used effectively to communicate with this receiver? The same words and ideas will at times have opposite effects on different receivers. For example, the words *liberal*, *conservative*, *intellect*, *abortion*, *welfare*, and *wealthy* will be received positively by some and negatively by others.

Among the many attributes that can affect receiver opinions are status, power, personality, expectations, nationality, and culture. Let us use the latter attribute—culture—as an example. Generally speaking, the Japanese prefer to communicate indirectly, only getting to the point after many introductory and preliminary comments. Germans, on the other hand, are direct and get to the point at the beginning or very early in the message.

Variations in receiver attributes also exist within countries. For example, the culture of the United States is comprised of many subcultures—Hispanics, Asian-Americans, African-Americans, American Indians, Polish-Americans, and many others. Each of these subcultures has its own values, attitudes, biases, and viewpoints that must be considered when analyzing a receiver for the you–viewpoint.

Receivers within countries and around the world use widely differing languages, dialects, accents, and nonverbal communication. If a sender wants his or her messages accepted and understood by receivers from differing cultures, the approach, words, and nonverbal signals used in each message must be adapted to the specific culture or subculture involved. For example, opinions vary widely on how nonverbal signals are appropriately used. See the communication note, "When Yes Means No," on page 17.

Let's return to the Wilson Brooks's communication situation described earlier. As the public accountant writing to contractor Brooks about an IRS tax audit, your analysis of his opinions reveals the following:

Analyze the receiver's opinions—values, attitudes, biases, and viewpoints.

Status, personality, expectations, and culture affect opinions.

Opinions: Mr. Brooks values honesty and free enterprise; he dislikes paperwork and paying taxes.

Based on this analysis of his opinions, your letter should reinforce these facts: (1) the deductions he took were permitted in prior years, but the law has changed; (2) the paperwork related to filing an amended return can be handled entirely by you; (3) all he will need to do is sign the amended return; and (4) only those taxes due should be paid.

Emotional State.

Analyze the receiver's emotional state—happy? angry? neutral?

Finally, the receiver's emotional state should be considered. Is the receiver going to receive this message in a happy state, a neutral state, or an angry state? The answer to this question will assist you in determining whether you should use a direct or an indirect approach. In most cultures, a happy or a neutral person will accept and understand your message when you give the main point in your opening (direct). An angry person, however, might better accept and understand your message if you provide an explanation, reason, or other supporting information before you give your main point (indirect).

Analysis helps determine message approach.

Communication Notes

When Yes Means No

Most of us think signaling yes or no is just a matter of nodding the head up and down or shaking it from side to side. This may be true enough for the U.S. culture, but not in other parts of the world. According to Desmond Morris in his book *Manwatching,* the head nod we use for yes means no in Greece, Cyprus, Turkey, Yugoslavia, Malta, some Arab countries and southern Italy. And if you shake your head for no in Bulgaria, parts of Greece, Yugoslavia and Iran, it will be interpreted as yes. The old English nay means yea in Greece. And our slangy yeah is no in Japan.

Another affirmative signal—our famous OK gesture of circled thumb and forefinger—has a variety of positive meanings to us, ranging from precision to perfection to agreement to praise. But not everywhere. In France it signifies worthlessness, no good, zero. In Tunisia—especially when combined with a chopping motion—it's taken as a death threat. In Sardinia or Greece, it's an obscene gesture. And in Japan it's a sign for money.

As reported in "That's Life," Woman's Day, *September 4, 1990, p. 132a.*

Using the communication situation again, your analysis of Wilson Brooks reveals the following about his emotional state:

Emotional State: Disappointment and possibly some anger. These emotions may be mixed with relief that he can turn to you for expert help.

Based on these findings regarding Mr. Brooks's emotional state, it is best to provide him with an explanation before you give your recommendation.

Each receiver in a group needs to be analyzed if you want to communicate with every member of the group.

This will help to prepare him for your recommendation and assist him in accepting it.

In any communication situation, an analysis of your receiver will be helpful to you. It will enable you to use effectively one of the most important concepts of business communication—the you–viewpoint.

USING THE YOU–VIEWPOINT

Using the you–viewpoint will achieve business communication goals.

Using the you–viewpoint requires understanding your receiver's point of view. Your receiver's knowledge, interests, opinions, and emotional state are given primary consideration in the development and transmission of the message. To achieve the goals of business communication—understanding, response, favorable relationship, and goodwill—the sender should always use the you–viewpoint.

Your receiver will understand and accept the you–viewpoint message.

Your analysis of the receiver will enable you to use the you–viewpoint. You can use your understanding of the receiver's knowledge to influence your selection of ideas and the amount of explanation to include in the message. In addition, you will be able to use words in the receiver's vocabulary that are understandable and acceptable to him or her.

Also, the message can be directed toward meeting the receiver's interests, that is, his or her concerns, needs, and motivations. Your determination of your receiver's opinions will assist you in avoiding negative situations or, at least, in handling them carefully. Finally, analysis of your receiver's emotional state will influence whether you use the direct or indirect approach in your message.

Members of a group of receivers must be individually analyzed.

If you are sending the same message to a group of receivers and you want to achieve the business communication goals with every member of that group, each individual in the group—to the extent possible—must be analyzed. Then the message must be composed for the members of the group with the least knowledge about the subject, the least interest, and the most opposed emotionally.

The opposite of the you–viewpoint is the I–viewpoint.

The opposite of the you–viewpoint is the I–viewpoint, which includes the me–, my–, our–, and we–viewpoints. The **I–viewpoint** means the sender composes messages from his or her point of view instead of the receiver's point of view. Poor communicators use the I–viewpoint and choose the content for their messages based on their own knowledge, interests, opinions, and emotional states. Most of the time, the I–viewpoint type of message does not achieve the goals of business communication.

Examine these contrasting examples of sentences from opposite viewpoints:

Contrasting examples of viewpoints are shown here.

I–Viewpoint	You–Viewpoint
We shipped your order Friday.	You will receive your order Monday.
We can sell each unit to you for $10, and you can charge your customers $15.	You can make a $5 profit on each unit when you buy them for $10 and sell them for $15 each.
I am happy to tell you I have approved your application.	You will be glad to know that your application has been approved.
We manufacture seven different kinds of Haircare shampoo.	So that you may select the shampoo that is just right for your hair, Haircare makes seven special blends.
You simply do not understand what I am saying.	I am not making myself as clear as I should.

As these examples show, the you viewpoint message is directed toward the receiver's perceptions and feelings. Note that *we* and *I* in many of the I–viewpoint examples have been changed to *you* and *your* in the you–viewpoint examples. This type of simple, obvious change generally is important to make; but the you–viewpoint requires much more than simple word changes. It requires that you focus your message's content on the receiver rather than on yourself. It requires that in your messages you emphasize the receiver's interests and benefits rather than your interests and benefits. When you use the you–viewpoint, the receiver will likely respond positively both to you and the content of your message.

Be honest and forthright in all your messages.

The recommendation that you use the you–viewpoint in your messages does not suggest in any way that you ignore basic values. Honesty and forthrightness are basic to all successful business communication.

Review poor and good letters that could be sent to Wilson Brooks.

It will be helpful now to look at two examples of letters that could be sent to Wilson Brooks, the contractor. As you will recall, Mr. Brooks asked you to review the IRS audit of his last year's tax return and to give him advice in writing on what he should do. Figure 1•5 is an example of a **poor** letter to Mr. Brooks written from the I–viewpoint—the sender's viewpoint. Figure 1•6 is an example of a **good** letter to Mr. Brooks written in the you–viewpoint—the receiver's viewpoint. It is the good letter you might have written based on your analysis of Mr. Brooks as a receiver.

Mills Associates, CPAs

1700 Mesquite Avenue ■ Las Vegas, NV 89100-1234 (702) 555-1030

Needs Work

August 25, 199-

Mr. Wilson Brooks, President
Best Homes Construction Company
6600 Commercial Way
Boulder City, NV 89005-1001

Dear Mr. Brooks:

In regard to my review of the Internal Revenue Service (IRS) audit report dated August 15, 199-, the Audit Division correctly identified several errors you made. Therefore, to avoid violations of the income tax laws and the concomitant potential penalties, an amended return must be filed before the specified IRS deadline.

The errors you made when you prepared your own return involve very technical sections of the IRS Code (particularly Sections 1.000.23.0 through 1.000.45.9 and Section 4.712.11.5) covering provisions of the newly promulgated 199- tax law dealing with partial or complete eliminations of previously allowable deductions for such expenditures as personal interest, state and local sales taxes, and many other deductions. The IRS correctly claims—assuming that your taxes were calculated properly and accurately—that you owe $3,750 in additional taxes.

But the IRS does not and is not required to try to search out in your records other deductions you could have claimed or errors or omissions in your possible favor and to recompute your tax burden. It is my recommendation that you seek professional assistance in the preparation of an amended return for the determination of an accurate specification of your 199- taxes. I and my colleagues at Mills Associates, CPAs, can review your records and possibly determine deductions that you failed to claim or otherwise reduce your tax burden. As I will have to accommodate this review in my schedule, please let me know your decision as soon as feasible.

Sincerely,

Joshua Allen

Joshua Allen, CPA
Manager

ar

I–viewpoint message uses direct approach and words not in receiver's vocabulary.

Does not consider receiver's interests, is negative, and is too technical.

Word choice is inappropriate. Sentences are too long and involved.

Figure 1•5 Example of a **Poor** Letter to Wilson Brooks Written from the I–Viewpoint—the Sender's Viewpoint

Mills Associates, CPA

1700 Mesquite Avenue ■ Las Vegas, NV 89100-1234 (702) 5

GOOD

August 25, 199-

Mr. Wilson Brooks, President
Best Homes Construction Company
6600 Commercial Way
Boulder City, NV 89005-1001

Dear Mr. Brooks:

As you requested, I have reviewed the Internal Revenue Service
(IRS) audit of your last year's tax return.

The IRS states that you claimed deductions that are not permitted
under the new 199- tax law. The new law removed or reduced some
deductions that had been permitted before. These include personal
interest, sales tax, and a number of others. The IRS found some
of these items on your return. The IRS further states that you
owe $3,750 in additional taxes.

To be sure that you claim all the tax deductions the IRS now
allows and to determine the correct amount of your taxes, I recommend that we review your records. We could then file an amended
return. This action will ensure that you are obeying the law.
Also, you would pay only the taxes that are due.

Please let me know if you have any further questions. If you
agree with my recommendation, I will be glad to review your
records and prepare the amended tax return for you to sign.

Sincerely,

Joshua Allen

Joshua Allen, CPA
Manager

ar

> You–viewpoint message uses indirect approach and prepares receiver for the recommendation.

> Word choice and sentence length appropriate for this receiver.

> Receiver's interests are emphasized.

> The you–viewpoint message is positive.

Figure 1•6 Example of a **Good** Letter to Wilson Brooks Written Using the You–Viewpoint Based on an Analysis of Mr. Brooks as a Receiver

PROVISION FOR FEEDBACK

Sender should provide for feedback.

The sender's role in implementing the communication process includes providing for **feedback**—response from the receiver. Providing for the necessary response from the receiver is one of the four goals of business communication. To achieve this goal, you should:

- ask directly or indirectly for the response
- assist the receiver in giving that response

If the sender is applying for a job using a letter and a resume, the desired receiver response is that an interview is granted. In the letter the sender should (1) ask for an interview, and (2) provide the receiver with a telephone number and address where the sender can be reached easily. In a written sales message, the sender should ask for the order and provide a toll-free telephone number or easy-to-use order form for placing the order.

If the communication is oral, the sender can ask the receiver tactfully if the message is understood or if the receiver has any questions. In critical situations the receiver might be asked to repeat the message and explain his or her understanding of it. If the sender is giving a speech to a group, feedback can be gained by observing the audience, asking questions, or administering an evaluation instrument.

Feedback is essential to confirm receiver understanding.

Since the most important goal of business communication is that the receiver understand the message, feedback from the receiver to the sender is essential to confirm that understanding.

COMMUNICATION BARRIERS

Communication barriers interfere with the communication process and must be removed.

Although knowledge of the communication process and skill in implementing it are basic to communicating effectively, the sender must also deal with barriers that interfere with the communication process. A **communication barrier** is any factor that interferes with the success of the communication process. (See Figure 1•4.) These barriers may occur between any two of the communication process steps or may affect all the steps in the process. Being aware of these barriers and removing them is necessary for successful communication to take place. The most crucial barriers are discussed in the next sections.

WORD CHOICE

Communication Barrier 1: poor word choice.

Choosing words that are too difficult, too technical, or too easy for your receiver can be a communication barrier. As you will recall, the analysis of the receiver should include a determination of the receiver's vocabulary level. The message must then be composed and transmitted at the appropriate level.

CONNOTATION VERSUS DENOTATION

Communication Barrier 2: differing connotations.

A receiver and a sender may attach different meanings to the words used in a message. Although there is a specific meaning, or **denotation,** for each word given in the dictionary, these same words may have other meanings in the minds of the communicators. A different meaning is the **connotation.** Connotative meanings are those other meanings suggested to communicators based on their own experiences, interests, opinions, and emotions. Connotative meanings can also be the result of slang or sarcastic usage. Senders should analyze their receivers as thoroughly as possible to determine what connotations those receivers might attach to specific words.

If you as a sender said to one of your subordinates, "Well, that certainly was fast work!" you may have meant the work was completed in less time than you expected. The receiver, however, may attach a different meaning to the statement. This other meaning is the connotative meaning—or the connotation. Based on what he or she is thinking and feeling at the moment, the receiver may connote that you meant the work was slow, was done too quickly, or was done improperly. Other specific examples of connotations versus denotations include the following:

Word	Sender Denotes	Receiver Connotes
cheap	inexpensive	poorly made
liberal	fair	radical
compromise	adjust	give in
determined	committed	stubborn
aggressive	energetic	pushy
proposal	suggestion	decision

INFERENCES

Communication Barrier 3: inappropriate inferences.

A sender should guard against a receiver making inappropriate inferences from a message. An **inference** is a conclusion the receiver may draw from the facts contained in the message. That conclusion may or may not be true, depending on the situation. For example, a manager might say to a secretary, "Please make five photocopies of this memo for distribution to the employees in our unit." The secretary might infer—make an inference—from the facts in the message that the manager not only wanted the copies made but also distributed to the employees. The manager, however, may have wanted the copies to be attached to other material being distributed, held for distribution at a later time, or distributed at the time of a conference with the unit's employees.

Another example of an inappropriate inference is a sender who says, "Be sure to finish this job as soon as you can." The receiver interprets the message as, "Work overtime to get this job done," while the sender intended that the job be completed during regular working hours.

Inferences may be drawn from actions as well as words. For example, suppose that as a supervisor passes two subordinates, they laugh. The supervisor may infer that they are happy, satisfied employees or that the employees are laughing at him or her. Both inferences may be wrong.

Of course, much business and individual activity is based on inference. Intelligent and appropriate inferences are essential to initiative and follow-through on the job. The sender is responsible for seeing that the receiver's inferences are appropriate. Inappropriate inferences can be avoided if the sender conveys clear and explicit messages. As with other communication barriers, the barriers caused by unintended inferences can be eliminated by a careful analysis of the receiver.

GRAMMAR, SPELLING, PUNCTUATION, AND SENTENCE STRUCTURE

Incorrect grammar, spelling, punctuation, and sentence structure will hinder the receiver's understanding and acceptance of a message. The sender can lose credibility with the receiver if these communication barriers are permitted to exist.

For example, incorrect sentence structure can cause misinterpretation of the message. Assume that a sender wants to say that there will be a price increase effective January 1 on all product modifications. The sentence should not be structured "There will be a price increase on all product modifications effective January 1." Is the increase only on product modifications that are effective January 1? That is not the meaning the sender intended the receiver to understand. A better way to structure this sentence would be, "Effective January 1 there will be a price increase on all product modifications."

As another example, assume that employees have requested that they be allowed longer coffee breaks and management attempts to respond. Note the miscommunication in the following incorrectly punctuated sentence: "For a while longer, coffee breaks will not be permitted." The message management intended was, "For a while, longer coffee breaks will not be permitted."

TYPE OF MESSAGE

Selecting the wrong type of message may lead to communication failure. For example, communicating detailed job instructions orally will most likely fail. A written message is more appropriate for such a complex message. Oral communication, however, is more effective for the resolution of a personal conflict between two employees.

If the message is a report on an evaluation of alternative manufacturing processes, the type of message will depend on who the receiver will be. The message may be written or oral, a long report or a short report, a report with or without technical terms, or a report with or without graphic aids. There often are many different types of messages that can be used for any one communication situation.

Generally, the higher the level in an organization to which a message is sent, the shorter the message should be. The time of top managers is extremely valuable; therefore, a brief summary is more useful than a long, detailed report. Managers at lower levels, who are close to the actual operational procedures, derive greater benefits from long, technical messages.

Communication Barrier 4: incorrect grammar, spelling, punctuation, and sentence structure.

Communication Barrier 5: wrong type of message.

APPEARANCE OF THE MESSAGE

Communication Barrier 6: poor appearance of written message.

The readability and acceptance of a written message will be reduced if its appearance is poor. Communication barriers caused by poor appearance include smudges, sloppy corrections, light print, wrinkled paper, and poor handwriting. The sender should not send any messages containing these types of communication barriers.

APPEARANCE OF THE SENDER

Communication Barrier 7: poor appearance of sender of oral message.

The credibility of an oral message can be reduced if the appearance of the sender is unattractive or unacceptable to the receiver. In addition, unintended nonverbal signals can distract a receiver and influence the way an oral message is received. For example, if you smile when you sympathetically give bad news, your motives may be suspect.

If the credibility of the message is questioned, the quality of the receiver's understanding, acceptance, and response will be reduced. For success in oral business communication, senders should maintain required standards of appearance in dress, cleanliness, and facial and body movements.

ENVIRONMENTAL FACTORS

Communication Barrier 8: distracting environmental factors.

Another common communication barrier is any environmental condition that distracts the sender, the receiver, or both, from the successful transmission and reception of the message. One such example of a distracting environmental factor is a noisy machine in an area where a supervisor is trying to communicate with an employee. Another example is the boss's desk—a symbol of authority—between a supervisor and a worker. The desk can intimidate the worker and limit his or her ability to respond to a message. Other examples of environmental factors that can serve as barriers to effective communication include room temperature, odor, amount of light, area colors, and distances.

The sender has the responsibility to try to eliminate any environmental factors that are communication barriers. If the room in which an oral presentation is to be given is too warm, the sender should try to get the thermostat turned down or have the windows opened. If the receiver cannot see to read a message because of limited light, the sender should arrange for more light. Environmental factors that are communication barriers can usually be eliminated or adjusted.

RECEIVER'S CAPABILITY

Communication Barrier 9: receiver incapable of receiving message.

If the receiver has a physical or mental disability that causes a communication barrier, the sender should attempt to assist the receiver in overcoming it. The receiver may have a hearing impairment, a reading disability, or other disability. The sender can remove or compensate for such barriers in the communication process by carefully selecting the form of the message and providing for appropriate feedback mechanisms. Most of the solutions are clear choices.

For the hearing impaired, the volume of an oral message should be amplified or the message should be in written form. A good example of assisting the hearing impaired is the closed captioning that is now available on many television programs with the use of a special receiver. For the visually impaired, the print of a written message should be enlarged or the message should be transmitted orally.

In recent years considerable progress has been made in providing for full participation of persons with disabilities in all fields of human endeavor. Effective communicators draw on the resources available or devise their own ways to overcome a limitation of the receiver's capability.

LISTENING

Communication Barrier 10: poor listening.

The failure of the receiver to listen is a common barrier to successful oral communication. Listening effectively is not easy. One reason it is difficult for a message receiver to listen is that an average speaker talks at a rate of 100 to 200 words a minute while the average person can listen at a rate of 500 or more words a minute. This difference allows listeners' minds to wander to topics other than the message. In addition, listeners—instead of listening—may be worrying about the type of response that they will make. Listening is a skill, and it must be learned. Some persons have not developed the listening skill as fully as others.

Senders can use several methods to overcome poor listening as a communication barrier. Receivers can be requested to listen carefully, or they can be asked questions periodically to determine the extent of their listening. In some circumstances a poor listener may be encouraged to study and learn improved listening skills. One of the most effective ways to remove poor listening as a barrier to communication is to improve the quality of the message and its conveyance. Short, interesting, clear, organized messages that are presented enthusiastically are more likely to be listened to by receivers.

OTHER COMMUNICATION BARRIERS

Several of the most important communication barriers and ways to remove them have been discussed in the preceding sections. In attempting to improve your communication effectiveness, you must eliminate other important barriers. For example, some receiver-related communication barriers include lack of interest, lack of knowledge needed to understand, different cultural perceptions, language difficulty, emotional state, and bias. You, the sender, will want to do everything possible to remove these receiver-related communication barriers.

Several other important barriers exist.

The sender should try to eliminate all barriers.

AN IMPORTANT CONCLUDING COMMENT ON BARRIERS

You can achieve success in communicating if you use the you–viewpoint.

The major way that you as a sender can create a communication barrier is to fail to use the you–viewpoint in your communication. Many of the barriers listed in this chapter can be removed by a careful analysis of the receiver's knowledge, interests, opinions, and emotional state. Based on this analysis, you can achieve effective communication if you use the you–viewpoint in composing and conveying your messages.

DISCUSSION QUESTIONS

1. Define business communication. Explain the definition.

2. Discuss the importance of your being able to communicate effectively.

3. Discuss why communication is important to businesses.

4. Describe how a sender achieves the business-communication goal of receiver understanding.

5. The second goal of business communication is receiver response. Discuss techniques the sender can use to achieve this goal.

6. What are the benefits to the sender and receiver of achieving the third goal of business communication, favorable relationship? How can this goal be achieved?

7. What does organizational goodwill mean? How can organizational goodwill, the fourth goal of business communication, be gained?

8. Discuss the patterns of business communication by briefly describing (a) internal communication patterns, and (b) external communication patterns.

9. What is the difference between formal and informal communication? Give an example of each.

10. What special precautions can be taken to ensure accuracy and understanding in serial communication?

11. Describe the communication environment.

12. What is the sender's role in the communication process? Discuss.

13. Describe the receiver's role in the communication process.

14. Give examples of the main types of messages—written, oral, and nonverbal. What kinds of communication situations are appropriate for each type of message?

15. Explain why the sender should analyze the receiver. Tell how the analysis of the receiver can improve communication.

16. Discuss analyzing the knowledge of the receiver. Indicate what you can learn from this analysis that is helpful in composing and transmitting a message.

17. Describe the interests of the receiver. Tell how the sender and receiver's differing positions and levels of authority influence interests.

18. Explain receiver opinions and indicate how they should influence the composition of a message.

19. Discuss how the culture of the receiver influences his or her opinions.

20. What is meant by the emotional state of the receiver? How does the emotional state of the receiver help determine the approach that will be used in the message?

21. What is the you–viewpoint? Give examples of (a) the use of the I–viewpoint, and (b) the use of the you–viewpoint.

22. Is it possible to use the you–viewpoint and transmit ethical messages? Discuss.

23. Discuss the differences between connotations and denotations. Give examples of how senders and receivers attach different meanings to the same words.

24. Define an inference. Describe the appropriate role of inferences in business.

25. Describe how the sender's use of incorrect grammar, spelling, punctuation, and sentence structure can interfere with a communication.

26. Explain how environmental factors can be communication barriers. Give three examples of environmental factors and tell how they could be communication barriers.

27. What is the major, overriding communication barrier and how does a sender overcome it?

APPLICATION EXERCISES

1. Interview a manager and ask the following questions:

   a. How important is communication to the successful performance of your job?

   b. What is an example of a successful communication experience you have had?

   c. What is an example of an unsuccessful communication experience you have had?

   d. What communication barriers do you commonly experience?

   e. What does organizational goodwill mean to you?

   f. What recommendations do you have for someone who wants to improve his or her communication skills?

   Share the answers to these questions with the class.

2. Analyze as message receivers the students in your business communication class. Do this analysis on a group basis. Be sure to

give attention in your analysis to the students' knowledge, interests, opinions, and emotional states.

3. Select an international leader and describe how he or she communicates. Evaluate the effectiveness of the communication.

4. Select a poor communicator (you need not name the person) and analyze why he or she is poor. Explain corrective actions this communicator could take to improve.

5. Select a culture other than your own and gather information on that culture's values, attitudes, biases, and viewpoints. Use the library or interview a student or faculty member from the culture selected to obtain information. Share your findings with the class.

6. The communication environment is defined in this chapter as including "all things perceived by the participants in that environment." Describe the communication environment in your classroom.

7. Describe a rumor (an informal communication) that you have heard that influenced the behavior of members of a group with whom you are familiar.

8. Observe and record communication barriers for a 24-hour period. Indicate how each barrier could have been removed.

9. Explain how successful students appropriately use the you–viewpoint in their classwork.

Text 1A

10. Rewrite the following sentences so that they are in the you–viewpoint. Be sure not to change the meaning of the sentences in your revised versions.

   a. Be quiet and listen to these important instructions.

   b. He always seems to interrupt while others are talking.

   c. Make no mistakes. The report must be completely accurate.

   d. I have enclosed a postage-paid reply card for you to use for an order.

   e. We have received your order and a check for the amount you owe for the merchandise.

   f. I am sorry that you did not get a pay raise this month.

   g. Your request for a promotion is denied. Talk to me again next month.

   h. We have to charge you $200 to repair the CD player.

   i. That is not true. The meeting is at 3 p.m., not 4 p.m.

   j. Don't be late again. Give the monthly reports to Amanda by no later than the 20th of the month.

11. Interview a manager and ask the following questions:

   a. Are the businesspersons you deal with generally ethical in their communication?

b. Is business communication becoming more or less ethical today than in the past?

c. What recommendations do you have for dealing with unethical communication?

Share the answers to these questions with the class.

12. Describe a situation in which an inappropriate inference was made. Tell how the communication error could have been avoided.

13. For each of the following words give a denotative meaning and a possible connotative meaning: (a) reasonable, (b) trendy, (c) believe, (d) rare, (e) French fries.

14. Bring to class an example of a written message whose poor appearance reduces its readability and acceptability. Point out to the class how the message's appearance is a communication barrier.

15. Give an example of a speaker (a sender of a message) whose appearance is inappropriate for his or her audience (receivers of the message).

16. Describe three different networks in which you participate.

17. List the nonverbal messages that are sent and received in a classroom.

18. Give an example you have observed of an environmental barrier that interfered with the successful transmission of a message from a sender to a receiver.

MESSAGE ANALYSIS

Text 1B

This letter is being sent to several sophomore students who are business majors. Each letter is individually addressed. Using what you have learned from this chapter about the you–viewpoint, rewrite the letter so that it communicates effectively with the receivers. Your major tasks will be to shorten the sentences, lower the vocabulary level, and emphasize the benefits to the receivers. An analysis of the receivers reveals the following:

Knowledge: Possess a tenth-grade vocabulary level.

Interests: Want to improve chances for success after graduating.

Opinions: Believe that they can learn from doing.

Emotional State: Neutral.

Do you aspire to success upon your graduation from Western College and upon acceptance of your chosen career entry position and during your subsequent career chronology?

Would you be interested in associating with a viable organization known for its facility to assure students that kind of success—an organization that provides opportunities for leadership and informational sources of career value?

Then associate with Phi Beta Lambda now!

You can do so by attending an informational meeting to be held at 3:30 p.m. on Wednesday, October 20, 199-, in the Pryor Conference Room of the Business Building.

Phi Beta Lambda, a professional business fraternity, has facilitated the growth of other students like you by providing: (1) leadership opportunities as an officer or committee chairperson, (2) competitive events to hone your career skills and to achieve awards, and (3) informative meetings with outstanding speakers from the business world.

I anticipate that you will officially associate with Phi Beta Lambda and become a member of the Western College Chapter at the October 20 informational meeting!

CHAPTER 2

Principles of Business Communication

Learning Objectives

Your learning objectives for this chapter include the following:

- To choose words that your receiver(s) will understand and that will gain the receiver reaction you need
- To develop clear, concise, and effective sentences
- To form clear, concise, logical, coherent, and effective paragraphs
- To use your own composing style to give uniqueness and life to your messages

Compose effective messages by using the principles of business communication.

Successful managers communicate concisely and clearly.

The best way to improve your ability to compose effective business messages is to learn and use the principles of business communication. This chapter will provide the principles you need for choosing words, developing sentences, and forming paragraphs.

Keep business messages short and simple.

The basic principle of business communication is to keep your message short and simple. Some communicators remember this principle by its initials, KISS, which stands for Keep It Short and Simple. Application of this principle means composing your business messages using short and simple words, sentences, and paragraphs. Your messages, as a result, will be concise, easy to understand, and straightforward.

> *If I'd had more time, I'd have written a shorter book.*
>
> **Mark Twain**

As Mark Twain implies, it may take extra time to compose a shorter, better message, but it will be worth it to you and your receiver. To be an effective, successful business communicator, you will want to adopt the businesslike KISS principle.

Most of the 15 principles of business communication that are discussed in the following sections apply to both written and oral messages. A few apply only to written messages. As in Chapter 1, readers and listeners will be called receivers.

CHOOSING WORDS

Choose effective words.

Words are the smallest units of messages. You will want to give attention to each word you choose to be sure it is the most effective one. An **effective word** is one that your receiver will understand and that will gain the receiver reaction you want. You can improve your ability to choose words by (1) using a dictionary and a thesaurus, and (2) following some important principles of business communication.

USE A DICTIONARY AND A THESAURUS

The two most valuable resources for the business communicator are a dictionary and a thesaurus. These important reference tools are discussed next.

Use a dictionary to select words.

A **dictionary** is a word reference book. You can use it to determine a word's meaning(s), acceptable spelling(s), hyphenation, capitalization, pronunciation(s), and synonym(s). Many word processing software packages have a spell-check feature that can assist you in determining the correct spelling for words.

A dictionary is also helpful in choosing correct words. Some words are easily confused and, therefore, at times misused. Examples of such words are *effect* and *affect, capital* and *capitol, principal* and *principle, continuous* and *continual,* and *further* and *farther.* See Appendix A for an extensive list of easily confused words.

Use a thesaurus to find synonyms.

A **thesaurus** provides additional synonyms and different shades of meanings. Thesauruses are available in book form or as software; the latter is usually a part of a word processing software package. If you have an idea you want to express, you can look up words in a thesaurus that represent that idea and find several alternative words that can be used to express the idea. Each choice usually has a slightly different connotation. Using a thesaurus is a way to find the simplest and most precise words for your message. It is also a way to find synonyms to use so that you can avoid repeating a word.

Use a dictionary and a thesaurus to select appropriate words.

A dictionary and a thesaurus should be at your side when you are attempting to compose effective messages. Your use of them can increase your power to choose the most appropriate words for each of your messages.

In addition to using a dictionary and a thesaurus, you will want to follow some important principles of business communication when you are choosing words for your messages. These principles are discussed next.

PRINCIPLE 1: CHOOSE UNDERSTANDABLE WORDS

Choose words your receiver will understand.

The first principle of word selection is to choose words that will be understood by your receiver. Prior to composing your messages, you will have analyzed your receiver's knowledge, interests, opinions, and emotional state. Considering the information you gathered in this analysis and keeping in mind the importance of the you–viewpoint, you will want to choose words that the receiver will understand.

An **understandable word** is one that is in your receiver's vocabulary. Consider your receiver's educational level and experience as they relate to your message when choosing words. The words that will communicate best are those slightly below the receiver's vocabulary level. For most receivers, you should select the more understandable words in the following examples rather than the less understandable ones:

Less Understandable	More Understandable
verbalize	say
utilize	use
decrement	decrease
equitable	fair
facetious	joking
procrastinate	delay
expeditious	quick
gesticulate	gesture
forbearance	patience
configuration	shape
debilitated	weak
emulate	copy
demonstrate	show
finality	end
foremost	first
perforate	punch
reverberate	vibrate
perspiration	sweat

Understandable words are words that are in your receiver's vocabulary.

Understandable words are generally simpler and shorter.

Appropriate technical words can be efficient.

Notice that the more understandable words are the simpler words normally used in everyday conversations. Also, words that are more understandable are usually shorter.

Using appropriate technical words is a special consideration in choosing understandable words. A **technical word**—sometimes referred to as *jargon*—is one with special meaning in a particular field. Technical words can assist in conveying precise, meaningful messages among certain receivers and senders. For example, between two accountants the use of the words *accrued liabilities* will be understandable. The use of such technical words for the accountants will be more precise and efficient than using nontechnical language. For most of us, though, *accrued liabilities* is not as understandable as *debts that have not yet been recorded on our books*. Here are some other examples of technical and nontechnical words:

Technical Words	Nontechnical Words
generate	develop
de facto	actual
generic	general
format	arrangement
quarantine	confine
extremity	hand or foot
expectorate	spit
seminar	course
deciduous	sheds leaves annually
ferment	sour

Appropriate technical words are those in your receiver's vocabulary.

You will want to use only those technical words that are in your receiver's vocabulary. To do otherwise reduces the receiver's understanding of your message. If you are not sure whether a technical word is in your receiver's vocabulary, do not use it.

In summary, you can best choose understandable words by selecting simple words, short words, and appropriate technical words. The examples that follow assume that the receiver is a typical high school graduate who has no particular technical knowledge.

Less Understandable	More Understandable
The canine pursued the feline.	The dog chased the cat.
Scott formulated the proclamation.	Scott prepared the announcement.
An optometrist provided periodic examinations of the employees' eyes predicated on the premise that their environmental circumstance required monitoring.	An eye doctor regularly examined the employees' eyes because of workplace conditions.
The altercation commenced following dissension.	The fight began after a quarrel.
The economic prognosticator speculated that recession was imminent.	The economist predicted that soon there would be a downturn in business.
The cinema was a credible depiction of matriculation.	The movie was a believable story of going to college.
The tabulations of our quantitative measures of refrigerator production reflect increases during the current fiscal year as compared with the immediate past fiscal year period.	Our records show that we are making more refrigerators this year than we did last year.

PRINCIPLE 2: USE CONCRETE WORDS

Use concrete words. They are specific and precise.

A **concrete word** is one that is specific and precise. In your business messages use concrete words—words that are so clear that there will be no question in your receiver's mind as to the meaning you intended.

Abstract words are less clear in meaning.

An **abstract word** is a general word. Abstract words are the opposite of concrete words. Their meanings are less clear than the meanings of concrete words and are more likely to create wrong or confusing connotations in your receiver's mind. Abstract words are appropriate for literary compositions, but you will want to use primarily concrete words in your business messages. Here are examples of abstract words and ways to make them more specific:

Abstract Words	Concrete Words
soon	3.00 p.m., Wednesday
occasionally	10 percent of the time
often	18 times out of 20
loyal	would give his/her life
office furniture	wooden desk
computer	Model 486X Zenith Notebook
holiday	Thanksgiving
cold	0 degrees Fahrenheit
good student	Has 3.25 grade point average (4.0 = A)
car	Toyota Camry LE
woman	Micaela Alvarez

Notice in the preceding examples that sometimes a few more words are needed to be concrete. These additions to the length of your message are worth the clarity you gain.

PRINCIPLE 3: PREFER STRONG WORDS

Verbs and nouns are strong words. Adjectives and adverbs are weaker.

A **strong word** in the English language will be either a verb or a noun. Verbs are the strongest words, and nouns are next in strength. Adjectives and adverbs, while needed for concreteness at times, are generally weaker, less objective words. (See Chapter 6 for a review of the parts of speech.)

You will want to give preference to verbs and nouns in your business messages and avoid the use of subjective adjectives and adverbs. Adjectives and adverbs tend to distract the receiver from the main points of the message. Reducing your use of them will help keep you from overstating a point or position. To have an impact, business messages should convey objectivity by avoiding exaggeration.

Prefer strong words for power and objectivity.

Descriptions are often applied to senders who communicate with clarity and forcefulness. For example: person of a few words; strong, silent type; straight to the point; and clear as a bell. A short, powerful message composed of strong words will more likely get the attention of your receiver.

Note these examples:

Weak Words	Strong Words
situation	problem
invoice	bill
male parent	father
passed away	died
dismissed	fired
requested	ordered
I feel that probably we will want to take action on this some time late next week.	We should take action on this matter before next Friday.
Following this excellent recommendation will solve all our problems.	Following this recommendation will solve our problem.
You can be assured that the difficult personnel problem we discussed will never happen again as long as this company exists.	The personnel problem we discussed has been corrected.

Use weak words to soften messages.

While Principle 3 advocates a preference for strong words, there will be times when you will want to soften a message with weaker words. This is particularly true for a message that is bad news for your receiver. If you have to discuss a problem with a coworker, you will build better human relations and more acceptance of your message if you use the weaker word, *situation,* instead of the stronger word, *problem.* (This use of weak words is fully discussed in Chapter 12.)

PRINCIPLE 4: EMPHASIZE POSITIVE WORDS

Emphasize positive words and avoid negative words.

A positive, *can do* attitude is one of the most important attributes you can have in business. Possessing that attitude is just the first step; you will want to communicate it to your receivers by selecting positive words and avoiding negative words. A **positive word** is one that conveys optimism and confidence. Negative words trigger unpleasant emotional feelings in most of your receivers.

Positive words are more likely to achieve business communication goals.

Positive words in a message help to achieve the business communication goals of securing the needed response, maintaining a favorable relationship, and gaining goodwill. Here are examples of negative words you should avoid using when possible:

Negative Words		
no	criticism	bad
cannot	accuse	ill timed
do not	weakness	discouraging

Negative Words, *Continued* _____

problem	sad	won't
impossible	apologize	unfortunate
never	error	sorry
failed	mistake	delayed
concern	improper	wrong

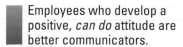

In some situations, negative words can be used for emphasis.

These examples show that unpleasant and negative words are often strong words. There will be occasions when you will want to use negative words for emphasis. (An example is a claim letter to a vendor to get a piece of defective equipment repaired or replaced; see Chapter 11.)

Employees who develop a positive, *can do* attitude are better communicators.

As the next examples show, however, you will more effectively convey a positive attitude and the you–viewpoint if you emphasize what can be done rather than what cannot be done. Both your professional and personal relationships will be served well by selecting positive words and avoiding negative ones.

Negative Phrasings	**Positive Phrasings**
Do not be negative.	Be positive.
I cannot today.	I can tomorrow.
We can't ship the order until Friday.	You will receive the order Monday.
You will not regret your decision.	You will be happy with your decision.
We close at 9 p.m.	We are open until 9 p.m.

I don't agree with your position, but let's discuss it tomorrow.	I hear what you are saying; let's discuss your points in more detail tomorrow.
The necessary equipment cannot be purchased until the next budget period.	The necessary equipment can be purchased during the next budget period.
I am sorry to say that we cannot accept the return of the defective lawn mower.	Please let our expert staff repair your lawn mower at your convenience.

PRINCIPLE 5: AVOID OVERUSED WORDS

Avoid overused words because they have lost their effectiveness.

An **overused word** is one used so much in normal conversations or in business messages that it has lost its effectiveness. The continued use of such words makes messages less precise and less understandable. Because we have heard them over and over, their use makes messages less interesting. Avoid these and similar overused words:

Overused Words and Phrases	
good	right on
awesome	the bottom line
A number 1	great
you know	a done deal
state-of-the-art	interface
hands-on	okay
in due course	per se
very	you know what I mean
really	is *that* right
super	Not!!

PRINCIPLE 6: AVOID OBSOLETE WORDS

Avoid obsolete words because they are pompous, dull, or stiff.

An **obsolete word** is one that is out-of-date, pompous, dull, or stiff. Some of these obsolete words were used years ago in business messages and have been adopted by younger managers. Such words are not normally used in everyday conversation and should not be used in business communication.

Sometimes individuals tend to use obsolete words and become formal, stilted, and pompous when writing messages or speaking before groups. They fail to use the desirable conversational language that communicates best with receivers. Some examples of obsolete words we should avoid are:

Obsolete Words and Phrases	
aforementioned	as stated previously
attached herewith	enclosed herewith
enclosed please find	hoping to hear from you soon
contents duly noted	under separate cover
advised	kindly advise
as per	trusting to hear
in closing	as stated above

As you read through these examples, you quickly realize that most people do not use obsolete words in their everyday conversations. Some do, however, in their writing or public speaking. Such obsolete words should be avoided in all business messages.

Communication Quotes

Communication is Basic to any Business

Words, memos, and unwritten and unspoken messages shape the substance of our jobs and the quality of our relationships. We all communicate, but how clearly, honestly, and how much affect our health and company success.

Clear, honest communication also is a pivotal point of respect. It tells people they are important and have a right to know what you are thinking and feeling. Good communication does more than enhance the feeling of respect in the workplace; it also boosts motivation and productivity.

Robert H. Rosen, The Healthy Company, Los Angeles: Jeremy P. Tarcher, Inc., 1991, p. 41.

DEVELOPING SENTENCES

In the first part of this chapter you learned how to choose effective words. Now you are ready to study the principles that will guide you in combining those words into effective sentences.

Businesspersons prefer concise, efficient, effective communication. To be successful, you will want to use clear, short sentences that are in the active voice and that emphasize your most important points. The principles of business communication for developing clear sentences are in the following sections.

Use short, clear sentences that are in the active voice and that have appropriate emphasis.

PRINCIPLE 7: COMPOSE CLEAR SENTENCES

Clear sentences are composed by following the principles for choosing words that were discussed in the preceding sections. A **clear sentence** uses words that are understandable, concrete, strong, and positive. In addition, clear sentences have unity; that is, they normally contain one main idea. Finally, clear sentences are logically composed by keeping related words together.

Compose clear sentences with understandable, concrete, strong, and positive words.

GIVE SENTENCES UNITY

Clear sentences have unity.

Sentence unity means a sentence that communicates one main idea—one thought. At times you may also want to include ideas that support the main idea. The general rule, however, is: one thought, one sentence. If you have two main thoughts, construct two separate sentences. Examine these contrasting examples of sentences without unity and with unity:

Lack Unity	Have Unity
The employees were informed that the summer work schedule would be changed from last year and the summer payroll dates would conform to the new summer schedule.	The employees were informed that the summer work schedule would be changed from last year. The summer payroll dates will conform to the new summer schedule.

By separating the two subjects—*summer work schedule* and *summer payroll dates*—each sentence is clearer and is given more emphasis.

KEEP RELATED WORDS TOGETHER

Related words are together in clear sentences.

Modifiers are words, phrases, or clauses that describe or limit other words, phrases, or clauses. Modifiers should be placed close to the words they modify. For the sentence to be clear, the word or words that are being described or limited by the modifier must be obvious. In each of the following examples, a modifier has been placed in italics:

Unclear Relationship	Clear Relationship
When I give you the test and raise my hand, *start taking* it.	When I raise my hand, *start taking* the test I have given you.
For last month the manager discovered that quality control was down.	The manager discovered that quality control *for last month* was down.
I am *immediately* approving your proposal effective so that you can act quickly.	So that you can act quickly, I am approving your proposal effective *immediately*.
Eva, our marketing manager, will hold for all salespersons *a training conference* on Monday, April 5.	Eva, our marketing manager, will hold *a training conference* for all salespersons on Monday, April 5.

USE CORRECT GRAMMAR

Clear sentences are grammatically correct.

Clear sentences are grammatically correct. All parts of a sentence should agree. The subject and verb should agree in tense and number. Pronouns should agree with their antecedents in three ways—number, gender, and clear relationship. Another important form of agreement is parallelism—

using the same grammatical form for parts of sentences that serve the same purpose. Correct grammar is discussed in Chapters 6 and 7.

PRINCIPLE 8: USE SHORT SENTENCES

A short sentence is more effective than a long sentence. Generally, short sentences are easier to understand.

The average length of your sentences will depend on the ability of your receiver to understand. For a middle-level receiver, short sentences should average 15 to 20 words. Generally, you should use sentences of longer average length for receivers with more knowledge about the subject and sentences of shorter average length for receivers with less knowledge about the subject.

Vary the length of your sentences to provide interest and to eliminate the dull, choppy effect of too many short sentences. However, you may need a long sentence simply to cover the main idea or the relationship of ideas.

Sentence fragments are used in business messages; they can be as short as one word, for example, *Yes*. A complete sentence will have at least two words—a subject and a predicate; for example, *Penny laughed*. Any sentence that is 30 words or longer is considered a long sentence and should be examined for clarity. The criteria of a **short sentence** for a middle-level receiver follow:

> **How Long Is a Short Sentence?**
> - A sentence fragment can have 1 WORD.
> - Complete sentences will have at least 2 WORDS (a subject and a verb).
> - Short sentences will average 15 TO 20 WORDS.
> - Long sentences are 30 WORDS OR LONGER.

Short sentences are preferred because of the following advantages. They are less complex and, therefore, easier to understand. They are efficient and take less time to listen to or read. Short sentences are businesslike—concise, clear, and to the point. Sentences can be shortened by omitting unnecessary words and by limiting sentence content to one major idea.

OMIT UNNECESSARY WORDS

An **unnecessary word** is one that is not essential to the meaning of the sentence. Clear and concise sentences are lean. They have only *essential* words. When composing sentences, try to omit words that are not essential. Compare these examples:

Wordy	Lean
Tell the production manager that all of the critical component parts will be received and on the assembly line on time.	Tell the production manager the critical parts will be on the assembly line on time.

Margin notes:

Use short sentences. They are more understandable.

Short sentences should average 15–20 words.

Vary sentence length for interest.

Examine sentences with 30 words or more for clarity.

Compose short sentences by omitting unnecessary words.

In the near future we will meet to confer and establish our goals and aims.	We will establish our goals soon.
As the current time seems to be ripe for action, it appears it would be a very good idea to make the decision to sell now.	Now is the time to sell.
In the field of marketing, each and every customer must be given individualized, personalized attention.	Each customer must be given personalized attention.
The accountant is in the process of reviewing the reports.	The accountant is reviewing the reports.
The little personal microcomputer sold for the price of $999.	The microcomputer cost $999.

LIMIT CONTENT

As you will recall, clear sentences convey one main idea. If you have a sentence that is 30 words or longer, you may want to divide it into two or more sentences. Examine the unity of the sentence to see if it is appropriate to divide it further. Remember, you want just one thought unit for most sentences.

Limiting content is another way to achieve short sentences.

Excessive Sentence Content	Limited Sentence Content
When the president decided we would purchase a computer, the director of the computer center developed bid specifications, and the company treasurer sent out requests for bids; the vendors who received the bid requests were selected by the purchasing department, which maintains lists of vendors for that purpose.	The president decided we would purchase a computer. As a result of the decision, the director of the computer center developed bid specifications. The company treasurer sent out the specifications with requests for bids. The vendors who received the bid requests were selected by the purchasing department. The purchasing department maintains lists of vendors for that purpose.

Never be so brief as to become obscure.

Tyron Edwards

One technique for developing short sentences from long ones is to change commas and semicolons to periods when possible. In the preceding illustration you can see that this was done. Often phrases and dependent clauses can be modified so that they can stand alone as short sentences.

PRINCIPLE 9: PREFER ACTIVE VOICE IN SENTENCES

Prefer active voice. It is clear, concise, and forceful.

Sentences using the active voice of the verb will communicate more clearly, concisely, and forcefully than those in the passive voice. In the **active voice** the subject does the acting; in the **passive voice** the subject is acted on. For example, *Joyce submitted the report* (active voice) versus *The report was submitted by Joyce* (passive voice). The active voice emphasizes Joyce and the action.

The active voice is more direct, stronger, and more vigorous than the passive voice. The active voice usually requires fewer words and results in shorter, more understandable sentences. You will want to make the active voice predominant in your sentences. Look for the advantages of the active voice over the passive voice in these contrasting examples:

Passive	Active
The principles of business communication were learned by the students.	The students learned the principles of business communication.
The agreement was voted for by the union members.	The union members voted for the agreement.
Profits have increased this year.	UPS reported increased profits this year.
Applications for the job will be reviewed by a committee.	A committee will review applications for the job.

Passive voice can be used for variety and for de-emphasizing ideas.

While these examples clearly show the power, liveliness, and conciseness of the active voice, there are appropriate uses of the passive voice. Use the passive voice when the doer of the action is unknown or unimportant or when you want to de-emphasize negative or unpleasant ideas. For example, when a customer's order is more important than who shipped it, the passive voice is appropriate:

Active: Aldridge's shipped your order on schedule.

Passive: Your order was shipped on schedule.

In the passive voice the customer's order is emphasized, thus permitting use of the you–viewpoint. Further, in the passive voice, the doer of the action— the vendor—is de-emphasized and appropriately left unnamed.

In the next example you can see how to reduce a negative impression of a doer by using the passive voice. It permits you to leave the doer unnamed.

Active: Aldridge's shipped your order late.

Passive: Your order was shipped late.

You will also sometimes want to use the passive voice to provide variety and interest in your messages. Because of its many advantages, however, the active voice should be dominant in your business messages.

PRINCIPLE 10: GIVE SENTENCES APPROPRIATE EMPHASIS

Give sentences appropriate emphasis using sentence design.

Giving your sentences **appropriate emphasis** means emphasizing the important ideas and de-emphasizing the unimportant ideas. Every speaker or writer wants a particular message transmitted to the receiver. As you develop each sentence in a message, ask yourself, "Should the main idea of this sentence be emphasized or de-emphasized?" Then design the sentence to give the appropriate emphasis.

There are several ways to emphasize or de-emphasize an idea: use length of sentence, use location within the sentence, use sentence structure, repeat key words, tell the receiver what is and what is not important, be specific or general, use format, and use mechanical means. Each of these ways is discussed and illustrated in the following sections.

USE LENGTH

Length: Short sentences emphasize; long sentences de-emphasize.

Short sentences emphasize content and long sentences de-emphasize content. Most of the time you will want to use shorter sentences to give your ideas greater emphasis. Compare these examples:

> All of us know that effort will bring success if we are persistent.
>
> Effort will bring success.

Location: Beginnings and endings emphasize; middles de-emphasize.

The important content of the message—*effort brings success*—receives far more emphasis in the short sentence. The longer version not only changes the main idea to a dependent clause, but also surrounds the main idea with excessive, distracting words.

> ### The more you say, the less people remember. The fewer the words, the greater the profit.
>
> **Fénelon**

USE LOCATION

Beginnings and endings of sentences are the locations of greatest emphasis. What ideas are stressed in these sentences?

> Nancy received a promotion.
> Nancy received a promotion from assistant manager to manager.
> Outstanding performance resulted in a promotion for Nancy.

Nancy is emphasized in all three sentences. Nancy's promotion also receives emphasis in the first sentence by its location at the end. The fact that Nancy is now a manager receives emphasis in the second sentence. Finally, in the third sentence Nancy's outstanding performance is emphasized.

Sentence beginnings compete for attention with the words that follow them; endings compete for attention with words that precede them. However, words in the middle of sentences have to compete with both the preceding and following words and, therefore, are de-emphasized. For example:

The new position requires a change in residence, but it affords an excellent opportunity for advancement.

Maria received the stereo; the speakers, which are on back order, will be delivered next Tuesday.

In the first sentence, the *change in residence* is de-emphasized by its location. In the second sentence, *which are on back order* is de-emphasized. Location is an excellent way to give appropriate emphasis.

USE SENTENCE STRUCTURE

Structure: Ideas in independent clauses are emphasized; in dependent clauses, de-emphasized.

You give the greatest emphasis to an idea by placing it in a short, simple sentence. If you want to show a relationship between ideas, it is possible to emphasize main ideas by placing them in independent clauses and de-emphasize other ideas by placing them in dependent clauses. The independent clause is similar to the short sentence; it can stand alone. Dependent clauses are not complete thoughts; they do not make sense standing alone. (See Chapter 7 for a discussion of sentence structure.)

The two short sentences that follow give approximately the same emphasis to two main ideas: the finality of the sale and the later delivery of the merchandise:

The sale is final. The merchandise will not be delivered until later.

Ideas share emphasis in a compound sentence.

If you want the two ideas to share emphasis—each receiving a reduced amount—you can organize them into a compound sentence:

The sale is final, but the merchandise will not be delivered until later.

However, by organizing these two ideas into one complex sentence, one idea can be emphasized and one de-emphasized. This sentence structure arrangement is called **subordination.** Organizing your sentences using subordination of ideas gives you flexibility in composing your messages. Examine the varying emphases in the following examples:

Although the sale is final, the merchandise will not be delivered until later.

Although the merchandise will not be delivered until later, the sale is final.

In the first example, the idea of later delivery of the merchandise is emphasized by being placed in an independent clause. In the second sentence, the primary idea of the finality of the sale gets the attention as an independent clause.

REPEAT KEY WORDS

Repetition: Emphasize ideas by repeating key words.

Main ideas represented by key words can be emphasized by repeating those words within a sentence. Note the emphasis given *defective* and *radio* in this sentence from a customer complaint:

The radio I purchased from you is defective; please replace this defective radio immediately.

Here is another example of emphasis through repetition of the same root word in different forms:

Alfredo, who is graduating with honors, graduates in May.

Repetition of key words also provides coherence and movement in a sentence. Coherence and movement will be discussed later in this chapter.

TELL RECEIVER WHAT IS IMPORTANT

Explicitness: You can tell what is important and unimportant.

You can tell your receiver that an idea is important or unimportant by your word choice. For example:

The *most important point* is that the sale is final.
Of less concern is that the merchandise will not be delivered until later.

Of course, there are many words and constructions you can use to indicate the importance of an idea. You can refer to ideas with such words as *significant, of (no) consequence, (not) a concern, high (or low) priority, (not) critical, fundamental, (non)essential*. Your thesaurus will be helpful in choosing words to tell your receiver that one idea is important and another unimportant.

BE SPECIFIC OR GENERAL

Specification: Specific words emphasize; general words de-emphasize.

Another way to give appropriate emphasis is to use concrete words (specific words) to emphasize ideas and to use abstract words (general words) to de-emphasize ideas. Here are examples of how this works:

Specific:	Sarah bought a new *Sprint convertible*.
General:	Sarah bought a new *car*.
Specific:	The employee *suffered from severe heart problems, arthritis, and diabetes*.
General:	The employee *was in poor health*.

USE FORMAT

Format: Emphasize ideas with punctuation and listings.

The way you arrange and punctuate a sentence can give emphasis to selected ideas. One way to highlight an idea is to separate it from other information in the sentence. Consider this example:

Marty Brooks—an Olympic Gold Medal winner—has agreed to endorse our products.

"An Olympic Gold Medal winner" stands out because it is set off with dashes. Dashes, colons, and exclamation points are strong punctuation marks and can be used to emphasize ideas. Ideas can be de-emphasized by setting them off with commas or parentheses, which are weaker punctuation marks.

A vertical numbered or lettered list attracts more attention than a list of items simply set off by commas in regular sentence format. This example shows how you can emphasize points by putting them in a numbered list.

The primary findings of the study reveal the following:

1. Prices are going to increase.
2. Supplies are going down.
3. Demand will level off.

USE MECHANICAL MEANS

There are several ways you can give emphasis to ideas through mechanical means. You can <u>underline</u> or use **boldface** type. You can use a different color to highlight selected ideas. The previous sentence and the illustrations and marginal notes in this book are examples of the effective use of color. Other mechanical means include type size, typeface, uppercase letters, bullets, arrows, and circles.

Overuse of format or mechanical means to emphasize ideas will reduce their effectiveness and can be distracting. Their use in letters and memos should be very limited and reserved for special situations. The use of mechanical means to emphasize ideas is more common in advertisements, reports, and visual aids.

There are many ways to emphasize and de-emphasize ideas as you develop effective sentences. You will want to practice and use these techniques to strengthen your business communication skills.

FORMING PARAGRAPHS

Paragraphs organize the receiver's thoughts.

Combining sentences into paragraphs is an important part of composing a message. Paragraphs help your receiver organize his or her thoughts and see where your message is going. You can form effective paragraphs by following five basic principles of business communication. These principles will guide you in determining paragraph length, unity, organization, emphasis, and coherence.

PRINCIPLE 11: USE SHORT PARAGRAPHS

Use short paragraphs. They are easier to understand.

You will want to use short paragraphs in your business messages. A **short paragraph** is easy to understand, helps your receivers organize their thoughts more easily, and appears more inviting to the receiver. Receivers are more likely to read short paragraphs.

Long paragraphs are more complex, appear more difficult to read, and are harder to comprehend. Readers are less likely to read them.

In letters and memos, paragraphs should average four to five lines. Paragraphs with eight lines or more should be examined.

In business letter and memo writing, short paragraphs average four to five lines. If any paragraph in a letter or memo is eight lines or more, it is long and should be examined carefully to see if it can be shortened or divided. Business letters and memos are likely to be read quickly, and short paragraphs aid receiver understanding.

In reports, paragraphs should average six to seven lines. Paragraphs with twelve lines or more should be examined.

Business reports are more likely to be studied carefully, and the paragraphs can be somewhat longer, but not much longer. In business report writing, short paragraphs should average six to seven lines. Twelve lines or more in any paragraph in a report is a signal that it is long, and its unity (see

Principle 12) should be examined carefully. Criteria of a short paragraph for business letters and memos and for business reports follow:

How Long Is a Short Paragraph?

Business Letters and Memos
- A short paragraph can have 1 LINE.
- Short paragraphs will average 4 TO 5 LINES.
- Long paragraphs are 8 LINES OR MORE.

Business Reports
- A short paragraph can have 1 LINE.
- Short paragraphs will average 6 TO 7 LINES.
- Long paragraphs are 12 LINES OR MORE.

Paragraph lengths should vary from one line to many.

These guidelines for the lengths of paragraphs in business messages are recommended averages and maximums. The lengths of paragraphs should be varied to accommodate content and to promote reader interest. Paragraphs can and should vary from one line to many lines. They can consist of one sentence or a number of sentences.

First and last paragraphs are usually shorter for greater emphasis.

In most business letters, memos, and reports, the first and last paragraphs are shorter than the middle paragraphs. Often the first and last paragraphs in letters and memos are one to three lines long and consist of only one or two sentences. In reports the first and last paragraphs may be somewhat longer. Short opening and closing paragraphs are more inviting to the reader. They add emphasis to the message's beginning and ending ideas. In Parts 3 and 4 of this book, there are several examples of letters, memos, and reports in which paragraph size can be examined.

PRINCIPLE 12: GIVE PARAGRAPHS UNITY

Clear paragraphs have unity.

Paragraphs should have unity. **Paragraph unity** means that all the sentences in a paragraph relate to one topic. The topic should be covered adequately; however, if the paragraph becomes too long, it should be divided into two or more logical parts. Examine these paragraphs:

Lacks Unity: Thank you for your order. You will receive the shipment of Everwear shoes before your sale begins on Monday, June 14. During your sale you may want to promote the comfort of these long-wearing shoes. The flex-sole design makes Everwears feel like they are already broken in the first time they are worn. In addition, they will feel the same way years later. They do truly seem to wear forever. Good luck with your sale!

Has Unity: Thank you for your order. You will receive the shipment of Everwear shoes before your sale begins on Monday, June 14.

During your sale you may want to promote the comfort of these long-wearing shoes. The flex-sole design makes Everwears feel like they are already broken in the first time they are worn. In addition, they will feel the same way years later. They do truly seem to wear forever.

Good luck with your sale!

Giving unity to paragraphs is sometimes more difficult than the preceding examples imply. The following example lacks unity. Can you determine why?

Lacks Unity: In order to save money, the Employee Benefits Committee has proposed that a new medical and hospitalization insurance plan be developed for our employees. The new plan should provide essential services our employees need but at a lower cost than the old plan. Consideration should be given also to reducing or eliminating some of the old plan's less essential services. Other savings might be realized through reduction of other fringe benefits, such as life insurance, bonuses, and vacation allowances. The development of a new medical and hospitalization insurance plan is important to the company's financial well-being.

Did you note that the fourth sentence did not relate directly to the paragraph's main topic? If you did, you are right. The main topic was saving money with a new medical and hospitalization insurance plan. The fourth sentence shifted the topic to saving money by reducing other fringe benefits. The fourth sentence is a separate topic that requires its own paragraph or paragraphs.

PRINCIPLE 13: ORGANIZE PARAGRAPHS LOGICALLY

Organize paragraphs logically using direct or indirect plans.

Paragraphs can be organized logically using one of two basic plans: the direct plan (deductive approach) or the indirect plan (inductive approach). In the **direct plan** the main idea is presented in the first sentence of the paragraph, and details follow in succeeding sentences. In the **indirect plan** details are presented first, and the main idea is presented later in the paragraph.

Present positive or neutral news using the direct plan.

Present negative news or persuasion using the indirect plan.

The content determines which plan—direct or indirect—you will use. Positive news and neutral news can best be presented using the direct plan. Getting directly to the main point and following it with details helps orient the reader to the content. Negative news or persuasive news can best be presented using the indirect plan. This approach enables you to provide details at the beginning of the message that pave the way for an unpleasant main point, an unfavorable recommendation, or a request for action.

The topic sentence presents the main point of the paragraph.

The sentence that presents the main point of a paragraph is called the **topic sentence.** The topic sentence will either announce the main idea to the reader, or it will summarize the content of the main idea. The topic sentence is like the headline on a newspaper story. In using the direct plan, the topic sentence will be the first sentence, as it is in this paragraph. With the indirect plan, the topic sentence will be placed later in the paragraph.

As a general rule, the first sentence in a paragraph should be either the topic sentence or a transitional sentence. How to provide transition (movement) in a first sentence will be explained later under Principle 15. Unless there is an important reason to locate it elsewhere in the paragraph, the topic sentence should be placed first in business messages. Here are examples of the two basic plans with the topic sentences underlined:

Neutral news.

Direct Plan (Topic Sentence First): <u>Most chief business executives rate business communication as the most important skill a manager can possess</u>. A recent survey of business executives showed that 80 percent of the respondents thought business communication was a manager's most important skill. The remaining 20 percent of the respondents rated business communication second to technical skill. The survey was conducted using a random sample of the presidents of the Fortune 500 companies.

Negative news.

Indirect Plan (Topic Sentence Within): You are a valuable employee to the manufacturing division. You are the only employee with a high level of expertise in statistical quality control. <u>Although I cannot approve your request for transfer to the marketing division at this time, it may be possible to do so soon</u>. The timing of your transfer depends on our success in replacing you by (1) recruiting a qualified new employee, or (2) upgrading the skills of a current employee.

Persuasion.

Indirect Plan (Topic Sentence Last): Spring is just around the corner. This means that vacation time is almost upon us. When you think about planning your vacation for this year, think of us. <u>Call the Farlands Travel Agency at (502) 555-1234, and let us send you the "Ideal Vacation Planner's Guide."</u>

In summary, paragraphs can be organized logically using the direct or the indirect plan. Generally, the direct plan is recommended for good news and neutral news; and the indirect plan is recommended for bad news and persuasion.

PRINCIPLE 14: GIVE PARAGRAPHS APPROPRIATE EMPHASIS

Give paragraphs appropriate emphasis using paragraph design.

As you will recall from the section on sentences in this chapter, giving *appropriate emphasis* means emphasizing the important ideas and de-emphasizing the unimportant ideas. Many of the same ways for giving appropriate emphasis to sentences apply to giving appropriate emphasis to paragraph content. The applicable ways are summarized here:

Design paragraph emphasis using length, location, repetition, explicitness, format, and mechanics.

Length	Short paragraphs emphasize content and long paragraphs de-emphasize content.
Location	Beginnings and endings of paragraphs are the locations of greatest emphasis. The middle of a paragraph is the location of least emphasis.
Repetition	Repeating key words throughout the paragraph can emphasize the ideas represented by those words.

Explicitness	You can tell your reader that an idea is important or unimportant.
Format	The way you arrange and punctuate a paragraph—set ideas off with punctuation, listings, wider margins, etc.—can give emphasis to selected ideas.
Mechanics	You can emphasize ideas using mechanical means: underlining, boldface type, color, type size, typeface, uppercase letters, bullets, arrows, and circles.

PRINCIPLE 15: PROVIDE PARAGRAPH COHERENCE

Provide for flow of thought with paragraph coherence.

Providing **coherence** between and within paragraphs means providing for a flow of thought. You want to encourage the logical movement of your receiver's mind from one idea to the next. The primary way to assure coherence is to organize paragraphs logically using the direct or indirect plans as discussed in Principle 13.

You can also provide for coherence between and within paragraphs by using transitional words and tie-in sentences. Hints for successfully adopting these latter suggestions follow.

USE TRANSITIONAL WORDS

Provide coherence with transitional words.

A **transitional word** is a helpful bridge from one idea to the next. Transitional words help receivers see where you are leading them, why you are leading them there, and what to expect when they get there. Transitional words provide coherence by holding ideas together logically.

For example, suppose you present an idea in one sentence and you want to expand on that idea in the next sentence. By using transitional words such as *in addition, furthermore*, and *also* at the beginning of the second sentence, you can help receivers see the relationship between ideas. The following example shows this kind of bridging between two sentences:

Adding Information: Michi is a proficient writer. *In addition,* she is an excellent speaker.

There are other transitional words that provide coherence for different situations. Here are some examples:

Contrasts:	but, however, by contrast, nevertheless, on the other hand, from another viewpoint
Examples:	for example, to illustrate, for instance, that is, as follows, like, in illustration
Sequence:	first (second, third), next, then, finally, last, to sum up, in conclusion
Emphasis:	primarily, most importantly, particularly, especially, in fact, indeed, above all
Conclusions:	therefore, thus, so, consequently, as a result, accordingly, hence

Exclusions:	except, neither . . . nor, except that, all but, except for, all except
Additions:	in addition, furthermore, also, and, similarly, moreover, as well as, too

USE TIE-IN SENTENCES

A **tie-in sentence** helps your receiver move from one aspect of the subject to the next. When using the tie-in sentence technique for coherence, repeat the same subject one or more times. To develop tie-in sentences, you can paraphrase the subject, repeat key words that describe the subject, or use pronouns that refer to the subject. Examples of tie-in sentences using these approaches are as follows:

Paraphrasing: The information system in the MN2-O Company is *used extensively* for decision making. Because of this *high rate of use,* it is imperative that the data in the information system be up to date.

Repeating Key Words: Oscar Cruz found that direct mail is a *cost-effective technique* for selling magazine subscriptions. Telemarketing is another proven *cost-effective technique* for promoting subscription sales.

Using Pronoun Reference: *Judy* will complete the required research within two months. *She* will report *her* findings no later than December 1.

COMPOSING WITH STYLE

The most effective business communicators use the principles that have been reviewed in this chapter. You, too, should find them effective. There is one other important dimension of your communication—your personality. Your writing and speaking should reflect the interesting, unique person you are.

Be yourself. Use words and combinations of words that not only are understood by your receiver but also reveal who you are—words that give life and distinction to your message. There are many combinations of words that will send the same basic message to your receiver. Use the words that communicate clearly and concisely and that reflect your personality.

One of America's outstanding orators, Patrick Henry (1736–1799), showed what can be accomplished with style. The first sentence shows how he might have made one of his famous statements; the second sentence is what he actually said:

Not This: If I can't have freedom, then I would rather not live.

But This: Give me liberty, or give me death!

Provide coherence with tie-in sentences.

Compose with style—include your personality.

President William Jefferson Clinton (1946–) is a highly skilled communicator. What he could have said and what he actually said during his 1993 inaugural address are contrasted in the following example and communication quote:

Not This: What this country does a good job of and what we ought to do is provide additional opportunity for everybody and expect additional responsibility from everybody.

But This:

Communication Quotes

We must do what America does best: offer more opportunity to all and demand more responsibility from all. (*1993 Inaugural Address*)
President William Jefferson Clinton (1946–)

One of the leaders in advocating full rights for women, Susan B. Anthony (1820–1906), was extremely effective in awakening the American nation to inequities based on gender. Contrast the way she might have expressed her basic belief in equality for women with the way she actually expressed it:

Not This: There is no reason to give women fewer rights than we give men.

But This: Men, their rights and nothing more; women, their rights and nothing less.

Another powerful communicator who moved Americans, Martin Luther King, Jr. (1929–1968), used the principles of communication coupled with his own unique selection of words. What he could have said and what he did say are sharply contrasted in the following illustration:

Not This: It is hard for others to hold you down if you never give them the chance.

But This: A man can't ride your back unless it's bent.

Finally, from an effective writer and speaker, John F. Kennedy (1917–1963), we have this contrast in what could have been said and what was said:

Not This: Do not inquire about what you can get the government to do for you; instead find out what you can do for the government.

But This: Ask not what your country can do for you; ask what you can do for your country.

Be a powerful business communicator. Use the you–viewpoint and the principles of business communication, and be yourself.

Effective communicators give thought and time to what they say and write. You, too, with study and effort, can improve your ability to be an effective communicator in your professional career and your personal life. Remember to use the you–viewpoint, apply the principles of business communication, and be yourself—you will then be a powerful business communicator.

The following checklist will help you use the Principles of Business Communication. When drafting and revising messages, refer to this list to be sure you have used each principle.

Checklist—Principles of Business Communication

When Composing the Message, Did I:
- ☐ 1. Choose Understandable Words?
- ☐ 2. Use Concrete Words?
- ☐ 3. Prefer Strong Words?
- ☐ 4. Emphasize Positive words?
- ☐ 5. Avoid Overused Words?
- ☐ 6. Avoid Obsolete Words?
- ☐ 7. Compose Clear Sentences?
- ☐ 8. Use Short Sentences?
- ☐ 9. Prefer Active Voice in Sentences?
- ☐ 10. Give Sentences Appropriate Emphasis?
- ☐ 11. Use Short Paragraphs?
- ☐ 12. Give Paragraphs Unity?
- ☐ 13. Organize Paragraphs Logically?
- ☐ 14. Give Paragraphs Appropriate Emphasis?
- ☐ 15. Provide Paragraph Coherence?

DISCUSSION QUESTIONS

1. Define the KISS principle of business communication and discuss the advantages of its use.

2. Explain how the use of a dictionary can help you be a more effective communicator.

3. Explain how a thesaurus can be helpful when composing messages.

4. What are understandable words?

5. What are appropriate technical words? Give an example.

6. Discuss the differences between concrete and abstract words. Which should you use in your business messages?

7. Tell how to implement Principle 3: Prefer Strong Words.

8. What are the relative merits of using positive and negative words in messages?

9. Define overused words. Explain why senders should avoid using them in their messages.

10. Explain how a sender applies Principle 6: Avoid Obsolete Words.

11. Define what is meant by the term *clear sentences*.

12. Describe what is meant by the following guideline for forming sentences: Keep Related Words Together.

13. Explain what must be done to assure that sentences are grammatically correct.

14. Why are short sentences preferred in business communication? How can sentences be shortened?

15. Discuss the advantages of using the active voice and of using the passive voice in sentences.

16. Discuss each of the following ways to emphasize or de-emphasize sentence content (include examples in your discussion): repeat key words, tell receiver what is important, and be specific or general.

17. Explain how you can give emphasis to sentence content using sentence structure.

18. Give two examples of how you can give emphasis to sentence content by using format.

19. Describe what is meant by giving emphasis to sentence content by (a) using length, and (b) using location.

20. What is the role of paragraphing in a written message?

21. Explain why a sender should use short paragraphs in business messages. Tell what the average length of short paragraphs should be for (a) letters and memos and (b) reports.

22. What is meant by Principle 12: Give Paragraphs Unity?

23. Explain the direct and indirect plans for organizing paragraph content? Include in your explanation how a sender would decide which plan to use.

24. How does a sender provide for paragraph coherence?

25. How can you follow the principles of business communication in your composing efforts and still reflect your own personality in your messages?

APPLICATION EXERCISES

PART A

Instructions: For each principle of business communication listed, follow the directions given for its exercises. Keep the basic meaning contained in each of the exercises, and use examples that are different from those in this chapter. Use a dictionary and a thesaurus to assist you in these exercises. Assume that your receiver is a high school graduate with a tenth to eleventh grade vocabulary level and no particular technical expertise.

PRINCIPLE 1: CHOOSE UNDERSTANDABLE WORDS

1. Select Simple Words. Select simpler words to replace these difficult words: (a) captivate, (b) exemplary, (c) amass, (d) folio, (e) propriety, (f) illicit, (g) proponent, (h) jeopardy, (i) sequester, (j) intrinsic.

2. Use Short Words. Select short words to replace these long words: (a) capricious, (b) homogenous, (c) incorporate, (d) reproduction, (e) reasonable, (f) amalgamate, (g) vacillation, (h) prerogative, (i) surreptitious, (j) gregarious.

3. Use Appropriate Technical Words. Select nontechnical words to replace each of these technical words: (a) premium, (b) jurisprudence, (c) liability, (d) hypothesis, (e) asset, (f) invoice, (g) accounts receivable, (h) system configuration, (i) exempt employee, (j) debug.

PRINCIPLE 2: USE CONCRETE WORDS
Select concrete words to replace these abstract words: (a) college, (b) industry, (c) building, (d) equipment, (e) computer, (f) tree, (g) soda, (h) morning, (i) transportation, (j) periodically.

PRINCIPLE 3: PREFER STRONG WORDS
Select strong words to replace these weak words: (a) recommenda-

tion, (b) remiss, (c) inexpensive, (d) request, (e) comply, (f) overlooked, (g) ask, (h) refrain, (i) purchase, (j) withstand.

PRINCIPLE 4: EMPHASIZE POSITIVE WORDS
List five positive words that would be good to use in business messages and five negative words a sender should avoid using.

PRINCIPLE 5: AVOID OVERUSED WORDS
List five overused words or phrases a sender should avoid using.

PRINCIPLE 6: AVOID OBSOLETE WORDS
List five obsolete words or phrases a sender should avoid using.

PRINCIPLE 7: COMPOSE CLEAR SENTENCES
1. Give Sentences Unity. Rewrite the following long sentence. Divide it into a number of sentences each of which possesses unity.

The new product was online to be produced by October 1, but the necessary parts inventory was not available on time to start production as scheduled; to solve this problem, the purchasing agent and the expediters located alternative vendors.

2. Keep Related Words Together. Revise the following sentences so that there is a clear relationship between the modifiers and the words they modify:

    a. Time cards are due at 4 P.M. each Monday promptly.
    b. To all employees the cards must be given before Monday.
    c. All of the reports were submitted from the committees.
    d. The employee was too ill to come to work because he sent his report by mail.
    e. The information was not available needed to complete the project.

PRINCIPLE 8: USE SHORT SENTENCES
Shorten the following sentences by omitting unnecessary words and limiting content:

    a. Be really sure to bring all of your applicable reports to the place where we are holding the meeting of the committee.

    b. The public transportation system, the city buses, was the very best and most efficient way for employees to come to work.

    c. Most managers and administrators not only want to do a good and adequate job, but also, in addition, want to be admired and liked.

    d. The commitment and dedication of most businesspersons lead them to do everything they can to increase productivity.

    e. The time of the meeting will be determined, set, and announced on May 1.

PRINCIPLE 9: PREFER ACTIVE VOICE IN SENTENCES

Change the following sentences from the passive voice to the active voice:

    a. A contract was prepared by the lawyer.

    b. All contracts must be signed by the parties involved.

    c. Telephone calls should not be personal in nature.

    d. A decrease in income for the quarter has occurred.

    e. Reports are to be prepared in duplicate.

PRINCIPLE 10: GIVE SENTENCES APPROPRIATE EMPHASIS

Following the guideline instructions for emphasis, create one to three sentences for each situation:

1. Use Length. You want to call your regular customers' attention to a special sale designed for them. Emphasize this point by the length of your sentence(s).

2. Use Location. You want an employee to stop coming to work late. Emphasize this point at the beginning of your sentence(s).

3. Use Sentence Structure. You have to say no to a request for a promotion. Use sentence structure to de-emphasize the *no* in your sentence(s).

4. Repeat Key Words. Repeat key words in your sentence(s) to emphasize that a car gets high gas mileage.

5. Be Specific or General. Be general in your sentence(s) to de-emphasize the slightly below average miles per gallon rating for a new model car.

6. Use Format. Use format in your sentence(s) to emphasize the number of games your school's football team has won this season.

7. Use Mechanical Means. Use mechanical means in your sentence(s) to emphasize the time of a personnel committee meeting.

PRINCIPLE 11: USE SHORT PARAGRAPHS

Indicate the recommended average number of lines for short paragraphs in (a) letters and memos and (b) reports. Also indicate the number of lines for paragraphs that are considered long for (c) letters and memos and (d) reports. Finally, indicate (e) the number of lines in the shortest possible paragraph.

PRINCIPLE 12: GIVE PARAGRAPHS UNITY

Indicate the sentence that does not belong in each of the following paragraphs:

    a. Business communication instruction offers students an important opportunity. That opportunity is a chance to strengthen the most critical skill they can possess—the ability to communicate. Most managers, when asked, say that strong communication skills are essential to success. Specifically, this success depends on several subskills. Included in these subskills is knowing how to develop a business message. Also, understanding how to delegate and how to provide constructive criticism are crucial to managerial success. Basic to managerial achievement, however, is understanding how to analyze the receiver for the you–viewpoint.

b. Parents of today's youth are faced with an increasing dilemma: how to pay for their children's higher education. The cost of college is going up. Over the past five years, this cost has increased 50 percent. Student interest in college is also on the rise. Finding innovative ways to pay the rising cost of a college education is one of today's major challenges.

PRINCIPLE 13: ORGANIZE PARAGRAPHS LOGICALLY
Using the direct plan, indicate the most logical order of these sentences by listing their letters in that order:

a. This new marketing plan should increase sales significantly.

b. The increased sales will justify the intensive planning effort.

c. The VP for Sales approved the new marketing plan.

d. I think you will agree that the planning effort was worth it.

PRINCIPLE 14: GIVE PARAGRAPHS APPROPRIATE EMPHASIS
Create a paragraph that emphasizes the importance of getting a college education and de-emphasizes the time commitment that is required.

PRINCIPLE 15: PROVIDE PARAGRAPH COHERENCE
Using the indirect plan, indicate the most coherent order for these sentences by listing their letters in that order:

a. Why should you join the Management Association (MA)?

b. Don't wait. Join MA today!

c. You will receive valuable publications.

d. In addition, you can exchange ideas with other managers.

PART B

Instructions: Use your creativity to rewrite the following sentences. While retaining the basic meaning of the original version, be sure to draw on your own unique personality in determining the wording of the revised versions.

1. Last year was the best ever for the Remco Corporation.

2. Communication skills are important for success in business.

3. You should believe in yourself.

4. The book cannot be returned to the bookstore; you have marked it up.

5. We have won.

6. Being ethical is important for many reasons.

MESSAGE ANALYSIS

Text 2A

Rewrite the well-intended but poorly written memo that follows. Apply the principles of business communication you have studied in this chapter. Include in your memo only the information you think is important for the bank employees to know about the new marketing program.

It is with a great deal of delight that I announce that the Milroy National Bank is initiating a new marketing effort called the "Bank Marketing Program" that should cause an expansion of our services to materialize in the near future over the next few months in our market area of Milroy and the surrounding counties. To internalize this plan through each employee learning his or her role in its implementation, we will all attend a Milroy State University special course in the bank's Community Services Room designed exclusively for our employees that explicates the promotional concept and strategy. This course will begin soon. Now I know that it goes without saying that many of you do not want "to go to school" again, but attending this seminar is the only way that you can be adequately informed and enabled to support our important new effort that is vital to the sustenance of our bottom line position. On another topic, summer is just around the corner and many of you will be taking accumulated vacation leave time; and we should not schedule those during June when the Bank Marketing Course will be conducted.

Banking Promotions, Inc., designed this new program especially for us. They have been extremely successful in over 50 other communities. As per the previously stated comments, our efforts to cooperate and support and participate in the new marketing effort can result in strengthening our competitive position which, in turn, will stabilize and enhance our relative financial position, assure continued employment opportunities for all employees, and improve the picture for the employee profit sharing program. Trusting that I can count on your best efforts, good luck with the new "Bank Marketing Program."

Developing Business Messages

CHAPTER 3

Learning Objectives

Your learning objectives for this chapter include the following:

- To use a three-step process for planning and composing effective business messages
- To describe how the vocabulary level of business messages can be determined
- To write successfully in groups
- To describe how to choose ethical content for business messages
- To explain how to assure the legality of business messages
- To use available alternatives to assure unbiased language in business messages

T he planning and composing process for developing all types of written and oral business messages is the same. The process consists of the following three tasks:

Use the same planning and composing process for all messages.

- determine the message's purpose(s)
- analyze the receiver(s) for the you–viewpoint
- compose the content of the message

Carrying out this process may take from a few seconds for a simple oral message to several days for a long written report. Following the process is essential for developing effective business messages.

Individuals or groups develop messages.

Most business messages are developed by individuals working alone. Sometimes, however, a larger or more complex project requires a team of writers working together. Such an effort is called **collaborative writing.**

Analyze your messages.

Message analysis is a related aspect of developing effective business messages. Control the vocabulary level of your messages so that they fit your receivers. In addition, be sure that your messages are ethical, meet legal requirements, and contain unbiased language.

This chapter discusses how to develop effective business messages. The *how-to* of planning, composing, and analyzing business messages is presented.

PLANNING AND COMPOSING BUSINESS MESSAGES

The three-step process for planning and composing business messages is simple but critical to your success in communicating. The process incorporates and applies topics covered in Chapter 1, Business Communication Foundations, and Chapter 2, Principles of Business Communication.

The process: Determine purpose, analyze receiver, and compose content.

STEP 1: DETERMINE PURPOSES

The primary and secondary purposes for a specific business message will vary depending on the communication situation.

Message purpose will vary.

ANALYZE THE COMMUNICATION SITUATION

Your first task in determining the purpose or purposes of a message is to decide what is involved in a specific communication situation. When analyzing the communication situation, you will want to ask yourself: Who will receive the message? Will the message be positive, neutral, negative, or persuasive for my receiver(s)? On preliminary examination, what will be the main content of the message—the main idea and the supporting ideas? Figure 3•1 shows the parts of the communication situation analysis.

First: Analyze the situation.

Who is the receiver? Does the message contain positive, neutral, negative, or persuasive information? What is the main content?

The specific questions you might ask yourself when analyzing the communication situation include the following: Can I say yes to an employee's request for a vacation during the first two weeks in August? How can I initiate a communication to my customers to promote a summer clearance sale?

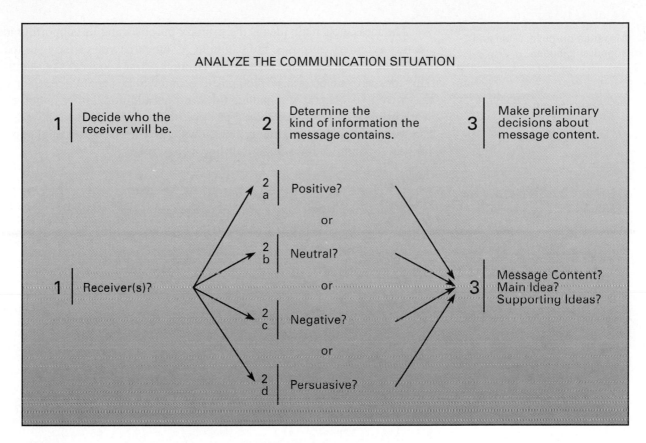

ANALYZE THE COMMUNICATION SITUATION

1 | Decide who the receiver will be.

2 | Determine the kind of information the message contains.

3 | Make preliminary decisions about message content.

1 | Receiver(s)?

2 a | Positive?

or

2 b | Neutral?

or

2 c | Negative?

or

2 d | Persuasive?

3 | Message Content? Main Idea? Supporting Ideas?

■ **Figure 3•1** Analyzing the Communication Situation

How do I say no to a customer who wants to return a microcomputer for a full refund of its purchase price?

Analysis may take a few seconds or several days.

The analysis of the communication situation may be done mentally in a few seconds before you write a memo or place a telephone call. On the other hand, the communication situation analysis may involve collecting extensive information and may be written. This would be the case for an involved business report to be submitted to a board of directors.

ESTABLISH PRIMARY AND SECONDARY PURPOSES

Second: Establish purpose within framework of goals.

Following the analysis of the communication situation, your second task is to establish the primary and secondary purposes of your message. This will be done within the framework of the four business communication goals of receiver understanding, necessary receiver response, favorable relationship, and organizational goodwill.

> *A word to the wise is enough, and many words won't fill a bushel.*
>
> **Benjamin Franklin**

Message purpose: Main and
supporting ideas.

Purposes can be:
• Simple

The message's main idea is the primary purpose, and its supporting ideas are the secondary purposes. For example, assume that you can say yes to an employee's request to take a vacation during the first two weeks of August. This message can be oral, will be positive, and will be sent to a receiver you know well. Its content will include the yes, plus additional information about work priorities—work that should be done before the vacation and work that can wait until afterwards. Figure 3•2 shows how your purposes might appear for this communication situation if they were written.

Figure 3•2 Simple Message Purposes

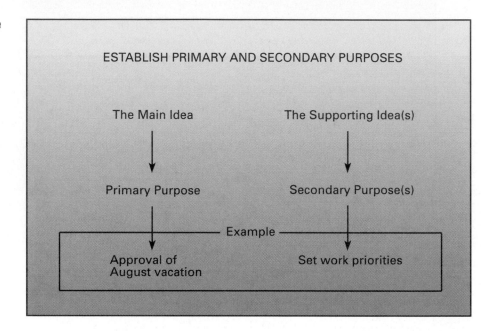

Another example shows how establishing primary and secondary purposes for a specific message can be more involved. Assume that the message you are developing is a written annual departmental report. The message category will likely be mixed. There may be some positive information, some neutral information, some negative information, and some persuasive information in the report. The receivers of the report could include employees who report to you, managers at your level in other departments, and upper management of the organization. The primary and secondary purposes for your departmental report might be as shown in Figure 3•3.

• Involved

When you have analyzed the communication situation and have determined the primary and secondary purposes of the message, you are ready to analyze your receivers to enable you to use the you–viewpoint.

STEP 2: ANALYZE THE RECEIVER FOR THE YOU–VIEWPOINT

The second step in planning and composing an effective written or oral business message is to analyze the receiver or receivers for the you–viewpoint. Since this step is discussed fully in Chapter 1, only a brief summary of it is given here.

Figure 3·3 Involved
Message Purposes for
Departmental Report

INVOLVED MESSAGE PURPOSES

Primary Purposes

1. To document clearly the department's accomplishments for 199-.
2. To persuade upper management to meet the department's future needs.

Secondary Purposes

1. To instill pride of accomplishment in the department's employees.
2. To inform managers at your own level of the department's activities and needs.
3. To inform upper management of the contributions your department and its employees have made.
4. To convince upper management to finance the department's continuing operation and proposed projects.
5. To maintain favorable relationships with others.
6. To build organizational goodwill for the department.

ANALYZE THE RECEIVER

For some communication situations, you will know the receiver of your message quite well. Little or no analysis of the receiver may be necessary. By contrast, it may be necessary for you to do a careful, detailed analysis of the receiver in other communication situations. Whether your analysis of the receiver requires a limited or an extensive amount of research, the approach is the same. You analyze your receiver in four areas—knowledge, interests, opinions, and emotional state—as shown in Figure 3·4.

Analyze receiver's knowledge, interests, opinions, and emotional state.

If you have multiple receivers of your message, you need to analyze each receiver in the group. For example, if you are giving a speech to a Rotary Club, you should visualize the various members of the audience. If you are writing a memo to five other people in your office, analyze each receiver. To achieve the goals and purposes of your message with all your receivers, the message must be understandable to the receiver in the group with the least amount of knowledge about the subject, the lowest vocabulary level, and the most emotional opposition to the message.

If you have multiple receivers, analyze each one.

A message must be composed so all receivers can understand it.

Your analysis of the receiver will give you better information on the receiver's vocabulary, interests, possible biases, and emotional state. You can determine from your analysis the ideas, words, and approach that will communicate best in each situation. This kind of information is essential if you are to use the you–viewpoint.

USE THE YOU–VIEWPOINT

Based on the analysis of your receiver, you will be able to use the powerful you–viewpoint in developing your message. When using the you–viewpoint, give highest priority to what you think will be your receiver's perception of the message. You are trying to communicate receiver understanding and to obtain appropriate receiver reaction. The receiver's perception of your message *is* your message.

Use the you–viewpoint for receiver understanding and action.

The receiver's perception is the message.

Using the you–viewpoint means choosing words that are understandable and acceptable to your receiver. It also means considering the receiver's

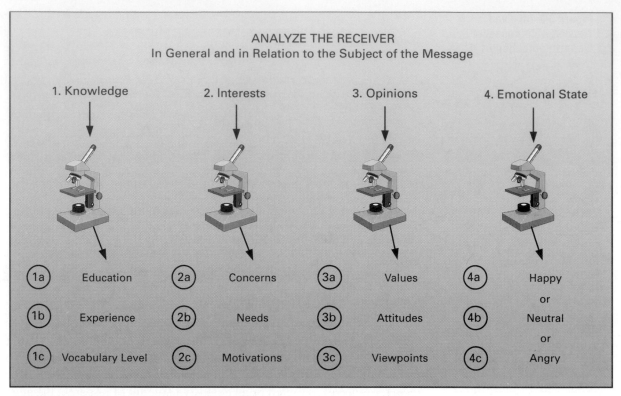

ANALYZE THE RECEIVER
In General and in Relation to the Subject of the Message

1. Knowledge	2. Interests	3. Opinions	4. Emotional State
1a Education	2a Concerns	3a Values	4a Happy
1b Experience	2b Needs	3b Attitudes	4b Neutral
1c Vocabulary Level	2c Motivations	3c Viewpoints	4c Angry

Figure 3•4 Analysis of the Receiver

Using the you–viewpoint is critical to success.

knowledge, interests, opinions, and emotional state. Using the you–viewpoint in composing the content of your message is critical to the success of your message.

STEP 3: COMPOSE MESSAGE CONTENT

The third step in developing an effective business message is to compose the content of the message. Composing the message content includes the following tasks: selecting the type of message, selecting the organizational plan, outlining the content, drafting the message, editing and revising the message, and proofreading the final product. See Figure 3•5 for the six tasks involved in composing message content.

Six tasks are involved in composing message content.

Many of the composing tasks may be done mentally for simple, short messages. The tasks you do on paper will depend on the complexity and the length of the message.

Composing tasks can be done mentally or on paper.

SELECT THE TYPE OF MESSAGE

First: Select type of message.

Your initial task is to decide whether to use a written message or an oral message. Once you make this choice, you have many variations of either type of message to consider. For example, written messages can be handwritten, typed, or printed. They can take the form of electronic mail, diskette, letter, memo, written report, fax, or many other forms. Oral messages include telephone calls, voice mail, face-to-face meetings, small group presentations, and public speeches. Each of these messages varies in the way it can be composed and transmitted.

Figure 3·5 Composing the
Message Content

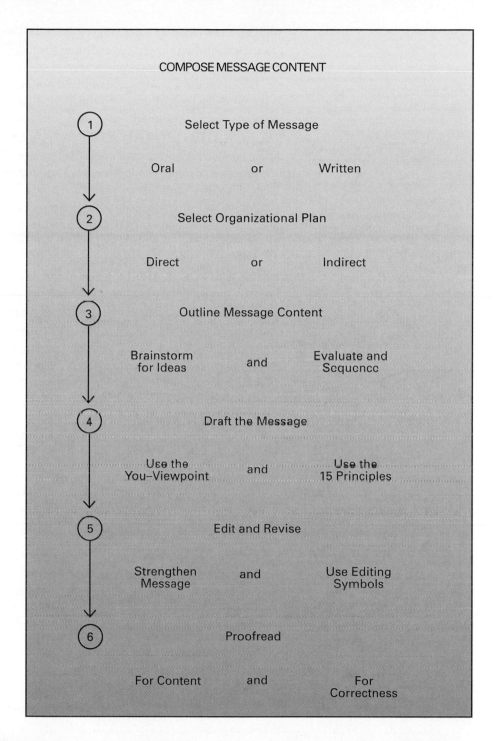

COMPOSE MESSAGE CONTENT

1. Select Type of Message

   Oral   or   Written

2. Select Organizational Plan

   Direct   or   Indirect

3. Outline Message Content

   Brainstorm   and   Evaluate and
   for Ideas   Sequence

4. Draft the Message

   Use the   and   Use the
   You–Viewpoint   15 Principles

5. Edit and Revise

   Strengthen   and   Use Editing
   Message   Symbols

6. Proofread

   For Content   and   For
                                       Correctness

The advantages of oral messages are that they (1) can be quickly transmitted, (2) are more personal, and (3) allow immediate feedback. The disadvantages are that they (1) lack a permanent record, (2) are unsuitable for highly complex material, and (3) permit only limited reflection by the receiver.

The advantages of written messages are that they (1) provide a permanent record, (2) accommodate lengthy and complex content, (3) can be reread and studied, and (4) can be edited and revised. The disadvantages are that they (1) are transmitted slowly, (2) are more formal, (3) delay and reduce feedback, and (4) require storage.

Select the best type of message for the situation.

Based on the advantages and disadvantages of oral and written messages, you can select the type of message that will best achieve your purposes and best communicate with your receiver.

SELECT THE ORGANIZATIONAL PLAN

Second: Select an organizational plan.

Use the direct plan or the indirect plan.

There are two organizational plans that are used for both oral and written messages—the direct (deductive) plan and the indirect (inductive) plan. There are many variations of these two plans. In Part 3 and Part 4 of this text, alternative ways to use the direct and indirect approaches are discussed. These alternative ways apply to both written and oral messages. The direct and indirect plans for messages are shown in Figure 3•6.

The direct plan is best for positive or neutral information; the indirect plan is best for negative information or persuasion.

The **direct plan** attempts to achieve the primary purpose (main idea) of the message immediately by placing the main idea in the opening. The details supporting or explaining the primary purpose follow the opening. The **indirect plan** opens on neutral ground or on a point of agreement. The opening is followed by supporting reasons or explanations and moves to the primary purpose later in the message. Research has shown that in most situations the direct plan is more effective for positive information or neutral information, and the indirect plan is more effective for negative information or persuasion.

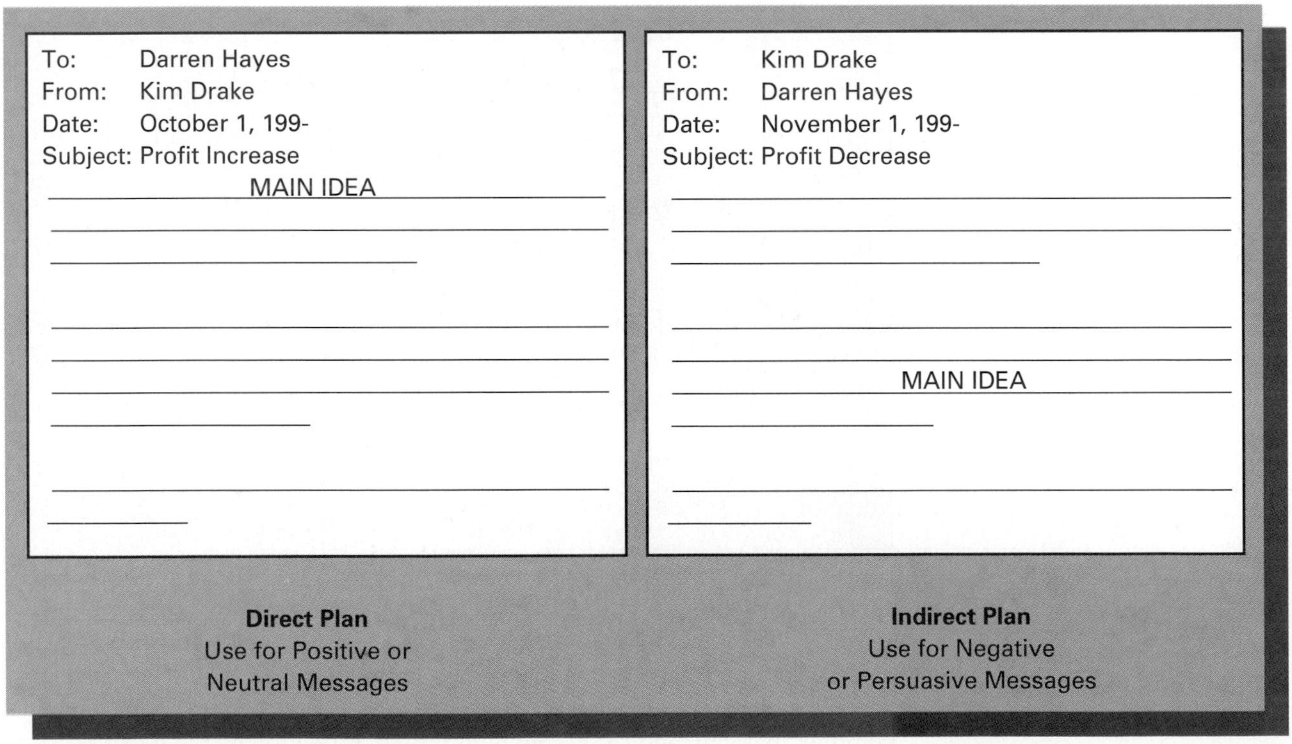
To: Darren Hayes
From: Kim Drake
Date: October 1, 199-
Subject: Profit Increase
MAIN IDEA
To: Kim Drake
From: Darren Hayes
Date: November 1, 199-
Subject: Profit Decrease
MAIN IDEA
Direct Plan
Use for Positive or Neutral Messages
Indirect Plan
Use for Negative or Persuasive Messages

Figure 3•6 Organizational Plans for Messages

When developing international business messages, keep in mind that many cultures around the world communicate almost exclusively using the indirect plan. Included in the cultures that respond more positively to the indirect plan are Asian, Spanish speaking, Middle Eastern, Southern European, and cultures located near the equator. Northern American and Northern European cultures will respond more positively to the direct plan.

After selecting the type of message you will use—written or oral—and the organizational plan for your message—direct or indirect—you are ready to outline message content.

OUTLINE THE MESSAGE CONTENT

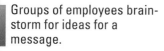
Third: Outline the message content.

In outlining message content, you are simply organizing your ideas for the message in your mind or on paper, diskette, or other medium.

Keeping purpose(s) and receiver(s) in mind, brainstorm content.

Start the outlining process by brainstorming for ideas. **Brainstorming** involves (1) concentrating on both the purpose(s) of your message and your receiver(s), and (2) listing all the ideas that you think should be included in the message. Let this activity take place randomly. Do not evaluate the ideas in detail; just record them. As you do this, you may find it necessary to gather helpful information from files, other employees, or other sources.

Assume, for example, that you have received a claim letter from a customer asking for a refund for a ski boat that was bought on sale. Although the customer's letter is not very well written, the message is clear—she wants her money back. You will have to tell her no—send her a negative message—because you do not give refunds for items bought on sale. You

Groups of employees brainstorm for ideas for a message.

brainstorm ideas for the content of your response. Your notes, written on the claim letter you received, might appear as in Figure 3•7.

Evaluate and sequence ideas.

The second part of the outlining task is to evaluate and sequence the ideas you developed during your brainstorming session. Arrange the ideas you want to use in a logical order following the organizational plan you chose. In your response to the claim letter, you will want to use the indirect plan because you must give the customer negative information. The order in which you would sequence ideas for the positive message is shown in Figure 3•7 by the number in parentheses following each idea. After completing the sequencing of ideas, you are ready to draft the message.

DRAFT THE MESSAGE

Fourth: Draft the message.

Using your mental or recorded notes from the outlining process, your next task is to draft the message. You may draft the message by dictating,

Figure 3•7 Brainstorming the Message Content on Claim Letter

Purposes of Message:
Reject request for refund on boat.
Maintain customer's business.
Increase organizational goodwill.

Ideas for Content: *Express appreciation for purchase. (1)*

Neutral opening—"do all we can." (2)
Repair at cost or $39.95 kit. (7)
Wish many happy hours of skiing. (8)

Amount of savings—$2,000. (4)

3132 First Street
Oxford, MS 38655-2284
April 28, 199-

Mr. Roscoe Lopez
Store Manager
The Boatwright, Inc.
4000 West Broadway Avenue
Jackson, MS 39200-1712

Dear Mr. Lopez:

I want my money back on the defective boat I bought from you during your "Save 33 Percent" Sale. I found a hole in the hull the first time I put the boat in the water.

Please send me the refund check for $4,020, and I will bring the boat back.

Yours truly,

Carrie Hagen

Carrie Hagen

Volume purchases/cut overhead. (5)

Reinforce purchase decision. (3)
No—All sales final during 33% sale. (6)

keyboarding, or handwriting. It is important to use the 15 principles of business communication given in Chapter 2 when drafting messages. Also, be sure to use the you–viewpoint. Put yourself in the place of your receiver.

You may have one or more drafts.

Word processing makes second and succeeding drafts easier to do.

For simple messages your first draft may be the final version of the message. For difficult messages you may have a rough first draft and then one or more improved draft versions of the message. With the development of word processing, it is much easier to have multiple drafts of messages because only the changes need to be keyed. Word processing technology and its advantages are more fully explained in Chapter 4.

You may or may not prepare a complete draft for an oral message. You may transmit oral messages from mental notes or written notes. If you prepare a complete draft of a speech, you should use notes for the actual presentation of the speech. Reading an oral message from a complete, written draft is not recommended except in circumstances where you must be extremely cautious in what you say. An example of this would be reading a prepared statement for a news release.

If you know you can edit and revise, just get something in writing at the start.

If you are drafting a message that you know you will edit and revise, it is more important to get something down in writing than it is to get the initial copy perfect. Experienced writers know that the clearest, most effective communication results from editing and revising drafts of messages.

The clearest messages come from editing and revising drafts.

You will, of course, prepare complete drafts of your written messages. For example, the first rough draft of the negative message to Carrie Hagen about the defective boat is shown in Figure 3•8.

After reviewing the first draft of a message, you can either decide that it becomes your final version or that you will edit and revise it. Prior to the advent of word processing technology, business communicators usually sent first drafts of letters, memos, and reports to avoid the time and cost of retyping. With the advantages of word processing, it is recommended that first drafts of most messages be edited and revised to assure clarity and effectiveness.

EDIT AND REVISE THE MESSAGE

Fifth: Edit and revise the message.

When editing and revising, keep the primary and secondary purposes of the message in mind. Edit the message from your receiver's point of view using the principles of business communication to guide your improvements.

Keep purpose(s) and receiver(s) in mind while editing and revising.

Editing and revising are the best ways to strengthen the quality of your messages so that they achieve their purpose in the most effective manner. The results of editing and revising can be seen in Figure 3•9. Note the clarity, power, and you–viewpoint that have been added in this second draft of the letter.

To aid communication between message preparer and originator, use editing symbols.

Standard symbols for editing and revising are shown in Appendix B and are used in Figure 3•9. Editing symbols are helpful devices for communication between the originator and the preparer of messages. It is suggested that you learn to use these symbols in your editing, revising, and proofreading efforts.

Give the editing and revising task highest priority.

Give the editing and revising task the highest priority for important or lengthy, complex messages. This is your opportunity to strengthen your word choice, sentence development, and paragraph formation. You can

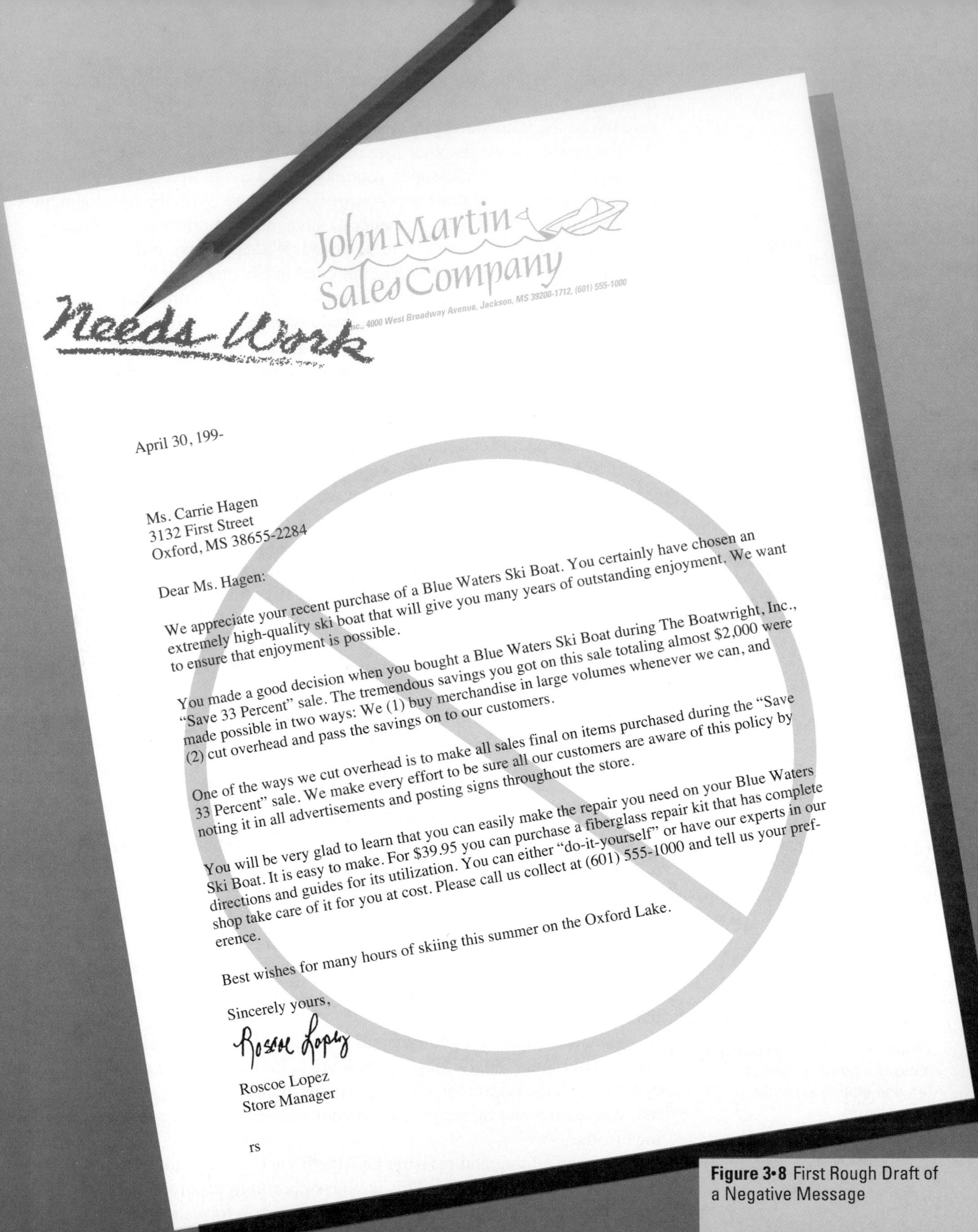

John Martin Sales Company

Inc., 4000 West Broadway Avenue, Jackson, MS 39200-1712, (601) 555-1000

Needs Work

April 30, 199-

Ms. Carrie Hagen
3132 First Street
Oxford, MS 38655-2284

Dear Ms. Hagen:

We appreciate your recent purchase of a Blue Waters Ski Boat. You certainly have chosen an extremely high-quality ski boat that will give you many years of outstanding enjoyment. We want to ensure that enjoyment is possible.

You made a good decision when you bought a Blue Waters Ski Boat during The Boatwright, Inc., "Save 33 Percent" sale. The tremendous savings you got on this sale totaling almost $2,000 were made possible in two ways: We (1) buy merchandise in large volumes whenever we can, and (2) cut overhead and pass the savings on to our customers.

One of the ways we cut overhead is to make all sales final on items purchased during the "Save 33 Percent" sale. We make every effort to be sure all our customers are aware of this policy by noting it in all advertisements and posting signs throughout the store.

You will be very glad to learn that you can easily make the repair you need on your Blue Waters Ski Boat. It is easy to make. For $39.95 you can purchase a fiberglass repair kit that has complete directions and guides for its utilization. You can either "do-it-yourself" or have our experts in our shop take care of it for you at cost. Please call us collect at (601) 555-1000 and tell us your preference.

Best wishes for many hours of skiing this summer on the Oxford Lake.

Sincerely yours,

Roscoe Lopez

Roscoe Lopez
Store Manager

rs

Figure 3•8 First Rough Draft of a Negative Message

John Martin Sales Company

The Boatwright, Inc., 4000 West Broadway Avenue, Jackson, MS 39200-1712, (601)...

GOOD

April 30, 199-

Ms. Carrie Hagen
3132 First Street
Oxford, MS 38655-2284

Dear Ms. Hagen:

We appreciate your recent purchase of a Blue Waters Ski Boat. You certainly have chosen an extremely high-quality ski boat that will give you many years of outstanding enjoyment. We want to ensure that enjoyment is possible.

You made a good decision when you bought a Blue Waters Ski Boat during The Boatwright, Inc., "Save 33 Percent" sale. The tremendous savings you got on this sale totaling almost $2,000 were made possible in two ways: We (1) buy merchandise in large volumes whenever we can, and (2) cut overhead and pass the savings on to our customers.

One of the ways we cut overhead is to make all sales final on items purchased during the "Save 33 Percent" sale. We make every effort to be sure all our customers are aware of this policy by noting it in all advertisements and posting signs throughout the store.

You will be very glad to learn that you can easily make the repair you need on your Blue Waters Ski Boat. It is easy to make. For $39.95 you can purchase a fiberglass repair kit that has complete directions and guides for its utilization. You can either "do-it-yourself" or have our experts in our shop take care of it for you at cost. Please call us collect at (601) 555-1000 and tell us your preference.

Best wishes for many hours of skiing this summer on the Oxford Lake.

Sincerely yours,

Roscoe Lopez

Roscoe Lopez
Store Manager

rs

Figure 3•9 Edited and Revised Negative Letter

check that you have used the chosen organizational plan effectively. In addition, it will be another chance to add distinctiveness—a part of your personality—to the message.

You may edit and revise some messages many times. Long business reports often are revised three, four, or more times. Keep editing and revising until you have a version of the message in the you–viewpoint that is clear, concise, and businesslike.

PROOFREAD THE MESSAGE

Sixth: Proofread the message.

Proofread to catch all spelling, punctuation, and grammar errors and to check format.

The proofreading task is different from the editing and revising task. Proofreading is checking each word to be sure that it is spelled correctly. It is assuring yourself that proper punctuation and grammar have been used, that your sentences are complete and properly constructed, and that your format meets appropriate standards.

Careful proofreading involves (1) reading the message for content and, (2) reading it again for correct grammar, spelling, and punctuation. Some proofreaders can find more spelling errors by reading the copy backwards. If you are using word processing, you may have a spell-check feature to assist you in finding errors. You may also have document analysis software (style checker) to help you detect possible errors. Spell checkers and style checkers do not eliminate the need for proofreading; they just make the task easier.

Spell checkers and style checkers assist with proofreading.

Errors detract from the clarity of the message and reduce your credibility in the mind of the receiver. Therefore, you or some other competent person should proofread each message carefully. As the one who submits the report or signs the letter or memo, you have the ultimate responsibility for both the content and its accuracy. Several proven procedures and techniques for effective proofreading are given in Appendix C.

After completing the tasks involved in composing the content of your message, you arrive at its final version. This version should be understood clearly by your receiver, stimulate the action you want, build a favorable relationship between you and the receiver, and increase organizational goodwill. In addition, your message should achieve its specific purposes for the communication situation.

Following the planning and composing process will achieve the goals and purposes of your message.

DETERMINING VOCABULARY LEVEL

Message analysis includes determining vocabulary level to assure receiver understanding.

As you know, one of your primary concerns in composing effective business messages is using a vocabulary level that your receiver will understand. **Vocabulary level,** as used in this book, refers to the level of difficulty of the words and combinations of words in messages.

READABILITY FORMULAS

Readability formulas can be used to check vocabulary levels.

There are several readability formulas that can be used to calculate vocabulary levels for your messages. These formulas—such as the Gunning, Flesch, Dale-Chall, and Fry—are available in most libraries. They generally measure the average length of sentences and the percentage of "difficult" words. While the counting necessary to use the formulas can be done manually, several of the formulas have been computerized and can be easily used with electronic media.

READABILITY RATINGS

Readability ratings show approximate grade level.

The vocabulary level ratings obtained from readability formulas generally reflect the approximate grade level a person would need to understand the written material. For example, a rating of 12 would mean that a person would have to be able to read at the twelfth-grade level to fully comprehend the material.

Readability analysis does not check the actual words you use or the manner in which you combine those words into sentences. An analysis will not show if the writing is accurate or inaccurate, interesting or dull, valuable or not valuable to a receiver. Use readability ratings as guides, and use common sense in their application.

Common sense must be used with readability ratings.

A message may have a low readability rating because it uses short words and short sentences even though it uses difficult technical words. By contrast, a message may have a high readability rating because it uses long words and long sentences even though the sentences are easy to understand and the words are familiar. In addition, an appropriate grade level for a message does not necessarily guarantee that the message will communicate effectively. An inappropriate grade-level rating for a message, however, does mean that the message should be examined for word choice and sentence length.

VOCABULARY LEVELS

As you compose a message for a given communication situation, keep in mind the estimated vocabulary level of your receiver. A message at too high a vocabulary level will not be understood clearly by your receiver. A message at too low a vocabulary level will insult your receiver or not hold his or her attention and interest.

A message at too high a level will not be understood; too low is insulting.

The middle-level receiver's vocabulary level will fall between grades 8 and 12. Most high school graduates have vocabulary levels between grades 10 to 12. A rule of thumb: Business messages written at the 8th to 12th grade levels will communicate clearly with most receivers.

The middle-level receiver is between grades 8 and 12. Most high school graduates read at grade levels 10 to 12.

Readability formulas are important tools for analyzing your messages. Use these tools regularly to analyze the vocabulary levels of form letters or memos, newsletters, speeches, magazines, books, and similar materials that will be read (or heard) by many receivers. Use these tools periodically to check the vocabulary levels of your messages to only one receiver.

WRITING IN GROUPS

Collaborative writing is group writing.

For most business messages, an individual working alone performs the three-step planning and composing process. Sometimes, however, a writing project is too large for one person. Or, it may require special knowledge that would only be available within a group of persons. Typical messages written by a team of writers are long reports or complex proposals. When a group of two or more persons cooperates to develop a message, the process is called **collaborative writing.**

THE COLLABORATIVE WRITING PROCESS

In collaborative writing the planning and composing process is usually carried out in the following manner:

The group does some of the tasks; individuals do others.

Step 1:   Determine purposes. Step 1 is performed cooperatively by the group. The group analyzes the communication situation and establishes the primary and secondary purposes to be achieved in the message.

Step 2:   Analyze the receiver for the you–viewpoint. Step 2 is also a cooperative effort of the group.

Step 3:   Compose message content. Part of Step 3 is performed by the group and part by individuals as follows:

1. Selecting the type of message and organizational plan usually are done in group meetings.
2. Outlining the message content is usually divided. Brainstorming for the major ideas in the message and the evaluation and sequencing of those ideas are done by the group.
3. Brainstorming for the subsections of the major ideas and the evaluation and sequencing of those ideas are done by individuals working alone or in subgroups.
4. Drafting, initial editing, and revising the subsections of the message are performed by individuals.
5. Final editing and revising of the total message are generally group responsibilities.
6. Proofreading the message usually is delegated to one individual; for some writing projects, the entire group may proofread.

THE WRITING TEAM

The composition of the collaborative writing group—the writing team—varies considerably. The team for a particular message could consist of you and your boss. On the other hand, some large collaborative writing teams consist of several persons from sales, manufacturing, purchasing, personnel, and other departments, along with computer and research specialists and an editor. The size and composition of the group will depend on the nature of the report, proposal, or other message that must be developed.

The size of the writing team depends on the nature of the message.

SUCCESSFUL COLLABORATIVE WRITING

Successful collaborative writing depends on several factors. The writing team members should be able to speak and write clearly. Effective group dynamics have to prevail during team meetings. In a shared writing effort, team members must be open to constructive criticism and able to disagree with each other without being disagreeable. A group loyalty must develop.

Team members must understand the writing process and be able to implement it. They have to agree on a schedule and adhere to it.

Successful collaborative writing depends on effective team effort.

Productive collaborative writing depends on an effective team effort that competently implements the planning and composing process. In the appropriate communication situation, collaborative writing can result in a message that is comprehensive, accurate, and concrete—a message that is more powerful than an individual could develop.

BEING ETHICAL

Being ethical is essential for success.

Being ethical in your communication is essential to a successful personal life and business career. Effective interpersonal relationships are built on trust, honesty, and fairness. Promises made are kept. Fair disclosure of information is provided.

> *Truth has no special time of its own.*
> *Its hour is now—always.*
>
> **Albert Schweitzer**

Unethical messages are costly.

Being ethical is enlightened self-interest. You will pay far more in time, money, and effort to repair the damage caused by false messages than truthful, forthcoming messages would cost in the first place. In addition, it is not always possible to repair the damage caused by an unethical message. Your credibility is lost, interpersonal relationships are destroyed, and your career is impaired.

ETHICS IN BUSINESS

Unethical behavior receives much publicity.

Today we frequently read in the newspaper or hear on television about unethical behavior in business and government. Insider trading, bribery, misleading advertising, misrepresentation of facts, cover-ups, and stonewalling are seemingly common.

Most people are ethical.

In fact, only a small percentage of business and professional people behave in unethical ways. Those who are unethical do not succeed in the long run, and most of them are not successful even in the short run. Millions of business transactions based on trust and honesty are successfully completed each day. Merchandise is fairly advertised, orders are received, quality products are shipped, and payment is made on time. If businesses and their customers did not relate this way, businesses could not exist.

Today, about 90 percent of large U.S. companies have codes of ethics.

The most successful businesses are managed and operated by ethical employees. Research shows that today about 90 percent of large U.S. companies have codes of ethics to help guide their employees' behavior. Many of these companies have training sessions in which the codes are discussed and procedures for assuring compliance throughout the company are explained. After a number of years of inattention, most businesses now realize the importance of a strong sense of individual and corporate values. Several examples of ethical communication will illustrate this trend.

GENERAL MOTORS

When there is a downturn in the economy or an increase in world competition, companies may find it necessary to restructure and reduce the size of their operations. Fairness requires such companies to ethically communicate their plans well in advance to employees, suppliers, local communities, and other concerned persons. General Motors, faced with continuing losses, did this in 1991 when it announced that it would close 21 plants and cut 74,000 jobs by 1995. This particular GM announcement was an ethical communication because it allowed significant lead time so that employees could attempt to find other jobs, suppliers could plan for the loss of orders, and local communities could look for new employers.

General Motors' ethical behavior in this case went beyond its announcement. The corporation offered early retirement packages and outplacement services to thousands of employees affected by the plant closings.

PERRIER GROUP

Perrier, a French mineral water company, has plants located in several countries and sells water all over the world. Perrier had an excellent reputation for purity and was used as a control in tests of other water. Perrier was faced with a crisis in 1990 when minute traces of benzene were discovered in a half-dozen bottles of its water during tests in North Carolina. Perrier's U.S. subsidiary immediately issued communications to withdraw the product from the American market. Within a week, all Perrier products were withdrawn from the market worldwide. Full-page newspaper advertisements were run in over 100 countries informing the public about the withdrawal. These prompt, ethical communications by Perrier illustrate responsible action by a large corporation.

The contamination, caused by a filter in a bottling plant, was discovered in February, and Perrier had pure water back on the market by May. It regained half its market share the first month, and shortly thereafter exceeded its previous sales. Ethical communication was not only the right thing for this company to do, it also resulted in quickly restoring public confidence in Perrier.

HERMAN MILLER, INC.

Herman Miller, manufacturer of office furniture in Zeeland, Michigan, is an environmentally concerned company. Its research director determined in 1990 that the use of Honduran mahogany and rosewood to construct its high-line, profitable "Eames" chair was helping to destroy rain forests. The company directed that the chair be discontinued. Other similar environmentally ethical decisions included the construction of an $11 million waste-to-energy heating and cooling plant and two $800,000 incinerators used to burn toxic solvents.

Exemplifying the many ethical communications related to its responsible behavior, Miller eliminated employee use of over 800,000 styrofoam cups each year and issued 5,000 mugs to employees imprinted with "On spaceship earth there are no passengers . . . only crew."

GENERAL ELECTRIC

• Employee involvement

In 1992 and 1993, General Electric faced low-wage competition from Japan, Mexico, and the southern United States. It informed its employees in the Fort Wayne, Indiana, and Louisville, Kentucky, plants that costs had to be reduced or the plants would have to close. Union employees overwhelmingly approved changes in work procedures that kept their plants open. GE ethically communicated with its constituencies—employees, suppliers, local community, etc.—in solving problems that affected them all.

GOODY'S MANUFACTURING CORPORATION

• Product tampering

In December 1992, the Federal Bureau of Investigation reported it was investigating a cyanide-poisoning death of a man who had taken Goody's headache powder. Two packets of the powder were found to have been emptied and the contents replaced by sodium cyanide. Goody's ethically announced an immediate nationwide recall of all its headache powders. The FBI later said that suicide, not criminal tampering, was responsible for the man's death.

Ann Lewallen Spencer, President of Goody's, said, "Johnson & Johnson kind of led the way for us to know how to proceed."[1]

JOHNSON & JOHNSON

Johnson & Johnson provides a classic example of an ethical communication.

A review of a classic example of the ideal way Johnson & Johnson and its managers faced an ethical situation may make it clearer how most businesses try to operate today. In 1982 an unknown criminal poisoned Tylenol capsules. This then caused the deaths of seven people. Unaware of the cause of the deaths, Johnson & Johnson managers based their ethical and decisive

A company credo guides ethical behavior.

reactions to this crisis on the company's 45-year-old credo shown in Figure 3•10. This credo is based on the belief that business is a moral undertaking for the benefit of society with responsibilities that go far beyond sales and profits.

Johnson & Johnson believes it exists to benefit society.

Communications were developed to alert the public and medical community. All Tylenol capsules were removed from stores, production was

Communication Quotes

As a leader in health care, we believe we have a special responsibility to enhance the quality of life for our customers, employees and the community at large. This responsibility goes beyond producing high quality products. It also involves conducting our business in accordance with the highest ethical standards, treating our employees sensitively and fairly, and helping to meet critical community needs.

Ralph S. Larsen, Chairman and Chief Executive Officer of Johnson & Johnson, stresses the importance of the company credo.

---

[1]"Goody's Learned from Tylenol Case in Relieving Crisis Headaches," *The Courier-Journal,* Louisville, Kentucky, February 1, 1993, p. B5.

Figure 3•10 Johnson & Johnson Company Credo

First responsibility is to customers.

Second responsibility is to employees.

Third responsibility is to communities.

Fourth responsibility is to stockholders.

Our Credo

We believe our first responsibility is to the doctors, nurses, and patients, to mothers and fathers and all others who use our products and services. In meeting their needs, everything we do must be of high quality. We must constantly strive to reduce our costs in order to maintain reasonable prices. Customers' orders must be serviced promptly and accurately. Our suppliers and distributors must have an opportunity to make a fair profit.

We are responsible to our employees, the men and women who work with us throughout the world. Everyone must be considered as an individual. We must respect their dignity and recognize their merit. They must have a sense of security in their jobs. Compensation must be fair and adequate, and working conditions clean, orderly and safe. We must be mindful of ways to help our employees fulfill their family responsibilities. Employees must feel free to make suggestions and complaints. There must be equal opportunity for employment, development and advancement for those qualified. We must provide competent management, and their actions must be just and ethical.

We are responsible to the communities in which we live and work and to the world community as well. We must be good citizens—support good works and charities and bear our fair share of taxes. We must encourage civic improvements and better health and education. We must maintain in good order the property we are privileged to use, protecting the environment and natural resources.

Our final responsibility is to our stockholders. Business must make a sound profit. We must experiment with new ideas. Research must be carried on, innovative programs developed and mistakes paid for. New equipment must be purchased, new facilities provided and new products launched. Reserves must be created to provide for adverse times. When we operate according to these principles, the stockholders should realize a fair return.

Johnson & Johnson

Printed with the permission of Johnson & Johnson, One Johnson & Johnson Plaza, New Brunswick, NJ 08933

The Tylenol crisis was handled ethically.

halted, and complete cooperation was given to the media and public health officials. Society was well served by this private company. Its managers' ethical behavior was the foundation for the comeback of Tylenol in new tamper-proof containers. Less than six months after the tragedy, Johnson & Johnson had regained 70 percent of its previous market; and Tylenol was again available to the public. The Johnson & Johnson story is a model of ethical managerial decisions and communications.

HOW YOU CAN BE ETHICAL

How can you be sure you are an ethical communicator? First, you determine exactly what ethical communication is. Second, you adopt principles or develop systems that work best for you in choosing ethical content for your messages.

WHAT ETHICAL COMMUNICATION IS

Being ethical means:
• Doing what is right

• Achieving the highest good

Being ethical means doing what is right to achieve what is good. In business communication what is right refers to the responsibility to include information in your messages that ought to be there. What is good refers to the end result of the communication. The ethical end result is to strive for the highest good attainable for all of those involved in the communication. Therefore, **ethical communication** strives for the highest good for all involved and provides information that is fully adequate for the circumstance, truthful in every sense, and not deceptive in any way.

CHOOSING ETHICAL CONTENT FOR YOUR MESSAGES

Choosing ethical content requires analytical skills.

Choosing ethical content for messages requires the same analytical and practical skills as does sound business leadership. Being ethical in your communication requires that you determine—from among all the alternatives—the right and good information in given situations. Figure 3•11, A **Poor** Example—An Unethical Message, and Figure 3•12, A **Good** Example—An Ethical Message, show contrasting choices for message content.

You will be faced with gray areas and competing interests.

In many communication situations, you will be faced with gray areas. Very few situations in the real world are entirely right or entirely wrong. There may be competing interests among your superiors, subordinates, customers, suppliers, stockholders, and others. Principles and systems that can help you make decisions on ethical content for your messages are presented following the next section, An Example of an Ethical Situation—Communicating About a Plant Closing. Examine the ethical situation, and then study the principles and systems.

AN EXAMPLE OF AN ETHICAL SITUATION—COMMUNICATING ABOUT A PLANT CLOSING

Reflect on this communication situation as you review the ethical principles and systems.

As you study the principles and systems for making ethical decisions, think about the following example: Assume that you are the manager responsible for developing and transmitting messages that will announce to various receivers that one of your corporation's plants is closing. The plant employs 3,000 people and is one of three major plants in a community of 25,000.

The receivers of your messages will include the plant's current employees, businesspersons in the communities where the plant is located and where the employees live, suppliers to the plant, local and state government officials, managers and supervisors within the corporation, the corporation's stockholders, the corporation's customers, and the general public.

Reflect on the receivers' needs in this communication situation. The employees need to know about the plant closing several months in advance so they can search for other jobs. The local community and government officials need to know so they can seek other industry to replace the lost jobs and tax income. The suppliers need to know so they can seek replacement customers. The corporate managers and stockholders want a smooth transition and need the plant to be cost effective until the day it closes. The corporation needs to maintain a positive image with its customers and the general public.

Bikes, Inc.
INTEROFFICE MEMO

Needs Work

Date: February 15, 199-

To: All Employees

From: Danielle M. Mohr, President *D.M.*

Subject: New Shift

Beginning February 17, 199-, and for an indeterminate time, there will be a newly established third shift running from 12 midnight to 8 a.m. One third of the employees in each department on the 8 a.m. to 4 p.m. shift and one third on the 4 p.m. to 12 midnight shift will be assigned to the new midnight shift. The employees who will have their shifts changed will be notified via a paycheck insert tomorrow.

> Lacks consideration of what is good for the employees.

> Lead time is unreasonably short.

> No explanation for the action is given.

Figure 3•11 A **Poor** Example—An Unet
Message

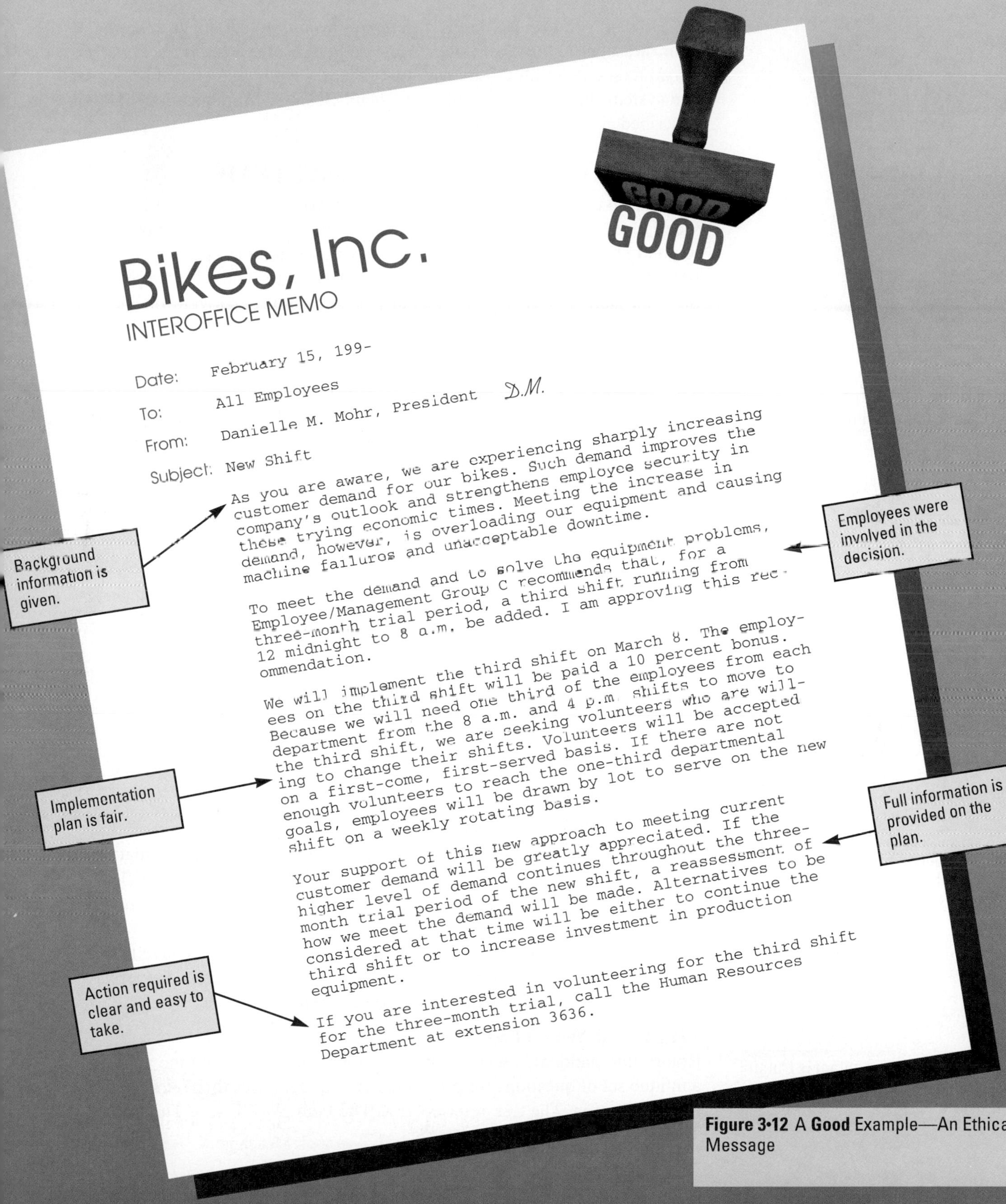

Bikes, Inc.
INTEROFFICE MEMO

GOOD

Date: February 15, 199-

To: All Employees

From: Danielle M. Mohr, President   D.M.

Subject: New Shift

As you are aware, we are experiencing sharply increasing customer demand for our bikes. Such demand improves the company's outlook and strengthens employee security in these trying economic times. Meeting the increase in demand, however, is overloading our equipment and causing machine failures and unacceptable downtime.

Background information is given.

To meet the demand and to solve the equipment problems, Employee/Management Group C recommends that, for a three-month trial period, a third shift running from 12 midnight to 8 a.m, be added. I am approving this recommendation.

Employees were involved in the decision.

We will implement the third shift on March 8. The employees on the third shift will be paid a 10 percent bonus. Because we will need one third of the employees from each department from the 8 a.m. and 4 p.m shifts to move to the third shift, we are seeking volunteers who are willing to change their shifts. Volunteers will be accepted on a first-come, first-served basis. If there are not enough volunteers to reach the one-third departmental goals, employees will be drawn by lot to serve on the new shift on a weekly rotating basis.

Implementation plan is fair.

Your support of this new approach to meeting current customer demand will be greatly appreciated. If the higher level of demand continues throughout the three-month trial period of the new shift, a reassessment of how we meet the demand will be made. Alternatives to be considered at that time will be either to continue the third shift or to increase investment in production equipment.

Full information is provided on the plan.

If you are interested in volunteering for the third shift for the three-month trial, call the Human Resources Department at extension 3636.

Action required is clear and easy to take.

Figure 3·12 A **Good** Example—An Ethical Message

How do you decide what is the *right information* that ought to be in your messages to these receivers? How do you resolve what is the *highest good* attainable for all those involved? After the following ethical principles and systems have been presented, the plant closing communication situation described above will be analyzed.

ETHICAL PRINCIPLES AND SYSTEMS

The ethical principles and systems that have worked well for others are provided in the following sections. These principles and systems can be helpful to you in being an ethical communicator. Choose among these suggestions to find the one or the combination that works best for you. Use the principles and systems you choose on a daily basis to assure that your business messages are ethical.

THE GOLDEN RULE

The Golden Rule is "Do unto others as you would have them do unto you." This simply stated, fundamental moral imperative is a helpful ethical principle for many business communicators. They analyze the communication problems facing them. Then they analyze the alternative content they could select for their messages. They choose content that will provide the full disclosure, truth, and straightforwardness that they would want to have if they were the receiver(s).

THE SOCIAL-UTILITY CONCEPT

The concept of social utility provides a higher level system than does the Golden Rule principle. To determine ethical content for a message using this approach, you first list all the alternative content from which you could choose. You then consider the positive and negative impacts of each of the alternatives on all those affected by your message. Those content alternatives that produce the greatest good and the least harm for all affected are chosen for inclusion in the message. Using this approach, self-interest is overridden by the requirement that everyone's good be counted equally.

THE UNIVERSAL-LAW CONCEPT

Using the universal-law approach, the actions and the alternatives that could be chosen for message content are categorized as good or evil for society as a whole. The question the business communicator asks is, "Would I be willing to require all others in the same circumstances to send the same kind of message I am sending?" The answer has to be yes. You would have to be willing, for the welfare and betterment of society, to establish a universal law requiring all others to behave as you are behaving.

THE FOUR-WAY TEST

Rotary International, a service club with members throughout the world, has a unique set of questions for promoting ethical decisions, behavior, and communication. The test, referred to as The Four-Way Test of Things We Think, Say or Do, is as follows:

1. Is it the TRUTH?
2. Is it FAIR to all concerned?
3. Will it build GOODWILL and BETTER FRIENDSHIPS?
4. Will it be BENEFICIAL to all concerned?

Printed with the permission of Rotary International, One Rotary Circle, Evanston, IL 60201

This test stresses truth, fairness, goodwill, good interpersonal relationships, and benefits to all concerned. It becomes a helpful, practical way for many to implement the social utility and universal law concepts.

OTHER PRACTICAL APPROACHES

Two other classic systems for making ethical decisions—one from the business world and the other from an ethics resource center—may be helpful to you.

Donald V. Seibert of the JCPenney Company suggests that the following questions be asked to assure ethical decisions:

1. Am I personally proud of this action?
2. Am I comfortable with this decision?
3. Would I feel comfortable if it were known by my associates, my friends, my family, the public in general?

"Morality Can Be Contagious," address by Donald V. Seibert, Chairman of the Board, JCPenney Company, Inc., before the Religious Heritage of America, Washington, D.C., October 9, 1978.

Examine your values, conscience, and the potential reactions of others.

The above questions help you analyze message content in three important ways. Question 1 helps you apply your personal values to the message content. Question 2 encourages you to examine your conscience. Question 3 enables you to analyze what the reactions of those other than you and your receiver would be if they were to hear or read the message. This simple, straightforward system may work well for you.

Another practical approach has been developed by Ivan Hill of the Ethics Resource Center in Washington, D.C. Hill suggests using this method to analyze situations involving ethics until you get in the habit of telling the truth and trying to be ethical. He offers these four guidelines for dealing with ethical questions:

1. Look at the community in which you live and society in general. What is the normal behavior in this society? Relate your question to this normative standard of conduct. How does it fit the social norms that reflect the ethical principles society has developed as its core guidelines?

Test your content against community standards, the law, your conscience, and a higher power.

In using this system, first, you make sure your message content meets applicable community and society standards of behavior. Second, you make sure your message is legal. Third, you apply your own personal values to the content. Fourth, you seek guidance from a higher power. This system emphasizes using acceptable standards of conduct in ethical decision making.

An excellent source of information on business ethics and ethical communication is the following nonprofit organization:

Ethics Resource Center, Inc.
1120 G Street, NW, Suite 200
Washington, DC 20005-4302
(202) 737-2258

Communication Quotes

Excellence in Ethics

Some cynics insist that business ethics is an oxymoron and that any commercial venture must emphasize survival over ethics. This belief is based on the assumption that the pressures of competition, short-term profits, and constant change create an atmosphere in which the ends justify the means.

However, evidence shows that profits don't have to be sacrificed in order to be ethical. Well-known companies such as Cadbury Schweppes, Corning Glass Works, Diamond Shamrock, Digital Equipment Corporation, IBM, Motorola, 3M, and Southwestern Bell have established reputations for strong ethics and healthy finances. Lower revenues and profits and damaged future earning capacity are the ultimate consequences of unethical behavior.

Robert H. Rosen, The Healthy Company, Los Angeles: Jeremy P. Tarcher, Inc., 1991 pp. 51-52.

AN ANALYSIS OF THE EXAMPLE ETHICAL SITUATION—COMMUNICATING ABOUT A PLANT CLOSING

Let's apply the ethical principles and systems given in the preceding section to the plant closing situation described earlier. As you will recall, you are the manager responsible for developing messages to various receivers in which you announce a plant closing.

The plant closing communication situation involves competing interests.

The ethical issues in this communication situation involve competing interests. The corporation's managers and stockholders will want a cost-effective plant closing that does not involve employee turmoil. The plant's employees will need to find other jobs. Government officials will be concerned about lost tax revenue and community development. Suppliers will be concerned about replacing lost business. The corporation's customers will need a new source of supply. Finally, the public at large will have a general interest.

When do you send the messages? What information do you include in different messages for different receivers? How do you best achieve the highest good for all those involved in the communication?

Seek the greatest good for all receivers.

The principles and systems can guide you to develop ethical messages that contain full information and provide the greatest good to all receivers. With some assumptions about detailed facts in this communication situation, here are logical, ethical decisions regarding your messages:

1. The messages will go out at the same time. They will be sent several months in advance of the closing to give the large number of people who will be hurt time to try to take corrective actions.

2. Regret will be expressed to all receivers that the plant has to be closed. A truthful, open explanation of why the action had to be taken will be given.

3. Information will be provided to the plant's employees and managers to assist them in the transition. Information will also be provided to the employees to help them find other jobs.

4. The corporation's stockholders and managers will be reminded of how the timing and content of your messages—to employees, customers, the general public, and others—best serve the corporation's long-term interests. Even if the actions do not result in increased profits, the actions ought to be taken because they are the right things to do and benefit the greatest number of people.

FINAL COMMENTS ON BEING ETHICAL

Being ethical is contagious.

Being ethical in your communication is not only essential and the right thing to do, it is also contagious. Others will follow your lead when they observe the success you experience in interpersonal relationships and in your career. All will benefit from being ethical.

ASSURING LEGALITY

Learn the legal requirements that relate to your work.

You and your organization could be sued or prosecuted if you violate the law in your business messages. Thousands or even millions of dollars could be lost. Prison terms might have to be served. To assure the legality of your written or oral messages, you must be aware of the laws, court decisions, and administrative regulations that apply to those messages. Ignorance of the law and related information does not excuse violators.

If you are considering content for a message and are not sure about its legality, you should consult with an attorney or other competent authority. Many companies have attorneys who are available to employees. In addition, some company officials—personnel officers, purchasing agents, and others—have specialized knowledge of legal requirements in their areas of responsibility.

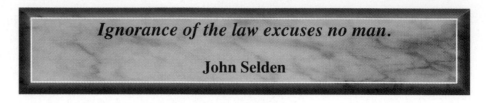

> *Ignorance of the law excuses no man.*
>
> **John Selden**

A review of some of the most important legal considerations will assist you in assuring the legality of your messages.

CONTRACT COMMUNICATION

The oral and written communication with the customers of your company must meet the requirements of several laws. Among the most important forms of communication is the contract.

PLAIN ENGLISH LAWS

Plain English laws are common.

Several states have "plain English laws" requiring that contracts be written so consumers can understand them. Some states specify readability levels, average number of syllables per word, layout, size of print, and many other content details. These laws require careful analysis of a contract's content. Other states have more general guidelines such as requiring contracts to contain understandable words, short sentences, and short paragraphs. If the principles of business communication given in Chapter 2 are followed, the requirements of plain English laws would be met.

WARRANTIES AND GUARANTEES

Warranties can be express or implied.

The Uniform Commercial Code, the Consumer Product Warranty Act, the Federal Trade Commission Improvement Act, and similar legislation cover express warranties (promises made willingly by the seller) and implied warranties (promises created by law). An example of an express warranty is a manufacturer's written promise to replace a product during the first year if it proves defective due to quality of construction or materials. An example of an implied warranty provided by law is that the product must be satisfactory for the purpose intended. Promises to consumers and others can be made orally or in writing, so be sure you only warrant to the extent you intend.

CREDIT AND COLLECTION COMMUNICATION

Many state and federal laws specify the responsibilities of businesses in issuing credit and collecting debts. Here are some of the more important federal laws.

Businesspersons must be sure they use plain English in their contracts.

EQUAL CREDIT OPPORTUNITY ACT

Credit must be equally available.

This law requires that credit be equally available to all creditworthy customers. It also covers how credit worthiness is determined. The content of credit applications and any oral questioning of credit applicants must not include references to race, color, religion, or national origin. Credit decisions cannot be based on age, marital status, or future personal plans. Credit refusals must be in writing.

FAIR CREDIT BILLING ACT

This law protects credit card users against false charges made to their accounts. The act specifies in detail those procedures that consumers and creditors must follow to resolve problems.

Billing and collection procedures must be specific.

FAIR DEBT COLLECTION ACT

This law specifies in detail what bill collectors can and cannot do. What you can and cannot say, how many times you may call the debtor, and to whom you may write (not relatives or employers) are among the requirements included.

FEDERAL TRUTH-IN-LENDING ACT

Credit terms must be clear.

Requirements for full disclosure of credit terms to consumers are stated in this law. Lenders and creditors must clearly disclose service charges, finance charges, and the effective annual interest rate. How the terms and conditions of loans must be specified—such as number of payments and due dates of payments—is covered in this law. It also provides that the borrower has the right to cancel within three business days after signing the contract.

EMPLOYMENT COMMUNICATION

Managers, supervisors, and employees need to know the legal requirements affecting employment communication. Much of what can and cannot be said or written about employees is specified in the following laws.

THE CIVIL RIGHTS ACT

This law and its amendments prohibit discrimination in employment. Hiring, firing, compensation, and other conditions of employment cannot be based on race, color, religion, gender, or national origin. This act, first passed in 1964 and since amended, is landmark legislation: every business communicator should be aware of its requirements. Affirmative action programs have evolved from the Civil Rights Act, the Equal Employment Opportunity Act, and other extensive federal, state, and local employment regulations.

LABOR-MANAGEMENT RELATIONS ACT

Communications between managers and workers, particularly concerning unions, are guided by this law. Details regarding the implementation of this law are provided by the National Labor Relations Board.

THE PRIVACY ACT

This law gives employees access to information about themselves. It also limits the use of personnel information to the purpose for which it was collected. For example, it is important when serving as a reference that you respond only to specific requests that have been approved by the employee. Further, your comments should relate only to documented job performance. Any reference should be objective, given in good faith, and without malice.

AMERICANS WITH DISABILITIES ACT

This 1990 act, covering some 43 million Americans with disabilities, is referred to as the most important employment legislation since Title VII of the Civil Rights Act. This act makes it unlawful to discriminate against disabled individuals in regard to hiring, firing, compensation, training, and advancement. Communicators must be aware of language that the courts might rule discriminatory, such as job descriptions and advertisements calling for *high energy level, able bodied, etc*. Both physical and mental disabilities are covered by the law. Persons with disabilities are qualified applicants and employees if they "can perform the essential functions of the job." If so, employers must reasonably accommodate their disabilities.

COPYRIGHT AND FAIR-USE COMMUNICATION

Copyright laws vary throughout the world, and managers must be aware of the laws within the country where they are communicating. In the United States the copyright laws, with limited exceptions, prohibit copying material without the owner's permission. The related fair-use doctrine permits the making of single copies for noncommercial purposes. Material does not have to be registered with the U.S. Copyright Office to be copyrighted.

Copyright laws protect the originators' interests in their ideas, writings, and other creations. You may have to obtain permission to use the information, and you will be required to give credit to the originator as the source. In addition, the originator may require you to pay a fee for its use. Even if the information is excluded from the coverage of the copyright laws, ethical standards require that you give credit to the originator as the source. (How to give credit to a source is shown on page 462 in Chapter 16.)

Discrimination in employment communication is illegal.

Communications between labor and management must meet legal requirements.

Information about employees must be kept private.

Disabled persons must be treated fairly.

Copyright laws prohibit copying most materials.

The fair-use doctrine permits limited copying.

Secure permission for sources; give them credit.

You do not have to cite a source for information that is general knowledge such as "communicators should be sure their messages are ethical and legal." You can say that on your own even though you might have read it in this book or in some other publication. Copyright laws and the fair-use doctrine are complex. Most libraries have the material published by the copyright office on these topics. Business communicators must make themselves aware of the laws and guidelines that apply to their messages.

Using others' materials without giving credit is called *plagiarism* or *paraphrasing,* depending on the manner in which the material is used. These two terms are defined as follows:

- **Plagiarism** means stealing and using someone else's ideas or words as your own without giving the other person(s) credit as the source.
- **Paraphrasing** means restating (in your own words) and using the ideas belonging to another without giving the other person(s) credit as the source.

Plagiarism and paraphrasing can cause communicators serious legal and ethical problems. Avoid these problems (1) by understanding and obeying the copyright laws, (2) by giving credit to others when using their ideas or words, or (3) by not using others' ideas and words.

OTHER INTERPERSONAL COMMUNICATION

Common law and other legislation cover such important legal considerations as defamation and fraud.

DEFAMATION

The law does not permit you to make statements that injure the reputation or character of another person. Such statements, called *defamation,* are libelous (written) or slanderous (oral). To be considered defamation, the statements must be false, made to or read by a third person, and cause some injury. True statements can be considered defamation if they are made with the intent of harming the other person.

FRAUD

Lying that causes another person monetary damage is called *fraud*. Fraud exists when these conditions are proven: (1) a communicator misrepresents or conceals a material fact, (2) the misrepresentation was made knowingly or with a reckless disregard for the truth, (3) the misrepresentation was made with the intent to deceive, (4) the deceived person relied on the false statement, and (5) monetary damage was incurred by the deceived person. Fraud can be committed by words or conduct and includes false advertising and false endorsement of products or services.

USING UNBIASED LANGUAGE

The use of unbiased language is a final and important consideration in the composition of business messages. Fair and balanced treatment of all individuals regardless of race, gender, culture, age, ability, religion, or

Plagiarism is stealing and using another's ideas.

Paraphrasing is restating another's words.

Libel and slander are statements that injure a reputation.

Fraud is lying that causes another person monetary damage.

Message analysis includes assuring unbiased language for fair and balanced treatment of all individuals.

socioeconomic status is essential in a democracy. Such treatment is vital to the maintenance of favorable human relationships.

You will want to avoid all words that have unfavorable denotations or connotations in their reflection on any individuals. The use of such language will offend not only those to whom the references are made but also many other persons. Respect for the dignity and worth of all persons is compatible with being a responsible citizen. To increase your effectiveness as a business communicator, analyze your messages to eliminate any biased language.

AVOID GENDER-BIASED LANGUAGE

Using unbiased gender language is a special challenge because of the structure of the English language. The English language implies stereotyping of males and females because of (1) the generic use of masculine singular pronouns—pronouns used to represent both men and women; (2) the generic use of the word *man*; (3) the existence of masculine marker words; and (4) the use of certain words, phrases, and constructions that involve stereotyping. Fortunately, the structure of our language does not stereotype individuals on the basis of race, age, religion, etc.

Some English language listeners and readers, however, tend to subconsciously picture a male when words such as *man, he,* or *chairman* are used. This is true even though such words are used generically—used to represent both men and women. These images should be avoided in your business messages. The examples that follow suggest that many alternatives to gender stereotyping are available.

Biased	Unbiased
businessman	businessperson, business executive, manager
chairman	chairperson, moderator, chair, group leader,
cameraman	camera operator
foreman	supervisor
lady or female doctor	doctor
The student should determine which principle of business communication gives him the most difficulty and then practice using it.	The student should determine which principle of business communication gives the most difficulty and then practice using it.
When an individual travels by plane, he is able to work en route.	When individuals travel by plane, they are able to work en route.
If he is not sure he wants what buying, he should not buy it.	If you are not sure you want what you are buying, you should not buy it.

Sidebar notes:

Using biased language offends not only those referred to but also many others.

The English language structure is biased as to gender stereotyping.

Listeners and readers tend to picture a male when *man, he,* or *chairman* is used.

You should avoid these male-only images.

Biased	Unbiased, *Continued*
the ladies and the men	the women and the men, the ladies and the gentlemen

Gentlemen:
  Dear Sirs:
  (letter salutations)
	Ladies and Gentlemen: (or avoid salutation by using the Simplified Block Letter style shown in Chapter 10)

Avoid Other-Biased Language

Avoid negative stereotypes.

To be sure that you treat persons of different races and cultures in a bias-free manner, avoid all negative stereotypes of any group. Instead of using a name that may have unfavorable connotations, refer to groups by the name they prefer. For example, African-Americans prefer the name *African-American* to *Negro, black, colored,* or other terms used years ago. Many Hispanics prefer *Hispanic* to *Chicano* or *Mexican-American*.

Terms can be omitted to achieve unbiased language.

Avoid emphasizing religion or race when it is not essential to the main point of the message. For example, leave out the terms in italics in the following two sentences: "The *Jewish* investor from New York City funded the construction of the regional mall." "The *white* teacher spoke to the inner-city youth."

Substitute unbiased language for biased language.

To avoid biased language when referring to age, for example, use *older person* or *senior citizen* instead of *elderly person* or *old man* or *old woman*. When referring to persons with disabilities, use people-first language and focus on the person, not the disability. Use *person with AIDS* instead of *AIDS patient* and *person with mental illness* instead of a *mentally ill woman (or man)*.

Do not imply that people are less or more because of their status.

Do not use any language that belittles, offends, embarrasses, or denigrates other persons. Do not imply that a person of a different status (race, gender, religion, culture, age, socioeconomic level, physical or mental condition) is inferior simply because he or she is of that status. Do not imply by your language that a person of another status is rigid, lazy, stupid, slow, devious, shrewd, dishonest, fanatical, or cold. In addition, do not attribute superior qualities to persons of a certain status.

Conclusion

You can develop effective business messages by using the planning and composing process, controlling vocabulary level, being ethical, assuring legality, and using unbiased language.

You can develop effective business messages by following the process and guidelines outlined in this chapter. The process for planning and composing business messages—determine the purposes, analyze the receiver, and compose the content—is a proven approach. The recommendations for determining vocabulary level, being ethical, assuring legality, and using unbiased language can assist you further in developing business messages that communicate effectively with your receiver.

1. Describe how to analyze the communication situation.

2. Explain how to establish primary and secondary purposes of a business message.

3. Explain how to analyze the receiver for the you–viewpoint.

4. When you have multiple receivers of the same message—for example, a speech to a group—how do you analyze the receivers for the you–viewpoint?

5. Explain how you can select the correct type of message.

6. When should you use the direct plan, and when should you use the indirect plan for messages?

7. Describe how to brainstorm for ideas to include in a message.

8. Discuss the evaluation and sequencing of ideas for a message.

9. Discuss editing and revising in the composition of business messages.

10. Explain how to proofread a message.

11. Define collaborative writing; tell when it would be appropriate to write a message collaboratively.

12. What are the factors necessary for a collaborative writing effort to be successful?

13. Explain how readability formulas can be of value in developing business messages.

14. Discuss the status of ethics in business today.

15. Discuss what ethical communication is.

16. Describe how you could use the ethical principles and systems given in this chapter in choosing ethical content for your business messages.

17. Describe (a) the social utility concept and (b) the universal-law concept.

18. Explain how you can assure the legality of your messages.

19. Describe what is meant by (a) plagiarism and (b) paraphrasing.

20. Explain how you can use alternative wording to assure unbiased language in business messages. Give an example.

APPLICATION EXERCISES

T Text 3A

1. Read the following case problem and follow the instructions for planning and composing the required business message.

For years Raymond Bowling has been a regular mail-order customer of Houghton's Big Man's Clothing. Recently, he became quite angry at Houghton's and told them so. He had requested that a pair of hiking shoes be specially ordered for him (they were not a standard catalog item). Lesley Jones, a new order clerk, trying to be efficient, promptly dropped a handwritten postcard to him saying, "The shoes you want are not available; they are not in the catalog." The clerk did not know that Houghton's had a policy of gladly ordering special items for an additional fee. Mr. Bowling wrote to you, Houghton's marketing manager, and said, "I have spent over $5,000 with you in the past ten years. If you have quit special ordering, you have just lost a good customer! In fact, you will never hear from me again!"

a. Analyze this communication situation. What should be the primary and secondary purposes for your response to Mr. Bowling? What would be included in your content outline?

b. Analyze the receiver, Raymond Bowling, in the four areas of knowledge, interests, opinions, and emotional state.

c. Specify the type of message—written or oral—that you would send to Mr. Bowling. Give reasons for your selection.

d. Select the organizational plan you would use for Mr. Bowling's message and tell why.

e. Edit, proofread, and rewrite the following message to Mr. Bowling.

Dear Mr. Boling:

I am glad to tell you your past business is very much appreciated and I am glad to tell you that Houghton's is steel glad to order special for you. Lesley Jones, a new order clerk, didn't no about our policy and got carried away. She knows now looks forward to getting your next order. The shoes you wanted have been ordered and you can get them sent to you in two weeks. Write us another letter if you still want them. Thank you for your many years of association with Houghton's.

2. Briefly describe (a) two situations in which you would use oral messages, and (b) two situations in which you would use written messages.

3. Interview a manager and ask the following questions:

a. When you have to communicate with a person (or persons), how do you decide whether to send a written message or an oral message?

b. In what communication situations do you use the direct plan (getting directly to the main point in your opening)?

c. In what communication situations do you use the indirect plan (making comments in the first part of the message that prepare your receiver for the main point)?

d. How much editing and revising of your messages do you do?

e. Who proofreads the final versions of your messages?

Report your findings to the class.

4. Briefly describe (a) five situations in which you would use the direct plan for messages, and (b) five situations in which you would use the indirect plan for messages.

5. Interview a person of another culture. Describe for the interviewee the direct and indirect plans for organizing messages as they are explained in this chapter. Ask the interviewee the following questions:

a. Which organizational plan is used for most messages in his or her culture?

b. What types of messages use the direct plan?

c. What types of messages use the indirect plan?

Report your findings to the class.

6. Assume that you are writing a memo to your instructor to recommend that student oral reports be videotaped. List four ideas for content for this memo in a logical sequence for an indirect plan.

7. Edit and revise the following message so that it communicates more clearly and concisely to a middle-level American receiver:

It is excruciatingly clear that in order to ascend to the new heights of sales to achieve the new sales quotas the salesmen and saleswomen must dramatically and definitely increase their efforts. Here are the things they must do whenever: (a) Get out in the field more of the time (b) practice, practice, practice and improve their presentations that they make. This will ultimately result in more—more commissions for them and more income over expenses, or profit, for the company organization.

8. Report to the class an actual example from business of each of the following: (a) ethical behavior and (b) unethical behavior. Do not use the examples in this chapter.

9. Form teams to brainstorm for ethical content of messages in each of the following communication situations:

a. A department manager is being denied a budget request important to the department's success.

b. An employee who does not have the aptitude for the work is being fired.

c. A company is developing an advertisement for its newly discovered hair restorer that works for some bald people but not all.

10. Bring to class an advertisement with content that appears to be unethical—not fully truthful or not in the best interests of consumers.

Explain why you think the advertisement is unethical.

11. Over a 48-hour period, record all reports of illegal business communication that you find in newspapers or magazines or hear on television or radio. Report your findings to the class.

12. Get together with five or six other students in your class and discuss the topic, "Businesses are more ethical today than they were ten years ago." Appoint one student in your group to report a summary of the group's discussion to the class.

13. Change the language in the following sentences so that it is unbiased as to race, gender, culture, age, or disability, as appropriate.

a. Helen is confined to a wheelchair. (*Hint:* Avoid emphasizing the limitations of the disability.)

b. Gilbert is the black man standing by the water fountain. (*Hint:* Avoid emphasizing race when it is not essential to the main point of the message.)

c. The exercise program was developed for old people. (*Hint:* Avoid unflattering language.)

d. As you know, Italians tend to be emotional. (*Hint:* Avoid implying that persons have limitations because of their culture.)

e. This is obviously man's work. (*Hint:* Avoid language that is demeaning, patronizing, or limiting.)

MESSAGE ANALYSIS

Text 3B

Using what you have learned in this chapter, edit and revise the following letter to assure that it is accurate, ethical, legal, and unbiased. Also, be sure that the vocabulary is appropriate for a person who is a high school graduate.

The balance on you're credit card has exceded it's limit, and you cannot make any more purchases at this time. The waye you can correct you're problematic situation is to supply aditional information to us to show that youhave an aditional ability to pay based on increased earning power. Other wise, once you have payed the balance down below it's limit, you can feel free to start using the card again for convient, easy-charge shopping.

We might have to report you're attempt to the authorities if you try to buy above you're limit again. I know that over charging on a credit card is probably not really a problem for someone whom live in a rich suburb of Chicago.

You're business is greatley appreciated! We are glad you choose AmericaFirst for you're credit card. For your convient in replying, enclose is a postage-payed, addressed form. Let us know if you're annual salrey has increased you're affluence by at least 10 percent form the $18,000 that you reported to us at the time of your application two years ago.

CHAPTER 4

Communication Technologies and Techniques

Learning Objectives

Your learning objectives for this chapter include the following:

- To demonstrate understanding of communication technology by defining terms related to computing
- To explain how technology can be used to improve business communication
- To identify message situations as routine and/or repetitive and recommend preparation and distribution methods

Written and oral communication are essential in business; they are also expensive. Labor, materials, and postage affect the cost of written communication. Labor, equipment, lodging, and transportation contribute to the cost of oral communication.

Technology can help reduce the cost of communicating.

To reduce communication costs and increase worker productivity, businesses are turning to technology. Because the technology used in business communication is related to computers, you must be familiar with the vocabulary of computer technology. Figure 4•1 contains terms commonly used in discussing computer technology; other terms are included within the text of this chapter.

USING TECHNOLOGY TO STREAMLINE WRITTEN COMMUNICATION

To recognize the impact that technology can have on reducing correspondence costs, a business communicator must understand the document cycle. The cycle has six steps: (1) creation; (2) production; (3) reproduction; (4) distribution; (5) filing, storage, and retrieval; and (6) destruction. Each step takes time; the longer the time, the higher the cost.

The document cycle has six steps.

Document creation begins when a businessperson dictates or keys a document. Production occurs when a support staff member transcribes the dictation or formats and edits the document. He or she may use a typewriter or a computer with word processing software to accomplish this task. The production portion of the cycle is repeated partially or totally every time the document is revised. Once the writer approves the format, content, and mechanics of the document, it is reproduced. Photocopiers are generally used for this purpose. Distribution occurs when the document is sent to the receiver by using a messenger (internal distribution), a computer network (internal or external distribution), or the postal service (external distribution). Copies of the document are then filed for later use and for eventual destruction in accordance with the company's records retention policy.

STREAMLINING INPUT

Input is the process of transferring images (numbers, letters, symbols, drawings, etc.) to a computer. Devices

---

Communication Notes

One Step Closer to the Paperless World

The TV in your hotel room may soon be a powerful business tool. By mid-1994, hotels that have Spectradyne pay-per-view movies will be able to deliver faxes to their guests via TV sets.

A new digital video network, the product of Spectradyne and Electronic Data Systems, will make the service a reality in over 600,000 hotel rooms. A blinking light on the telephone or TV will signal that a fax is waiting. Guests will be able to press a button on the TV remote control to read the fax and, if they wish, order a printout to be picked up at the front desk. Faxes can also be deleted using the remote.

Figure 4·1 Technology
Vocabulary

BPS	Bits per second. Used when referring to storage and retrieval speed.
baud rate	The speed at which a modem can transmit data; 2400 BPS is a standard baud rate, and 9600 BPS is a fast baud rate.
bit	Binary digit, 0 or 1, used for data representation.
byte	A group of bits, usually 8, used to represent a character.
cache	An area of memory where frequently accessed instructions are stored to achieve greater processing speed.
CD-ROM	Compact disk with read-only memory. A laser disk that can be read repeatedly but written to only once.
chip	An integrated circuit (electronic circuit) embedded in a nonconducting material such as silicon.
CPS	Characters per second. Used when referring to the speed at which printers and other output devices operate.
cursor	Symbol (blinking line, arrow, box, or other symbol) used to indicate where the next character that is keyed will be displayed.
DOS	Disk operating system. Command instructions for IBM and IBM-compatible microcomputers.
GIGO	Garbage in, garbage out. A reminder that computer output is only as valid and meaningful as the data and processes used to create it.
K	Kilobyte; 1024 bytes. Used when referring to memory or disk capacity.
MB or meg	Megabyte; approximately 1 million bytes. Used when referring to memory or disk capacity.
MHz	Megahertz; 1 million cycles (or pulses) per second. Used to refer to the speed at which computers perform operations.
menu	Monitor-displayed listing of options available.
modem	Short for modulator/demodulator. Device used to connect a computer to a telephone line so that data can be sent and received. Modems may be either internal or external.
OCR	Optical character recognition. Using a light source to read and convert characters to electrical signals to be sent to the central processing unit (CPU).
port	A connector used to attach input/output devices to a computer. Ports may be parallel (1 character at a time) or serial (1 bit at a time).
ppm	Pages per minute. Term used to refer to speed of output devices such as laser printers.
pps	Pages per second. Term used to refer to output rate of high-speed printers.
RAM	Random access memory. Memory that can be written to or read from by the user.
ROM	Read-only memory. Computer memory on which instructions are stored permanently.
VDT	Video display terminal; another name for a screen or monitor.
virus	Destructive or intrusive instructions embedded within computer programs. The virus is designed to spread by copying itself onto other program disks.
WYSIWYG	What you see is what you get. Desirable feature of word processing and desktop publishing software that allows users to see on their monitors exactly what will be printed as output.

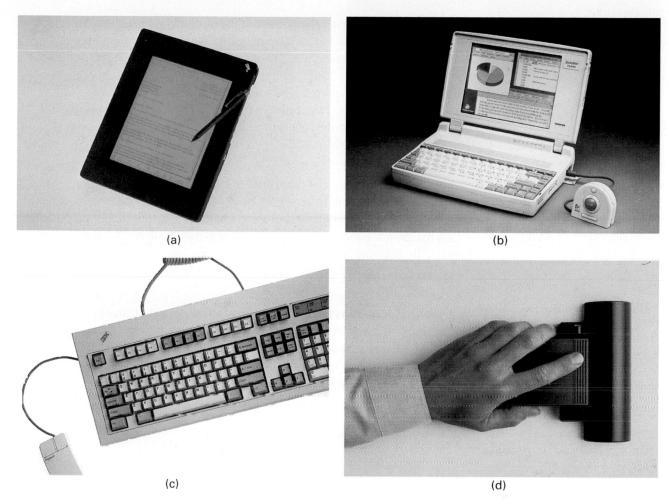

Input Devices: (a) Pen-based Portable Computer; (b) Laptop and Trackball; (c) Mouse and Keyboard; (d) Hand-held Scanner.

currently being used to input to a computer include the keyboard, mouse, trackball, touchscreen, pen, microphone, fax, and scanner.

THE KEYBOARD

Keyboards are the most common input devices.

The most widely used input device is the keyboard. The standard typewriter keyboard (named *qwerty*—the key sequence in the upper left row of alphabetic characters) doesn't have enough keys to accommodate the extensive number of commands computers use. Therefore, keyboards have been expanded to include function keys (F1, F2, Esc, Ctrl, Alt, etc.), cursor keys (arrows), and a numeric key pad. Some keys, if programmed, can perform functions other than those printed on them. Such programming can be useful when international or mathematical character sets are needed.

THE MOUSE

A mouse is a hand-held pointer.

Another item that is part of today's microcomputer systems is a hand-held pointing device called a **mouse.** The standard mouse has two buttons. To make the mouse feed information or issue commands, users click one of the buttons after positioning the pointer at the appropriate place on the screen. A mouse may be wired to a computer or be battery powered and use infrared light to transmit data. The mouse is ideal for users who don't key, key slowly, or use the "hunt-and-peck" method of keying, It is also extremely useful when using software that runs under a Windows environment (discussed later in this chapter). Some users, however, have difficulty adjusting to the fact that a slight hand movement can cause a large on-screen pointer movement.

THE TRACKBALL

Another pointing device is the **trackball.** Users roll a stationary ball with the tips of their fingers to move the pointer on the screen. The advantage of a trackball over a mouse is that the trackball can operate in a fixed position. This makes it a good device when work space is limited. The trackball is especially popular among portable computer users.

Trackballs are stationary.

THE TOUCHSCREEN

A user may make choices and enter data by touching his or her fingertip to a sensitized **touchscreen.** Fingertip position is the key. Libraries have made good use of these systems to help patrons locate materials. Restaurants and retail businesses with limited product lines may also use touchscreens. A fast-food restaurant clerk might enter a customer's food choice by pressing an icon (symbol) of a hamburger; if condiments are desired, icons of a ketchup bottle or an onion might be touched.

Input may be made by touching a sensitized screen.

THE PEN

A special pen (stylus) and tablet may be used to capture images and transfer them to a computer. In older systems, light pens were used; these systems worked only with cathode ray tubes (CRTs). Today, **pens** have transmitters and tablets have receivers (the opposite may also occur). Although handwriting recognition continues to be a problem, pen systems have potential for use in industries such as sales, insurance, and transportation.

Special pens are used to write on sensitized screens.

THE MICROPHONE

Microphones are used as part of voice input devices. These devices compare the patterns produced by the speaker's voice to a set of prerecorded patterns. If the patterns match, the computer accepts the words.

Voice is an emerging input device.

THE FAX

Facsimile (fax) transfer, generally associated with sending and receiving hardcopy documents, is becoming a popular method of generating input to computers. The introduction of fax modems has made the change possible. Computers with fax modems can receive transmissions directly; no paper copy is created.

Fax modems enable computers to send and receive messages.

THE SCANNER

The **scanner,** an optical character recognition (OCR) device, enables communicators to transfer images from paper to a computer. Doing so eliminates the need to rekey documents. Once stored on the computer, the documents can be edited, revised, or manipulated using whatever software is appropriate.

Scanners use optical character recognition.

Scanners may be either desktop or hand-held. With desktop units, a page of information is placed on the glass plate of the scanner. With a hand-held unit, the operator moves the scanner across the document; a barcode reader is a hand-held scanner.

Barcode readers are hand-held scanners.

STREAMLINING PROCESS

In today's dynamic business world, communicating clearly and quickly is essential. Computer hardware and software help business communicators streamline the message creation process.

HARDWARE

In the broadest sense, computer **hardware** consists of the physical elements necessary to perform computing. The most basic piece of hardware is the central processing unit (CPU)—the circuitry that connects components for storage, manipulation, and retrieval of data. The CPU may be a large, powerful unit called a **mainframe computer,** or it may be a smaller but still powerful unit called a *microcomputer*. Because microcomputers are so widely used in business, they will be the focus of the discussion in this chapter.

Computers may be either mainframes or micros.

The CPU is housed in a case with one or more **drives**—devices that allow computers to read from or write data to disks or diskettes. A monitor, an input device, and an output device complete the most common microcomputer system.

Microcomputers. **Microcomputers** are available in three styles—desktop, laptop, and notebook. Each style derives its name from its size and weight. Desktop computers usually consist of three separate pieces of equipment: CPU, monitor, and keyboard. Laptop computers contain the CPU, monitor, and keyboard in one unit and are small and light enough to be used while placed on a person's lap. Notebook computers are also one-piece units but are even smaller than laptops and can fit into a briefcase. Both laptop and notebook computers have broad appeal among business travelers. Both can be operated using battery power or AC current. Both can be linked to (docked with) desktop units. Docking allows users to take advantage of the larger monitors, keyboards, and storage capacity of desktop models.

Laptop and notebook computers are portable.

Monitors. A **monitor** is a screen on which an operator views what has been entered. Desktop microcomputers typically use cathode ray tube (CRT) monitors; laptop and notebook computers typically use liquid crystal display (LCD) monitors. All three microcomputer types are available with either monochrome (one-color) or full-color monitors. **Resolution** (image clarity) will vary with the type of monitor.

Monitors vary in size and resolution.

SOFTWARE

Software is the name for the instructions that make computers do what users want. Business communicators frequently use the following types of software: word processing, document analysis, desktop publishing, graphics, spreadsheet, database, utility, and Windows. Word processing, document analysis, and desktop publishing software are discussed in detail in this chapter; spreadsheet, database, utility, and Windows software are given less attention. Graphics software is discussed in Chapter 16.

Software is a set of instructions.

Word Processing Software. **Word processing software** is the software business communicators use most often. Keyed characters are displayed on a monitor. Errors in content and mechanics can be corrected without rekeying the entire document. Two common features of microcomputer word processing software that benefit business writers are the thesaurus and the spell checker.

A **software thesaurus** is the computer version of the word-choice book that writers use to bring variety to their word choice. The user may highlight a word within a document or key a new word. The computer searches for and displays alternatives on the screen. The user may reject all alternatives, select one, or direct the computer to search for substitutes for one of the alternatives.

By using a **spell checker,** a writer can direct the computer to match each word in a document against words contained in the word processing software dictionary. If a word in the document is not in the dictionary, the word is highlighted, and a list of possible alternatives is displayed. The user may choose one of the alternatives, reject all the alternatives, or edit the highlighted word. Most word processing software packages allow the user to add words to a dictionary or to create an additional dictionary.

Using a spell checker does not eliminate the need for proofreading. Spell checkers do not detect content errors. Keying or word-choice errors such as using *then* for *than, of* for *if,* or *you* for *your* will go unnoticed.

Document Analysis Software. **Document analysis software** programs, often called *style checkers*, use artificial intelligence to help writers improve the quality of their messages. Style checkers detect possible errors in grammar, punctuation, spelling, capitalization, abbreviation, and number display. They also detect possible violations of the principles of business communication, such as the use of weak words or passive voice. Possible errors and violations are highlighted, and corrections are suggested. Summary statistics for items such as readability and tone are presented in numeric and graphic form.

Because of the complexity of the English language and the nature of software programs, some items identified by document analysis software are actually correct. The writer must decide whether a change is needed and which, if any, of the suggested alternatives is most appropriate. In addition, the creator of the message must verify that the content of the message is accurate. The software doesn't know if $15 should be $51 or if May 12 should be May 19.

Document analysis software is improving. Until the software is perfected, however, message creators must remember that software is not a replacement for good writing skills—it is a powerful supplement to them.

Desktop Publishing Software. When a computer using **desktop publishing software** is linked to a laser printer, users have the tools needed to produce newsletters, brochures, reports, and a variety of other business messages with the quality of a professionally typeset document. Text may be organized into columns of varying length and width. Type styles and type sizes may be varied within or among pages. Charts, graphs, or clip-art illustrations can be used to enhance text; photographs can also be

---

Two popular word processing features are:

• computerized thesaurus

• spell checker

Spell checkers do not eliminate proofreading.

Document analysis software helps writers check for errors in:
• grammar
• punctuation
• spelling
• style

Document analysis software supplements good writing skills.

With desktop publishing, professional quality documents can be created "in-house."

incorporated. Advanced word processing software programs currently offer some desktop publishing features.

Desktop publishing and word processing are merging.

Spreadsheet Software. Writers who need to incorporate financial data or other types of numeric calculations into their text will find **spreadsheet software** helpful. Data are entered into locations called cells. Mathematical formulas can then be applied to the cells. Tables, graphs, and charts can be created using this type of software. Most word processing and desktop publishing packages allow users to bring in (import) documents created on compatible spreadsheet software packages.

Spreadsheet software is useful when doing calculations.

Database Software. **Database software** is designed to organize data. Individual data elements (e.g., names, addresses, prices, quantities) are entered into the computer. Users may then select and group the elements having desired features. For example, select those students whose GPA is greater than or equal to 2.50 and list them in alphabetical order by the first letter of their last names. The lists, tables, and other documents created using database software may be incorporated into documents created using word processing or desktop publishing software.

Database software helps users select and group data.

Utility Software. **Utility software** is used to perform maintenance tasks associated with computer use. These tasks include diagnosing problems, backing up and restoring data, converting files from one storage medium to another, detecting and eliminating viruses, and coding/decoding files to protect them from access by unauthorized users. Utility software programs may be furnished by the computer manufacturer or purchased through independent companies.

Utility software is used to do maintenance tasks.

Windows Software. Designed to maximize productivity, **Windows software** allows several applications to run at the same time and provides a simple method of exchanging information between applications. This software has made it easier to use computers and to do applications on them. Windows (framed regions on the monitor) and icons (symbols) guide users through various operations. Windows of varying sizes and shapes can be on the screen at the same time. A keyboard may be used with Windows software, but greater efficiency is achieved when a mouse is used.

Windows show activity in several applications at once.

Communication Notes

Questions? Call 1-900-PAY A FEE

If you have ever called a toll-free number for help with a computer software problem, your life is about to change. Most of the major software companies are eliminating unlimited support on at least some of their products and introducing pay-as-you-go plans.

Although the plans vary from company to company, $2 per minute seems to be the going rate. Users who anticipate needing a great deal of assistance may choose to pay an annual fee for unlimited calls. Unlimited-use fees range from $129 to $20,000 per year, with the larger fees being assessed to big businesses. In some cases, users are given a 90-day grace period during which they may receive personalized assistance without charge.

Excerpted from Walter S. Mossberg, "Talk is Cheap? Not If You're Calling for Software Support." The Wall Street Journal, 14 October 1993, B1.

STREAMLINING OUTPUT

The most common computer output device used by business communicators is the printer. Voice, video, and microform output are also possible.

PRINTERS

Printers come in two basic types, impact and nonimpact. Each type has advantages and disadvantages.

Impact Printers. **Impact printers** create images by striking an inked ribbon that then makes contact with paper. Dot matrix printers and electronic typewriters are two examples of impact printers. Dot matrix printers may be able to print graphics; electronic typewriters are unlikely to be able to do so. The advantage of impact printers is that they are inexpensive; the primary disadvantage is that they are noisy. Another disadvantage is speed. Electronic typewriters produce letter-quality type slowly. Dot matrix printers produce draft-quality type fairly quickly but operate slowly when producing "near letter-quality" type.

Nonimpact Printers. **Nonimpact printers** come in three styles. Thermal printers use heat to create images; special paper is required. Ink jet printers spray ink onto paper. Laser printers use light beams to record images on a light-sensitive drum; the images are then transferred to paper using a special toner. Print quality varies among the three printer styles. The poorest quality is produced by thermal printers; the highest quality is produced by laser printers. High speed and quiet operation are advantages of nonimpact printers; purchase price and supply costs are disadvantages.

VOICE OUTPUT

Speech synthesizers are used to generate **voice output.** Early synthesizers created output that sounded artificial. Today's units, however, produce voices similar to those of humans. Voice output has several business applications. Telephone companies use it to respond to directory assistance inquiries, telemarketers use it to sell their products, and auto manufacturers use it to warn drivers that the speed limit has been exceeded. Computers for those with visual impairments are still another application.

VIDEO OUTPUT

Graphics, sound, and movement have been merged to produce computer **video output.** As a result, still photographs, graphs, and diagrams can be replaced by music, voice, sound effects, and full-action video clips. The video is captured from VCRs, camcorders, or CD players and stored in a microcomputer. Once retrieved from storage, the video can be edited to create attention-getting, informative output. Training is a natural application for this technology; sales presentations are another possibility.

COMPUTER OUTPUT MICROFORMS (COM)

Paper output can be slow to produce and expensive to store; monitor and voice output are not appropriate for all applications. The alternative is **computer output microforms** (COM). COM can be generated at speeds much faster than those of powerful laser printers. COM is also much smaller; information from as many as 100 sheets of paper can be stored on one

Impact printers use pressure to create images.

Nonimpact printers are quiet.

Voice output devices use synthesizers to replicate the human voice.

Video display is available on microcomputers.

COM is small, fast, and cost effective.

Fax equipment helps businesses send and receive messages.

microfiche sheet. Production and storage costs are also lower. There is a downside, however; special equipment is needed to read COM.

STREAMLINING DISTRIBUTION

The computer has had a dramatic effect on communication distribution. With computer distribution, neither time nor distance are obstacles to communication. Messages may be sent or received at any time of any day. Fax systems and networks play an important role in communication distribution.

FAX SYSTEMS

Facsimile systems transmit copies of documents over telephone lines at costs lower than overnight mail, express mail, or messenger service. These systems can send accurate copies of text, graphs, illustrations, photographs, signatures, drawings, or other information. Receivers then have a paper copy as a permanent record of the message. Documents may vary in size and may be sent to unattended facsimile equipment.

Facsimile systems can send accurate copies of original documents.

Facsimile equipment is used often in business: orders are placed and acknowledged; contract proposals are sent, and signed contracts are returned; and restaurants accept "fax-food" orders and deliver products to their customers' offices. Fax has also made inroads into the home- or personal-use market.

Fax is found in both the business and the personal-use market.

The introduction of fax modems (discussed earlier) has encouraged wider use of facsimile. Fax modems are standard in most microcomputer systems. They enable communicators to create and send documents using their computers rather than printing documents and then inserting them into a stand-alone fax machine. Computer fax messages can be read and destroyed, saved, edited, and/or printed.

Fax and video are now being integrated. This union will allow transmission of camera images for viewing and, if desired, printing at the receiver's location.

NETWORKS

When computers are connected using optical fibers, radio waves, or wire, a **network** is formed. A network may be used to link computers within an office or building; this linkage is called a **local area network** or LAN. A network also may be used to link computers operated by users in distant locations; this linkage is called a **wide area network** or WAN. Networks can be helpful in many ways, including facilitating collaborative writing projects. Coauthors can communicate with one another and send draft versions of their work to one another via a network. After the parts of the

Networks link computers.

document have been combined, the network can be used to share the final version with all team members.

Networks have made it possible for people to communicate with one another using **electronic messaging systems.** These systems—also referred to as *electronic mail* or *E-mail*—are often used as substitutes for traditional letters and memos. The sender uses a computer to create a message that is then transmitted to and stored in the computer of one or more receivers.

Because the goal is to get the message out quickly, E-mail is generally informal. Phrases are used more frequently than sentences; grammar, spelling, and punctuation errors are typically overlooked. Keyboard-created icons such as the (*view sideways*) happy face :) or frown :(may be imbedded within a message. Comments such as (WOW!) or [not!] may be added to give feedback or clues to meaning that are normally absent in written communication. Not all E-mail messages should be casual; the audience for each message must be considered.

> *The fantastic advances in the field of electronic communication constitute a greater danger to the privacy of the individual.*
>
> **Earl Warren**

USING TECHNOLOGY TO STREAMLINE ORAL COMMUNICATION

Technology can help those who wish to speak with or leave messages for one or more receivers. Wireless messaging systems, picture telephones, voice mail, and audio conferencing are among the more popular communication methods; less popular, but also valuable, are video conferencing and group decision support systems.

WIRELESS MESSAGING SYSTEMS

Cellular telephones and pagers are two forms of wireless messaging systems. Because physical connections are impossible, other methods of signal transmission are used.

CELLULAR TELEPHONES

Cellular telephones are portable units that allow business professionals to make and receive calls from isolated locations. Radio signals are used to transmit messages. The trade-off for the convenience of cellular telephones is cost; users are billed for both calls they make and calls they receive. People who spend long periods of time out of their offices will find cellular telephones helpful.

PAGERS

Use pagers when telephone calls are impractical or impossible.

Another method of locating people when telephone calls are impractical or impossible is the *pager*. Basic systems are activated by dialing a telephone; advanced systems are activated by computer. When a connection is made, the pager beeps. Basic systems display the telephone number the receiver is to call; more advanced systems display several short lines of text.

PICTURE TELEPHONES

Picture phones add nonverbal cues to telephone communication.

A **picture telephone** has a small monitor on its base set that permits senders and receivers to view one another as they speak. The ability to view nonverbal cues raises the quality of telephone communication to a level near that offered by face-to-face communication. Callers no longer have to rely exclusively on volume, pauses, and intonation; facial expressions, gestures, and posture can be seen and interpreted.

VOICE-MAIL SYSTEMS

Voice-mail systems combine a computer and a telephone.

Automated message systems that combine a computer and a telephone are known as **voice-mail systems.** The features of these systems can include message storage and retrieval, message forwarding, group messages, delivery verification, delayed messaging, and password protection. Such systems help avoid the "telephone tag" caused by schedule differences. Messages may be left at the convenience of the caller and retrieved at the convenience of the receiver. Most systems permit receivers to access their mailboxes from remote locations. Some systems use keypad numbers to route callers. A voice-output device will direct callers by instructing, *If you are calling about your account, press 1; if you are calling to place an order, press 2;* and so on.

CONFERENCING

Conferencing is a way for people in different locations to hold meetings without having to travel. The two most common forms of conferencing are audio conferencing and video conferencing.

AUDIO CONFERENCING

Audio conferencing permits timely, inexpensive meetings for people who are at different locations.

When two or more people at different locations confer by telephone, they have an **audio conference.** The date and time of an audio conference are typically prearranged. One caller is designated as the originator. The originator telephones the audio conference participants one at a time. As each receiver answers, he or she is added to the conference group. Participants may be added at any time during the conference. Similarly, they may end their involvement at any time simply by hanging up.

VIDEO CONFERENCING

In video conferencing, both sound and pictures are transmitted.

Video conferencing, the most advanced form of conferencing, uses specialized, costly equipment to transmit both sound and pictures. Video cameras enable participants to see one another and whatever visual aids are used. Many corporations, hotels, and conference centers now have video conferencing rooms. Organizations that have implemented video conferencing report that they have been able to keep travel costs to a minimum while improving managerial productivity and involving more people in the decision-making process.

GROUP DECISION SUPPORT SYSTEMS

Group decision support systems (GDSS) draw on people and computers to make decisions. Meetings (often called *sessions*) may be held at common or distant locations. When sessions are held at a common location, participants share a public computer screen to view both input and output. When sessions are held at distant locations, each participant views the public screen on a window at his or her computer.

GDSS participants share a public screen or view the screen on a computer window.

USING TECHNOLOGY TO STREAMLINE BUSINESS PRESENTATIONS

Technology is helping businesspersons give more effective large- and small-group presentations. Two computer-based aids for oral presentations are electronic imagers and desktop slidemakers.

ELECTRONIC IMAGERS

Computer displays can be projected for viewing.

Units that project computer monitor images onto larger screens are called **electronic imagers.** Communication and decision making are enhanced because data can be manipulated while the speaker is with the audience. By using a special LCD palette that fits onto the top of a standard overhead projector, a speaker can project images from a personal computer to a display screen. No special software is required, but an interface card is needed. LCD units work especially well in small-group settings. For large-group settings, such as a small auditorium or a lecture hall, a wall- or ceiling-mounted projection unit will provide greater versatility.

DESKTOP SLIDEMAKERS

Computer images may be converted into 35-mm slides.

Images displayed on a computer screen may be duplicated onto 35-mm slides. A **desktop slidemaker** links a computer, a camera, and a film recorder. A special computer board is required, and internal storage capacity standards must be met; film is developed by traditional methods. For the most dramatic slides, the computer should have a color monitor. By choosing colors carefully and using them wisely, communicators can create slides that are visually appealing and easy to read.

CREATING ROUTINE AND REPETITIVE MESSAGES

Routine messages have a similar content and purpose each time they are sent.

Repetitive messages are those sent to many receivers at the same time.

Most organizations have some correspondence that can be classified as routine or repetitive. A **routine message** is prepared on a regular basis and has the same or nearly the same content and purpose each time it is created. A **repetitive message** is sent to many people at the same time. A message that is regularly sent to a large number of receivers is both routine and repetitive.

Image projectors help speakers make effective presentations.

Choose form messages, guide messages, or form paragraphs for routine and repetitive messages.

Writers often use *form messages, guide messages, or form paragraphs* for routine or repetitive messages. These message types, described in the following sections, make good use of the time of both the message creator and the message preparer. In addition, using them helps to maintain consistency; similar situations are handled in similar ways. All three message types are appropriate for positive or neutral messages. Guide messages and form paragraphs are better choices for negative messages because they can be personalized.

FORM MESSAGES

Form messages are preprinted.

A **form message** is a preprinted letter or memo. The entire supply may be distributed immediately, or the copies may be kept until needed for routine use. Form messages may be designed in any of four basic styles: plain, fill-in, checklist, or reference.

PLAIN FORM MESSAGES

No additional items are added to plain form messages.

The **plain form message** (Figure 4•2) is keyed, printed, proofread, and signed before being duplicated. No additional information is added when the form is used.

Internal plain form messages generally are printed on an organization's interoffice memo stationery. Brief external messages may be printed on a postal card that has the organization's name in the return address area; formal or lengthy external plain form messages are printed on the company letterhead. The salutation is very general: *Dear Customer, Dear Subscriber,* and *Dear Friend* are examples. Because plain form messages will probably be sent to both men and women, all gender references are omitted.

Salutations are very general.

Figure 4•2 Lengthy External
Plain Form Message

TWO CONVENIENT LOCATIONS

Prairie View Bank
452 Prairie View Road
Lancaster, TX 75134-3520
214-555-1876

Southside Center
141 Chester Parkway
Lancaster, TX 75146-2607
214-555-1130

```
January 4, 199-


Dear Customer

On December 31, 199-, Liberty Bank and Alamo Bank merged to
become Lone Star Bank (LSB), the largest independent commer-
cial bank in the Lancaster area.

Bank ownership has not changed; therefore, policies affect-
ing you and this community will continue to be set by people
who know this area well. In addition, the same people who
greeted you so warmly and worked with you so effectively at
Liberty and Alamo will serve you at LSB.

The real benefit, though, is improved access to services.
The services that were available to you at each individual
bank are now available at both LSB locations. No longer do
you have to decide whether to bank where you live or bank
where you work. There will be an office of Lone Star Bank
where you need it, when you need it!

Thank you for your continued patronage and support; as
always, it is deeply appreciated.

Sincerely
```

Melanie Klatt

```
Melanie Klatt
President

rt
```

FILL-IN FORM MESSAGES

The difference between a plain form message and a fill-in form message is that the **fill-in form message** allows the writer to add variables (information that changes). Figure 4•3 shows a fill-in form message. The dots in the letter address area and the blank lines within the text are optional. The dots are reference points used to ensure that the address will be visible through the opening of a window envelope. The blank lines help the person who prepares the message align the variables with the text. Such space must be adequate to hold the largest number of characters possible for each variable.

A fill-in form message is more expensive to produce than a plain form message because each variable item must be keyed individually. Therefore, the date and letter address should be variables only when the information will be needed later.

Fill-in form messages contain variables.

Fill-in form messages may be inserted into window envelopes.

Figure 4•3 Fill-in Form
Message

Figure 4•3 Fill-in Form Message

DBK *Industries*   1031 Placid Road   Human Resources Department
Chicago, IL 60606-2420   (312)555-8027

•   •

•   •

Dear

_____ has submitted an application for employment with DBK
Industries as a _____ and has listed you as a reference.

To enable us to assess this application for employment, we need
your help. Please complete the enclosed reference form and
return it in the postage-paid envelope that is also enclosed.

A response by _____ will be appreciated.

Very truly yours

D. B. D'Medico

D. B. D'Medico
Manager

ks

Enclosures

bu-2

With checklist form messages, users select from a listing of possible options.

CHECKLIST FORM MESSAGES

Another variation of the plain form message is the **checklist form message** (Figure 4•4). The text of the message is preprinted; the date and the letter address are optional fill-ins. The checklist consists of several items, any or all of which may apply. The person who prepares the message places a check-mark or an *X* before each item that applies to the receiver of the message. These forms often are completed in handwritten rather than typewritten form. Each checklist form message should be designed to meet one particular need. Combining messages into a multipurpose checklist could confuse the reader.

REFERENCE FORM MESSAGES

The reference form message and the checklist form message are similar because they both refer the reader to one or more optional items. In the

Figure 4·4 Checklist Form
Message

The B.R. Steiner Company
213 Colony Place
Fort Worth, TX 76185-3272 (817) 555-4311

Date _____

Dear Customer

_____ Your order is complete; enjoy your merchandise!

_____ Item _____ is currently unavailable but
         is on order. If the item cannot be shipped
         within three weeks from the date of this notice:

         _____ Your account will be credited.

         _____ A full refund will be issued.

_____ Item _____ has been discontinued.

         _____ Your account will be credited.

         _____ A full refund will be issued.

_____ Item _____ is not available in the size
         requested. A credit memo is enclosed; please
         resubmit your order or request a refund.

Thank you for placing an order with us; we hope we may serve
you again in the near future.

Very truly yours

L.L. Patite

L. L. Patite
Distribution Manager

htd

Enclosure

OIF.1

reference form message, however, the reference numbers or statements are printed on the back of the letter or on a separate sheet. Readers are asked to match the reference number(s) with the appropriate statement(s). Long distance telephone bills often include reference codes.

With reference form messages, codes are used to refer readers to explanations.

GUIDE MESSAGES

A **guide message** is used for internal and external routine correspondence that has to be modified to fit special circumstances. A guide message is also used when a writer wishes to personalize a message more than is possible with a preprinted form.

The content of a guide message is prepared in advance, but the document is not preprinted. Instead, each piece of correspondence is individually prepared. Guide messages are often used in conjunction with the mail-

Guide messages are individually prepared.

merge feature of word processing software. The message and the file containing the variables are created separately, each using codes common to both. When the files are merged, the codes are matched and a completed document is created. A guide message with variable codes is shown in Figure 4•5. Notice that the receiver's first name, surname, city, state, and ZIP Code are coded as separate variables. This coding scheme allows the first name to be used in both the letter address and the salutation; it also makes sorting by surname, city, state, or ZIP Code easier.

FORM PARAGRAPHS

Form messages and guide messages save time, but they do not offer a great deal of content flexibility. In order to gain more flexibility, a writer may use **form paragraphs**—a series of paragraphs that are prewritten but not

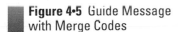
Form paragraphs are prewritten but not preprinted.

Figure 4•5 Guide Message with Merge Codes

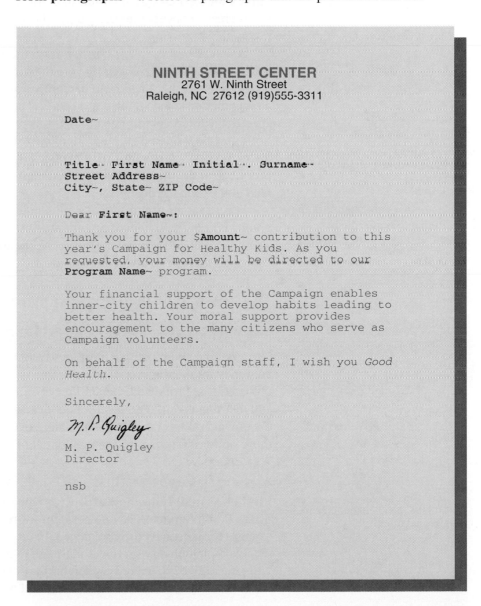

preprinted. When an appropriate situation arises, the writer selects the combination of paragraphs appropriate for the message and supplies the necessary variables. Each message is then individually prepared. Time is saved because the paragraphs do not have to be recomposed each time similar situations arise. The entire message should be proofread to be sure that the correct paragraphs have been selected and that the variables have been keyed accurately. Figure 4•6 contains a sample set of form paragraphs.

PREPARING ROUTINE AND REPETITIVE MESSAGES

Individually prepared, personalized messages create a more positive impression than preprinted messages.

The process used to prepare routine and repetitive messages is linked to the impression desired by the writer. Individually prepared, personalized messages create a positive impression; photocopied messages create a less favorable impression.

As noted earlier in this chapter, form messages are always preprinted. Photocopying and offset printing are the most common duplication methods. Guide messages and form paragraphs are usually keyed, then stored on a computer disk and recalled as needed. The message creator may dictate specific instructions for preparation of the correspondence, or the instructions may be written on a preprinted form. The operator follows these instructions when keying variables. Because the messages were carefully proofread at the time they were stored, only the variables need to be proofread at the time the document is printed.

Variable information must be proofread.

Code numbers are used to identify form messages, guide messages, and form paragraphs.

Whenever a form message, a guide message, or a set of form paragraphs is created, an identifying number or code should be assigned to it. The creator and the preparer of the correspondence refer to the material by using this number or code.

DISTRIBUTING ROUTINE AND REPETITIVE MESSAGES

Once routine and repetitive messages have been created and prepared, they are ready for distribution. If the message is a memo, internal distribution procedures are followed. Generally, personnel are hired to collect mail from and distribute mail to predetermined locations within the organization. If the document is to be distributed externally, several options exist. Some of those options are described in greater detail in the following sections.

FIRST-CLASS MAIL

First-class mail is expensive, but delivery is prompt.

First-class mail is the most expensive type of service offered by the United States Postal Service. The rate per item for first-class business mail is the same as for personal correspondence. In return for the higher rate, mailers receive rapid delivery service. First-class mail to locally designated cities will generally be delivered overnight; first-class mail to locally designated states (usually those within 600 miles) will be delivered in two days. The

■ Figure 4·6 Form Paragraphs

Number	Paragraph (variables underlined)
1	Your copy of the sales report for the number quarter is attached. Please review the report and share its contents with your staff.
2	Congratulations! Your area was the sales leader for the number quarter.
3	The figures for this quarter reflect an increase in sales of $ amount for your area.
4	Please review the attached sales report for the number quarter and share it with your staff.
5	The figures indicate that your area had an increase in sales of $ amount. This increase represents a fine recovery.
6	The sales summary for the number quarter has been completed, name of sales manager, and we are concerned about what the figures indicate.
7	Your area has once again suffered a loss in sales. The figures show that your area experienced a decrease in sales of $ amount.
8	The sales figures for the number quarter show that your area experienced a decrease in sales of $ amount.
9	The sales figures for the number quarter show that your area experienced an increase in sales of $ amount. This is the number consecutive quarter in which you have shown an increase.
10	Thank you! Keep up the good work.
11	Your area has a great sales potential, and you have done well with it.
12	Your area has a great sales potential, and we want you to do well with it. If there is anything this office can do to help you, please let us know.
13	Plan to attend the sales managers' meeting on date in location. Sales strategies will be the primary agenda item.

No. 306

standard for delivering mail to U.S. locations more than 600 miles from the mailing point is three days.

A somewhat reduced postage rate is available to organizations that pre-sort their outgoing mail by ZIP Code or carrier route. A customer service representative of the U.S. Postal Service can provide complete details about the specific quantity, weight, sorting, and coding requirements associated with this option.

First-class mail should always be used when prompt delivery is needed. First-class mail should also be used by writers who have chosen to personalize and individually prepare their external messages. These writers will not want to risk creating an unfavorable impression by choosing a less

By pre-sorting mail, postal patrons can reduce their first-class mailing costs.

Use first-class mail for individually prepared, personalized messages and for those requiring prompt delivery.

expensive delivery option. The desire to create a favorable impression will also prompt writers to key individually rather than to use labels on the envelopes in which their messages are inserted.

THIRD-CLASS MAIL

Third-class "bulk" mail is the least expensive way to mail. Third-class mail is used when cost savings are more important than overall impression or timely delivery. This distribution method is often used for messages inserted in envelopes addressed with mailing labels. It is also used for messages folded to simulate an envelope.

Mailers must realize, however, what they are trading for cost savings. First, bulk mail is processed after all types of first-class mail; therefore, delivery may be delayed. Also, additional labor charges may be incurred in preparing mail to meet the Postal Service requirements for quantity, weight, sorting, and coding. Finally, readers may give less attention to or ignore bulk mail.

ENVELOPES VERSUS FOLDED PAPER

If the sender wishes to create a businesslike impression, the form message is folded and inserted in a No. 10 envelope. For a less formal effect, the sender can single- or double-fold 8 ½- by 11-inch letter size paper and tape the ends. The folding may be done manually or with equipment designed for that purpose. When documents are sent by third-class mail, the bulk mail permit is printed on the form or the envelope before duplication.

INDIVIDUALLY KEYED ADDRESSES VERSUS LABELS

A personalized appearance will be created by having each mailing address individually keyed. This is the most expensive method of addressing envelopes. Individually keyed envelopes are, however, more likely to be opened by receivers.

Prepared labels are an alternative to individually keyed addresses. The labels may be prepared from a computer listing or with the aid of word processing or photocopying equipment. Labels may be quickly and easily affixed to envelopes or folded documents by hand or with automated equipment. Prepared labels are less costly than individually keyed envelopes; in addition, they may be prepared in ZIP Code sequence thereby reducing the time needed to sort the items for bulk mailing.

SUMMARY

As an effective business communicator, you should strive to use communication technology to reduce the cost and to improve the quality of correspondence. Managers and administrative support staff should work together to select appropriate communication technologies and to establish cost-effective procedures for their organization.

Use third-class mail when cost savings are more important than a positive impression or timely delivery.

Third-class mail is inexpensive, but postal service restrictions apply.

Envelopes are not the only way to distribute messages externally.

Mailing addresses may be individually typed.

Labels may be prepared.

Increase the cost-effectiveness of your messages by using communication technology and techniques.

DISCUSSION QUESTIONS

1. Name two factors that contribute to the cost of written communication and two that contribute to the cost of oral communication.

2. What are the six steps in the document cycle?

3. How do computer keyboards and typewriter keyboards differ?

4. What two types of scanners are available?

5. What four components typically form a microcomputer system?

6. List three styles of microcomputers.

7. Define the following computer-related terms:

   a. resolution   d. icon
   b. byte   e. modem
   c. RAM   f. OCR

8. List three types of software commonly used by business professionals.

9. What two word processing features discussed in this chapter can assist business writers in creating messages?

10. Explain why spell checkers and document analyzers are not replacements for proofreading.

11. What software should be used to perform the following tasks?

    a. check for grammar errors   d. sort a mailing list
    b. run two applications at once e. detect a virus
    c. use pictures in a newsletter f. calculate payroll

12. Name one advantage and one disadvantage of (a) an impact printer, and (b) a nonimpact printer.

13. What advantages does COM have over paper output? What disadvantages does it have?

14. Identify and explain the two types of networks.

15. Describe the features and benefits of voice-mail systems.

16. List and explain the two forms of conferencing.

17. How has technology improved a communicator's ability to make a small- or large-group oral presentation?

18. What makes a message routine? What makes it repetitive?

19. List the four types of form messages.

20. Compare the cost and service differences of first-class and third-class mail.

APPLICATION EXERCISES

1. The spell-check feature of a popular word processing program was used to search for errors in the following paragraph—no errors were detected. Proofread the paragraph, and underline any errors the spell checker missed.

   Jane was working a loan in the luggage department. For shoppers approached the counter while he was rapping an other customers' package. Jim, the accessory department clerk, was able too assist here and offered to help. Jan excepted. All six customers were   served   quickly.

2. Use a thesaurus (paper or electronic as your instructor directs) to find an appropriate substitute for each word below:

   a. antiquated   f. structure

   b. exemplary   g. momentum

   c. preposterous   h. conservative

   d. disintegrate   i. veritable

   e. regime   j. irritable

3. Visit a business that uses an electronic messaging system. Interview a manager and secure the following kinds of information: (a) benefits derived from the system, (b) system arrangement, (c) system costs, and (d) any plans for changing the present system or installing a new system. As your instructor directs, prepare an oral or written report summarizing your findings.

4. Visit or phone a U.S. Postal Service office and inquire about the quantity, weight, sorting, and coding requirements of "bulk" mail. As your instructor directs, prepare an oral or written report summarizing your findings.

5. Assume that you are a business communication consultant who has been hired by Metropolis University (MU) to make suggestions for streamlining the creation and preparation of the school's routine and repetitive messages. Read each situation below and give advice in the areas outlined. Justify your recommendations.

   a. In August of each year, the school sends materials about Metropolis to the guidance department of every high school in the state. The explanatory letter that accompanies the packet is changed each year, but all schools receive the same letter.

      (1) Is the letter routine or repetitive?

      (2) What message type should be used? Be specific.

      (3) What would be an appropriate salutation?

   b. A representative from MU attends education fairs in major cities in this and nearby states. Information about students who attended an education fair is sorted and sent to the heads of the appropriate MU departments. Information about a student interested in accounting, for example, would be sent to the head of the business department. The department heads write to the students and try to maintain the prospect's interest in MU.

(1) Are the department head messages routine or repetitive?

(2) Should the messages be sent by first- or third-class mail?

c. To be admitted to MU, a student must complete an application form, pay a $50 fee, submit a high school transcript, and forward his or her ACT scores. The admissions office continually updates each applicant's file and notifies the student of what remains to be done.

(1) Is this a routine or repetitive message?

(2) What type of form message would be most appropriate?

(3) Should the sender use mailing labels or individually keyed envelopes?

6. Business Leaders of the Future, a club for business students, will hold its annual state conference in your community next July. As Program Committee Chair, you are to locate and schedule speakers, introducers, and recorders for each of the ten small-group meetings held during the conference. You have decided that creating guide messages with variables would be the most efficient way to correspond with the individuals who have agreed to participate in the conference.

Select from the list of variables below those you think should be incorporated into a message to be sent to each group. Some items will be used in more than one message; others may not be used in any message.

Group	Variables
Speakers	a. conference registration fee
	b. current date
	c. hotel room rates
	d. introducer's name
Introducers	e. letter address
	f. meal costs
	g. presentation date
	h. presentation room
	i. presentation title
Recorders	j. presentation time
	k. recorder's name
	l. salutation name
	m. speaker's name

Text 4B

Change the formal message below to an informal one that might be sent using E-mail.

Dear Samantha:

Thank you so much for your gracious invitation to join you for lunch at the Rich Valley Country Club on Thursday, April 11.

The date you suggest is very near the end of the tax season, and the activity level in my office will be at its peak. Much as I would like to leave for a few hours and drive to Rich Valley to meet you, I cannot do so until later in April.

Are you free on Tuesday, April 25? Mama's Pasta in Kirkland has received wonderful reviews for both its food and its atmosphere. Dining there would allow both of us to break away for a few hours and enjoy a peaceful drive to Kirkland.

Let me know if the April 25 date is workable.

Very truly yours,

International and Cross-Cultural Business Communication

CHAPTER 5

Learning Objectives

Your learning objectives for this chapter include the following:

- To describe the challenges of international and cross-cultural business communication
- To use the guidelines for cross-cultural communication
- To identify cultural attributes of the major trading partners of the United States
- To analyze the American mainstream culture and its subcultures
- To identify key resources in international and cross-cultural business communication

125

International business opportunities are increasing.

Increased profit is motivation for increased world trade.

The rapidly increasing involvement of American businesses in international trade and the growing number of job opportunities in multinational businesses are reasons for you to develop skill in international and cross-cultural business communication.

The motivation for American firms to expand their involvement in world trade is increased profits. Businesses increase profits in their foreign operations by achieving increased productivity of high-quality products at lower costs. Also, American companies increase profit margins by exporting their products to other countries or importing foreign products for sale in the United States.

Communication Quotes

Communication with other individuals in similar professions in foreign countries and understanding their cultures is vital to all businesspersons. Realizing the differences in thinking creates opportunity and lifelong understanding essential to our ability to conduct ourselves properly in business and private life.

Denis M. Frankenberger, President and Chief Executive Officer of Advance Machinery Company, Inc. (Louisville, Kentucky), one of the largest machine tool companies in the United States.

International business success depends on effective cross-cultural communication.

Success in international and cross-cultural business communication depends on understanding other cultures and on skill in using the techniques of cross-cultural communication. The definitions of the following two terms will help you focus your study of this chapter. **International business communication** refers to the transmission of information between businesspersons from two different countries. **Cross-cultural business communication** refers to the transmission of information between businesspersons of two different cultures whether they reside in the same or different countries.

A company and its employees can benefit from a properly managed international business operation. Success in managing cultural diversity depends on the ability to communicate effectively. There is little doubt that

> *We shall never be able to remove suspicion and fear as potential causes of war until communication is permitted to flow, free and open, across international boundaries.*
>
> **Harry S. Truman**

most students studying this chapter will be involved sometime during their careers in international and cross-cultural business communication.

In addition to communicating internationally, communicating effectively with the various subcultures within the United States is important for business communicators. To sell products and services, businesses and other organizations communicate with African Americans, Hispanics, American Indians, and members of other subcultures.

This chapter discusses the challenges of international and cross-cultural communication, ways to communicate successfully in international and cross-cultural business situations, the American mainstream culture and its subcultures, and key resources in international and cross-cultural business communication.

THE CHALLENGES OF INTERNATIONAL AND CROSS-CULTURAL BUSINESS COMMUNICATION

Cultural variations create communication challenges.

The challenges of international and cross-cultural business communication are similar to the communication challenges within a culture—analyzing receivers and using the you–viewpoint—with one major difference. That difference is found in the striking variations among cultures throughout the world. Cultural variations exist in languages, values and attitudes, symbols and gestures, laws, religions, politics, educational levels, technological development, and social organizations.

There are cultural differences within countries.

As many as 20,000 cultures exist in the world. The cultural diversity even within some countries is striking. This diversity, while possibly more subtle than that between two countries, must be considered when analyzing receivers.

Americans (a term used throughout the world to refer to citizens of the United States) recognize cultural differences within their own country. These differences include variations in behavior between the faster-paced North and the slower-paced South. Persons from Chicago talk faster than persons from Alabama. The more formal, more reserved people of Maine can be contrasted to the less formal, less reserved people of southern California.

In Kentucky, for example, someone might say, "I would be proud to carry you to the office." For that person the word *proud* would mean "glad" and the word *carry* would mean "transport." Although this would be readily understood by others from the same state, people from some other areas of the country could easily be confused.

Great cultural differences are found among countries.

The amount of cultural diversity within the United States, however, is small in comparison with the cultural diversity throughout the world. A direct message composed in businesslike terms sent to a German businessperson may be extremely successful for you and your company. The same message sent to a Japanese businessperson—because of its directness—may fail miserably. The difference in the success of the two communications lies in the cultural differences of the two countries. The next sections describe examples of cultural differences and the challenges these differences present to the business communicator.

LANGUAGE DIFFERENCES

There are 3,000 languages and 10,000 dialects in the world.

More than 3,000 different languages are spoken throughout the world. More than 200 different languages are spoken in India alone. Considering all the various dialects in the world, some linguists estimate that there are at least 10,000 variations of languages. If you are not skilled in the use of your receiver's primary language, you are facing your first major challenge in international business communication.

Word choice can be a problem.

American auto companies have experienced many difficulties because of lack of knowledge of another culture's language. Chevrolet's Nova was not received well in Spanish-speaking countries. Its name sounded like *no va*, which in Spanish means "it doesn't go." Ford's Comet was named Caliente for the Mexican market. Unfortunately, even though *caliente* means "hot" in a literal translation, it also is a slang word for "streetwalker" in Mexico, and poor sales resulted there.[1]

There are other examples of a word being appropriate in one country and not in another. A U.S. trade magazine promoting gift sales in Germany used the English word *gift* in its title. Unfortunately, the word *gift* in German means "poison." The trade magazine did not effectively achieve its objective of selling gifts in Germany. A foreign company inappropriately selected *EMU* for the name of its airline that flew to Australia. An emu is an Australian bird that cannot fly. Finally, *Esso* means "stalled car" in Japanese—hardly an appropriate name for gasoline and oil products that were being sold in Japan.

Communication Notes

Do You Know What We Mean? (Signs in English)

Sign in Moscow, Russia . . .

"You are welcome to visit the cemetery where famous Soviet composers, artists, and writers are buried daily except Thursday."

Sign in Budapest, Hungary . . .

"Please do not feed the animals. If you have any suitable food, give it to the guard on duty."

Languages are structured differently.

Even the way parts of speech are used in different languages varies culturally. In Japanese, the verb is at the end of a sentence. This enables the Japanese to begin to express a thought and watch the receiver's reaction. Depending on how the receiver is reacting to the message, the verb may be changed, thereby changing the whole meaning of the sentence. For example, a Japanese might start to say, "Please go away from me now," but end

---

[1]David A. Ricks, *Big Business Blunders,* Homewood, IL: Dow Jones-Irwin, 1983, pp. 38–39.

up saying "Please stay with me now" by changing the verb, which is said last.

An American company caused itself considerable communication problems in Germany by insisting that all its employees call each other by their first names. This made the Germans uncomfortable, because they do not use first names with even close business associates with whom they have worked for years. In Germany, the use of first names is reserved for intimate friends and relatives. Forcing the Germans to adopt an American custom caused stress that seriously reduced the quality of communication in the German-based American operation.

NONVERBAL COMMUNICATION DIFFERENCES

A sender's nonverbal signals—facial expressions, body movements, and gestures—influence the receiver's understanding and acceptance of a message. In international and cross cultural business communication, nonverbal signals vary as much as spoken languages do.

The cultural diversity in nonverbal communication can be shown by an examination of worldwide differences in the way people greet each other. As can be noted in Figure 5•1, nonverbal greetings vary from a bow to a handshake to a hug to an upward flick of the eyebrows depending on the country and the culture involved.

Not understanding cultural differences in nonverbal messages causes communication problems. For example, if in Germany an American were to signal *one* by holding up the index finger, it would be understood as *two*. Germans signal one by holding up the thumb and *two* by extending the thumb and index finger. An American ordering a train ticket in Germany by raising the index finger, therefore, would likely get two tickets instead of one.

Also in Germany, smiles are reserved mostly for close friends or relatives. The American who laughs often and smiles at everyone would overwhelm many Germans. Such unacceptable nonverbal behavior by an American would definitely interfere with any accompanying verbal communication.

In Japan it is considered impolite or vulgar for people to cross their legs by placing one foot or ankle on the knee of the other leg. The preferred way of sitting in Japan is with both feet on the floor with knees held fairly close together. It is acceptable to cross the legs by placing one knee directly over the other, or to cross the ankles.

In Italy a person waves goodbye by raising one hand with the palm facing the body and moving the hand back and forth to and from the body. In Korea, it is acceptable for men to hold hands in public, but it is frowned on to touch the opposite sex in public. In Lebanon, while *yes* is signaled by nodding the head as Americans do, *no* is indicated by an upward movement of the head or raised eyebrows.

In France, continual eye contact with someone with whom you are speaking is appropriate. In most Asian countries, however, limited eye contact, with the eyes diverted most of the time, is more acceptable.

Figure 5•1 Cultural Differences in Greetings

Country	Nonverbal Method of Greeting
Argentina	Shaking hands while slightly nodding heads (After long absences, women kiss each other on the cheek and men may embrace.)
Australia	Warm handshake between men (A man shakes hands with a woman only if she extends her hand first.)
Belgium	Shaking hands with everyone, using a quick shake with light pressure
Chile	A handshake and a kiss to the right cheek
China	A nod or slight bow (In addition, a handshake is also acceptable.)
Fiji	A smile and an upward flick of the eyebrows (A handshake is also appropriate.)
France	A handshake (A firm, pumping American handshake is considered impolite.)
Greece	An embrace and a kiss on both cheeks or a handshake
India	The *namaste*—bending gently with palms together below chin
Japan	A bow, as low and as long as the other person's
Portugal	A warm, firm handshake for everyone
Russia	A handshake and sometimes, among older people, the traditional three kisses on the cheeks
Saudi Arabia	A handshake (Frequently, males will also extend the left hand to each other's right shoulders and then kiss the left and right cheeks.)
Thailand	The *wai*—placing both hands together in prayer position at chest and bowing slightly
United States	A warm, firm, pumping handshake

Adapted with permission from the Culturgram©, Provo, UT: David M. Kennedy Center for International Studies, Brigham Young University, 1992.

A person involved in cross-cultural communication must be aware of the wide variation throughout the world in the meaning of nonverbal signals. These differences in nonverbal signals, however, are only illustrative of more important underlying cultural differences in the ways people think and feel.

> *A world community can exist only with world communication, which means something more than extensive shortwave facilities scattered about the globe. It means common understanding, a common tradition, common ideas, and common ideals.*
>
> **Robert M. Hutchins**

OTHER CULTURAL DIFFERENCES

Underlying the cultural variations in verbal and nonverbal communication are many other deep-seated cultural differences that affect communication. The most important differences are in the ways people in other cultures *think* and *feel*. These differences are grounded in such things as values, attitudes, religions, political systems, and social orders. Your understanding of these other cultural differences is vital to your success in cross-cultural communication. A few examples of some of them will illustrate this point.

The friendly, outgoing, competitive, informal American who primarily uses the direct plan for communicating may not be received well in Asian or some European countries. In most of these countries people are more reserved and less direct in their human relations than are Americans. Most Japanese, for example, need to build a personal relationship of trust and friendship before entering an important business relationship. On the other hand, most Americans are willing to do business with a limited or nonexistent personal relationship with their customers or vendors. In successfully relating to the Japanese, therefore, Americans must be willing to build the necessary personal relationships first. This requires more patience than most Americans normally need to use in their business dealings in the United States.

Deeply-rooted cultural attitudes toward the appropriate roles of women vary markedly throughout the world. While gender differences are de-emphasized in business in the United States, women—simply because they are women—find conducting business in some countries practically impossible. As Barbara Marsh indicates in an article in *The Wall Street Journal*, American businesswomen face special communication challenges when they travel to conduct business in other countries.

Generally, developed nations are more accepting of women as equals in business, while opportunities for women in lesser developed nations are practically nonexistent. Businesswomen must analyze cultural attitudes toward females

Communication Notes

Gender Gap: Businesswomen Face Formidable Barriers When They Venture Overseas

In many foreign countries, business is still more of a man's world than in the U.S.; and women face problems being accepted as professionals. This leads to cultural conflicts that can be hard to handle when an American businesswoman is on unfamiliar turf and doesn't know the rules. For example, a Saudi Arabia religious law forbids women from mixing with unrelated men. In 1991 police, citing the law, requested two American businesswomen to leave the premises of a trade show—and the women complied. In another example, an American businesswoman in Japan found it impossible to be taken seriously by a Japanese businessman. He took her to a romantic restaurant, tried to hold her hand, and even wanted to kiss her afterward. Her protests did not bring an apology or get the discussion focused on business.

As reported in, "Gender Gap: Businesswomen Face Formidable Barriers When They Venture Overseas," The Wall Street Journal, April 16, 1992, p. R20.

The way people think and feel is the most important cultural difference.

Most cultures are more reserved than the American culture.

American businesswomen have special challenges in international business.

in those countries where they want to do business. Then adjustments in language and nonverbal behavior must be made. A less aggressive approach may be required. Indirectness may be essential. Women have even used men as intermediaries to do business in some countries.

On a completely different level, a simple example of cultural diversity that affects business communication is business hours. You cannot, for instance, telephone a business if that business is not open. Figure 5•2 shows this variation.

Business hours and days limit contact time.

Figure 5•2 Common Business Office Hours Around the World

Country	Business Office Hours
Australia	8:30 a.m. to 5:30 p.m.
Brazil	8 a.m. to 12 noon; 2 p.m. to 6 p.m.
Canada	9 a.m. to 5 p.m., or 8 a.m. to 4 p.m.
China	8 a.m. to 12 noon; 1 p.m. to 5 p.m.
Greece	8 a.m. to 1:30 p.m.; 5:30 p.m. to 8:30 p.m.
Hong Kong	9 a.m. to 5 p.m., weekdays; 9 a.m. to 1 p.m., Saturday
Northern Ireland	9 a.m. to 5 p.m.
Italy	8 or 9 a.m. to 1 p.m.; 3:30 or 4 p.m. to 7 or 8 p.m.
Norway	8 a.m. to 4 p.m.
Romania	7 a.m. to 3 or 4 p.m.
Spain	9 a.m. to 1:30 p.m.; 5 p.m. to 8 p.m.
Russia	8 a.m. to 5 p.m.
United States	8 a.m. to 5 p.m.
Zimbabwe	8 a.m. to 5 p.m.

Adapted with permission from the Culturgram©, Provo, UT: David M. Kennedy Center for International Studies, Brigham Young University, 1992.

Note in Figure 5•2 that many countries in warmer climates close offices in the middle of the day. That time is used for the main meal and a rest or, as they call it in Spanish-speaking countries, a *siesta*. There is also, of course, variation in business hours due to time differences in international time zones. The six- to nine-hour difference in time between European or Asian countries and the United States allows little or no overlap in normal business hours.

Days in the workweek vary.

It is also interesting to note that the days of the week that businesses operate vary around the world. In the United States most business offices operate Monday through Friday, with Saturday and Sunday off. In Korea the workweek is Monday through Saturday, and possibly Sunday. In contrast, the workweek in Saudi Arabia and other Islamic countries is Saturday through Wednesday, with Thursday and Friday off. Friday is the Islamic day of rest and worship.

Countries also have different currencies. In addition, currency exchange rates change continuously. Differences in money are another factor with which the international traveler must contend. Figure 5•3 shows some of the major currencies in the world and their exchange rates on the referenced date against the U.S. dollar.

Business office hours around the world vary considerably, making it difficult to transact business. For example, when it is 8 a.m. in New York City, it is 10 p.m. the *next day* in Beijing, China.

Figure 5·3 Currency Exchange Rates Around the World

CURRENCY TRADING EXCHANGE RATES
Monday, February 1, 1993

Country	Currency	U.S. $ Equivalency
Argentina	Peso	$1.01
Australia	Dollar	.675
Austria	Schilling	.08686
Brazil	Cruzeiro	.0000577
Britain	Pound	1.4595
Canada	Dollar	.7915
China	Renminbi	.171233
France	Franc	.18067
Germany	Mark	.6114
India	Rupee	.03453
Japan	Yen	.007994
Kuwait	Dinar	3.2563
Mexico	Peso	.3221649
Norway	Krone	.1437
Spain	Peseta	.008606

As reported in, The Wall Street Journal (Midwest Edition), February 2, 1993, p. C17.

The cultural diversity described in this section is indicative of some of the challenges of international and cross-cultural business communication. Guidelines for meeting these and other cross-cultural communication challenges are given in the next section.

GUIDELINES FOR SUCCESSFUL CROSS-CULTURAL COMMUNICATION

You can be successful in cross-cultural communication if you follow proven guidelines. Use of the information given previously in Chapters 1 and 2 on business communication foundations and principles will be essential to your success. In addition, follow the special guidelines for international and cross-cultural business communication given in this section.

Goal of Cross-Cultural Communication
To achieve normal business communication without cultural prejudice.

Goal: Communicate without cultural prejudice.

Your goal for effective cross-cultural communication is to achieve normal business communication without cultural prejudice. This means having the ability to communicate comfortably and naturally while eliminating barriers that might be caused by cultural differences.

The guidelines for successful cross-cultural communication are presented in three groups. These consist of basic guidelines for cross-cultural communication, guidelines for cross-cultural communication in English, and guidelines for using an interpreter or translator.

The basic guidelines will assist you in gaining the necessary general information and perspective for cross-cultural communication in the international business environment. The guidelines for communicating cross-culturally in English are provided because most of the world's business is conducted in English. Finally, the guidelines for using an interpreter or translator cover those special situations where a bilingual person is employed to bridge the language barrier.

BASIC GUIDELINES FOR CROSS-CULTURAL COMMUNICATION

The basic guidelines presented in this section should be followed to prepare for cross-cultural communication in the international business environment.

GUIDELINE 1: REVIEW THE FOUNDATIONS AND PRINCIPLES OF BUSINESS COMMUNICATION

Use foundations and principles of business communication.

In any cross-cultural communication situation, the basic business communication knowledge you have already gained will apply. A review of that knowledge should be your first step in preparing to communicate in the international business environment.

As you will recall, the goals of business communication given in Chapter 1 include receiver understanding, necessary receiver response, a favorable relationship between you and your receiver, and goodwill for your organization. These goals will be a part of your cross-cultural business communication effort.

In addition, the communication process will be the same—you need to analyze your receiver and use the you–viewpoint, select the appropriate form of message, provide for feedback, and remove communication barriers. Finally, application of the KISS principle of business communication (Keep It Short and Simple) will enhance your effectiveness in international and cross-cultural business communication.

GUIDELINE 2: ANALYZE YOUR OWN CULTURE

Understanding your own culture is essential.

A starting point in relating effectively to others is to know your own culture. Then, understanding how others view your culture is vital for success in cross-cultural communication. As Robert Burns wrote, seeing ourselves as others see us is a powerful capability.

> *Oh, wad some Pow'r the giftie gi'e us*
> *To see oursels as ithers see us!*
>
> **Robert Burns, "To a Louse on a Lady's Bonnet," 1786.**

People throughout the world use comparisons, evaluations, and categories to assimilate and understand the messages they receive. They use stereotypes of other peoples to help them understand the messages those peoples are sending. Although individuals within one culture may vary considerably, many have similar tastes in food and clothing. They may also hold common values and possess similar attitudes, opinions, and beliefs.

Cultural relativism refers to varying standards of right and wrong.

Cultural relativism is the term used to describe the fact that different cultures have somewhat different standards of right and wrong. As people grow up, they tend to suppose that the ways they do things in their cultures are normal and that the ways of other cultures are not. The ways of others seem peculiar, strange, and even wrong. As you study other cultures, however, you may realize that there is not necessarily one right or wrong way to do something—merely many different, but equally correct, ways.

Understanding the practices of your own culture will enable you to understand and relate more successfully to the practices of other cultures. The American mainstream culture and subcultures are described later in this chapter in the section entitled, "Analysis of the American Mainstream Culture and Its Subcultures," on page145.

GUIDELINE 3: DEVELOP THE ABILITY TO BE OPEN TO AND ACCEPTING OF OTHER CULTURES

Be open to and accepting of others' cultures.

As you think about your own culture, you begin to sense that it represents one way to believe and to do things. It is important to accept that this is not the only way. This understanding is essential in order to communicate successfully with people of other cultures who believe and do things differently. With your involvement in the international and cross-cultural business environment, you will want to adopt an open, accepting attitude toward the differences in others.

Cross-cultural involvement can be an exciting, new adventure. You may be (or have been) apprehensive the first time you meet with persons from another culture. You may feel deficient in some ways and superior in other ways. You will no doubt have many mixed emotions. The guideline that directs you to be open to and accepting of other cultures will serve you well in the international business environment.

How can you be open and accepting? Be open to learning about the other culture with which you are dealing. Be open to different foods, to different ways of doing things, to different beliefs—beliefs, for example, about the value of time (a clock "runs" in the United States; it "walks" in Spanish-speaking Latin America). Be accepting of other people's needs for indirectness in communicating (as in Asia), and for the use of titles and last names instead of first names (as in Europe). Be open to and accepting of the different ways people of other cultures think and feel.

Be patient, but do not be condescending. Be tolerant of differences. Do not rush to an early judgment about the way a conversation or business deal is going. You may be misreading a communication situation because of cultural differences. Ask questions. Ask if you are being understood. Obtain feedback.

Your success in cross-cultural communication will depend largely on your ability to be open to and accepting of differences in others. Only in that way can you communicate in the you–viewpoint without cultural prejudice.

GUIDELINE 4: LEARN ALL YOU CAN ABOUT THE OTHER CULTURE AND APPLY WHAT YOU LEARN

This is the *key guideline* for effective cross-cultural communication. There is, of course, much to be learned about another culture. Do not let the volume of information overwhelm you. Anything you learn will be helpful and will

strengthen your ability to communicate. The last section of this chapter provides several good sources of information for learning about other cultures.

A basic recommendation in learning about another culture is to learn as much as you can of that culture's language. Ideally, you would be able to speak and write the other culture's language fluently. That may not be possible. In any case, learn as much as you can. Learn at least greetings, courtesy words, and the basic positive and negative signals. Learn the few basic phrases that represent typical words used in regard to the subject of your communication. For example, learn how to say "We want to do business with you," if that is appropriate.

• Use what you learn.

You should not only learn as much as possible of the other culture's language, but you should also use what you know in your oral and written messages. Your receivers will appreciate your efforts. They will be understanding and accepting of any deficiencies in your use of their language.

A second aspect of learning about another culture is to learn as much as possible about the people of that culture. This aspect of learning includes a wide range of information from how the people think to the foods they eat. For example, there is considerable evidence that Americans think in an explicit, linear manner, while Asians think in an implicit, intuitive manner. Americans are more likely to think in terms of facts and dichotomies—black-white, right-wrong, good-evil, and true-false. Asians, in contrast to Americans, are likely to think in terms of feelings, relationships, and continuums.

In addition to the way people think, understanding other aspects of the culture you are studying is also important. You should try to learn about how the people relate to each other, what their preferences are in foods and how they eat, what their preferences are in apparel, what hours comprise their workday, how they negotiate, what their business ethics are, what topics of discussion are acceptable and what topics are unacceptable, and what gestures are acceptable and what gestures are unacceptable. The list goes on and on. You should try to learn about their religion, politics, educational system, economy, government, and history.

When you have acquired information about the other culture, analyze it in the following ways: How is it similar to your culture? How is it different? How can you best bridge these differences? By applying the information gained in this analysis—and with practice—you can become an effective cross-cultural communicator.

The preceding four basic guidelines are important for success in any cross-cultural communication in the business environment. There are two other categories of guidelines. The category to apply depends on whether your cross-cultural communication will be in English or in two languages.

GUIDELINES FOR CROSS-CULTURAL COMMUNICATION IN THE ENGLISH LANGUAGE

Fortunately for Americans, most cross-cultural business communication is conducted in the English language. This is true throughout the world.

While the extensive use of English as the primary cross-cultural language is fortunate for Americans, it is important to recognize that for most persons in the world, English is a second language. Non-Americans' facility with the English language and their understanding of its context will limit communication effectiveness. Some Americans mistakenly equate a lack of ability to speak English fluently with a lack of intelligence in non-Americans. That serious error becomes a communication limitation for the Americans because they will analyze their receivers incorrectly. These two guidelines will assist you in overcoming any such limitations.

GUIDELINE 5: KEEP YOUR MESSAGE SHORT AND SIMPLE WHEN USING ENGLISH WITH MEMBERS OF ANOTHER CULTURE

Use the KISS principle in cross-cultural communication in English.

This guideline reminds you to use the KISS principle of business communication (*keep it short and simple*) when communicating in English with people from another culture. Use short words and short sentences. In addition, it is especially important to avoid jargon, slang, and colloquial expressions such as "the bottom line," "operating by the seat of your pants," and "do you read me?" Most of your receivers will have learned only formal English in their schools.

Except for the use of technical words appropriate for your receiver, the readability level of your message should be at about eighth- to tenth-grade level. Be sure to provide for feedback so that you can confirm receiver understanding of the message.

GUIDELINE 6: ENUNCIATE SOUNDS AND PRONOUNCE WORDS PRECISELY

Pronounce words precisely.

If the communication in English is oral, be sure to enunciate sounds and pronounce words precisely. Try to overcome any accents or speech mannerisms that may be distracting and may create communication barriers. While you will not want the slowness to appear exaggerated, speak somewhat more slowly. Be sure not to speak more loudly than necessary for normal hearing.

GUIDELINES FOR CROSS-CULTURAL COMMUNICATION USING AN INTERPRETER OR TRANSLATOR

If English is your only language and your receiver does not know English, then you must use an interpreter for oral communication and a translator for written communication. All previous guidelines apply when using an interpreter or a translator. Four additional guidelines should be followed as well.

GUIDELINE 7: USE SHORT, SIMPLE PHRASES AND SENTENCES WHEN USING AN INTERPRETER

Use short, simple sentences when using an interpreter.

Avoid long introductory phrases, parenthetical elements, interjections, and complex and compound sentences. As you prepare to use an interpreter, give special attention to the parts of your message that may be difficult to convey. Develop clear illustrations of these difficult parts to help ensure your receiver's understanding.

Avoid talking to the interpreter.

Avoid talking to your interpreter. Talk directly to your receiver while keeping your interpreter in the corner of your eye. Permit your interpreter to explain your remarks if necessary, and encourage your receiver to ask questions if you sense you are not being understood clearly. Remain calm and poised. Concentrate on your receiver's interests and not on yourself or your interpreter.

GUIDELINE 8: PRACTICE WITH YOUR INTERPRETER

Practice using an interpreter.

If possible, learn your interpreter's preferred ways of operating—in complete thought units, in short phrases, or word by word. You and your interpreter will be a team. Since practice improves any team effort, you will want to rehearse your cooperative effort with an interpreter.

GUIDELINE 9: SELECT ONLY TRANSLATORS WHO ARE QUALIFIED TO TRANSLATE THE TYPE OF WRITTEN MESSAGE YOU ARE SENDING

Most people who have read instructions accompanying foreign-made products know the difficulty of translating from one language to another—generally, languages cannot be translated verbatim.

Translators must know the subject matter.

The translator must be both competent in the languages involved and qualified in the subject matter so that the *meaning* of the message is conveyed to the receiver, not just the words. As you will recall, insufficient knowledge resulted in the naming of American cars Nova and Caliente for Spanish-speaking markets.

Computerized language translation software can be of value when translating letters, memos, sales literature, and other business messages. Globalink (Fairfax, Virginia) is a company that has software for a wide range of languages. Based on an ASCII format, the Globalink programs translate about 20,000 words per hour at an 80 to 95 percent accuracy rate.

Communication Notes

Excerpts from Product Instructions from Southeast Asia

For assembling a small cabinet . . .

"Please up-side-down the cabinet and screw in the 4 pvc studs."

For operating a stop watch . . .

"Hold B about 3 seconds or push B once by once."

Communication Quotes

At my restaurants, the Emperor of China and the Empress of China, cultural diversity isn't just a management philosophy; it's a way of life. . . . For example, my cooks are all Chinese, but most of the rest of the staff is not. Initially, this posed a problem because many of the servers (from more than a dozen countries) did not speak or write Chinese, while the cooks could read only Chinese. . . . I finally overcame the problem by installing a computer system that allows orders to be entered in English on one station and printed in Chinese in the kitchen.

Ai-Ling Kuo Wang, owner and manager of two successful Chinese restaurants, the Emperor of China and the Empress of China, in Louisville, Kentucky.

GUIDELINE 10: PROVIDE FOR BACK TRANSLATION OF YOUR WRITTEN MESSAGES

Check for translation errors; that is, have a second translator translate the message back into English for verification of its meaning. Back translation is a technique for obtaining essential feedback. Many translation errors have been caught this way.

COMMUNICATING SUCCESSFULLY WITH MAJOR TRADING PARTNERS OF THE UNITED STATES

Brief examples of analyses of other cultures will help show the value of the previous guidelines. For these examples, the cultures of four major trading partners of the United States are examined—Japan, Germany, Canada, and Mexico.[2]

COMMUNICATING SUCCESSFULLY WITH JAPANESE BUSINESSPERSONS

Americans involved in international business can improve communication with the Japanese by taking into consideration Japanese cultural attributes. Remember that these are only stereotypes, and that individuals within cultures vary considerably. Nonetheless, these guidelines can help Americans work more effectively with the Japanese in many business enterprises.

JAPANESE CULTURAL ATTRIBUTES

Japanese tend to be modest, respectful of superiors, loyal to their organizations, contemplative and holistic in their thinking, and traditional in terms of their society. They are achievement oriented. They value human relationships above business relationships and practice situational ethics; i.e., moral judgments based more on the merits of the situation than on some absolute ethical standard. Their privacy is important to them, and direct questioning about their personal lives is resented. "Losing face" is their worst catastrophe. The shame of losing face reflects not only on the individual but also on the family.

COMMUNICATION WITH THE JAPANESE

When communicating with the Japanese, American businesspersons should be gracious and diplomatic. In business meetings in Japan, bowing when greeting your hosts and then shaking hands are important gestures. Do not be surprised if the Japanese, who value punctuality less than Americans do, are somewhat late for the start of a meeting. Because status and hierarchy are important in Japan, an exchange of business cards upon meeting will be helpful to them in sorting out relationships. The American belief in the equality of all does not prevail in Japan.

---

[2]These cultural analyses were adapted with permission from *Culturgram*©, Provo, UT: David M. Kennedy Center for International Studies, Brigham Young University, 1992.

In business meetings in Japan, American businesspersons should bow when greeting their hosts and then shake hands.

Primarily use the indirect organizational plan with the Japanese.

During meetings, confrontations should be avoided. The Japanese will prefer indirectness in approaching business transactions. They may seem to agree with you in order to avoid offending you. Do not be misled by this courtesy into believing that the agreement is set. The agreement will not be finalized until it is in writing and signed.

Japanese businesspersons will want to spend most of the meeting time clarifying the relationships of the trading partners and discussing the details of the business arrangement. Many times the actual terms will be agreed to in informal social gatherings.

Patience is the watchword. If sufficient trust in the Americans and their firm is developed through these negotiations, final approval of the transaction may be achieved. It is important for the Americans not to feel compelled to win points in the negotiations. The Japanese will prefer to share equally the points of agreement. Courtesy and humility should be an American's bywords in communicating with the Japanese.

COMMUNICATING SUCCESSFULLY WITH GERMAN BUSINESSPERSONS

The German cultural attributes are quite distinctive. Remember, however, that the description that follows is a stereotype and will not fit all Germans.

GERMAN CULTURAL ATTRIBUTES

Germans are generally reserved, inquisitive, and conservative.

Compared with Americans, German businesspeople are more formal, reserved, and restrained. Germans tend to be inquisitive and want to hear the supporting evidence for a new idea or procedure. They enjoy vigorous discussion based on logical reasoning. They value intelligence and education. Like Americans, Germans value individualism and the success of the individual.

Germans are basically conservative and prefer discipline and order to informality and change. They may seem to move slowly in their business operations, but they are strong and enduring. Germans take a more serious approach to their business affairs than do Americans. Smiles and laughter are likely to be reserved for celebrations with intimate friends and loved ones. Germans are punctual. They believe it is offensive to waste another person's time by being late.

Germans approach relationships and communication directly. While some Americans might think they are too outspoken or blunt, Germans would see their behavior as simple honesty. Germans have opinions about most things and express those opinions freely. They reserve compliments for only the most outstanding achievements. Germans are a determined people who set goals and tenaciously accomplish them.

COMMUNICATION WITH GERMANS

This generalized thumbnail sketch of German businesspeople provides important information which, if used by American businesspeople, will help them avoid some communication barriers. Fortunately, Americans have much in common culturally with Germans. Building on these commonalities and adapting to the differences are the marks of a good cross-cultural communicator.

Communicating with Germans calls for formality and seriousness.

When communicating with German businesspersons, Americans should generally be formal, serious, impersonal, and thorough. In meeting with Germans, titles and last names should be used; and greetings should include firm handshakes with all those present. Avoid questions such as *How are you?* and *What do you do?* Such questions may be considered too personal. As time passes and the Germans become better acquainted with you, you can establish relaxed, friendly, and personal relationships.

If you are presenting new information or a business proposal, be prepared to answer questions about it. Germans will demand supportive evidence based on solid research or logical reasoning. You may want to present your proposal privately to the top German executive for approval first. Then, that executive can either present the proposal to other Germans on your behalf or endorse your presentation after you have made it. This approach can increase the credibility of your proposal with other Germans and reduce the amount of time spent justifying it.

Directness can be used effectively in communicating with German businesspersons in the same way that it can be used with Americans. Avoid humor at business meetings with Germans; it will be distracting. Also, avoid giving minor compliments; they will be perceived as frivolous and will make your sincerity questionable. Be businesslike, and focus on the agreed-upon goals of the meeting.

At the end of the meeting you will likely know where you stand with your German receivers. Be on time for your meetings, adjourn them precisely at the agreed time, and be sure to shake hands with everyone as you depart.

COMMUNICATING SUCCESSFULLY WITH CANADIAN BUSINESSPERSONS

The Canadian culture, while similar to the United States culture, has some diversity based on the origins of its citizens. Again, keep in mind that the following is a stereotype of the Canadian cultural attributes.

CANADIAN CULTURAL ATTRIBUTES

The Canadian people's ancestry is basically French and English, although some Canadians have their origins in Germany, the Netherlands, and Ireland. Canadians value their diversity. Twenty-eight percent of all Canadians are of French origin, and 81 percent of the population of the province of Quebec speak French as their first language. Although French is the official language of Quebec, English is used in parts of Montreal, eastern Quebec, and throughout the rest of Canada. The Canadian economy is strong, and the standard of living is virtually the same as that of the United States.

Canadians generally are more reserved and formal than the people of the United States. Most are friendly, kind, open, and polite. They follow more formal rules of etiquette than do Americans. The use of courtesy titles and last names is common, and coats and ties are required for dining in some restaurants. In addition, Canadians dress well and conservatively for formal and semiformal occasions such as business meetings; they dress casually at other times. Western Canadians are likely to be less formal and reserved than eastern Canadians.

Canadians are a conservative, law-abiding people. Their conversations are to the point, intelligent, and polite. As in the United States, eye contact is important. Greetings include a firm handshake and a sincere "hello." Many other cultural attributes are shared by the people of Canada and the people of the United States.

COMMUNICATION WITH CANADIANS

Successful communication with Canadian businesspersons requires using basically the same approaches as are used in the United States. Some important differences, however, should be noted.

You can use the direct organizational plan with Germans.

Canada is bilingual.

Canadians are somewhat more reserved, formal, and conservative than are U.S. citizens.

Canada shares many cultural attributes with the U.S.

When communicating with Canadians, businesspersons from the United States should be more formal and reserved than when dealing with those from the United States. Until told differently, last names and titles should be used. Politeness and courtesy are essential. Directness can be used, but the "hard sell" approach will not appeal to most Canadians. Be sincere, warm, and friendly. Your dress should be formal business attire.

Communicating with Canadians calls for politeness and courtesy. The direct plan can be used.

Although Canada is officially a bilingual country, French should be spoken, if possible, when doing business in Quebec. Fortunately for most U.S. businesspersons, English is used in the rest of Canada and can be spoken in Quebec if necessary. In Canada some words are used differently than in the United States. For example, school grades are called *marks* in Canada, tennis shoes are called *running shoes,* and sofas are called *chesterfields*. Some words are pronounced differently, such as, *aboot* for *about, vahz* for *vase,* and *tomahto* for *tomato.*

Some language variations exist between Canada and the U.S.

Communicating successfully with Canadians is important. Canada is the United States' largest trading partner. A recent agreement will gradually eliminate all trade barriers between the two countries by 1999, so contact and communication with Canadians will increase for American businesspersons.

COMMUNICATING SUCCESSFULLY WITH MEXICAN BUSINESSPERSONS

The Mexican culture is quite different from that of the United States. While the Mexican stereotype is extremely valuable, remember that individual Mexicans differ one from another.

MEXICAN CULTURAL ATTRIBUTES

Mexicans are a very warm, friendly, gracious people. They greet another person with a handshake and stand very close while talking, possibly touching the other person or his or her clothing.

Mexicans are considered warm, gracious, and people oriented.

Their time is your time. In fact, although they know most Americans will be punctual for appointments, Mexicans give time much less importance. They rank people at a much higher level than time and may be quite late for appointments. They mean no disrespect by this behavior.

While an American defines success in terms of efficiency, achievement, money, and material possessions, a Mexican may be more likely to define success as adapting to the status quo and to the position into which he or she was born.

Mexican graciousness reflects itself in several ways. Their messages are generally indirect and elaborate. Sometimes favorable relationships of the moment are more important than the truth. Mexican businesspeople may seem to make a business commitment that they later do not keep. Their intention was not to deceive you; rather, their commitment was to be courteous to you and to make the current moment pleasant.

Business transactions in Mexico may depend on the development of personal favors and friendships. In order to receive a benefit—something as simple as a public service—some businesspeople have reported that they had to pay money or give gifts to key people. This method of getting things done in Mexico is not considered dishonest because the services provided are not illegal. Some American businesspersons have considerable difficulty with this way of operating.

Mexicans achieve self-esteem primarily through their friendships and personal relationships rather than through promotions or recognition for job performance. Mexicans will not necessarily be loyal to their employers and their jobs, but rather to superiors at work whom they like. They gain self-esteem through the ways their friends treat and respect them. They tend to trust only their friends.

COMMUNICATION WITH MEXICANS

Many American firms have been disappointed in their business dealings in Mexico because they did not understand the differences between the cultures. In attempting to communicate effectively with Mexicans, it should be emphasized that building personal relationships and friendships will be important. Close friends in Mexico are more open with each other than Mexicans are with strangers or acquaintances.

Use indirectness in communicating with Mexican businesspersons. In your meetings, plan to visit socially at first in order to accommodate their need for indirectness. Expect your Mexican counterpart to stand or sit very close to you and maybe to touch you while talking with you. Expect your Mexican associate to be very gracious, courteous, and respectful. To build the necessary relationship, you must be the same. Your meetings with Mexican businesspersons will likely start quite late, well after the appointment times.

Because there may not be follow-through on commitments made early in your relationship, patience must be the foundation of your business ventures in Mexico. If Mexicans are working for your organization, realize that they may value job performance less than you might expect in the United States. These kinds of situations will improve as you build a trusting and mutually respectful personal relationship with your Mexican business associates.

In many ways there are greater differences between the cultures of Mexico and the United States than there are between the United States and Japan, Germany, and Canada. The Japanese, Germans, and Canadians are achievement oriented—more like Americans; this common underlying philosophical goal facilitates communication. The Mexican culture is changing as Mexico increases its industrial development.

ANALYSIS OF THE AMERICAN MAINSTREAM CULTURE AND ITS SUBCULTURES

Both a *mainstream* culture and many *subcultures* co-exist in the United States. Successful communicators understand that, while common cultural attributes are shared by Americans, overlapping subgroups have their own

Mexicans value friendships and personal relationships.

Communicating with Mexicans calls for personal relationship development.

Primarily use the indirect communication plan with Mexicans.

distinctive languages, nonverbal signals, values, social systems, religions, and other cultural characteristics. Understanding the American mainstream culture is essential for successful communication with American subcultures.

THE AMERICAN MAINSTREAM CULTURE

Over 255 million people live in the United States. The people of the world call them *Americans*. Interestingly enough, even the people who live in Canada and Mexico call the people who live in the United States *Americans,* while referring to themselves as *Canadians* or *Mexicans*.

The American mainstream culture consists of persons who prefer to communicate in the English language. Although they primarily use the direct plan of communication (versus the indirect plan), they tend to do so politely. Americans are generally friendly and informal. They are likely to greet you by your first name and shake your hand with a firm grip and pumping action. They have a strong sense of humor and laugh and smile frequently.

Americans are time conscious and efficiency oriented. They tend to be impatient. They do not need to have personal friendship as a basis for business relationships. They have limited respect for rank and authority.

Eye contact while conversing is a sign of strength and honesty to Americans. They have a greater need for personal space than do some other peoples—at least two to three feet minimum distances between themselves and others. Americans tend to limit personal touching of each other in public.

Americans value highly an individual's freedom to achieve. Work, activity, and progress are valuable in their own right. Americans tend to put an individual's needs above an organization's needs. They believe rather firmly that the "American way" is the "right way."

Americans value material possessions and have many more of them than do most people of the rest of the world. Americans support an open economy, are predominantly Christian, and believe in democracy.

The foregoing is a limited analysis of the American culture. It can be seen, however, how this stereotype can be helpful to you in cross-cultural communication. As you communicate with subcultures in the United States and other cultures around the world, you will quickly note that while there is much in common, there are sharp differences in values, tastes, and attitudes. For example, Japanese Americans have greater respect for rank and authority and greater loyalty to organizations than does the American mainstream culture. Hispanics are warmer and more gracious. Around the world, we find that Latin Americans and peoples of the Middle East need and desire much less personal space than do Americans. Germans and many other Europeans are more reserved and formal than Americans.

AMERICAN SUBCULTURES

A subculture is a distinctive segment of a culture that thinks and behaves in unique ways. A subculture, while adopting many of the larger culture's

Sidebar notes

Americans tend to be:
• friendly and informal

• time conscious, impatient, and independent

• direct in eye contact and space conscious

• supportive of an individual's rights and needs

• materialistic and capitalistic

The American culture differs from other cultures.

Subcultures are a mix of attributes.

attributes, may have its own values, language, customs, geographic location, and social systems. Subcultures can be based on race, religion, age, gender, national origin, or any number of other distinctions. Individuals can be members of many overlapping subcultures. For example, an individual can be a black African-American male who is 70 years old, lives in the Northeast, and is a member of the Jewish faith.

Subcultural analysis helps the business communicator transmit messages that are more understandable and acceptable to the members of that subculture. As examples, three American subcultures—African Americans, Hispanics, and American Indians—are discussed briefly in the following sections.

It is important to recognize that any description of a subculture is a stereotype, and few members of that subculture will possess every attribute mentioned. While stereotypes can be quite helpful, communicators should remember that every receiver has his or her own personal culture.

AFRICAN AMERICANS

The African-American subculture is the United States' largest minority.

Over 35 million black African Americans comprise about 15 percent of the United States' population—a sizeable minority. These Americans are of all ages, religions, and social classes; they all differ. Some members of this minority culture, however, speak a dialect of English that differs from American mainstream English. Sometimes they show more emotion and

Members of American subcultures represent a wide variety of nationalities, races, ages, regions, and religions.

maintain less reserve—loud voices and hearty laughter may be observed in social settings. An underlying concern most African Americans have is that they be treated fairly by the majority.

HISPANICS

Hispanics—approximately 30 million live in the United States—comprise America's fastest-growing subculture. While there is great variation among Hispanics, a stereotype of this subculture shows its distinctiveness as a group. Hispanics in the United States are more likely than persons of other subcultures to continue to use their first language, Spanish. An estimated one-fourth use only Spanish, while three-fourths are bilingual. Hispanics, as compared to members of the American mainstream culture, are more gentle and considerate, more fatalistic and pessimistic, and more present-time oriented. They are less technically oriented, less reserved, and less team-oriented.

Hispanics come to the United States primarily from Mexico (sometimes referred to as Chicanos), Cuba, and Puerto Rico. Each country of origin constitutes a subgroup within the subculture.

AMERICAN INDIANS

Over 1.5 million American Indians live in the United States; approximately one-half of these native Americans have become integrated into the American mainstream culture, and one-half live on reservations.

American Indians on reservations have distinctive attributes.

Indians who live on reservations are more group-oriented than members of the mainstream American culture, preferring consensus decision making. They have many customs and traditions, tend to live for the moment, are not concerned with time schedules, and do not aspire to private property ownership. American Indians, generally, are reserved and possess great dignity.

> ### When they are in Rome, they do there as they see done.
>
> **Robert Burton,** *Anatomy of Melancholy,* Vol. 3, 1621.

Respect other cultures. When in Rome, do as the Romans do.

There is no need to offend or alienate another person by not respecting his or her cultural beliefs. The Americanized adage that will serve international and cross-cultural business communicators best is, *When in Rome, do as the Romans do.*

As the guidelines for successful cross-cultural communication given earlier in this chapter indicate, you must know yourself, be open, learn all you can about the other culture, apply what you learn, and keep your messages short and simple. The key guideline is to learn all you can about the other culture and then use that knowledge in your communication. The last section of this chapter provides sources of information for enhancing your cross-cultural communication.

SOURCES OF INFORMATION ON INTERNATIONAL AND CROSS-CULTURAL BUSINESS COMMUNICATION

This chapter presents basic information on the challenges of international and cross-cultural business communication and on communicating successfully in the international business environment. As you prepare yourself further in this area, you will find that an increasing amount of high-quality information is available for study and reference.

Further information is available:

Basic to your study should be a review of one or more of the several good international business textbooks now on the market. For more specific information on cross-cultural business communication, the following books are recommended:

• in specialized books

Copeland, Lennie, and Lewis Griggs. *Going International: How to Make Friends and Deal Effectively in the Global Marketplace*. New York: Random House, 1985.

Do's and Taboos Around the World. Compiled by The Parker Pen Company. New York: Wiley, 1990.

Gudykunst, William B., and Young Yun Kim. *Communicating with Strangers: An Approach to International Communication*, 2d ed. New York: McGraw-Hill, Inc., 1992.

Hall, Edward T. *Beyond Culture*. New York: Anchor Books, 1989.

Ricks, David A. *Big Business Blunders*. Homewood, IL: Dow Jones-Irwin, 1983.

Terpstra, Vern, and Kenneth David. *The Cultural Environment of International Business*, 3d ed. Cincinnati: South-Western Publishing Co., 1991.

The following organizations are good sources of information on communication generally and international and cross-cultural business communication specifically:

• from professional organizations

Association for Business Communication
Baruch College — C.U.N.Y.
Department of Speech
17 Lexington Avenue
New York, NY 10010

International Association of Business Communicators
Suite 940, 870 Market Street
San Francisco, CA 94102

A key to success in cross-cultural communication is learning all that you can about the other culture. A good source of extensive publications on other cultures and how to relate effectively to them is the following center:

• from international centers

David M. Kennedy Center for International Studies
Publications Division
Brigham Young University
P.O. Box 24538
Provo, UT 84602-4538
Telephone: (800) 528-6279

Many institutions of higher education are giving increased attention to preparing businesspersons for effective leadership and service in international and cross-cultural business situations. Most of these programs include information on cross-cultural communication.

International business offers opportunities for achievement and success.

There are many employment opportunities available to you today in the international and cross-cultural business environments. Traveling to other countries and working with another culture are broadening and exciting. International and cross-cultural business experience not only provides excellent opportunities for achievement and success in your chosen field, but it also prepares you to communicate effectively and to achieve success in your own culture.

DISCUSSION QUESTIONS

1. Why should students study international and cross-cultural business communication?

2. Describe how the challenges of international and cross-cultural business communication differ from the challenges of communicating within a culture.

3. Give three examples of how differences in the use of languages throughout the world cause difficulties in cross-cultural communication.

4. Give three examples of cultural differences in nonverbal signals.

5. Describe what is meant by the statement, "The most important differences are in the ways people in other cultures think and feel."

6. What is the goal of cross-cultural communication? Discuss the meaning of this goal.

7. Define and explain cultural relativism.

8. What does "being open to and accepting of other cultures" mean?

9. Explain what one should try to learn about another culture in preparation for cross-cultural communication.

10. Explain what is meant by Guideline 5: Keep Your Message Short and Simple When Using English with Members of Another Culture.

11. What does Guideline 6: Enunciate Sounds and Pronounce Words Precisely mean?

12. How can you use an interpreter effectively?

13. What are important qualifications for a translator?

14. List five features of the Japanese culture that are distinctively different from the American culture.

15. What are five features of the German culture that are different from the American culture?

16. Discuss the similarities and differences between the Canadian and U.S. cultures.

17. What basic advice regarding cross-cultural communication would you give to a manufacturer who wanted to operate a plant in Mexico?

18. Analyze the American mainstream culture and list several of its attributes.

19. Give two attributes for each of the following American subcultures: (a) African American, (b) Hispanic, and (c) American Indian.

20. List resources for the international/cross-cultural business communicator as specified in the following items: (a) three books, (b) two professional associations, and (c) one international center.

APPLICATION EXERCISES

1. Gather information at the library that will enable you to analyze a culture other than the cultures (American, Japanese, German, Canadian, and Mexican) analyzed in this chapter. Give particular attention in your analysis to the way the people of the culture think and how that would affect their communication with Americans. Report your findings as directed by your instructor.

Text 5A

2. Interview a foreign student or businessperson currently residing in your area and ask the following questions:

   a. How do the people of your country perceive Americans?

   b. What was the most difficult adjustment you had to make when you moved into this culture?

   c. What advice would you give to someone going to your country to live and work?

   Write a report that contains the answers to your interview questions.

3. Develop a list of at least three advantages and three disadvantages of using stereotypes to assist you in strengthening your ability to communicate cross-culturally. Debate the value of the use of stereotypes in cross-cultural communication.

4. Interview a foreign language instructor and ask, "How does studying a foreign language strengthen one's effectiveness as an international businessperson?"

5. Analyze the distinctive features of your regional culture. Give attention to language, nonverbal signals, and the ways people think and feel. Compare your culture to those in other regions of your country.

6. Form groups of four to seven students each. Assign each group a specific culture from among the following: American, Canadian, German, Japanese, Mexican. Each group is responsible for describing its assigned culture by answering these questions.

   For your assigned culture, how important is/are:

   a. time?

b. groups versus individuals?

c. eye contact?

d. rank and authority?

e. personal relationships?

Write a report of your conclusions.

7. Research the attributes of the following American subcultures and report your findings as directed by your instructor: (a) older Americans, and (b) residents of a region other than your own.

MESSAGE ANALYSIS

Assuming that your receivers can read English, revise the following message for: (a) Mr. Danjiro Hayashi, a Japanese receiver living in Japan, and (b) Ms. Gundel Herbig, a German receiver living in Germany. You can use part or all of the information below for your messages, and you can add information you think appropriate for the situation.

Dear (appropriate courtesy title and name):

Contracting with you to ship you the American Rock Group T-shirts, as we discussed by phone, will not be possible. The price is simply not high enough.

We have enjoyed doing business with you in the past. The world business climate continues to improve.

Our source of blank T-shirt supply has increased its cost to us by 33 percent. In addition, the royalty charge for each Rock Group has increased by varying amounts.

Sincerely,

(Your name)

Sales Manager

PART 2

Business English

COMMUNICATION NEWS

Writing and Speaking Well Are Important Tools

John Mack Carter has been editor-in-chief of Good Housekeeping since 1975. Under his leadership, the magazine has won two National Magazine Awards in the Personal Service category, in 1989 and again in 1993. Mr. Carter was named to the additional post of director of magazine development for Hearst Magazines in October 1979. Under his aegis, Country Living, Victoria, and SmartMoney magazines were created. Country Living is recognized within the industry as the most successful new magazine launched in the 1980s. Mr. Carter says:

> As one who lives in the worlds of both business and communications, I can make a strong case for the importance of developing the communication skills of business students. My current working practice requires me to read eight different business and financial journals on a regular basis, everything from The Wall Street Journal to Fortune, and more than 30 other publications a month.
>
> The most important thing I have learned is that the essence of business is people, not balance sheets, and success depends on communications: Board of Directors and shareholders. Management and employees. Sellers and buyers.

I believe that writing well and speaking well may be the two most important tools for getting ahead in business. Basic to these tools are business English and business communication skills. There are no shortcuts or easy solutions to the development of these skills. But then, neither are there any shortcuts to success.

John Mack Carter knows well what is essential for success; he has experienced the highest levels. In

---

I believe that writing well and speaking well may be the two most important tools for getting ahead in business. Basic to these tools are business English and business communication skills.

January of 1990, he received the 1989 Henry Johnson Fisher Award—the magazine industry's highest honor—from the Magazine Publishers of America for his lifetime of achievement. In May 1990, Carter was elected to a two-year term as president of the American Society of Magazine Editors. Currently, he serves as an ex-officio member of the board of directors.

During his distinguished career, Carter has received many awards and honors for his achievements in publishing, television, and journalism. His words provide important real-world guidance to today's business communication students.

John Mack Carter

Editor-In-Chief, Good Housekeeping, and Director of Magazine Development, Hearst Magazines

It's Your Turn

How can a sound knowledge of business English make you a more effective communicator?

What are the important grammar skills you need to strengthen?

CHAPTER 6

Parts of Speech

Learning Objectives

Your learning objectives for this chapter include the following:

• To define and identify the eight parts of speech
• To describe the function of each part of speech
• To use the parts of speech correctly

E very word in a sentence has a use or function. Knowing the functions of words will enable you to select the right word, which in turn will help you communicate your ideas effectively. Your understanding of the parts of speech will aid you in selecting the right word at the right time. The eight parts of speech are as follows:

1. **Verb.** A word or phrase that describes the action or state of being (or condition) of the subject
2. **Noun.** A word that names a person, place, or thing
3. **Pronoun.** A word that takes the place of a noun
4. **Adjective.** A word that describes or modifies a noun or pronoun
5. **Adverb.** A word that describes or modifies a verb, an adjective, or another adverb
6. **Preposition.** A word that connects a noun or pronoun to other words in the sentence
7. **Conjunction.** A word that joins words, phrases, or clauses
8. **Interjection.** A word that expresses surprise, emotion, or strong feeling and is not related to other words in the sentence

VERBS

The verb is the most important part of speech in a sentence. It expresses an action or a state of being. Every complete sentence must have a verb. Some sentences, compound and complex, have more than one verb. (Compound and complex sentences are discussed in Chapter 7.) When you are constructing sentences, remember that you should build each sentence around the verb.

VERB TYPES

Sentences are constructed using two types of verbs. The two types of verbs are action verbs and state-of-being verbs.

ACTION VERBS

An **action verb** expresses acts. It adds power and precision to your communication. *Promote, negotiate, organize, praise, report, liquidate,* and thousands of other words are action verbs. The action verb is italicized in the following examples:

> Sonia *solicited* comments about the policy from her employees.
>
> The marketing managers *organized* their distribution plans.
>
> Emmitt *praised* the volunteers for their work.
>
> Paul accidentally *erased* the diskette.

STATE-OF-BEING VERBS

A **state-of-being verb** expresses the five senses (*hear, smell, see, taste,* and *touch*). A state-of-being verb is also called a *linking verb*. These verbs join or link one part of a sentence to another. State-of-being verbs are less powerful and less precise than action verbs. Other state-of-being verbs include *is, am, are, was, were, seem, appear, will be,* and *have been.* The state-of-being verbs are in italics in the following examples:

The room *smells* of cigar smoke.

The pie *tastes* too sweet.

Teresa *is* a good employee.

Yesterday *was* a cold, windy day.

VERB TENSE

Verb tense indicates the time that action occurs. Six verb tense forms are used to indicate time. The six tenses are categorized into two groups—simple tense and perfect tense.

SIMPLE TENSE

Simple tense includes present, past, and future. The time of action or state of being of each simple tense is designated by its name.

Present Tense. A **present tense verb** expresses action that is going on at the present time or action that is continuing or habitual. Present tense verbs may also be used to indicate general truths. Verbs showing present tense are in italics in the following examples:

The sales representatives *are displaying* their products. (present time)

Dave Wright, our office manager, *edits* all outgoing correspondence. (continuing)

Telephones *expedite* business transactions. (general truths)

Past Tense. A **past tense verb** indicates action that has been completed. Verbs in the past tense have two forms—regular and irregular. The past tense of regular verbs is formed by adding *d* or *ed.* The past tense of irregular verbs is formed by changing their root word. Regular and *irregular verbs* in the past tense are shown in italics in these examples:

Anne *performed* better than William in sales last month. (regular—*perform* [root word] + *ed*)

Anne *sold* more than William last month. (irregular—root word is *sell*)

Mr. Pai *traveled* to the conference in an automobile. (regular—*travel* [root word] + *ed*)

Mr. Pai *went* to the conference in an automobile. (irregular—root word is *go*)

Roberta *mailed* the check to Gene. (regular—*mail* [root word] + *ed*)

Roberta *sent* the check to Gene. (irregular—root word is *send*)

Verb tense indicates the *time* that action occurs.

The three simple tenses are present, past, and future.

Present tense expresses current and continuing action or general truths.

Past tense expresses completed action.

> *Everything that can be said can be said clearly.*
>
> **Ludwig Wittgenstein**

Future Tense. A **future tense verb** is used to indicate actions that are expected to occur in the future. Future tense is formed by using *shall* or *will* before the present tense form of the verb. Most business communicators use *will* to express future tense. *Shall* is used sparingly; it is used mainly to express legal or strong obligation. The following sentences show verbs in the future tense in italics:

> Terry *will sell* his duplex when he retires.
>
> *Will* you *attend* the convention?
>
> I *will vote* on election day.
>
> The protestors *will demonstrate* in front of the White House.
>
> I *shall look* forward to hearing from you by next week.
>
> You *shall rise* when the judge enters the room.

PERFECT TENSE

A **perfect tense verb** shows action that has been completed at the time the statement is made. The perfect tense requires a form of the verb *have*, along with the past participle of the main verb. (Participles are discussed at the end of this section.) The perfect tenses are present perfect, past perfect, and future perfect.

Present Perfect Tense. A **present perfect tense** verb refers to an action begun in the past and completed in the present. Present perfect tense may also refer to habitual or repeated past action. This tense is formed by adding *has* or *have* to the past participle of the main verb. The following examples show verbs in the present perfect tense in italics:

> Nancy *has repaired* our cash register many times.
>
> The band *has practiced* long hours for this parade.
>
> Martha and Diane *have dined* here for the past 14 months.
>
> Nate *has called* his mother every day since school began.

Past Perfect Tense. A **past perfect tense** verb refers to an action that was completed before another event in the past occurred. This tense is formed by adding *had* to the past participle of the main verb. The verbs in the past perfect tense are in italics in the following examples:

> Nancy *had repaired* our cash register before we closed last night.
>
> The band *had practiced* long hours earlier in the semester.
>
> Martha and Diane *had dined* here earlier in the week.
>
> Nate *had called* his mother before she left for the weekend.

Future Perfect Tense. A **future perfect tense** verb is used to express an action that will be completed before a stated time in the future. This tense is formed by adding *shall have* or *will have* to the past participle of the main verb. Examples of verbs in the future perfect tense are in italics in the following sentences:

> Nancy *will have repaired* our cash register by the time we close.

Future tense expresses expected action.

Will is used more than *shall* in business communication.

The three perfect tenses are present perfect, past perfect, and future perfect.

Present perfect tense = *has* or *have* + past participle

Past perfect tense = *had* + past participle

Future perfect tense = *shall have* or *will have* + past participle

The band *will have finished* practicing for the parade before the Thanksgiving holidays.

By then, Martha and Diane *shall have dined* here for 14 months.

By the end of the semester, Nate *will have called* his mother fifty times.

VERB VOICE

Voice is the term used to indicate whether the subject is doing or receiving the action. Sentence meaning and emphasis are communicated through the proper use of verb voice. The two voices of verbs are active and passive.

ACTIVE VOICE

When the subject of the sentence is performing the action, the verb is in the **active voice.** In business communication the active voice usually is preferred because it is more direct and concise. Sentences that use verbs in the active voice identify the one performing the action. The following examples demonstrate how the verbs, shown in italics, are used in the active voice:

Tanya *addressed* the needs of the community at the political rally.

Troy *is designing* a new office layout for the accounting section.

Frank *has flown* to Europe to coordinate the international sales promotion.

Alisha *will audit* the books at the end of the year.

They *work* for Allspice, Inc.

PASSIVE VOICE

A verb is in the **passive voice** when the subject of the sentence receives the action. The passive voice is used sparingly in business communication. It is used when the subject is unknown or when the writer wants to soften the message to avoid making an accusation. Another use of the passive voice is to emphasize the action rather than the person who performed the action. The passive voice can also be used to eliminate a gender pronoun.

Passive voice verbs require a form of *be* (*am, is, are, was, were, been*) as a helping verb, along with a past participle of the verb. Uses of verbs in the passive voice are shown in italics in the following examples:

The computers *were left* on over the weekend. (The person who left the computer on is unknown, or the speaker did not want to accuse anyone. Softened from "One of you left the computers on over the weekend.")

Several suspicious incidents *have been reported*. (Communicator does not want to identify who did the reporting.)

Progress *was made* by the negotiation team. (Emphasis is on what—progress, not whom—negotiation team.)

The books *were audited* prior to the holidays. (A biased statement was avoided by not saying, "He audited the books prior to the holidays.")

Changing the verb voice from active to passive does not change the verb tense from present to past. The tense in the passive voice is expressed by its auxiliary (helping) verb. The following examples show verbs (in italics) in the passive voice in several different tenses:

The rehearsals *are conducted* daily at 3 p.m. (*passive voice*, present tense)

The director *conducts* rehearsals daily at 3 p.m. (active voice, present tense)

The rehearsals *were conducted* in the evening last season. (*passive voice*, past tense)

The director *conducted* the rehearsals in the evening last season. (*active voice*, past tense)

The rehearsals *will be conducted* during the morning in the spring. (*passive voice*, future tense)

The new director *will conduct* the rehearsals during the morning in the spring. (*active voice*, future tense)

VERB MOOD

Communicators use verb moods to express facts, commands, or conditions. The three moods are indicative, imperative, and subjunctive.

The three verb moods are indicative, imperative, and subjunctive.

INDICATIVE MOOD

The **indicative mood** is used to make statements or to ask questions involving facts. Business writers use verbs in this mood more than in the imperative or subjunctive moods. Examples are in italics in these sentences:

Use indicative mood to ask questions or make factual statements.

Fred *will travel* to Houston after the wedding.

Who do you think *will be promoted*?

How many application letters *did* you *submit*?

The new employee *appears* to like her job.

IMPERATIVE MOOD

The **imperative mood** is used to give commands, give instructions, or make requests. Sentences in the imperative mood usually have *you* understood as the subject and, therefore, it is omitted. Verbs used in the imperative mood are shown in italics in the following sentences:

Commands, instructions, and requests are in the imperative mood.

Phone Mr. Riley before you leave.

Take this package to the post office before noon.

Please *complete* editing the report before the three-day weekend.

Sit down and *discuss* your problem.

SUBJUNCTIVE MOOD

The **subjunctive mood** is used to express a wish, a doubt, or a situation that is contrary to fact. This mood is rarely used today. Many people find its use difficult because in the subjunctive mood the verb *were* replaces the verb *was* and the verb form *be* replaces *am, are,* and *is.* Here are some examples; the subjunctive mood verbs are in italics:

The subjunctive mood is rarely used.

I wish Sherry *were* here. (wish)

Should Sherry *arrive,* we would go to a movie. (doubt)

If Sherry *were* here, I would not be studying. (contrary to fact—Sherry is not present)

If I *were* Sherry, I would go to Las Vegas. (contrary to fact—I am not Sherry)

I suggest that his trip *be* canceled. (wish—*be* replaces *is*)

Erika insisted that her automobile be completely rebuilt. (contrary to fact—*be* is used for *is*)

VERBALS

A **verbal** is a verb form used as a noun, an adjective, or an adverb. Verbals cannot function as verbs and do not express action or state of being. The three verbals are the infinitive, the gerund, and the participle.

INFINITIVE

The **infinitive** is formed by placing the word *to* in front of the present tense of the verb. Several examples are *to rent*, *to program*, and *to hire*. An infinitive can function as a noun, an adjective, or an adverb, but it can never be used as a verb. The infinitive is in italics and its use is in parentheses in each of the following sentences. (Some parts of speech are identified in examples in Chapter 6 and are discussed in depth in Chapter 7.)

> *To win* an election is the goal of every politician. (noun—subject)
>
> Ricardo plans *to save* his bonus for a trip next summer. (noun—direct object)
>
> Her desire is *to be president*. (noun—predicate nominative)
>
> Dixon's plan *to renovate* his house is costly. (adjective)
>
> The Sales Department advertised *to attract new customers*. (adverb)

GERUND

A **gerund** is a verb form that can function only as a noun. It is formed by adding *ing* to a verb. *Typing, hiring,* and *manufacturing* are examples of gerunds. Gerunds may be used in phrases consisting of a gerund, an object, and words modifying the object. In the following sentences the phrases are in italics, the gerunds are in bold, and their uses are in parentheses:

> ***Winning*** *an election* is the goal of every politician. (subject)
>
> Judy likes ***teaching*** *school*. (direct object)
>
> Gina's hobby is ***decorating*** *cakes*. (predicate nominative)
>
> Teri made most of her money by ***selling*** *automobiles*. (object of preposition)
>
> Don, ***acting*** *as president*, began the meeting. (appositive)

PARTICIPLE

A **participle** is a verb form that can be used as an adjective or as part of a verb phrase. The three types of participles are present, past, and perfect.

Present Participle. The **present participle verb** is always formed by adding *ing* to the present tense of a verb. The verb phrase is in italics, and the present participle is in bold in each of the following examples:

> The ambulance did not stop at the ***blinking*** *light*. (adjective)
>
> The sales force has a ***driving*** *desire* to be number one in its region. (adjective)
>
> Carl, my neighbor, is ***raking*** *my leaves*. (verb phrase)
>
> The factory is ***producing*** *too many defective doors*. (verb phrase)

The three verbals are the infinitive, the gerund, and the participle.

Infinitive = *to* + present tense of verb.

Infinitives are used as nouns, adjectives, or adverbs.

Gerunds are used only as nouns.

Gerund = verb + *ing*.

Participles are used as adjectives or as parts of verb phrases.

Present participle = present tense verb + *ing*.

Past Participle. A **past participle verb** is usually formed by adding *d* or *ed* to the present tense of a regular verb. Irregular verbs form their past participles by changing their root words. The past participle is in italics in each of the following examples:

The horses will be *brought* in air-conditioned trailers. (verb phrase—irregular verb)

The monument honors all *decorated* soldiers. (adjective—regular verb)

Tom *bought* five copiers from the new office supply store. (verb phrase—irregular verb)

The preacher is a soft-*spoken* individual. (adjective—irregular verb)

Perfect Participle. A **perfect participle verb** is always used as an adjective and is formed by combining *having* with the past participle. The perfect participles are in italics in the following sentences:

Catherine, *having changed* her major to veterinary medicine, will have to attend another university.

Candice, *having completed* the secondary research, began on the survey.

Having located the missing papers, Ms. Hughes proceeded with the meeting.

Having finished watching the news broadcast, Karen walked four miles.

NOUNS

A noun is a person, place, or thing. The two main groups of nouns are proper nouns and common nouns.

PROPER NOUNS

A **proper noun** is a particular person, place, or thing. Proper nouns are always capitalized. *Washington Monument, Charlie Buchanon, St. Louis,* and *USA Today* are examples of proper nouns.

COMMON NOUNS

A **common noun** identifies a general class of persons, places, things, or ideas. Common nouns are not capitalized. Examples of common nouns are *manager, bowl, stock, happiness,* and *deposits.* The three classes of common nouns are concrete, abstract, and collective.

Concrete Nouns. A **concrete noun** identifies those things that you can see, touch, hear, taste, or smell. Words such as *receptionist, automobile, cat, water, teacher,* and *examination* are concrete nouns. Concrete nouns are precise and easily understood, which makes them effective for business communication.

Abstract Nouns. An **abstract noun** identifies an idea, emotion, quality, or belief. Examples of abstract nouns are *charity, disappointment, love, resentment, attitude,* and *happiness.* People's opinions and feelings differ in degree; therefore, abstract nouns are less precise than concrete nouns. They should be used infrequently in business communication because they are more difficult to understand.

Past participle usually = present tense verb + *d* or *ed*.

Sometimes the root word is changed.

The perfect participle is always an adjective.

Perfect participle = *having* + past participle.

Nouns are words that identify persons, places, and things.

Proper nouns are specific.

Common nouns are general.

Concrete nouns are precise.

Abstract nouns are vague.

Collective Nouns. A **collective noun** is a group of persons or a collection of things. It is normally treated as a singular noun because the group is acting as one; however, a collective noun would be treated as a plural noun if the group members were acting as individuals. Collective nouns include *flock, audience, board of directors, team, nation, staff,* and *committee.*

Collective nouns identify a group.

COMPOUND NOUNS

Compound nouns are multiple words used to name singular nouns.

A **compound noun** is two or more words used to identify one person, place, or thing. A compound noun may be written as one or more words, or it may be hyphenated. When in doubt, consult a dictionary for the correct spelling. Compound nouns can be classified under any of the three classes of common nouns. Examples of compound nouns in each class are:

Concrete: flight attendant, vice president, mother-in-law
Abstract: self-esteem, common sense, goodwill, life cycle
Collective: booster club, board of directors, civil service

PLURAL FORMS OF NOUNS

A plural noun is normally formed by adding *s* or *es* to a singular noun.

A **plural noun** is used to identify two or more persons, places, or things. The plural of most nouns is formed by adding *s* or *es* to the singular form of the noun. Because there are so many ways of forming plurals, consult a dictionary if a question arises. Examples of different ways that nouns are formed as plurals include computer, *computers;* dress, *dresses;* company, *companies;* portfolio, *portfolios;* sister-in-law, *sisters-in-law;* deer, *deer;* and shelf, *shelves.*

POSSESSIVE FORMS OF NOUNS

Possessive nouns show ownership.

A **possessive noun** is used to show possession or ownership. The possessive form of a noun is indicated by using an apostrophe. The following general guidelines will help you correctly form possessive nouns in written communication:

1. The possessive of a singular noun not ending with an *s* or a *z* sound is formed by adding *apostrophe s.*

    singer's guitar   instructor's class

Placement of apostrophe and addition of *s* to show possession depends on the noun and the ending sound.

2. The possessive of a singular noun ending with an *s* or a *z* sound is formed by adding *apostrophe s* to a noun with one syllable and by adding only an *apostrophe* to a noun with more than one syllable.

    Hawks's notepad   Kirkpatz' house

3. The possessive of a plural noun ending with an *s* or a *z* sound is formed by adding an *apostrophe.*

    a players' coach   all employees' vacations

For compound nouns, possession is shown after the last word.

4. The possessive of a compound noun is formed by placing the *apostrophe* or *apostrophe s* after the final word or word element.

    ambassador-at-large's house   all major generals' aides

5. When two or more people share ownership of an object or objects, add an *apostrophe* or *apostrophe s* to the final name.

   Brian and Amy's cat   Ted and Agnes' automobile

6. When two or more people each own separate objects, possession is indicated by adding an *apostrophe* or *apostrophe s* to each noun.

   Brian's and Amy's cats   Ted's and Agnes' automobiles

> *Next to the originator of a good sentence is the first quoter of it.*
>
> **Ralph Waldo Emerson**

PRONOUNS

Pronouns are used in place of nouns. Pronouns make your writing more interesting because you do not repeat the noun. There are seven types of pronouns: personal, relative, interrogative, indefinite, demonstrative, reflexive, and intensive. Each type of pronoun performs a different function in a sentence.

PERSONAL PRONOUNS

A **personal pronoun** is a substitute for a noun that refers to a specific person or thing. Personal pronouns change their form when they perform different functions and appear in different parts of a sentence. The different forms are called *cases*. The three types of personal pronoun cases are nominative, possessive, and objective.

NOMINATIVE CASE

The **nominative case** is used when the pronoun functions as the subject of a sentence or a clause. The nominative case is also called the *subjective case*. Singular personal pronouns in the nominative case are *I, you, he, she,* and *it*. Plural personal pronouns in the nominative case are *we, you,* and *they*. The nominative case is also used when the pronoun follows a linking verb. The italics in the following sentences illustrate the uses of nominative case pronouns:

> *He* is making a speech. (subject of sentence)
>
> After *they* leave for school, Mary Beth goes back to bed. (subject of clause)
>
> It was *she*! (*it*—subject of sentence; *she*—follows linking verb)

POSSESSIVE CASE

The **possessive case** is used when the pronoun shows possession or ownership. The possessive case does not need an apostrophe. Singular possessive pronouns are *my, mine, your, yours, his, her, hers,* and *its*. Plural possessive pronouns are *our, ours, your, yours, their,* and *theirs*. Several examples of pronouns in the possessive case are shown in italics in the following sentences:

Is this sweater *mine*? (shows whose sweater)

Your application was submitted too late. (shows whose application)

If the notebook is not *yours*, it must be *his*. (shows whose notebook)

Our spring break comes a week after *theirs*. (shows whose spring break)

William will make *your* room reservation for the trip. (shows whose reservation)

The students support *their* mascot. (shows whose mascot)

The car lost *its* shine. (shows what lost its shine)

OBJECTIVE CASE

The **objective case** is used when the pronoun functions as an object in a sentence, clause, or phrase. Singular pronouns in the objective case are *me*, *you*, *him*, *her*, and *it*. Plural objective pronouns are *us*, *you*, and *them*. The following sentences show in italics pronouns that are performing these functions:

Did Ross see *him* make that dive? (direct object of a sentence)

I received the fax from *her*. (object of preposition)

If Jose hits *him*, Tim will call the police. (direct object of a clause)

RELATIVE PRONOUNS

A **relative pronoun** connects a group of words containing a subject and verb (a clause) to a noun or pronoun. *Who, whom, whose, which,* and *that* are the relative pronouns. If the word to which the pronoun refers is a person, use *who, whom, whose,* or *that*. Use *who* when the pronoun referring to a person is in the nominative case and *whom* when the pronoun is in the objective case. Use *which* or *that* if the pronoun refers to a thing. Relative pronouns are in italics in the following sentences:

The representative *who* sells the most furniture will win a trip to Hawaii.

George is not sure for *whom* he will vote.

Any athlete *whose* ability is great should try out for the Olympics.

The road, *which* was recently repaved, is much smoother.

The plan *that* was approved will be implemented next spring.

INTERROGATIVE PRONOUNS

An **interrogative pronoun** is used within a question. *Who, whose, whom, which,* and *what* are the interrogative pronouns. Pronouns precede verbs in questions. Like other pronouns within sentences, they function as subjects, objects, modifiers, and subject complements. The italics in the following sentences illustrate how interrogative pronouns are used:

Who told you to use my credit card number? (subject)

Whose dog won the field trials? (modifier)

Whom do I call? (object)

Which picture should be used in the advertisement? (modifier)

What was the reason for the audit? (subject complement)

INDEFINITE PRONOUNS

Indefinite pronouns do not specify a particular person or thing.

An **indefinite pronoun** is used to make a general statement about individuals or things. Indefinite pronouns include *each, anyone, one, anything,* and *nobody.* The indefinite pronouns are in italics in the following sentences:

Each of the lawyers took careful notes.

Does *anyone* plan to work on Saturday?

One of the administrators left a briefcase on the train.

Is there *anything* that I can do?

Nobody saw Mr. Jackson leave the building.

DEMONSTRATIVE PRONOUNS

Demonstrative pronouns substitute for specific nouns.

A **demonstrative pronoun** is used to indicate a specific person, place, or thing. The four demonstrative pronouns are *this, these, that, and those.* Demonstrative pronouns are in italics in these sentences:

This is the expansion plan to be used.

These are state-of-the-art CD players.

That is the reason Sally was promoted.

Are *those* the chairs that we ordered?

COMPOUND PERSONAL PRONOUNS

Compound personal pronouns are *intensive* or *reflexive.*

A **compound personal pronoun** has the suffix *self* or *selves.* A compound personal pronoun may be an intensive or reflexive pronoun. *Intensive pronouns* are used for emphasis, while *reflexive pronouns* reflect the action of the verb to the subject or to a noun or pronoun in the sentence. Examples of intensive and reflexive pronouns, in italics, follow:

He *himself* checked all visitors who entered the facility. (intensive—emphasizes a pronoun)

The ladies *themselves* made all the plans for the trip. (intensive—emphasizes a noun)

Marilyn saw *herself* as the most dedicated mother at the ceremony. (reflexive—refers to the subject)

The management thinks that he praised *himself* too much for making that one sale. (reflexive—refers to the pronoun)

ADJECTIVES

Adjectives modify nouns and pronouns and make them more precise.

An **adjective** provides additional information about a noun or a pronoun. Adjectives make the meaning of the noun or pronoun more exact by answering such questions as *which one, how many,* and *what kind.* Adjectives also are called *modifiers.*

Adjectives may be regular or irregular. *Regular adjectives* generally are one-syllable words with *er* or *est* added when making comparisons.

Irregular adjectives usually contain two or more syllables and use *less*, *least*, *more*, or *most* when making comparisons.

DEGREES OF COMPARISON IN ADJECTIVES

Adjectives change form to show degrees of comparison. There are three degrees of comparison: positive, comparative, and superlative. Examples of the degrees of comparison of adjectives are shown in Figure 6•1.

POSITIVE DEGREE

The **positive degree** is used to describe one item or one group of items. The positive form is the form used in dictionary definitions. The adjective in the positive form is in italics in the following examples:

> That computer is *small*.
>
> Henry is a *capable* manager.
>
> Their sales were *large*.
>
> Pistol Pete is a *fast* horse.

The three degrees of comparison for adjectives are positive, comparative, and superlative.

Positive degree describes one noun.

Figure 6•1 Degrees of Comparison of Adjectives

Positive	Comparative	Superlative
slow	slower	slowest
happy	happier	happiest
intelligent	more intelligent	most intelligent
considerate	less considerate	least considerate

COMPARATIVE DEGREE

The **comparative degree** is used to show the difference between two items. The comparative degree is formed by adding *er* to a regular adjective or by adding the words *more* or *less* to an irregular adjective. The adjectives used in the above examples in positive degree are shown in the comparative degree:

> That computer is *smaller* than the typewriter.
>
> Henry is a *more capable* manager than Rudolph.
>
> Rudolph is a *less capable* manager than Henry.
>
> Their sales were *larger* this quarter than last.
>
> Pistol Pete is a *faster* horse than No Risk.

Comparative degree compares two nouns.

SUPERLATIVE DEGREE

The **superlative degree** is used to compare three or more items. It can also be used for emphasis. The superlative degree is formed by adding *est* to a regular adjective or by adding *most* or *least* to an irregular adjective. The adjectives used in the previous two examples are now shown in the superlative degree:

> That computer is the *smallest* one available.
>
> Henry is the *most capable* manager.

Superlative degree compares three or more nouns.

Rudolph is the *least capable* manager.

Their sales were *largest* in the fourth quarter.

Pistol Pete is the *fastest* horse in the race.

ABSOLUTE ADJECTIVES

An **absolute adjective** is always in the superlative degree. Therefore, it cannot be compared. For example, if the design of a building is *perfect*, another building cannot have a *more perfect* design. Some absolute adjectives are *essential*, *unique*, *right*, *final*, *full*, *square*, *round*, *correct*, *never*, *dead*, and *empty*.

COMPOUND ADJECTIVES

A **compound adjective** is two or more adjectives used together to describe a single noun or pronoun. Usually, compound adjectives are hyphenated if they are placed before the noun or pronoun that they modify; they are not hyphenated if they are placed after the noun or pronoun they modify. Both rules are demonstrated by the compound adjectives in italics in the following sentences:

Carmen is a *well-respected* artist.

According to the art critics, Carmen is *well respected*.

State-of-being verbs are less powerful than action verbs.

A verb is a word that expresses an action or a *state of being*.

The astronauts are on a *one-week* voyage.

The astronauts' voyage is for *one week*.

See also "The Hyphen" section in Chapter 8 where the use of hyphens in compound adjectives (and other compound words) is discussed in detail.

ARTICLES

Although classified as adjectives, *a*, *an*, and *the* are also called **articles.** The article *the* is used to denote specific nouns or pronouns. The articles *a* and *an* are used to denote general nouns or pronouns. The articles are in italics in the following examples:

Ron read *the* best-selling novel.

Ron read *a* novel.

Ron read *an* exciting novel.

When the word following the article begins with a consonant sound (*s*tore, *b*each, *c*ar, etc.), you use *a*; use *an* if the word begins with a vowel sound (*h*our, *e*gg, *exciting*, etc.). Examples of articles and consonant and vowel sounding words are shown in italics:

Mr. Riegle is chief executive officer of *a retailing* business.

Jim gave Martha *an hourglass* for Christmas.

It is difficult to turn around *an industry*.

It is difficult to turn around *a failing industry*.

Leann earned *an A*, *a B*, and *an F*.

ADVERBS

Adverbs are used to modify verbs, adjectives, or other adverbs.

Adverbs are modifiers that restrict, limit, or describe verbs, adjectives, or other adverbs. They answer questions such as *how, when, where, why, in what manner,* or *to what degree*. Many end in *ly*. Examples of adverbs used as modifiers are shown in italics in the following sentences:

> The stock market rose *dramatically* after the announcement. (rose *how*?)
>
> Roger answered the request *promptly*. (answered *when*?)
>
> Plant the rose bushes *here*. (plant *where*?)
>
> The *extremely* bright student had all *A*'s. (*how* bright?)
>
> The building deteriorated *very quickly*. (deteriorated *how*? quickly; *to what degree*? very)

PLACEMENT OF ADVERBS

The placement of an adverb depends on how it is used in the sentence.

An adverb may be a single word (drive *carefully*), a phrase (drive *in a careful manner*), or a clause (drive *as carefully as you can*). A single-word adverb can be placed before or after the word it modifies. Prepositional and infinitive phrases and clauses that function as adverbs usually follow the word they modify. An **adverbial clause,** which is a dependent clause that acts as an adverb, precedes the independent clause in a sentence. Chapter 7 contains a detailed discussion of phrases and clauses.

DEGREES OF ADVERBS

Adverbs also have positive, comparative, and superlative degrees.

Some words that are used as adverbs as well as adjectives have positive, comparative, and superlative degrees of comparison. Examples of the degrees of comparison of adverbs are shown in Figure 6•2.

Figure 6•2 Adverb Degrees of Comparison

Positive	Comparative	Superlative
good	better	best
high	higher	highest
likely	more likely	most likely
efficient	less efficient	least efficient

PREPOSITIONS

A preposition is a connector that needs an object.

A prepositional phrase contains the preposition and its object.

A **preposition** connects a noun or pronoun to another word in a sentence. The noun or pronoun that follows the preposition is called the **object of the preposition.** A word group containing a preposition and the object of the preposition is called a **prepositional phrase.** The following sentences illustrate prepositional phrases. The prepositions are in italics, and the object of each preposition is in bold.

A letter *of* **appreciation** will be sent *to* each **member** *of* the **committee**.

Erik studied journalism *in* **1990** before he went *to* **work** *for* the local **newspaper.**

Most *of* the **people** you know are happy *with* their **positions**.

For further **information** *about* the **discount**, call Jamie.

FUNCTIONS OF PREPOSITIONAL PHRASES

Prepositional phrases work as units in a sentence. They perform the functions of adjectives and adverbs and provide variety within the sentence. Examples of prepositional phrases that act as adjectives and adverbs are in italics in these examples:

An employee *of Bob's* was arrested last night. (The prepositional phrase as adjective modifies the noun *employee*.)

Kara listened intently *to Steve's comments*. (The prepositional phrase as adverb modifies the verb *listened*.)

The receptionist, apologetic *about the phone call*, continued our conversation. (The prepositional phrase as adverb modifies the adjective *apologetic*.)

Hillary is *in a really nice time in her life*. (Both prepositional phrases act as adverbs. They modify the verb *is*.)

OBJECT OF PREPOSITION

As previously mentioned, the object of a preposition is a noun or pronoun that follows the preposition. The object of a preposition can be modified by an adjective; for example, "Curt looked at the *beautiful* sunset."

Personal pronouns and *who* have unique objective forms. The objective form of *who* is *whom*. The personal pronouns are *me, us, you, him, her,* and *them*. The objects of the prepositions are in italics in these sentences:

For *whom* are you buying the valentine?

Please give the raise to *me*.

Please reserve the rooms for *us*.

The promotional matter is between *you* and *him*.

Will you give this coat to *her*?

Why must we send it to *them*?

UNNECESSARY PREPOSITIONS

Although prepositional phrases can be used effectively to make communication more interesting, a communicator must be careful to avoid unnecessary and, therefore, incorrect prepositions. Effective business communicators avoid inserting extra prepositions within a sentence or ending a sentence with a preposition. However, ending a sentence with a preposition is acceptable in oral communication if rearranging the sentence is awkward. Use only those prepositions that clarify a sentence. The prepositions *to, of, at, for,* and *up* are frequently used unnecessarily. Examples of these uses are shown in italics in the following sentences:

The secretary asked Ralph where he was going *to*. (unnecessary preposition)
The secretary asked Ralph where he was going.

Margin notes:

Prepositional phrases work as adjectives and adverbs.

Objects of prepositions are nouns or pronouns and can be modified by adjectives.

Omit unnecessary prepositions within sentences.

Avoid ending a sentence with a preposition.

The letters fell off *of* the desk. (unnecessary preposition)
The letters fell off the desk.

Laura asked Joy where the phone book was *at*. (unnecessary preposition)
Laura asked Joy where the phone book was.

What did you do that *for*? (incorrect)
Why did you do that?

Donna will climb *up* to the top. (unnecessary preposition)
Donna will climb to the top.

Does Alice know about what it is? (awkward)
Does Alice know what it is about? (preferred)

CONJUNCTIONS

A **conjunction** is used to join words, phrases, and clauses. Conjunctions are also used to introduce clauses. Conjunctions are similar to prepositions in that they serve as connectors but are different in that they do not have objects. The three kinds of conjunctions are coordinate, correlative, and subordinate. Coordinate and correlative conjunctions join grammatically equal word elements; subordinate conjunctions join grammatically unequal word elements.

COORDINATE CONJUNCTIONS

A **coordinate conjunction** joins words, phrases, and independent clauses that are of equal importance or rank. Of equal importance or rank means that similar elements are connected; for example, adjectives are connected to adjectives and nouns are connected to nouns. The coordinate conjunctions are *and, but, or, nor, for, as,* and *yet.* The following examples show coordinate conjunctions (in italics) joining words, phrases, and independent clauses:

Their basset hounds were named J.R. *and* Myrtle. (joins nouns)

Hurriedly *but* correctly Suzy audited the books. (joins adverbs)

I hope it will not rain *or* snow for the homecoming parade. (joins verbs)

From Chicago to Cleveland *and* from Cleveland to New York City will be long drives. (joins prepositional phrases)

The dentist had a difficult time cleaning Jay's teeth, *for* the plaque had accumulated. (joins independent clauses)

CORRELATIVE CONJUNCTIONS

A **correlative conjunction** is paired with another correlative conjunction to connect two parallel words, phrases, or clauses. The most common correlative conjunction pairs are *both . . . and, either . . . or, neither . . . nor, not . . . but, not only . . . but also,* and *whether . . . or.* Examples, shown in italics, follow:

Neither Clara *nor* Jack knew about the new truck. (connects nouns)

The pie *not only* looks good *but also* tastes delicious. (connects verb phrases)

Both Jill *and* Marie are personnel directors. (connects nouns)

Either chair the committee *or* find someone who is willing. (connects clauses)

Be sure that connected elements are parallel.

A common difficulty with using correlative conjunctions involves *parallelism*. Be sure that connected elements are equal or parallel in grammatical form or rank. A detailed discussion of parallelism is in Chapter 7. The following sentences demonstrate a few parallelism errors. The correlative conjunctions are in italics.

Leon should *either* get rid of his cold *or* he should stay home. (Incorrect—*either* precedes the verb *get*, but *or* precedes the pronoun he.)

Leon should *either* get rid of his cold *or* stay home. (Correct—both conjunctions precede verbs.)

Jason plans *either* working at the office *or* to play golf this weekend. (Incorrect—*either* precedes the gerund *working* but *or* precedes the infinitive *to play*.)

Jason plans *either* to work at the office *or* to play golf this weekend. (Correct—both conjunctions precede infinitives.)
or
Jason plans *either* working at the office *or* playing golf this weekend. (Correct—both conjunctions precede gerunds.)

Gloria *not only* accepted the pay cut *but also* the contract. (Incorrect—*not only* precedes the verb *accepted* and *but also* precedes the noun *contract*.)

Gloria accepted *not only* the pay cut *but also* the contract. (Correct—both conjunctions precede nouns.)

SUBORDINATE CONJUNCTIONS

Subordinate conjunctions connect clauses of unequal rank.

A **subordinate conjunction** joins a subordinate clause to the main clause; that is, a dependent clause to an independent clause. Some subordinate conjunctions are *after, although, because, before, since, when, while, where, if, whether, though,* and *until*. The subordinate conjunctions are in italics and the main clauses are in bold in the following examples:

Since George has been ill, **he has worked only four hours a day.**

Andrea was promoted to plant manager *because* she was the best engineer.

We will continue operating under these guidelines *until* the new regulations are published.

INTERJECTIONS

Interjections express strong emotions.

An **interjection** expresses strong emotion or feeling. It is not related grammatically to any other words in a sentence. Most interjections do not have any meaning if they are taken out of the message context. An interjection is normally punctuated with an exclamation point. Interjections are seldom used in business writing. They are used sparingly in oral communication and in written advertising material. The interjections are in italics in the following examples:

Wow! That was a beautiful dive.

Help! Our warehouse is full.

Ouch! That hurts.

My goodness! How can our sales improve that much?

1. List and define the eight parts of speech.

2. Compare active and passive voices. Give an example of each.

3. Describe how verb tense is changed when using passive voice.

4. Identify the three simple tenses. Explain the use of each tense.

5. Describe the uses of the three verb moods.

6. Identify the three types of participles and explain how each is constructed.

7. Discuss the two main groups of nouns.

8. Compare the three classes of common nouns.

9. What type of verb should be used with a collective noun? Why?

10. When are pronouns used to replace nouns?

11. Distinguish between compound nouns and plural nouns, and give an example of each.

12. Explain how a singular noun ending with an *s* or a *z* sound is changed to show possession.

13. Define an interrogative pronoun and state where it is placed in a sentence.

14. Describe the three degrees of comparison used with adverbs and adjectives.

15. What is an absolute adjective? Give an example.

16. Compare the uses of the articles *a, an,* and *the.*

17. What is the difference between an adverb and an adjective? Construct a sentence that uses at least one adjective and one adverb.

18. What is an object of a preposition, and what can be used to modify it?

19. Describe how prepositions are used unnecessarily. Give examples.

20. Identify and describe the three types of conjunctions. Give an example of each.

21. What is an interjection? Give an example.

APPLICATION EXERCISES

1. Identify each verb and indicate whether it is an action or a state-of-being verb. Also indicate if the verb is in active or passive voice.

   a. What more can you do?

   b. If we get the contract, we will have to increase our production.

   c. Consolidate daily errands to eliminate unnecessary driving.

   d. The Cowboys are a good football team.

   e. The cottontail rabbit has an established home range of approximately five acres.

   f. The luggage was sent to the wrong city.

   g. The proposed regulation establishes limits on how long an airplane can be exposed to snow or freezing rain before being deiced again.

   h. Are you going to the company picnic?

   i. Antique collectors cherish things from the past.

   j. The results of the vote of the union members were taken into consideration by management.

   k. If their marriage survived this past week, it surely is solid enough for anything the future has in store.

   l. Ms. Jimenez was recommended for promotion by the committee.

   m. Steve put the proposal on Ginny's desk after he completed reading it.

2. Identify each verb or verb phrase and indicate whether it is in the indicative, imperative, or subjunctive mood.

   a. Go to Personnel on Monday.

   b. The contractors worked together extremely well after the accident occurred.

   c. If I were you, I would investigate changing insurance companies.

   d. Who brought the doughnuts for the morning break?

   e. Send my mail to Kerrie while I am attending the convention.

   f. Ted, take the video camera to the repair shop.

   g. Should you drop the class, you must repay the tuition.

3. Identify each verbal and indicate its form (infinitive, gerund, or participle).

   a. Charlotte agreed to refund the money for the cracked cup.

   b. Hiking is a relaxing and healthful pastime.

   c. I appreciate your collecting donations for the relief fund.

   d. The striking clock woke me at midnight.

   e. Talking with friends, Fred missed the results of the race.

f.   Adolph is expected to announce his decision.

g.   Instead of asking for help in unjamming the printer, Mindy broke it.

4.   Verbs and verb phrases are in italics in the following sentences. Determine the correct verb form and indicate the tense. Example: The announcement of the resignation *shake* the building. *Shook— past tense*

a.   He *has came* to this golf course for the past three years.

b.   Late last night Candace *answers* the telephone.

c.   The boy *say* he *has saw* three deer in his back yard.

d.   I *sent* the package to you next week.

e.   The dog *bark* each time that a cat *cross* the yard.

f.   By the end of the decade, all of Bill and Cindy's children *will have went* to college.

g.   *Will* you *cut* the orange for my lunch?

h.   Economic numbers *are* pretty gloomy last month.

i.   Tomorrow Betty *will spoke* to our marketing division.

j.   I *visited* the museum every week since moving to Chicago.

k.   The workers *will struck* if their demands are not met.

l.   Honest negotiations *have brought* more benefits in the future.

m.   The dog *will lay* on the rug in front of the fireplace.

5.   Identify each adjective and adverb in the following sentences and indicate how the word is used (adjective or adverb). Indicate the word that each adjective or adverb modifies.

a.   Trade analysts called the U.S. sanctions mild.

b.   The University's pride was obvious after the overwhelming victory.

c.   You always get more accomplished when you are in a crisis.

d.   Mrs. Baty's secretary really enjoys using the new laser printer.

e.   The credit card will have no annual fee.

f.   The most successful managers are those who are most concerned about their employees.

g.   Networks buy new shows from Hollywood studios and later resell them to local television stations.

h.   Glyn and Heather almost always bring their lunches to work.

i.   The law was carefully designed to prevent discrimination against disabled people.

j.   Profits were rapidly sliding, and stockholders were becoming increasingly alarmed.

k.   All employees will follow the enclosed schedule for the summer.

l.   One good sign is that revenues have picked up dramatically.

m. The silver market fell rapidly when the tycoon quickly sold his assets.

6. Common errors occur in the following sentences. Find and correct the errors. Explain each correction.

a. James attempted a trick by jumping off of the bridge.

b. Between the two secretaries, Eddie is the best typist.

c. Where are you taking the horse to?

d. Leann drove the race car too rapid on the curve.

e. The workers will either accept the contract or they will strike.

f. The shrub growed well in the open office.

g. If I was in charge of this operation, we would close on Thursday for the holiday.

h. The employee will be expected to create a database, enter data, save and retrieve files, edit, search, sort.

i. John shaped and molded the image of African Americans worldwide.

j. The company president has came by every day this week.

k. Kendall left for Europe next Tuesday.

7. Identify the part of speech for each word in the following sentences.

a. A new employee is expected to read the manual.

b. Josh raked the leaves and put them into large bags.

c. Dr. Johnson finished his rounds, and then he went to the spa to jog and to play racquetball.

d. The government should do a thorough economic analysis of the deal's effect on farmers.

e. Hurry! The sale ends Friday.

f. Today's hike was longer and required some tricky footwork crossing a beaver dam.

g. Wow! Aren't that deer's antlers magnificent?

h. Prior to investing in stocks, an individual should have a thorough understanding of economics.

i. Jim and Kaye did the inventory completely and accurately.

j. The Racers did really well.

k. Although the monthly report is accurate, changes have been made recently.

l. Nowhere will you find a state with more pride in its history than Texas.

m. If our products sell well, dividends will be distributed to stockholders.

Text 6C

Correct all grammatical errors in the following letter.

Congratulations! We observe in this morning's paper that your company will be selected last week by the Kellogg Corporation to remodel the Hallway Hotel.

We please to learn that you have been award the contract. By remodeling the Hotel, you helped bring a modern atmosphere for all visitors to downtown Battle Creek.

Our city are fortunate that your organization are handling the remodeling. We is confident that this project made the downtown area more appealing for visitors.

Sentence Structure

CHAPTER 7

Learning Objectives

Your learning objectives for this chapter include the following:

- To identify and understand the parts of sentences
- To assure grammatical agreement in sentences including subject and verb agreement, pronoun and antecedent agreement, and parallelism
- To identify and avoid the common sentence errors of dangling modifiers, double negatives, and split infinitives
- To define and give examples of the functions of sentences
- To describe and use the four basic sentence structures

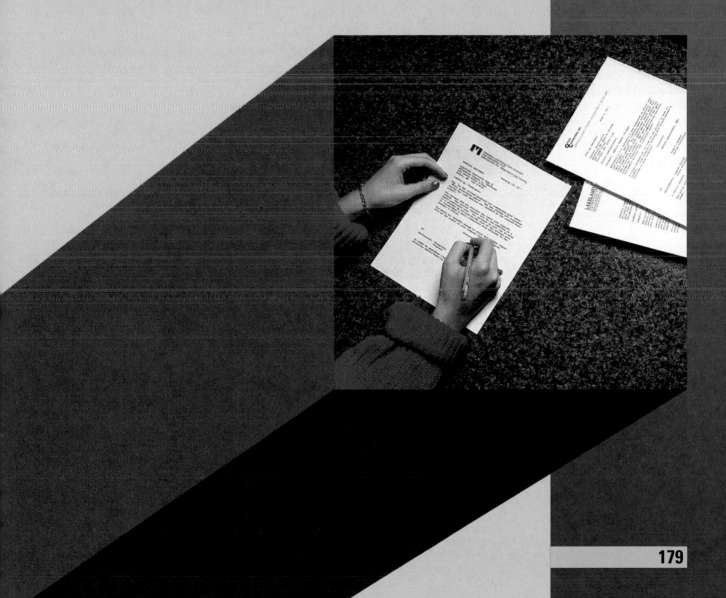

A **sentence** is a group of related words that expresses a complete thought. A sentence always contains a subject and a predicate. It is the basic unit for organizing messages.

You can improve your ability to communicate by becoming familiar with sentence construction and learning how to organize sentences.

Importance of Constructing Grammatically Correct Sentences

• Your messages will be clearer

• Your messages will be more precise

• Your credibility will be increased

PARTS OF SENTENCES

The starting point in developing your understanding of how to structure sentences is to know their two essential parts. These parts are the subject and the predicate.

THE SUBJECT

The **subject** is the part of a sentence that tells who or what is being discussed.

THE COMPLETE SUBJECT

The **complete subject** includes all words related directly to the subject. The complete subject is italicized in the following examples:

   David writes.

   Young, energetic David writes.

   She left in a hurry.

   The check, which was for over $100, was received on Monday.

THE SIMPLE SUBJECT

The **simple subject** is the main noun or pronoun in the complete subject. The simple subject in a sentence is the *who* or the *what* that performs the action or is in the state of being described in the sentence. In the following examples, the simple subject is in bold print and the complete subject is in italics:

   *Young, energetic **David*** writes. (David is the *who* that performs the action of writing.)

   *The **check**, which was for over $100,* was received on Monday. (The check is the *what* that was received.)

   *The basketball **game*** was exciting. (The game is the *what* that was exciting.)

COMPOUND SUBJECT

A compound subject is formed when two or more simple subjects are connected by a coordinate conjunction.

When two (or more) simple subjects are connected by a coordinate conjunction, a **compound subject** is formed. The coordinate conjunctions are *and, or, but, nor, for, yet,* and *so.* The compound subject is in bold print in the following examples of italicized complete subjects:

Rita and Tim went to the dance.

The *office and plant* closed for the holiday.

The *Eagles or* the *Wildcats* will win the tournament.

THE PREDICATE

The predicate tells something about the complete subject.

The **predicate** is the part of a sentence that tells something about the complete subject. The predicate may be complete, simple, or compound.

THE COMPLETE PREDICATE

The complete predicate includes the verb and all words directly related to it.

The **complete predicate** includes the verb and all the words directly related to it. The complete predicates are in italics in the following examples:

David *writes*.

She *left in a hurry*.

The memo *was printed on white paper*.

Were you *pleased with the gift?*

THE SIMPLE PREDICATE

The simple predicate is the main verb in the complete predicate.

The **simple predicate** is the main verb in the complete predicate. The verb expresses action or a state of being. The simple predicate is in bold print in these examples of complete predicates:

She **left** *in a hurry*. (*left* expresses action)

The memo **was printed** *on white paper*. (*was printed* expresses action)

They **seem** *happy*. (*seem* expresses a state of being)

COMPOUND PREDICATE

A compound predicate is formed when two or more simple predicates are connected by a coordinate conjunction.

A **compound predicate** is formed when two (or more) simple predicates are connected by a coordinate conjunction. The compound predicate is in bold print in these examples of italicized complete predicates:

She *works hard and learns well*.

The accounting report *was prepared, reviewed, and accepted*.

SUBJECT AND PREDICATE IDENTIFICATION

Analyze sentences by first locating the simple predicate and then finding the subject.

Practice in recognizing subjects and predicates will strengthen your understanding of sentence structure. It is easier to analyze sentence structure if you start by locating the simple predicate (the verb); then ask *who* or *what* to identify the subject. The following examples illustrate this approach:

The office closed at 4:30 p.m. (The action *closed* is the verb. What closed? *The office* is the subject.)

Jose manages the jewelry store. (The action *manages* is the verb. Who manages? *Jose* is the subject.)

They are good friends. (The state of being *are* is the verb. Who are? *They* is the subject.)

The rainbow was beautiful. (The state of being *was* is the verb. What was? The *rainbow* is the subject.)

Before leaving, Sally and Joyce said goodbye to everyone. (The action *said* is the verb. Who said? *Sally and Joyce* is the compound subject.)

In the mornings, George rises early and exercises. The action *rises and exercises* is the compound predicate. Who rises and exercises? *George* is the simple subject.)

In the usual sentence arrangement, the subject precedes the verb.

In inverted sentences, the verb precedes the subject.

The most common sentence arrangement is for the subject to be followed by the verb; e.g., *Reba bought a car.* A sentence in which the subject follows the verb is called an **inverted sentence.** Examples of inverted sentences include sentences beginning with *Here* or *There,* some questions, and a few other instances. The following examples, in which the subject is in bold print and the verb is in italics, illustrate this inverted arrangement:

There *are* 20 **employees** in the front office.

Here *is* the **report.**

Why *was* **she** absent?

In back *is* **Millie.**

To locate the subject and verb more easily in these cases, restate the sentence in the standard order—subject, then verb. For example:

Inverted order:	There *are* 20 **employees** in the front office.
Standard order:	Twenty **employees** *are* in the front office.
Inverted order:	Here *is* the **report.**
Standard order:	The **report** *is* here.
Inverted order:	Why *was* **she** absent?
Standard order:	**She** *was* absent why?
Inverted order:	In back *is* **Millie.**
Standard order:	**Millie** *is* in back.

In some of the previous examples, there were words or groups of words that were ignored when the predicate and subject were being located. These parts of sentences will be considered in the next sections.

OBJECTS AND SUBJECT COMPLEMENTS

Objects and complements help complete the sentence thought.

Objects and subject complements are important parts of sentences. They help to complete the thought expressed by the subject and the simple predicate. Understanding the functions of objects and subject complements will assist you in avoiding grammatical errors.

OBJECTS

An object is a noun, pronoun, or a phrase or clause that is used as a noun. Objects may be direct or indirect.

Direct objects receive the action of the verb.

A **direct object** receives the action of the verb and helps complete the thought of the sentence. The direct object answers the what? or whom?

question raised by the subject and verb. Examples of direct objects are shown in italics in the following sentences:

David writes a *memo*. (David writes what?)

If you feel qualified, you can enter the *competition*. (You enter what? Note that only action verbs can take direct objects; feel is a linking verb [see page 157 in Chapter 6].)

He studied *business communication* one semester. (He studied what?)

The instruction helped *Raymond*. (The instruction helped whom?)

An **indirect object** receives the action that the verb makes on the direct object. The indirect object usually answers the question, To whom is the action being directed? Indirect objects are always located between the verb and the direct object. You cannot have an indirect object if you do not have a direct object. Neither the direct object nor the indirect object ever appears as a prepositional phrase. You can locate the indirect object by inverting the sentence and mentally inserting the word *to*. In the following two sentences the indirect object is in bold print and the direct object is in italics:

Ritsuko reads **Genaro** the *book*. (The book was read by Ritsuko *to* Genaro.)

We sold the **customer** a *new car*. (A new car was sold by us *to* the customer.)

SUBJECT COMPLEMENTS

The **subject complement** is (1) a noun or pronoun that renames the subject, or (2) an adjective that modifies the subject. In both cases, the subject complement follows a linking verb in the sentence. A **linking verb** (such as, *is, was, has been, am, are*, and *seem*) does not show action. In each of the following examples, the subject and the subject complement are in italics and the linking verb is in bold print:

Robert Burton **is** an excellent *communicator*. (*Communicator* is a noun that renames *Robert Burton*.)

The *letter* **was** *long*. (*Long* is an adjective that modifies *letter*.)

He **is** a leading *CEO*. (*CEO* is a noun that renames *he*.)

I **am** the *president*. (*President* is a noun that renames *I*.)

PHRASES, CLAUSES, AND FRAGMENTS

Being able to identify groupings of words—referred to as *phrases* or *clauses*—is important for understanding sentence structure. Also, you should know what sentence fragments are and make conscious decisions on whether you will use them.

PHRASES

A **phrase** is a group of related words that functions as a part of speech. Phrases do not contain both a subject and a verb; some phrases contain one or the other, some contain neither. Here are some examples of phrases:

Verb phrases:	can sell/have keyed/is considered
Noun phrases:	the home office/a fast car/an excellent proposal
Prepositional phrases:	to the store/by the beginning/in the past

Adjective phrases:	bright and articulate/ready to wear/above aveage
Participial phrases:	having been promoted/seeing clearly/keying rapidly
Infinitive phrases:	to know/to call/to have told/to be congratulated

Phrases can strengthen and add life to writing.

Using phrases as parts of speech—as adjectives, adverbs, and nouns—can make your writing more interesting. They can add variety and color. Phrases are a way to add strong words to your sentences and bring power to your writing. Finally, they can strengthen your writing by providing helpful details and showing relationships. Note how the italicized phrases in the following examples add detail, variety, color, interest, power, and liveliness:

John manages. (no phrases)

John manages employees *in the plant*. (prepositional phrase)

John manages *better than the average person*. (adjective phrase)

John, *a better-than-average manager*, oversees *40 employees*. (adjective phrase, noun phrase)

John seems *to be a natural at managing*. (infinitive phrase)

A capable manager, John oversees *40 employees*. (adjective phrase, noun phrase)

Managing effectively, John oversees *40 employees*. (participial phrase, noun phrase)

Understanding the purpose of the phrase is also important. For example, prepositional phrases can serve as adjectives and adverbs. If a phrase is serving as an adjective, it should be placed close enough to the noun it modifies so that the relationship is clear.

Wrong:	The members present were of the union.
Right:	The members of the union were present.

The phrase *of the union* serves as an adjective and modifies the noun *members*. This relationship is more clearly understood if the modifying phrase is close to the noun.

CLAUSES

A clause has both a subject and a verb.

Independent clauses can stand alone.

A **clause** is a group of related words that contains both a subject and a predicate. There are two kinds of clauses: independent and dependent. An **independent clause,** sometimes referred to as the *main clause,* expresses a complete thought and has a subject and a predicate. It can stand alone as a separate sentence. In the following examples of independent clauses, the simple predicates are shown in bold print, and the subjects are shown in italics:

both *the telephone and the fax* **are** important communication tools

the *environmental group* **fought** the change

A **dependent clause,** also called a *subordinate clause,* does not express a complete thought and cannot stand alone. The dependent clause contains both a subject and a predicate; but, because of its construction, it depends upon another clause for the thought to be complete. The dependent clause is almost always introduced by a subordinate conjunction (such as, *because, as soon as, if,* or *when*) or by a relative pronoun (such as, *who, which,* or *that*). Look at the subordinate conjunction or relative pronoun (shown in bold print), the simple subject (in bold italics), and the simple predicate (in regular italics) in these examples of dependent clauses:

when the ***report*** *has been received*

because the ***factory*** *is* now open

The basic difference between dependent and independent clauses is the use of a subordinate conjunction or relative pronoun. If you add a subordinate conjunction to an independent clause, you make it a dependent clause. On the other hand, if you were to omit the subordinate conjunction or relative pronoun at the beginning of the previous illustrations of dependent clauses, those clauses would become independent clauses:

the report has been received

the factory is now open

One other point related to clauses—the word *like* should not be used to introduce a clause. Grammar rules permit using *like* as a verb, adjective, or preposition, but *as* should be used to introduce clauses.

Wrong: The message is short *like* you wanted it to be.

Right: The message is short *as* you wanted it to be.

SENTENCE FRAGMENTS

A **sentence fragment** is a group of words that may or may not have meaning. *Sentence fragment* is another name for an *incomplete sentence*. Note the following examples:

if the offer is on the table (lacks meaning)

Congratulations! (has meaning in context)

Pat, having been transferred (lacks meaning)

Best wishes for success. (has meaning in context)

While the use of sentence fragments that have some meaning in context is fairly common in business communication, the acceptability of their usage is debated. Some business communicators think the infrequent, selective use of meaningful sentence fragments gives life and personality to their messages. Other business communicators do not use sentence fragments because, technically, they are grammatically incorrect. You will need to make your own decision on this issue.

SENTENCE PATTERNS

A helpful approach to understanding sentence construction for many students is to examine the most common basic sentence patterns. While the English language is extremely flexible, the following patterns are the most frequently used:

Dependent clauses are introduced by subordinate conjunctions or relative pronouns; they cannot stand alone as sentences.

Sentence fragments are incomplete sentences and may or may not have meaning.

Some writers selectively use sentence fragments; others never use them.

A common sentence pattern is subject → verb → object or complement.

1. Subject → Verb
   David → writes.
2. Subject → Verb → Direct Object
   David → writes → memos.
3. Subject → Verb → Indirect Object → Direct Object
   David → writes → Joshua → a memo.
4. Subject → Verb → Subject Complement
   Ed → is → fine.
5. Here (or There) → Verb → Subject
   Here → is → your purchase order.

SUBJECT AND VERB AGREEMENT

One of the basic rules of sentence construction is that the subject and the verb must *agree in number*. If the subject is singular—refers to just one person or one thing—then the verb must be singular. If the subject is plural, the verb must also be plural. Your ability to identify the subject is essential to determining whether it is singular or plural. The subject and the verb are in italics in the following examples:

Singular:	The *accountant was* in the office.
Plural:	The *accountants were* in the office.

Singular:	The *pilot flies* the plane.
Plural:	The *pilots fly* the planes.

Recall that adding an *s* to most subjects makes them plural and adding an *s* to most verbs makes them singular. If you are not sure whether the subject is singular or plural (for example, a word like *athletics*), look it up in a dictionary. Then use the verb that agrees with the number of the subject.

Words between the subject and the verb (intervening words) must be ignored when determining the correct number of the subject. In the following examples the subject and the verb are in bold print, and the word or words to be ignored are in italics:

Singular:	The **man** *with the books* **is** the salesperson.
Plural:	The **men** *with the books* **are** the salespersons.

Singular:	The **computer,** *as well as the printers,* **was** new.
Plural:	The **players,** *other than Tim,* **were** on time for the golf game.

Recall that a compound subject is two (or more) subjects connected by a coordinate conjunction. Some compound subjects take singular verbs and some take plural verbs.

There are four possibilities:

1. When compound subjects are connected by *and,* they are plural and require a plural verb.
2. When compound subjects are connected by *or* or *nor,* and both are singular, they take singular verbs.

3. When compound subjects are connected by *or* or *nor,* and both are plural, they take plural verbs.

4. When compound subjects are connected by *or* or *nor,* and one of the subjects is plural and one singular, the verb should agree with the number of the subject which is closer to it.

The compound subjects are in bold print, and their correct verbs are in italics in these examples:

Plural:	**Aurelia and Esteban** *are* students.
Plural:	The **purchasing agent,** the **sales manager,** and the **accountant** *attend* all the departmental meetings.
Singular:	Either **Bill or Erika** *is* to go first.
Singular:	Neither **Sheila nor David** *is* going.
Plural:	Neither the **cabins nor** the **tents** *are* available for shelter.
Singular:	The **tents or** the **cabin** *is* available for shelter.
Plural:	Neither the **cabin nor** the **tents** *are* available for shelter.

Notice in the last two examples that the plural verb sounds better. In sentences with both singular and plural subjects, this is almost always true. It will be best for you, therefore, to try to put the plural subject closer to the verb.

Some subjects appear to be plural but are singular.

Some words used as subjects are singular even though they may give the appearance of being plural. Examples of these words are *everybody, everyone, anybody, anyone, somebody, someone, nobody,* and *neither.* With these singular subjects, use singular verbs:

Singular:	Anyone is (not *are*) invited.
Singular:	Everybody is (not *are*) welcome.
Singular:	Each of the managers attends (not *attend*) a conference.
Singular:	Neither was (not *were*) at work yesterday.

Also, some words that end in *s* are singular. Use singular verbs with those words:

Singular:	Athletics is an extracurricular activity.
Singular:	Mathematics is my favorite subject.
Singular:	Economics is an important field of study.

The name of one song, book, company, magazine, or article is singular even though the name is plural:

Singular:	*People* is an interesting magazine.
Singular:	Furniture Movers, Inc., is located in Los Angeles.
Singular:	"Heartaches" is an old song.

Subjects in plural form that are considered as a single unit or as a whole take singular verbs. Amounts, distances, and some compound subjects are examples of this guideline:

Singular:	Twenty-five miles is the distance to Syracuse.

Singular:	Seven to nine pounds is the normal weight for a minia-ture dachshund.
Singular:	Turkey and dressing is a Thanksgiving favorite.

Some subjects appear to be singular but are plural.

The words *few*, *both*, *many*, and *several* are considered plural and take plural verbs. For example:

Plural:	Few think that the economy is in a deep recession.
Plural:	Both were promoted after only one year.
Plural:	Many are pleased with the company's progress.
Plural:	Several are contributing time to the United Fund.

Collective nouns may be singular or plural.

Collective nouns such as *committee*, *faculty*, and *audience* may be singular or plural. If the group is acting as one, the verb should be singular. If the group members are acting as individuals, the verb should be plural:

Singular:	The committee has met four times this week.
Plural:	The faculty are teaching their classes in spite of the noisy construction project.

PRONOUN AND ANTECEDENT AGREEMENT

Pronouns and their antecedents should agree.

Pronouns are noun substitutes.

Pronouns replace antecedents.

To be grammatically correct in your communication, you will want to know and use another form of agreement—the *agreement of pronouns and their antecedents*. Recall that pronouns are noun substitutes. The pronouns used as subjects, objects, or complements are *he, she, I, we, you, it, her, him, them*, and *they*. As a possessive, a pronoun is used as a modifier. Examples of possessive pronouns are *my, mine, our(s), your(s), his, her(s)*, and *their(s)*. An **antecedent** is a word, phrase, or clause that is replaced by the pronoun. An antecedent is most likely to be a noun.

Pronouns and their antecedents should agree in number.

Pronouns and their antecedents must agree in three ways: (1) in number, (2) in gender, and (3) in clear relationship. In the following examples of agreement in number, the antecedent is in italics and the pronoun is in bold print:

Singular:	*Dan* reported on Friday, and **he** said the sale is final.
Plural:	*Dan* and *Yoko* reported on Friday, and **they** said the sale is final.
Singular:	*Anna* found **her** coat in the conference room.
Plural:	*Anna* and *Frieda* found **their** coats in the conference room.
Singular:	*Everybody* sat at **his or her** desk.
Plural:	The *employees* sat at **their** desks.
Singular:	*Coats, Inc.*, is opening **its** fourteenth store.
Plural:	All Coats, Inc., *employees* believe **their** company will continue to grow.
Singular:	Either *Edward* or *Jonathan* will sell **his** quota this month.
Plural:	*Edward* and *Jonathan* will sell **their** quotas this month.

| Singular: | The *number* is high; **it** exceeds 100. |
| Plural: | A *number* of employees have voted **their** convictions. |

Pronouns and their antecedents should agree in gender.

The next set of examples of pronouns and their antecedents shows agreement in gender. The antecedent is in italics and the pronoun is in bold print:

Masculine:	*Alan* will key **his** memo today.
Feminine:	*Nancy* keyed **her** memo yesterday.
Mixed:	Every *man* and *woman* must key **his** or **her** memo before the meeting on Wednesday.
Neuter:	A *project* is completed when **its** recommendations are finalized.

Pronouns and their antecedents should clearly relate.

Finally, there must be a clear relationship between a pronoun and its antecedent. Examples of unclear relationships and clear relationships follow:

Unclear:	Luis spoke with the president, and he said the plan would work. (Antecedent not clear; who said the plan would work?)
Clear:	Luis spoke with the president, and Luis said the plan would work.
Unclear:	Vincent wrote Atsushi when he was in Texas. (Who was in Texas?)
Clear:	When Vincent was in Texas, he wrote Atsushi.

PARALLELISM

Sentence constructions should be parallel.

One other important form of agreement you will want to use in constructing correct sentences is parallelism. **Parallelism** means having balance and consistency between or among parts of sentences that serve the same function.

The same grammatical form should be used for parts that serve the same function.

Parallelism is achieved by using the same grammatical form for the two or more parts of sentences that serve the same function. Using the same grammatical form means using noun with noun, adjective with adjective, verb with verb, adverb with adverb, phrase with phrase, or clause with clause. Parts of sentences serve the same function if they serve as a part of a series, a contrast, a comparison, a choice, or an expression of equality.

Different examples of parallelism are shown in the following illustrations. The parts of these sentences that are not parallel are shown in bold print.

SERIES

Parts of series should be parallel.

Not parallel:	Jane is responsible for finance, production, and **to oversee marketing.** (Two parts of the series, *finance* and *production,* are nouns; one part, *to oversee marketing,* is an infinitive phrase.)
Parallel:	Jane is responsible for finance, production, and marketing. (All parts of the series are nouns.)
Not parallel:	He completed the accounting report quickly, accurately, and **with a neat appearance.** (The parts, *quickly* and *accurately,* are adverbs; *with a neat appearance* is a prepositional phrase.)

Parallel:	He completed the accounting report quickly, accurately, and neatly. (All parts of the series are adverbs.)
Not parallel:	Judy is bright, **a hard worker,** and personable. (While other parts of the series are adjectives, *a hard worker* is an adjective-noun combination.)
Parallel:	Judy is bright, tireless, and personable. (All parts of the series are adjectives.)

Parts of contrasts should be parallel.

CONTRAST

Not parallel:	Vicky speaks clearly but **writes with many errors.** (The part *speaks clearly* is a verb-adverb combination, but *writes with many errors* is a verb-prepositional phrase combination.)
Parallel:	Vicky speaks clearly, but writes poorly. (Both parts are verb-adverb combinations.)

Parts of comparisons should be parallel.

COMPARISON

Not parallel:	Your selling season is longer than **the Youngblood RV Center.** (The comparison is not clear—selling season is longer than Youngblood RV Center? The necessary information to complete the comparison is omitted.)
Parallel:	Your selling season is longer than the Youngblood RV Center's selling season. (Both parts of the comparison now contain clarifying adjective-noun combinations.)

Expressions of equality should be parallel.

EXPRESSION OF EQUALITY

Not parallel:	Mary Lea hired an assertive salesperson and **accountant.** (The use of the adjective *assertive* as a modifier for *salesperson* and *accountant* produce the unlikely meaning that they are to be one person.)
Parallel:	Mary Lea hired an assertive salesperson and an accurate accountant. (The use of appropriate articles and modifiers in both places clarifies that two people were hired.)

Parallel constructions are both correct and clear.

The parallel constructions in these illustrations are generally shorter, clearer, and stronger than the constructions that are not parallel. Achieving parallelism in your sentences improves their readability and maintains their momentum. Because of their balance and consistency, parallel constructions communicate effectively as well as correctly.

COMMON SENTENCE ERRORS

Avoid common sentence errors.

Dangling modifiers and double negatives are common sentence errors you will want to avoid. English language grammarians are currently debating whether splitting an infinitive is an error; your decision on splitting an infinitive should be a conscious one.

DANGLING MODIFIERS

Avoid dangling modifiers; modifiers must be placed correctly.

A **dangling modifier** exists in a sentence when a phrase that limits or slightly changes the meaning of a word is not placed so that its relationship to that word is clear. In other words, the modifying phrase is *dangling* if it is too far removed from the word it modifies. For clarity in your messages, avoid dangling modifiers. In each of the following examples, the modifier is in italics and the word to be modified is in bold print:

Incorrect: The personnel **manager** hesitated to explain the policy to the employee, *seemingly confused.* (Who is *seemingly confused?*)

Correct: The personnel **manager,** *seemingly confused,* hesitated to explain the policy to the employee. (Moving the modifier closer to **manager** clarifies the relationship.)

Incorrect: *When still a new employee,* my supervisor gave **me** a major report writing assignment. (Who was the *new employee?*)

Correct: *When still a new employee,* **I** was given a major report writing assignment by my supervisor. (Modifier *When still a new employee* now clearly modifies the subject, **I,** in the rephrased sentence.)

DOUBLE NEGATIVES

Avoid double negatives; do not use negative adverbs and negative verbs together.

A **double negative** is formed when a negative adverb (*no, not, hardly, barely, scarcely,* etc.) is used in the same sentence with a negative verb (*can't, couldn't, won't, didn't,* etc.). Such constructions are illogical because their use actually forms a positive. Double negatives are grammatically unacceptable and should be avoided. In the following examples the negative adverbs are in bold print and the negative verbs in italics:

Incorrect: I *don't* **hardly** know how to tell her. (The negative adverb **hardly** and the negative verb *don't* are used in the same sentence.)

Correct: I *don't* know how to tell her. (The negative adverb **hardly** has been removed from the sentence.)

Incorrect: It *won't* do **no** good to suggest another time. (The negative verb *won't* and negative adverb **no** are used in the same sentence.)

Correct: It *will* do **no** good to suggest another time. (The negative verb *won't* has been changed to the positive verb *will.*)

SPLIT INFINITIVES

Avoid split infinitives when possible; do not place adverb between *to* and a verb.

An infinitive is formed by placing the word *to* before a present tense verb (*to accept, to agree, to feel,* etc.). A **split infinitive** is formed when an adverb is placed between the *to* and the verb (to *bravely* accept, to *barely* agree, to *warmly* feel, etc.). Although the trend is toward accepting split infinitives, many receivers still believe they are ungrammatical. It is best to avoid them when possible. Avoid, too, using several words to divide the infinitive. In the following examples, the infinitives are in bold print and the adverbs or other words that split the infinitives are in italics:

Incorrect: The manager wants you **to** *carefully* **consider** the decision. (The infinitive **to consider** has been split by the adverb *carefully.*)

Correct:	The manager wants you **to consider** *carefully* the decision. (The adverb *carefully* has been placed after the infinitive.)
Incorrect:	The manager wants you **to** *as carefully as possible* **consider** the decision. (Several words, *as carefully as possible*, split the infinitive **to consider.**)
Correct:	The manager wants you **to consider** the decision *as carefully as possible*. (The words *as carefully as possible* have been moved to the end of the sentence so they do not split the infinitive.)

Some split infinitives seem to sound better than do technically correct versions. In these cases you should either use the split infinitive or reword the sentence to avoid the problem. For example:

Technically Correct:	He seems to feel barely the cold wind. (The wording *to feel barely* is awkward.)
Split Infinitive:	He seems to barely feel the cold wind. (When the infinitive *to feel* is split with the adverb *barely*, the sentence sounds better.)
Revision:	The cold wind does not seem to bother him. (The revision avoids the problem of a split infinitive.)

FUNCTIONS OF SENTENCES

Sentences can serve one of four basic functions. These four functions are:

1. *To state a fact.* A statement or **declarative sentence** is followed by a period. For example:

   The store held open house on December 1.

   Penny spoke with Karen about the request.

2. *To ask a question.* A question or **interrogative sentence** is followed by a question mark. For example:

   Have you finished your report?

   Are you going to the office?

3. *To issue a command or make a courteous request.* A command or request, also known as an **imperative sentence,** is followed by a period. Usually *you* is understood as the subject in a command or request. For example:

   [You] Please bring the file to our next meeting.

   [You] Send the application form to Ai-lien Chang.

4. *To express strong emotion.* An exclamation or **exclamatory sentence** is followed by an exclamation point. For example:

   Congratulations on your promotion!

   It's raining!

> *It is my ambition to say in ten sentences, what others say in a whole book.*
>
> **Nietzsche**

TYPES OF SENTENCE STRUCTURES

There are four sentence structures.

Finally, for you to know how to construct correct sentences, it is essential that you know the four basic sentence structures. The technical names of these sentence structures are *simple sentence, compound sentence, complex sentence,* and *compound-complex sentence.* Sentence structures are classified on the basis of the number and kinds of clauses they have. The two kinds of clauses—independent (main) and dependent (subordinate)—were discussed earlier in this chapter.

Your messages will be more interesting if you vary the sentence structures you use. You can also emphasize an idea by placing it in an independent clause or de-emphasize it by placing it in a dependent clause. The effective communicator understands and uses all four sentence structures.

THE SIMPLE SENTENCE

Simple sentences contain one independent clause.

The **simple sentence** contains one independent clause and no dependent clauses. You will recall that independent clauses contain both a subject and a predicate and are not introduced with a subordinate conjunction or a relative pronoun. Also, simple sentences can have compound subjects or compound predicates and can include phrases. Here are some examples of typical simple sentences:

> David writes. (simple sentence)
>
> Ms. Crawford and Mr. Sams approved the proposal. (simple sentence with compound subject)
>
> Sales of personal computers doubled last year. (simple sentence with prepositional phrase)
>
> Because of the extension of the reporting date, we can edit and proofread our report again. (simple sentence with introductory prepositional phrase and compound predicate)
>
> Mr. Frederickson is the fifth president of Swanger Company. (simple sentence with prepositional phrase)

Simple sentences are businesslike, but overuse results in choppy speaking or writing.

You can make your communication of an idea more powerful by using a simple sentence. This sentence structure gives the greatest emphasis to the idea because there are no distracting dependent clauses. The simple sentence is especially effective in composing business messages. It is a clear, concise, and efficient way of communicating—the simple sentence is businesslike. Overuse of simple sentences in a message, however, can result in choppy, singsong monotony—particularly if the sentences are all short. Note the choppiness in the following paragraph:

> The catalog was received. The order was placed. The machine and the conveyor were received. Both worked at first. We started production. But the machine failed. The supervisor tried to fix it. The engineer tried to fix it. They both were unsuccessful. We called the manufacturer. Repair service can be performed in two weeks.

To make your writing more interesting and possibly to de-emphasize some ideas, you will want to use sentence structures other than simple sentences.

THE COMPOUND SENTENCE

Compound sentences contain two or more independent clauses.

The **compound sentence** contains two or more independent clauses and no dependent clauses. In this sentence structure, two or more ideas share emphasis. By pairing the ideas in one sentence consisting of independent clauses of similar strength, the ideas receive somewhat less emphasis than they would in separate simple sentences.

In the following examples, the subjects are in italics and the verbs are in bold print. Note in these examples that the independent clauses in each compound sentence are joined with a coordinate conjunction, a conjunctive adverb, or a semicolon:

> *Laurie* **will fly** to the conference, and *she* **will speak** on communication at the 9 A.M. session.

> *Birgit* **worked** for International Importing for three years; *Michele* **worked** for Cosmopolitan Company for five years.

> *Mr. Riley* **was offered** the position, but *he* **did not accept** the offer.

> The *applicants* **appeared** to be equally qualified; however, *most* of the managers **believed** that Mr. Riley was the best choice for the job.

Here is the example paragraph from the top of this page modified to show the use of compound sentences:

> The catalog was received, and the order was placed. The machine and the conveyor were received, and both worked at first. We started production, but the machine failed. The supervisor and the engineer tried to fix it, but both were unsuccessful. We called the manufacturer, and we were told that repair service can be performed in two weeks.

Compound sentences can convey a close relationship of two or more ideas.

The use of the compound sentence structure enables you to show that two or more ideas are of equal importance. By putting them together in one sentence, you indicate a close relationship which constitutes another, larger idea.

THE COMPLEX SENTENCE

Complex sentences contain one independent clause and one or more dependent clauses.

The **complex sentence** contains one independent clause and one or more dependent clauses. Remember that a dependent clause depends on the independent clause to make a complete thought— hence, the term *dependent clause*.

In the *complex sentence* structure, one or more ideas are subordinated to the main idea. The less important or negative ideas can be de-emphasized by placing them in dependent clauses; the main idea can be emphasized by placing it in the independent clause. Another advantage of the complex sentence is that the dependent clause can be used to further explain, clarify, and strengthen the main idea. The dependent clauses commonly used in complex sentences are the following kinds:

Ideas can be emphasized and de-emphasized in complex sentences.

- Noun clauses—used as subjects and objects
- Adjective clauses—used to modify nouns and pronouns
- Adverb clauses—used to modify verbs

As you know, a dependent clause contains both a subject and a verb and is introduced with a subordinate conjunction (such as, *because, although, while, as soon as, if, whether,* or *when*) or a relative pronoun (such as, *who, which,* or *that*). In the following examples the dependent clauses are in italics:

> *Although 99 percent of American retail stores stay open all year,* most of them make more than half their profit during the November-December holiday season.

> *While it is important that you be on time for work,* "flextime" permits you to choose your starting time.

> You will want to know *that many call the independent clause the main clause.*

> The independent clause is either preceded or followed by the dependent clause, *which may be referred to as the subordinate clause.*

> All *who are being promoted* will receive raises.

> *When new graduates seek employment,* they should be sure to use their networks of friends, acquaintances, and relatives.

Here is the example paragraph using complex sentences:

> The order was placed when the catalog was received. Since the machine and conveyor were received in working order, production was started. When the machine failed, the supervisor and the engineer tried to fix it. Because they both were unsuccessful, we called the manufacturer who told us that repair service can be performed in two weeks.

Complex sentences are more complicated than simple sentences in that they carry more than one idea. By its design, this structure causes some ideas to be de-emphasized and some ideas to be emphasized.

To help you more fully realize the importance of correct grammar and sentence structure in your communications, review two examples of messages. Figure 7•1 is an example of a **poor** memo. Its writer will lose credibility because of the grammatical errors and poor sentence structure. Figure 7•2 is a **good** version of the same memo, a message that will gain credibility because of its correctness.

FACTORY DIRECT SALES, INC.

Interoffice Memorandum

TO: Charles Murray, Manager
Distribution Services

FROM: Vincent Harrison, Supervisor V.H.
Shipping Department

DATE: September 25, 199-

SUBJECT: Improvement of Shipping Turnaround Time

Needs Work

As you know, the average time it takes for us to ship an order is 4.2 days. All of them in the shipping department thinks that this amount of shipping turnaround time is too much.

> Pronoun is incorrect; subject and predicate do not agree.

> Sentence is incomplete.

I estimate that the shipping turnaround time of 4.2 days could be reduced. By at least two days with the hiring of an additional employee for the shipping department. A new employee's salary would be approximately $22,000. Their fringe benefits would be approximately $6,500.

> Short, choppy, simple sentences; pronoun is incorrect.

The benefits to Factory Direct Sales, Inc., include shipping time, improved morale, and fewer complaints. Specifically, the benefits are:

> Series is not parallel.

1. Competitive shipping time with other direct sales and catalog sales companies.

2. The morale of the shipping department workers would improve.

3. Fewer customer complaints about our shipping time.

> List is not parallel.

Because of these benefits I recommend the hiring of one additional employee for the shipping department. As the holiday season is quickly approaching. I recommend that we hire before October 1.

> Sentence is incomplete.

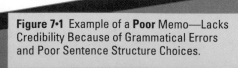

Figure 7-1 Example of a **Poor** Memo—Lacks Credibility Because of Grammatical Errors and Poor Sentence Structure Choices.

FACTORY DIRECT SALES, INC.

Interoffice Memorandum

GOOD

TO: Charles Murray, Manager
Distribution Services

FROM: Vincent Harrison, Supervisor   V.H.
Shipping Department

DATE: September 25, 199-

SUBJECT: Improvement of Shipping Turnaround Time

As you know, the average time it takes for us to ship an order is 4.2 days. All of the shipping department employees think that this amount of shipping turnaround time is too much.

> *Pronoun error is eliminated; subject all and predicate think agree.*

I estimate that the shipping turnaround time of 4.2 days could be reduced by at least two days with the hiring of an additional employee for the shipping department. A new employee's salary would be approximately $22,000, and his or her fringe benefits would be approximately $6,500.

> *Sentence is complete and shows relationship of ideas.*

> *Sentence combines related ideas; pronouns agree with antecedent.*

The benefits to Factory Direct Sales, Inc., include reduced shipping time, improved morale, and fewer complaints. Specifically, the benefits are:

1. Competitive shipping time with other direct sales and catalog sales companies.
2. Improved morale in the shipping department.
3. Fewer customer complaints about our shipping time.

> *Series is parallel; all parts are adjective-noun combinations.*

> *List is parallel; item No. 2 changed to be compatible.*

Because of these benefits I recommend the hiring of one additional employee for the shipping department. As the holiday season is quickly approaching, I recommend that we hire before October 1.

> *Sentence is complete and shows relationship of ideas.*

Figure 7·2 Example of a **Good** Memo—Gains Credibility Because of Grammatical Correctness and Appropriate Sentence Structure Choices.

THE COMPOUND-COMPLEX SENTENCE

Compound-complex sentences contain two or more independent clauses and one or more dependent clauses.

The **compound-complex sentence** contains two or more independent clauses and one or more dependent clauses. The compound-complex sentence structure offers a business communicator the advantages of both the compound and complex sentences. Ideas can be related, emphasized, and de-emphasized in this complicated structure.

Compound-complex sentences are used infrequently in business messages because of their length.

The compound-complex sentence structure, however, can become long and cumbersome. Business readers want to be able to understand a sentence on the first reading. For this reason this sentence structure is used infrequently in business messages. In the following examples of compound-complex sentences, the dependent clauses are in italics and the independent clauses are in bold print:

> *Because many businesses are in isolated areas,* **volunteer fire fighting organizations are important to them;** *in addition to fighting fires effectively,* **these volunteer organizations help keep insurance rates low.**

> *Although Gail and Robert are going on vacation,* **their work must go on;** *fortunately,* **Eva and Paul are experienced and can do the work in their absence.**

Here is the example paragraph using compound-complex sentences:

> When the catalog was received, the order was placed; the machine and conveyor were received in working order, so production was started. When the machine failed, the supervisor and the engineer tried to fix it; because they both were unsuccessful, we called the manufacturer who told us that repair service can be performed in two weeks.

In your development of business messages, you have the opportunity to increase your effectiveness significantly by giving attention to sentence construction. In this chapter you have studied material that will assist you in composing correct, interesting, and powerful sentences. You have increased your ability as a business communicator.

DISCUSSION QUESTIONS

1. Define a *sentence*. Explain the difference between a complete sentence and a sentence fragment.

2. Define the *subject* of a sentence, and explain the difference between the complete subject and the simple subject.

3. Define the *predicate* of a sentence, and explain the difference between the complete predicate and the simple predicate.

4. Why are some subjects called *compound subjects*? Give an example of a compound subject.

5. Why are some predicates called *compound predicates*? Give an example of a compound predicate.

6. What is a good technique for identifying verbs and subjects in sentences?

7. What is an inverted sentence? Give an example.

8. What is the difference between direct objects and indirect objects? Give an example of a sentence that contains both a direct object and an indirect object.

9. Describe subject complements. Give an example of each type of subject complement.

10. Define the term *phrase*. Give an example of (a) a verb phrase, (b) a noun phrase, (c) a prepositional phrase, (d) an adjective phrase, (e) a participial phrase, and (f) an infinitive phrase.

11. Define the term *clause*. What is the difference between an independent clause and a dependent clause? Give an example of each.

12. Discuss the pros and cons of using sentence fragments in business communication. Give an example of a sentence fragment.

13. Create a correct sentence for each of the following sentence patterns:

    a. Subject → Verb
    b. Subject → Verb → Direct Object
    c. Subject → Verb → Indirect Object → Direct Object
    d. Subject → Verb → Subject Complement
    e. Here (or There) → Verb → Subject

14. What does the term *agreement* in sentence construction mean? In your answer, explain subject-verb agreement, pronoun-antecedent agreement, and parallelism.

15. Give examples of:

    a. subject and verb disagreement and agreement

b. pronoun and antecedent disagreement and agreement

c. lack of parallelism and parallelism

16. Describe the following sentence errors: (a) dangling modifier, (b) double negative, and (c) split infinitive.

17. What are the four functions of sentences? Give an example sentence for each function.

18. Describe and give an example of a simple sentence.

19. Describe and give an example of a compound sentence.

20. Describe and give an example of a complex sentence.

21. Describe and give an example of a compound-complex sentence.

22. Explain why business communicators should vary the sentence structures they use. Give the advantages and disadvantages of each structure discussed.

APPLICATION EXERCISES

1. On a separate sheet of paper write each of the following sentences. Identify the complete subject by underlining it once and the complete predicate by underlining it twice.

a. The house will be moved by Movers, Inc.

b. Cecil was able to talk to Fred about the new product.

c. Joe initiated the new product line.

d. Jean, the plant manager, also was active in politics.

e. Jan, who was just promoted, is now supervisor of the Information Processing Center.

f. All of the merchandise was replaced.

g. The sun and the moon were all that he wanted.

h. Productivity in the plant was up 55 percent.

i. There were seven employees on vacation at the same time.

j. Why can't you return the stereo?

Text 7A

2. Circle the simple subject and the simple predicate in each sentence in Application 1.

3. List the letter for each sentence in the following paragraph. Write the complete subject for that sentence beside the letter.

(a) Many types of businesses can be profitable. (b) Among the most profitable are restaurants. (c) But there can also be business failures. (d) It comes down to quality—quality food and quality management. (e) Constantine and Norma opened a

Greek restaurant. (f) The two of them bought only the best food, and they oversaw its careful preparation. (g) Although Constantine and Norma charged high prices, many customers were served; and excellent profits were made.

4. List the letter for each sentence in Application 3. Write the complete predicate for that sentence beside the letter.

5. List the letter of each of the following sentences. Write the direct objects and any indirect objects for that sentence beside the letter.

   a. Ping-lin drove the car to Tony's house.
   b. Ping-lin gave Tony the car.
   c. The supervisor evaluated the worker.
   d. The supervisor offered the worker a promotion.
   e. Every employee gave a donation to the United Fund.

6. List the letter for each of the following sentences. Identify and explain the purpose of the italicized phrases in each sentence:

   a. Juan *is clearly* in charge of the office.
   b. She likes *to sleep late* in the morning.
   c. Will Sarah own *the main plant*?
   d. The supervisor is *an excellent manager*.
   e. *Understanding clearly,* Karen did her job.

7. Identify the subject complement in this sentence: Our customers are strong supporters.

8. List the letter for each of the following sentences. Beside each letter, write any dependent clause the sentence may contain, and indicate the sentence structure (i.e., simple, complex, compound-complex, or compound).

   a. When the question of ethics arose, the supervisor stated clearly that all the accurate information would be provided.
   b. The accounting records will be audited beginning November 1.
   c. Effective communication is critical; without it both individuals and organizations will fail.
   d. Roxine is well liked because she is warm and friendly when relating to others.
   e. If the time seems right, I plan to see my manager tomorrow about a raise in my salary.
   f. The Computer Center is a full-service communication facility; when you need word processing, E-mail, fax services, etc., all you have to do is request them.
   g. The work on the report was completed after the clerk photocopied and distributed it to the company officers and board members.

h. Jane was glad she attended the workshop; she learned how to develop powerful proposals, which is knowledge she needs for her job.

i. Graphic aids are an important way to make complex information understandable.

j. While all of the salespersons did not agree, the home office changed the structure of the sales commissions.

9. List the letter for each sentence in Application 8. Write the independent (main) clause(s) beside each letter.

10. Write the correct verb form for each of the following sentences:

a. Forensics (is, are) the study of debate.

b. Each of the employees (serve, serves) on at least one committee.

c. *Communication Notes* (contain, contains) articles helpful to business persons.

d. The professor or the students (is, are) responsible for the discussion.

e. The board, other than the officers, (vote, votes) on increasing fees.

f. Neither Dale nor Teresa (is, are) ready to report.

g. The committee (has, have) decided to proceed with the project.

h. Each member of the group, however, (think, thinks) the project should be done a different way.

i. Most of the tasks (is, are) challenging.

m. "Hurry up and wait" (seem, seems) to describe project progress.

11. Indicate the correct pronoun in each of the following sentences:

a. All of the students had (their, his or her) resumes.

b. Either Linda or Betty left (their, her) coat at Brian's house.

c. The college opened (their, its) school year on August 20.

d. Each of the students introduced (their, his or her) designated partner.

e. Every woman and man must introduce (their, his or her) partner.

12. Explain how each of the following sentences lacks parallelism. Rewrite the sentence correcting the lack of parallelism.

a. Wal-Mart's prices were lower than the Corner Store.

b. The manager encouraged the plant employees, and the office employees were motivated by her.

c. Judy was strong, optimistic, and a woman of courage.

d. Diane works as a nurse and is volunteering as a firefighter.

e. The student's paper was brief and clearer.

13. Examine the following sentences for the common sentence errors of dangling modifiers, double negatives, and split infinitives. List the letter of each sentence and write a corrected version of that sentence beside the letter.

   a. Lu wasn't never a team player.

   b. Anxiously waiting for the interview, Carlos could see the prospective employee.

   c. Mr. Davenport wants you to quickly fill the order.

14. Write a short paragraph that includes an example of each of the four functions of sentences—statement, question, command or request, and exclamation.

15. Write a short paragraph that includes an example of each of the four basic sentence structures—simple sentence, compound sentence, complex sentence, and compound-complex sentence.

MESSAGE ANALYSIS

Examine the following message. Rewrite the message and correct any grammatical errors you find:

All *The Daily Times* employees was suppose to come to work at the same time under the old plan. The new plan (referred to as "flextime"), however, permit employees to choose his or her starting and ending times for their workdays.

Flextime allow employees to work according to his or her own biological clocks. If them workers what are "night" people wants to come in late in the morning. Them can come at 9, 10, or even 11 a.m. Them employees what are early risers. Them can come in at 6, 7, or 8 a.m.

There is really three basic kinds of people: late nighters, early risers, and the other kind is the average sleepers. Everybody are in one of these categories. *The Daily Times* are concerned about their employees and they want them to be happy, as satisfied as possible, and productive.

CHAPTER 8 Punctuation

Learning Objectives

Your learning objectives for this chapter include the following:

- To review and use correctly the terminal punctuation marks—period, question mark, and exclamation point
- To review and use correctly the comma and the semicolon as internal marks of punctuation
- To review and apply the guidelines for using the following punctuation marks:

Apostrophe	Hyphen
Colon	Parentheses
Dash	Period
Diagonal	Quotation marks
Ellipsis points	Underscore

When you speak, the tone of your voice, the gestures you make, and the pauses you insert help your listeners understand what you are saying. When you write, punctuation helps your readers understand your message. Punctuation tells your readers where one thought ends and the next begins. Punctuation adds emphasis and clarifies. Writing without punctuation is comparable to traveling from South Carolina to Oregon without road signs.

This chapter reviews the punctuation that occurs most often in business writing. It is not designed to eliminate the need for reference manuals. Experienced writers freely consult reference sources about punctuation usage. When you have a question about punctuation, do not leave the answer to chance. Take the time to check this chapter, a reference manual, or a similar source. Incorrect punctuation can cause your reader more confusion and frustration than using no punctuation at all.

Punctuation marks add emphasis and clarity to a message.

Check reference sources when you are uncertain about punctuation.

TERMINAL PUNCTUATION

The three punctuation symbols that are used to signal the end of a complete thought are the period, the question mark, and the exclamation point.

THE PERIOD

The **period** is the most frequently used ending mark of punctuation. It is used at the end of a declarative or an imperative sentence:

Periods are used to end:
• declarative and imperative sentences

> Miller's Hardware Store sustained nearly $500,000 in damages from the fire. (declarative)
>
> Emi has decided to campaign for the presidency. (declarative)
>
> Try the Model 6 free of charge for 30 days. (imperative)
>
> Take the package to the post office. (imperative)

A request that requires *action* rather than an oral or written response also ends with a period. This type of request is often referred to as a **courteous request.** The writer would rather have the reader devote time to doing what has been requested than to writing or calling to say yes or no:

• courteous requests that require action

> Won't you let us know the color you prefer.
>
> Will you please return my call before 3 p.m. today.

The period is also used when the writer asks an **indirect question.** A question is indirect when it is a statement about a question:

• indirect questions

> I wonder where the picnic will be held.
>
> Manuel asked whether you and I are related.

THE QUESTION MARK

A **question mark** should be used with an interrogative sentence. An interrogative sentence asks for or requires a definite response. The response may be a single word, or it may be one or more sentences:

Question marks are used to end direct questions.

Do you have a key to the building? (one-word response)

What arrangements have you made for your trip to Seoul? (a response of one or more sentences)

When a series of questions has a common subject and predicate, the questions may be treated as part of a single sentence.

Have we determined when? where? why?

Shall we visit Paris? Berlin? Rome?

THE EXCLAMATION POINT

Exclamation points show strong emotions.

An **exclamation point** is used with an exclamatory sentence. Although it is not used frequently, the exclamation point can do a great deal to bring life to business correspondence. Strong emotion such as surprise, enthusiasm, or anger is expressed in an exclamatory sentence:

Yes! Nikki won the award.

Hurry! Make your reservation today.

Welcome!

BPR **will not** sacrifice quality to increase profits!

CHOOSING TERMINAL PUNCTUATION

Deciding whether to use a period, a question mark, or an exclamation point is easy. Simply ask yourself the following questions. If your answer to both questions is no, the period is the appropriate mark of punctuation.

Am I expressing a strong emotion? (If you are, use **!**)

Am I asking the reader to give me a response? (If so, use **?**)

PRIMARY INTERNAL PUNCTUATION

Using the appropriate terminal punctuation mark is one step toward achieving message clarity, but appropriate internal punctuation is also important. The comma and the semicolon are the most frequently used internal punctuation marks.

THE COMMA

Commas separate items in sentences.

The comma plays an important role in business writing. A **comma** separates items in a sentence and helps the reader correctly interpret each thought. By learning how commas are used and by mastering the rules for their placement, you will become a more effective business writer. Using commas incorrectly—omitting them where needed or adding them where they are not needed—can hamper communication. Consider these examples:

Too few or too many commas can hamper message clarity.

After you have eaten the leftover meat the vegetables and the dairy products should be placed in the refrigerator. (commas have been omitted)

In this sentence, the absence of commas makes the reader wonder what is to be eaten and what is to be put into the refrigerator. Confusion results, and additional communication is necessary. The message becomes clear when a comma is inserted after the word *eaten* and between each item in the compound subject:

> After you have eaten, the leftover meat, the vegetables, and the dairy products should be placed in the refrigerator.

In the following sentence, message clarity is lost because four commas are used where none are needed.

> This afternoon, we will meet with the chair of the board, while her staff members, tour the new addition, to the factory. (commas are used where they are not needed)

The sentence should read:

> This afternoon we will meet with the chair of the board while her staff members tour the new addition to the factory.

Although the original versions of these sentences are extreme examples of comma omission and misuse, they illustrate the need for caution in using commas. The best way to assure correct use of commas is to be able to justify the placement of each comma.

CALENDAR DATES

A **complete calendar date** consists of a month, a day, and a year. Whenever a complete calendar date occurs within the body of a sentence, the year is set apart from the rest of the sentence by commas. Incomplete calendar dates require no punctuation. When a complete calendar date occurs at the end of an independent clause or a sentence, the final comma is replaced by a semicolon or terminal punctuation. If the military or international date form is used, however, no commas are needed:

> On *June 17, 1932,* the time capsule was sealed. (The calendar date is complete.)
>
> In *June 1932* the time capsule was sealed. (No commas are needed since the date is incomplete.)
>
> The time capsule was sealed on *June 17, 1932.* (The calendar date is complete and ends the sentence.)
>
> On *17 June 1932* the time capsule was sealed. (The military or international date form does not need commas.)

A calendar date used to clarify the noun that precedes it is also set off by commas. The calendar date may be complete or incomplete:

> On *Monday, October 23,* the Bloodmobile will be at Village Mall. (The incomplete calendar date *October 23* is needed to clarify Monday.)
>
> On Thursday, *November 17, 1992,* three sets of twins were born at Sidney General Hospital. (The complete calendar date *November 17, 1992,* is needed to clarify Thursday.)

COMPLEX SENTENCES

When a dependent clause *introduces* an independent clause in a complex sentence, a comma is used to separate the clauses. When the dependent clause does not introduce the independent clause, a comma is *not* used:

Before you leave, please verify your address. (The dependent clause introduces the independent clause.)

After we receive your check, we will process your order. (The dependent clause introduces the independent clause.)

Phone Isabel Parry *if you would like more information.* (No comma is needed; the dependent clause does not introduce the independent clause.)

COMPOUND SENTENCES

When the independent clauses in a compound sentence are joined with a coordinate conjunction, use a comma before the conjunction:

> The credenza is attractive, *but* it is too large for my office. (The coordinate conjunction joins independent clauses.)

> The trees and wild flowers in the forest were beautiful and created a peaceful atmosphere, *but* Leona and Signe longed for the noise and activity of the city. (The coordinate conjunction *but* joins the independent clauses.)

> Ilene and Ted rode with Karen. (No comma is needed because the coordinate conjunction *and* does not connect two independent clauses.)

When two independent clauses are joined by a conjunction, place a comma before the conjunction.

COORDINATE ADJECTIVES

When two or more adjectives in a series independently modify the same noun, they are called **coordinate adjectives.** Commas are used to separate coordinate adjectives.

> Avery is a patient, caring, sincere foster parent; Dyanne is a well-known, well-respected office automation consultant.

The adjectives in the first series independently describe Avery as a foster parent; those in the second series independently describe Dyanne as a consultant. The writers could have said:

> Avery is a patient and caring and sincere foster parent; Dyanne is a well-known and well-respected office automation consultant.

A comma replaces the word *and* between adjectives.

Combining the adjectives, however, is more efficient for the writer and more pleasing to the reader. A good test of the need for commas and where they should be placed is to insert the word *and* between the adjectives. If the word *and* can be inserted without altering the meaning of the sentence, a comma should be used.

Sentence without punctuation:	We arrived on a cold stormy night.
Test:	We arrived on a cold (and) stormy night.
Correctly punctuated:	We arrived on a cold, stormy night.

The following example needs no commas. If we try to insert the word *and* between the adjectives, the sentence becomes awkward.

Sentence without punctuation:	Robert drove a shiny blue sports car. (The words *shiny, blue,* and *sports* describe the car, but they do so collectively, not independently.)

Test:	Robert drove a shiny (and) blue sports car.
Correctly punctuated:	Robert drove a shiny blue sports car.

GEOGRAPHIC LOCATIONS

A **complete geographic location** consists of a city and a state, province, or nation. When such a geographic location occurs within a sentence, the name of the state, province, or nation is set apart from the rest of the sentence by commas. When an incomplete geographic location is named in a sentence, no commas are necessary:

> The convention will be held in *Honolulu, Hawaii,* next December. (Honolulu, Hawaii, is a complete geographic location.)

> Our largest warehouse is in *Portland*. (The geographic location is incomplete.)

> Have you ever visited *Acapulco, Mexico*? (The geographic location is complete; the question mark replaces the ending comma because the name of the country is the last item in the interrogative sentence.)

Use commas with complete geographic locations.

NONESSENTIAL ELEMENTS

Words, phrases, or clauses that are not necessary to the meaning or structure of a sentence are considered **nonessential elements.** Appositives, introductory words, introductory phrases, nonrestrictive clauses, parenthetical expressions, and transitional expressions are all nonessential elements.

Each nonessential element requires one or more commas. A nonessential element that begins a sentence is followed by a comma. A nonessential element that ends an independent clause is followed by a comma or a semicolon; one that ends a sentence is followed by the appropriate terminal punctuation mark. A nonessential element that does not end an independent clause or a sentence is preceded and followed by commas.

To determine if an item is nonessential, omit it from the sentence. If the meaning and structure of the sentence are complete without the item, it is considered nonessential.

Place commas before and after nonessential information.

Appositives. An **appositive** is a word or a phrase that immediately follows a noun and provides additional information about it. When this additional information is not necessary to the meaning of the sentence, it is separated from the rest of the sentence by commas:

> My oldest son, Nathan, ran in the Boston Marathon. (The name *Nathan* is not essential to the meaning of the sentence; only one of the writer's sons may be the oldest.)

> My son Nathan ran in the Boston Marathon. (The name is needed to indicate which of the writer's sons ran the marathon.)

Use commas with nonessential appositives.

Introductory Words. An **introductory word** is the first word in a sentence; it leads the reader to the independent clause and is separated from the clause by a comma. *Obviously*, *generally*, and *unfortunately* are examples of introductory words; others are used in the following examples:

> *Yes,* Ms. Armandoza was employed as a clerk in our office. (The introductory word is not essential to the meaning or structure of the sentence.)

An introductory word is followed by a comma.

Currently, I am a student at City College. (The introductory word is not essential to the meaning or structure of the sentence.)

When the receiver is named as the opening word(s) of a sentence, the writer has used a **direct address.**

Mr. Wilson, you'll receive many hours of enjoyment from your new treadmill.

Georgia, your work on the Fox audit was excellent.

Introductory Phrases. An **introductory phrase** is a group of words that begins a sentence and introduces an independent clause. Introductory phrases may or may not be separated from an independent clause by a comma; the deciding factor is readability. If omitting the comma could cause reader confusion, include it. Some writers use a comma after an introductory phrase that has five or more words. You, too, may find this technique helpful:

To confirm your reservation phone Chris. (No comma is necessary; the message is clear without the comma.)

By working together we achieved our goal. (No comma is necessary; the message is clear without the comma.)

Before leaving, Mildred thanked Ed and Mary for their hospitality. (Message clarity is improved by placing a comma after the introductory phrase.)

After entering your five-digit authorization code and hearing the progression tone, enter the area code and number. (Message clarity is improved by placing a comma after the long introductory phrase.)

Nonrestrictive Clauses. Earlier in this section, you learned that an appositive provides additional information about a noun; a **nonrestrictive clause** has the same function. One feature distinguishes an appositive from a nonrestrictive clause: An appositive is a word or a phrase—not a clause.

Nonrestrictive clauses, which frequently begin with *who* or *which,* are separated from the rest of a sentence by commas. Some writers prefer to use the word *which* to begin a nonrestrictive clause and the word *that* to begin an essential clause.

The north wing of the hospital, which was funded by a grant from the Barrows Foundation, will increase our ability to provide high-quality medical care to the people of Adler. (The clause is not essential to the meaning of the sentence.)

The payment *that was due March 15* is now three weeks past due. (The clause is essential to the sentence.)

The artist *who donated the sculpture* wishes to remain anonymous. (The clause is essential to the sentence.)

Please inform Senator Barjo that, *although we have supported him in the past,* we will oppose him on the sales tax issue. (The clause is not essential to the meaning of the sentence. Note that this nonrestrictive clause does not begin with *who* or *which.*)

Mr. Wong, *who took his oath of citizenship last May,* will carry the national flag in the parade. (The clause does not restrict the meaning of the sentence.)

Commas are optional after introductory phrases.

Nonrestrictive clauses provide additional information and are set apart by commas.

Parenthetical Expressions. When one or more words interrupt the flow of a sentence, a **parenthetical expression** is created. The expression is separated from the rest of the sentence by commas:

> The operation will, *therefore,* be postponed. (The word *therefore* interrupts the flow of the sentence.)
>
> The white blossom, *although less common,* is as beautiful as the red. (The words *although less common* interrupt the flow of the sentence.)
>
> Will you, *B. J. Sutherland,* accept our invitation to join PPT? (The name *B. J. Sutherland* interrupts the flow of the sentence.)
>
> The review was, *to say the least,* unfavorable. (The words *to say the least* interrupt the flow of the sentence.)

Transitional Expressions. A word or phrase that links sentences or independent clauses is a **transitional expression.** When a transitional expression is used to link two independent clauses, it is preceded by a semicolon and followed by a comma. When a transitional expression is used to link two sentences, it is followed by a comma:

> Most of the passengers preferred fast food; *therefore,* the driver stopped at Hillberg's Hamburger Haven. (A transitional expression links two independent clauses.)
>
> Your newest catalog had not yet arrived when we placed our order. *As a result,* we were unable to use the new price in calculating the total cost of our order. (This transitional expression links two sentences.)

Words such as *however* and *therefore* and phrases such as *of course* and *as a result* may be either parenthetical or transitional. The key is how they are used in the sentence.

> The invoice, *therefore,* has been approved for payment. (The word *therefore* interrupts the flow of the sentence—it is parenthetical.)
>
> The remaining items in the order were delivered yesterday; *therefore,* the invoice has been approved for payment. (The word *therefore* is used as a transitional word linking two independent clauses.

SERIES

When three or more words, phrases, or clauses are to be taken as one unit to form a subject, a verb, or an object, a **series** is formed. Items in a series should be separated by commas. The final item is usually set apart from the others by the word *and* or the word *or.* For clarity, a comma should be used before the conjunction as well as between each of the items:

> *Dot matrix, ink jet,* and *laser* are types of computer printers. (The three names are part of a compound subject.)
>
> Jason bought *shirts, shoes,* and *socks* to complement his new suit. (The items are the direct object of the verb *bought*.)
>
> The campers will *canoe, hike,* and *swim.* (The verbs describe the actions of the campers.)
>
> *One and won, hear and here,* and *piece and peace* are examples of homonyms. (Each *pair* of words in the series is part of a compound subject.)

THE SEMICOLON

The **semicolon** is used to separate. It may also be used to join.

COMPOUND SENTENCES WITHOUT CONJUNCTIONS

A semicolon is used to join two independent clauses that are not joined by a coordinate conjunction. The semicolon makes the reader aware of the close relationship between the independent clauses. Although each clause could be written as a separate sentence, a smoother writing style is achieved by joining them with a semicolon:

> Please sign and return the enclosed card; it requires no postage. (The clauses are closely related; no conjunction is used.)

> Dawn finished the audit in Benson on Monday; on Tuesday she traveled to Kapel. (The clauses are closely related; no conjunction is used.)

When a comma is mistakenly used to join independent clauses where no conjunction is present, a **comma splice** is created. Writers should be careful to avoid this error.

> Larry has asked for a one-month leave of absence, he and his wife plan to tour the Orient. (incorrectly punctuated; comma splice)

> Larry has asked for a one-month leave of absence; he and his wife plan to tour the Orient. (correctly punctuated; semicolon joins independent clauses)

COMPOUND SENTENCES WITH CONJUNCTIONS

When independent clauses are joined by a coordinate conjunction and either or both of the clauses contain commas, clarity is achieved by using a semicolon (rather than a comma) before the conjunction that joins the two independent clauses. In the example that follows, the second sentence uses a semicolon and is clearer and easier to read:

> Mr. Abelson, Ms. Skurla, and Mrs. Newstrom will leave for Detroit on September 10, but Mr. Yukita, Mrs. Zollar, and Mr. Nelson will not leave until September 12.

> Mr. Abelson, Ms. Skurla, and Mrs. Newstrom will leave for Detroit on September 10; but Mr. Yukita, Mrs. Zollar, and Mr. Nelson will not leave until September 12.

SERIES ITEMS CONTAINING COMMAS

Using commas to separate items in a series could result in confusion when one or more items within the series contain a comma. By using semicolons to separate the items in this type of series, the message is easier to interpret. In the example that follows, the second sentence—the one that uses semicolons to separate the series items—is much clearer:

Semicolons may be used to separate or to join.

Semicolons join independent clauses when no conjunction is used.

Semicolons should be used to join independent clauses that contain commas.

Use semicolons to separate long, complex series items that contain commas.

Our Canadian offices are in Medicine Hat, Alberta, Thunder Bay, Ontario, Sherbrooke, Quebec, and Digby, Nova Scotia.

Our Canadian offices are in Medicine Hat, Alberta; Thunder Bay, Ontario; Sherbrooke, Quebec; and Digby, Nova Scotia.

The comma and the semicolon are two punctuation marks that influence the clarity and readability of a message. Use them effectively to help your reader better understand your message.

SECONDARY INTERNAL PUNCTUATION

Several other punctuation marks are used within sentences to bring clarity, emphasis, and variety to writing. Those punctuation marks are discussed in this section.

APOSTROPHE

As you write letters, memos, and reports, you will use the apostrophe in two ways: to form possessives and to form contractions.

Apostrophes are used to form possessives and contractions.

POSSESSIVES

A **possessive** shows ownership. Both nouns and pronouns may be expressed as possessives. Figure 8•1 shows the possessive form of several nouns and pronouns. Recall that only nouns use an apostrophe in their possessive form. The apostrophe is placed either before the *s* ('s) or after the *s* (s') depending on the noun. The context of the sentence will often provide a clue to placement of the apostrophe. Detailed information on forming possessives is in Chapter 6.

Figure 8•1 Possessive Forms

Word	Possessive	Word	Possessive
she (pronoun)	her vacation	employee (noun)	employee's desk
we (pronoun)	our pets	employees (noun)	employees' lounge
they (pronoun)	their class	Sue (noun)	Sue's memo
he (pronoun)	his computer	window (noun)	window's reflection
month (noun)	a month's rest	Douglas (noun)	Douglas' stapler
months (noun)	three months' salary		

CONTRACTIONS

Contractions are seldom used in business correspondence.

A **contraction** is a combination of two words in a shortened form. An apostrophe is used to signal the omission of one or more letters in the contraction. Contractions such as *can't, won't,* and *you're* are seldom used in business writing because they lack the formality desired in a permanent record. The opposite is true of *o'clock;* this contraction for "of the clock" is seldom used because it is too formal. If you are unsure about whether to use an apostrophe, remember this: A contraction *always* has an apostrophe.

There are several contractions that, when spoken, sound the same as possessive pronouns. These potentially confusing words are listed in Figure 8•2.

Figure 8•2 Possessive and Contraction Soundalikes

Word	Meaning
its	possessive form of pronoun *it*
it's	contraction of *it is*
their	possessive form of pronoun *they* (before noun)
they're	contraction of *they are*
theirs	possessive form of pronoun *they* (not before noun)
there's	contraction of *there is*
whose	possessive form of pronoun *who*
who's	contraction of *who is*
your	possessive form of pronoun *you*
you're	contraction of *you are*

COLON

Colons alert the reader that something of importance will follow.

The **colon** is often used as a clue to the reader that a *list*, an *explanation*, or an *example* will follow. The words that introduce the listing should contain a subject and a predicate. The items following the colon may be in words or in complete sentences, in paragraph form, or in a list. Items in paragraph form or in a list may or may not be numbered. The writer makes the placement decision based on the space available and the amount of emphasis to be placed on the items. A list will receive more attention than items presented in paragraph form.

Items in paragraph form are capitalized only if they are complete sentences or proper nouns. Items in list form are always capitalized.

Bretta's reason for missing the meeting was simple: She was one of three passengers in the elevator when it stopped between the sixth and seventh floors. (explanation in paragraph form)

Here is an example of how to use boldface type to emphasize important words: Suzanna and Karl **must** submit their expense reports before June 30. (example in paragraph form)

Several factors influenced our decision: personnel, space, and equipment. (listing in paragraph form; common nouns)

Paragraph form

Three factors influenced our decision: (1) Additional personnel would be needed. (2) Space for expansion does not exist. (3) Our equipment is old and fragile. (explanatory listing in paragraph form with numbered sentences)

Verticle list form

The decision was influenced by the following factors:
1. The need for additional personnel
2. The lack of space for expansion
3. The condition of our equipment

Our decision was influenced by personnel, space, and equipment factors. (No colon is used because the portion of the sentence before the series is not an independent clause.)

The colon has several other applications that occasionally occur in business writing. Those uses and an example of each are presented in Figure 8•3.

Figure 8•3 Other Uses of the Colon

Use	Example
Ratio	15:1 (15 to 1)
References	17:55-62 (volume:page numbers)
Reference Initials	PAM:sf (author:keyboard operator)
Salutations	Dear Mrs. Tompkins: (mixed punctuation)
Times	4:45 p.m. (hour:minutes)

DASH

Dashes separate.

Unlike a hyphen, which is used to bring things together, a **dash** is used to separate. A dash shows a sudden change in thought or places emphasis on what follows. There are no spaces before, between, or after the two hyphens that form the dash. Because of its strength and the impact it creates, the dash should be used less frequently than other marks of punctuation.

One thing is very clear—the members oppose an increase in dues. (emphasis)

The response to the ad has been excellent—much better than we expected. (emphasis)

Ann—a B+ student—is the catcher for the softball team. (sudden change of thought)

DIAGONAL

The **diagonal** (also called the *slant* or *slash*) is frequently used to indicate a choice or an alternative, to mean *per*, or to abbreviate the words *with* and *without*. The diagonal is also used in creating fractions and may be used in displaying reference initials. No space is used before or after the diagonal.

The diagonal indicates choice, means *per*, and helps to abbreviate *with* and *without*.

Cyndi and/or Garth will attend. (Cyndi may attend; Garth may attend; both may attend)

The individual we hire will prepare our annual report; his/her workstation will be equipped with a computer, desktop publishing software, and a laser printer. (the gender of the new employee is unknown)

S/he will file the report by the end of February. (S/he is used to mean she or he and to eliminate gender bias)

By the year 2000 automobile mileage should exceed 60 miles/gallon. (miles *per* gallon)

I arrived in Memphis on time but w/o my luggage. (without)

The decorator advised us to use beige w/maroon as our color scheme. (with)

3/4 (fraction)

1 2/3 (mixed number; space before fraction)

DKH/ssb (author/keyboard operator)

When completing business forms, writers often use the diagonal as part of a date. The standard format is month/day/year; two character positions are allocated to each part. The emerging popularity of the international date style (day/month/year) and the confusion that could result make this format inappropriate for use in correspondence.

11/10/97 (November 10, 1997? October 11, 1997?)

In correspondence avoid using the diagonal with a date.

ELLIPSIS POINTS

Ellipsis points indicate that words have been omitted.

An **ellipsis** is an omission of words from a direct quotation. As you prepare business messages, you may find it necessary to include only part of what another person said or wrote. When this occurs, use ellipsis points. **Ellipsis points** are a series of three periods separated from the quote and from each other by one space. When the ellipsis occurs at the end of a sentence, the ellipsis points follow the terminal punctuation. Ellipsis points are used in advertising and personal business correspondence to indicate a pause. In other forms of business writing, ellipsis points are used to indicate that words have been omitted from a direct quotation:

> In your letter of July 10 you stated, ". . . the deadline for payment was July 7."
>
> The fluctuations in currency exchange rates are interesting . . . and worth watching.
>
> Ethyl choked back tears as she began her acceptance speech by saying, "I am truly honored. . . ." (end of sentence)

HYPHEN

Hyphens bring items together.

The **hyphen** is used to bring things together, to show that two items are related. Because the purpose is to join, there is no space before or after a hyphen. Hyphens are commonly used in four ways: (1) to form compound words, (2) to join prefixes and suffixes to root words, (3) to join numbers or letters in a range, and (4) to indicate where a word has been divided. The first three uses are more common and are explained in this section.

COMPOUND WORDS

Hyphens form compound words.

The most frequent use of the hyphen is to form compound words. A **compound word** is two or more words used as one. Compound words may be nouns, verbs, or adjectives. Writing experts do not always agree on whether compound words should be hyphenated, written as two words, or written as one word; style preferences are continually changing. The best source of information about compound nouns and verbs is a current dictionary. The information presented in this section will help you determine when and how to hyphenate compound adjectives.

Hyphens join some compound adjectives.

Compound adjectives may be formed in several ways. Figure 8•4 lists the various types of compound adjectives, gives an example of each, and indicates when each should be hyphenated.

Kind of Compound Adjective	Example	When Usually Hyphenated
noun + adjective	*tax-free* bond	if listed in a dictionary *or* before a noun
noun + present participle	*time-consuming* task	before a noun
adjective + participle	*free-wheeling* attitude	before a noun
adjective + noun + *ed*	*able-bodied* person	before a noun
cardinal number + noun	*10-minute* break	before a noun
adverb + participle	*well-organized* proposal	only before a noun; only if adverb does not end in *ly*
adverb + adjective	*more entertaining* show	never
participle + adverb	*filled-in* form	only before a noun

Figure 8•4 Hyphenating Compound Adjectives

The sentences below are examples of how some of the information presented in Figure 8•4 is applied:

Dan Rather is a *well-known* broadcast journalist. (adverb + participle before noun)

Dan Rather is *well known* as a broadcast journalist. (adverb + participle not before noun)

You are a *well-trained, highly skilled* worker. (coordinate adjectives adverb + participle and *ly* adverb + participle—before noun)

The workshop will focus on *team building*. (noun + present participle not before noun)

Sometimes two or more hyphenated compound words with the same base word appear in a series. In this case the hyphen is used, but the base word may be omitted in all except the last item of the series:

Your resume should state your *short-* and *long-range* goals. (The word *range* is omitted in the first compound word.)

The announcement can be repeated at *5-, 15-,* or *30-minute* intervals. (The word *minute* is omitted in the first two compound words.)

PREFIXES AND SUFFIXES

A **prefix** is a syllable(s) added to the beginning of a word; a **suffix** is a syllable(s) added to the end of a word. Prefixes and suffixes are generally *not* separated from their root words. There are a few exceptions to this rule, however, and they are explained in this section. The only suffix preceded by a hyphen is *elect,* and it is used only as part of a compound title:

President-elect Mason

Vice President-elect Marks

Prefixes are followed by hyphens in a variety of situations. Figure 8•5 lists those situations and gives an example of each.

Prefix/Prefix Ending	Hyphenated	Example
prefix ending in *i*	before word beginning with *i*	quasi-intellectual
prefix ending in *a*	before word beginning with *a*	ultra-ambitious
prefix ending in *e*	seldom; consult dictionary	de-emphasize, deactivate, preelection
prefix ending in *o*	seldom; consult dictionary	coworker, microchip microorganism
self	always when a prefix	self-assured
re (to do again)	to distinguish from word with different meaning	re-form/reform

Figure 8·5 Hyphenating Prefixes

There is an additional rule of which you should be aware. Whenever a prefix is added to a proper noun, the prefix is separated from the word by a hyphen:

> mid-October
>
> trans-Alaska

RANGES

A hyphen is used between the high and low numbers or first and last letters in a range. The hyphen indicates that the items are related and takes the place of *to* or *through*.

Hyphens are used between points in a range.

> The range of scores on the first test was 51-93.
>
> Students whose last names begin with A-F will order yearbooks on Monday.
>
> When main floor seating is nearly full, open balconies A-C.
>
> The reunion will be held August 15-17 in Dallas.

PARENTHESES

Items that are very unimportant may be placed in parentheses.

Parentheses, like commas, may be used to separate nonessential information from the rest of a thought. If parentheses and commas were compared according to their strength, however, parentheses would be rated as weaker marks of punctuation. The information they contain may be so unimportant that the writer should consider eliminating it entirely. Names, dates, times, amounts, references, abbreviations, area codes, phone numbers, addresses, and editorial comments are just a few of the items that may be enclosed within parentheses. If an author chooses to use parentheses, certain requirements must be met:

1. Both left and right parentheses must be used.

   Baron Clothiers, Inc. (BCI) accepts telephone orders between 7 a.m. and 4 p.m. (EST) Monday through Friday.

2. Commas, semicolons, periods, or other punctuation marks should be used as needed within the parentheses.

   The entree (salmon) will be served with a baked potato, broccoli with cheese sauce (or, if you prefer, lemon butter), and a colorful fruit garnish.

3. The presence of parentheses should not affect the use of punctuation elsewhere in the sentence or question:

> After she retired (lucky woman!), Elsa moved to Idaho.

PERIOD

Earlier in this chapter, you reviewed the use of the period as a mark of terminal punctuation. While that use of the period is certainly the most common, it is by no means the only use. Additional uses are covered in this section.

ABBREVIATIONS

Abbreviations are shortened forms of words, names, or phrases; their primary purpose is to save time and space. As a general rule, business writers restrict their use of abbreviations to those they are confident their receivers will recognize.

The capitalization, punctuation, and spacing of abbreviations vary widely. Chapter 9 covers some of these issues; the most comprehensive source of information about abbreviations is a reference manual.

DECIMALS

A **decimal** is one method by which writers may express fractional components of a whole number. In business, it is common to use decimals when expressing money or measurements. No spaces are used before or after the decimal.

> The starting wage is $7.50 an hour.
>
> Each package should contain 14.5 ounces of cereal.
>
> Our new office is 5.8 miles north of town.
>
> All units that vary from specification by more than .0025″ must be rejected.

LISTINGS

When items in a listing are identified by numbers or by letters, a period is used. Listings may be formatted in three ways; all three apply to either numeric or alphabetic listings.

> 1. In one format, the number is indented and the text wraps to the left margin. This is true whether the text runs over one line or many.
>
> 2. In another format, both the number and any runover lines of the text begin at the left margin. This, also, is true whether the text runs over one line or many.
>
> 3. Still another option is to key the number at the left margin and hang indent the text. This is true whether the text runs over one line or many.

A minimum of two spaces should follow the period. With word processing equipment, it is common to tab to the next position on the preset tab grid.

Ideas are the root of creation.

Ernest Dimnet

QUOTATION MARKS

Quotation marks show exact wording, give special emphasis, or identify literary or artistic works.

A **quotation mark** may serve three different purposes in written messages: (1) to indicate that the writer is using the exact words of another individual, (2) to emphasize words that are unique or have a special meaning in a particular message, or (3) to identify literary and artistic works. In all cases, quotation marks are used in pairs—one is placed at the beginning of the quote or item of information, the other is placed at the end.

QUOTATIONS

The length of a quote influences how it is displayed.

The length of a direct quotation determines whether it will be set off by quotation marks or emphasized in a separate, indented paragraph. If a direct quotation occupies less than four lines of type, the copy is placed in quotation marks and is not indented:

> In his inaugural address, Governor Snellgrover told the citizens of the state, "Education, jobs, and the environment are high-priority items."

If the quoted material occupies four or more lines of type, it should not be displayed in quotation marks. A quotation of this length should be displayed as a separate, single-spaced paragraph and should be indented on the left and right sides. This indented format, together with information about the source of the material, makes quotation marks unnecessary.

> In his inaugural address, Governor Snellgrover told the citizens of the state:

> During my campaign I promised to work to maintain the quality of life that has made this state such a fine place in which to live. Education, jobs, and the environment are high-priority items. We must not lose what we have worked so hard to achieve; we must strive to make further gains.

Notice that the preceding paragraphs have emphasized *exact words* and *direct quotation*. These terms are important because only materials that meet these standards should be included in quotation marks. If you use your own words to describe another person's idea (paraphrasing), quotation marks are not needed; but credit should be given to the originator of the idea. The sentences below illustrate this principle:

> Mrs. Perea said, "The issue will be referred to the Finance Committee."

> Mrs. Perea said that the issue will be referred to the Finance Committee.

EMPHASIS

Words in quotation marks receive emphasis.

Whenever you wish to emphasize a word or phrase, even if it is not part of a direct quote, consider displaying it in quotation marks. Humorous items, definitions, and technical terms used in nontechnical ways are good candidates for this type of emphasis. If words are emphasized with quotation marks too frequently, however, the benefits of this display are lost.

> "Shorty" is an unlikely nickname for someone six feet tall!

Is "data" singular or plural?

Etc. is the abbreviation for the Latin phrase meaning "and so forth."

LITERARY AND ARTISTIC WORKS

Use quotation marks to set off the title of any *section* of a *published* work. Also use quotation marks to enclose the title of a song or the title of a television or radio show.

> Martin's article, "Bigger Isn't Always Better," has been accepted for publication in *The Entrepreneur*. (article in a magazine)
>
> Chapter 8 in *Business Communication* is "Punctuation." (chapter in textbook)
>
> Billy giggled when his grandpa told him his grandma's favorite song was "Material Girl." (song title)
>
> Channel 4 recently announced that it would begin showing reruns of "Star Trek" daily at 11:30 p.m. (television show)

WITH OTHER PUNCTUATION MARKS

Because quotation marks may be used to begin, end, or set off material within a statement or question, some guidelines must be set regarding the use of other punctuation when quotation marks are present. Figure 8•6 will be a helpful reference.

Figure 8•6 Quotation Marks with Other Punctuation Marks

Punctuation Mark	Placement
period	inside quotation marks
comma	inside quotation marks
colon	outside quotation marks
semicolon	outside quotation marks
question mark	inside *if* quotation is a question
	outside *if* the entire item is a question

There are three additional rules concerning the use of punctuation and quotation marks that business writers should remember:

1. Punctuation may be included in a quotation. If the quote is taken from a printed source, the punctuation should be included where the original author inserted it—even if it is incorrect.

2. Ending punctuation may be placed before or after the quotation marks, but never in both places. When a conflict exists, use the stronger mark of punctuation. Exclamation points are the strongest, followed by question marks and periods.

3. Direct quotes that occur in the middle or near the end of other statements or questions are introduced by either a colon or a comma.

Here are some examples of how the placement guidelines and rules may be applied:

Did the evaluation report contain this statement: "Her work is exceptional; she can be relied upon to complete her work quickly and accurately"? (The entire item is a question.)

Theo asked: "Did I miss anything?" (Only the quote is a question.)

One of the golfers in the foursome behind us yelled "Fore!" (Only the quote is an exclamation.)

This badly damaged package was marked "Fragile"! (The entire sentence is an exclamation.)

UNDERSCORE

The underscore gives special emphasis.

The underscore is used to give special emphasis. When preparing manuscript for typesetting by a printer, for example, the underscore signals that what is above it should be set in italics.

Underscores may be used as a substitute for italics.

Because typewriters and computer printers may not be able to print italicized characters easily or well, the underscore has become an acceptable substitute. The underscore is used to emphasize the titles of *complete* literary and artistic works. Literary works include books, magazines, and newspapers; artistic works include movies, plays, paintings, and sculptures. Displaying the titles of complete works in uppercase letters is also acceptable. As noted earlier in this chapter, titles of *sections* of these works are displayed within quotation marks.

For faster service, call <u>1-800-555-CASH</u> (printing instructions)

For faster service, call *1-800-555-CASH* (after printing)

Have you read <u>Downsizing or Rightsizing</u> by P. C. Wiltery? (book title)

The next issue of *Buyer Beware* will contain an article comparing color monitors for computers. (magazine)

<u>Window on the World</u> is just one of the watercolors in Calley's show. (painting)

PUNCTUATION REVIEW

Punctuation helps a writer convey a message clearly and concisely. Figure 8•7 contains a list of the punctuation marks discussed in this chapter. A brief description of how each punctuation mark may be used is also included. Refer to Figure 8•7 whenever you have a question about punctuation. If more information is needed, review the section of this chapter that discusses the specific punctuation mark.

Punctuation Mark	Use(s)
apostrophe	to form the possessive of a noun to form a contraction
colon	to introduce a listing, an explanation, or an example in expressing ratios in literary references in reference initials after the salutation when mixed punctuation is used in expressing time
comma	with a complete calendar date to separate an independent clause in a complex sentence from the dependent clause that introduces it to separate two independent clauses joined by a coordinate conjunction in a compound sentence to separate coordinate adjectives with a complete geographic location to identify nonessential elements: appositives, introductory words, phrases, nonrestrictive clauses, parenthetical expressions, and transitional expressions to separate items in a series
dash	to add emphasis to show a sudden change in thought
diagonal	to indicate a choice, *per, with,* or *without* to construct fractions in reference initials with caution, to separate month/day/year in a numeric date
ellipsis points	to show that words have been omitted
exclamation point	to end an exclamatory sentence to signal a pause
hyphen	to form a compound word, especially a compound adjective to join a prefix or suffix to a root word to join points in a range
parentheses	to separate nonessential information
period	to end a declarative sentence to end an imperative sentence to end a courteous request to end an indirect question with abbreviations to form decimals in listings
question mark	to end an interrogative sentence
quotation marks	to identify a direct quotation to highlight an unusual item or word with a meaning unique to the message
semicolon	to join closely related independent clauses when no conjunction is used (compound sentence) to join independent clauses when one or both clauses contain commas (compound sentence) to separate items in a series when those items contain commas
underscore	to signal the need for italicized type to emphasize when italicized type is impossible or impractical

Figure 8·7 Frequently Used

DISCUSSION QUESTIONS

1. How is a courteous request different from an interrogative sentence?

2. When may a series of questions be treated as part of a single sentence?

3. What determines whether items in a series should be separated by a comma or by a semicolon? Give an example of each.

4. What determines whether a comma is used following an introductory phrase?

5. When should a comma be used to separate independent clauses?

6. What test may a writer use to determine whether a comma is needed between adjectives?

7. List two ways in which a colon may be used; give an example of each.

8. Distinguish between a direct quotation and a paraphrased thought with respect to the following:

   a. The use of quotation marks
   b. The need to give credit to the originator of the idea

9. Why would a writer use parentheses rather than commas to separate nonessential elements from the rest of the sentence?

10. How can you distinguish between a contraction and its sound-alike possessive pronoun?

11. What is the difference between an essential appositive and a nonessential appositive? Use an example to illustrate the difference.

12. What items constitute a complete geographic location? How should such a location be punctuated within a sentence?

13. Distinguish between a parenthetical expression and a transitional expression. Using the word *therefore,* construct a sentence to illustrate each type of expression.

14. Write a sentence to show how the diagonal is used in each of the following situations. Be sure to use examples other than those shown in the chapter.

    a. choice or alternative
    b. to mean *without*

15. What is an ellipsis? What are ellipsis points?

16. Explain how the use of a hyphen differs from the use of a dash.

17. List two ways (other than terminal punctuation) in which the period is used in business writing.

18. Indicate whether the punctuation marks listed below should be placed *inside* or *outside* an ending quotation mark.

    a. period   d. question mark

    b. comma   e. exclamation point

    c. semicolon   f. colon

19. If a writer does not have access to typewriters or printers that can create italics, how should she or he give special emphasis to text?

20. Indicate whether the following titles should be placed in quotation marks or underscored.

    a. magazine article   c. song

    b. book   d. painting

APPLICATION EXERCISES

Text 8A

1. Carefully read each item below. Insert the terminal mark of punctuation that would be best in each situation. Choose periods, question marks, or exclamation points.

   a. Thank you for bringing the error to our attention

   b. Where is Ruth Washington's office

   c. Will you please be sure Debra gets the file before noon

   d. You're our *best* sales representative

   e. Andres has agreed to chair the committee

   f. Your order will be shipped on March 27

   g. When will your novel be available in paperback

   h. The fire alarm is sounding

   i. Bill Danjor called to ask whether you are having difficulty accessing the network

   j. When will R. J. be released from the hospital

   k. The bids will be opened in my office

   l. Will you please insure the package before mailing it

   m. Act now

2. Read each sentence below and insert commas where necessary in each series or between coordinate adjectives.

   a. A file cabinet an executive desk and three large boxes were strapped to the pallet.

   b. The person we hire must be a poised confident individual.

c. The house has a new roof new carpeting and a fresh coat of paint.

d. Place an order for two chairs three desks and two magazine racks.

e. People attending the concert may park in lot A D or F.

f. Pascal BASIC and C are computer programming languages.

g. The clean basic lines of the design give the garment its appeal.

h. Mark Abernathy is a witty humorous entertainer.

i. Sarah and Ryan named their triplets Sandy Andy and Melody.

j. Your resume should include information about your work experience your educational qualifications and your activities.

k. Ms. Atwood is a knowledgeable articulate spokesperson for this charity.

l. The script calls for devious sinister characters.

m. The successful applicant must be a proficient typist an accurate proofreader and a cooperative worker.

3. Locate the dates and geographic locations in the sentences below. Determine if commas are needed, insert them where necessary, and give the reason for their use.

a. Was Myrtle born in Lexington Alabama or Lexington Massachusetts?

b. A video camera brought to us for repair by noon on Tuesday May 18 should be returned to you in time for your daughter's wedding on Saturday May 30.

c. Stephen's art collection is insured through the Lloyds of London office in New York City.

d. The original patent was registered on November 30 1913.

e. The restaurant will be closed for remodeling from June 28 through July 9.

f. The United States celebrated its bicentennial on July 4 1976.

g. In June I will attend the five-year reunion of my graduating class.

h. Their journey began in Seattle Washington on August 17.

i. The board will reconvene at 8 a.m. on Wednesday October 9.

j. In September 1990 Naples Florida formalized its Sister City agreement with Piemonte Italy.

4. Locate the nonessential elements in each of the following sentences and insert punctuation where needed. Indicate whether the nonessential element is an appositive, an introductory word, an introductory phrase, a nonrestrictive clause, a parenthetical expression, or a transitional expression.

a. You Roberta are one of the most talented cartoonists in the Midwest.

b. Mo said that he would be working late every night this week; he indicated however that he will not be working this Saturday.

c. Thank you Dr. Byman for writing a letter of reference for me.

d. Therefore you are entitled to a full refund.

e. Interstate 94 which passes through Chicago is the best way to reach your destination.

f. Sandy Jasper a fourth grade student at Park School won the city Spelling Bee.

g. For an exciting vacation visit Monterey.

h. Thomas Hoffman a well-respected poet is gaining popularity as a photographer.

i. The condominium is spacious and conveniently located; we will therefore make an offer on it.

j. Naturally we will cooperate with you on the project.

k. The results seem promising however additional testing will be done.

l. Your mortgage payment including an escrow for taxes and insurance will be $670 per month.

m. Yes two pedestrians witnessed the accident.

5. Insert commas and semicolons where necessary in each of the following sentences. Explain the reason for each punctuation mark.

a. Polyester was popular in the 60s today buyers prefer natural fibers.

b. After lunch proofread the document print it and deliver it to the vice president.

c. Because he did not want to miss any calls Rodger bought a cellular phone and printed both its number and his desk phone number on his business card.

d. When Catherine Powers phones tell her that Melissa McLean has accepted the position and will begin work on Wednesday July 7.

e. Word processing has increased our ability to produce written messages rapidly yet the demand for office personnel has not declined.

f. Do you mean Taylor Texas Taylor Michigan or Taylor Pennsylvania?

g. Sharon was disappointed by the tone of Seth's remarks and she asked him to take a more positive approach to the issue.

h. The chairs were the wrong color the style was ideal.

i. The story captured my attention and when I read the last word I found that I did not want it to end.

j. Because you will be the first to arrive at the hotel I am enclosing a copy of our reservation confirmation.

k. Constance is 18 her brother is older.

l. Last year the choir toured France this year it will travel through Germany.

m. The train will arrive at 9 p.m. today it will depart at 4 a.m. tomorrow.

6. Exercises 1-5 focused on either internal or terminal marks of punctuation. In this exercise, however, some of the items require no punctuation; others require terminal punctuation, commas, and/or semicolons. Insert punctuation where appropriate.

a. Sylvan questioned why Henrietta had withheld information about the merger.

b. Carley Aspen who played on Broadway in *A Chorus Line* is our landlord.

c. Since your invoice does not include an adjustment for damaged goods we are withholding payment.

d. He removed his jacket and left it lying on the table.

e. Andy Prospect who is legally blind competes in races designed specifically for people with disabilities.

f. Have you spoken with Harley about the loud distracting noises coming from the ventilation system?

g. I enjoyed viewing the film but the book provided more detail about the characters.

h. The sum of 4 8 12 and 24 is 48 the average of the numbers is 12

i. Please Mr. Todd make an appointment for a checkup.

j. When the guests had finished eating the band began to play music with a faster tempo

k. This program is designed for persons with no credit questionable credit or bad credit.

l. Linda asked that her mail be forwarded to her brother's home in Pinckneyville Illinois.

m. Casey was the successful bidder because his estimate included not only parts but also labor.

n. Neatness accuracy and clarity are important factors.

o. After the instructions were given I started working on the test.

p. Mrs. Adamczak will phone you when she returns from vacation.

q. Todd is the shorter more slender of the twins

r. You must use a pencil to record your responses otherwise the scanner will not be able to read them

s. Meteorologists do not control the weather they simply predict what is likely to occur.

t. The first part of the test went fairly well I think but I will need to review my English spelling and mathematics before returning for the next section of the examination.

u. Place the shipment on the truck tonight so that it will be ready when the driver arrives in the morning.

v. The new tax laws which were enacted during the current legislative session will take effect on July 1.

w. Your request for permission to convert to a month-to-month lease must therefore be referred to the Residents' Council.

x. The brochure should be redesigned before additional copies are ordered

y. Congratulations Michael

z. Robert Brown president of Brown Brothers Albert Pyroz personnel director at Dataform Sylvia Jacobsen owner of a consulting firm and Amanda Newel records manager at BZP Corporation were all members of the panel discussing mid-life career changes.

7. Carefully read each sentence below. Decide whether the quotation marks and other marks of punctuation have been used correctly. Make the necessary corrections.

a. Mr. Rothchild asked me, "Why don't more of our workers attend the holiday party"?

b. The visitors from abroad had difficulty understanding what Marvin meant when he said, "Fat chance".

c. According to the minutes, the motion was "tabled" I disagree.

d. "The day will come, said my mother, when you will be rewarded for your hard work."

e. *The Wizard of Oz* is my niece's favorite movie.

f. What did Dad mean when he said the book was a "lulu?"

g. As the President approached the podium, the delegates began to yell Four more years!

h. When she finished City 2000 Sue said: "Reading that article was as much fun as watching grass grow".

i. Did the shopper shout "Goodbye! or Good Buy!"

j. Everyone on the plane laughed when the youngster yelled, "Are we there yet?"

k. The sign on the boat read, For Sail.

l. Why are people who live in Nebraska called "Cornhuskers"?

m. Fairy tales usually begin with the words "Once upon a time;" they often end with the words "And they lived happily ever after."

8. Decide whether the secondary internal punctuation marks have been used correctly in the following sentences. Make all changes that are necessary.

a. The components were broken and had to be refused before shipping.

b. Hans Jensen is best known for the spine tingling mysteries he has written.

c. Three options are available. 1—Enter into a contract with a service bureau. 2. Hire temporary workers. (3). Ask our employees to work overtime.

d. The General Management Aptitude Test/GMAT will be given again in January.

e. A postage-paid, selfaddressed envelope has been enclosed to encourage a speedy reply.

f. Faye (and-or) Mark will witness the will.

g. Karen Abernathy is a self-motivated, energetic student who will certainly become a successful office worker.

h. The installation instructions are on pages 2 . . . 6.

i. Chapter 2, Sinks and Faucets, is contained on pages 126/134 of *Home Improvement Hints.*

j. Did you try the two, three, or four-step process?

MESSAGE ANALYSIS

Text 8C

Insert commas where needed in the following letter. If you think that two sentences are closely related, replace the period and the capital letter that follows it with a semicolon and a lowercase letter.

This letter will confirm information shared during our telephone conversation on April 29.

Your accounting internship will begin on Monday June 4 and conclude on Friday August 31. For the first part of the summer you will work in the Payroll Department under the supervision of Darren DeForest. During the last five weeks of your internship you will work with Janet Lummar in Internal Audit. Each of these individuals is a dedicated talented accountant from whom you should learn a great deal.

Please report to our Personnel Department Room 323 at 8 a.m. on June 2. Stephanie Fritz will explain company rules and procedures as they apply to your internship.

Henry I'm pleased that you have chosen to spend your summer with Central Power and Light. By working together we can make the experience pleasant and beneficial for everyone.

CHAPTER 9

Learning Objectives

Your learning objectives for this chapter include the following:

- To demonstrate an understanding of the importance of style guidelines in business writing
- To apply correctly the suggested style guidelines for:

  Expressing numbers
  Capitalizing words
  Dividing words
  Using abbreviations

T he word *style* is used in several different ways in business writing. A person's ability to organize and express ideas is called style. The format of a letter, memo, or report may be referred to as style. Reference manuals are sometimes called style manuals. In this chapter, **style** is used to mean the basic rules for number display, capitalization, word division, and abbreviation that apply to business writing.

Writers should be as concerned about correct usage as they are about their basic writing skills. Correct usage—usually called *mechanics*—and good writing skills work together to:

- minimize the number of distractions in a message
- bring consistency to communication
- reflect well on the writer
- have a positive effect on the reader

Style may mean different things in business writing.

Here style refers to rules for correct usage.

NUMBERS

Numbers play a major role in our lives. They are used to represent, describe, and locate people and objects. Because numbers are so widely used, attention must be given to expressing them correctly in business writing.

Business writers use general style when expressing numbers. **General style** is a blend of two styles known as *formal* and *technical*. In general style, numbers are represented in words when formality is needed and in figures when the clarity of technical style is appropriate.

General style is used for expressing numbers in business writing.

GENERAL GUIDELINES

There are several guidelines related to the way numbers are expressed. Some of these guidelines are used frequently in business writing, others are used rarely. This section describes those guidelines that have frequent application in business correspondence and reports.

WRITING WHOLE NUMBERS

Whole numbers greater than ten are written in figures. This guideline applies only to whole numbers—those that have no decimal or fractional parts.

Write whole numbers greater than ten in figures.

Sam purchased *ten* tickets to the play.

Make *eight* copies of the report and mail them to Rochelle.

The new restaurant has a seating capacity of *225*.

WRITING ROUND NUMBERS

Round numbers may be expressed in figures, words, or a combination of the two. To reduce the emphasis placed on a round number, words are used. When emphasis is desired, a figure is used. Figures are often used in advertising for emphasis. Because numbers greater than a million may be difficult to read when expressed in figures, a writer may combine words and figures to achieve greater clarity.

Using figures to represent large round numbers draws attention to those numbers.

Sachi has flown over *20,000* miles this year.

Only *five hundred* tickets are available.

The population of the country is over *15 million*.

BEGINNING A SENTENCE WITH A NUMBER

Express numbers that begin sentences in words.

Numbers that begin a sentence are expressed in words. If the number is large, rewrite the sentence.

Three inches of rain fell last night.

Two thousand entries have been keyed.

Thirteen thousand two hundred seventy-seven people attended the convention. (Awkward. See the following sentence.)

The convention attendance was *13,277*. (Improved version)

WRITING NUMBERS CONSISTENTLY

Express numbers consistently.

Be consistent in expressing numbers, and strive for easy reading. When numbers greater than *and* less than ten appear in the same sentence, use figures for all numbers. If two numbers are adjacent to one another, as in a series, punctuation and proper spacing are important to make the numbers easy to read. When one of two adjacent numbers is part of a compound modifier, the smaller number is written in words.

A discount is offered for payment made within *ten* days, and the full amount is due within *30* days. (inconsistent)

A discount is offered for payment made within *10* days, and the full amount is due within *30* days. (consistent)

The following items were ordered: 12 two-button vests, 8 four-button sweaters, 9 pairs of slacks, and 1 coat. (adjacent numbers; compound modifier.)

In 1993, 23,677,102 orders were filled. (easy to read)

PUNCTUATING NUMBERS

Use commas in numbers with four or more digits.

In numbers with four or more digits, a comma is usually used. The comma is optional in round numbers less than 10,000 and is omitted in identification, model, serial, and house numbers.

1,000,000

7,000 or 7000

1,113

ID No. 10558

7246 West Monroe Avenue

SPECIFIC GUIDELINES

The general guidelines just presented will help you through many writing situations involving numbers. There are some specific guidelines, too, that should be mastered. As you read the material, you will encounter the term *ordinal*. **Ordinal** words or numbers show position in a series. *First, second, third, tenth*, and *seventy-fifth* are examples of ordinal words; *1st, 2d, 3d,*

Ordinals show position in a series.

10th, and *75th* are examples of ordinal numbers. Note that *d* is used in place of both *nd* and *rd* in ordinal numbers.

ADDRESSES

All house or building numbers over one are written in figures when they are used within the text of a message. When part of a mailing address in a letter or on an envelope, all house and building numbers are displayed in figures; *one* is no longer an exception. Numbered streets are written as words if ten or below and as figures in all other cases. When figures are used for both house number and street name, place a hyphen between them.

> One Winston Place (when used in text)
>
> 1015 North Sixth Street
>
> 3648 - 141st Street
>
> 10 West 157 Avenue

Notice that in the last two examples the street names are expressed in different ways; one (141st) uses an ordinal ending, the other (157) does not. When a word appears between the house number and the street name, the ordinal ending may be omitted.

DATES

Figures are used for the day and the year. If the day is used without a month or if the day precedes the month, ordinal numbers or words may be used.

> March 1996   February 28   January 1, 2000
>
> the 1st and 15th (ordinal without a month)
>
> the 2d of June (ordinal number)
>
> the second of June (ordinal word)

Some writers use the international (military) date form, but it has not received widespread acceptance in American business correspondence. The international date form should be used in correspondence sent to receivers outside the United States. Select the form used in the country to which you are writing. Here are two common international date forms.

> 23 March 1997   1997.3.23

FRACTIONS

When a fraction is used by itself, it is expressed in words. Use a hyphen between the numerator (top number) and denominator (bottom number) of a fraction written in words unless one part already contains a hyphen. When a fraction is part of a mixed number, it is expressed in figures.

> one-third of the class (noun)
>
> a one-third share (adjective)
>
> one sixty-fifth
>
> 7 1/4

Notice the space in the mixed number between the fraction and the whole number. Unless a typewriter or keyboard has a special key for fractions, this space is necessary for readability. Without the space the figure could be misread as 71/4 (seventy-one fourths).

MONEY

Express money amounts in figures.

Money amounts are expressed in figures. If the money amount is a whole number, the decimal and zeros are omitted. A comma is used in most money amounts of four digits or more. The comma is optional in even money amounts less than $10,000. An indefinite amount of money should be written in words.

Indefinite money amounts are written in words.

$5,079.32	$450
$3000 or $3,000	several thousand dollars

For amounts of money less than $1, use figures and spell the word *cents*:

1 cent	98 cents

On orders, invoices, and other business forms, the symbol ¢ may be used. If definite amounts of money greater and less than $1 occur in the same sentence, use the $ symbol and a decimal where necessary:

We were quoted prices of $1.03, $1, and $.97 per item.

ORDINALS

Only one- or two-word ordinals should be used in sentences; they should be spelled in full.

If an ordinal can be expressed in one or two words, it should be spelled in full. If the ordinal exceeds one or two words, the sentence should be rewritten to avoid the need for an ordinal. This restriction applies only to ordinals that appear within the body of a sentence. Refer to the sections on addresses and dates under the Specific Guidelines heading in this chapter for the proper use of ordinals in those items.

The *first* award will be presented by Martin Miliken.

The company's *seventy-fifth* anniversary celebration was well attended.

Dilton's one-hundred seventeenth Customer Appreciation Sale will begin Monday, August 12. (Long ordinal; hard to read when displayed in words.)

Dilton's has held a Customer Appreciation Sale for 117 years; this year's sale will begin Monday, August 12. (Improved version; sentence has been rewritten to avoid the need for an ordinal.)

PERCENTAGES

In nontechnical business writing, *percent* is written as a word, and the number is expressed as a figure.

Percent is usually spelled out.

50 percent	18 1/2 percent	10.5 percent

At the beginning of a sentence, spell out the number or reword the sentence.

Sixty-five percent of the voters cast ballots in favor of the referendum.

The referendum was favored by 65 percent of those voters casting ballots.

TIME

To designate time with a.m. (midnight to noon) or p.m. (noon to midnight) use a figure; zeros are not needed for on-the-hour times. For formality, use a word before *o'clock*; for emphasis, use a figure before *o'clock*. Approximate time and time on the half hour are expressed in words.

> The stores in the mall close at *9 p.m.*
>
> The flight will depart at *6:07 a.m.*
>
> The doors will be opened at *7 o'clock* each morning. (emphasis)
>
> The reception will begin at eight o'clock this evening. (formality)

In all cases, be sure the time of day is clear:

> The train will arrive at six-thirty. (six-thirty in the morning or six-thirty in the evening?)
>
> The train will arrive at six-thirty this evening. (clear)

To avoid confusion, writers usually use *midnight* rather than 12 a.m. and *noon* rather than 12 p.m.

CAPITALIZATION

Early in your education, you were taught to capitalize the first letter of a word that begins a sentence and the first letter of a proper noun. Few, if any, writers have difficulty with these practices. This section, therefore, will present other basically accepted rules for capitalization.

ACADEMIC COURSES

When referring to a *specific* course, capitalize the first letter of the main word(s). Do not capitalize general subjects other than languages.

> *Issues in Global Ecology* is a very popular course on this campus.
>
> Are you taking an *ecology* course this term?
>
> Dr. Whiterabbit teaches *Psychology* 101, 103, and 256.
>
> Dr. Whiterabbit teaches *psychology* courses.
>
> Sandra is enrolled in her third *French* class.

COMPASS DIRECTIONS

Specific names of geographic locations (sections, places, continents, countries, states, cities, rivers, mountains, lakes, and islands) are capitalized. Do not capitalize general directions.

> She was born in the *South*.
>
> Their business will expand to the *Far East*.
>
> The parking lot on the *north* side of the building is being repaired. (a direction)
>
> She drove *west* on I-94 to the North Dakota border. (a direction)

GOVERNMENT

The names of domestic and foreign government agencies, units, and organizations are capitalized.

Environmental Protection Agency

Royal Canadian Mounted Police

United Nations Security Council

Short forms of the names of national and international government bodies and their major divisions should also be capitalized. Writers should use short forms only when they are certain their readers will understand them.

the Court (United States Supreme Court)

the Division (Wage and Hour Division of the Department of Labor)

the Corps (United States Corps of Engineers)

The short forms of the names of state and local government bodies are not capitalized.

the city   the state   the department

When in doubt about the capitalization of government and judicial bodies, consult a reference book such as *The Chicago Manual of Style*, published by The University of Chicago Press.

INSTITUTIONS AND ORGANIZATIONS

The full names of institutions (churches, libraries, hospitals, and schools) and organizations (associations, companies, committees, and clubs) and their divisions or departments are capitalized. The word *the* is capitalized only when it is part of the official title. Follow the style established by the organization or institution as shown on its letterhead or other written communication.

Memorial Hospital has released the plans for its new addition.

Temple Israel has been selected as the site for the dinner.

Are you a member of the Association of Records Managers and Administrators?

Katy plans to enroll at The Ohio State University next fall.

Publicity Committee	*but*	the committee
Intensive Care Unit	*but*	the unit
Accounting Department	*but*	the department

TIME

The most common reference to time in business writing is a date, but time can also be a reference to seasons, holidays, or events. The names of days, months, holidays, religious days, and historical events are *always* capitalized. The names of seasons are capitalized only when they are part of a specific title or are personified, as in poetry.

Thursday, February 3	Martin Luther King Day
Rosh Hashanah	World War II
Winter Carnival	this spring

TITLES

Titles are divided into two categories—occupational titles and official titles. An occupational title is capitalized only when it is a specific job title. An official title is capitalized when it comes before a personal name, unless the personal name has been added for clarification or description (nonessential element set off by commas). An official title is generally not capitalized when it follows a personal name or is used in place of a personal name. The titles of state, national, and international officials are an exception; these titles are capitalized when they come before, come after, or are used in place of personal names.

> The treasurer, Myron Backstrom, gave the keynote address. (occupational title)
>
> Marketing Manager Ellen Francis has announced her resignation. (specific job title)
>
> Josefina Ortiz, city manager, reported on economic development activities. (title following name)
>
> After speaking, President Smith returned to New York. (national title before a personal name)
>
> The Emir hosted the dinner. (international title used in place of name)

> *Proper words in proper places, make the true definition of a style.*
>
> **Jonathan Swift**

WORD DIVISION

When traditional typewriters are used to produce business documents, it *may* be necessary to divide a word at the end of a line of type in order to achieve a balanced right margin. Note the emphasis on the word "may." Word division is an option—not a requirement.

Word processors have minimized the need to make decisions about when and how to divide words. The decision about whether words are to be divided is made as the document is formatted. When hyphenation is selected and a word would extend beyond the right margin, the software searches its dictionary. If the word is in the dictionary, a hyphen is inserted at an appropriate location and the rest of the word is wrapped. If the word is not in the software dictionary, the keyboard operator will be prompted to insert the hyphen. Even with a word processor, a writer may elect to divide a word. Therefore, it is important for all business writers to know how to divide words properly.

Two reference books that are helpful when writers need to know where to divide a word are a word book and a dictionary. A word book is a better reference because it shows not only syllables but also preferred word division points. A dictionary will indicate only syllables; writers must then determine where the word is best divided.

If you decide to divide a word, the following guidelines should be used. Note that the guidelines are for those who use typewriters and word processors. The rules are not as strict for typesetters, i.e., those who produce such things as books and magazines.

1. Divide a word only between syllables.

2. Divide between two vowels if they are pronounced separately. (e.g., punctu-ation, cha-otic, evalu-ation).

3. Divide after a one-syllable vowel unless the one-letter syllable *a* or *i* is followed by *ble, bly, cle, or cal*. When this occurs both syllables should be carried to the next line. (e.g., med-ical).

4. Divide before a suffix. (e.g., commence-ment)

5. Divide between two parts of a compound word. If the word is hyphenated, divide at the hyphen. (e.g., well-known)

6. Avoid dividing names, dates, and addresses. If these items must be divided, follow these guidelines:
   a. Do not use a hyphen to show that the item has been divided.
   b. Keep a personal title with the name. (e.g., Mrs. Pat/Jones)
   c. Divide a date between the day of the month and the year. (e.g., June 20,/ 1991)
   d. Divide an address between the city and the state. (e.g., Cincinnati,/Ohio)

7. No fewer than two letters of the word should be left on the first line, and no fewer than three letters should be carried to the next line. The goal is to give the reader an idea of the word before it is divided. Therefore, if it is possible to divide a word in more than one place, select the division point that places the larger part of the word on the upper line.

These guidelines refer to what should be done when words are divided. There are some times, however, when a word should not be divided:

1. Words of five or fewer letters should not be divided even if they have two or more syllables.

2. The last word on a page should not be divided. Avoid dividing the last word in a paragraph.

3. Divide as few words as possible; avoid ending two consecutive lines with divided words.

4. Do not divide figures, abbreviations, contractions, or items containing symbols.

ABBREVIATIONS

Abbreviations are a simple way to save space and time in business writing. Their use should be limited, however, to those that the reader will recognize and understand. If an abbreviation is to be used several times within a letter or report, the complete form—followed by the abbreviation in parentheses—should be used at the first instance. The reader will then understand the abbreviation when it occurs again.

Use only those abbreviations that your reader will recognize.

> The Student Conduct Committee (SCC) has filed its report. After the vice president has reviewed the SCC report, she will submit it to the Board of Governors.

ACRONYMS

Acronyms are a special form of abbreviation. They are *words* formed by using the first letter of each major word of a compound item.

Acronyms are pronounced as words.

Cost of Living Allowance	becomes	COLA
Random Access Memory	becomes	RAM
Computer Assisted Retrieval	becomes	CAR
North Atlantic Treaty Organization	becomes	NATO

BUSINESS AND ASSOCIATION NAMES

Business firms, government agencies, and professional groups are often known by their initials. Therefore, their abbreviated names are sometimes called *initialisms*. The standard format for initialisms is all capital letters, no periods or spaces:

Some business organizations are known by their abbreviated names.

> IBM (International Business Machines)
>
> AT&T (American Telephone and Telegraph)
>
> FCC (Federal Communications Commission)

Abbreviated words are often part of the name of a business firm. Assn. for Association, Co. for Company, Corp. for Corporation, Ltd. for Limited, and Inc. for Incorporated are just a few examples. Abbreviate these items only when they are part of a business name; spell them in full when used independently within a sentence.

> Brown and Bowen Co.
>
> Financial analysts report that the company is sound.

MEASUREMENTS

Measurements may be abbreviated when they occur frequently in tables or business forms. When used, they are displayed in lowercase letters and do not have periods. In most business writing, measurements are spelled in full rather than abbreviated. Common measurements and their abbreviations are shown in Figure 9•1.

Spell out measurements in general correspondence.

MONTHS/DAYS

Each of the months of the year and days of the week has a standard abbreviation (see Figure 9•2). These abbreviations should be used only to save

Figure 9•1 Measurements

Measure	Abbreviation
centimeter	cm
foot	ft
gallon	gal
kilogram	kg
miles per hour	mph
pound	lb
pages per minute	ppm
words per minute	wpm

Figure 9•2 Month/Day Abbreviations

Days		Months	
Sun.	Thurs.	Jan.	July
Mon.	Fri.	Feb.	Aug.
Tues.	Sat.	Mar.	Sept.
Wed.		Apr.	Oct.
		May	Nov.
		June	Dec.

Use abbreviations sparingly for months and days.

space on business forms; they should not be used in business reports or correspondence.

PERSONAL NAMES

Names may be abbreviated by using initials or a shortened form of the name.

Abbreviations for personal names may take the form of an initial or a shortened form of the name. Before abbreviating a person's name, be sure that the individual will not object to the use of the abbreviated form.

A. J. Dillon	C. Luisa Diaz
Patricia D. Seiler	Geo. Rafferty

Nicknames are different from abbreviations.

An abbreviation is different from a nickname. An abbreviation is always shorter than its given name; it always ends with a period. Nicknames may be modifications of a given name (Vicky for Victoria), or may be totally unrelated to the given name (George Herman "Babe" Ruth). Some of the more widely used abbreviations and nicknames for names are shown in Figure 9•3. Personal names should not be abbreviated unless space is limited, as in tabulations or enumerations. Use of nicknames in business writing should be restricted to those that are modifications of given names.

PERSONAL TITLES

Personal titles should be abbreviated when they occur before a name.

Personal title abbreviations such as *Mr., Mrs., Ms.,* and *Dr.* are used before a personal name:

Mr. Juan Estrada　　Ms. Edith Owens

Mrs. Clara Goers　　Dr. Victor Cruz

The individual preference of the person should be respected when using titles.

Unless a woman's specific title is known, *Ms.* should be used before her name. It is the woman's responsibility to let her correspondents know her personal preference. When the person's preference is known, that title should be used. If a writer's first name may be used by members of either gender (Pat, Terry, Fran), the writer should include a personal title in the signature line. This procedure should also be followed if a writer uses only initials (A. K. Jones; B. W. O'Brien) This technique, as well as other options, is illustrated in Chapter 10.

The titles Junior and Senior are abbreviated when they follow a personal name:

Kenneth Langford, Jr.　　Fred Larmer, Sr.

Figure 9•3 Abbreviated Names

Abbreviation	Name	Possible Nicknames
Chas.	Charles	Charlie, Chuck
Eliz.	Elizabeth	Liz, Beth
Marg.	Margaret	Maggie, Meg, Peg
Robt.	Robert	Bob, Rob, Bobby
Thos.	Thomas	Tom, Tommie
Wm.	William	Bill, Will

PROFESSIONAL TITLES, DESIGNATIONS, AND DEGREES

Many people choose to use their professional titles, designations, or degrees when conducting business. Whenever possible, write professional titles (e.g., Professor, Reverend, Vice President) in full; however, abbreviate designations and academic degrees.

Abbreviate designations and academic degrees.

Certification programs offered by professional associations allow individuals to earn designations to signal their accomplishments. Accountants, for example, may earn the designation CPA when they become certified public accountants. While the specific requirements for each designation vary, each generally involves some combination of a test and work experience. Designation abbreviations contain no periods, follow an individual's name, and are separated from the name by a comma. Several common designations are shown in Figure 9•4.

Academic degrees are awarded by educational institutions to individuals who complete the requirements for various programs of study. When academic degrees are abbreviated, periods are used. Some of the most common academic abbreviations and the degrees they represent are shown in Figure 9•5.

Use either a title or an academic degree abbreviation—not both.

When referring to a person who has the academic or medical credentials to be addressed as doctor, use either the title or the abbreviation for the

Figure 9•4 Designation
Abbreviations

Abbreviation	Designation
CPA	Certified Public Accountant
CMA	Certified Managerial Accountant
CDP	Certified Data Processor
CPS	Certified Professional Secretary

Figure 9•4 Designation Abbreviations

degree, but not both. If the title is used, the abbreviation *Dr.* is placed before the name. If the abbreviation for the degree is used, it is placed after the name, and a comma separates the name from the abbreviation.

Dr. Jane Alexander   Jane Alexander, D.D.S.

Figure 9•5 Degree
Abbreviations

Abbreviation	Degree
A.A.	Associate of Arts
A.S.	Associate of Science
B.S.	Bachelor of Science
B.Ac.	Bachelor of Accounting
B.B.A.	Bachelor of Business Administration
M.A.	Master of Arts
M.B.A.	Master of Business Administration
Ed.D.	Doctor of Education
Ph.D.	Doctor of Philosophy
D.D.S.	Doctor of Dental Science
D.Pharm.	Doctor of Pharmacy
D.V.M.	Doctor of Veterinary Medicine

STATES/TERRITORIES/PROVINCES

The official two-letter postal abbreviations for state, territory, and province names should be used when part of a complete address. In all other cases, the name of the state, territory, or province should be spelled in full. A complete list of the two-letter postal abbreviations used in the United States and Canada is in Appendix D. Be sure to secure the postal address requirements of any other countries to which you write.

Spell out names of states, territories, and provinces unless they are part of a complete address.

Symbols are a form of abbreviation.

Use only those symbols that your reader will recognize and understand.

SYMBOLS

Symbols are a form of abbreviation. Some standard business symbols, a brief definition of each, and an example of its use are shown in Figure 9•6.

Symbols should be used sparingly in business writing. Only those symbols that are certain to be interpreted correctly should be used.

Figure 9·6 Standard
Business Symbols

Symbol	Definition	Example
&	ampersand (meaning *and*)	Cole & Parks
*	asterisk (refers reader to a note)	Price*
		*subject to change without notice
@	at, each, per	17 @ $2.25 each
©	copyright	© South-Western Publishing Company
®	registered trademark	Kodak®
°	degree	77°
/	diagonal, slash	and/or, s/he, 2/3, 12/31/99
¢	cents	59¢
$	dollars	$13
'	feet (apostrophe)	6'
"	inch (quotation mark)	9"
:	ratio (colon)	4:1
#	number (before figure)	#10
#	pounds (after figure)	100#
%	percent	66%
x	*by* or *times* (lowercase *x*)	2 x 4, 3 x 5
K	thousand	640K, $20K

TIME ZONES

The world is divided into time zones. In Canada and the United States, each zone has its own abbreviation. In addition, one character in that abbreviation is changed to indicate whether those residing in the region are observing standard or daylight saving time. Figure 9·7 lists time zone abbreviations and definitions. Telephone directories typically include a map of North America and show the areas covered by each zone.

When writers ask receivers to phone them, the time zone is often included in the message. Typically, the time zone is displayed in parentheses following the hours during which telephone calls are received. For example: 9 a.m. to 4 p.m. (EST).

OTHER ABBREVIATIONS

So many abbreviations are used in business that it is impractical to include all of them in this text. A brief listing of some of the most commonly used terms is, however, included in Figure 9·8. Notice that some of the abbreviations use capital letters; others use lowercase letters. Some of the abbreviations use periods, others do not.

Because abbreviations are often associated with particular fields (e.g., education, law, medicine, transportation), you may encounter abbreviations

Time zones for both standard and daylight saving time are abbreviated.

Consult references before abbreviating unfamiliar terms.

with which you are unfamiliar. When this situation arises, consult a dictionary or reference manual.

Figure 9·7 Time Zone Abbreviations

Time Zone	Abbreviation
Atlantic Standard Time	AST
Atlantic Daylight Time	ADT
Eastern Standard Time	EST
Eastern Daylight Time	EDT
Central Standard Time	CST
Central Daylight Time	CDT
Mountain Standard Time	MST
Mountain Daylight Time	MDT
Pacific Standard Time	PST
Pacific Daylight Time	PDT

Figure 9·8 Other Commonly Used Abbreviations

Term	Abbreviation	Term	Abbreviation
account	acct.	maximum	max.
affidavit	afft.	merchandise	mdse.
also known as	a.k.a.	month/months	mo.
amount	amt.	money order	MO
as soon as possible	ASAP	national	natl.
attached	att.	net weight	nt. wt.
average	avg.	not applicable	N/A
balance	bal.	number	No.
care of	c/o	overnight	o/n
charge	chg.	optional	opt.
collect on delivery	COD	organization	org.
continued	cont.	original	orig.
credit	cr.	out of stock	OS *or* o.s.
hundredweight	cwt.	package	pkg.
department	dept.	page/pages	p./pp.
destination	dest.	paid	pd.
discount	dis.	parcel post	PP
division	div.	part, point	pt.
extension	ext.	port of entry	POE *or* p.o.e.
for example	e.g.	prepaid	ppd.
free on board	FOB *or* f.o.b.	purchase order	PO

Other Commonly Used Abbreviations, *Continued*

freight	frt.	quantity	qty.
government	gvt.	quarter	qtr.
gross weight	gr. wt.	received	recd.
headquarters	hdqrs.	requisition	req
hour	hr.	returned	retd.
institute	inst.	shortage	shtg.
interest	int.	standard	std.
inventory	invt.	statement	stmt.
invoice	inv.	wholesale	whsle.

DISCUSSION QUESTIONS

1. Why are style guidelines important to a business writer?

2. Why is the general style for writing numbers especially good for business?

3. List three of the five general guidelines for writing numbers. Give an example of each.

4. What technique should a business writer use to emphasize a round number? To de-emphasize a round number?

5. What advice would you give to a writer about using numbers greater and less than ten in the same sentence?

6. What are the guidelines for using figures to display house numbers and street names?

7. When should dates be expressed in figures? in words? Give an example of each.

8. When should fractions be expressed in figures? in words? Give an example of each.

9. Explain and give an example of how each of the following money amounts should be expressed:

   a. A definite amount

   b. An indefinite amount

   c. An amount less than one dollar

   d. Money amounts less than and greater than one dollar that appear in the same sentence

10. What are ordinals? What should be done when ordinals exceed one or two words?

11. Explain how percentage figures should be written in nontechnical business documents.

12. Give an example of how each of the following should be written:

   a. Time expressed with a.m. or p.m.

   b. Time expressed with o'clock

   c. Approximate time and time on the half hour

13. When should each of the following be capitalized?

   a. Academic courses

   b. Compass directions

14. When should the short form of state and local government bodies be capitalized?

15. When should the word *the* be capitalized in the name of an institution or organization?

16. In what ways may time be expressed other than a date? Which, if any, should be capitalized?

17. When should titles of international, national, and state government officials be capitalized?

18. Which reference book is preferred when a writer must decide where to divide a word?

19. Explain where each of the following items should be divided:

    a. A word containing a suffix (e.g., workable)
    b. A compound word (e.g., textbook)
    c. A compound word containing a hyphen (e.g., twenty-seven)

20. If it is possible to divide a word in more than one place, how should a writer determine where to insert the hyphen?

21. List two of the conditions under which a word should not be divided.

22. When should personal names be abbreviated?

23. In what two ways may a personal name be abbreviated?

24. How is an abbreviated name different from a nickname? Give one example of each type of name.

25. Assume that you wish to use CBEC to represent Columbia Business Executives Club within the text of a message. How and when would you introduce the abbreviation?

26. Give two examples other than those in the text of businesses that are known by their abbreviated names or by initialisms.

27. What title should be used when a writer doesn't know the marital status of a female message receiver?

28. Pat Carter and Gayle Jorgenson want to know how to ensure that receivers of the messages they write know they are men. What advice would you give them?

29. In what way is the abbreviation display for a professional designation different from the abbreviation display for an academic degree?

30. Is it permissible to use both the title *Dr.* and the abbreviated form of the academic degree with the same personal name?

31. When should measurements, months, and days of the week be abbreviated?

32. When should the two-letter postal state abbreviation be used within business messages?

33. When a writer wishes to include his or her time zone in a business message, how should the time zone be displayed?

34. When a writer is uncertain of the meaning of an abbreviation, what should he or she do?

35. List three symbols that are commonly used in business and give their meanings.

APPLICATION EXERCISES

Text 9A

1. Select the appropriate expression for each number in the items below:

a. (Thirty-six/36) inches equal (one/1) yard.

b. We expected to pay less than ($500/$500.00/5 hundred dollars).

c. Effective January 1, your salary will be increased by (twenty-five dollars/$25/$25.00) a week.

d. The (first/1st/1) (100/one hundred/1 hundred) people to enroll will receive a ($10/$10./ten dollar/$10.00) discount.

e. Be sure to have a dental checkup every (six/6) months.

f. (Fifty/50) percent is (1/2/one-half), but it is not a majority.

g. Will the contract take effect on May (31/31st/thirty-first) or on the (1/1st/first) of June?

h. Because it was nearly (noon/twelve p.m./12:00), the committee recessed until after lunch.

i. Please change my address from (763 - Fifth Avenue/763 - 5th Avenue/763 5th Avenue/763 Fifth Avenue) to (376 - Fifth Avenue/376 - 5th Avenue/376 5th Avenue/376 Fifth Avenue).

j. Bobby has grown almost (two/2) inches since his last visit.

k. The entire process will take only (10/ten) or (15/fifteen) minutes.

l. The average price was (93¢/93 cents/$.93) a unit.

m. Officials estimate that more than (2,000,000/2 million/two million) people will attend the (three-/3-) day event.

n. The auto dealer reported that there were (fifteen/15) (two-door/2-door) sedans left in stock.

o. Their grandchildren's ages are (2, 6, 10, 13, and 19/two, six, ten, thirteen, and nineteen/two, six, ten, 13, and 19).

p. Our forwarding address is (710/Seven Ten/Seven Hundred Ten) West (Six/6/Sixth) Street.

q. We have a (one/1) in (1,000,000/1000000/a million) chance of winning the sweepstakes.

r. The serial number on the Model (1222/1,222/twelve 22/twelve twenty-two) laser printer is (736,921-G/736921-G).

s. Minnesota has about (twenty-five percent/25%/25 percent/

twenty-five %) of the nation's peat supply but less than (five percent/5%/5 percent/five %) of the growing market.

Text 9B

2. Each sentence below requires corrections in capitalization. Some words shown in lowercase should be capitalized; some shown in capital letters should be in lowercase. Correct the errors.

a. according to a recent Report from the American Council on Science and Health, fluoridation of drinking water is a very effective weapon against tooth decay.

b. The applicant earned a master's Degree in geology at Albrook college in New Mexico.

c. The department of Public Works is located in city hall.

d. The Civil war pitted the North against the south.

e. The vice president will represent the President at the Nato meeting.

f. The department of the navy has given the science research Institute a grant of $600,000.

g. What grade did you earn in Contemporary persuasion?

h. The centers for Disease Control (cdc) reported an outbreak of german measles in the Western Suburbs of Dallas.

i. The "Metro business index" is available from the Atlanta chamber of commerce.

j. The Commencement speaker will be Mayor Barbara Pandy.

k. Rita P. Quirk, the treasurer of the Association, received the Group's annual distinguished service Award.

l. the senate has adjourned for its Holiday break; sessions will resume in four weeks.

m. Last night we saw a french film with english subtitles.

n. The west end Summer spree will begin Sunday, august 3.

o. the director's comments were well received; her Staff applauded.

p. The Chair of the City's Finance committee resigned two weeks after the Auditing firm issued its Final Report.

3. Several company, organization, agency, and program names are listed below. By what abbreviation is each name most commonly known?

a. Beginner's All-purpose Symbolic Instruction Code

b. Federal Deposit Insurance Corporation

c. General Electric

d. Individual Retirement Account

e. Common Business Oriented Language

f. Federal Insurance Corporation of America

g. Central Intelligence Agency

h. American Automobile Association

i. National Football League

j. Cable News Network

4. Use a telephone book or other reference source to indicate the standard time zone abbreviation for each of the following locations:

a. Cheyenne, Wyoming
b Shreveport, Louisiana
c. Thunder Bay, Ontario

d. Santa Rosa, California
e. Raleigh, North Carolina
f. Halifax, Nova Scotia

5. Each item below contains at least one abbreviation. Decide whether each has been used correctly. If the abbreviation is incorrect, change it.

a. Milicent @ Hugh Rolle, Insurance Agents

b. Dr. Karla Ives, C.P.A. was called as an expert witness.

c. The Buffalo team outscored its opponents 3/2.

d. The maximum weight is 15,000#.

e. Fitness centers were recently opened in Seattle, WA; Montgomery, Alabama; Wichita, KS, and Regina, Saskatchewan.

f. Tmos. G. Galdwin will replace M.S. Sloan as our representative in your area.

g. MS Edith Port has been named ceo at Player, ltd.

h. The new pc has 640K of memory.

i. Ron Zefirov, Jun., recently visited Ecuador.

j. You and-or your spouse should attend the meeting on long-term health care insurance.

k. Is it G.M. or Honda that will open an assembly plant in Kapus next Sept.?

l. On a Fahrenheit scale, the freezing point is 32° and the boiling point is 212°.

m. Mr. Milo Carver, Mrs. Niko Osi, and Doctor Marg. O'Donnell will be our representatives.

6. Indicate *if* and *where* each of the following items should be divided. Some items may be divided in more than one place; indicate *all* acceptable dividing points.

a. advisement
b. certifiable
c. everywhere
d. March 21, 199-
e. eager

f. fast-paced
g. strenuous
h. willing
i. quantity
j. transition

Text 9C

Edit the following message to reflect correct use of numbers, capitalization, abbreviations, and symbols.

thank you for bringing to our attn. the error in your most recent shpt. As you noted, there was a shtg.

4 boxes of our No. three greeting cards and 11 pkgs. of our numb. 45C all-occasion gift wrap were sent to you on Mon., 4/16. You should receive them within a wk. Enclosed with that package is a complimentary set of recipe cards. These 3X5 cards fit all std. recipe boxes.

The Summer edition of our catalog will be mailed in May. When ordering from it, you may wish to place your order by calling our toll-free number (1-800-555-1905); phones are answered from 7 a.m. to 10 p.m. pst every weekday.

PART 3

Correspondence Applications

Make Your Complaints Effective

Business correspondence is used for messages that are positive, neutral, negative, persuasive, or goodwill. One frequently used application of persuasive correspondence is a complaint message. Effective use of the following guidelines for complaining will result in your complaints being more productive.

Get a grip on your emotions. Use tact and diplomacy; not sarcasm, cursing, screaming, or nasty letters. Give the organization an opportunity to correct the problem. When your complaining to a sales clerk is getting nowhere, you must take your complaint to a supervisor or manager. Maintain your composure in stating your complaint. Always write down the name of the individual to whom you have spoken, and document your efforts to resolve the complaint. Inform each new person what steps you have already taken to solve the problem. When telephone calls and personal visits do not produce positive results, you will need to write a letter.

Prepare a letter. The most effective letter will be concise, well-documented, and filled with facts. State what you want done, and give a date as to when you would like a response. The receiver of the letter will prefer a short explanation—one or two pages.

In the letter do not repeat yourself or resort to name-calling or sarcasm. Writing a nasty letter that contains vulgarities will reduce the likelihood that the correspondence will be read in its entirety. Evidence that can substantiate your claim—such as receipts, canceled checks, proof of purchase, and bills—should be enclosed with the letter. Send copies of the evidence, not the originals.

Include your name, address, daytime and evening telephone numbers, and the address of the store or dealer. Identify the defective product or unsatisfactory service that has led to the complaint. Many businesses will not spend much time reading a sloppily written letter. Type or write it neatly.

Complaints that are legitimate and reasonable usually are responded to positively.

Send the letter. Ensure that the letter gets to the appropriate person. Find out the name of the person in charge of a particular department or company. Your letter should be directed to the person responsible for assistance. It may help to send the letter by certified mail, return receipt requested.

Set reasonable goals. Complaints that are legitimate and reasonable usually are responded to positively. Complaints should be filed without delay. Waiting for months or years to register your complaint will decrease the chances for it to be settled to your satisfaction.

The basic rule of effective complaining: Make your complaint timely, make it to the proper person, and make it compelling with important details.

As reported in "The Lemme Doit Guide to Effective Complaining," *The Courier Journal*, Louisville, Kentucky (December 13, 1993), pp. C1 and C5.

It's Your Turn

When an unsatisfactory meal is received at a restaurant, what is the best way to register a complaint? At what level should a complaint be submitted?

CHAPTER 10

Formats of Letters and Memos

Learning Objectives

Your learning objectives for this chapter include the following:

- To identify and describe the seven standard parts of a letter
- To identify and describe the appropriate use of supplementary parts of a letter
- To format business letters using the block, modified block, and simplified block styles
- To format a memo properly
- To discuss the characteristics of appropriate stationery for letters, memos, and envelopes

Your reader's first impression of your letters and memos has a lasting effect.

Ⓣhe initial impression made by your letters or memos will have a lasting effect on the receivers of your messages. The energy expended in writing good letters or memos is well spent when you select appropriate stationery and formats. The receiver will assume that you care and that you are knowledgeable about letter and memo writing when you use proper grammar, punctuation, spelling, stationery, and formats.

LETTERS

Letters are used to transmit formal written messages.

A **letter** is used to communicate a formal written message. The appearance of a letter is important because it makes the first impression on the reader; the content is important because it ensures that the reader understands and fully accepts your message. The appearance of a letter depends on the parts of a letter, punctuation style, letter format, and stationery. In this chapter, you will learn how to improve the appearance of a letter; you will be taught how to organize and write the content of a letter in Chapters 11, 12, 13, 14, and 22.

USES OF LETTERS

Letters are used for both internal and external communication.

Letters are used to communicate written messages to individuals outside an organization. Letters are also used to communicate formal written messages to employees within an organization.

STANDARD PARTS OF A LETTER

Letters normally contain seven standard parts.

The number of letter parts and their location depend on the format you select. As shown in Figure 10•1, most letters contain seven standard parts: heading, letter address, salutation, body, complimentary close, signature block, and reference initials.

HEADING

Dateline and letterhead or return address make up the heading.

The first standard part of a letter is the **heading,** which consists of the letterhead and the dateline or the return address and a dateline. All business organizations should use letterhead stationery for the first page of a letter. A **letterhead** contains the name of the company and its complete address. It may contain a phone number, fax number, originating department, originator's title, founding date, organizational slogan, emblem, or logo, and other information that the organization deems appropriate. The amount of information in a letterhead will depend on the type of organization sending the letter. However, a letterhead should use no more than two inches of stationery space. Usually a letterhead is placed at the top of the page but part of the information may be at the bottom of the page. For example, the street address and telephone number or another location may be shown at the bottom of letterhead stationery. The letterhead may be printed in more than one color. Examples of letterheads are shown in Figure 10•2.

The letterhead should be limited to 2″ of vertical space.

The **dateline** contains the month, day, and year that the letter is written. The month should be spelled out. Figures are not used for the month (e.g.,

The date of the letter is part of the heading.

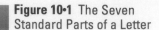

Figure 10·1 The Seven
Standard Parts of a Letter

1. HEADING

ROADRUNNER COURIER

327 Sherman Street
Lexington, KY 40502-3251
(606) 555-4275
FAX (606) 555-6464

Dateline

2. LETTER ADDRESS
XXXXXXXXXXXXXXXXX
XXXXXXXXXXXXXXXXX

3. SALUTATION:

X X X X X X X X X X X X X X X X X X X X X X X X X X X X X X X X XXXXXX
X   X
X   X
X   X
X   4. BODY   X
X   X
X   X
X   X
X X X X X X X X X X X X X X X X X X X X X X X X X X X X X X X XXXXXX

5. COMPLIMENTARY CLOSE,

6. SIGNATURE BLOCK
XXXXXXXXXXXXXXXXXXXX

7. REFERENCE INITIALS

2/10/95) because there is no universal agreement as to whether the day or month appears first. Dates may be in one of the following two styles:

September 3, 199-

3 September 199-

Notice that there is no punctuation when the day appears before the month in the dateline. Placing the month before the day is the style used by most American business organizations. Placing the day first is the preferred style for international and military use.

The horizontal placement of the dateline (or the keyed return address and dateline) depends on the letter format. The vertical placement of the dateline varies depending on the length of the letter. The dateline usually is

The letter length determines where the date is placed.

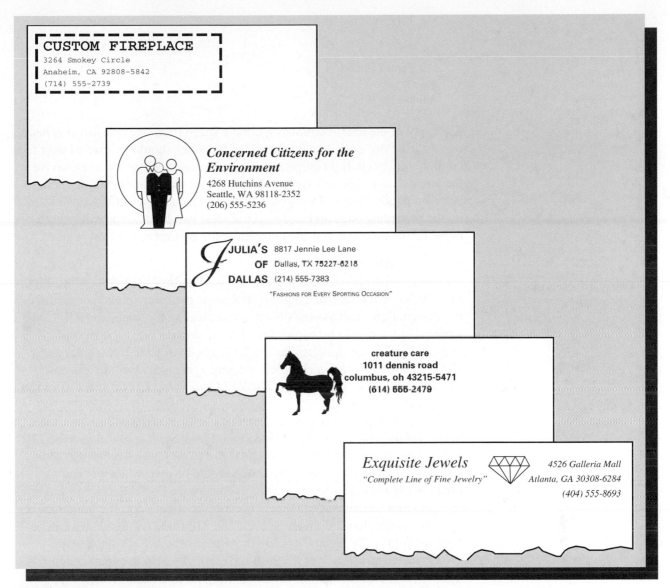

Figure 10·2 Examples of Letterheads

keyed two or more lines below the printed letterhead. It may "float" from 14 to 18 lines from the top of the page.

When a return address is keyed at the top of a personal business letter, the dateline is keyed on the line below it. When the return address appears below the signature block of a personal business letter, the date usually is placed between lines 10 and 15.

Letterhead stationery is used only for the first page of a letter. Stationery of the same color and quality, but without the letterhead, is used for continuation pages. The heading on each additional page begins on line seven, leaving a top margin of one inch (six lines). The continuation page heading should contain the first line of the letter address, the page number, and the date. Two popular formats for continuation page headings are:

Only the first page should be on a letterhead.

or

Ms. Teresa Underhill
Page 2
August 15, 199-

The body of the letter continues a double space (two lines) below this heading. At least one complete paragraph of the letter should be carried over to a continuation page. If a complete paragraph cannot be carried over, revise the letter so that it is only one page. Individual words are never divided between pages. Divide a paragraph only if you can leave at least two lines on the preceding page and carry over at least two lines to the following page. Leave at least a one-inch margin at the bottom of the first page.

LETTER ADDRESS

The letter address is the receiver's address.

The **letter address** includes the addressee's courtesy title (Ms., Miss, Mrs., Mr., Dr., etc.), name, street number and name (or some other specific mailing designation, such as post office box number), city, state, and ZIP Code. Abbreviations should be avoided in street addresses (e.g., use *Avenue* instead of *Ave.*; use *Road* instead of *Rd.*). The two-letter U.S. postal abbreviation should be used in complete mailing addresses. A list of the postal abbreviations is in Appendix D. The ZIP Code is keyed one space after the postal abbreviation.

The **ZIP Code** is a five-digit code that identifies areas within the United States and its possessions. In 1985 the U.S. Postal Service introduced the **ZIP + 4** system. This system uses the original ZIP Code plus a hyphen and four additional numbers. This expanded code should be used when it is known because it speeds the delivery of mail. It enables the Postal Service to sort mail on high-speed automated equipment for specific streets, specific buildings, or even to specific floors within buildings. The ZIP Code for an address can be obtained from a ZIP Code Directory provided by the U.S. Postal Service.

Other countries such as Canada and Germany also use mail codes. Canada's six character codes use alternating numbers and letters; e.g., T2K5S3. In Germany the city identification code is keyed prior to the name of the city; e.g., 53105 Bonn.

The letter address begins at the left margin at least four lines below the date.

The letter address is always keyed flush with the left margin. The first line of the letter address is keyed four spaces (lines) below the date.

SALUTATION

The salutation is the greeting of the letter.

The **salutation** is the greeting that begins the message. Examples of correct and incorrect salutations for letters to specific individuals include:

Correct	Incorrect
Dear Ms. Elam:	Dear Amy Elam:
Dear Amy:	Dear Ms. Amy:
Dear Brian and Amy:	Dear Harrisons:

Examples of correct and incorrect salutations in writing the same letter to many people include:

Correct	Incorrect
Dear Customer:	Dear Gentlemen:
Ladies and Gentlemen:	Dear Ladies and Gentlemen:

Salutation content depends on first line of letter address.

The content of the salutation depends on the first line of the letter address. When a letter is addressed to a company and contains an attention line (discussed on page 262), the salutation is directed to the company and not to the person in the attention line. The formality of the salutation depends on the relationship between the sender and the receiver of the letter. A general guide is to use the name that you would use if you met the person or persons face to face. If the first line of the letter address is singular, the salutation must be singular; if the first line is plural, the salutation must be plural.

The salutation begins two lines below the letter address at the left margin.

The salutation is keyed flush with the left margin and placed a double space (two lines) below the last line of the letter address. A colon follows the salutation in a business letter if mixed punctuation is used; no punctuation follows the salutation if open punctuation is used. Mixed and open punctuation are discussed on page 265. The salutation is omitted in the simplified block letter format (see page 268).

BODY

The message is contained in the body of the letter.

The **body** is the message section of the letter. It begins a double space (two lines) below the salutation. The body is single-spaced within paragraphs and double-spaced between paragraphs. The paragraphs may be indented or blocked, depending on the letter format selected. Normally, the first and last paragraphs of a letter are shorter than the other paragraphs.

COMPLIMENTARY CLOSE

The complimentary close ends the message.

The **complimentary close** is a phrase used to end the message. Frequently used complimentary closes include:

Sincerely,   Sincerely yours,   Yours truly,

The complimentary close is placed two lines below the body.

The complimentary close is keyed a double space (two lines) below the last line of the body of the letter. The first character of the close should begin at the same horizontal point as the first character of the date. Only the first character of the first word in the complimentary close is capitalized. The complimentary close is followed by a comma if mixed punctuation is used and by no punctuation if open punctuation is used. The simplified block letter omits the complimentary close.

SIGNATURE BLOCK

The sender's name and title appear in the signature block.

The **signature block** contains the writer's keyed name and title. The name is keyed four spaces (lines) below the complimentary close. A courtesy title in the signature block is optional. It may be included, in parenthesis, when the gender of the writer is unclear; e.g., Pat, Kim, or Lynn. The position title of the sender is keyed a single space (line) below the keyed name. If the name and position title are on the same line, they are separated by a comma. The sender of the message signs the letter in the space between the complimentary close and the keyed name. The signature normally does not include the courtesy title even if it is keyed in the signature block.

REFERENCE INITIALS

Reference initials are those of the writer and the keyboard operator.

The initials of the message originator and the keyboard operator make up the **reference initials.** If the originator is the same person who signs the letter, his or her initials are optional. If the originator's initials are given, they are separated from those of the keyboard operator by a colon or a diagonal. The originator's initials should be capitalized and the keyboard operator's lowercased. The reference initials are flush with the left margin on the line below the sender's title. Examples of reference initials are:

    rs   JGN:db   JFB/kel

> ## *Simplicity is the glory of expression.*
>
> ### Walt Whitman

SUPPLEMENTARY PARTS OF A LETTER

In addition to the seven standard parts, letters may contain one or more supplementary parts. These parts include the attention line, subject line, company name in signature block, enclosure notation, copy notation, and postscript.

ATTENTION LINE

When a company name is used as the first line of the letter address, the **attention line** can be used to direct the letter to a person, position title, or department within the company. Using a person's name in the first line of the letter address is preferred over using an attention line.

The attention line is part of the letter address.

When used, the attention line should be the second line of the letter address. It may be keyed with initial capitals or with all capitals. The word *Attention* should not be abbreviated, and it should not be separated from the rest of the attention line with a colon. The salutation agrees with the first line of the address and not the attention line. An example of a letter address with an attention line is:

    Guardian Savings
    Attention Loan Officer
    2157 Lavon Drive
    Cascade, ID 83611-5283

    Ladies and Gentlemen:

SUBJECT LINE

The subject line is a synopsis statement of the message.

The **subject line** identifies the main topic of the letter. It is considered part of the body of the letter. The subject line should be short—less than one line—and it should not be a complete sentence. The key words contained in a subject line help office personnel to sort and route incoming mail and to code documents for storage and retrieval.

The subject line is keyed a double space (two lines) below the salutation. It may be centered, flush with the left margin, or indented the same number of spaces as the paragraphs. It may be keyed in all capitals or keyed with initial capitals. If the word *Subject* is used, it is followed by a colon. A letter that includes a subject line is shown in Figure 10•3a.

Figure 10•3a Block Letter Format, Mixed Punctuation

Heading

Letter Address

Salutation

Subject Line

Body

Complimentary Close

Signature Block

Reference Initials

——————— PROFESSIONAL OFFICES ———————
Regency Center 1265 Westgrove Drive
Raleigh, NC 27611-3426
(919) 555-9132   FAX (919) 555-7584
"Your Success Is Our Business"

October 12, 199-

Ms. Marilyn Barry
Rosie's Embroidery & Monogramming
2436 Mockingbird Lane
Asheville, NC 28603-7234

Dear Marilyn:

LETTER USING BLOCK FORMAT

This letter is in block format. All lines begin at the left margin. The letterhead uses less than two vertical inches of stationery, and the date is placed approximately a double space (two lines) below the letterhead.

The letter address is keyed flush with the left margin and is the same as the address on the envelope. The position title may be keyed after the name on the first line or a single space (one line) below the name on the second line, depending on its length.

The salutation is on the second line below the inside address. The name used in the salutation should be the same as would be used if the sender met that person on the street. Notice the colon after the salutation (mixed punctuation).

The subject line is keyed flush with the left margin a double space (two lines) below the salutation and is considered part of the body. The body is single-spaced within paragraphs and double-spaced between paragraphs.

The complimentary close is keyed a double space below the body and is flush with the left margin. A comma follows the close (mixed punctuation). The signature block (writer's name and title) is keyed four spaces below.

Sincerely,

Carlos

Carlos Eubanks
Office Consultant

rfs

A **reference line** is sometimes used instead of a subject line (Re: Contract 1065-940). It is used to direct the reader to source documents or files. A reference line is keyed a double space (two lines) below the letter address.

COMPANY NAME IN SIGNATURE BLOCK

The name of the company may be keyed in all capital letters a double space (two lines) below the complimentary close. A company name is not commonly used with letterhead stationery. The company name is placed in the signature block when the letter is in the nature of a contract, or plain paper is used rather than letterhead stationery. The first character of the company name is aligned with the first character of the complimentary close. An example of a company name in the signature block is:

Sincerely,

CAPITAL ENGINEERING

Carlos Jimenez
Manager

ENCLOSURE NOTATION

An enclosure notation is used when an item accompanies a letter.

Any item included in the envelope other than the letter, such as a check, invoice, or photograph, is considered an **enclosure.** When something is included with a letter, an enclosure notation should be keyed a single or double space (one or two lines) below the reference initials (flush with the left margin). The enclosures may be identified, or the number of enclosures may be put in parentheses. Examples of enclosure notations are:

Enclosure: Contract   Enclosures (4)   Enc. 4

COPY NOTATION

Copy notations list other persons who will receive a copy of the letter.

A **copy notation** is used when a copy of a letter is being sent to someone other than the addressee. The copy notation is keyed as a "c" flush with the left margin and a double space (two lines) below the reference initials (or enclosure notation if used). The names of the individuals or groups to receive the copies should be keyed after the notation. Examples of copy notations include:

c   Norman Winder

c   Raymond Talmon
     Felix Marshall

c   Planning Committee

POSTSCRIPT

Postscripts are used for personal messages or points needing re-emphasis.

A **postscript** may be used to add a personal comment or to emphasize an important point discussed in the body of the letter. It should *not* be used to add an important point omitted from the body of the letter. The postscript should follow the last notation and be formatted in the same style as the paragraphs of the message. If the paragraphs are indented, the postscript should also be indented. A postscript may be handwritten. The notation "P.S." is usually omitted.

PUNCTUATION STYLES

The two styles of punctuation commonly used in business letters are mixed and open. The most popular style is mixed punctuation. **Mixed punctuation** requires a colon after the salutation and a comma after the complimentary close.

Letters using **open punctuation** omit the colon after the salutation and the comma after the complimentary close. Open punctuation is becoming more accepted but is still less popular than mixed punctuation.

LETTER FORMATS

The format is part of the reader's first impression of your letter. Organizations usually designate the format of their letters, but in some circumstances they may permit the originator to select the format. The most frequently used formats are block, modified block, and simplified block.

BLOCK

The **block format** is becoming very popular. It can be keyed rapidly because none of the parts of the letter are indented. Figure 10•3a shows a block format letter.

MODIFIED BLOCK

The date (or the return address and date), complimentary close, and signature block begin at the horizontal center of the page in the **modified block format.** There are two versions of the modified block format: (1) body of the letter with block paragraphs, and (2) body of the letter with indented paragraphs. Letters using the modified block format are shown in Figures 10•3b and 10•3c.

SIMPLIFIED BLOCK

The **simplified block format** is a modern, efficient letter format similar to the AMS Simplified Letter that was developed several years ago by the Administrative Management Society. The simplified block letter eliminates the use of a salutation and a complimentary close. It is often used when gender or marital status of female receiver is unknown. Figure 10•3d shows a letter in the simplified block format.

PLACEMENT

A carefully arranged letter resembles a picture in a frame. The letter should have a border of blank space to form a frame. The width of this frame will vary with the length of the letter, but it should normally be at least one inch on each side. Today, with many offices using word processing equipment, a letter can be adjusted easily to give it an attractive appearance. Some organizations are justifying their line lengths (making the right margin even). This gives an attractive but somewhat more formal appearance.

Figure 10•3b Modified Block
Format, Blocked Paragraphs

OFFICE
DOCUMENT
DESIGNERS

1418 Slocum Road
Phoenix, AZ 85018-0231
(602) 555-4274 FAX (602) 555-6684

March 2, 199-

North Health Care
Attention Personnel Director
525 S. Bishop Avenue
Denver, CO 81035-4123

Ladies and Gentlemen

You asked for information about the modified block letter format. This letter is in the modified
block format with block paragraphs. A pamphlet with additional information about letter formats
is enclosed.

Notice the date in the heading begins at the horizontal center of the page. The letter address is
flush with the left margin. The addressee's name is unknown so an attention line is used. The
salutation is plural because the first line of the letter address is the name of a company; the use of
a singular title in the attention line has no effect on the salutation. There is no punctuation after
the salutation because open punctuation is used.

The body of this letter uses block paragraphs but could have used indented paragraphs. As in
most letters, the body is single-spaced within paragraphs and double-spaced between paragraphs.

The complimentary close is keyed a double space (two lines) below the body and at the horizontal center of the letter. Notice that it is in line with the date and is followed by no punctuation
(open punctuation).

The reference initials contain the originator's and keyboard operator's initials because the individual signing the letter did not originate the document. The enclosure notation is used to ensure
that the person mailing the letter includes the pamphlet and that the person receiving the letter is
aware that it was included.

The modified block is a well-accepted format that is popular in many organizations.

Sincerely

Pat Manlego

(Mr.) Pat Manlego
Document Designer

PZ:pd

Enclosure

PERSONAL BUSINESS LETTERS

A personal business letter is written by an individual when conducting business of a personal nature. An application for employment, a request for
information, and a comment about services received are examples of personal business letters. A good grade of paper should be used for this type of
letter. A block style or modified block style with mixed or open punctuation
is suitable. While the trend is to key the sender's address a single space (one
line) below the signature block, it is currently more commonly a part of the
heading. The simplified block letter format is not recommended for application letters because many individuals interpret the lack of a salutation as
being impersonal. Figure 10•4 , on page 269, shows a personal business letter.

There is no specific format for a
personal business letter, but
standard parts and placement
are the same as in a business
letter.

OFFICE
DOCUMENT
DESIGNERS

1418 Slocum Road
Phoenix, AZ 85018-0231
(602) 555-4274 FAX (602) 555-6684

March 2, 199-

North Health Care
Attention Personnel Director
525 S. Bishop Avenue
Denver, CO 81035-4123

Ladies and Gentlemen

You asked for information about the modified block letter format. This letter is in the modified block format with indented paragraphs. You will notice that it is identical to the modified block except that the first word is indented one-half inch. When a subject line is used, it may be centered or indented one-half inch to match the paragraphs.

The date in the heading begins at the horizontal center of the page while the letter address is flush with the left margin. No punctuation is used after the salutation because open punctuation is used.

The body of this letter uses indented paragraphs but could have used blocked paragraphs. As in most letters, the body is single-spaced within paragraphs and double-spaced between paragraphs.

The complimentary close is keyed a double space (two lines) below the body and at the horizontal center of the letter. Notice that it is in line with the date and is followed by no punctuation (open punctuation).

The reference initials contain the originator's and keyboard operator's initials because the individual signing the letter did not originate the document. The enclosure notation is used to ensure that the person mailing the letter includes the pamphlet and that the person receiving the letter is aware that it was included.

The modified block is a well-accepted format that is popular in many organizations.

Cordially

Pat Manlego

(Mr.) Pat Manlego
Document Designer

PZ:pd

Enclosure

INTERNATIONAL BUSINESS CORRESPONDENCE

Business letter formats used by writers in other countries are similar to those used by business letter writers in the United States. When corresponding with someone in a foreign country, you must be knowledgeable about differences in letter formatting that may cause misunderstandings. For instance, the month should be spelled out because in the United States the date March 9, 1994, would be written 9.3.1994 in Germany. Figure 10•5, on page 270, shows a sample business letter written in German and Figure 10•6, on page 271, shows the same letter written in English.

There are other differences in German letter formatting: the street name comes before the house numbers, the city name follows the mailing code,

Figure 10·3d Simplified
Block Format

CREATIVE
CONSULTANTS

48 Preston Center
Ann Arbor, MI 48107-7382
(313) 555-9263

24 July 199-

MRS MONICA PEREZ
PRESIDENTS RACQUET CLUB
2710 SOUTHWELL LANE
DEARBORN MI 48128-7214

SIMPLIFIED BLOCK LETTER FORMAT

This letter, Mrs. Perez, is in the Simplified Block Letter format. It is modern and time saving. The letter should be constructed using these guidelines:

1. Use block format. Omit the salutation and complimentary close. Use the addressee's
name in the first sentence to personalize the message.

2. Use a subject line keyed in all capital letters. The subject line is keyed a double space
below the address; the body is keyed a double space below the subject line.

3. Key all enumerations at the left margin.

4. Key on one line the writer's name and title in all capital letters flush with the left margin and four spaces (lines) below the body of the letter.

5. Key the keyboard operator's initials in lowercase letters a double space (two lines)
below the writer's name. Enclosure notations and copy notations are keyed a double space
below the keyboard operator's initials.

Mrs. Perez, you will enjoy using this format once you become familiar with it. A brochure
describing future writing workshops is enclosed.

Tammie Greene

TAMMIE GREENE, COMMUNICATION CONSULTANT

sj

Enclosure

c April Lane

the dateline is always flush right, and the salutation is a double space below
the subject line. Germans are more formal than Americans in their communication; writers include titles such as Dr., Mr., Mrs., or Ms. in the salutation and never address someone by his or her first name.

ENVELOPES

The envelope should be appropriate for the letter.

Envelope paper should be the same color and quality as the letterhead stationery. The envelope must be of adequate size to hold the letter and any
enclosures or attachments without unnecessary folding. The return address,
mailing address, and envelope notations are the three things that may be
included on an envelope. Correctly addressed envelopes are shown in
Figure 10·7, on page 272.

529 Vanlea Drive
Grafton, ND 58237-3364
April 1, 199-

Ms. Yolanda Robertson
Quality Engineers
675 Chaucer Drive
Grand Forks, ND 58201-9314

Dear Yolanda:

This is a personal business letter keyed in modified block format with indented paragraphs. The personal business letter may use any of the three accepted formats.

The heading contains the sender's address immediately above the date. This address is keyed and not printed as it would be in letterhead stationery. Notice that the individual sending the letter omits his or her name in the heading. A general guide is to place the heading on lines 10 to 12, but this varies with the length of the letter.

The letter address is flush with the left margin about four to six lines below the dateline. The letter address is the receiver's address, which also appears on the envelope.

The salutation is a double space below the letter address. When mixed punctuation is used, key a colon (not a comma) after the salutation because this letter is business and not personal in content.

Supplementary parts (attention lines, subject lines, enclosures, etc.) are used as in regular business letters. The body of the letter contains the message that the sender is transmitting to the receiver. The body should be single-spaced within paragraphs and double-spaced between paragraphs.

The writer signs in the space between the complimentary close and the signature block. Normally, a personal business letter does not contain reference initials because the sender keys the letter.

Sincerely,

Reed White

RETURN ADDRESS

The **return address** is the sender's address. It is keyed in capitals in the upper left corner of the envelope. It should contain the sender's address as shown on the letterhead. Often the sender's name will be keyed immediately above a pre-printed business return address. For personal business letters, return addresses should be keyed on plain envelopes.

Return address goes in upper left corner of an envelope.

MAILING ADDRESS

The **mailing address** contains the receiver's name and address as shown in the letter address. The address should not exceed five lines, and all lines should be blocked. The ZIP Code or ZIP + 4 (preferably) should be used in

The envelope (mailing) address should be the same as the letter address.

Figure 10·5 Sample German Business Letter

Heading

SPIEL MIT KG
SPIELWAREN
Postfach 3478
100 Berlin 13

Letter Address

City Spielwaren
z.Hd. Herrn Peter Schacht
Georgenstr. 84

4000 Düsseldorf 32

Location, Date

Berlin, den 05.03.1993

Subject Line

Ihr Schreiben vom 01.03.1993

Salutation

Sehr geehrter Herr Schacht,

Body

vielen Dank für Ihr Schreiben vom 01.03.1993, in dem Sie Ihr Interesse an unserer neuen Serie von Spieluhren zum Ausdruck bringen. Wir erlauben uns, Ihnen mit getrennter Post unverbindlich einige Muster zur Ansicht zu senden.

Wir freuen uns über Ihr Interesse an unseren Produkten und stehen für eventuelle Rückfragen gerne zur Verfügung.

Complimentary Close

Mit freundlichen Grüßen

Signature Block

Inge Fuchs

SPIEL MIT KG
Inge Fuchs
Vertriebsleiterin

Enclosure

Anlage: Gesamprospekt 1993

all addresses. The Postal Service recommends using all capital letters and no punctuation on the envelope to facilitate use of optical scanning equipment. The last line of the letter address must contain only the city, state, and ZIP Code.

The first line of the address should be keyed one-half inch to the left of the horizontal center of the envelope and on line 14 of a No. 10 envelope or on line 12 of a No. 6 3/4 envelope.

ENVELOPE NOTATIONS

Two types of envelope notations are used. Special mailing instructions should be keyed in all capital letters a double space (two lines) below the

Envelopes may have two types of notation.

Figure 10•6 English
Translation of German
Business Letter

**PLAY-WITH US, Ltd.
TOYS**
P.O. Box 3478
1000 Berlin 13

City Toys
C/O Mr. Peter Schacht
George Street 84

4000 Dusseldorf 32

Berlin, the 5th of March 1993

Your letter dated 1 March 1993

Dear Mr. Schacht,

Thank you for your letter from 1 March 1993 in which you showed an interest in
our new line of playwatches. We have taken the liberty to send you a few samples,
at no obligation, of our product for your approval.

We are pleased that you are interested in our products and are at your disposal to
answer any further questions.

With friendly greetings,

PLAY-WITH US, Ltd.
Inge Fuchs
Sales Manager

Enclosure: 1993 Catalog

postage stamp. These Postal Service requirements permit electronic scanning and sorting of mail. Mailing instructions include SPECIAL DELIV-
ERY, SPECIAL HANDLING, REGISTERED, CERTIFIED, and so on.

Instructions for individuals handling the receiver's mail are keyed in all
capital letters a double space (two lines) below the return address. These
notations include CONFIDENTIAL, HOLD FOR ARRIVAL, PERSONAL,
or PLEASE FORWARD.

MEMOS

Memos are the primary form of
internal written communication.

The most common form of written message for communication within an
organization is the **interoffice memorandum,** or *memo* as it is usually
called. Memos have grown in popularity as organizations have become

Figure 10·7 Correctly Addressed Envelopes

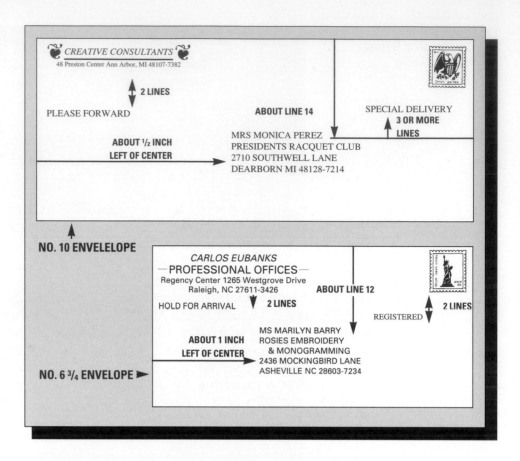

larger and as communications within organizations have become more complex. Memos are normally less formal and shorter than letters.

USES OF INTEROFFICE MEMOS

Memos have a wide variety of uses.

Memos are used in a variety of ways. They may be used to communicate upward to superiors, downward to subordinates, laterally to peers, and diagonally to other members of a network. Information of all kinds can be conveyed from one department to another through the use of memos. They are used to announce such things as times and dates of upcoming meetings as well as results of previous meetings, proposed or actual changes in policies or procedures, reports of activities, and instructions.

ADVANTAGES OF MEMOS

Advantages of memos include:
* *being able to reach multiple addressees*

The use of memos has several advantages. One advantage is that the same memo can be addressed to several individuals. If you want to send the same memo to specific employees, you can list all the names and place a check mark after a different name on each copy. Or, you can list all the names and request that the memo be "routed" from the first-named person through the last-named person. Entire groups can be addressed in a memo and individual copies given to each member of the group, or the memo may be placed on a bulletin board. Examples of ways to properly address memos are:

Specific Individuals	Entire Groups
TO: Todd Shupe, John Waldman, and George Nichols	TO: Sales Department Employees
TO: See Distribution List Below	

- saving time

A second advantage of using memos is that they are less formal than letters and may require less time to compose. Memos should be clear and accurate, but they usually do not have to be as polished as formal letters. Memos may be handwritten to save time.

- providing a written record

Another advantage of using a memo is that it provides a written record of the message. Written messages make a more lasting impression than do oral messages.

FORMATS OF MEMOS

Formats for memos vary.

Memos may be prepared using a formal or a simplified format. The same organization may use more than one format for its memos, or it may specify the format that will be used throughout the organization.

A **formal memo** may be prepared on a pre-printed form that contains the headings **TO:, FROM:, DATE:,** and **SUBJECT:** or on letterhead stationery with headings keyed when the memo is keyed. A **simplified memo** may be keyed on plain paper or letterhead stationery. The format of a simplified memo is the same as a simplified block letter, except that the address is omitted. A formal memo is shown in Figure 10•8; a simplified memo appears in Figure 10•9.

SPECIAL FORMS OF MEMOS

Special forms of memos perform specific functions.

Business firms have developed various kinds of memo forms to perform specific functions within an organization. One is a **round-trip memo,** which is also called a *message-reply memo.* It usually consists of multiform paper, carbon or carbonless, on which the sender can complete the heading and the message portion. The sender can then remove a carbon copy for her or his files before sending the memo. The receiver may add a reply and remove a copy before returning the memo to the original sender. An example of this kind of memo is shown in Figure 10•10 on page 276.

Another frequently used special memo form is a **telephone memo.** It is designed so that minimal effort is needed to relay a telephone message. An example of a telephone memo is shown in Figure 10•11 on page 276.

STATIONERY

The purpose of the message must be determined so the proper stationery can be selected.

Stationery used for letters or memos will influence the impression formed by the receiver of the message. The type of stationery that is used will be determined by the purpose of the message. For example, the stationery used for closing a major business transaction should be of a higher quality than the stationery used for announcing an upcoming sale to credit card customers.

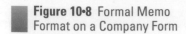

Figure 10•8 Formal Memo Format on a Company Form

Continental **D**oors

Heading

TO:	All Employees
FROM:	Benji Nozaki, Publications Coordinator
DATE:	August 16, 199-
SUBJECT:	Characteristics of Formal Memos

BN

Many questions have arisen concerning proper construction and use of formal memos. The following guidelines should answer these questions.

Formal memos contain several characteristics which are unique. Some of these characteristics are:

1. A preprinted or keyed memo heading is used consisting of **TO:**, **FROM:**, **DATE:**, and **SUBJECT:**.

2. The individual sending the memo may or may not use a business title. The sender normally does not use a complete signature. An individual's first name or initials are usually written after the keyed name on the **FROM** line in the heading.

Body

3. The memo is not centered vertically as is a letter.

4. Memos, whether formal or simplified, are normally short and contain only one topic; that topic is indicated in the subject line. If more than one topic is needed, separate memos are sent.

5. The body of the memo is in block style beginning a double space below the heading. The body is single-spaced.

6. Informal writing style is appropriate for memos. First person, I, is commonly used along with inferences and jargon.

7. Reference initials, enclosure notations, copy notations, and second page headings are used as in letters.

Remember that memos should be concise and easy to read; they should not contain any irrelevant information. Please let me know if you think of any other characteristics of formal memos.

Reference Initials

gs

WEIGHT

The weight of paper plays a part in impressing the receiver of your message. The stationery most commonly used for business letters is 20-pound bond. The weight measurement is determined by the weight of four reams of 8 1/2″ × 11″ paper. One ream usually contains 500 sheets.

> The weight of the paper is a factor in selecting stationery.

> The most commonly used weight is 20-pound paper.

SIZE

Most business letters are prepared on **standard size paper,** 8 1/2″ × 11″. Letters from business executives are sometimes placed on 7 1/2″ × 10″ high-quality stationery called **executive stationery.** Standard size paper (8 1/2″ × 11″) and **half-sheet paper** (8 1/2″ × 5 1/2″) are the two most common sizes of paper used for formal memos. The paper-saving advantage of using half sheets is often outweighed by the disadvantage of locating the

> Letters are normally prepared on 8 1/2″ × 11″ paper.

> Memos are normally printed on standard size or half-sheet paper.

Figure 10•9 Simplified Memo Format on Plain Paper

August 16, 199-

All Employees

CHARACTERISTICS OF SIMPLIFIED MEMOS

Many questions have arisen concerning proper construction and use of memos. The following guidelines should answer these questions.

Simplified memos contain several characteristics which are unique. Some of these characteristics are:

1. Full sheets are used to prepare simplified memos; either plain paper or letterhead stationery can be used.

2. All spacing guidelines for a simplified block letter apply also to the simplified memo. The only difference is that no address is used in the simplified memo.

3. Personal titles are not used, but a business title or department name may be used.

4. Memos, whether formal or simplified, are normally short and contain only one topic; that topic is indicated in the subject line. If more than one topic is needed, separate memos are sent.

5. Informal writing style is appropriate for memos. First person, I, is commonly used along with inferences and jargon.

6. Reference initials, enclosure notations, copy notations, and second page headings are used as in letters.

Remember that memos should be concise and easy to read; they should not contain any irrelevant information. Either the formal memo or simplified memo format is acceptable for our interoffice communication.

Benji Nozaki

Benji Nozaki, Publications Coordinator

gs

smaller sheet when it is filed with standard size paper. Simplified memos are prepared on standard size paper.

COLOR

Color is another important consideration in selecting business stationery. White is the most popular color and is acceptable for all correspondence. Recently, there has been a trend toward using other paper colors. Selecting the appropriate stationery color is extremely important to the image of the company. The type of industry certainly must be a determining factor in selecting paper color. For example, Mary Kay Cosmetics, which caters exclusively to a female clientele, uses pastel pink, on the other hand, a lumber company may very effectively use light wood-grained stationery. Some companies use different colored memo forms to identify originating departments.

White stationery is always appropriate; other colors may be used.

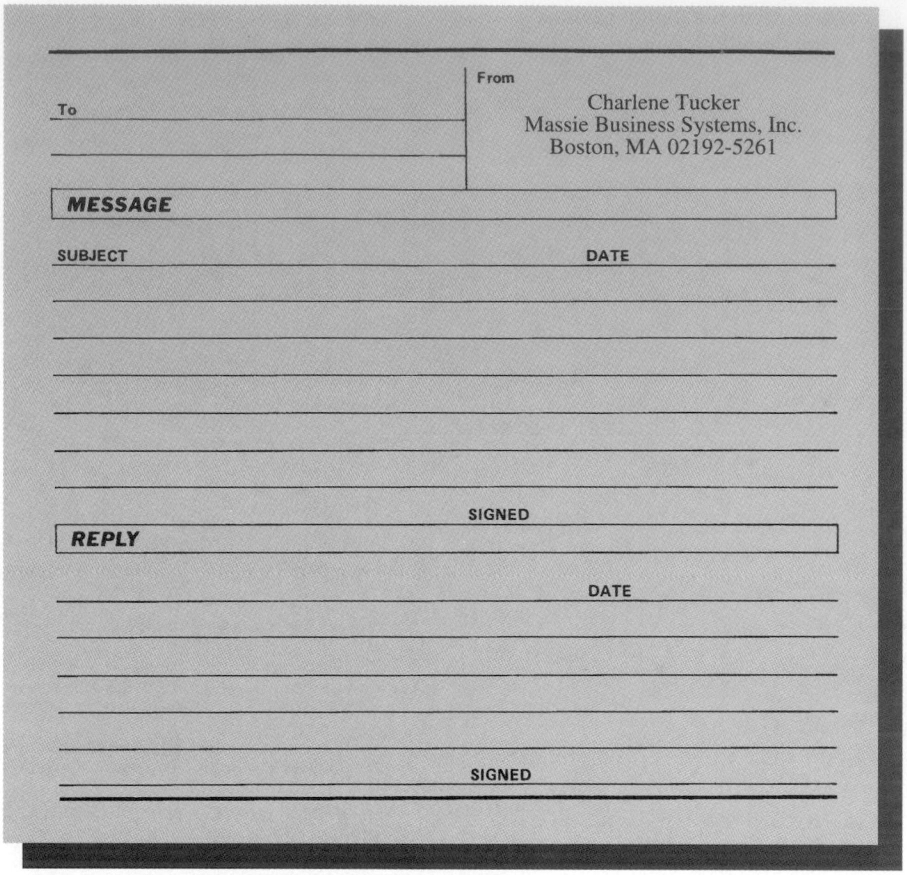

Figure 10•10 Round-Trip Memo

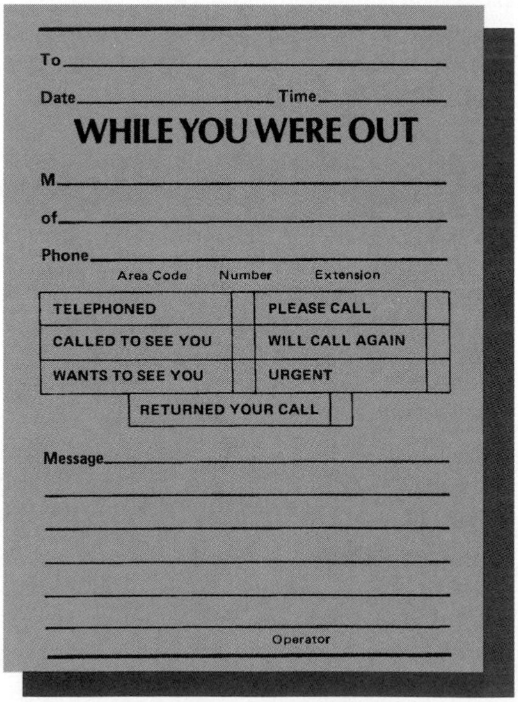

To _____

From

Charlene Tucker
Massie Business Systems, Inc.
Boston, MA 02192-5261

MESSAGE

SUBJECT _____ DATE

_____

_____

_____

_____

_____

_____

SIGNED

REPLY

DATE

_____

_____

_____

_____

SIGNED

Figure 10•11 Telephone Memo

To _____

Date _____ Time _____

WHILE YOU WERE OUT

M _____

of _____

Phone _____

Area Code   Number   Extension

TELEPHONED	PLEASE CALL	
CALLED TO SEE YOU	WILL CALL AGAIN	
WANTS TO SEE YOU	URGENT	
RETURNED YOUR CALL	

Message _____

_____

_____

_____

_____

Operator

QUALITY

The quality of stationery is determined by the amount of rag content in the paper. The **rag content** is the amount and type of fiber (usually cotton) used in the composition of the paper. High-quality stationery usually has 25 percent or more rag content. High-quality stationery also has a watermark showing the name of the company that manufactures the paper or the emblem of the organization that uses the stationery. Letters should be prepared on high-quality stationery; all pages should be of the same weight, color, quality, and size. The advantages of using high-quality stationery for letters include superior appearance, excellent texture, and long life without chemical breakdown. Memos should be prepared on less-expensive grades of paper.

ENVELOPE PAPER

While the previously cited factors are important, they do not represent the end of the stationery selection process. Envelopes, too, must be given consideration. Envelope paper should be of the same weight, color and quality as the letterhead stationery. Also, envelopes should be in proportion to the size of the stationery. For example, standard 8 1/2″ × 11″ stationery requires No. 10 (9 1/2″ × 4 1/8″) envelopes; executive stationery is 7 1/4″ × 10″ and requires No. 7 (7 1/2″ × 3 7/8″) envelopes.

An organization may convey a positive or a negative image by its written messages. The stationery selected to carry these messages should share importance with the composition of the messages.

High-quality stationery has high rag content and a watermark.

Paper used for second and successive pages should match the color, quality, and size of letterhead stationery.

Paper for memos can be of lesser quality.

Envelope paper should match the stationery.

DISCUSSION QUESTIONS

1. List and explain the seven standard parts of a business letter.

2. Distinguish between the uses of memos and business letters.

3. Discuss the use of a subject line in a business letter.

4. What is an attention line, and why is it not used extensively in today's business letters?

5. Define *enclosure* and describe how you indicate that a business letter has one.

6. Identify information that is essential and information that is optional in a letterhead. Explain why information included in a letterhead may vary among organizations.

7. What is an appropriate use of a postscript in a letter and what is an inappropriate use?

8. What two punctuation styles may be used in letters. What are their differences?

9. Describe a situation where simplified block format is more appropriate than block or modified block letter format.

10. Which letter format do you prefer? Why?

11. Why is a copy notation used in a business letter?

12. Distinguish between the two types of envelope notations and give examples of each.

13. Explain why most personal business letters are not written on letterhead stationery.

14. What formatting differences should be considered when corresponding with individuals in other countries?

15. Discuss the differences between formal and simplified memo formats.

16. Why are memos a popular means for internal communication in an organization?

17. List the parts that normally comprise the heading of a formal memo.

18. Describe two types of special form memos.

19. What is rag content? How does it affect stationery?

20. What types of envelopes should be used with (a) standard size stationery and (b) executive stationery?

1. Visit two business firms and obtain copies of memos used in their organizations. Identify the purpose of each memo and the job levels of the communicators. Describe the formats of the memos.

2. Find a business letter written in block or modified block form. Reformat the letter in simplified block style. In a brief paragraph explain the changes that you made.

3. Write a memo to your instructor explaining the advantages of using the simplified block letter format when the name of the addressee is unknown.

4. Visit your Postal Service office and obtain information about rates for different classes of mail. Write a memo to your instructor conveying this information.

5. Bring to class three envelopes that you have received from business organizations. Identify keying and formatting errors.

6. Obtain three or four samples of business letterheads. Describe the characteristics of the paper and the differences in the letterheads.

7. Correct the following personal business letter headings.

   a. Sept. 21, 199-
      Ricardo Morales
      8819 Riverway Cir.
      Oxford, Miss. 38655

   b. Marlboro, Vermont 05344-1124
      173 Scenic View Dr.
      9 Mar., 199-

8. Correct the following formal memo headings.

   a. TO: Isako Iwasaki:
       DATE: June 9 199-,
       SUBJECT: Fringe Benefits Meeting.

   b. TO: Departmental Employees,
       FROM: Chad Palmer,
       WORK SCHEDULE FOR HOLIDAYS.

9. Correct the following business letter addresses and salutations (assume mixed punctuation).

   a. Ms. Anita Seymour,
      301 N. Frost St.
      Minot, N.D. 58701-1357

      Dear Anita,

   b. Dr. Victoria Sanchez, D.D.S.
      8814 Ballymote Ave.
      El Paso, Tex. 79943-1435

      Dear Dr. Sanchez, D.D.S.:

c. Mr. Kurt Reeves
1108 Hillside Dr.
Van Horne, Iowa 52346-1157

Dear Kurt Reeves;

d. Heine Electric Company
173 Conductor Circle
Marion, Ill. 62959-1134

Attn: Personnel Manager

Dear Sir

10. Correct the following business letter headings, letter addresses, salutations, and complimentary closes (assume mixed punctuation).

a. November 4, 199-
119 Rodeo Drive
Cheyenne, WY 82001-0104

Mr. Garth Hardin
1712 Yellowstone Ave.
Billings, Montana 59102-9865

Dear Garth,

Sincerely:

b. April, 17 199-

Ms. Vanessa Evans
5534 Pershing Street
Lincoln, Neb. 68504-1345

Dear Ms. Vanessa:

Sincerely

Text 10B

Correct all errors in the memo that follows. Use the formal memo format that was discussed in this chapter.

Cathy's Candy Company　　　　　　　　　　　　**INTEROFFICE MEMO**

18 May, 199-

TO: All Employees

FROM: Lisa Monroe, Personnel Director

CHANGE IN INSURANCE BENEFITS

You receive some of the best insurance coverage that is available.

This outstanding coverage is getting extremely expensive. The management of Cathy's has evaluated all of its employees' benefits and has decided to change the insurance coverage it provides.

A representative of Investors Mutual Insurance Company will be here on May 25 to discuss the coverage of our new insurance plan. A meeting to discuss the new coverage will be held at 10 a.m. in the conference room.

Sincerely,

Lisa Monroe
Personnel Director

CHAPTER 11

Positive and Neutral Messages

Learning Objectives

Your learning objectives for this chapter include the following:

• To describe positive and neutral messages
• To list the advantages of using the direct plan for effective communication of positive information, requests, inquiries, claims, and adjustments
• To describe the four specific guidelines for using the direct plan
• To identify the differences between poor and good positive and neutral messages
• To use the direct plan competently for a variety of positive and neutral messages

Positive and neutral messages
give favorable or neutral information.

A **positive or neutral message** conveys pleasant, favorable, or neutral information to the receiver. Such a message may (1) inquire about a service, a product, or a person; (2) grant a request that has been made of you or your organization; (3) announce an upcoming sale or a new product; or, (4) may be used in internal communication to announce promotions, expansions, salary increases, or improvements in fringe benefits. The receiver will be getting information that is favorable or neutral and will accept the contents of the message easily. The message should be constructed using the direct plan so the receiver can readily see the benefits.

Claim messages will also be discussed in this chapter because they follow a plan similar to that used for positive information. Even though claim messages may be communicating bad news—the sender is indicating that he or she has been wronged—receivers should welcome them because they assist in improving products or services. Claim messages are strengthened when written in the direct plan format.

USE THE DIRECT PLAN FOR POSITIVE AND NEUTRAL MESSAGES

The direct plan immediately
gives receiver positive or neutral
information

The *direct plan* should be used in transmitting all positive and neutral messages. The direct plan will immediately give the good or neutral information to the receiver, who will then respond favorably to the remainder of the message. An advantage of this plan is that the receiver will know at once that the message is conveying information that is going to be beneficial (or at least not harmful). If the positive or neutral information—the purpose of the message—is not at the beginning, the receiver may lose interest and may not finish the message.

Direct plan increases the likelihood that receiver will read
entire message.

Direct plan gets receiver in positive frame of mind.

Another advantage of giving the positive or neutral information at the beginning of the message is to put the receiver in an agreeable frame of mind before presenting an explanation of the conditions related to the positive or neutral information. The explanation will have a much better chance of acceptance if the receiver is in a good mood rather than in an apprehensive state.

HOW TO USE THE DIRECT PLAN

The direct plan has specific
steps.

You should incorporate into your positive and neutral messages the business communication fundamentals that were presented in the first three chapters. In particular, analyze your receiver and use the you–viewpoint as discussed in Chapter 3. The four stages in the direct plan for presenting positive or neutral information are detailed in Figure 11•1.

Direct plan should be used for messages presenting positive information, neutral information, and claims.

The direct plan is used for a variety of positive messages—approved adjustments, requests, credit applications, and employment applications; favorable decisions; or any other favorable information. The direct plan is also used for neutral information and claim messages. The content of the message must be decided before the direct plan can be implemented.

Figure 11•1 Direct Plan Outline

DIRECT PLAN

I. The **Opening**
   A. Give the positive or neutral information
   B. Be optimistic
   C. Provide coherence
   D. Use emphasis techniques
   E. Stress receiver interests and benefits

II. The **Explanation**
   A. Present related information
   B. Be objective
   C. Be concise
   D. Be positive

III. **Sales Appeal** (if appropriate)
   A. Personalize appeal
   B. Suggest alternatives if appropriate
   C. Aim for quick action

IV. The **Friendly Close**
   A. Build goodwill
   B. Be concise
   C. Be positive
   D. Express appreciation

DETERMINING CONTENT

Content of message is developed after purposes are determined.

The situation must be analyzed and the primary and secondary purposes of the communication determined before any message can be composed. If the primary purpose is transmitting positive or neutral information, the direct plan should be used in organizing the message. Before composing a positive or neutral message, the following questions on content must be answered: What is the most favorable information? How will this information benefit the receiver? What additional information should be given to the receiver? Would a convincing sales appeal in this message be appropriate? What friendly message can be transmitted in the close to build goodwill?

Once you have determined the purposes and content, you are ready to implement the direct plan. The parts of the direct plan outline are discussed in the following sections, and the most important considerations are reviewed.

OPENING

In the direct plan, the memo or letter should give the positive or neutral information in the **opening**—the first paragraph of the message. Give the positive information immediately, be optimistic, provide coherence, use emphasis techniques, and stress receiver interests or benefits.

The first sentence of the first paragraph should contain the information that will be most beneficial to the receiver. Only positive words should be used in describing the information. The paragraph should be short for emphasis. The receiver's interest will be aroused if the benefits of the good information are stressed in the opening. For coherence, information should be provided so that the receiver will know which request, order, contract, or previous transaction is being discussed. This identification may be placed in a reference line.

In the direct plan, messages begin with positive or neutral information.

EXPLANATION

The second part of a message using the direct plan should contain the explanation. The **explanation** presents any additional information that relates to the positive or neutral information presented in the first paragraph. The explanation is factual and, therefore, needs to be presented in an objective manner. It should be concise but still contain all the details the receiver needs. The explanation should be written in an optimistic manner.

The supporting explanation should follow the positive or neutral opening.

SALES APPEAL

The **sales appeal** is a portion of a message in which the writer attempts to persuade the reader to take a specific desired action. It can be effective in many positive and neutral messages, but is not appropriate in all of them. Situations in which a sales appeal should be used include letters approving charge accounts, letters informing students that they have been accepted into a program, and messages approving claims. Situations in which a sales appeal would not be appropriate include claim letters and messages agreeing to speak at a meeting.

The sales appeal, if used, should come after the explanation. Depending on its length and nature, it may be placed in a paragraph by itself or combined with the closing paragraph. Adapt the appeal to the situation; if possible and desirable, provide alternatives for the receiver. The sales appeal may tell about an upcoming sale or a new product. Personalize the appeal to convince the receiver that it is in his or her best interest to take immediate action.

The sales appeal should be used when appropriate.

The sales appeal should follow the explanation.

FRIENDLY CLOSE

The **friendly close** is the final paragraph of a message. Its primary purpose is to build goodwill. Goodwill is built by being personal and optimistic. The close may express appreciation for an employee's past service or for a customer's business. The close may move to a related subject, or it may unify

A properly written close builds goodwill.

the message by referring to the good information given in the first paragraph. The close in a positive or neutral message is normally short and avoids clichés.

IMPLEMENTING THE DIRECT PLAN

The direct plan will be illustrated through the development of a positive information letter to a customer. Here are the details of the communication situation:

> You are vice president of customer services for Merchants State Bank in Paris, Tennessee. Matt Brockway has requested that your bank loan him $200,000 to open a hardware store. Matt worked as a salesclerk in a hardware store before moving to Paris. He has good credit references and also has saved $25,000 for a down payment. You will write a letter to Matt informing him that his application for the $200,000 loan has been approved. He will need to repay the loan in 20 years at a variable interest rate. The rate for the first year will be 9 percent, and the rate for subsequent years will be 1/2 percent above the average treasury rate set by the federal government. You want to express appreciation for his business and invite him to conduct all his financial transactions with Merchants State Bank.

DETERMINE APPROPRIATE CONTENT

The first step in writing a message is to analyze the situation and determine the message purposes and content that will most effectively accomplish the objective of the communication. In the Matt Brockway letter, the objective is to transmit positive information—the approval of a loan. In this situation the ideas should be developed and organized using the direct plan. The

Hardware Store Similar to the One That Matt Wants to Open.

following sections illustrate how the content of the positive information letter may be developed. Each section discusses a stage of the direct plan and presents an example of *poor writing* and an example of *good writing*.

OPEN WITH THE POSITIVE INFORMATION

A **poor** opening presenting the positive information is:

> It has come to my attention that you will need to stop by my office to sign the necessary papers for your loan. Our credit committee approved it yesterday in its weekly meeting.

This poorly written opening stresses the writer's interest instead of the receiver's interest and benefits. Note that the good information, the loan approval, is not given until the second sentence and the loan is not clearly identified. The paragraph is also written in a stiff, impersonal manner rather than in a positive, friendly style. After reading the opening, Matt will be neither excited nor eager to read the explanation giving the conditions of the loan.

The following would be a **good** opening for this case problem:

> Your application for a $200,000 loan has been approved. This money should provide the necessary capital for you to open your hardware store.

In contrast to the poorly written opening, this paragraph meets all the requirements of properly presenting positive information in a message. It immediately gives the positive information. The you–viewpoint is emphasized—the benefit that the receiver will realize from the loan is given. The loan is specifically identified in the two sentences, thus providing coherence. Because this first paragraph has a positive, personal tone, Matt should have an open mind toward Merchants State Bank.

PROVIDE AN EXPLANATION

The next step in composing a message using the direct plan is to present an explanation of the conditions under which the positive information—the loan approval—will be carried out. A **poor** way to present an explanation to Matt is:

> The loan is for a 20-year period. Merchants State Bank makes loans only at a variable interest rate because of the uncertainty of inflation rates. The interest rate for your loan for the first year will be 9 percent, but the rate will probably be higher for subsequent years. The monthly payment is due by the fifth day of each month. There is a 1 percent penalty for late payment.

The style of this poor explanation is similar to the style of the poor opening; it stresses the writer's interests rather than the receiver's benefits. Lack of a you–viewpoint and the tone of the message make the explanation negative. The explanation should contain all relevant facts so that the receiver will not have any questions. In this example, no information is given concerning how the monthly payments are to be made or when the money will be available. The explanation could be made more concise by stating that the details of the loan would be furnished when Matt came in and signed the loan agreement.

In contrast, a **good** explanation follows:

> This loan is for a 20-year period. The rate for the first year is the lowest available from any local financial institution—9 percent. The interest rate on your loan after the first year is at a low 1/2 of 1 percent above the average treasury rate set by the federal government. We can arrange the payment dates and method of payment when you come in to sign the loan agreement and pick up your check. At that time, I will also discuss with you other agreement details.

The good example meets all requirements for a positive explanation.

This explanation presents the facts in an objective way and answers the receiver's questions. The paragraph is written positively. It contains enough information so that the receiver understands the conditions of the positive information, yet it remains concise by indicating that details of the loan will be furnished at a later time. After presenting the explanation, the writer should consider using a sales appeal.

CONSIDER SALES APPEAL

A sales appeal should be used whenever a writer attempts to obtain additional business from the receiver. The sales appeal, depending on its length and nature, may be written as a separate paragraph(s) or as part of the final paragraph of the letter. In this case the following is an example of a **poor** appeal for additional business from Matt:

> I want to invite you to use our bank for all your financial business. We will consider giving you additional loans as soon as you have more equity in your store.

The example of a poor sales appeal is cold and impersonal.

Note the impersonal tone of the message. There is no you–viewpoint in the sales appeal and the second sentence is more likely to discourage than encourage additional business.

The following is an example of a **good** sales appeal for this case:

> Mr. Brockway, you are on your way to becoming a successful businessperson. You may be interested in using the many financial services offered by Merchants State Bank. Your preferred customer rating entitles you to free checking if you maintain a $1,000 balance in your passbook account, a low-interest revolving credit account, preferred status on additional loans, free photocopying, and other banking services. A brochure describing all the Merchants State Bank customer services is enclosed. Please ask about these benefits on your next visit to Merchants.

The good example of a sales appeal is positive and personalized.

This example of a sales appeal is written in a personalized way; it encourages Matt to use other financial services at Merchants State Bank. It mentions additional services that Matt can receive at the bank, and it encourages quick action on Matt's part without appearing pushy.

END YOUR LETTER WITH A FRIENDLY CLOSE

A positive or neutral message should conclude with a friendly close that builds goodwill. A **poor** close, such as the one that follows, would guarantee ill will:

> Don't forget to come to Merchants and sign the loan papers. We cannot release the money until the paperwork is completed and signed. Thanks for doing business with us. If there is anything else I can do, please call.

An example of a **good** friendly close that will do much to establish goodwill follows:

> You may stop in at your convenience and complete the necessary paperwork for your loan. Your business is certainly appreciated, Mr. Brockway; our staff is available to help meet all your financial needs.

This friendly close is written in a positive, personalized, and concise way. Appreciation is shown for Matt's business. It reinforces the sales appeal section of the letter.

SUMMARY—POOR AND GOOD MESSAGES TO MATT BROCKWAY

Poor and good examples are used to demonstrate how effective positive messages are written. The *poor* example paragraphs are combined as a letter in Figure 11•2. This **poor** example fails to use the direct plan for positive information and to incorporate the communication fundamentals that are presented in Chapters 1, 2, and 3.

Customer goodwill is promoted in the positive letter shown in Figure 11•3. This letter combines the **good** example paragraphs. It integrates communication fundamentals into the direct plan message to produce an effective business communication.

An approval of a loan request has been used to illustrate how the direct plan is used to communicate a positive message. To further demonstrate how the direct approach is used in actual business correspondence situations, several other examples of good and poor positive and neutral messages are presented in the following pages.

INQUIRIES

Businesspersons periodically make routine requests for information. Routine **inquiries** are neutral messages that require no persuasion and, therefore, should be written using the direct plan. These inquiries may be about a product, a service, or a person.

A message of inquiry must be written so that the writer will obtain all the information necessary to make a decision about a product, service, or person. Consider what you or your company needs to know and ask specific questions. Your letter of inquiry should be written so that the receiver can reply easily, quickly, and completely.

The example of a poor close is negative and does not build goodwill.

The good example of a close is friendly and builds goodwill.

Contrasting poor and good letters to Matt Brockway are presented in Figures 11•2 and 11•3.

Use direct plan with inquiries because persuasion is not needed.

Inquiries should ask specific questions.

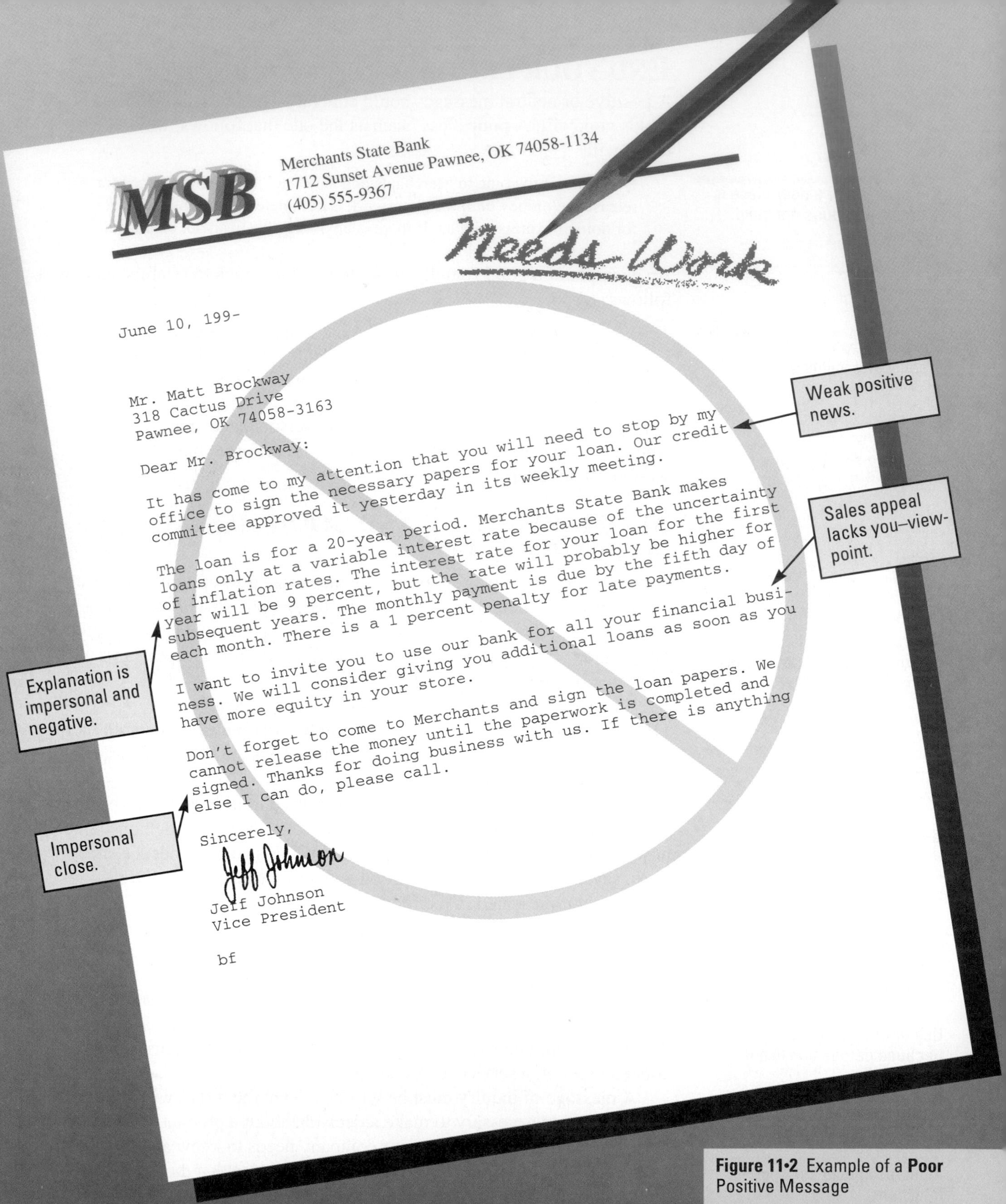

Merchants State Bank
1712 Sunset Avenue Pawnee, OK 74058-1134
(405) 555-9367

Needs Work

June 10, 199-

Mr. Matt Brockway
318 Cactus Drive
Pawnee, OK 74058-3163

Dear Mr. Brockway:

It has come to my attention that you will need to stop by my
office to sign the necessary papers for your loan. Our credit
committee approved it yesterday in its weekly meeting.

> Weak positive news.

The loan is for a 20-year period. Merchants State Bank makes
loans only at a variable interest rate because of the uncertainty
of inflation rates. The interest rate for your loan for the first
year will be 9 percent, but the rate will probably be higher for
subsequent years. The monthly payment is due by the fifth day of
each month. There is a 1 percent penalty for late payments.

> Sales appeal lacks you–view-point.

> Explanation is impersonal and negative.

I want to invite you to use our bank for all your financial business. We will consider giving you additional loans as soon as you
have more equity in your store.

Don't forget to come to Merchants and sign the loan papers. We
cannot release the money until the paperwork is completed and
signed. Thanks for doing business with us. If there is anything
else I can do, please call.

Sincerely,

Jeff Johnson

> Impersonal close.

Jeff Johnson
Vice President

bf

Figure 11·2 Example of a **Poor** Positive Message

Merchants State Bank
1712 Sunset Avenue Pawnee, OK 74058-1134
(405) 555-9367

GOOD

June 10, 199-

Mr. Matt Brockway
318 Cactus Drive
Pawnee, OK 74058-3163

Dear Mr. Brockway:

Your application for a $200,000 loan has been approved. This money should provide the necessary capital for you to open your hardware store.

[Positive good information.]

This loan is for a 20-year period. The rate for the first year is the lowest available from any local financial institution—9 percent. The interest rate on your loan after the first year is at a low 1/2 of 1 percent above the average treasury rate set by the federal government. We can arrange the payment dates and method of payment when you come in to sign the loan agreement and pick up your check. At that time I will also discuss with you other agreement details.

[Facts presented in positive manner.]

Mr. Brockway, you are on your way to becoming a successful businessperson. You may be interested in using the many financial services offered by Merchants State Bank. Your preferred customer rating entitles you to free checking if you maintain a $1,000 balance in your passbook account, a low-interest, revolving credit account, preferred status on additional loans, free photocopying, and other banking services. A brochure describing all the Merchants State Bank customer services is enclosed. Please ask about these benefits on your next visit to Merchants.

[You–viewpoint used to sell additional services.]

You may stop in at your convenience and complete the necessary paperwork for your loan. Your business is certainly appreciated, Mr. Brockway; our staff is available to help meet all your financial needs.

[Friendly close expressing appreciation.]

Sincerely,

Jeff Johnson

Jeff Johnson
Vice President

bf

Enclosure

Figure 11·3 Example of a **Good** Positive Message

An inquiry about products or services should make the receiver of the message glad to respond. The inquiry may include only one sentence requesting a pamphlet or catalog; or it may have several paragraphs in which questions are asked. If several questions are asked, listing and numbering them will aid the receiver in responding. Use the direct plan outline by presenting your request and stating the reason for it (if necessary) in the opening paragraph. In the second part of your message give enough information so that the receiver can respond intelligently. Close your message by requesting action. Inquiries usually do not have a sales appeal section.

Message receiver should be glad to receive inquiry about products or services.

Figure 11•4 is an example of a **poor** inquiry requesting details about information processing workshops. The inquiry is not specific enough to enable Ms. Hernandez to send the information Mr. Hudson needs to make a decision. It would be difficult for Ms. Hernandez to answer the two questions unless she knows for which software programs instruction would be needed, the location of the training, the number of hours of training that would be needed, etc.

The letter in Figure 11•5 is an example of a **good** inquiry about information processing workshops. The letter starts by presenting the reasons for the request. Sufficient information is provided to Ms. Hernandez so that she can provide the necessary details in her reply. The listed and numbered questions make it easier for Ms. Hernandez to respond. The close is positive and encourages a prompt reply.

An inquiry about a person must be made carefully to protect the rights of the individual. You should ask only questions that are relevant to the situation. Information obtained should be kept confidential. State whether or not the person about whom you are inquiring authorized your request. Begin your inquiry by clearly identifying the person and stating your need for the information. The explanation should contain relevant facts—pertinent information that the individual shared with you, requirements that must be met (job, loan, award, etc.), or questions that you need answered. Close by stating that you would appreciate the receiver's sharing the information and by promising to keep the information confidential.

Inquiries about persons should ask only relevant questions and should promise confidentiality.

REQUESTS

A **request** is a message expressing the writer's needs or desires and usually asks for a response. Managers of business organizations receive requests from their customers, their employees, and others. These requests may include, for example, a request from an employee for six months' parenting leave or a request from a civic organization for the manager to speak at a conference. Requests should be carefully considered and approved whenever feasible.

Businesses receive many requests.

Most requests are approved.

The proper handling of a request can build goodwill for an organization. For instance, approval of a parenting leave will gain goodwill for the organization. The employee taking the leave will have a sense of obligation to the company and will return refreshed and enthusiastic about the job. Goodwill, no doubt, will spread throughout employee groups when they

Goodwill can be improved with proper handling of requests.

observe the company's humanistic philosophy. Accepting an invitation to speak at a meeting of a civic organization can build goodwill for the company among those attending the meeting. The acceptance letter should convey enthusiasm about the prospect of appearing before the group; it should in no way indicate a duty to perform a community service. The acceptance letter should emphasize the positive aspects of accepting the invitation to speak.

Request approvals should stress the positive news.

To illustrate how the direct plan can be used in a positive message communicating approval of a request, assume that you are the human resources manager of Diamond Brakes, Inc. Chamene Phillips, an assembly line worker, has requested a change from the day shift to the night shift. This change will allow Chamene to eliminate babysitting services and enable her husband to take care of their children while she is at work. Because you want to build goodwill and because there is a shortage of workers on the night shift, you would write a memo to her approving this change and providing details about it.

A **poor** approval memo for this request is shown in Figure 11•6. It does little to build employee morale and goodwill for the company. Note the absence of the you–viewpoint. Also, notice that the positive information is not given until the second paragraph.

The **good** memo in Figure 11•7 uses the direct plan and should influence positively Chamene's attitude toward the company. It gives Chamene the positive information in the first sentence. The second paragraph presents an explanation that is factual, positive, and concise. A friendly close is given in the final paragraph. A sales appeal—the optional third step in the direct plan—is not appropriate for this situation.

CLAIMS

Claims take many forms.

Claims include requests for merchandise exchange, for refunds on defective or damaged merchandise, for refunds for unsatisfactory service, and for correction of work. Your complaint receives greatest emphasis when the complaint is the first item in the message. Generally, the receiver wants the claim information so that he or she can make necessary corrections as soon as possible. For this reason, and to give strength to your claim, use the direct plan.

Claims are presented by using the direct plan.

The plan for claim messages can easily be adapted from the direct plan used for positive and neutral information shown in Figure 11•1 on page 284. The claim should be presented in an objective way, without a display of anger and without placing blame on the receiver. The *opening* should present immediately the claim and its impact. The impact could include the inconveniences suffered and identification of specific damages. The *explanation* should provide any necessary additional background that relates to the claim. In this section provide facts supporting the claim and describe actions that have been taken. In addition, you should specify actions that you want the receiver to take; set a deadline by which corrective action should be taken. There would be no *sales appeal* in a claim letter. Finally, the *friendly close* should be optimistic.

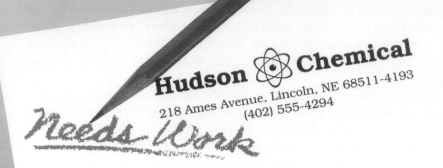

Hudson ⚛ Chemical
218 Ames Avenue, Lincoln, NE 68511-4193
(402) 555-4294

Needs Work

July 19, 199-

Ms. Isabel Hernandez, Manager
Business Computer Systems
4210 Conroe Lane
Seward, NE 68434-2317

Dear Ms. Hernandez

Hudson Chemical has been serving eastern Nebraska for 75 years. We have stores in more than 50 communities.

Last year we started modernizing our stores. We put computer systems in each store. Now we must teach the personnel how to use the equipment. Can your company provide training for our personnel? How much will it cost?

I am looking forward to your reply.

Sincerely

Garin Hudson

Garin Hudson
Owner

sr

> The poor opening does not present the request.

> The explanation does not provide the receiver with necessary information.

> Weak close.

Figure 11·4 Example of a **Poor** Inquiry

Hudson ⚛ Chemical

218 Ames Avenue, Lincoln, NE 68511-4193
(402) 555-4294

July 19, 199-

Ms. Isabel Hernandez, Manager
Business Computer Systems
4210 Conroe Lane
Seward, NE 68434-2317

Dear Ms. Hernandez

Hudson Chemical is modernizing its operation and needs computer training for its personnel. Approximately 125 employees will need training on word processing, spreadsheet, and marketing software programs. Our personnel would be available for training between September 1 and December 1. Specifically, we need answers to these questions:

The good opening presents reason for request.

Facts are given to permit reader to respond properly.

1. What would be the optimum size for each class section?
2. Would the instruction be more effective if taught at your location or in one of our regional offices?
3. For which software packages can you provide training?
4. How many hours of instruction would be necessary for each software package?
5. Could your organization provide this type of training?
6. How much would this type of training cost?

Specific questions help receiver provide the necessary information.

Your prompt reply to the above questions would be appreciated so that we may begin planning an effective training program.

Sincerely

Garin Hudson

Garin Hudson
Owner

sr

Closes with request for prompt reply.

Figure 11•5 Example of a **Good** Inquiry

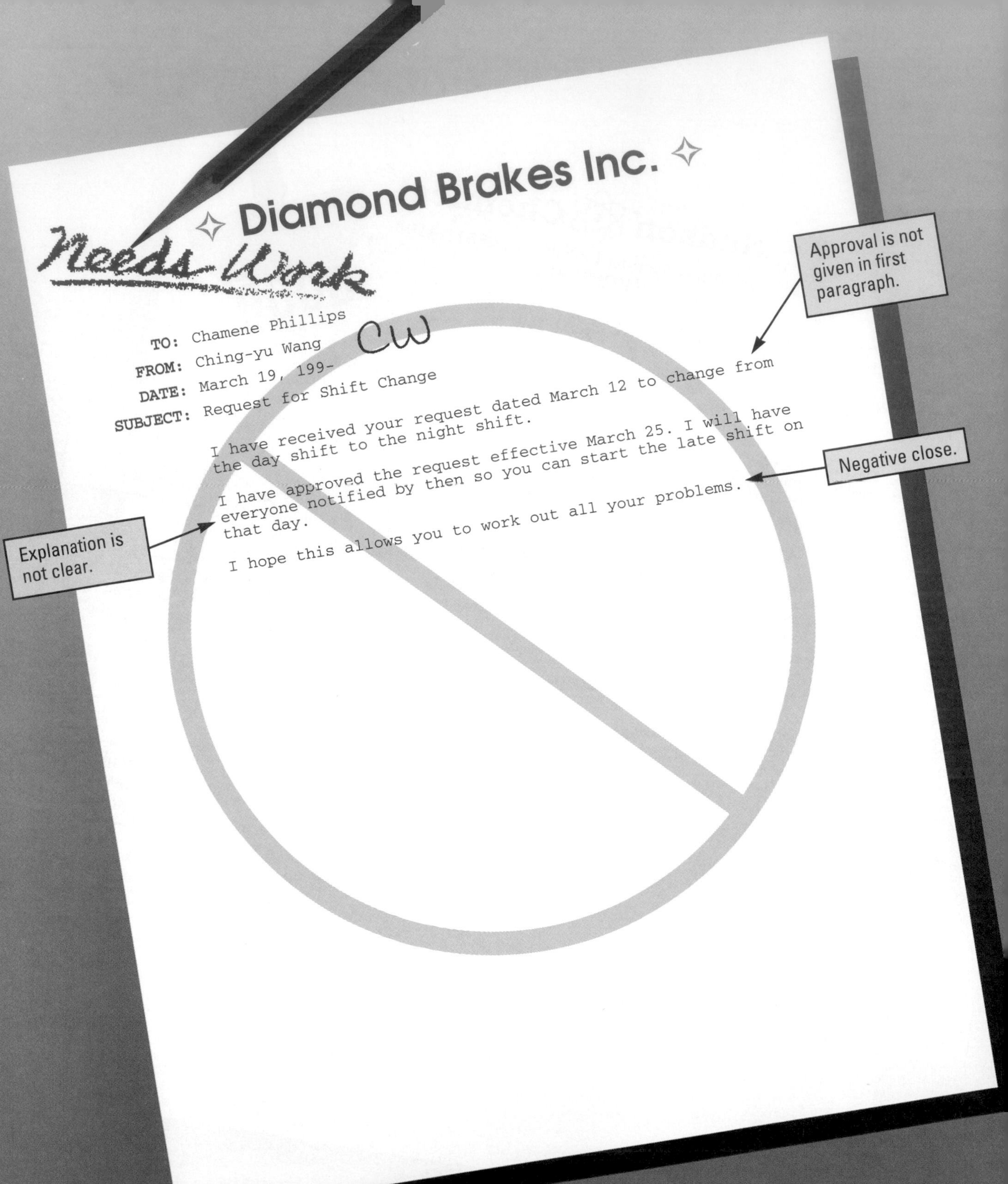

✧ Diamond Brakes Inc. ✧

Needs Work

TO: Chamene Phillips
FROM: Ching-yu Wang   CW
DATE: March 19, 199-
SUBJECT: Request for Shift Change

I have received your request dated March 12 to change from the day shift to the night shift.

I have approved the request effective March 25. I will have everyone notified by then so you can start the late shift on that day.

I hope this allows you to work out all your problems.

> Approval is not given in first paragraph.

> Negative close.

> Explanation is not clear.

Figure 11•6 Example of a **Poor** Request Approval Memo

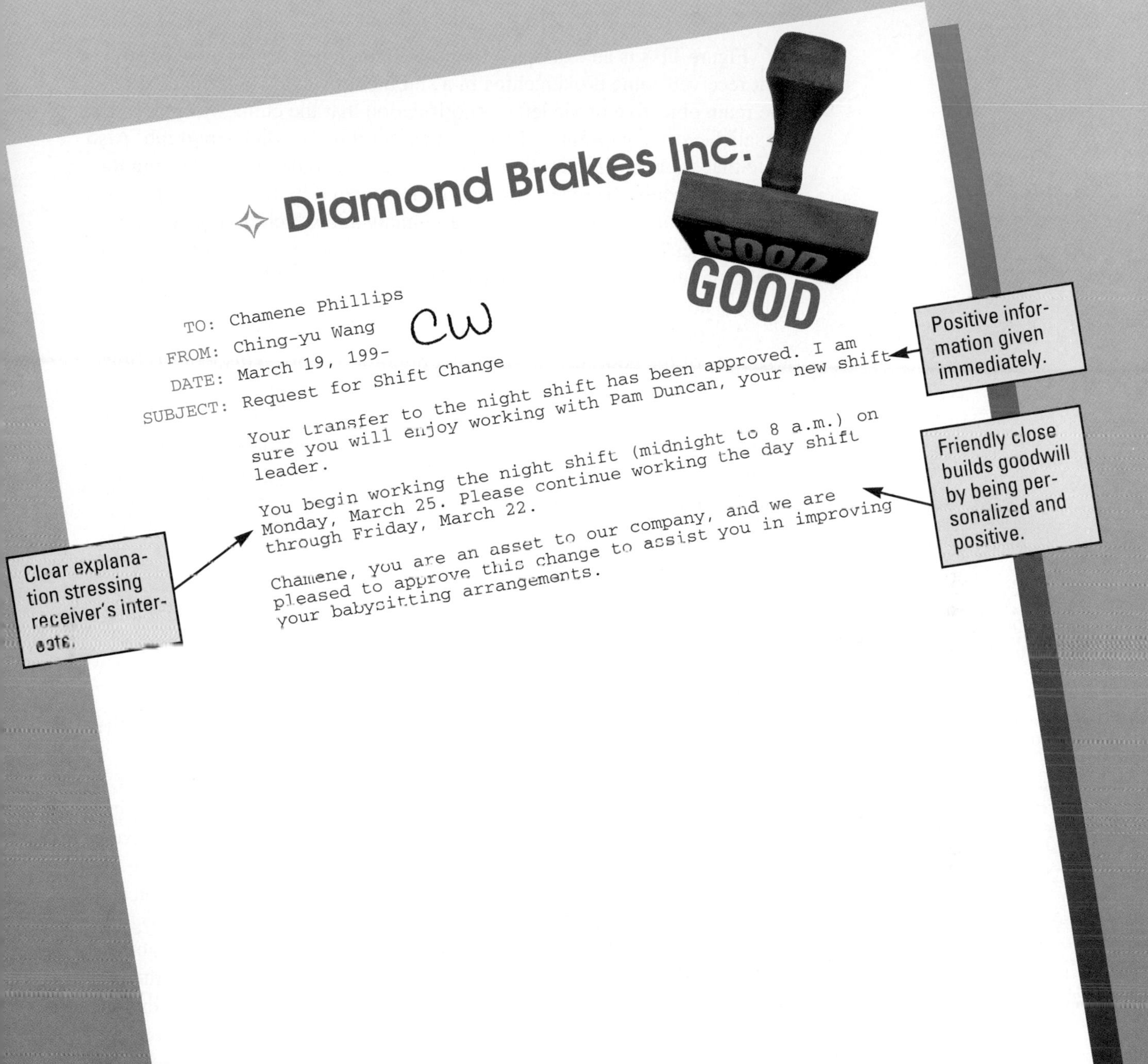

◇ Diamond Brakes Inc.

GOOD

TO: Chamene Phillips
FROM: Ching-yu Wang   CW
DATE: March 19, 199-
SUBJECT: Request for Shift Change

Your transfer to the night shift has been approved. I am sure you will enjoy working with Pam Duncan, your new shift leader.

You begin working the night shift (midnight to 8 a.m.) on Monday, March 25. Please continue working the day shift through Friday, March 22.

Chamene, you are an asset to our company, and we are pleased to approve this change to assist you in improving your babysitting arrangements.

> Positive information given immediately.

> Friendly close builds goodwill by being personalized and positive.

> Clear explanation stressing receiver's interests.

Figure 11·7 Example of a **Good** Request Approval Memo

Figure 11•8 is an example of a **poor** claim letter from a jewelry store that received some broken china in a shipment from a wholesaler. Note that the main objective of the letter—notification that the china was received in unsatisfactory condition—did not appear until the second paragraph. Also note that the letter implies blame; the claimant should avoid accusing the receiver because the receiver will only be angered by this approach. The claim was not clearly identified—how many and which pieces of china were broken? The receiver needs this information, but is not interested in sender-related details such as the claimant's order number. And lastly, this letter is not written in a considerate tone.

A superior letter for the same situation is shown in Figure 11•9, an example of the **good** use of the direct plan for a claim. This letter is objective and courteous. The problem and its impact are specified in the opening. The damaged items are clearly identified. A concise explanation of the circumstances is given in the second paragraph. A deadline as to when replacement china is needed is given politely in the third paragraph. The close is friendly and optimistic.

ADJUSTMENTS

Business firms that receive claim messages should respond to them quickly in order to maintain the goodwill of the customer. A positive response to a claim is known as an **adjustment.** If there is any doubt about the legitimacy of a claim, the customer usually receives the benefit of the doubt.

A letter approving a claim is positive information and should use the direct plan. The letter should begin with the positive information—the adjustment. This immediate positive information will aid in eliminating any negative feelings the customer has toward the company. The explanation should be convincing to regain the customer's confidence. An effective, personalized sales appeal gives the company an opportunity to emphasize to the customer the quality of the product or service. To avoid ending on a negative note, an adjustment letter should never close with an apology.

An example of a **poor** adjustment response to the claim letter about the broken china is shown in Figure 11•10. This letter does not get to the positive information until the third paragraph. The explanation places the blame on the delivery company and is not convincing. The repeated references to the trouble and inconvenience caused continually remind the receiver of the negative aspects of the situation. Details as to when the replacement items are to arrive are omitted. The hollow apology in the close does not build the goodwill of the customer. The you–viewpoint is absent from the letter.

An example of a **good** letter granting an adjustment is shown in Figure 11•11. Note that this letter begins immediately with the positive information. The explanation emphasizes not the wrong itself but what was done to correct the wrong. This explanation should help regain the customer's confidence. In the third paragraph, the writer uses a personal approach when describing an item that Mr. Brannon may be interested in selling. The close ends the letter on a happy, positive note.

Legitimate claims should be approved quickly.

Use direct plan for adjustment letters.

New Employees Receiving Unsolicited Positive Information—Orientation on Employee Benefits.

UNSOLICITED POSITIVE AND NEUTRAL MESSAGES

Businesses send both internal and external unsolicited positive or neutral messages.

An **unsolicited positive** or **neutral message** is a communication initiated by an organization. Examples of unsolicited positive or neutral messages to customers may include an announcement of new products or services, notification of new hours of operation, reductions in prices of merchandise, relocation to a new building, or employment of new customer representatives. Unsolicited positive messages to employees may announce new fringe benefits, an unscheduled pay increase, or a promotion.

Unsolicited positive or neutral messages should employ the direct approach. In the example in Figure 11•12, Ms. Bailey misses an opportunity to build on the goodwill that was gained when she gave Ms. Burns the $500. The letter is written from the savings and loan's viewpoint rather than from Ms. Burns'.

In the example of a **good** unsolicited positive information letter shown in Figure 11•13, Ms. Bailey increases Ms. Burns' enthusiasm for doing business with South Central Savings and Loan. Note how the you–viewpoint is used to enhance the positive information.

Use of direct plan in positive and neutral messages increases their effectiveness.Illustration

Skillfully used, the direct plan is appropriate for messages that request information, convey favorable information, convey neutral information, or make or settle claims. With the direct plan, effective messages can increase employee morale, promote customer goodwill, and positively affect those who receive them.

Classic Gems and Jewels

518 Prescott Center
Atlanta, GA 30321-4137
(404) 555-4291

Needs Work

October 22, 199-

Priscilla Brooks
Quality Crystal Importers
8319 Elm Street
Dallas, TX 75217-3184

Dear Priscilla:

As your records will show, on September 28 I ordered three complete sets of Corigan China (my Order 2174). The units were shipped to me by All State Van Lines (your Invoice 527T) and arrived at my store October 19.

At the time of delivery the receiving clerk noticed that two of the boxes were smashed in on the side. Further inspection showed that your organization used cheap cartons to ship expensive china. As a result of the inferior cartons and the rough handling of the china, over half of the shipment is broken.

It is hard for me to understand how a wholesaler who handles china could permit such inadequate treatment of its products. I do not accept this shipment of china. Further, I want this broken china taken off my hands and replaced with new pieces. Because I will be holding my annual Thanksgiving sale in November, I insist that the replacement Corigan China reach me by November 10.

Sincerely,

Nick

Nicholas Brannon
Owner

jt

Annotations:

While providing transition, the poor opening does not clearly identify the damages.

The explanation is not written in a considerate tone.

Negative and demanding close.

Figure 11•8 Example of a **Poor** Claim Letter

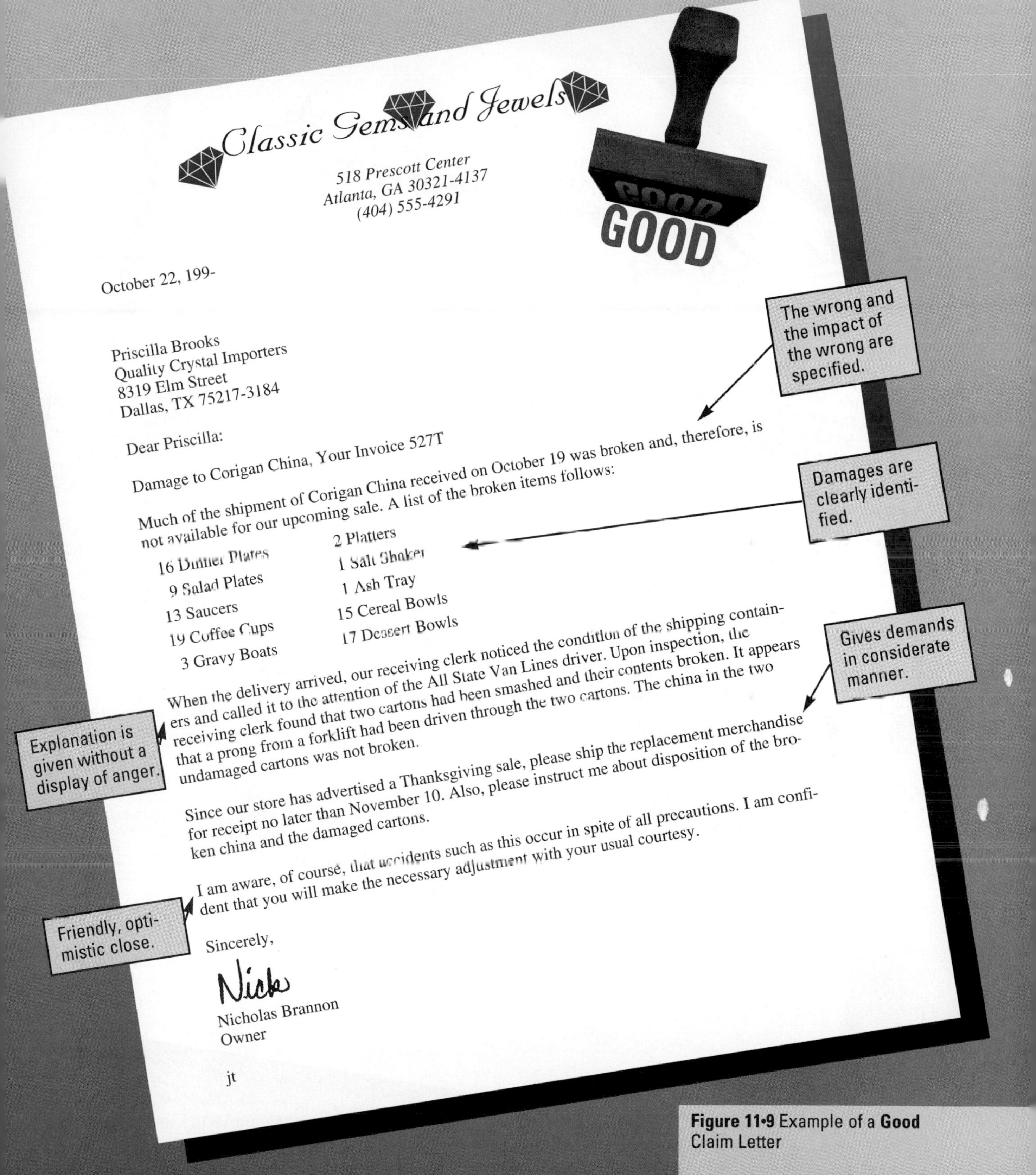

Classic Gems and Jewels

518 Prescott Center
Atlanta, GA 30321-4137
(404) 555-4291

GOOD

October 22, 199-

Priscilla Brooks
Quality Crystal Importers
8319 Elm Street
Dallas, TX 75217-3184

Dear Priscilla:

Damage to Corigan China, Your Invoice 527T

Much of the shipment of Corigan China received on October 19 was broken and, therefore, is not available for our upcoming sale. A list of the broken items follows:

16 Dinner Plates	2 Platters
9 Salad Plates	1 Salt Shaker
13 Saucers	1 Ash Tray
19 Coffee Cups	15 Cereal Bowls
3 Gravy Boats	17 Dessert Bowls

When the delivery arrived, our receiving clerk noticed the condition of the shipping containers and called it to the attention of the All State Van Lines driver. Upon inspection, the receiving clerk found that two cartons had been smashed and their contents broken. It appears that a prong from a forklift had been driven through the two cartons. The china in the two undamaged cartons was not broken.

Since our store has advertised a Thanksgiving sale, please ship the replacement merchandise for receipt no later than November 10. Also, please instruct me about disposition of the broken china and the damaged cartons.

I am aware, of course, that accidents such as this occur in spite of all precautions. I am confident that you will make the necessary adjustment with your usual courtesy.

Sincerely,

Nick

Nicholas Brannon
Owner

jt

Figure 11·9 Example of a **Good** Claim Letter

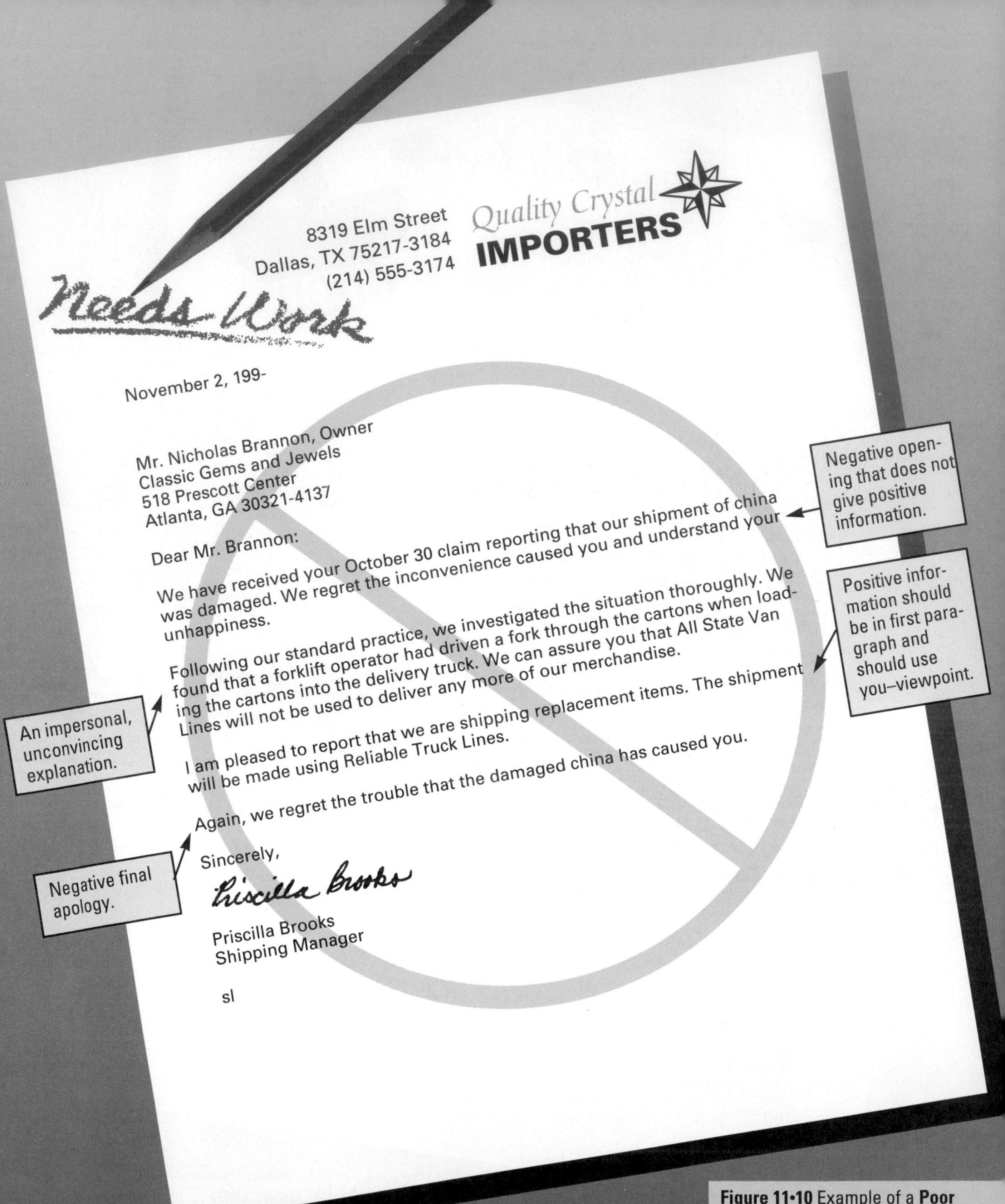

8319 Elm Street
Dallas, TX 75217-3184
(214) 555-3174

Quality Crystal
IMPORTERS

Needs Work

November 2, 199-

Mr. Nicholas Brannon, Owner
Classic Gems and Jewels
518 Prescott Center
Atlanta, GA 30321-4137

Dear Mr. Brannon:

We have received your October 30 claim reporting that our shipment of china was damaged. We regret the inconvenience caused you and understand your unhappiness.

> Negative opening that does not give positive information.

Following our standard practice, we investigated the situation thoroughly. We found that a forklift operator had driven a fork through the cartons when loading the cartons into the delivery truck. We can assure you that All State Van Lines will not be used to deliver any more of our merchandise.

> An impersonal, unconvincing explanation.

> Positive information should be in first paragraph and should use you–viewpoint.

I am pleased to report that we are shipping replacement items. The shipment will be made using Reliable Truck Lines.

Again, we regret the trouble that the damaged china has caused you.

Sincerely,

Priscilla Brooks

Priscilla Brooks
Shipping Manager

> Negative final apology.

sl

Figure 11•10 Example of a **Poor** Adjustment Letter

8319 Elm Street
Dallas, TX 75217-3184
(214) 555-3174

Quality Crystal
IMPORTERS

November 2, 199-

Mr. Nicholas Brannon, Owner
Classic Gems and Jewels
518 Prescott Center
Atlanta, GA 30321-4137

Dear Mr. Brannon:

Your replacement china will reach you by November 10, in time for your annual Thanksgiving sale. This fast delivery of the replacement china is our way of proving to you that we value your business.

Because your continued business is important to us, we have carefully examined the handling of your order. It was determined that a forklift operator for All State Van Lines accidentally drove a fork through two of the cartons. The manager of the van lines assures me that the forklift operator has been given additional training and will be more careful in the future.

Mr. Brannon, jewelry stores throughout the United States are having excellent sales with our new add-a-pearl necklace. The necklace chain is made of 14-karat gold and comes in 16-, 18-, 24-, or 30-inch lengths. The pearls are white and of the highest quality. A sample necklace containing six pearls is enclosed. Also enclosed is a convenient order form listing prices for your use. Why not order now so you will have this new profit-making item in your store for your sale.

Best wishes for a successful Thanksgiving sale.

Sincerely,

Priscilla Brooks

Priscilla Brooks
Shipping Manager

sl

Enclosures

> Gives positive information immediately.

> Convincing explanation.

> Announces a new item for sales appeal.

> Positive close.

Figure 11·11 Example of a **Good** Adjustment Letter

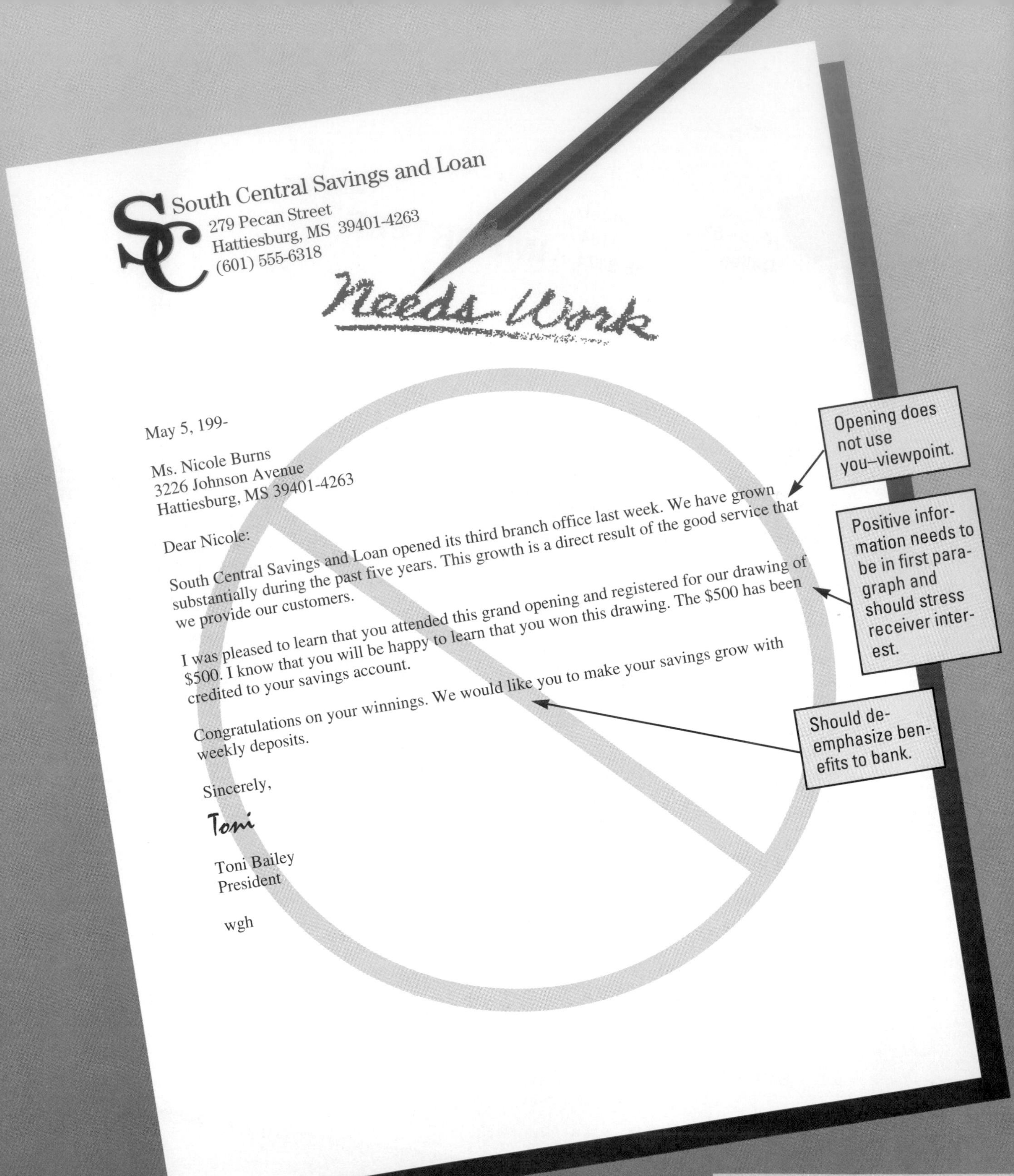

South Central Savings and Loan
279 Pecan Street
Hattiesburg, MS 39401-4263
(601) 555-6318

Needs Work

May 5, 199-

Ms. Nicole Burns
3226 Johnson Avenue
Hattiesburg, MS 39401-4263

Dear Nicole:

South Central Savings and Loan opened its third branch office last week. We have grown substantially during the past five years. This growth is a direct result of the good service that we provide our customers.

I was pleased to learn that you attended this grand opening and registered for our drawing of $500. I know that you will be happy to learn that you won this drawing. The $500 has been credited to your savings account.

Congratulations on your winnings. We would like you to make your savings grow with weekly deposits.

Sincerely,

Toni

Toni Bailey
President

wgh

> Opening does not use you–viewpoint.

> Positive information needs to be in first paragraph and should stress receiver interest.

> Should de-emphasize benefits to bank.

Figure 11•12 Example of a **Poor** Unsolicited Positive Letter

South Central Savings and Loan

SC
279 Pecan Street
Hattiesburg, MS 39401-4263
(601) 555-6318

May 5, 199-

Ms. Nicole Burns
3226 Johnson Avenue
Hattiesburg, MS 39401-4263

Dear Nicole:

Congratulations! You have won $500 in a drawing held at the grand opening of our third branch office.

The $500 has been deposited in your savings account and has begun earning interest at a 3.5 percent annual rate. At your earliest convenience, please come to the branch office and have the $500 recorded in your passbook.

Thank you, Nicole, for participating in our grand opening. Staff at each of our three locations look forward to serving you in the future.

Sincerely,

Toni

Toni Bailey
President

wgh

> Positive, you–oriented, strong beginning.

> Stresses benefits to customer.

> Continues building goodwill.

Figure 11·13 Example of a **Good** Unsolicited Positive Letter

DISCUSSION QUESTIONS

1. Identify a type of bad news message that should use the direct plan. Explain why this message should be constructed using the direct plan.

2. Where should you place the positive information in a request approval? Why?

3. List four characteristics of the opening section of the direct plan.

4. List three characteristics of the sales appeal section of positive or neutral messages.

5. What is the purpose of a friendly close? How is this purpose accomplished? Give an example of an effective friendly close.

6. Compare a request approval written to an external audience with one written to an internal audience.

 7. Describe the process of gathering information about a person that should be followed to ensure that the individual's rights are protected.

8. Discuss five communication fundamentals presented in Chapters 1 through 3 that should be used in positive or neutral messages.

9. Identify three types of positive messages that could be referred to as unsolicited. Use examples other than those in the text.

APPLICATION EXERCISES

1. Describe the various types of information that a customer would like to receive in addition to the notification that his or her claim has been approved.

2. Visit two retail stores in your community and ask how they handle adjustment messages. Get copies, if possible, of their letters and share this information with the class.

3. Obtain an example of a positive message used by a business in your community. Present an analysis of this message to the class.

4. Inquire at several organizations about the various situations in which they use a neutral message. Determine the frequency of its use. What organizational plan is followed for presenting the neutral message?

5. Develop a form letter that could be used as an inquiry for obtaining information from prospective members of a student organization. Assume that this student organization requires a 3.0 GPA, completion of 45 semester hours of general education courses and 15 semester hours of business courses, and recommendations from two instructors.

CASE PROBLEMS

INQUIRIES

1. You own a VCR that was given to you upon graduation from high school. You are interested in purchasing a camcorder so you can take movies. Write a letter to Video World requesting information about the camcorders it sells, so that you can make an intelligent purchase. You want to know if the equipment Video World sells has features such as wide angle lens, telephoto lens, warranty, rechargeable batteries, etc. Supply details to make your letter complete.

2. Your garden club is sponsoring a community-wide symposium on wild flowers. Mr. David Minulcik, a noted horticulturist, will conduct several of the sessions. You are responsible for preparing the promotional material about the activities. Write a letter to Mr. Minulcik requesting information about his background. The deadline for delivering the brochure to the printer is approaching. It is important that all necessary data are obtained with this one letter to Mr. Minulcik.

3. Stars Cinema wants to build a movie theater in a neighboring state. Form a committee of four students and develop a plan to find the best town for the new theater. Remember that information will be needed from this state on town populations, community interests, and cost of land. Write a memo to your instructor detailing the results of the project. Attach letters that could be sent to agencies requesting information needed to make the final decision for building the movie theater.

4. Pepper Stokes would like to take her husband, Pearce, on a vacation to Germany for their tenth wedding anniversary. She is doing all the planning for this event so she can surprise him with the trip. She will need to contact the Tourist Information Office, Schumannstrasse 27, 50201 Salzburg, Germany, for information. Write a letter that Pepper Stokes could use to obtain pertinent information. Be sure to include necessary details to make this a complete inquiry.

5. As a recent college graduate entering the business world, you are interested in building an investment portfolio. Many of your friends recommend Southland Investments. Write a letter to Southland asking about its investment programs. You would like information about minimum initial investment, types of investments (stocks, bonds, mutual funds, etc.), withdrawal penalties, tax shelters, etc.

6. As human resources manager of Joshua's Electronics, you frequently must obtain information about prospective employees from their references. You must gather sufficient information on each individual to enable your company to make hiring decisions. Develop the body of a form letter that could be used to obtain the necessary information.

REQUESTS

7. You are the supervisor at the Safety Tire Company responsible for approving employee vacations. Bill Barnett works on the assembly line and is entitled to two weeks of vacation each year. He has been planning a one-week wedding trip in August, but had to use his two weeks of vacation in March to settle an uncle's estate. Bill has requested an additional week of paid vacation. You are restricted by company policy from approving this request; however, because the company's fiscal year begins September 1, you can allow Bill to draw on one week of his next year's vacation.

   Write a memo informing Bill of your decision. You want Bill to accept this compromise without bitterness toward the company. He has been a faithful, loyal employee for the past five years; it is your wish that he continue to be a good employee.

8. You are the credit manager for Kevin's, a family clothing store, in Paducah, Kentucky. Amanda Hyde has applied for a Kevin's charge card. Write Amanda a letter approving her request. Assign her a $5,000 credit limit, and explain the details of the charge card. Add necessary facts to make the letter complete.

9. As director of customer service for Treetop Airlines, you receive the following letter from Rosanna Simpson:

   I purchased a round-trip airline ticket ($250) from Nashville, Tennessee, to Houston, Texas. While in Houston, an emergency caused me to change my plans for returning on your airline.
   I am returning the unused portion of my ticket. I would appreciate a $125 refund.

   Write a letter to Rosanna and approve her request for a refund. Be sure to thank her for using Treetop Airlines.

10. You are vice president of your college's Future Business Leaders student organization. One of your responsibilities is to coordinate the organization's public service activities within your community.

Jeremy Cole is organizing the Special Olympics for the region. He has asked your organization to provide seven members to assist in judging events. Future Business Leaders normally does not commit itself to activities that are not directly related to business; however, the Special Olympics is very important to the community and your organization will receive excellent exposure. You believe that your organization should participate in this activity. Write Mr. Cole a letter expressing appreciation for being considered to participate in such a worthwhile event. Tell him that you will have seven individuals there and can assist with more persons if necessary.

11. You are the Pulaski County judge and have the authority to perform marriage ceremonies. However, the large number of time-consuming duties of a county judge has forced you to initiate a policy of not performing marriage ceremonies. Mr. and Mrs. Carl Thompson, strong supporters of your last campaign, have requested that you officiate at their daughter's wedding. You will make an exception to your policy and perform the ceremony. Write a letter to the Thompsons and inform them of your decision. Supply necessary details to make your message complete.

12. Drexel Pharmaceutical maintains a two-bedroom houseboat on Barkley Lake for use by its employees. You are responsible for processing reservations to use this houseboat. Develop a form memo to confirm reservations. Include approved dates of use, rules of occupancy, and other pertinent details.

CLAIMS

13. Mr. Al Sams was vacationing in Milroy, New York, when he had tire trouble and purchased four blemished tires from Browning Tire Sales, Inc., in Milroy. Blemished tires are usually perfect, except for some small defect that does not affect their usability. The defect could be a misprint on the labeling of the tire, imperfect whitewall coloring, or irregular tread pattern.

While driving home (about 600 miles), Mr. Sams began experiencing tire trouble. The tires caused his car to handle improperly because they were out-of-round. Mr. Sams is upset with Browning Tire Sales. He is aware that the sales agreement stipulated that all sales were final and that no adjustments would be made, but he is convinced that an exception should be allowed since the tires have less than a thousand miles on them.

Write a claim letter for Mr. Sams requesting an adjustment on the tires. Organize the letter in a polite way so as not to antagonize anyone at Browning Tire Sales, Inc.

Text 11A

14. You are the store manager of Boyd's Office Supplies, Inc. For many years you have ordered the majority of your merchandise from Wholesale Office Supplies, Inc.

Recently, you were speaking with a competitor and learned that the competitor receives a 45 percent discount from Wholesale Office Supplies, Inc. This competitor has been in business for only one year.

Write a claim letter to Wholesale Office Supplies, Inc., requesting that your discount be increased from 40 to 45 percent and that the new rate be applied on your last purchase of $3,167.83. Add the facts necessary to make your letter complete.

15. You are the store manager of Tabitha's Apparel. Last week you received a shipment of 48 dresses. You inspected the dresses on their arrival, and all of them seemed to be in excellent condition. Yesterday, as one of your valued customers was trying on a size 12 dress, it was apparent that the dress was no larger than a size 8. Upon closer inspection of the remaining 39 dresses, you found five others that appear to have been sized incorrectly. You would like six replacement dresses as quickly as possible. Write a letter to Connie's Collections requesting these replacements within two weeks. Make the claim message complete by adding necessary facts.

16. You are the director of Westside Shopping Mall. This mall was built by Perrin Construction Company and completed nine months ago. Last week the roof of the mall was damaged by a severe hailstorm. It is your opinion that the roof should have been sturdy enough to withstand the storm. Insurance on the building covers this type of claim, but you do not want your premiums to be increased because the damage appears to be due to poor workmanship on the part of the construction company. Write Perrin Construction Company a claim letter requesting that the roof be repaired immediately to avoid further damage to merchandise in the stores.

17. This past summer you purchased by mail order from MicroCompu an Executive 900 microcomputer for home use. The microcomputer has a 486DX, 50MHz processor with 4 MB of RAM. You purchased this microcomputer primarily for its speed. While using a statistical package on the computer, you find that it does not make the calculations faster than the 286 microcomputer you replaced. Write a letter to MicroCompu explaining that you want to return the microcomputer and be refunded the $1,575 that you paid for it. Supply any additional details that are necessary to make a complete claim letter.

 18. You are the administrative manager of Robert's Lamp Post, a retail store specializing in lighting fixtures. Frequently, you receive shipments of lamps in which several of the fixtures are broken. You would like to develop a claim form letter that could be stored in your word processor and used when returning damaged merchandise. Write this form letter.

ADJUSTMENTS

19. You are the service manager for Bates Heating and Air Conditioning Co. You have just received a letter from Brian Davis, 3197 Poplar Street, Marvell, Arkansas, stating:

I purchased an 11,000 BTU air conditioner from your company two months ago. This unit was guaranteed to cool a 500-square foot room. I am trying to get it to cool a 12- by 20-foot room and have been unsuccessful.

I paid over $475 for this unit, but it will not do the job. I want you to immediately send someone to pick up the unit. Credit my account for the purchase amount.

Write a letter to Mr. Davis informing him that you will have the unit picked up. Explain that next Friday is the earliest date the truck can be there. Because Marvell is 95 miles away, deliveries and pickups are made there only once a week. Express disappointment that the air conditioner did not work, but remind Mr. Davis that at the time of the sale you mentioned that he might need to have his home insulated in order to obtain maximum service from the unit.

20. Dixie Lee Collins purchased a recliner that was manufactured by Comfty Seats. After using it for four months, a tear was noticed in a seam on the armrest. Dixie Lee has written requesting either new upholstery or a full refund for the purchase price of the recliner. As a customer relations specialist for Comfty Seats, write a letter to Dixie Lee asking her to take the recliner to any upholstery shop and get it re-covered. Explain in the letter that the upholstery shop should send you the bill for its services. In addition, you should ask Dixie Lee if she is interested in purchasing a love seat that would complement the recliner and mention that she would receive 40 percent off the regular price.

21. You are owner of Mountain Crafts in Asheville, North Carolina. Deeanna Roberts lives in Broken Arrow, Oklahoma, and purchased an expensive handmade quilt at your store when she was vacationing in Asheville. Ms. Roberts has returned the quilt because she noticed some stains on it when she got home. She has requested that you replace her quilt with a similar one that does not contain any stains.

Write a letter to Ms. Roberts approving her request and informing her that you have received some beautiful handmade baskets that she might be interested in purchasing. Supply any additional details that are necessary to make a complete adjustment.

22. Westrup's Nursery landscaped Pat Freeman's home last fall. Four beautiful 15-foot trees were planted for $575 per tree. A winter storm broke three of the main branches on one of the trees. Pat has requested a replacement tree or a refund for one tree.

As manager of Westrup's Nursery, write a letter to Pat stating that a replacement tree will be planted for her this fall. Suggest that she stop at the nursery and look at a different variety of tree that can withstand more weight on its branches. Of course, there will be no charge to her for the replacement tree.

23. You are Chuck Morgan, operator of Chuck's Catering Service. Recently, you catered a dinner for the Better Health Insurance

Company. Pheasant had been ordered for the main course, but influenza struck your supplier's farm and killed all the pheasants. The company agreed to accept Cornish hens as a substitute. There was no difference in the cost of the two entrees. Better Health Insurance Company has now requested an adjustment of $2 a dinner ($850 total) because it believes the Cornish hens were of lesser value.

Write a letter to Better Health Insurance Company approving the claim for $850. Enclose a check with your letter. Explain the circumstances that led to the change in the entree.

24. Hermitage Coins of Nashville, Tennessee, conducts most of its business by mail order. Periodically, customers return coins stating that the coins do not meet their specifications. This is understandable, since grading of coins is an inexact science. You need to prepare a form letter that could be used in processing these adjustments. Hermitage is willing to make refunds but would prefer to send customers replacement coins.

UNSOLICITED POSITIVE AND NEUTRAL MESSAGES

25. You are initiating a new program to try to reduce the number of sick days that your employees use each year. Employees who complete the year without missing work will have their names entered for a drawing in which one person will win a five-day cruise for two to the Caribbean. Write a memo that could be sent to all employees announcing this program. Add necessary information.

26. American Quality Paper has sales representatives throughout the United States. It has set a goal of increasing its sales 25 percent during the next 12 months. As an incentive to the sales representatives, the company is offering to send the three representatives who increase their sales the most during the 12-month period on an all-expenses-paid trip to Hawaii for five days. Each representative would be permitted one guest. Write a letter to the sales representatives informing them of the promotion. Add any necessary details.

27. You were the chairperson of the fund-raising committee of Ranch for Teens, a nonprofit recreational facility. This year's fund-raising drive collected $100,000 more than the previous year's drive.

Because of this highly successful effort, the directors of the ranch approved the construction of an additional bunkhouse that will allow ten more teenagers to use the facility. Write a letter to the major contributors informing them of this positive news.

28. Clarksville Progressive Business Leaders (CPBL) has been actively involved with Clarksville's educational system. To show its support for higher education, it has decided to award $1,000 scholarships to five Clarksville High School graduates. As the CPBL president, write a letter to the principal, Ms. Louise Hendricks, informing her of the five scholarships and explaining

to her the procedure that will be used to select the winners. Add necessary information.

29. All-Wood Furniture Company makes a line of fine furniture for home use. The company was forced to lay off 34 employees one year ago due to lack of sales. During the past 60 days sales have improved, and warehouse inventories have decreased. This condition has made it possible to recall the 34 employees effective the first of next month. Write a letter to the employees informing them of their recall.

30. Parker Super Mart is a thriving food store with very civic-minded management. It would like to give a free turkey to every senior citizen for Senior Citizen Week. A list of the town's senior citizens has been obtained from the Senior Citizen Organization.

A form letter needs to be written that will announce the program. Write the letter telling each senior citizen that he or she may pick up the turkey or call to have it delivered. Add any necessary information.

MESSAGE ANALYSIS

Correct the following message that has been written to Stan and Sharon Robertson who have been accepted as members of the Cavalier Country Club.

Text 11B

I am extremely pleased to have received your application for membership in the Cavalier Country Club. We are always looking for new members.

We have one of the best country clubs in the area, and we are quite inexpensive. All of our members enjoy playing golf on this wonderful course and relaxing with friends in the comfortable club house.

If we are fortunate enough to continue getting new members, we will be able to expand our course to 18 holes within three years. You need to contact your friends and try to get them to join our club.

Don't forget to send your $50 check for monthly dues by the first of each month. We charge only $550 for an annual membership. You may prefer sending us a $550 check for the entire year.

CHAPTER 12

Negative Messages

Learning Objectives

Your learning objectives for this chapter include the following:

- To describe the nature of negative messages
- To list the advantages of using the indirect plan for effective communication of negative information
- To use the indirect plan competently for a variety of negative messages
- To use the direct plan for negative messages when it is appropriate

A **negative message** is one that is likely to be viewed as unpleasant, disappointing, or unfavorable by the receiver. A negative message, for example, may refuse a request that has been made of you or your organization. The message may provide information about a change in policy that employees do not particularly favor, or a price increase that customers prefer to avoid.

A negative message is a challenge to compose. At the same time, it is an opportunity for you as a writer or speaker to resolve a common business problem successfully. You can even win a friend for yourself or a customer for your organization with an effectively conveyed negative message.

Negative messages give unfavorable information.

USE THE INDIRECT PLAN

The general strategy for conveying all types of negative messages is to use the indirect plan. With the indirect plan, the sentence or the section of the message that conveys the disappointing idea follows reasons that explain why you must refuse a request or why you must provide unfavorable information. The indirect plan prepares your receivers for the negative information. Research has shown that preparing receivers to receive negative information will assist them in accepting it.

Important advantages of the indirect plan are that it enables receivers (1) to accept the negative information you must give them and (2) to maintain a satisfactory relationship with you.

The indirect plan has these advantages because it maintains calm through its gradual approach. It gives time for the receiver's anxiety to subside. The indirect plan affords the opportunity for reason to prevail and for understanding to develop. If the negative information is given first, the receiver may ignore the rest of the message; even a fair, reasonable explanation following the bad news may never be accepted.

If your message is written or spoken thoughtfully and carefully in the you–viewpoint, the receiver may even agree that the negative information is appropriate and acceptable. An effective presentation of the message may clearly show that the negative information is, in fact, in the best interest of the receiver. It may represent a decision that benefits the receiver. The achievement of a positive receiver reaction is your goal in preparing negative messages.

The indirect plan prepares receiver for negative.

Research supports effectiveness of indirect plan.

The indirect plan enables receivers to accept negative information and maintain their relationship with you.

The indirect plan:

• *Maintains calm*

• *Permits reason to prevail*

• *Changes a negative situation to a positive one*

HOW TO USE THE INDIRECT PLAN

In this section specific guides for using the indirect plan for writing negative messages are given. In addition, you will want to use the fundamentals of effective business communication that are presented in Chapters 1, 2, and 3. Figure 12•1 outlines the steps and specific guides for using the indirect plan to present negative information.

There are specific steps in the indirect plan.

Figure 12·1 Indirect Plan
Outline

INDIRECT PLAN FOR NEGATIVE MESSAGES

I. The **Opening Buffer**
  A. Provide coherence.
  B. Build goodwill.
  C. Be positive.
  D. Maintain neutrality.
  E. Introduce the explanation.

II. The **Logical Explanation**
  A. Relate to opening buffer.
  B. Present convincing reasoning.
  C. Stress receiver interests/benefits.
  D. Use de-emphasis techniques.
  E. Be positive.

III. The **Negative Information**
  A. Relate to logical explanation.
  B. Imply or give negative information explicitly.
  C. Use de-emphasis techniques.
  D. Give negative information quickly.
  E. Be positive.
  F. Say what can be done (not what cannot).
  G. Avoid an apology.

IV. The **Constructive Follow-Up**
  A. Provide alternative solution and/or
  B. Give additional reasoning.

V. The **Friendly Close**
  A. Build goodwill.
  B. Personalize the close.
  C. Stay off negative subject.
  D. Be warm.
  E. Be optimistic.

The indirect plan can be used effectively for a variety of different kinds of both written and oral negative messages—refused claims, refused requests, unfavorable decisions, or any unpleasant information. Written messages are shown in this chapter to illustrate clearly the use of the indirect plan for negative messages.

DETERMINING CONTENT

The situation must be analyzed before the indirect plan is implemented.

Each communication situation must first be analyzed to determine (1) primary and secondary purposes, and (2) the basic content of the message. The following questions must be answered for negative messages: What ideas can I use in the opening to establish coherence and build goodwill in this particular situation? Why is it in the receiver's interest for me to refuse the request or present the unfavorable information? Is there an alternative course of action that I can recommend to this receiver? What friendly message can I convey in the off-the-subject close?

Once you have determined the purposes and content of the negative message, you are ready to implement the indirect plan. In the following sections, the indirect plan outline is discussed; and the most important considerations are reviewed.

OPENING BUFFER

Use the opening buffer to:

• Provide coherence

• Build goodwill

• Be positive

• Maintain neutrality

• Introduce the explanation

In the indirect plan, the opening buffer should meet the following requirements: provide coherence, build goodwill, be positive, maintain neutrality, and introduce the explanation. The opening buffer usually will consist of one to three sentences. It will serve as the first paragraph in a memo or a letter.

To provide coherence, the opening buffer puts you and your receiver on the same wavelength. The negative message is tied to some common ground—a previous conversation, a point of agreement, a memo or letter received earlier, a prior transaction, or some other common ground.

You will want to build goodwill by using courteous, polite words such as *thank you, please,* and *appreciate,* and by keeping the receiver's interests central to your opening buffer. Use positive words; avoid negative words. Using positive words helps set a favorable tone and makes your message more acceptable to the receiver. It is possible, in fact desirable, to compose negative messages without using a single negative word.

The two final requirements for a good opening buffer—maintain neutrality and introduce the explanation—are closely related. You will want your receiver to read through the opening buffer into the logical explanation that follows. You do not want to give away the negative information in the opening. Therefore, the opening buffer should not imply either a yes or a no. It should not lead the receiver in either direction; it should be neutral.

The final requirement of the opening buffer is to set the stage for the explanation, that is, introduce the explanation. In the last sentence of the buffer, give your receiver some indication of the thrust of the explanation. In effect, give the receiver the "headline" for the explanation that follows in the next paragraph(s). This sets up the strategy for the logical explanation, which is the next part of your message, and it assists in providing coherence.

LOGICAL EXPLANATION

Logical explanation follows the opening buffer and precedes the negative information.

The second part of the indirect plan is the logical explanation. In a memo or letter, the logical explanation usually begins after the opening buffer and often can be handled in one paragraph. If the explanation is short, the negative information may be included in the same paragraph. In some situations the constructive follow-up can immediately follow the negative information in the same paragraph. This buries the negativeness in the middle of a paragraph. In other written message situations the logical explanation may be so long that it requires two or more paragraphs.

The logical explanation:
- Justifies the negative information.

One of the most important aspects of the indirect plan is that the reasoning that justifies the negative information is presented *before* the negative information. After the opening buffer, you present the reasons explaining why you must convey the negative information. If at all possible, these reasons should show how the negative information will be in the best interest of your receiver. This reasoning, in order to be effective, must be presented in a calm, convincing, and pleasant manner using the you–viewpoint.

Communication Quotes

When people are informed and understand the reasons for a course of action, they are more likely to both accept and support the action. If they have been a part of the process, they may be able to help move a course of action that will result in more positive news.

Mrs. Ellen R. Gordon, President of Tootsie Roll Industries, Inc.

The specific requirements for the logical explanation are that it relates coherently to the opening buffer, presents convincing reasoning, stresses receiver interests/benefits, uses emphasis techniques, and is positive.

- Provides coherence

The opening buffer will have introduced the explanation. The beginning of the logical explanation should use coherence techniques to relate it to the opening and facilitate the flow of thought. You may use repetition of key words, a tie-in sentence, or some other coherence technique to ensure that the logical explanation follows the opening.

- Presents convincing reasoning

The convincing reasoning, which supports the unfavorable information, should be composed with the receiver's interests or benefits as the focal points. The receiver's favorable reactions to the words you choose will be your goal. In fact, if at the end of the reasoning the receiver agrees that the negative information represents the best alternative in this situation, you will have composed the ideal negative message.

Although the ideal logical explanation presents the reasoning in terms of receiver benefit, circumstances will not always permit you to compose the ideal message. You may have to base your reasoning on what is fair for all concerned. Also, there may be occasions when confidentiality precludes giving any specific reasons. In these situations, you will want to communicate convincingly and persuasively that the matter was carefully considered in the interest of the receiver before the decision was reached.

- Uses rules of emphasis

You will want to use rules of emphasis in the logical explanation. Start with the points that are most favorable to your receiver; and, as you move deeper into the paragraph, deal with the least favorable aspects of your reasoning.

- Accents positiveness

Finally, the logical explanation should be positive. Avoid all negative words, if possible. For example, use *situation* instead of *problem* and *needed change* instead of *correction*. In referring to the problem, avoid such words as *failure, cannot, trouble, inadequate,* and *defective.*

NEGATIVE INFORMATION

After the opening buffer and the logical explanation, you are ready to present the negative information. This step in the indirect plan consists of the request refusal, unfavorable decision, or other disappointing information. If the opening buffer and the logical explanation have been effective, receivers will be expecting the negative information. In fact, in most circumstances, it is possible for you to prepare your receivers so well that they will easily accept the information, refusal, or decision.

The primary goal in presenting negative information is to be sure that the receiver clearly understands this part of your message. In communicating with Americans, Europeans, Australians, and others with similar cultures, you will want to clearly imply or explicitly state your decision. Wording such as ". . . therefore, it would seem better for you to follow the company policy" may leave a question in the mind of your receiver. With this lack of clarity, the receiver may think that the decision is still up for discussion or that he or she could decide what to do. However, in many parts of the world—Asia and Latin America, for example—people prefer a lack of clarity because it makes the moment more pleasant.

> ### Communication Notes
>
> #### They Don't Say "No" in Asia
> In Thailand, there is no word for *no.* In Japan, there are over 20 ways to avoid saying *no* directly. The Koreans try to avoid giving bad news. Asians answer practically all questions either with *yes* or *maybe.* If you ask, "Do you want to buy this product?" you may get a *yes* that means "I heard your question." *Yes* does not always mean *yes* in Asia.

Even with the cultures that prefer more directness and clarity, it is desirable in most circumstances to imply the negative information clearly. It softens the bad news and permits you to present negative information in a positive manner. For example, "Smoking is permitted in the hallways only" is much more acceptable to most people than "Smoking is prohibited in the classrooms and offices." These statements both say basically the same thing; the first just says it positively. For effective communication of negative information, it is better to say what can be done rather than what cannot be done.

There are situations when the negative information should be given in explicit terms. These are the times when you believe that an implied refusal would not be strong enough or might be misunderstood by your receiver. In the case of rejection of admission to a college, for example, it may not be possible to imply the refusal. In this type of situation, it is better to present the logical explanation and then explicitly state the refusal in clear terms, ". . . therefore, the committee has disapproved your application for admission." This wording can leave no doubt in the receiver's mind. In most cases, though, you will want to imply the negative information to reduce its emphasis.

The recommended placement of the negative information section of the message is immediately following the logical explanation. In a written

De-emphasize the negative
information by placing it in the
middle of a paragraph.

message, never place the negative information in a separate paragraph. In order to de-emphasize the negative information, it should be in the middle of a paragraph. It may be followed by an additional reason or suggested alternative(s). This placement would tuck the negative information inside the paragraph and de-emphasize it.

The negative information should be given quickly in as few words as possible. Ideally, you can further de-emphasize the unfavorable news by placing it in a dependent clause. As in all sections of a negative message, you will want to use positive words and avoid negative words—say what can be done and not what cannot be done. Also, in most cases you will want to avoid negative apologies throughout the message because they only call further attention to the negativeness of the situation. Do not use apologies such as, "I am sorry I must refuse your request."

In summary, negative information is implied clearly or stated explicitly, follows the logical explanation, uses techniques to de-emphasize it, is given quickly, is positive, says what can be done, and avoids apologies. After giving the negative information, your next step in the indirect plan is to provide constructive follow-up.

CONSTRUCTIVE FOLLOW-UP

Constructive follow-up consists
of other solutions or additional
justification.

In the constructive follow-up section of a negative message, you provide other solutions to the problem or, if that is not possible, you give an additional reason justifying the unfavorable news.

For example, one good way to strengthen your communication and to build improved human relations is to do more than is expected by offering an alternative solution to the receiver. If you were asked to return to your high school on October 24 to speak to seniors about attending college and your schedule would not permit you to do so, you could suggest an alternative speaker or an alternative date. Even though you have to refuse the request, your suggested alternative may solve the problem and maintain effective human relations. In the case of adjustment refusals, you can make a special offer or resell the customer on the product or service.

If you cannot suggest an alternative or offer a solution to the problem, it will be important for you to save part of the logical explanation and place it following the negative information. This helps the receiver accept the bad news by de-emphasizing its importance and giving him or her additional justification for it.

FRIENDLY CLOSE

The friendly close moves the receiver's mind away from the problem—the negative information—and provides an opportunity to build goodwill. If you must refuse a customer credit, you will want him or her to continue to buy with cash. If you have to refuse an employee's request, you will want to maintain good human relations and not reduce the employee's productivity.

• Builds goodwill

You can build goodwill in the friendly close by ensuring that it is personalized, off the subject, warm, and optimistic. The wording of the friendly close should fit the receiver and the particular situation. It could make further reference to the constructive follow-up, or it could express appreciation to a customer for his or her business.

• Is off the subject

The friendly close should not include anything that reminds the receiver of the negative information you have given. It should be off the subject of the negative information. The friendly close should not include a final negative apology such as, "Again, let me say how sorry I am that we cannot honor your claim." This only reminds the receiver of the problem. Off-the-subject possibilities can include any friendly remark appropriate to your receiver. The prime requirement for the friendly close is to regain the goodwill that may have been lost due to the negative information.

IMPLEMENTING THE INDIRECT PLAN

A communication situation will help illustrate ways to compose negative messages.

The step-by-step development of a memo to an employee who must be given negative information shows clearly how the indirect plan works. Although negative messages often are best sent orally, a written message will be developed for this case to clearly illustrate the content. Here are the details of the communication situation:

The Amy Mills Case: Amy Mills, an interoffice courier under your supervision, has written you a memo requesting that on a regular basis she be permitted to arrive for work at 9 a.m.—an hour late. She is having problems securing day-care services for her two children. An important part of Amy's job is regular courier service throughout the office. Since it is critical to the operation of the office that her first run start at 8 a.m., you must refuse her request. Your task is to write a memo conveying the negative information to her and, at the same time, to make that information acceptable and maybe even desirable for her. Amy is an excellent worker. You want her available during the regular working hours.

DETERMINE APPROPRIATE CONTENT

The first step in writing a message is to determine its purposes and content. The primary purpose of your memo to Amy Mills will be to convey clearly the negative information, and the secondary purpose is to make that information acceptable and maybe even desirable for her. The content of the memo must be developed and organized for each step in the indirect plan. Examples of poor and good content you could decide to use are illustrated in the following sections.

WRITE EFFECTIVE OPENING BUFFER

The five qualities of a good opening buffer described previously can best be illustrated for this communication situation through contrasting examples.

An example of a **poor** opening buffer for a memo in response to Amy's request is as follows:

> It would be very inconvenient for the company for you to come in late. Please make arrangements to be on time.

In analyzing this poor opening buffer, note the lack of you–viewpoint and absence of goodwill. Also, receiver interests are ignored. This poor example provides coherence in a negative way by referring to Amy's request as one ". . . to come in late." Finally, this opening buffer reveals the negative answer to the request immediately. There is no motivation for Amy to read the logical explanation which is to follow the opening.

An example of a **good** opening buffer for this situation is:

> Amy, thank you for your memo about your work schedule. You have been doing an excellent job as a courier, and resolving your situation so you can continue your effective service is important to all of us.

In contrast to the poor opening buffer, this paragraph effectively meets all the requirements of a good buffer for a negative message. It provides coherence by concretely acknowledging Amy's memo and its subject matter. It does this in a positive, appreciative way by thanking her for sending the ". . . memo about your work schedule."

Goodwill is further built through commending her for her work in the company. This good opening buffer is neutral—it does not say yes or no to her request. It introduces the logical explanation by suggesting that a discussion of Amy's situation and service will follow.

PROVIDE A CONVINCING LOGICAL EXPLANATION

The next step in the indirect plan is to build on the opening buffer with a logical explanation justifying the negative information. A **poor** logical explanation to Amy might read as follows:

> Company policy requires that all employees report to work at 8 a.m. Your pay would be docked if you were to come in late; and eventually you might be the subject of punitive action. We need you to be here on time.

> *You'll never get mixed up if you simply tell the truth. Then you don't have to remember what you have said, and you never forget what you have said.*
>
> **Sam Rayburn**

This logical explanation shows—as did the poor opening buffer—a lack of positiveness and you–viewpoint. This poorly worded explanation illustrates a basic error commonly found in negative messages: it resorts to hiding behind company policy. In a negative message involving company policy, the justification for the policy and its existence should be stated as a part of the reasoning. Finally, the most positive part of this poor logical explanation, "We need you . . . ." is stated in the we–viewpoint!

Conversely, a **good** logical explanation for this communication situation could read as follows:

> The high quality of your work as a courier has been possible for at least three reasons: (1) your interest in and enjoyment of the work, (2) your commitment to promptness and thoroughness during your rounds, and (3) the scheduling of your work at the time it is most needed—during regular working hours. The flow of work in the office depends on this kind of courier service.

This logical explanation coherently follows the good opening buffer by picking up on the ideas ". . . doing an excellent job . . ." and ". . . continuing your effective service . . .." This good logical explanation concentrates on Amy's commitment to doing a good job and the need for her to be there during regular working hours. The most positive ideas are presented early in the paragraph with a gradual movement to less positive ideas. This is an effective use of the rules of emphasis. It is important to note that not a single negative word was used in this example.

After reading this logical explanation, Amy may feel that it is in her interest for you to tell her she has to be at work at 8 a.m. regularly so that she can continue to do a good job. At least, she will believe you have presented her with a fair, logical explanation. She will be prepared for the negative information that will be presented to her next.

GIVE NEGATIVE INFORMATION POSITIVELY

A **poor** way to tell Amy that you must refuse her request follows:

> I am sorry that I am forced to tell you that you have to be at work at 8 a.m.

This poor presentation states the negative information explicitly.

This is an explicit rather than an implied statement. It is written in the I–viewpoint rather than the you–viewpoint, and has overemphasized the problem by using negative words (*sorry, forced,* and *have to*) in an apology.

A **good** way to refuse Amy's request is:

This good presentation implies the negative information and stresses what can be done.

> Since your continued excellent performance requires that you be at work at 8 a.m., I want to assist you in any way I can in making the necessary arrangements to do so.

This presentation of negative information clearly implies the refusal. It also builds on the quality of Amy's work and your interest in helping her continue her service to the company. The refusal is de-emphasized by being placed in a dependent, introductory clause. The emphasis is on what can be done (not what cannot)—you are willing to assist her in making the arrangements to be on time. Instead of an apology, which would emphasize the negativeness of the situation, positive words express optimism that the problem can be solved.

Because you prepared Amy to receive negative information, this refusal will likely be acceptable to her. In fact, as suggested earlier, she may prefer the decision you have given her instead of the decision she originally requested. You have told her she is doing a good job, she is important, and she is needed at a particular time so that the work flow can function properly. She also knows you respect her because you took time to explain your refusal.

ASSIST RECEIVER WITH CONSTRUCTIVE FOLLOW-UP

Is there an alternative solution you can suggest to Amy Mills in the communication situation? The following is an example of a **poor** constructive follow-up section of your memo to Amy:

> I hope you can get your day-care problems worked out.

A **good** constructive follow-up section would be:

> Betty Marine, my secretary, uses the ABC Child Care Center in the building next to ours. She said it is highly respected, and her child likes the Center very much. Betty checked and found it has openings for additional children now.

This constructive follow-up suggests a possible solution for Amy Mills. If it is not the permanent solution she wants, it is at least one she could use temporarily. You will note the good suggested alternative is longer than the poor suggested alternative. This is often true of you–viewpoint writing or speaking. In order to achieve the overall goal of effective business communication, the additional effort and additional words are worthwhile.

BUILD GOODWILL IN FRIENDLY CLOSE

The last part of the indirect plan is the friendly close. A **poor** friendly close for Amy's memo might read this way:

The poor friendly close contains a negative final apology.

Again, Amy, let me say I am sorry I have to require you to be at work at 8 a.m. If I can be of any further help, please let me know.

Obviously, the apology serves no purpose other than to remind Amy of the negative information she has received. In fact, it is re-emphasized; and you do not want to do that. Also, the last sentence in the poor example appears to offer the kind of help she really does not need.

A **good** friendly close for Amy's memo is as follows:

Please contact Betty if you would like further information on the ABC Child Care Center. It appears to be a good alternative for you.

Your excellent work is appreciated, and I hope you stay with Worldwide Movers for many years to come!

The good friendly close is in the you–viewpoint and builds goodwill.

This friendly close meets all requirements. It builds goodwill. It is personalized, warm, and optimistic. It also meets the important requirement of being off the subject—it does not refer to the negative information.

SUMMARY—POOR AND GOOD MEMOS TO AMY MILLS

In reviewing how to write effective negative messages, two example memos—one poor and one good—have been presented. Both of these memos carry the refusal in response to Amy's request to begin work at 9 a.m. instead of 8 a.m. The **poor** memo (see Figure 12•2) shows a failure to use proven communication guides that enhance understanding and acceptance of negative messages. Also, the poor memo fails to use the indirect plan of presentation of the message.

Contrasting memos to Amy Mills are presented in Illustrations 12•2 and 12•3.

The **good** memo to Amy shown in Figure 12•3 incorporates recommended guidelines for effective business communication. The good memo shows how the indirect plan, properly implemented, builds goodwill and improves human relations.

To illustrate further how the guides apply to actual business situations, several other examples of poor and good negative messages are examined in the following pages.

REQUEST REFUSALS

Business firms frequently receive requests—for example, a request from a senior citizens' organization for a contribution to its greenhouse project or a request from a local Boy Scout troop to use a bank's community meeting room on the first Wednesday night of each month. Many of these requests are reasonable, and companies will want to respond positively.

Businesses receive many requests.

Sometimes, however, a **request refusal**—a denial of something asked for—must be sent when it is not possible to grant a request. For example, the company receiving the senior citizens' request may budget all charitable contributions once a year; therefore, no allocation is available at the time of the request. The company must then refuse this worthy request—at least at this time. The constructive follow-up in this negative message might be that

Some requests must be refused.

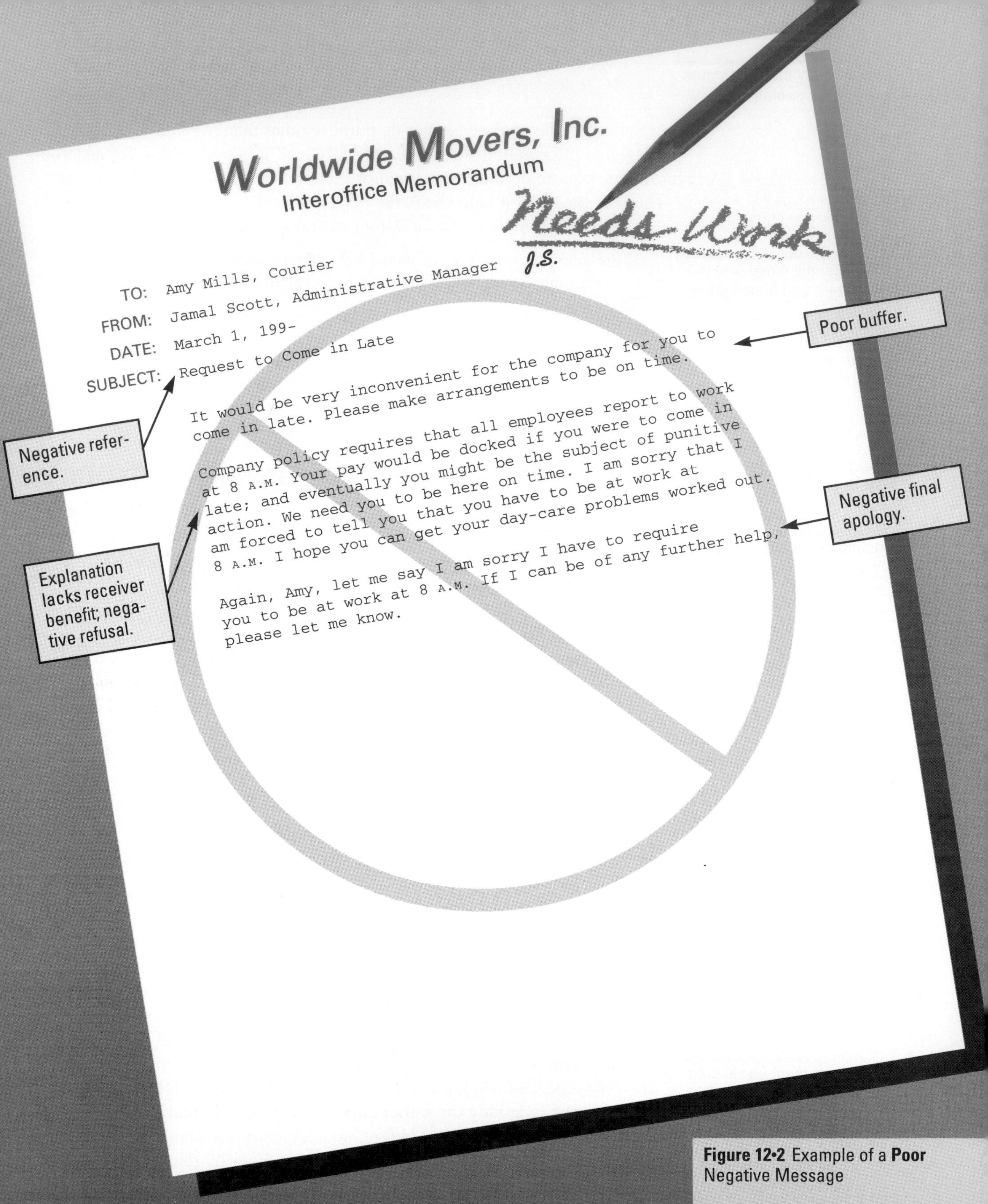

Worldwide Movers, Inc.
Interoffice Memorandum

Needs Work
J.S.

TO: Amy Mills, Courier

FROM: Jamal Scott, Administrative Manager

DATE: March 1, 199-

SUBJECT: Request to Come in Late

It would be very inconvenient for the company for you to come in late. Please make arrangements to be on time.

Company policy requires that all employees report to work at 8 A.M. Your pay would be docked if you were to come in late; and eventually you might be the subject of punitive action. We need you to be here on time. I am sorry that I am forced to tell you that you have to be at work at 8 A.M. I hope you can get your day-care problems worked out.

Again, Amy, let me say I am sorry I have to require you to be at work at 8 A.M. If I can be of any further help, please let me know.

[Annotation callouts:]
- Poor buffer.
- Negative reference.
- Explanation lacks receiver benefit; negative refusal.
- Negative final apology.

Figure 12·2 Example of a **Poor** Negative Message

Worldwide Movers, Inc.
Interoffice Memorandum

GOOD

TO: Amy Mills, Courier

FROM: Jamal Scott, Administrative Manager *J.S.*

DATE: March 1, 199-

SUBJECT: Your Work Schedule

Amy, thank you for your memo about your work schedule. You have been doing an excellent job as a courier, and resolving your situation so you can continue your effective service is important to all of us.

The high quality of your work as a courier has been possible for at least three reasons: (1) your interest in and enjoyment of the work, (2) your commitment to promptness and thoroughness during your rounds, and (3) the scheduling of your work at the time it is most needed—during regular working hours. The flow of work in the office depends on this kind of courier service. Since your continued excellent performance requires that you be at work at 8 A.M., I want to assist you in any way I can in making the necessary arrangements to do so. Betty Marine, my secretary, uses the ABC Child Care Center in the building next to ours. She said it is highly respected, and her child likes the Center very much. Betty checked and found it has openings for additional children now.

Please contact Betty if you would like further information on the ABC Child Care Center. It appears to be a good alternative for you.

Your excellent work is appreciated, and I hope you stay with Worldwide Movers for many years to come!

Annotations:
- Positive reference.
- Good opening buffer.
- You–viewpoint is reassuring.
- The negative information is de-emphasized.
- Alternative suggested.
- Goodwill and off-the-subject close.

Figure 12•3 Example of a **Good** Negative Message

the company will be glad to consider the request when the next budget is planned.

In the case of the local Boy Scout troop's request to use the bank's meeting room, this use may be exactly the type the bank intended for the meeting room. However, if the room is scheduled for use by the League of Women Voters on the first Wednesday night of each month, the bank must refuse the request. The bank, if possible, will suggest an alternative night for the Boy Scouts.

In any request refusal situation, it will be important to a business to maintain goodwill. At the same time, the business has to send a message that the receiver does not want to receive. Effective use of the indirect plan will make the refusal more acceptable.

Here is another situation that illustrates the use of the indirect plan for a request refusal: Assume you are a program coordinator of the Advanced Learning Center at your school. The Center sponsors educational seminars. A seminar entitled "Improving Your Business Writing Skills" is scheduled for the 15th of next month. The number of participants is limited to 25; more than 40 registrations have been received. You must write to those whose registrations cannot be accepted. A form letter is the easiest way to accomplish this task. Figure 12•4 shows a **poor** form letter for this situation.

The **good** form letter for this request refusal, shown in Figure 12•5, builds goodwill by explaining the situation and suggesting alternatives to the registrants.

ADJUSTMENT REFUSALS

Handling customer claims is a common problem for business firms. These claims include requests to exchange merchandise, requests for refunds, requests that work be corrected, and other requests for adjustments. Most of these claims are granted because they are legitimate. However, some requests for adjustment must be denied, and an **adjustment refusal** message, a rejection of a customer's claim, must be sent. Adjustment refusals are negative messages for the customer. They are necessary when the customer is at fault or the vendor has done all that can reasonably or legally be expected.

An adjustment refusal message requires your best communication skills because it is bad news to the receiver. You have to refuse the claim and at the same time retain the customer. You may refuse the request for adjustment and even try to sell the customer more merchandise or service. All this is happening when the customer is probably angry or at least inconvenienced.

You will want to use the indirect plan effectively for the presentation of this negative information. As a case in point, consider a customer who wants to return a defective boat that she bought on sale. Figure 12•6 shows a **poor** letter in which the boat dealer fails to implement the indirect plan and probably makes an enemy.

On the other hand, the same basic message can be written using the indirect plan and result in keeping a good customer. Figure 12•7 is a **good** example of how this letter refusing the return of the boat should have been written. (This is the letter that was developed in Chapter 3 on page 75.)

CREDIT REFUSALS

Buying on credit is common today. Most businesses permit and even encourage qualified customers to buy on credit. It is a strategy that increases sales.

Customers who have good credit ratings or who have sufficient assets for collateral will be granted credit. Customers who have problems paying their bills or who own nothing of sufficient value to use as backup may be refused credit. A message rejecting a request for credit is called a **credit refusal.** The receivers of credit refusals may be offended.

Business firms attempt to communicate credit refusals in a manner that makes the answer acceptable and helpful to the customer. Businesses want to do this out of common decency and also because they want to continue to serve the customer on a cash basis if possible.

Credit refusals are communicated in the following four basic ways: (1) personalized letters, (2) form letters, (3) telephone calls, or (4) face-to-face conversations. In all these cases the indirect plan is used for communicating the credit refusal.

Figure 12•8 is a **poor** example of a personalized letter in which a department store refuses to issue a customer a credit card. The indirect plan is not used in this letter.

An improved letter for this circumstance is shown in Figure 12•9, a **good** example of the use of the indirect plan for a credit refusal. A mutually

Advanced Learning Center
Georgeville College
One College Way/Galesburg, IL 61401-7723/(309) 555-7

Needs Work

March 1, 199-

Dear Registrant

Your check to cover the cost of registering for our seminar, "Improving Your Business Writing Skills," is enclosed. The check arrived after the class limit was reached.

Thank you for your interest in this program; we hope you will try to register for this seminar the next time it is offered.

Sincerely

Michelle Edwards

Michelle Edwards
Program Coordinator

dfm

Enclosure

> Poor request refusal lacks coherence and clearness.

> Explanation not logical or meaningful.

> Suggested alternative not helpful.

Figure 12•4 Example of a **Poor** Request Refusal (Form Letter)

Advanced Learning Center
Georgeville College
One College Way/Galesburg, IL 61401-7723/(309...

GOOD

March 1, 199-

Dear Registrant

Thank you for the interest you have shown in our seminar entitled, "Improving Your Business Writing Skills." The seminar is an extremely popular one; over 40 people have submitted registration forms.

One of the reasons this seminar is so popular is that the leaders believe in giving each participant individual attention. To be sure this occurs, seminar enrollment is limited to 25 participants. Registrations were processed on a first-come, first-served basis, and the 25-person class size limit was reached before your form and check arrived. Your check is, therefore, enclosed with this letter. Your name and phone number have been placed on our waiting list; if an opening becomes available, we will notify you immediately.

The Advanced Learning Center is committed to providing seminars that meet the needs of the business leaders in this area. The enclosed brochure lists the courses that will be offered during the next three months. If you would like additional information about any of them, please call collect (309) 555-7800.

Sincerely

Michelle Edwards

Michelle Edwards
Program Coordinator

dfm

Enclosures

> Good request refusal has coherence and a neutral opening.

> Logical explanation stresses receiver's interests and benefits.

> The negative information implied.

> Helpful alternative suggested.

> Off-the-subject, friendly close.

Figure 12-5 Example of a **Good** Request Refusal (Form Letter)

THE BOATWRIGHT, INC.
4000 West Broadway Avenue
Jackson, MS 39200-1712
(601) 555-1000

Needs Work

April 30, 199-

Ms. Carrie Hagen
3132 First Street
Oxford, MS 38655-2284

Dear Ms. Hagen:

We are sorry we cannot honor your request for a refund for the defective boat you recently purchased from us. Our sales policy, widely known in this area, has always been to refuse refunds for any items sold on sale.

It would cut our profit if we were to give refunds on sale items. We are always willing to give refunds on non-sale items. We have signs posted throughout the store on our sales policy. Also, our clerks are supposed to use our rubber stamp which says "Sorry, no refunds on sale items" on each sales slip during sales.

Again, let us say we are sorry that you didn't notice our policy and that we can't give you a refund for the defective boat. We would encourage you to come in and buy a repair kit from us.

Sincerely yours,

Roscoe Lopez

Roscoe Lopez
Store Manager

rs

> Poor letter gives negative information first (direct approach), is negative, talks down to receiver.

> Explanation not in you–viewpoint; not logical.

> Negative final apology; constructive follow-up poorly written and out of proper sequence.

Figure 12•6 Example of a **Poor** Adjustment Refusal Letter

THE BOATWRIGHT, INC.
4000 West Broadway Avenue
Jackson, MS 39200-1712
(601) 555-1000

GOOD

Good letter has coherence; builds goodwill.

Positive.

Neutral opening introduces explanation.

April 30, 199-

Ms. Carrie Hagen
3132 First Street
Oxford, MS 38655-2284

Dear Ms. Hagen:

Your recent purchase of a Blue Waters Ski Boat is appreciated. You have chosen a high-quality ski boat that can give you many years of enjoyment. We want to ensure that enjoyment is possible for you with your new boat.

You made a wise decision when you bought a Blue Waters Ski Boat during the "Save 33 Percent" sale. The tremendous savings of almost $2,000 that you realized on this purchase were made possible in two ways: (1) We buy merchandise in large volume, and (2) we cut overhead and pass the savings on to the customer. One of the ways we cut overhead is to make all sales final on items purchased during the "Save 33 Percent" sale. We make every effort to be sure all our customers are aware of this policy by noting it in all advertisements and posting signs throughout the store.

Convincing reasoning positively presented; receiver benefits stressed; negative information implied and de-emphasized.

You will be glad to know that the repair needed on your Blue Waters Ski Boat is easy to make. For only $39.95 you can purchase a fiberglass repair kit that has complete directions for its use. You can either "do-it-yourself" or have our expert shop take care of it for you at cost. Please call us collect at (601) 555-1000 and tell us your preference.

Alternative solution suggested; writer does more than expected.

Best wishes for many happy hours of skiing this summer on Oxford Lake.

Goodwill, off-the-subject close.

Sincerely yours,

Roscoe Lopez

Roscoe Lopez
Store Manager

rs

Figure 12·7 Example of a **Good** Adjustment Refusal Letter

Roth & Hilt

Clothing for the Entire Family

200 North Main Street   San Fernando, CA 01340-2277   (714) ___-___33

Needs Work

March 1, 199-

Ms. Fredericka Shepple
9872 South Rios Drive
San Fernando, CA 91340-3491

Dear Ms. Shepple:

I am sorry to inform you that Roth and Hilt cannot issue a credit card to you at this time. We would like to issue a credit card to you, but our store policy does not permit us to issue credit to college students.

College students do not have full-time employment and may not be able to pay their bills at the end of the month. The majority of students are temporary residents, and we cannot take a chance on someone leaving town with unpaid bills. We know that you may not be this type of individual, but we cannot take a chance.

Again, let me say that I am sorry that we cannot issue credit to you. If you are in need of school clothing or supplies, please stop at Roth and Hilt to do your shopping.

Sincerely,

Nancy Jones

Nancy Jones
Credit Manager

htc

Poor letter's negative opening gives bad news; not in you–viewpoint.

Not personalized or in you–viewpoint; negative.

No constructive follow-up to the negative news; negative final apology; poor reselling.

Figure 12•8 Example of a **Poor** Credit Refusal Letter

Roth & Hilt

Clothing for the Entire Family

San Fernando, CA 01340-2277

(714) 555-333█

200 North Main Street

March 1, 199-

Ms. Fredericka Shepple
9872 South Rios Drive
San Fernando, CA 91340-3491

Dear Ms. Shepple:

Your interest in obtaining a Roth and Hilt credit card is sincerely appreciated. Our aim is always to give you the best service possible.

Because your satisfaction is most important to us, your credit application was processed immediately. While processing your credit application, our credit department learned that you are a full-time student at California State University. The credit reference portion of your credit application was left blank. Roth and Hilt grants credit to individuals who are employed and who can provide a minimum of two good credit references. When you obtain part-time or full-time employment and resubmit an application listing two credit references, we will be most happy to reevaluate your request.

Roth and Hilt is always in touch with the latest in college fashions. A large shipment of the newest Easter fashions will be arriving next week. Please stop in to select a special outfit for the spring festivities.

Congratulations on being selected a cheerleader for California State. Your performance must be one of the reasons that CSU's football team has such an outstanding record.

Sincerely,

Nancy Jones

Nancy Jones
Credit Manager

htc

Annotation callouts:

- Good opening buffer builds goodwill; is neutral.
- Explanation logical; stresses receiver interests.
- Negative news implied.
- Alternative solution.
- Resells.
- Friendly, off-the-subject close; warm and personalized.

Figure 12·9 Example of a **Good** Credit Refusal Letter

satisfactory business relationship could develop from this credit refusal. The customer should not be offended by the credit refusal in Figure 12•9.

UNSOLICITED NEGATIVE MESSAGES

Sometimes businesses must initiate negative messages.

Not all negative messages are in response to a request or an inquiry. An **unsolicited negative message** is a bad news message initiated by the businessperson. Examples of such unsolicited negative messages include communications about price increases for products or services, budget reductions, and staff reductions (layoffs). These messages are especially difficult to compose because they initiate the bad news.

In Figure 12•10, you can feel the negative impact of the **poor** interoffice memo informing employees of a reduction in their insurance benefits. The indirect plan and the guides for its implementation were not used.

Figure 12•11, a **good** example of an unsolicited negative message, shows how the same information can be conveyed in a more acceptable manner. Employees are not going to be happy about the reduction, but at least the situation is more acceptable when the indirect plan is used. There is no need for a communicator to anger, disturb, or hurt receivers—intentionally or inadvertently—through poorly conveyed messages.

USE THE DIRECT PLAN WHEN APPROPRIATE

The direct plan gives negative information first.

You are already familiar with the direct plan for message preparation; that is, the main idea of the message is conveyed in the first sentences. There are occasions when the direct plan is used for negative messages—when the negative information is given first. Your analysis of the situation and the receiver will help you determine when you can use the direct plan.

The direct plan may be used:
• For some receivers

You may use the direct plan when you know your receiver prefers to learn the bad news first and the good news later. For example, if your receiver's personality is the type that prefers directness, use the direct approach.

• For routine information

You may also use the direct plan when the negative information is routine and will not be upsetting to your receiver. For example, a receiver will not be upset to learn that a nonessential meeting has been canceled.

• To emphasize sorrow

Another instance in which the direct plan may be used is when you want to emphasize how sorry you are about the negative situation. An example of this is a sympathy note sent regarding a death or tragedy.

• For situations involving ethics

In another situation, ethical behavior may be the issue and directness would strengthen a negative message and regain the trust of the customer. An example is an automobile service center billing for work that is covered by warranty. A message dealing with this ethical problem should use the direct approach and include an apology. Figure 12•12 is an example of a **poor** negative message using the direct plan that likely will not resolve the ethical problem or regain customer trust. Figure 12•13 provides an example of a **good** negative message using the direct plan that should regain trust and correct the problem.

• To emphasize negative information

Another instance in which the direct plan may be used for negative messages is when the negative information needs to be emphasized. Maybe you have previously told your receiver that you could not continue to sell to him or her if past-due invoices were not paid, but the message was misunderstood or not accepted. The direct plan will emphasize the negative message you must send in this situation.

In most negative message situations, however, you will want to use the indirect order of presentation because of its many advantages.

International Machine Tools, Inc.

Needs Work

Interoffice Memo

Employees of International Machine Tools

TO: Employees of International Machine Tools

FROM: Haru Okano, Personnel Manager *H.O.*

DATE: January 23, 199-

SUBJECT: Reduced Insurance Benefits

It is my unfortunate duty to inform you that insurance benefits for employees' dependents will be eliminated as of March 1.

I know that this reduction comes at a bad time since inflation is eating up so much of our paychecks. We must cut your benefits in order for our company to make a profit for our shareholders. This benefit reduction will reduce the company's insurance costs $250,000. This will give us the opportunity to pay higher dividends to our stockholders.

Again, let me say that I am sorry that you will have to provide your own insurance coverage for your dependents. If you need help in finding an insurance company that can provide you with coverage, please contact me.

gh

> Opening gives negative information explicitly and negatively.

> Lacks you—viewpoint (receiver's interest ignored); negative.

> Close not off-the-subject; limited offer to help.

Figure 12•10 Example of a **Poor** Unsolicited Negative Memo

Interoffice Memo

International Machine Tools, Inc.

TO: Employees of International Machine Tools

FROM: Haru Okano, Personnel Manager *H.O.*

DATE: January 23, 199-

SUBJECT: Your Insurance Benefits

The insurance benefits that you receive are superior to those of employees of most machine tool companies in this area. Since the fringe benefits that you receive are tax free, you have more take-home pay. In your interest, International Machine Tools plans to maintain this competitive position.

The nation's economy, however, is currently in a fluctuating period. Our company is facing the challenge of maintaining our quality products at a competitive price while providing adequate salaries and security for employees. To maintain our current number of employees and continue paying competitive wages, the dependents' hospitalization coverage must be discontinued. All employees will continue to have coverage under the $50,000 life insurance policy and the $100 deductible hospitalization plan.

Dependent hospitalization coverage will still be available from our same insurance company at a 25 percent savings for International Machine Tools' employees. An insurance representative will be available in the conference room all day on Thursday, January 30, to answer any questions you may have.

There are optimistic signs that the nation's economy is turning around. By working together we can all look forward to good years ahead.

gh

Good opening buffer builds coherence; is positive, neutral, and sets stage for explanation.

Negative information de-emphasized by position in paragraph and by being followed with positive information.

Convincing logical reasoning precedes the negative information.

Receiver's interests stressed in helpful alternative solution.

Friendly close is warm and optimistic.

Figure 12•11 Example of a **Good** Unsolicited Negative Memo

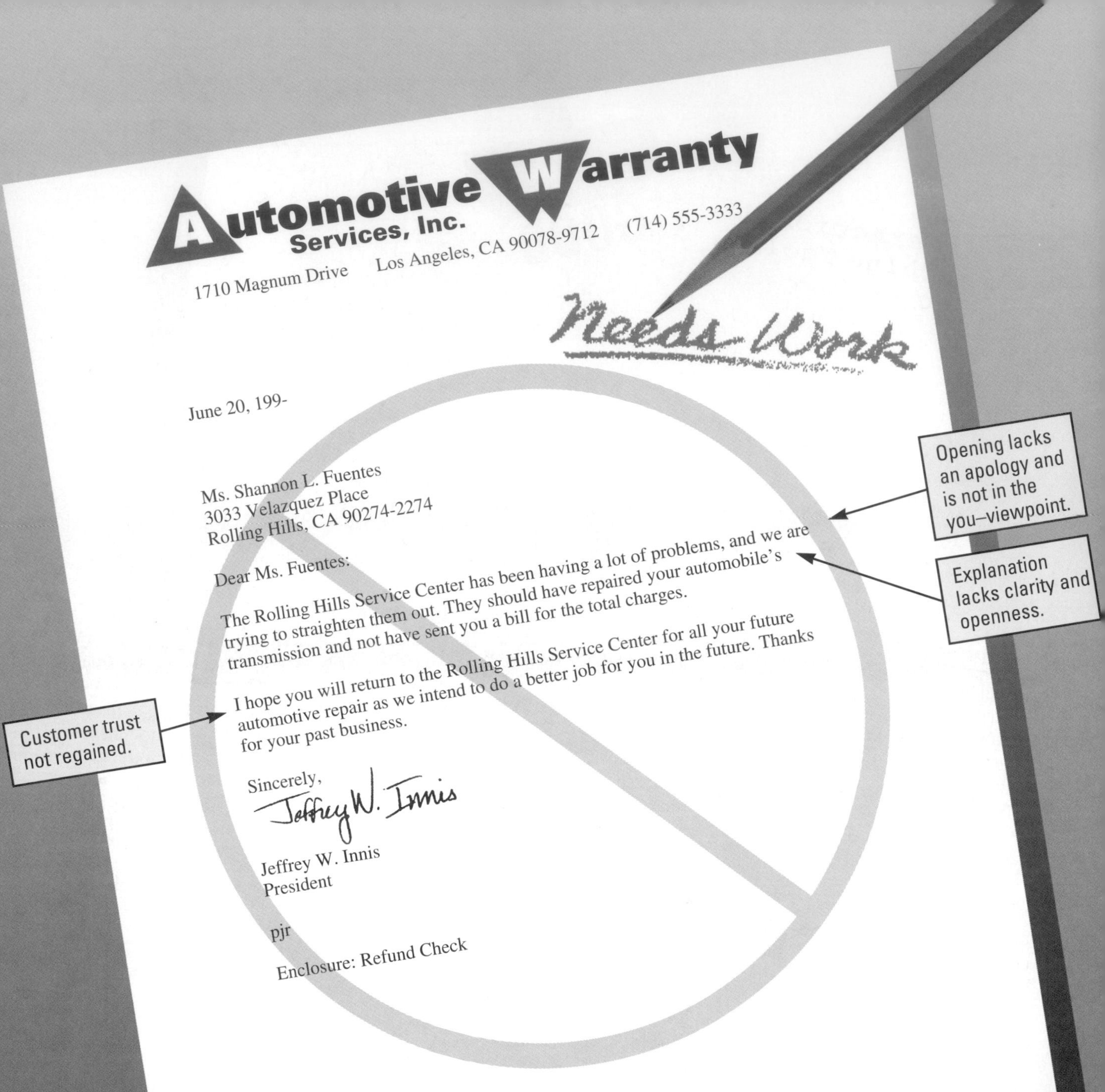

Automotive Warranty Services, Inc.

1710 Magnum Drive   Los Angeles, CA 90078-9712   (714) 555-3333

Needs Work

June 20, 199-

Ms. Shannon L. Fuentes
3033 Velazquez Place
Rolling Hills, CA 90274-2274

Dear Ms. Fuentes:

The Rolling Hills Service Center has been having a lot of problems, and we are trying to straighten them out. They should have repaired your automobile's transmission and not have sent you a bill for the total charges.

I hope you will return to the Rolling Hills Service Center for all your future automotive repair as we intend to do a better job for you in the future. Thanks for your past business.

Sincerely,

Jeffrey W. Innis

Jeffrey W. Innis
President

pjr

Enclosure: Refund Check

> Opening lacks an apology and is not in the you–viewpoint.

> Explanation lacks clarity and openness.

> Customer trust not regained.

Figure 12•12 Poor Negative Message Using the Direct Plan

Automotive Warranty Services, Inc.

1710 Magnum Drive   Los Angeles, CA 90078-9712   (714) 555-3333

GOOD

June 20, 199-

Ms. Shannon L. Fuentes
3033 Velazquez Place
Rolling Hills, CA 90274-2274

Dear Ms. Fuentes:

We apologize for the inconvenience you experienced when our branch service center in Rolling Hills billed you for the replacement of your transmission. Charging for work covered by one of our warranties is not good business practice, and steps have been taken to assure that this does not happen in the future. New management is now in place at this Center —managers committed to high-quality, ethical, economical service.

A refund check for $1,378.34, the cost for parts and labor incurred in the replacement of the transmission on your automobile, is enclosed. Your 10-year limited service warranty will be fully honored in the future.

Your business is greatly appreciated. Automotive Warranty Services assures you that any future needs you have for repair will be met promptly and fairly by the Rolling Hills Service Center.

Sincerely,

Jeffrey W. Innis

Jeffrey W. Innis
President

pjr

Enclosure

> Opening apologizes and deals directly with ethical issue.

> Appropriate correction of problem.

> Customer trust should be regained.

Figure 12·13 Good Negative Message Using the Direct Plan

DISCUSSION QUESTIONS

1. What are negative messages?

2. Explain why a negative message usually should be prepared using the indirect plan.

3. List and discuss the advantages of the indirect plan for negative messages.

4. List the five major parts of the indirect plan outline.

5. Discuss the importance of using the you–viewpoint for successfully communicating negative messages.

6. What are key questions to be asked when you are determining appropriate content for a negative message that will use the indirect plan?

7. What are the requirements for an effective opening buffer in a negative message that follows the indirect plan?

8. Describe how to assure that the logical explanation follows the opening.

9. Describe how to present convincing reasoning and use emphasis techniques in the logical explanation.

10. What are the benefits of following the guidelines for developing the logical explanation section of a negative message?

11. Give contrasting examples of conveying negative information (a) by saying what can be done, and (b) by saying what cannot be done. What are the relative benefits of each way?

12. Give an example of doing more than is expected for a message receiver. Discuss the advantages and disadvantages of doing more than is expected.

13. List several examples of content for off-the-subject, friendly closes for negative messages.

14. Define (a) a *request refusal,* (b) an *adjustment refusal,* (c) a *credit refusal*, and (d) an *unsolicited negative message.*

15. What is a businessperson's major goal when sending an adjustment refusal?

16. Why do businesses attempt to communicate credit refusals in a way that makes the message acceptable and helpful to customers?

17. Describe a circumstance where a businessperson would have to transmit an unsolicited negative message.

18. When is it appropriate to use the direct plan for a negative message?

APPLICATION EXERCISES

1. With four students on each side of the issue, debate the use of the indirect plan versus the direct plan for negative messages.

2. Observe and record over a 48-hour period oral and written communications that can be classified as negative messages—messages that are unpleasant, disappointing, or unfavorable to the receiver. Report your observations to the class so that the members can analyze the effectiveness and success of the communications. Use the indirect plan and its benefits as criteria for this analysis.

3. Interview a person from a culture other than your own and determine how negative information is transmitted effectively in the interviewee's culture. Report your findings to the class.

4. Analyze your personal experiences in receiving negative information. Record the strengths and weaknesses of the quality of these messages. Share your findings with the class.

5. Change the following statements to reflect what can be done instead of what cannot be done:

    a. Swimming is not permitted in Area A.

    b. No portion of your tuition will be refunded after the fourth week of the term.

    c. Time off cannot be taken without the permission of the manager.

    d. You do not qualify for a loan at this time.

    e. Vacation time not taken will be lost.

6. Interview a manager who supervises employees and ask (a) what is the most common negative information he or she has to give employees and (b) what is the most effective way he or she has found to convey negative information. Share your findings with the class.

7. Discuss the most effective ways you have observed for instructors to indicate to students that they have given the wrong answer during class discussion.

8. List the names of three major retail stores in your community. Analyze each of these stores in regard to its merchandise return and exchange policies and performance. Write a report.

REQUEST REFUSALS

1. You own approximately 100 acres of undeveloped property just north of a college campus. A student organization has asked your permission to hold a rock concert on your property. You must refuse this request because your property does not have developed roadways, connections to sewer systems, or liability insurance coverage.

   Refuse the student organization's request in a manner that will maintain goodwill and show the receivers how your denial benefits them. Supply any additional details that are necessary to make a complete letter.

2. Write a form letter that can be used to reject applications for employment at the Island River Mine, Bellville, Montana. The Island River personnel office is being deluged with letters of application, requests for application forms, and phone calls about employment possibilities. More than 50 percent of the miners in the area currently are unemployed. There is a need for a brief, courteous letter that maintains goodwill but refuses applications. Make this negative information as acceptable as possible for these persons who so desperately need and want work.

3. You are the international marketing manager for Global Sales, Inc., in New York City. One of your responsibilities is supervising the establishment of sales agencies that sell Global products in countries throughout the world. The standard agreement is that the foreign sales agency receive a 20 percent commission. You have negotiations under way with the Mohr Agency in Bamberg, Germany. Mohr has requested that a special dispensation be made and that its agency receive a 25 percent commission on sales. Say no to Mohr, but try to retain it as Global's sales agency in northern Bavaria. Add any necessary details to make your letter complete.

4. You have been out of school five years; they have been good years for you. You are now successfully established in your own computer service agency. Business is good; in fact, it is so good that you find it difficult to keep up with all the requests for your services.

   One of your best clients, the Matsumi Engineering Company, has just asked you to do a roadbed analysis for a new 3-mile section of Interstate I-674 through the mountains. It is a huge project—enough work to keep your whole facility busy for three months. However, you have other commitments; you must refuse this request from Matsumi for your services.

   Think through the indirect approach for refusing a request. Provide convincing reasons that the owners of Matsumi, natives of Japan who have been in the U.S. four years, will understand

and that will show the benefit to them of your decision not to undertake this particular project. You can commit your agency to complete other current projects for them in your usual quality fashion. One of the things that you refuse to do is accept more work than you can handle in an efficient, effective way for your clients. Write a letter to Matsumi telling them no and suggest an alternative that will possibly solve their problem.

5. A group of employees under your supervision has requested that you extend the number and length of their coffee breaks from two 10-minute breaks to four 15-minute breaks. Write a memo refusing their request. The additional coffee breaks would significantly lower production rates. Lower production rates would also mean lower bonuses for employees at the end of the year. Add any necessary details.

6. You have just learned that one of Replacement Windows, Inc., salespersons has been promising customers unrealistic installation dates that could not possibly be met. His unethical mode of operating, to get the sale, involved letting the customer request any date he or she wanted.

You, the sales manager, and four ethical salespersons on your staff meet to write a form letter suitable for sending to the customers involved. Your writing team's challenge is to compose an effective message that will convey the negative information that you cannot install the windows on the dates promised. In addition, you will try to keep their business. Your installation schedule will permit you to install the windows approximately three months after the promised date. Add any necessary details to make this a complete request refusal letter.

7. You are a student at the Rushville Academy in Arlington, Vermont. It is final examination time. Your employer has written you a memo requesting you to work overtime during the week of finals.

This is a very serious situation. You need the job desperately, for it will enable you to continue your education. Also, you especially need to study this week so that you can do well on the final examinations in your courses. It would be a wasted investment of time, having worked all semester to be unable to perform effectively on the final examinations. You could possibly lower your grades, or even fail a course, if you do not study for finals.

Your employer has implied to you on several occasions that once you graduate she would be interested in continuing your employment. Maybe this is one of the bases for your logical explanation as to why you must tell her you cannot work overtime during finals week.

Write your boss a memo that will convince her it is important to her (and to you) for you to study for finals and not work overtime this coming week. Also add any details that will make this a complete indirect memo that refuses a request. Be sure to include a suggested alternative(s) for your boss.

8. You are the manager of a franchise for Pizza Stores, Inc. An executive of a manufacturing plant near your restaurant has asked you if he could have his employees attend a pizza party at your restaurant at 9:00 p.m., Thursday. You would have to close your restaurant two hours early to accommodate the large number of his employees. Because you do not feel it is possible for you to close your restaurant to the public two hours early, you will have to turn down the request. You would be glad, however, to cater a pizza party at some other location. You can do this in the manufacturer's plant, at the community center, or at some other location of the executive's choosing. Write a letter to the executive that will turn down his request and keep the business. Add any necessary details.

ADJUSTMENT REFUSALS

9. You are sales manager for Browning Tire Sales, Inc., in Arlington, New York. Your most popular line of tires is the one that is rated "blemished." Blemished tires have some small defect that does not affect their usability. The defect may be a misprint on the labeling of the tire, imperfect whitewall coloring, or irregular tread pattern. In some instances, however—and these are rare—blemished tires may also have serious defects, such as being out-of-round. These tires do not ride well and may cause vibration inside the car.

   You sold some blemished tires to Al Sams when he was vacationing in Arlington. He has now returned to his home state, almost 600 miles away, and has written you that he wants a full refund on the blemished tires. Your policy, and the standard policy throughout the United States, on blemished tire sales is that there will be no refunds. The retail prices of blemished tires are considerably below those for unblemished tires. The fine print in the sales agreement with the customer specifies no refunds on blemished tires.

   Mr. Sams has stated in his letter that he intends to destroy the tires as soon as he receives your refund. He further states that all four tires seem to be out-of-round and that they cause his car to handle improperly. This, you believe, is an overstatement. In a threatening tone Mr. Sams tells you that he has several friends in the Arlington area to whom he will write to encourage them to discontinue their business with your company. In addition, he will ask them to encourage others to discontinue their business if a refund is not forthcoming promptly.

   You need to write a courteous adjustment refusal letter to Mr. Sams. The purposes of this letter will be (1) to resell Mr. Sams on the tires that he now has, (2) to convince him that it is to his benefit to continue to use those tires, and (3) to generally calm him down. His tires are obviously out-of-round. Equipment is available in almost every community to shave tires to correct such a problem. Could Mr. Sams take care of this locally? Suggest an alternative that might help him see that his problem is not hopeless. Furnish any necessary details to make this a complete adjustment refusal letter.

10. You operate a small, mail-order seed supply company. You frequently receive letters from customers asking your permission to return packets of flower seeds bought over a year ago. Your seed warranty, printed clearly on every packet, guarantees seeds for one year from date of purchase. Write a form adjustment refusal letter that will not only keep these customers' business but also sell them more seeds. It is likely that some of the seeds bought over a year ago are still good. Be sure to personalize this form letter because it will be prepared individually using word processing. Write the letter to one customer, but show how it can be modified to personalize it for other customers.

11. You are the claims manager for USA Airline, whose headquarters is in Atlanta, Georgia. You have just received a claim from Mrs. Norma Lawson, 123 Magnolia Drive, Jackson, Mississippi. Mrs. Lawson says in her claim letter:

. . . I am angry. I just opened my suitcase upon arriving home after flying on Flight 270 from Paris, France, to Atlanta, Georgia. Guess what I found? My $250 bottle of perfume was crushed. The perfume had soaked through my clothes and into the suitcase lining.

Had your luggage handlers been more careful, this would not have happened. I would still have my $250 bottle of perfume and many other happy memories of my trip, but your airline ruined this for me with the unhappy ending I experienced. Also, I would not have had the $75 clothes cleaning bill and $125 suitcase repair bill.

I want the $450 by return mail.

You investigated carefully what might have happened in this situation by talking with experienced luggage handlers at the Atlanta airport. What you found is what you suspected; for the perfume bottle to have broken, it must have been unprotected and probably near an outer cover of the suitcase. The airline does not take responsibility for glass items that are not packaged according to instructions and inspected prior to the flight. This policy is printed on the back of all tickets.

You must refuse this angry customer's request for an adjustment. Be sure to justify your airline's policy on glass items. At the same time you will want to encourage her to continue to fly on USA Airline. Your check of her flight record reveals that she has been a customer many times on the airline.

As a constructive follow-up, does she have personal property insurance coverage in a homeowner's insurance policy which may cover this loss?

12. Baseballs Limited is an American-owned company in Mexico that sells baseballs all over the world. As marketing manager at Baseballs Limited, you have just received a letter from Rinji

Nitobe, purchasing agent for Tokuda, Inc., Kushiro, Japan. In the letter he asks for a 50 percent refund of the purchase price for 10,000 baseballs Tokuda bought for resale to little league teams throughout northern Japan. His justification for this request is the complaint by some team managers that the balls are livelier this year than last. He says that, as a matter of goodwill, Tokuda would like to make 50 percent refunds to all their customers who bought from this shipment. Write a positive, courteous adjustment refusal letter. The team managers' complaints are without foundation. Newly manufactured balls are regularly subjected to random tests to assure the same degree of resiliency year-to-year. These tests are conducted by the International Baseball Association, a highly reliable organization.

13. As manager of Acme Landscaping Service you have just received a claim letter from one of your largest accounts—the Paris Country Club Golf Course. The letter reads as follows:

Dear Ms. Butterworth:

The replacement sod you placed on Greens 13, 14, and 15 is dying and is unsuitable for championship golf. I know that we have had an unusually hot and dry summer, but this grass should have survived it. Please make arrangements with me immediately to resod these greens. Of course, I expect this to be done at your expense in accordance with your warranty.

Sincerely yours,

Robert Ryan
Golf Pro

You will have to refuse this claim. First, the warranty Mr. Ryan refers to specifies that any claim must be entered within 90 days of purchase. The warranty expired 32 days ago. Second, the warranty also called for "adequate watering." There are generally recognized standards of what adequate watering means to golf greenskeepers. In fact, during the warranty period you became concerned about the limited watering being done by Gus Blakely, Paris's greenskeeper. As you passed the golf course on your way home each day, you noticed that he was not providing adequate watering. You finally made a special point to stop and give him specific advice on how much additional watering he needed to do.

Refuse the adjustment request. Provide the logical reasoning that justifies your refusal.

14. You are the owner and operator of a small gift shop with a policy of no refunds. You are glad to give credit toward another purchase if a customer wants to return an item. You have three signs that are clearly visible in your store which cite your no-refunds policy. Mildred Brown, a good customer who lives out of town, has written you asking for her first refund on a $125 vase. She believes the vase does not complement her decor. Refuse the adjustment. In your letter to Ms. Brown, explain and justify your

policies on refunds and credits. Can you suggest an alternative solution? Add any necessary details.

15. You have just received a letter from Sally DeFord who recently purchased a microcomputer from your store. Sally's letter to you is as follows:

Dear Mr. Quintero:

When you sold the Model IX Microcomputer to me, you said that there would be no strain on my eyes from looking at the screen. I have not found this to be the case. I find, instead, that after working three or four hours at the computer, my eyes begin to water and burn.

I must request that you permit me to return this microcomputer to your store for a full refund. It is just not satisfactory for my purposes.

Please let me know when I can return the microcomputer to you and pick up my refund check.

Yours truly,

Sally DeFord

You don't want to lose this sale. In fact, even though your warranty says that you will refund the money for any microcomputer which is not completely satisfactory to the customer, you have decided to refuse this particular request. It will be necessary in your logical explanation to convince the customer that she should keep the microcomputer. After all, there were several good reasons on which she based her decision to buy the microcomputer. Resell her on its benefits.

However, you still have the problem of Sally's eyestrain. Suggest to her that you can correct the problem. You can do this by attaching a green Plexiglas eye-ease cover to the front of the microcomputer screen at a cost of $14.95. In most cases this cover has solved the problem of eyestrain suffered by people using a computer. Do your best with this letter. If this negative message does not change the customer's mind, you will have to take the microcomputer back and refund $1,800.

16. It is spring. Sales of your leading fertilizer, Evergreen Brand, are at an all-time high. One of your recent customers, Mr. Harold Brown, has written to you saying that the Evergreen Brand fertilizer is not all that it is cracked up to be. His letter follows:

Dear Ms. Flintrock:

Recently, I purchased ten bags of Evergreen Brand fertilizer for use on my lawn. That was one of the biggest mistakes I ever made in my life. I spent more than 100 hours preparing the lawn bed for new seed and fertilizer. All that work was lost.

Your fertilizer killed my grass.

I am requesting that you reimburse me for the following items: 100 hours of labor at $10 an hour, $1,000; 10 bags of Evergreen Brand fertilizer at $8 a bag, $80; 5 bags of Evergrow grass seed at $20 a bag, $100; total $1,180.

Let me tell you this story. After preparing the lawn bed, sowing the grass seed, and watering it faithfully for five days, I then put what I thought was the finishing touch on it. I applied your fertilizer. It was, in fact, the finishing touch—it killed all my grass. Not only did your fertilizer not help my grass grow, it terminated the very existence of the grass.

Isn't my claim reasonable?

Sincerely,

Harold Brown

No, Mr. Brown's claim is not reasonable, and you must refuse it. Your warranty, which appears on every bag of Evergreen Brand fertilizer, warns that refunds will not be made if the fertilizer is applied to grass seed recently sown. In fact, the fertilizer warranty indicates that the grass should be at least an inch high and ten weeks old prior to the application of the fertilizer. Fertilizers that can be applied earlier than this are weaker and do not have the long-term value of Evergreen Brand.

Explain and justify your policy to Mr. Brown. Restore his goodwill so that he will come back to your store and buy additional grass seed to replace that which he has lost. The fertilizer that he placed on his lawn is still good, and it will have settled into the grass bed sufficiently by this time so as not to damage any newly sown grass seed. Write an adjustment refusal letter that assures the sale of additional grass seed.

CREDIT REFUSALS

17. You are the loan officer for the First National Bank of Bloomington, Ohio. You have just been approached by Sandra Morales who lives on a small farm at the edge of town. Her intent is to borrow money from the bank, buy 25 head of cattle, and make a little extra money on them. Her case to you is that she has plenty of land for grazing the cattle, and her job will permit her to feed them and care for them adequately.

    Her request for credit must be refused. First, she has had no experience in raising cattle. It is difficult, at best, for an experienced farmer or rancher to be successful at raising cattle and to make a profit in so doing. Second, the livestock market does not look good to you at this time. The costs of feed are excessive, and the market price for cattle is in a long downward trend. Write a letter that will maintain this customer's business with the bank but will refuse this particular loan.

18. Raymond Parker has just placed a sizable order, worth over $7,000, for home building supplies, with Contractor Supplies, Inc. Unfortunately, Mr. Parker's credit record with Contractor Supplies is so poor that management has decided that he must be refused further credit until he pays his current account of $14,200, which is

now 90 days overdue. As the manager of accounting services for Contractor Supplies, write a credit refusal letter to Mr. Parker using the direct approach. In your letter try to keep Mr. Parker as a customer. Of course, business with him will have to be on a cash basis until he pays his past-due account.

19. You are manager of Chapman's Fine Carpet Warehouse, Inc., in Sandusky, California. You have just received a letter from Fred Langemo, manager of the Triangle Restaurant in Grand Rapids, California, placing a large order for carpeting for his restaurant. In fact, this is the largest order you have received this month: more than $10,000 of commercial carpeting! You want this order.

   Unfortunately, Mr. Langemo has requested unreasonable credit terms. He suggests that he will pay you $500 down at the time the carpeting is installed satisfactorily. He wants to pay you the balance of approximately $10,000 (including a low rate of interest) over a ten-year period in installments of $1,000 a year. In an installation such as a restaurant, carpeting wears out in two to four years. It is important, therefore, that the carpeting be paid for within three years. Also, it is your standard practice to require that approximately one-half of the order be paid for before the carpeting is installed. This enables you, as the supplier, to obtain the carpeting and pay for it prior to installation.

   Write a credit refusal letter to Mr. Langemo that will keep his business. Explain the credit terms that you are willing to provide once his credit application has been approved.

20. A 17-year-old college student has requested that your credit union provide her with a $3,000 line of credit. State laws governing lines-of-credit do not permit granting such requests, so you will have to refuse. As an alternative you could suggest the possibility of a qualified co-signer. Add any necessary details.

21. A young married couple, Manuel and Bella Silva, are in the process of furnishing their first apartment. Because of their young ages, neither has established a credit record. They have come to your furniture store, HomeQuarters, to look at living room and bedroom furniture and kitchen appliances. Your advertised policy is to sell furniture and appliances for no money down, interest free, with no payments due for 90 days to customers with good credit records. Bella and Manuel have asked you if they qualify for this policy, but you must tell them no. Your objective is to ensure a sale to Manuel and Bella. However, because they lack a credit rating, they must pay one-third down on the purchase and start making payments within 30 days. Write what you are going to say to them. Use the indirect plan for this message.

22. You are one of the credit rating officers in the InternationalCard credit department. You have just received an application for a credit card from Joe Seymore, a college student at Brenham State College.

Your policy covering the granting of credit cards is that the card holder must be employed full time in a permanent position. Furthermore, an applicant's current financial condition must show assets exceeding liabilities at a ratio of at least 2 to 1.

Joe Seymore's application reveals that he has half-time employment and virtually no assets. Refuse his application at this time, but be sure to do so in a way that ensures his business in the future.

23. Fred Bowling is a young businessman who is really on the go. He is running several different enterprises—an ice cream store, an apple orchard, and a fishing bait business.

Fred has come to your bank with a plan for establishing yet another enterprise. He has submitted to you, along with his plan, his current financial statements, including a balance sheet, a profit-and-loss statement for the past year, and related documents. His plan is to build a new apartment complex that would cost $450,000. He has requested that you provide him with the entire financing for this project. His reasoning for this request is based on his success in all his other enterprises.

What Fred says is true to a degree. He does show an excellent profit picture on the small capital investment that he has in his various business projects; but therein lies the problem—his small capital investment capability. Fred currently has an overall 1-to-2 ratio of assets to liabilities, but at least a 2-to-1 ratio of assets to liabilities is required for any given project. Fred does not have that ratio on any of his current projects; therefore, you must refuse his request for credit because of insufficient capital.

Write a credit refusal letter that will maintain your relationship with Fred. He will be a good customer for the bank within the next few years. In fact, his current success in business indicates to you that he may very well qualify for the kind of loan he desires within three to four years. The rate of profit growth that he is showing in his current statement supports this analysis.

24. As manager of Wholesale Plumbing Company, you sell supplies to contract and home service plumbers. Many of these plumbers have established a line of credit with you that enables them to charge their purchases. You bill them once a month. A young woman, who is new to your area and who has just opened a plumbing service business, has asked you to establish a $3,000 line of credit for her. You must refuse this request for credit because she has not yet achieved a creditworthy record with your company. As an alternative arrangement, you can suggest that you could permit her purchases up to $300. These purchases would be paid for on a weekly basis. If your experience with her over the next three months is favorable, you could establish a higher line of credit for her that could be paid on a monthly basis.

UNSOLICITED NEGATIVE MESSAGES

25. As plant manager for the Vanderbilt Toy Company, you have the unfortunate responsibility to let your 76 employees know that there will be no holiday bonus this year. Your company has

consistently given generous bonuses for each of the past five years since the plant opened.

Provide convincing reasoning in a memo to your employees that will show them how they benefit by this negative information. The $38,000 that your company will save this holiday season by not giving the bonuses will be the difference between letting two employees go and keeping them on the payroll for the next year. You will admit, and you are proud of it, that the company has given each employee at least $500 for each of the past five holiday seasons. However, the economy is such this year that you are not going to be able to do it. Toy sales are down.

Convince the employees that your message is one they really want to receive. They have been depending on this $500. Add any additional details that will make your unsolicited negative message complete.

26. Write a form letter to the members of the Good Sam Campers' Club telling them that their dues will be increased by $5 next year. Costs to print the journal, operate national headquarters, and provide member hotline services have increased significantly over the past ten years, but there has been no increase in dues.

27. Write a memo to Marvin Boles telling him that he will be terminated as of March 1. The corporation has made a 10 percent across-the-board reduction in the number of employees, and your department's share of this is one employee. Terminations were based on length of employment. Marvin is an excellent employee. Maintain goodwill for the corporation and a favorable relationship for yourself with Marvin. You would like to see him come back to work for you when economic conditions permit. Add any necessary details to make this a complete memo.

28. You have over 2,000 wholesale dealers in Canada who regularly buy high school graduation rings from your American company. Price levels for these rings have not been changed in four years. Because of the increase in the world price of gold over the past 24 months, your company is going to have to increase the price level of your ring line by 12 percent. Appoint a writing team from management to write the form letter that will maintain the goodwill of your customers, keep their business, and help them accept your bad news. Add any additional details to make the letter complete.

29. Picture yourself as an insurance agent in Hopkinsville, Virginia. You have an affluent clientele of senior citizens in this retirement community. Many of these senior citizens have expensive jewelry collections. Insuring these collections has been an excellent source of income for your agency for many years.

Today, however, you received a letter from the home office of your company. This letter indicates that the increased crime rate in Hopkinsville and similar metropolitan areas makes it necessary for your company to discontinue this type of coverage. This will be negative information for many of your clients. It is bad news, of course, to you as well.

Write an unsolicited letter to your many senior citizen customers explaining the situation to them. Be sure that you do not alienate them from your insurance company. They will be disappointed. They may think immediately about shifting all their insurance to another company that will offer them jewelry insurance. Convince them through logical reasoning that they should stay with you as their agent and stay with the Reliable Insurance Company for all coverage except jewelry. Can you suggest to them an alternative source of coverage for their jewelry? Can you assist them in any way in obtaining this coverage? Use the indirect plan in a letter that will achieve your objective. Add any necessary details to make the letter complete.

30. As sales manager for Old English China, Inc., you have the sad duty of informing several hundred customers that your company is going out of business. Replacement dishes in various patterns have been available from Old English China for more than 82 years. Closing the business means these patterns will no longer be available from any source. The company's owner, Mr. Rudolph Budweiser, died recently. The heirs have decided that the patterns and manufacturing techniques used at Old English China all these years will not be sold to any other china manufacturer.

You do have one happy piece of information to convey. There is still a supply of almost all patterns, which will probably meet most customers' needs for the next four to five years.

Write to your customers explaining the circumstances and encourage them to order within 90 days to fill their anticipated needs for the next few years. Maintain the goodwill of your customers toward the Budweiser family because this family has several other enterprises from which these customers buy various kitchen and household items.

31. As a graduate of Murphy State College you know the value of cooperative education. In fact, as a student, you participated in cooperative education for three years while you earned your degree. Now you employ Murphy State College co-op students in your Christmas tree farm business. But, with the popularity of artificial Christmas trees, you are practically out of business. Twenty-five cooperative education slots that you have provided to Murphy State College will have to be discontinued.

Write the letter to the Murphy State College Cooperative Education Director, Dr. Ann Thompson, giving her the negative information. It will be important for you to maintain your relationship with the co-op education office because you may have other needs in the future as you develop other business interests. Also, as an alumnus of Murphy State College, you are interested in continuing friendly relations.

Write this unsolicited negative message in a manner that will (1) maintain goodwill, and (2) provide some direction to the cooperative education office for placement of the students you can no longer hire. Compile the necessary facts for a complete letter.

32. You are the public relations manager for a large manufacturer of breakfast cereals. It has just been learned that a batch of your leading brand, Fiber Munchies, was processed improperly. Due to a combination of machine failure and an inexperienced quality control inspector, this batch of Fiber Munchies has too few raisins and nuts and does not meet your high-quality standards. You must write to all the grocery stores that have bought Fiber Munchies and ask them to take the cereal off the shelf. Further, the store managers should return the cereal to you at your expense. Use the direct approach for this negative message and express your apologies up front. Most importantly, regain the confidence of these grocers. Assure them that there is nothing harmful in the cereal and that there is no need to recall the cereal from customers. Remind them that complaints should be graciously handled with replacement cereal and a discount-on-future-purchases coupon that you are providing the grocers. Your approach to handling this problem has been cleared with the National Public Health Service.

MESSAGE ANALYSIS

Text 12B

A new employee, who has been with your firm for three months, has requested vacation time during the firm's busy season. The company's policy does permit taking two weeks' vacation after three months employment if a commitment is made to return for at least an additional six months. The policy further states, however, that vacations cannot be scheduled between January 1 and April 15—the tax season. Edit and revise the following memo to assure that it is an effective negative message.

My answer is *no* to your request to take your vacation during the first two weeks of April. Policy prohibits your taking your vacation during the period January 1 through April 15. I know you are a new employee and probably do not fully understand that a significant part of our business involves preparation of tax returns. Most of these returns must be prepared between January 1 and April 15. That is when our clients have the necessary tax information available, and April 15 is the deadline for filing tax returns. Why don't you take your vacation the last two weeks of April?

CHAPTER 13

Persuasive Messages

Learning Objectives

Your learning objectives for this chapter include the following:

- To list the purposes of a persuasive message
- To describe how desire is built in a persuasive message
- To analyze a sales message and compare its parts to those of an indirect plan outline
- To write different kinds of persuasive messages using the indirect plan
- To write messages that are used for the various stages of collection

A **persuasive message** is a (1) request for action when you believe the receiver may be unknowing, disinterested, or unwilling, or (2) communication to try to change the opinion of a receiver. These messages will be viewed as neither positive nor negative by the receiver.

Persuasive messages are used to convince receivers to take action.

Communication Quotes

To be a successful leadership figure in a professional sports organization, I believe you have to be an effective communicator. Every message that you choose to convey must be well planned. I use the power of persuasive messages in several different means of communication.

I have sent strong messages to an individual player, or a group of players, with statements made through the newspaper or television. You can also drop subtle, but persuasive, hints through the media that are intended for a very narrow or broad audience.

As the owner of a professional sports franchise, you are also called upon to share your philosophies of success and winning through the spoken word—to a live audience. There is no greater means of transmitting a persuasive message than making direct eye contact with a room full of people who are interested in what you have to say.

Persuasive messages in the world of sports are sent every day. They are transmitted via the telephone, in person, and through the print and electronic media. Clear communication in the world of professional sports is just as critical as in any other business or professional enterprise.

Jerry Jones, Owner of the Dallas Cowboys

Persuasive messages are used for a variety of purposes in internal and external communication.

Persuasive messages are used in both internal and external communication. Examples of persuasive messages in internal communication include a speech asking employees to volunteer to work on upcoming weekends, an employee's memo to a manager requesting that the organization initiate a flextime policy, an employee's recommendation or proposal to establish a day care center, and a letter to employees requesting donations for a charity that has just been endorsed by the company.

A **sales message** is a communication about a product that includes a description of the product, its benefits, available options and models, price, and related services. It is the most common persuasive message in external communication. Other examples of persuasive messages used in external communication include a telephone call to ask the manager of another company to be the keynote speaker at an annual banquet, or a letter to persuade readers to respond to a questionnaire. Persuasive messages also include letters requesting employment with an organization.

Receivers will have to be convinced that it is in their best interests to take action.

Persuasive messages have to be designed to convince receivers that taking the requested action is in their best interest. The supporting facts in the message must be presented as useful or profitable to the receiver. Persuasive messages should be presented using an indirect approach.

USE THE INDIRECT PLAN FOR PERSUASIVE MESSAGES

The indirect plan assists in convincing a receiver to take action.

The *indirect plan* should be used for messages that attempt to convince the receiver to take an action. The advantage of using the indirect plan for persuasive messages is that it enables the sender to present first the benefits that receivers may gain from fulfilling the request. This puts receivers in the proper frame of mind to consider the request. If the request were given prior to the explanation, the receiver might form objections that would be difficult to overcome. The receiver also might not read the part of the letter that contains the benefits. The indirect plan does require the use of more words than the direct plan, but the result is worth the additional words.

The indirect plan conditions a receiver to accept the message.

You–viewpoint should be used.

If the message is positively constructed in the you–viewpoint, the receiver will more likely be in a positive mood to consider the value of the entire message and will more likely agree with its contents. An effective presentation will associate the message with the motivating factors in the receiver's mind.

HOW TO USE THE INDIRECT PLAN

Carefully analyze receiver to determine motivational factors.

Analyzing your receiver is especially important when planning a persuasive message. You will have to anticipate what motivates the receiver—his or her goals, values, and needs. You must then build your persuasive message around these factors using the you–viewpoint. Do this by stressing the receiver's interests and benefits.

Purposes of persuasive message are to have receiver consider entire message and then to take requested action.

The two primary purposes of a persuasive message are (1) to get the receiver to read or listen to the entire message, and then (2) to have the receiver react positively to the request. These purposes are more easily achieved when the indirect plan is used in constructing the message. The specific guides for using the indirect plan to construct persuasive messages are shown in Figure 13•1.

Persuasive messages include requests, recommendations, special claims, sales, collection, and employment.

The indirect plan can be used for a variety of persuasive messages— requests, recommendations, special claims, sales, collection, and employment. The organization and development of the first five types of persuasive messages are discussed in this chapter, and employment messages are covered in Chapter 22. An analysis of the indirect plan for persuasion will be helpful prior to discussing the construction of five sample persuasive messages.

ATTENTION

A receiver's attention must be gained to ensure message is read or heard.

The opening in any persuasive message must attract the receiver's attention. A persuasive message is successful only when the desired action is taken by the receiver. The desired action is not likely to be taken unless the receiver is motivated to read or to listen to the entire message. An attention-getting opening increases the chances that the receiver will read or listen to the entire message and then will take the desired action.

The receiver's attention must be captured in the opening sentence. It is

Figure 13•1 Indirect Plan
Outline for Persuasion

INDIRECT PLAN FOR PERSUASION

1. **Attention**
   A. Attract receiver's attention in opening sentence.
   B. Cause receiver to read or to listen to rest of message.
   C. Be positive and brief.

2. **Interest**
   A. Build on attention gained in the opening.
   B. Show benefits to receiver.
   C. Motivate receiver to continue reading.

3. **Desire**
   A. Build on receiver's attention and interest by providing proof of benefits.
   B. Re-emphasize benefits to the receiver.
   C. Downplay any negative points or obstacles.

4. **Action**
   A. Motivate receiver to take immediate action.
   B. Be positive.
   C. Make action easy.

Get receiver's attention immediately.

important that the opening be concise and positive. In a well-planned persuasive message, the receiver's curiosity is aroused when a message opens with an interesting point. When a positive emotion is aroused, the reader will continue reading.

Senders use different techniques to gain receivers' attention.

Many different methods have been used successfully by communicators to capture the receiver's attention. These methods include mechanical devices (such as color or drawings), using the receiver's name in the sentence, rhetorical questions, and interjections. The you–viewpoint must be considered when organizing the content of the message. Any method that gets the receiver's attention may be used if it is relevant to the topic of the message and is not trite or high pressured. Gimmicks may be used, but should not give the receiver the impression that an attempt is being made to mislead him or her. For example, beginning a letter with, "Your investment of $10 may grow to a million dollars by the end of the year," will probably cause the reader to read no further because the message is unrealistic.

INTEREST

To hold interest, make the receiver aware of the benefits of taking the action.

The receiver's interest must be held after his or her attention is gained. The topic of the first paragraph is expanded while maintaining the interest of the receiver. Interest will be maintained when benefits to the receiver are shown. When taking the requested action will result in several benefits to the receiver, the benefits may be emphasized by listing and numbering them. The receiver may hesitate to take the desired action unless he or she clearly sees the value of taking such action.

DESIRE

Once you have the receiver's attention and interest, proof of the benefits that the receiver can gain should be given so that he or she will be motivated to take the requested action. Remember, the purpose of the persuasive message is to move the receiver to take the desired action. Details of the message are used to intensify the interest and create desire within the receiver. Anticipate the receiver's negative reactions to taking the desired action; attempt to overcome these feelings by showing proof of the benefits to the receiver.

The *interest* and the *desire* sections of a persuasive message may be combined by listing a benefit and then immediately providing proof of that benefit. This arrangement would be used until all the benefits have been discussed.

ACTION

You are ready to ask the receiver to take immediate action once you have built his or her interest and desire. The action you request the receiver to take should be a logical next step. This action should be requested in a direct and positive manner.

The message sender must ensure that a minimum of effort is required for the receiver to take the necessary action. It is easier to ask for an action, such as checking a choice and returning an enclosed card, than to ask the receiver to write an entire letter.

When the desired action is required by a certain date, be sure that this date is clearly stated. If no time limit is involved, encourage the receiver to make a quick decision.

Many techniques can be used to influence the receiver to take the desired action immediately. A sales letter can offer coupons to be redeemed, specify a date that the offer ends, or suggest that supplies are limited. Collection letters can offer assurance that the receiver's credit will not be damaged if payment is received by a certain date. Including the receiver's name in a drawing for a free prize if he or she returns a questionnaire can be used with requests. All these techniques are effective if the receiver feels no undue pressure.

IMPLEMENTING THE INDIRECT PLAN

The use of the indirect plan for persuasion will be illustrated through the development of a request to a fellow member of a professional organization. Here are details of the communication case problem:

Garrett Ashburn has been a loyal member of Cajun Sales Managers (CSM) since his graduation from college ten years ago. He served as secretary two years ago. Recently, he was promoted to sales manager of Batteries Unlimited. In this position he is responsible for sales in 15 branch stores. Write him a letter informing him that he has been nomi-nated for president-elect of CSM. You realize that Garrett is busy in his new position at Batteries Unlimited but is highly deserving of the office in CSM. This position involves much public relations work. You may remind Garrett that he will have a

---

Providing proof of the benefits and values increases a receiver's desire to take action.

The receiver should feel that taking the action is a logical conclusion.

Make it easy to take the action.

If a deadline date is necessary, give it.

Various methods of getting the receiver to take action exist.

A communication case will help illustrate ways to compose persuasive messages.

year to prepare for the presidency. As benefits, both Garrett's contacts and reputation in the business community would be increased. Further, officers do not pay dues. Write a letter to Garrett convincing him that he should accept the nomination.

DETERMINE APPROPRIATE CONTENT

As is the case in developing all business messages, you must first analyze the situation to determine the content that will best accomplish the purpose of the communication. The following sections show how the content of the Garrett Ashburn letter may be developed. Each section discusses a stage of the indirect plan for persuasive messages and presents an example of poor writing and then an example of good writing.

CAPTURE THE RECEIVER'S ATTENTION

The first step in writing a persuasive message is to capture the receiver's attention. A **poor** way of gaining Garrett's attention is shown here:

The poor opening is negative and impersonal.

> The nominating committee has selected you as president-elect for the coming year. You would serve in this position for one year before assuming the duties of president.

This poorly written opening paragraph begins by immediately telling Garrett that he has inherited another responsibility. It may get his attention, but not in a positive way. The paragraph is impersonal and shows a lack of appreciation for Garrett's previous service. He may be reluctant to continue reading the letter because he immediately senses that this is just another job rather than an honor.

In contrast, a **good** opening to gain Garrett's attention follows:

The good opening is positive and personal.

> Your dedication and hard work over the past ten years have been among the principal reasons for the outstanding growth of Cajun Sales Managers. The nominating committee, therefore, shows its appreciation to you for this service by nominating you president-elect.

This good opening gains Garrett's attention by recognizing his long-time dedication to the organization. This paragraph uses both a positive approach and the you–viewpoint. It should interest him because it praises him for his previous service. Everyone likes to receive recognition, and this acknowledgment of his efforts should motivate Garrett to read the remaining portion of the letter with an open mind.

BUILD THE RECEIVER'S INTEREST

After you have captured the receiver's attention, concentrate on building interest in the receiver to accept the request. A **poor** way of building Garrett's interest is:

The poor message lacks a you–viewpoint.

> This responsibility should not be taken lightly because it will take many hours each week to carry out all the duties. I know you are busy with your

new position at Batteries Unlimited, but all of us have a lot of work. One of the primary functions of the office is to improve the public relations between our organization and the community. I know you can do an effective job with this.

This poor attempt to build the receiver's interest is similar to that of the poor opening in that it is impersonal and negative. The paragraph is cold and lacks a you–viewpoint; it is of no help in building Garrett's interest in accepting the nomination.

A **good** paragraph, which should build Garrett's interest, follows:

> As president-elect you would be able to observe the operation of the presidency and also would be able to assist the president with various duties. You might be asked to attend a few activities that the president could not attend; these functions would prepare you for assuming the position of president next year. The organization does not pay its officers, but the officers are exempt from paying dues.

The good message aids in building receiver's interest.

This good paragraph outlines the duties and one benefit of the office in a positive manner. Garrett's interest, now aroused, will peak in the next paragraph.

> *I sit here all day trying to persuade people to do the things they ought to have sense enough to do without my persuading them.*
>
> **Harry S. Truman**

STIMULATE DESIRE IN THE RECEIVER

In this section, emphasize the benefits that Garrett would receive by taking the requested action. Attempt to overcome any negative thoughts that Garrett may have. A **poor** attempt to stimulate desire is illustrated here:

> I know you are a busy person, but we certainly need someone to guide our organization. I feel you are the person who can do it. Our membership has grown significantly in the past two years; we feel you can maintain this growth pattern.

The arguments in this poor example are presented from a selfish point of view.

This approach will do little to motivate the reader to accept the nomination. The paragraph is written from the sender's point of view—not from the receiver's. Garrett will look at the nomination as nothing more than additional work with no corresponding benefits.

A **good** attempt to stimulate Garrett's desire to accept the nomination follows:

This good example points out the proof of the benefits to the receiver.

> Both your contacts and reputation in the business community would be increased. You would be consulted by the business leaders. Three of the

last four presidents of CSM have been promoted to upper-level management positions in their companies. Promoting CSM would take some of your time, but this time would be well spent.

The benefits that Garrett can gain from the position are clearly explained in the good example. Proof of the benefits that can result from being president are also shown. The negative aspect of the job—that it is time consuming—is handled in a positive way. Garrett should now be looking forward to accepting the nomination.

REQUEST ACTION FROM THE RECEIVER

Once Garrett has been motivated to accept the nomination, request that he do so immediately. Garrett's action of accepting the nomination should be made as easy as possible for him. A **poor** example of requesting action is shown here:

> Garrett, if you feel that you can spare the time to be president-elect, I would appreciate your writing a letter stating so. Make sure that you let me know because if you don't accept, I will have to find someone else.

This paragraph does little to motivate Garrett to accept the nomination. The you–viewpoint is absent. The paragraph is negative; it emphasizes the alternative that he does not have to accept the position.

A **good** example of requesting action may be written as follows:

> Please accept the nomination for president-elect of Cajun Sales Managers. Call me at 555-4185 with your decision by June 30 so that I may place your name on the ballot.

Notice the direct, positive approach used in this paragraph. Accepting the nomination is made easy for Garrett; he simply telephones his acceptance.

SUMMARY—POOR AND GOOD MESSAGES TO GARRETT ASHBURN

Good and poor persuasive messages have been illustrated. The **poor** paragraphs are combined as a letter in Figure 13•2. This persuasive request does not follow the indirect plan outline as shown in Figure 13•1.

The chances of Garrett's accepting the president-elect nomination are improved in the **good** message shown in Figure 13•3. This effective persuasive message follows the guidelines described earlier in this chapter.

This case problem shows how the indirect plan can be effective in communicating persuasive messages. To further assist in understanding the use of the indirect plan in organizing persuasive messages, several examples of both good and bad messages are illustrated in the following pages.

PERSUASIVE REQUESTS

Organizations use both simple requests and complex requests. The simple request was discussed in Chapter 11 and should be constructed with the

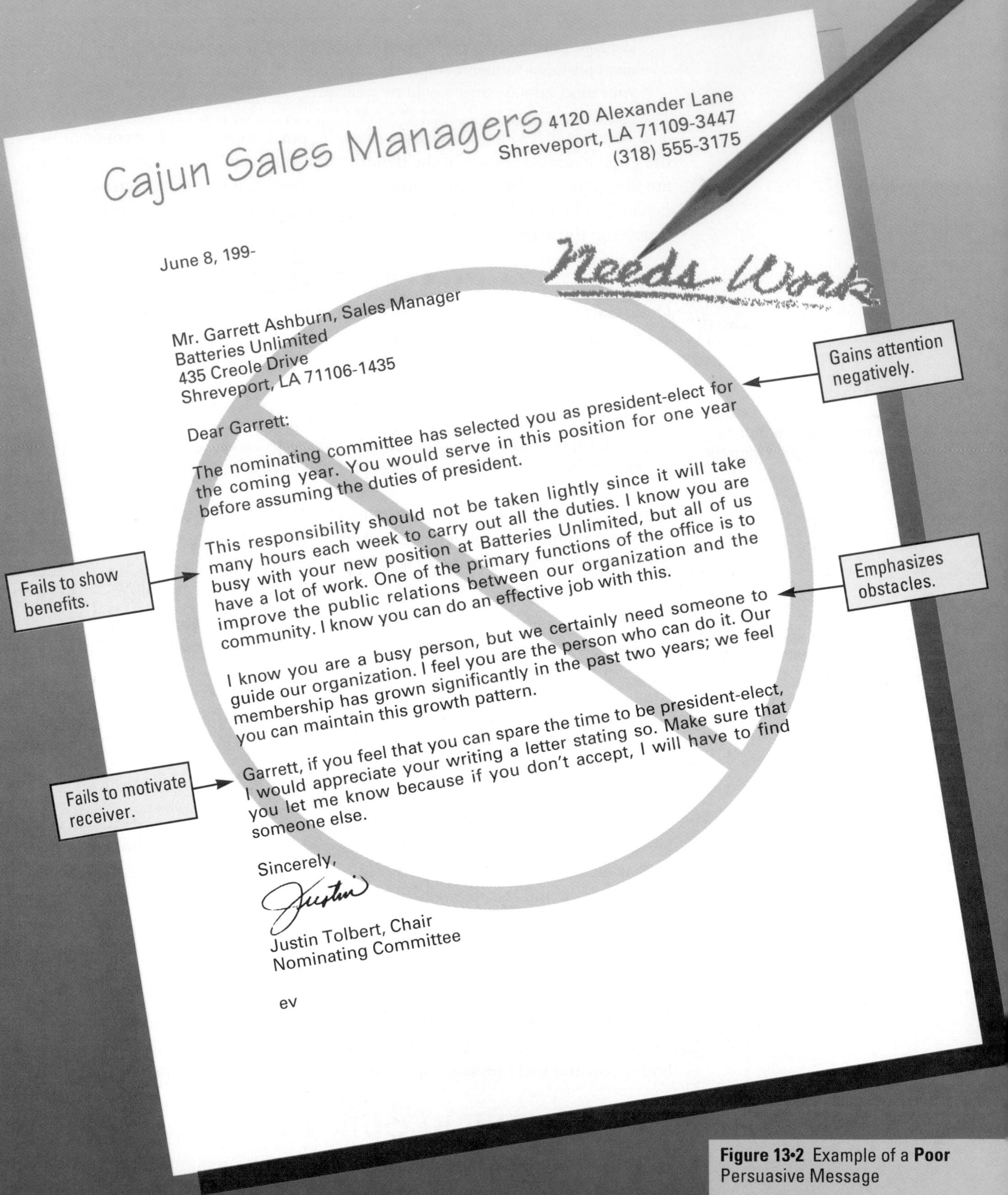

Cajun Sales Managers
4120 Alexander Lane
Shreveport, LA 71109-3447
(318) 555-3175

Needs Work

June 8, 199-

Mr. Garrett Ashburn, Sales Manager
Batteries Unlimited
435 Creole Drive
Shreveport, LA 71106-1435

Dear Garrett:

The nominating committee has selected you as president-elect for the coming year. You would serve in this position for one year before assuming the duties of president.

> Gains attention negatively.

This responsibility should not be taken lightly since it will take many hours each week to carry out all the duties. I know you are busy with your new position at Batteries Unlimited, but all of us have a lot of work. One of the primary functions of the office is to improve the public relations between our organization and the community. I know you can do an effective job with this.

> Fails to show benefits.

I know you are a busy person, but we certainly need someone to guide our organization. I feel you are the person who can do it. Our membership has grown significantly in the past two years; we feel you can maintain this growth pattern.

> Emphasizes obstacles.

Garrett, if you feel that you can spare the time to be president-elect, I would appreciate your writing a letter stating so. Make sure that you let me know because if you don't accept, I will have to find someone else.

> Fails to motivate receiver.

Sincerely,

Justin Tolbert, Chair
Nominating Committee

ev

Figure 13·2 Example of a **Poor** Persuasive Message

Cajun Sales Managers 4120 Alexander Lane
Shreveport, LA 71109-3447
(318) 555-3175

GOOD

June 8, 199-

Mr. Garrett Ashburn, Sales Manager
Batteries Unlimited
435 Creole Drive
Shreveport, LA 71106-1435

Dear Garrett:

Your dedication and hard work over the past ten years have been among the principal reasons for the outstanding growth of Cajun Sales Managers. The nominating committee, therefore, shows its appreciation to you for this service by nominating you president-elect.

As president-elect you would be able to observe the operation of the presidency and also would be able to assist the president with various duties. You might be asked to attend a few activities that the president could not attend; these functions would prepare you for assuming the position of president next year. The organization does not pay its officers, but the officers are exempt from paying dues.

Both your contacts and reputation in the business community would be increased. You would be consulted by the business leaders. Three of the last four presidents of CSM have been promoted to upper-level management positions in their companies. Promoting CSM would take some of your time, but this time would be well spent.

Please accept the nomination for president-elect of Cajun Sales Managers. Call me at 555-4185 with your decision by June 30 so that I may place your name on the ballot.

Sincerely,

Justin Tolbert, Chair
Nominating Committee

ev

> Focuses attention on receiver.

> Continues interest and keeps attention that was gained in first paragraph.

> Emphasizes proof of benefits to receiver.

> Motivates receiver and makes taking action easy.

Figure 13·3 Example of a **Good** Persuasive Message

Organizational plans for
requests may be:
• simple—direct
• complex—indirect

direct plan. The **complex request** is a persuasive message because in it you
will have to convince the receiver to take action. The complex request
should use the indirect plan.

> ***Business today consists of persuading crowds.***
>
> **Gerald Stanley Lee**

In this section we will be concerned only with complex (persuasive)
requests. Examples of persuasive requests are those that (1) seek an increase
in a department's budget, (2) want a donation to a community organization,
(3) look for participants for a research project, (4) desire a change in a work
schedule, and (5) want volunteers.

Figure 13•4 shows a **poor** persuasive request for employees to donate to
a company-sponsored charity. This example does not create any receiver
interest. The memo is written in the I–viewpoint rather than the you–viewpoint. The employees will have little motivation to support this year's fund
drive.

Figure 13•5 shows a **good** interoffice memo written in the you–viewpoint that creates receiver motivation for the same situation. The memo
gains attention, builds interest, stimulates desire, and makes taking action
easy.

The following table summarizes the approach used for the two types of
requests.

Request	Approach
Simple or routine	Direct
Persuasive or complex	Indirect

RECOMMENDATIONS

Recommendations are submitted
at all organizational levels.

Recommendations are best
when submitted in the indirect
persuasive plan.

A **recommendation** is a message that attempts to persuade the receiver to
take an action proposed by the sender. Individuals in business, government,
and civic organizations periodically submit recommendations to receivers
who are above, below, and at their same organizational level. They are most
effective when the indirect persuasive plan is employed. Examples that
should use the indirect plan include recommendations to a company officer
to advise the firm to replace obsolete equipment, to a manager to change a
company policy, and to a civic leader to use a tract of land for a city park
rather than a housing project.

Figure 13•6 shows a **poor** recommendation from Lynn Bowen, a supervisor, to Roger Musser, her manager, attempting to persuade him to give her

division responsibility for the manufacture of a new product. Lynn probably will not be successful in her recommendation if the poor memo is submitted. This memo is aimed at Lynn's desire to increase the size of her division, rather than at the advantages to the company of using her division to produce the new product. The memo is not written with the you–viewpoint. It also displays bitterness, which hinders communication. In addition, the memo is not written using the indirect plan—the key to successful persuasive messages.

The **good** memo in Figure 13•7 should increase the chances that Lynn's division will gain responsibility for the new product. Note how the indirect persuasive plan presents the *benefits*—of having Lynn's division produce the telephones—before the *recommendation*. This memo gains the manager's attention in the opening, uses the you–viewpoint in presenting the reasons supporting the recommendation, and presents the recommendation in a positive, professional manner. Note that this memo does not question the manager's decision to give another division responsibility for the telephones. Furthermore, it does not imply that another division is favored.

SPECIAL CLAIMS

Special claims are unique and should use the indirect persuasive plan. Routine claims use the direct plan and are discussed in Chapter 11. **Special or nonroutine claims** are those claims in which the fault is not indisputable and may require convincing the receiver that the sender is entitled to an adjustment or a refund.

Examples of special claims that should be organized as persuasive messages include the following: You want a roofing contractor, who has guaranteed his work, to replace the shingles on your office building because they are not aligned properly. A transportation company has purchased a fleet of 25 trucks, 20 of which have had their transmissions replaced rather than repaired in the first six months. The company wants the manufacturer to absorb the cost of the new transmissions. A work of art, which was purchased for $50,000, was found to be a forgery; the buyer demands reimbursement from the gallery that sold it.

Figure 13•8 is a **poor** special claim letter from Melba Preston Kennedy, owner of Preston Tower. Melba contracted to have wallpaper hung in the fifth floor office suites of the tower, but the contractor hung the wrong pattern. The writer of this letter is upset. The receiver's attention may be gained in the opening paragraph, but not in a way that will get the desired reaction. The writer clearly does not give the necessary details. The entire letter is negative, which will irritate the receiver and hinder getting the desired action—new wallpaper.

The letter in Figure 13•9 covers the same situation but is a **good** message. Notice how the writer shows the receiver the benefits to be gained by replacing the wallpaper. The writer of this letter remains calm and explains the necessary details for the receiver. The positive tone of the letter will encourage cooperation from the receiver. The writer is courteous throughout

comfy furniture
interoffice memorandum

F.D.

Needs Work

TO: All Employees
FROM: Felicia Downs, Human Resources Director
DATE: November 3, 199-
SUBJECT: Mountaintop Children's Home

The committee for selecting a charity for Comfy Furniture to sponsor has chosen Mountaintop Children's Home this year. We need you to send your donation no later than November 20.

We need to beat the $8,700 that we gave to Needline last year. We think that Mountaintop is in more need than was Needline. This year's goal is $10,000.

If you need more information, read the enclosed brochure that gives all the details.

tm

Enclosure

> **Impersonal—** does not gain attention.

> **Selfish—does** little to build interest.

> **Vague—difficult** for receiver to take action.

Figure 13-4 Example of a **Poor** Persuasive Request

comfy furniture

interoffice memorandum

TO: All Employees

FROM: Felicia Downs, Human Resources Director *F.D.*

DATE: November 3, 199-

SUBJECT: Mountaintop Children's Home

Imagine Thanksgiving without turkey or summer without a vacation. [Gains attention.]

The Mountaintop Children's Home makes sure that the 45 children who live there have those fun things. Mountaintop is a nonprofit organization that provides care for children who have lost their parents. A brochure describing the facilities and services provided at the home is enclosed. [Builds interest.]

Each year a committee consisting of one member from each department selects a charity for the Comfy Furniture employees to sponsor. This year we have pledged our support to Mountaintop. Last year the employees of Comfy generously gave $8,700 to Needline, and we know that you will help meet this year's $10,000 goal for the Mountaintop Children's Home. Your contribution is tax deductible. [Provides details that stimulate desire.]

Please return the enclosed pledge card by November 20. The amount you select will be deducted from your paycheck. The Mountaintop children will greatly appreciate and benefit from your generosity. [Makes taking action easy.]

tm

Enclosures

Figure 13·5 Example of a **Good** Persuasive Request

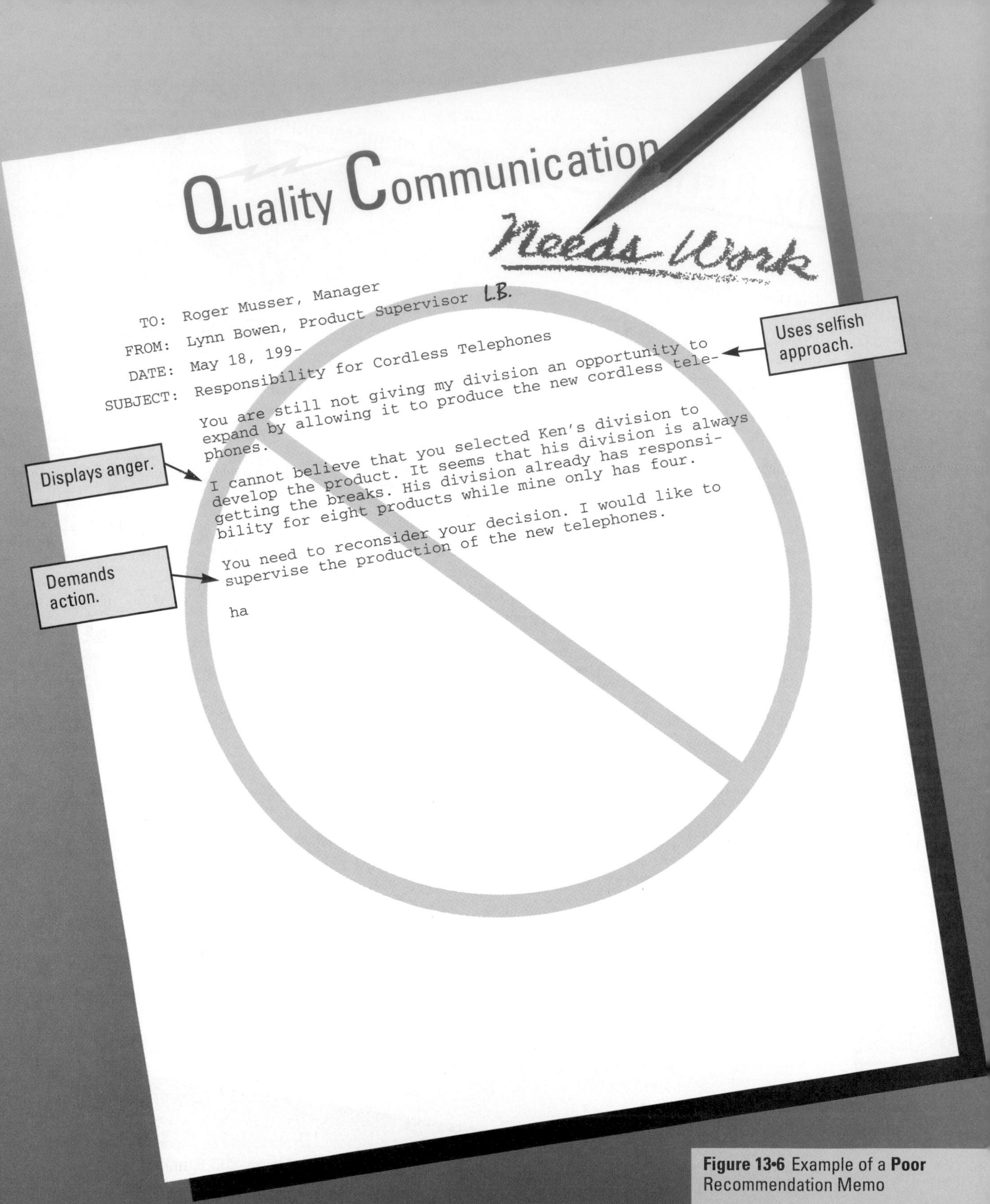

Quality **C**ommunication

Needs Work

TO: Roger Musser, Manager

FROM: Lynn Bowen, Product Supervisor L.B.

DATE: May 18, 199-

SUBJECT: Responsibility for Cordless Telephones

You are still not giving my division an opportunity to expand by allowing it to produce the new cordless telephones.

Displays anger.

I cannot believe that you selected Ken's division to develop the product. It seems that his division is always getting the breaks. His division already has responsibility for eight products while mine only has four.

Demands action.

You need to reconsider your decision. I would like to supervise the production of the new telephones.

ha

Uses selfish approach.

Figure 13•6 Example of a **Poor** Recommendation Memo

Quality Communication

GOOD

TO: Roger Musser, Manager

FROM: Lynn Bowen, Product Supervisor L.B.

DATE: May 18, 199-

SUBJECT: Responsibility for Cordless Telephones

Division C has been a leading profit center for Quality Communication for each of the last three years. The four products that it produces are in the top six of our most profitable products. One of the reasons that Division C is so profitable is that it produces its products in less time than our competitors do, putting us in a favorable cost position.

Gains the manager's attention.

Roger, you realize that there will be high demand for Quality's new cordless telephones. It will be critical that we mass produce these products quickly but with high quality. Division C had the lowest quality-control rejection rate of Quality's four divisions during the last three years.

Builds interest.

If Division C were to assume the task of cordless telephone production, it would need to add only five new employees—three temporary and two permanent. The other divisions would have to hire five permanent employees. In addition, the installation of the new equipment will be completed by July 1, reducing Division C's personnel requirements.

Stimulates desire.

I recommend that you give Division C responsibility for producing the new cordless telephones.

Gives a recommendation.

ha

Figure 13•7 Example of a **Good** Recommendation Memo

Preston Tower

1765 Sovereign Row   Topeka, KS 66631-1125   (913) 555-631_

Needs Work

July 12, 199-

Mr. Fred Klutts
K & S Designs, Inc.
218 Walnut Drive
Salina, KS 67401-0243

Dear Mr. Klutts:

You need to replace the wallpaper in Preston Tower because it is not what I ordered.

I did not pay $8,600 to redecorate and then not have the wallpaper properly match the carpeting. The tenant is threatening to leave due to your careless error.

I intend to have you replace all the paper on the fifth floor without charging me one dime. I need you to replace it promptly before the tenant leaves, creating another problem for me.

Sincerely,

Melba Preston Kennedy

Melba Preston Kennedy
Owner

rj

Is negative.

Shows anger.

Demands action rather than making a request.

Figure 13•8 Example of a **Poor** Special Claim Letter

July 12, 199-

Mr. Fred Klutts
K & S Designs, Inc.
218 Walnut Drive
Salina, KS 67401-0243

Dear Mr. Klutts:

You were selected to redecorate my fifth floor office suites because of your reputation as the best paint contractor in Kansas.

Attracts attention with praise.

You assisted me in selecting a wallpaper that would match the new carpet on the fifth floor. In fact, I paid an extra $4 a roll just to get perfect color coordination.

Gains interest by giving detail.

On the day we finalized the arrangements, I told you I would be out of town the week you would hang the paper. We agreed that my absence would create no problem, but it seems this was not true. Upon my return, I immediately noticed that the wallpaper that had been hung was not the color upon which we had agreed.

Adds details.

Because the paper is not the color that I had selected and does not match the new carpeting, please rehang the wallpaper using the proper color. The occupant of the suite needs the work completed by August 1.

Makes polite request and gives a deadline.

Sincerely,

Melba Preston Kennedy

Melba Preston Kennedy
Owner

rj

Figure 13·9 Example of a **Good** Special Claim Letter

the complaint but emphasizes that the contractor rehang the wallpaper and absorb the cost. Notice that a deadline for the completion of the job is given.

The following table summarizes the approach used for the two types of claims.

Claim	Approach
Simple or Routine	Direct
Special or Nonroutine	Indirect

SALES MESSAGES

Sales messages come in many different forms, such as letters, brochures, leaflets, catalogs, radio and television commercials, and billboards. Most of these messages are prepared by advertising professionals; however, you may one day be asked to compose one.

Before you compose a sales message, know the product or service you are going to sell. Know its strengths, its weaknesses, its competitors, and its market. As you compose the message, emphasize strengths and omit any mention of weaknesses. Your market should be researched carefully to determine how to appeal to your customers and to get their business.

Various techniques are used in sales messages to gain the receiver's attention: color, sentence fragments, catchy slogans, famous quotations, testimonials from celebrities, and descriptions of benefits. A salutation is frequently omitted from the message.

Once you gain the receiver's attention, you must maintain his or her interest to ensure that the entire message is read or heard. A careful analysis of the receiver is critical in preparing the message from the receiver's point of view. Extra care must be taken in the analysis of the receiver because sales messages are usually prepared for multiple receivers.

A **poor** sales message to retailers who may purchase from Custom Executive Computers is shown in Figure 13•10. This message is not written from the you–viewpoint. The letter fails to point out the benefits of the product. The microcomputer's features are given, but the writer does not explain why it is good that the machine has these features. The request for action is weak. How should the customer "let us know"?

A **good** sales letter is shown in Figure 13•11. Note how this letter stresses the benefits that retailers will receive if they purchase the Telecom Exec. The subject line is effective in gaining the reader's attention. Mentioning the retailer's profit will build interest. Notice how the letter integrates benefits and proof of those benefits. It not only points out the capabilities of the microcomputer but also explains how these capabilities will benefit the purchaser.

COLLECTION MESSAGES

A **collection message** is used by business firms to collect overdue accounts. The two purposes of collection messages are (1) to collect the money due, and (2) to retain goodwill with the customer.

Collection messages, generally, are written in three stages—reminder, appeal, and warning. Each stage is progressively more persuasive, and each stage has several steps within it. The number of steps in each stage will vary according to the type of business involved and the credit rating of the customer.

REMINDER STAGE

This stage is for customers who intend to pay but just need a reminder. The **reminder** is a simple and sometimes comical message intended to get a receiver to remember to pay a bill. Collection messages in this category are not considered persuasive and must never offend the receiver. These messages are normally only short notes or a sticker on a bill.

Examples of collection messages in the reminder stage include the following:

Past Due

Reminder

Please Remit

Messages in the reminder stage are very courteous because failure to make a payment is often only an oversight. A harsh reminder may well alienate a customer who had intended to pay on time. If the reminder fails, the collection process will proceed to the appeal stage.

Please don't make me beg.

APPEAL STAGE

An **appeal** is stronger than a reminder because the customer has failed to heed the reminder notice. You need to carefully analyze the customer before writing a letter of appeal. You will have to select the type of appeal that will persuade the customer to pay. You may appeal to the customer's pride, credit rating, morality, or reputation. Once you have selected the type of appeal to use, construct the message using the indirect persuasive outline.

A **poor** collection letter in the appeal stage is shown in Figure 13•12. This letter is too harsh. It is written from the writer's point of view and will cause anger, which will reduce rather than increase the chances of collection. Necessary details such as the amount due are not furnished.

The **good** collection letter in Figure 13•13 is recommended for the appeal stage. It is written in a positive, courteous tone. The opening paragraph will get the customer's attention by appealing to his pride. The customer should believe that the store is trying to help him maintain his

Custom Executive Computers

1763 SKILLMAN LANE   RALEIGH, NC 27618-2437
(919) 555-8319

Needs Work

April 10, 199-

Microsystems Center
789 Omega Road
Sparta, VA 22552-3125

Ladies and Gentlemen:

Custom Executive Computers has lowered its wholesale price on the Telecom Exec portable microcomputer from $2,199 to $1,459.

The Telecom Exec comes with one 3.5" high-density disk drive. It has a 13-inch color monitor which displays 25 lines of 80 characters. The Telecom Exec uses the Intel 486 microprocessor.

The Telecom Exec is a good portable microcomputer. It is compatible with all software packages for the IBM Personal Computer. Another good feature is that it can be expanded from a 80 Mb hard disk drive to a 120 Mb hard disk drive.

Let us know if you want any Telecom Exec at this reduced price. Remember our policy of a 5 percent discount if you order ten or more machines.

Sincerely,

Pauline Wombley

Pauline Wombley
Vice President for Sales

bc

Opening is not from the you–viewpoint.

Receiver's benefits are not re-emphasized.

Receiver's benefits are not pointed out.

Request for action is not positive.

Figure 13•10 Example of a **Poor** Sales Message

Custom Executive Computers
1763 SKILLMAN LANE   RALEIGH, NC 27618-2437
(919) 555-8319

April 10, 199-

Microsystems Center
789 Omega Road
Sparta, VA 22552-3125

TELECOM EXEC REDUCED TO $1,459

You can now purchase the Telecom Exec portable microcomputer with a 3.5" high-density disk drive for only $1,459. This low price allows you to earn $500 if you sell it at the suggested retail price of $1,959.

> Mention of profit gains attention.

The 13-inch color monitor of the Telecom Exec is small enough to make it portable but large enough to display 25 lines of 80 characters. The Telecom Exec's Intel 486 microprocessor ensures that the computer can outperform any 386-based machine. The 486 can process data twice as fast as can the 386. The Telecom Exec's storage capacity can easily be expanded from a 80 Mb hard disk drive to a 120 Mb hard disk drive. The wholesale price of the 120 Mb drive is only $275. This expansion will allow customers to have the same capabilities that they would have with desktop microcomputers.

> The value of the characteristics is given.

> Ease of expansion will interest some readers.

All software packages designed to run on the IBM Personal Computer will operate on the Telecom Exec. This compatibility allows the customer a wide selection of programs. In addition, many programs designed only for the Telecom Exec are available.

> The availability of software will build desire to purchase computer.

Please place your order for these low-cost, high-profit machines by calling our toll-free number, 1-800-555-9675. If you order ten or more machines before May 10, 199-, you will earn an additional 5 percent discount!

> Action can be taken easily.

Pauline Wombley

PAULINE WOMBLEY, VICE PRESIDENT FOR SALES

bc

Figure 13·11 Example of a **Good** Sales Message

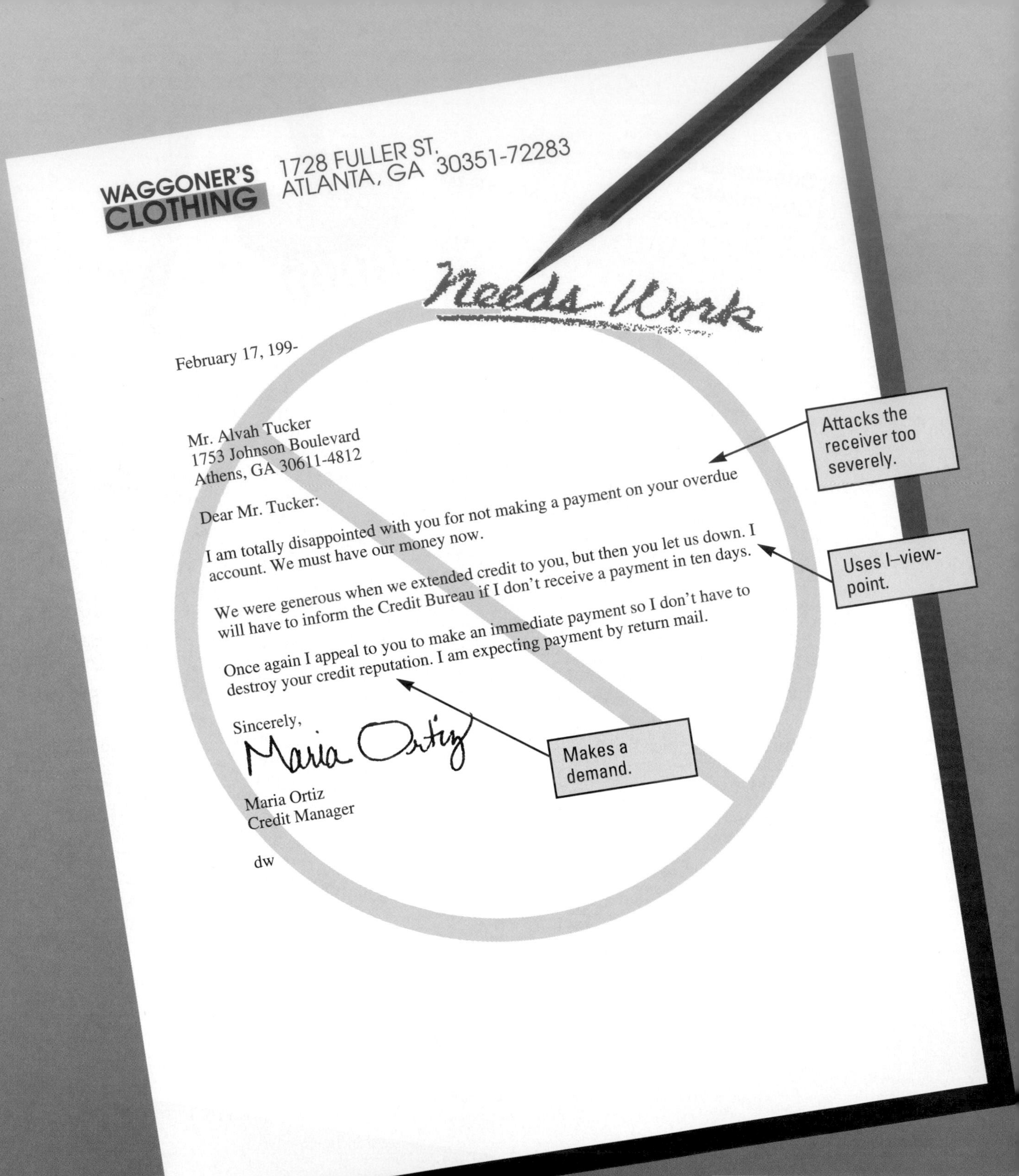

WAGGONER'S CLOTHING
1728 FULLER ST.
ATLANTA, GA 30351-72283

Needs Work

February 17, 199-

Mr. Alvah Tucker
1753 Johnson Boulevard
Athens, GA 30611-4812

Dear Mr. Tucker:

I am totally disappointed with you for not making a payment on your overdue account. We must have our money now.

We were generous when we extended credit to you, but then you let us down. I will have to inform the Credit Bureau if I don't receive a payment in ten days.

Once again I appeal to you to make an immediate payment so I don't have to destroy your credit reputation. I am expecting payment by return mail.

Sincerely,

Maria Ortiz

Maria Ortiz
Credit Manager

dw

Attacks the receiver too severely.

Uses I–view-point.

Makes a demand.

Figure 13·12 Example of a **Poor** Collection Message—Appeal Stage

WAGGONER'S CLOTHING 1728 FULLER ST.
ATLANTA, GA 30351-72283

GOOD

February 17, 199-

Mr. Alvah Tucker
1753 Johnson Boulevard
Athens, GA 30611-4812

Dear Mr. Tucker:

You take pride in your appearance because you selected our suits for your wardrobe. I know this pride extends to other aspects of your life.

You have been a valued credit customer of ours for many years, and we would like this relationship to continue. For some reason you have not responded to the reminders that were sent on December 20, January 20, and February 2. Your account is three months overdue.

Please send a check for $725.90 in the enclosed envelope by March 1 so that your credit reputation can remain in good standing.

Sincerely,

Maria Ortiz

Maria Ortiz
Credit Manager

dw

Enc.

Uses pride appeal.

Reviews past actions courteously.

Motivates receiver to take action.

Figure 13•13 Example of a **Good**
Collection Message—Appeal Stage

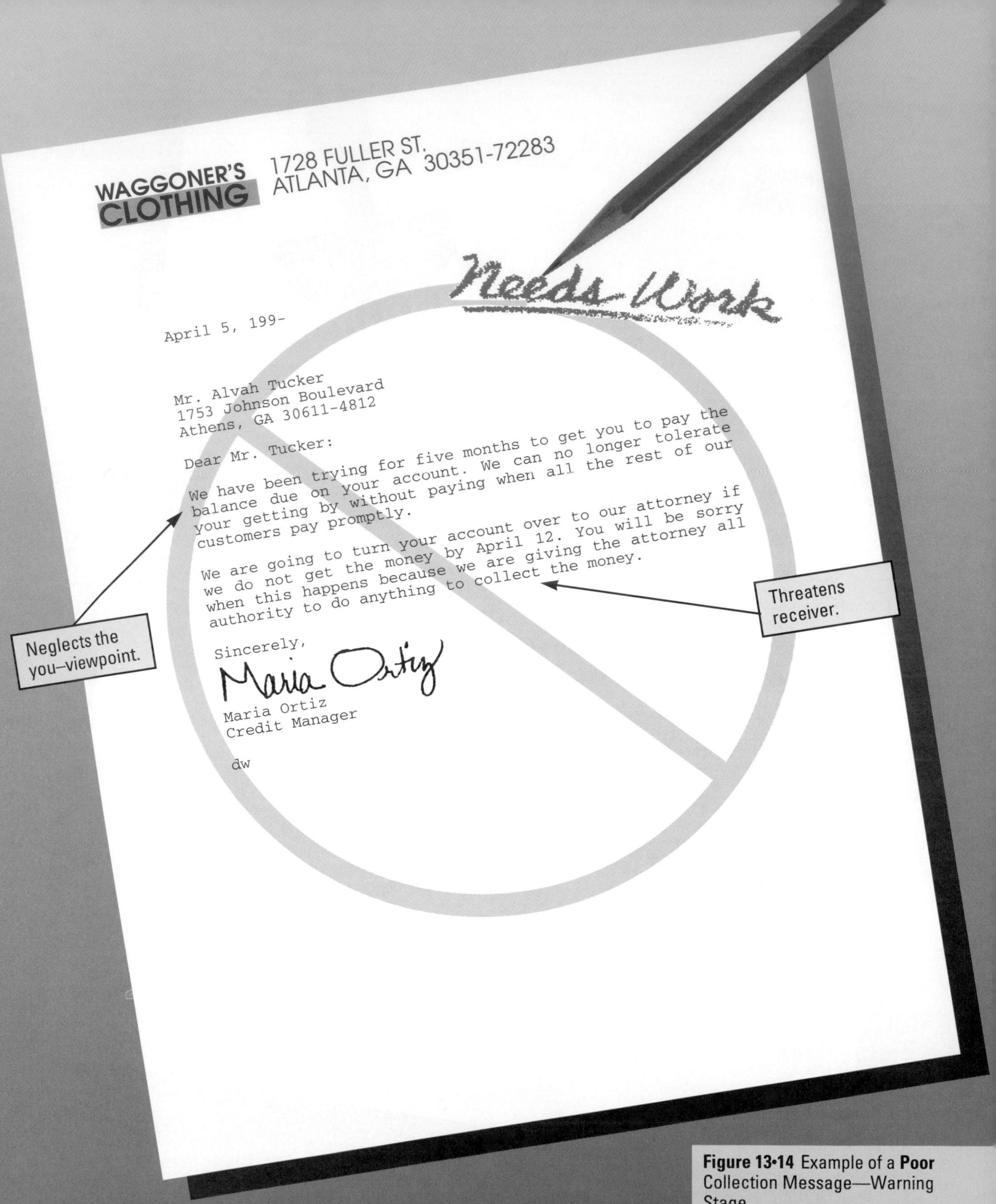

WAGGONER'S CLOTHING
1728 FULLER ST.
ATLANTA, GA 30351-72283

Needs Work

April 5, 199-

Mr. Alvah Tucker
1753 Johnson Boulevard
Athens, GA 30611-4812

Dear Mr. Tucker:

We have been trying for five months to get you to pay the balance due on your account. We can no longer tolerate your getting by without paying when all the rest of our customers pay promptly.

We are going to turn your account over to our attorney if we do not get the money by April 12. You will be sorry when this happens because we are giving the attorney all authority to do anything to collect the money.

Sincerely,

Maria Ortiz

Maria Ortiz
Credit Manager

dw

Neglects the you–viewpoint.

Threatens receiver.

Figure 13•14 Example of a **Poor** Collection Message—Warning Stage

WAGGONER'S CLOTHING 1728 FULLER ST.
ATLANTA, GA 30351-72283

April 5, 199-

Mr. Alvah Tucker
1753 Johnson Boulevard
Athens, CA 30611-4812

Dear Mr. Tucker:

Your account balance of $725.90 is five months past due, and you have ignored all our collection attempts. Your failure to respond leaves us no choice but to turn the account over to our attorney.

> Gains reader's attention.

Legal action is not pleasant for either of us, but it is necessary because of your failure to respond to our previous notices. A lawsuit will be expensive and embarrassing to you.

> Reminds reader of past actions.

Our attorney assures us that if your account balance is paid by April 12, no legal action will be taken; your credit reputation will be maintained. Please send the check in the enclosed envelope prior to April 12 to avoid this action.

> Motivates receiver to take immediate action.

Sincerely,

Maria Ortiz

Maria Ortiz
Credit Manager

dw

Enc.

Figure 13·15 Example of a **Good** Collection Message—Warning Stage

excellent credit reputation. The store's chances of collecting are greatly increased with this letter.

WARNING STAGE

The warning stage is used only when other stages have failed.

Reminders and appeals may not succeed in collecting all past-due bills. When these efforts fail, you must move into the final stage—warning. Until now you were interested in maintaining the customer's goodwill while trying to collect. When the warning stage is reached, you are interested only in collecting the past-due amount.

A **warning** is the last opportunity for a customer to pay an account before it is transferred to a collection agency, a credit bureau, or an attorney. Use the direct plan to develop your message for this stage. Sending the warning letter by registered mail—so signature is required—adds to the importance of the message and creates a sense of urgency.

A **poor** warning stage collection message is shown in Figure 13•14. Look back on pages 380 and 381. These pages show a letter with a poor warning stage and a letter with a good warning stage. In the poor example, the customer will be inclined to resist because of the anger shown here. The writer does not get directly to the warning in a firm manner without displaying anger. Notice that the amount due is never given. The use of threats is illegal and will not increase the writer's chances of collection.

Figure 13•15 shows how a **good** collection letter in the warning stage should be written. This letter gets directly to the main idea—the customer's account is past due, and no attempt is being made to correct the problem. Facts are presented in a positive tone with no sign of anger. In the last paragraph the customer is told exactly what must be done to avoid legal action.

Finally, let us summarize the approach that is used in each stage of collection messages.

Stage	Approach
Reminder	Direct
Appeal	Indirect
Warning	Direct

Your use of the indirect plan outline and examples in this chapter will enable you to compose effective persuasive messages. The ability to do so will serve you well throughout your career.

DISCUSSION QUESTIONS

1. What are the two primary purposes of a persuasive message?

2. Describe three characteristics of the interest section of the indirect plan for persuasion.

3. Describe how an effective communicator builds desire in a persuasive message.

4. Identify the organizational plan that should be used in recommendations, and explain why it should be used.

5. Identify the organizational plan that should be used by a grocery owner who wants the entire parking area resurfaced because asphalt is cracking after only three months. Explain why the organizational plan was selected.

6. Discuss the analysis that should be completed before a sales message is composed.

7. Explain why the following paragraph would be ineffective in opening a sales message. Rewrite the paragraph to be more effective.

We need to sell many Executive Typewriters. Our warehouse is full, and bills need to be paid.

8. Why is it especially important that a writer carefully analyze a customer before writing a collection letter in the appeal stage?

9. Why are collection letters written in stages? What are the three stages?

10. Discuss the circumstances under which a request should be written using (a) the direct plan, and (b) the indirect plan.

APPLICATION EXERCISES

1. Analyze a sales letter that has been received in your household. Identify the parts of the message that correspond to the parts of the organizational plan for persuasive messages.

2. Visit a business in your community and request copies of the various collection letters it uses. Compare the approach used by the business and the approach discussed in this chapter.

3. Outline the ideas to be included in the interest and desire sections of a message to send to your school's administration recommending that final examinations be eliminated.

4. Collect and review several advertisements from newspapers and magazines. Write a memo persuading your instructor to teach the approach of the ad that you believe is most effective.

5. Discuss your personal experiences in receiving persuasive information. Analyze the strengths and weaknesses of the quality of these messages.

CASE PROBLEMS

PERSUASIVE REQUESTS

1. Cleo's Barbecue was established as a restaurant three years ago. Since the opening of the first restaurant, 26 additional establishments have been started in your state. As marketing director of Cleo's, you are interested in determining whether the restaurant can expand to three neighboring states. Prepare a cover letter to be sent along with a questionnaire designed to determine consumer support if restaurants are opened in these three states. Your letter should persuade the individuals receiving the questionnaires to return them.

2. You are the business manager of Missouri Ostrich, Inc. The company's primary income comes from selling ostriches. The ostrich market, however, is not well established. A $25,000 payment on a loan is due on April 15, and you are unable to make the payment. Write a letter to Ruben Hurwitz, Loan Officer, Houston County Bank, Mountain Grove, Missouri 65711-1402, requesting that payment be postponed for three months. You have some good birds that will be ready for sale in three months. Ruben will need to be strongly persuaded because ostrich farming is new and high risk.

3. Ann Jacobs has been working for your organization for five years and has been doing an outstanding job. In fact, she has been doing such an excellent job that you immediately granted the vacation dates she requested. Since granting that request, you have learned that the company auditors have scheduled their annual audit during the period that Ann would like her vacation. You need Ann in the office during the auditors' visit, and the visitation date cannot be changed. Write Ann a memo requesting that she change her vacation dates. If she changes her plans to a future date, you will give her one additional week of paid vacation.

4. You are program director for the student economics organization on your campus. You have done such an outstanding job that you have been asked to obtain the keynote speaker for this year's state conference. You would like to get an economist from

Germany. Write a letter to the University of Heidelberg in Germany requesting that they furnish a speaker at no cost, except travel-related expenses, for the state conference. Add any details needed to make this a complete request.

5. You are the director of a wellness clinic at a local hospital. Doctors in the clinic wish to conduct a research project to help people lower blood pressure and cholesterol levels through diet and exercise rather than medication. Volunteers are needed to participate in the program. Write a personalized form letter to be sent to patients to persuade them to volunteer for the project. Note that no monetary compensation will be given, but that the weekly checkups are provided without cost.

RECOMMENDATIONS

6. You are the administrative office manager of the Professional Insurance Company (PIC) home office. The company has outgrown its present facilities. You would like the company to construct a new building that would be designed specifically for PIC. The present facility could be remodeled and expanded for less money, but it would not be so luxurious, functional, or efficient as a new building. Write a memo to the company's president recommending that a new office headquarters be built. Include necessary details to increase the chances of your recommendation being approved.

Text 13A

7. You are the president of the Student Government Association for your school. Numerous students have complained of difficulty in finding parking spaces on campus. You have noticed an empty parking lot behind a vacant building one block from campus. Write a letter to the owner recommending that students be permitted to park on the lot during the week.

8. Becky Wolf is an excellent clarinetist. She received many honors in high school. She is now working in Memphis, Tennessee, and has been identified as a potential member of the city's symphonic orchestra. She needs a personal letter of recommendation. Write a letter to the Memphis Symphony Orchestra Board of Directors telling them what an asset Becky would be.

9. You are the human resources director for Scurlock Department Store. Employees of your organization are in need of communication training. Izumi Mori, the training director, has informed you that she has two options for providing this training. She can conduct the training using personnel in her division, or she can hire an outside consulting firm. You have not been particularly pleased with the in-house training in the past and would like her to hire Communicators, Inc. Write a memo to Izumi giving her your recommendation. Add any details to make the memo complete.

10. Bellville Savings and Loan has a policy that customers may borrow money only for a home in which they will reside. Many

customers would like to purchase other property, such as rental houses or weekend homes. Bellville Savings and Loan cannot lend the money for these purchases but will recommend applicants to another financial institution. Write a personalized form letter that could be used to recommend these individuals. Supply necessary details.

SPECIAL CLAIMS

11. Rhonda Ragan bought her father an 1876 twenty-cent piece for $1,250. The coin was purchased from Ted's Numismatics as Uncirculated (MS-60). The coin showed wear on Liberty's kneecaps and hair, and there was wear on the eagle's breast on the reverse. Her father, an avid coin collector, graded the coin as Extremely Fine (XF) to About Uncirculated (AU). This coin in Grade XF-AU sells for about $275. Write a letter to Ted's Numismatics requesting a replacement coin or a check for $975. Add necessary details to make the letter complete.

12. You were recently involved in an automobile accident. As you were going to work early one morning, a deer jumped in your path. You were traveling at such a high rate of speed that you could not avoid hitting the animal. Damages to your car are estimated at $1,495. An accident report was filed, and you did not receive a ticket. Your insurance company will pay only $800; it feels you were partially responsible because you were traveling too fast. Write a letter to your insurance company asking it to pay the full amount less the $100 deductible.

13. You purchased a microcomputer from a mail order store and discovered when you unpackaged it that it did not work. You called the company's technical support division and spoke to Rebecca Manning. Upon hearing the symptoms, Rebecca stated that the power supply was faulty and recommended that you return the CPU. When the replacement unit arrived, the monitor would not work. Experiencing these problems, you decide to return the entire computer for a full refund. Write a letter to Compuco requesting a refund for the microcomputer, including shipping costs. Add details to make the letter complete.

14. Bill Porter owns an orchard containing 1,000 peach trees. This spring Bill purchased 100 peach trees that were later found to be diseased. Not only did these trees die but it also caused 500 other trees to die. Write a letter for Bill to Greenbriar Nursery requesting replacement trees or a $12,000 refund to cover the cost of the trees and the labor.

15. Holiday Tours is an agency that arranges package tours for clients. Often clients return from a tour and complain that accommodations did not meet the standards described in the brochures. Prepare a personalized form letter that could be sent to hotels and motels asking for a refund for a dissatisfied customer.

SALES MESSAGES

16. You are treasurer of your student business organization and have made arrangements with a local nursery for your organization to receive $2 for each mum corsage sold for homecoming. Write a form letter that could be sent to students promoting the sale of these corsages. Add the necessary details to make the letter complete.

17. You are a member of your school's Humanics Student Association, which has decided to organize a retired-persons tour to the Black Forest of Germany for its service project. Several tasks must be accomplished for this project. The tasks include:

    a. Contacting a travel agency to obtain airfare information.

    b. Writing a letter to a Tourist Information Office in one of the towns in the Black Forest area to obtain necessary information for developing a sales letter about the tour.

    c. Finding the exchange rate for German deutsche marks to U.S. dollars.

    d. Writing a form letter that could be sent to the retired people in the area advertising this tour. The letter should include the cost of the tour (airline tickets, lodging, food, and ground transportation). Have interested individuals send a deposit for the tour.

18. Ralph Dupont is building a new home in an exclusive neighborhood in New Orleans, Louisiana. Most homes in this neighborhood have tennis courts, swimming pools, sauna rooms, and hot tubs. Write a sales letter to Ralph convincing him to purchase a hot tub from your company, Relaxation Experts. Add the necessary details.

19. Reed's Furniture has been operating as a retail furniture store in your hometown for 25 years. Management recently decided to expand its stock to include waterbeds. The Comfort Sleep, which Reed's will sell, offers standard-, queen-, and king-size waterbeds. A complete waterbed with mattress, heater, and bed frame will start at $199.99. Write a letter to your customers announcing the addition of waterbeds to your inventory. Add details to make the letter complete and to gain the reader's attention.

20. A magazine sales clearinghouse offers sororities and fraternities an opportunity to make money through sales projects. The clearinghouse has a publication list of 300 nationally known magazines and a selection of more than 500 records and tapes. A participating organization earns 30 percent of the total proceeds from the project. Develop a form letter that could be sent to the presidents of professional and social organizations on college campuses throughout the country.

COLLECTION MESSAGES

21. St. Anthony Laundry permits its commercial customers to pay monthly. The Scenic Hills Lodge is four months past due in its

payments. This has just been brought to your attention. You would like to keep Scenic Hills as a customer, but you need to collect the past-due balance of $735. At a meeting with Scenic Hills' manager, Debbie Kramer, it was agreed that the motel would pay $50 per month on the past-due balance and cash for the laundry delivered each month. Since the meeting with Debbie, the motel has operated on a cash basis for each month, but has made no payments on the past-due balance. Write a letter to Debbie reminding her of the agreement to make payments on the past-due account.

22. Kent Fulsom has been a credit customer of Thurman Furniture Store for eight years. He is a good customer but periodically fails to make payments on his account. He is currently four months past due ($235.81); several reminders have produced no response. As credit manager of Thurman's, write an appeal collection letter to Kent requesting payment.

23. You are the branch manager of Northern Optical Center. Nine months have passed since you sold George Huckabay a pair of Softezee contact lenses for $275. George made a down payment of $50 but has not made any additional payments. You have sent him four reminders and five letters appealing for your money. You are no longer interested in maintaining a good customer relationship with Mr. Huckabay; you simply wish to collect your $225. Write a warning collection letter to Mr. Huckabay requesting immediate payment. If this payment is not received within 15 days, you will forward the account to a collection agency. Add details to the letter to make it complete.

24. Cosmetology Supplies Company sells beauty supplies to hair care shops in a six-state area. Credit is extended to each business after a credit check is conducted. Nanci's Salon accumulated a credit balance of $736.89 over a six-month period before Cosmetology Supplies revoked Nanci's credit privileges. Nanci's has been sent six collection letters, but no response has been received. Write a letter for the collection office informing Nanci's that it must pay the $736.89 balance within ten days or the account will be forwarded to an attorney.

25. Acme Finance Company's primary business is lending money to individuals who are purchasing used cars. Often individuals make payments for a period of time and then suddenly stop paying on their accounts. Sometimes a reminder will get them to continue their payments; sometimes it will not. Write a form letter that could be individualized for each customer requesting payment to update the account. Add necessary details.

MESSAGE ANALYSIS

Text 13C

Correct the errors in the following letter that has been written to Zachary Gibbs who has not made a payment on his motorcycle for the past three months.

I am tired of trying to get you to make payments on your motorcycle. You purchased your bike on June 12 and you have made only one payment on it.

The owner is on my back to collect the money from you. He wants me to go to your house and bring back the bike. I know that you were so happy to get it that I would hate to take it away from you. However, you must start making payments immediately or else I will have to confiscate the bike.

I will be expecting to get your $375 check to cover the three months of overdue payments by October 12 or I will have to take other action.

CHAPTER 14 Goodwill Messages

Learning Objectives

Your learning objectives for this chapter include the following:

- To be able to describe goodwill messages
- To explain when to use goodwill messages
- To compose the six common types of goodwill messages
- To describe the criteria for selecting the three styles of goodwill messages

Previous chapters have stressed the use of the you–viewpoint and the creation of goodwill. It has been suggested that you maintain good relationships with receivers by personalizing positive, neutral, negative, and persuasive messages. Certain messages have only one purpose, however, and that is to convey goodwill.

A **goodwill message** is written to communicate your concern and interest. Sending a goodwill message shows that you care about the receiver. Avoid canceling the positive effects by inserting statements that will cause the receiver to think you are simply trying to further a business relationship. Your goodwill messages should cause your receiver to form a positive opinion of you—the sender of the message. Timeliness is of utmost importance; goodwill can be lost if a message is received several weeks after an event.

TYPES OF GOODWILL MESSAGES

The types of goodwill messages are congratulations, condolence, appreciation, invitation, holiday greetings, and welcome.

CONGRATULATIONS

Everyone enjoys receiving praise. A message that praises the receiver for an accomplishment or an achievement is referred to as a message of **congratulations.** One of the reasons that congratulatory messages are so effective in building goodwill is that organizations and businesspersons do not use them very often. Congratulatory messages may be as formal as a typewritten letter about a promotion, or as informal as a handwritten note attached to a newspaper clipping of a birth announcement.

Congratulatory messages are sent to both individuals and organizations. The occasion that warrants such a message may be either personal or business in nature. A congratulatory message may be sent to an individual on the occasion of a business-related accomplishment, such as attaining the highest sales for the month, retiring after 30 years of service, or receiving a promotion. You also may send a congratulatory message to an individual for a personal event, such as a birthday, an engagement, a marriage, a birth, or an election to office in a social or civic organization. A business firm could receive a message of congratulations for expansion of its company,

The purpose of some messages is to promote goodwill.

Positive opinions are formed by goodwill messages.

Certain occasions call for goodwill messages.

Timely congratulatory messages are effective.

Congratulatory messages are sent for accomplishments or special occasions.

A letter of congratulations may be presented along with a plaque or pin.

relocation to a new building, announcement of a new product, or celebration of an anniversary.

Congratulatory business messages should be written in a personal, sincere manner. A direct approach should be used by immediately mentioning the honor or accomplishment. The message should focus on the receiver from start to finish. A closing that refers to the writer's assistance to the receiver in his or her achievement diminishes goodwill. A congratulatory letter to an individual for being elected to an office is shown in Figure 14•1.

A direct approach should be used in composing a congratulatory message.

CONDOLENCE

A letter of **condolence** or sympathy is difficult to write because it deals with misfortune; but when written properly, it should leave no doubt about your empathy and, more importantly, should help ease the pain felt by the receiver.

Messages of condolence must be sincere.

Messages of sympathy may be sent for an illness, death, natural disaster, or other misfortune. They may be typewritten or handwritten, or they may be in the form of a printed card. Handwritten messages are by far the most personal and will be the most appreciated.

The direct approach should be used for condolence letters. Begin with the purpose of the message—conveying sympathy. Only the necessary details need to be mentioned, and these should be treated positively and sincerely. For example, it is better to assure the survivor that she or he was appreciated and loved by the deceased person, in a letter of sympathy prompted by the death of a loved one, rather than eulogizing the deceased person. It is also appropriate to mention a personal detail of the deceased if such details are known to the writer; for example, "I remember your mention of the wonderful summer vacations you spent with your grandmother. I know that these memories will be even more precious to you now and in the future."

Make a sympathy letter short and positive.

Figure 14•1 Congratulatory Letter

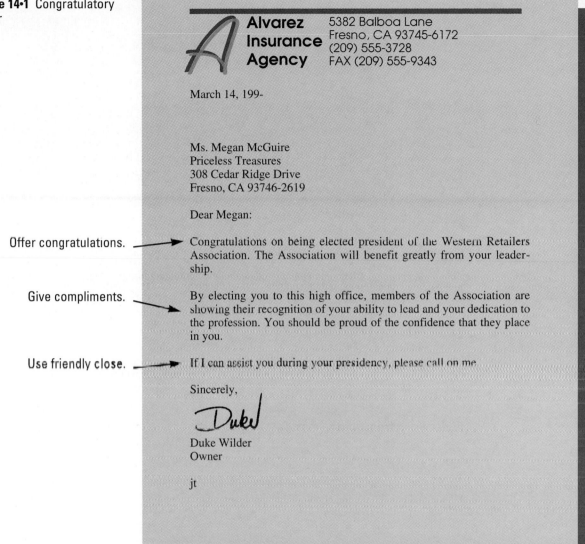

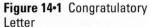
Alvarez
Insurance
Agency

5382 Balboa Lane
Fresno, CA 93745-6172
(209) 555-3728
FAX (209) 555-9343

March 14, 199-

Ms. Megan McGuire
Priceless Treasures
308 Cedar Ridge Drive
Fresno, CA 93746-2619

Dear Megan:

Offer congratulations. → Congratulations on being elected president of the Western Retailers Association. The Association will benefit greatly from your leadership.

Give compliments. → By electing you to this high office, members of the Association are showing their recognition of your ability to lead and your dedication to the profession. You should be proud of the confidence that they place in you.

Use friendly close. → If I can assist you during your presidency, please call on me.

Sincerely,

Duke

Duke Wilder
Owner

jt

If appropriate, a letter of condolence can offer assistance. Your message may be concluded by referring to the future in a positive way. Figure 14•2 shows a letter sent to a business friend whose building was destroyed by a tornado.

APPRECIATION

Most people do not expect rewards for acts of kindness or thoughtfulness; however, we all enjoy knowing that our efforts are appreciated.

Messages of gratitude show your appreciation.

A letter of **appreciation** may be sent for longtime thoughtfulness or for a onetime favor. Some examples of individuals who have shown sustained thoughtfulness include a long-standing, loyal customer; a faithful employee for many years; a friend who has consistently recommended a company and brought it many customers; and a volunteer who has generously contributed

Figure 14·2 Condolence
Letter

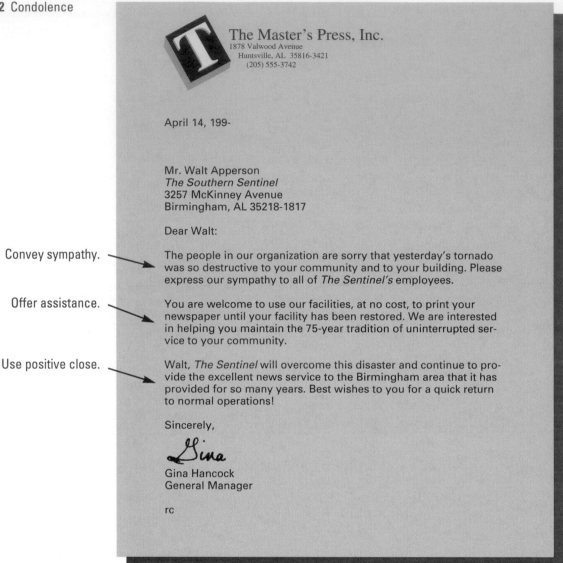

The Master's Press, Inc.
1878 Valwood Avenue
Huntsville, AL 35816-3421
(205) 555-3742

April 14, 199-

Mr. Walt Apperson
The Southern Sentinel
3257 McKinney Avenue
Birmingham, AL 35218-1817

Dear Walt:

Convey sympathy. → The people in our organization are sorry that yesterday's tornado was so destructive to your community and to your building. Please express our sympathy to all of *The Sentinel's* employees.

Offer assistance. → You are welcome to use our facilities, at no cost, to print your newspaper until your facility has been restored. We are interested in helping you maintain the 75-year tradition of uninterrupted service to your community.

Use positive close. → Walt, *The Sentinel* will overcome this disaster and continue to provide the excellent news service to the Birmingham area that it has provided for so many years. Best wishes to you for a quick return to normal operations!

Sincerely,

Gina

Gina Hancock
General Manager

rc

time and effort to charitable causes. Letters expressing thanks to such persons are always appropriate. Examples of letters of gratitude for one-time favors include a complimentary letter from a customer to a service department, a letter to a guest speaker who has given an excellent presentation, a letter to a new customer, a letter to a new member of an organization, and a letter to someone who has found a lost article and returned it to the owner.

Letters of appreciation should follow the direct approach. The good news—the expression of gratitude—should be given in the first paragraph and be followed by supporting evidence in a second or succeeding paragraphs. The letter should conclude with a comment of appreciation in the final paragraph. The thought of the letter, not the length of the letter, is the

Thank the receiver in the first paragraph.

Figure 14•3 Letter of Appreciation

POSTON REALTY

3152 Martin King Boulevard   Tempe, AZ 85283-1362   (602) 555-9315
FAX (602) 555-6269

August 8, 199-

Mr. Perry Shepherd
1735 Sunset Road
Tempe, AZ 85283-3521

Dear Perry:

Say thank you. →
Thank you for recommending Poston Realty to Ms. Valerie Thompson. You can be sure that we are doing our best to locate a home for Valerie in which she will be comfortable and proud to live.

Give supporting comments. →
Valerie is a welcome addition to our community. I know that you must be most pleased to have hired a person of such caliber.

Express appreciation →
Perry, your confidence in Poston Realty is appreciated. We welcome seeing any clients that you send us and will do everything we can to locate a residence that is right for them.

Sincerely,

Jeremy

Jeremy Poston
President

jd

important consideration. A letter thanking a client for recommending a prospective home buyer to a realtor is shown in Figure 14•3.

INVITATION

A business **invitation** is a request for an individual's presence and is used in various situations. Inviting employees to a small social gathering, asking prominent community members to attend a fund-raising event, inviting civic leaders and selected customers to a company open house are all examples of invitations that are currently used in the business community. A form letter inviting selected local citizens to a $15-a-plate dinner recognizing honor students is shown in Figure 14•4.

Figure 14•4 Letter of Invitation

ACADEMIC Booster Club
425 Quebec Street
Colfax, IA 50054-1362
(515) 555-5372

May 3, 199–

(Individualized
Inside
Address)

Dear (Name):

Extend invitation.

You are invited to join the Academic Booster Club for dinner at the Colfax Steak House on May 20 at 6:30 P.M. to honor the outstanding May graduates of Colfax High School.

Give details.

The $15 price per plate includes a steak dinner for you and your guests and helps to provide complimentary dinners for the honor students.

Through your commitment to the community, you have set a fine example for the students of Colfax High School. Your participation in this important community function will make possible the recognition of these students' high academic achievements.

Request reply.

Please send your reservations for yourself and your guests by May 15. Checks should be made payable to Academic Booster Club.

Sincerely,

Victoria Gomez
President

kb

An invitation may be formal or informal.

An invitation may be handwritten, it may be typed on company stationery, or it may be a formal, printed invitation. It should include all the necessary details such as the date, time, place, and suggested dress. In order to plan efficiently, an invitation should include an *RSVP;* that is, a request for a reply to the invitation.

HOLIDAY GREETING

Holiday greetings may be sent to celebrate festive seasons.

A **holiday greeting** message can be sent before or during any festive season. New Year's Day, Easter, Labor Day, Thanksgiving, Hanukkah, and Christmas are holidays generally celebrated in the United States. Businesses participating in international trade should be aware of and acknowledge appropriate holidays in the countries where they have employees, customers, or suppliers.

A greeting card is used often.

Many companies send season's greetings cards to customers or suppliers. The majority of letters and cards sent during December now say Holiday Greetings rather than Merry Christmas, because of diversity in the workplace. These greetings usually have the company name printed on the card. Executives and sales representatives may use a different kind of company card on which they can write personalized greetings to business friends and colleagues. Some companies send distinctively designed cards that bear the company name and logo. This type of card is impressive, because it is unique to the organization sending it. Individualized holiday greeting letters are sent by some business firms.

Figure 14•5 shows a company letter to employees that contains a holiday greeting and includes a token of appreciation for the employee's efforts during the past year. Along with wishes for a happy holiday season, the letter anticipates a prosperous year ahead.

WELCOME

Welcome letters are appropriate for new employees, new customers, or new community members.

A **welcome** message is used to greet new employees, new customers, and newcomers to a community. A new employee welcome is aimed at familiarizing new employees with the company and building goodwill. Many cities have organizations, such as the Welcome Wagon, that send welcome letters to persons moving into the community. These letters usually include special offers, coupons, small gifts, and other enticements from business firms wishing to attract new customers.

Welcome letters are sent frequently to new customers, particularly to those who are establishing credit with the business. These messages are used to congratulate the customer on opening a charge account with the business and to offer an incentive to the new customer to use the business' facilities in the near future. Figure 14•6 is an example of such a letter.

STYLE IN GOODWILL MESSAGES

A goodwill message is an effective way to build a positive relationship with a customer, an employee, or a supplier. Style is important in accomplishing the purpose of the communication.

HANDWRITTEN VERSUS TYPEWRITTEN VERSUS PRINTED MESSAGES

A goodwill message may be handwritten, typed, or printed.

You must decide whether a goodwill message should be handwritten, typewritten, or printed. A handwritten note is appropriate in times of sorrow; but

Figure 14•5 Holiday Greeting

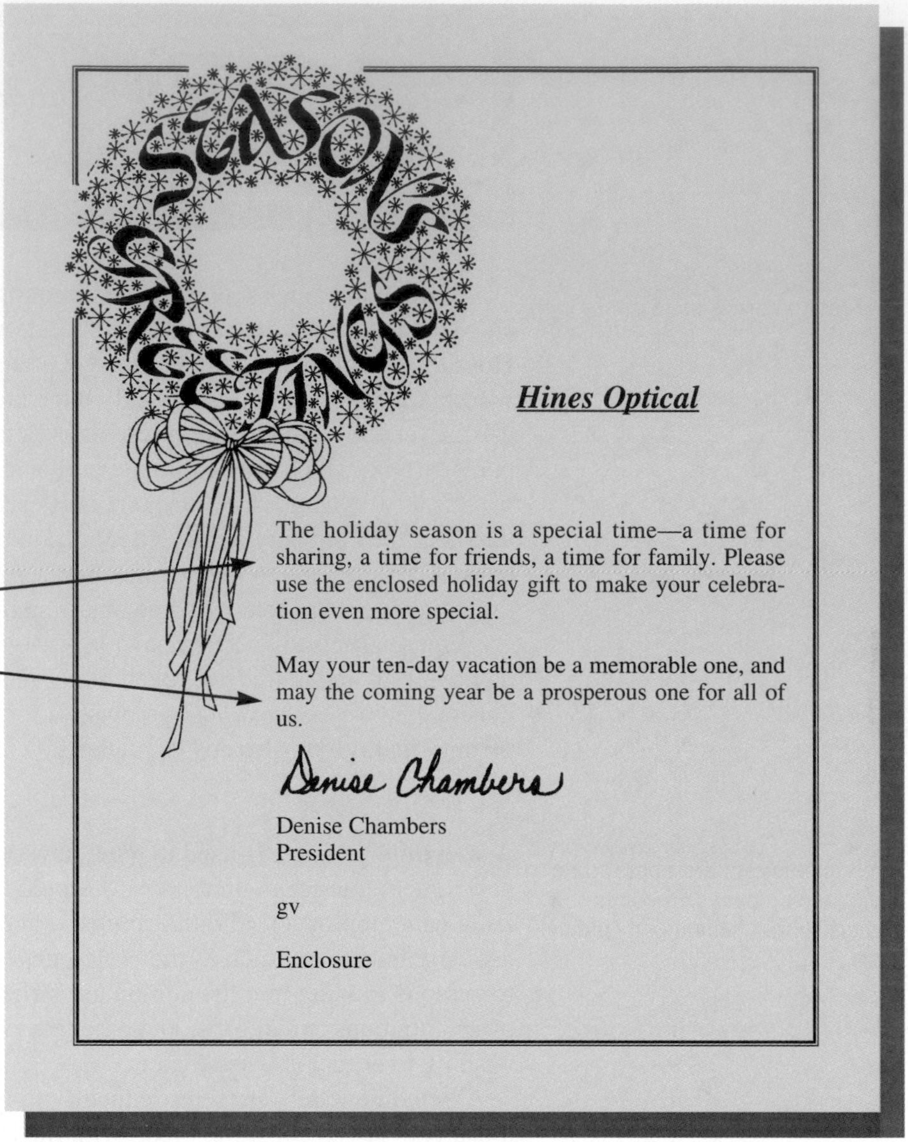

Hines Optical

Present gift.

Extend greetings.

The holiday season is a special time—a time for sharing, a time for friends, a time for family. Please use the enclosed holiday gift to make your celebration even more special.

May your ten-day vacation be a memorable one, and may the coming year be a prosperous one for all of us.

Denise Chambers

Denise Chambers
President

gv

Enclosure

a printed invitation to a social function is preferred, whether it is for a small wedding or a dinner and dance for several hundred people. A typewritten message is normally used to welcome a customer or employee to a business. The form that is most effective for conveying your message should be the basis of your decision.

CARD VERSUS LETTER

Whether to send a card or a letter depends on the occasion.

Using a commercially produced card is less time consuming and frequently is more suitable than a typed letter. A short, handwritten note on a holiday greeting card or a card of sympathy may mean more to the receiver than a long, formal letter. However, a typewritten welcome letter to a new credit customer is the preferred business procedure.

Figure 14-6 Welcome Letter for New Credit Customer

Waldman's
FURNITURE ✦ SHOWCASE

426 Beckley Road   North Prairie, WI 53153-2634   (414) 555-6384

September 18, 199-

Ms. Jacqueline Holsapple
546 Holly Drive
North Prairie, WI 53153-2634

Dear Jacqueline:

Welcome customer. → Welcome to the convenience of credit card buying at Waldman's Furniture Showcase. You will find this service an easy way to purchase home furnishings.

Provide information. → The credit agreement for your account is enclosed. Please take a moment to read it. If you have any questions, please call me. I will be happy to help you.

Show appreciation. → Waldman's is pleased to have you as a charge customer, and it truly appreciates your business. To show its gratitude, you will receive a 15 percent discount on your first credit purchase within 30 days.

Sincerely,

John

John Hickey, Finance Manager

bt

Enc.

FAMILIARITY VERSUS FORMALITY

How well you know the receiver dictates the formality of the message.

The formality of a goodwill message depends on the type of message you are sending and on how well you know the receiver. Put yourself in the place of the receiver and write a letter that you would like to receive—whether the message must, of necessity, be phrased in formal language or whether the nature of the message permits you to be relaxed and informal.

DISCUSSION QUESTIONS

1. Explain why a business or a businessperson should send goodwill messages.

2. Indicate two situations for which it would be appropriate to send congratulatory messages to an individual and two situations for which it would be appropriate to send congratulatory messages to a business.

3. Briefly discuss the different ways that an organization may transmit holiday greetings to its customers.

4. Describe how a condolence message should be composed.

5. Explain how welcome messages to new customers are different from welcome messages to new employees.

6. Describe three criteria that must be considered in selecting the style to use in goodwill messages.

APPLICATION EXERCISES

1. Visit a business in your community and determine the types of goodwill messages it uses. Obtain copies of the messages if possible. Report your findings orally to the class.

2. Describe to the class any unique holiday greetings that you have received from business firms. Discuss the effectiveness of these greetings in gaining your goodwill and encouraging you to patronize the company.

3. Design an invitation to participate in a charity golf tournament that your school is sponsoring. The proceeds from the tournament will go toward scholarships.

4. Divide into teams of three or four students and design an ad that could be placed in your school paper welcoming new students to campus on behalf of a student organization. This ad also needs to inform the students of the student organization.

CASE PROBLEMS

CONGRATULATIONS

1. You work for a restaurant supply company. Recently, one of the restaurants in your territory has been awarded a five-star rating by a dining association. Write a letter to this restaurant congratulating it on the accomplishment. Add any necessary details.

2. Charles Greenwell is the accountant for your employer, Purdom Motors. He has recently completed the requirements for the Certified Public Accountant (CPA) designation. Compose a message congratulating Charles on his accomplishment. Add any necessary details to make this a complete message.

3. Reed Cothern has recently driven one-million accident-free miles for Sunnyvale Bus Lines and will receive the Master Driver's award from the bus line. Fewer than ten percent of the drivers achieve this status. You are the public relations officer for the United Bus Drivers (a nationwide union). Write a letter to Reed congratulating him on his accomplishment. Add any necessary details to make this a complete letter.

4. Hudson Filters is moving into a new 50,000 square foot manufacturing plant. The modern-design building is an attractive addition to your community. The plant will contain the latest technology available. Write a letter to Hudson Filters congratulating it on the new building. Add any necessary details to make this a complete letter.

CONDOLENCE

5. You are president of a financial institution in a small community. Earlier this week a school bus transporting students to a conference in a nearby town was involved in an accident in which 14 children died. Many of the parents of these school children were customers of your organization. Write a form letter that can be sent to the parents expressing your sorrow.

6. Todd Ledbetter was a sales representative for your company for eight years. Yesterday, he died of AIDS. Write a letter to his family expressing your sympathy.

7. Vickie Toon is executive director of your community's industrial foundation. She has been trying for more than six months to get a company to relocate to your community. Yesterday, the company announced that it was relocating to another city. Vickie is extremely dejected and is giving consideration to resigning her position as executive director. Compose a condolence letter to Vickie that will show your support for her.

8. Heavy rains have caused the Mississippi River to go over its banks in many areas. Davenport, Iowa, is no exception; much

damage has occurred because of flooding waters. Your company, Industrial Plastics, has a plant in Davenport. Many of your company's Davenport employees have had excessive damage to their homes. As president of Industrial Plastics, write a form letter that can be sent to the Davenport employees expressing your condolences.

APPRECIATION

9. The photographer for your local newspaper took pictures at a field day for handicapped children that your student organization, Junior Business Leaders, sponsored. Yesterday, the newspaper had an entire page devoted to this event. You feel that the photographer was instrumental in getting this event so well publicized. Write the editor of the newspaper expressing your appreciation for the photographer's excellent work.

10. Mike Yee has been a faithful volunteer with the Needline Program for five years. He has given freely of his time and energy. Write a letter to Mike thanking him for his contribution.

Text 14A

11. Hans Gerhardt, a German high school soccer star, spent three weeks in your town visiting relatives. While he was in town, he held a one-week soccer camp for the recreational league. Your business sponsors one of the teams in the league. Hans has returned to Germany. Write a letter thanking him for conducting the soccer camp.

12. Many individuals donate their time as volunteers to the public library in your town. Eight of these individuals have been volunteers for more than ten years. You are the publicity chair for the Community Volunteer Association and would like to send each of them a letter showing your appreciation for their services. Compose a form letter that can be sent to each volunteer.

INVITATION

13. Your company, Thrifty Insurance Agency, owns a mountain cabin in Montana. Each year you invite several of your better customers to spend a week at the cabin. You would like to invite Waku Sumida and her family to spend a week at the cabin during the month of July. Write a letter inviting Waku and her family, and ask her to select the week that she would like to use the cabin.

Text 14B

14. Bluebonnet Electric is having an open house to celebrate moving into a new facility. Write a form letter that can be personalized and sent to all customers inviting them to the open house.

15. The art club at your school is displaying its art projects for the past year. Write a memo that the school can send to all parents inviting them to this art fair.

16. You belong to a community service organization that is sponsoring a fish fry to raise money to send underprivileged children to

summer camps. You are responsible for sending personalized invitations to businesspersons in your community inviting them to the fish fry. Prepare this invitation adding necessary details to make it complete.

HOLIDAY GREETING

17. Fidelity Central Insurance is renting a boat for its employees for a Fourth of July celebration. The company will provide refreshments and a live band as the boat cruises for five hours on the river. Prepare a memo that can be sent to the employees informing them of this holiday activity.

18. Guardian Savings and Loan Association closes to honor the memory of Martin Luther King, Jr. Design an ad that could be placed in a local newspaper informing its customers that Guardian Savings will be closed for the entire day.

19. Jack's Luxury Autos would like to extend holiday greetings to its customers for the new year. Prepare a letter that Jack's can send to express New Year's greetings to its clients.

20. Farmers Security Bank wishes to express its appreciation to its customers by presenting them with carving sets for Thanksgiving. It is your responsibility to compose a letter that a customer can present in exchange for a carving set. This is the bank's way of wishing customers a happy Thanksgiving.

WELCOME

21. You are the personnel manager for Creative Promotions. Tiffany Martinez recently was hired as a marketing analyst. Tiffany was an honor graduate of a prestigious university; she was highly recruited. You want to make Tiffany feel at home and consider Creative Promotions her place of employment for many years. Write a letter welcoming Tiffany. Add necessary details.

22. Dawn McCarty has opened a checking account at your financial institution. Write a letter to Dawn welcoming her as a customer.

23. The local Neighbor's Watch Committee is interested in the security of the neighborhood. It is planning to have a block party next Friday to meet residents who have recently moved into the neighborhood. The party will be held at the Community Center on Martin Street at 7:30 p.m. Soft drinks and snacks will be available. A representative from the local police force will give a presentation on home security at 8 p.m. Write a message welcoming newcomers to the neighborhood and inviting them to attend the party.

24. Panorama Cablevision has recently purchased another cablevision company. It would like you to write a memo to the employees of the newly acquired company welcoming them to Panorama. This memo needs to make the new employees feel as if they are equal to the original Panorama employees.

MESSAGE ANALYSIS

Text 14C Correct the following message that has been written to welcome a new resident to the community.

Tyler is the greatest small town in America. All of its citizens are friendly and willing to help you get settled.

Miller's Clothing is pleased that you selected Tyler for your residence. Miller's was established in 1905 and has been selling quality clothes since then. Some of the best buys in town are here at Miller's.

Customers enjoy shopping at Miller's. They can purchase the latest styles of clothing for children, ladies, or men. We have just received a large shipment of spring clothing and will give you a 20 percent discount since you are a new member of our community.

I know that you will be happy that you selected Tyler for your home.

PART 4

Written Report Applications

COMMUNICATION NEWS

Managers of business organizations receive more data than they can handle efficiently. In order for the data to become useful information, they must be organized and presented in an effective manner.

One method of dealing with text and gaining access to stored information that has proven to be effective is hypertext. Hypertext systems use the concept of a network of nodes and links to deal with nonlinear text.

Information in a hypertext system is stored as individual segments of text known as nodes. A node can be created using a word processor or editor. It can contain a single paragraph, many pages of text, tables, charts, and the like. A network is formed by connecting related nodes together using links and is referred to as a hypertext database. The links show the relationships among all the nodes in the system. With this system you can follow trails of thought or jump around the document rather than having to read an entire manuscript from beginning to end.

When preparing proposals and reports, hypertext enables you to organize your writing better while being more creative. It can assist you in the thinking and organizational process. Using the relationships among the pieces of information, hypertext permits you to link together segments of text. Thoughts can be expanded and presented in a logical manner by

> Hypertext assists you in managing information in a way that matches both your thinking processes and how you actually work.

creating an "idea" node and then linking it to a related node.

The structure of hypertext gives writers greater freedom and flexibility in developing thought patterns. Notes can be saved on specific subjects, references to data can be maintained, and solutions to model problems can be found using nodes and links.

The commercial hypertext software packages available today are designed for creating electronic documents. They permit the writer to integrate graphical images, video segments, and other media into documents. Hypertext software packages are available for a variety of computer systems.

Hypertext assists you in managing information in a way that matches both your thinking processes and how you actually work in preparing documents and presentations. As electronic publishing and multimedia presentations become more popular, so will hypertext systems.

As reported in "A New Way to Manage and Organize Information," *PC Today* (March 1993), pp. 46–49.

It's Your Turn

Should all employees in an organization be trained to use a hypertext system?
How does an organization determine which hypertext system to purchase?

CHAPTER 15

Business Studies and Proposals

Learning Objectives

Your learning objectives for this chapter include the following:

- To describe the importance of business studies and proposals
- To use the five steps for conducting a business study
- To write a successful proposal

Conducting studies and preparing proposals are frequent tasks in business.	$\boxed{F}$ requently, managers and employees in business conduct studies or prepare proposals. The systematic procedures used to conduct a business study are called **research methods.** These methods will be discussed in the first part of this chapter. The last part of this chapter provides guidelines for preparing proposals. Report preparation and graphic aids for reports and proposals are covered in Chapters 16 and 17.

BUSINESS STUDIES

Studies are made to find solutions for problems and to suggest improvements.

Business studies are conducted and reports written for many reasons. Such studies may result in new procedures, new products, new markets, or other new ways to increase profits. Studies are conducted to determine solutions to problems, make recommendations for improvements, or offer proposals for actions. Using the information from these studies, reports are written for the consideration of management. Conducting a study is a common activity, and everyone in business should know how to complete a study and record the results in a report.

THE STEPS IN A BUSINESS STUDY

There is a common, overall approach for conducting business studies.

The five steps in conducting a business study are:

1. Plan the study.
2. Gather information.
3. Analyze the information.
4. Determine solution(s).
5. Write the report.

Steps 1 through 4 are discussed in the next four major sections of this chapter. As mentioned previously, Step 5 is discussed in Chapters 16 and 17.

PLAN THE STUDY

The first major step is to plan the study.

Planning the study includes stating the problem, setting the boundaries, determining who are the readers of the report, and deciding on the procedures to be followed in completing the study.

STATING THE PROBLEM

Start planning by stating the problem.

The **statement of the problem** is a clear, accurate written agreement about what is to be studied. Prior to arriving at this statement, there may be discussions within the organization about what the study should accomplish. A preliminary investigation of the situation that prompted the study may be made to help define the problem. You may look at files, talk to employees, read other similar reports, talk to vendors, or make any number of preliminary inquiries to help you clarify what needs to be studied.

After this preliminary consideration, you can develop a statement of the problem. Here are examples of problem statements for studies:

To state the problem of a study clearly and accurately, a preliminary investigation is usually necessary.

1. To determine ways to improve the morale of ABC Company employees.

2. To design a new procedure for the company's annual inventory.

3. What is the best location for cash registers?

4. Should the company's microcomputers be networked?

Notice that the first two examples are infinitive statements while the last two examples are presented as questions. Either form is appropriate.

SETTING THE BOUNDARIES OF THE STUDY

A study needs to have boundaries. These boundaries are determined by defining the scope of the study, setting up a time schedule, and estimating budget allowances.

Defining the Scope of the Study. The **scope** of the study is defined by determining the factors that will be studied. It is best to limit the amount of information you will gather to the most needed and most important factors. The factors for one of the problem statements given previously might look like this:

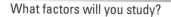

Statement of Problem: To determine ways to improve the morale of ABC Company employees.

Factors:

1. Salaries
2. Fringe benefits
3. Work assignments
4. Work hours
5. Evaluation procedures

You could study many other factors relative to improving employee morale. Some may be important, and you may want to consider them later. For any one study, however, a reasonable scope must be clearly defined by determining what factors will and will not be included.

Scheduling the Study. An agreement should be made on when the report of the study is needed or when it will be possible to complete the report. Working back from the report deadline, a **time schedule** should be set for the study indicating when each step is to be completed. Using the

Problem statements can use either the infinitive or the question form.

Next, set the study boundaries.

What factors will you study?

What time schedule will you follow?

steps for conducting a business study, a time schedule could look like the one in Figure 15•1.

Figure 15•1 Time Schedule

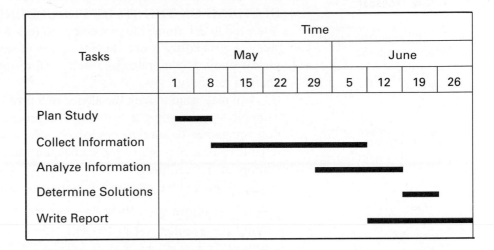

The time schedule shown is called a **Gantt chart.** It shows clearly when each major task will be worked on and completed. It also shows that several tasks can be worked on at the same time. For example, it is possible to write preliminary parts of the report while you are completing the analysis of the information. Time schedules should be as detailed as necessary, so that everyone understands exactly what is to be done and when.

Budgeting the Study. All studies cost money. Even studies that are conducted within an organization will have some costs above normal operating costs.

How much will the study cost?

A large organization may use a charge-back system to bill one department for having work done by another. For example, if you are doing a study for the human resources department, the computer department may charge the human resources department for processing the survey results. In addition, the printing department may charge the human resources department for printing the report.

There may be other study costs for such items as personnel time, supplies, and postage. All costs should be estimated and a budget approved before the study officially begins.

DETERMINING THE READERS OF THE REPORT

Analyze the receivers of the report.

Effective communication depends on using the you–viewpoint in all written and oral messages. This is certainly true for written reports. The way in which you write the results of your study should be determined by your readers' knowledge, interests, opinions, and emotional states—the key factors in analyzing readers.

When there will be primary and secondary readers of the report, both should be analyzed. If, for example, you are a financial manager writing a report for which colleagues in the field are primary readers, you can use the technical language of finance because it will be understood by other financial managers. If members of the general management staff, members of the production management staff, general employees, or stockholders are secondary readers, you may want to define your terms the first time you use them or include a list of terms and definitions as an appendix.

DECIDING ON THE STUDY PROCEDURES

Finally, in planning the report, decide on procedures.

You need to determine the procedures to follow in completing the overall study. A **procedure** is one step in a series of steps that are taken to complete a study. A comprehensive study will result if these procedures are planned carefully.

You may want to seek the advice of a professional consultant. If, for example, you are going to use statistical procedures to analyze the information you gather, be sure the procedures selected will give you valid and reliable results. A professional statistician can help with the selection of appropriate procedures.

Some procedural questions that must be answered may be:

- Will I use information about the topic that is already printed?
- Will I survey employees?
- Will I seek information from outside the company?
- Will I use a computer to analyze the information?
- Will the report be typed in the office or taken out to be printed?

Deciding on procedures for each step in your study simply means deciding exactly how to carry out that step. The procedures you actually select will vary from study to study.

GATHER INFORMATION

The second major step is to gather information.

You may gather information for your study from one or more sources. There are two basic types of information sources: secondary and primary. **Secondary sources** of information are the published materials on the topic. **Primary sources** include individuals, company files, observations, and experiments.

Information sources can be primary or secondary.

SECONDARY SOURCES OF INFORMATION

Secondary sources contain the published information about the topic.

Published materials on most topics are readily available in company, public, and college libraries. Experienced reference librarians can provide valuable assistance in finding published information that will be helpful in your study. They can direct you to indexes, catalogs, reference books, government documents, computer databases, and other helpful secondary sources of information.

Librarians can be helpful.

Of particular value to businesspersons today are computerized searches of published information on a given topic. Most reference librarians can assist you in searches that quickly give you an up-to-date bibliography of reference materials on your topic and sometimes abstracts of the materials. With this information you can go to microfilm files, book stacks, periodicals, or other appropriate locations to examine the available information in greater depth.

Computerized searches are effective.

Most published materials are copyrighted. You may have to obtain permission to use such information, and you will be required to give credit to

Computerized searches are helpful in finding secondary sources of information.

the originator as the source. (To avoid plagiarism and paraphrasing problems, see "Copyright and Fair Use Communication" on pages 92–93 of Chapter 3.) Be sure that you get complete bibliographic information on published materials while you are at the library so it will be available for footnotes and the bibliography.

If your study requires gathering information from both primary and secondary sources, you should gather secondary source information first. The published information may contain good ideas on what primary information you should gather and how you can gather it.

PRIMARY SOURCES OF INFORMATION

Primary sources provide unpublished information on the topic.

Your study may require gathering original information—information that has not been previously published on your topic. This primary information may come from an examination of original company records, a survey of knowledgeable individuals, an observation of an activity, or an experiment.

> *Get the facts, or the facts will get you. And when you get 'em, get 'em right, or they will get you wrong.*
>
> **Thomas Fuller**

Examining original records and files is an obvious source of historical information that may be helpful to you. The other ways to obtain primary information—surveys, observations, and experiments—are not such obvious sources of information.

Surveys. To get firsthand information from individuals, you can survey them. The basic ways to survey people are by mail, telephone, or face-to-face interview. Compared with other surveys, mail surveys are less expensive; the percentage of responses, however, will likely be lower. Telephone surveys outside the local calling area will cost more than mail surveys, but will get a higher percentage of responses. The most costly surveys are face-to-face interviews. They are a way, however, of assuring responses; the responses can be in greater depth than in mail or telephone surveys. Telephone surveys are the quickest way to obtain information. Mail surveys often require two months or more to get responses; face-to-face interviews are both time consuming to conduct and sometimes difficult to arrange.

Questionnaires are developed and used to obtain information by survey. With questionnaires, you can obtain opinions and facts from individuals. Here are some important guidelines to follow when developing questionnaires:

1. The survey questions should be developed from the factors being studied. In a survey of employees on employee morale, you might develop questions to seek opinions or facts about employee salaries, fringe benefits, work hours, etc.

2. The questions should be clear. They should mean the same thing to everybody. A question such as, "What kind of car do you own?" is not clear. Based on the respondents' interpretations, the answers could be convertible, Chevrolet, sports, foreign, etc. An example of a clearer way to obtain specific information is, "Please indicate the name of the manufacturer of your car."

3. Avoid leading questions. Leading questions influence readers to give a biased answer. Questions such as, "Would it be a good idea to improve the arrangement of our work hours?" will likely be biased toward a yes answer. A better version of this question is:

The present arrangement of our work hours is

_____ very satisfactory

_____ satisfactory

_____ unsatisfactory

_____ very unsatisfactory

4. Provide for all possible responses in the answer options; when it is not possible to be all inclusive, include an "other" option so that the respondent may answer appropriately.

5. Avoid skip-and-jump directions such as, "If your answer to Question 9 is no, skip Questions 10, 11, 12 and go directly to Question 13. If your answer to Question 9 is yes, also answer Question 10, but skip 11 and 12 if you do not have children. . . ."

Surveying people is a way to get primary information.

Questionnaires are used in surveys. They should be developed carefully.

The two basic types of questions are *open-ended* and *forced-answer.*

6. Choose the form of the questions carefully. The two basic types of questions are **open-ended** and **forced-answer.** Open-ended questions let respondents answer in their own words. These kinds of questions must be very carefully worded in order to receive comparable answers. If at all possible, use forced-answer questions. In this type of question you provide the possible answers to the questions, and the respondents choose among the alternatives given. More comparable and useful information can be obtained with forced-answer questions than with open-ended questions.

7. Sequence questions appropriately. Start your questionnaire with easy questions that will encourage respondents to continue. Group similar topics together. For example, put all questions on salaries in the same section of the questionnaire. Arrange questions in logical order—the way people commonly think of the topics.

Forced-answer questions are used commonly in mail and telephone surveys. Open-ended questions are more likely to be used in surveys conducted by personal interviews.

In designing forced-answer questions, be sure the "stem"—the question—is worded clearly. There should be no overlap in the possible answers; that is, use 25–29, 30–34, 35–39 instead of 25–30, 30–35, 35–40. Provide lines or boxes for easy check-mark answering. The lines or boxes for the responses should precede the possible answers.

Sample forced-answer questions are shown in Figure 15•2.

Examples of open-ended questions that may be asked in a personal interview are:

1. What do you think are the most important qualities a supervisor should have?

2. What do you think of the idea of a four-day workweek?

You will receive narrative-type answers to these questions. For several respondents, the answers will vary considerably and will be difficult to tabulate. However, if you interview only a few people and want to get all their ideas on selected topics, the personal interview approach, using open-ended questions, is best.

Questionnaires should encourage response

Questionnaires should be designed attractively to encourage response. A questionnaire should be accompanied by a covering letter or statement that explains it and motivates the recipient to fill in the questionnaire and return it to you.

Surveys are usually conducted using samples.

To save time and money, surveys are usually sent to a few people who are representative of a larger group. This type of survey is called a **sample survey.** Such surveys must be designed carefully so that the information gathered is reliable and valid. Unless you are an expert in survey design, it is recommended that you consult with a statistician on any sample survey you may be planning.

Observations may be used to gather primary information.

Observations. Observation is another way to gather primary information for a study. This technique involves one or more observers watching and recording facts about an activity. While the observation technique can incur high personnel costs, it is a way to obtain precise information.

Figure 15·2 Sample Forced-
Answer Survey Questions

1. Please check your age:
   _____ Under 25
   _____ 25–29
   _____ 30–34
   _____ 35–39
   _____ 40–44
   _____ 45–49
   _____ 50–54
   _____ 55–59
   _____ 60–64
   _____ Over 64

2. Please check your department:
   _____ Accounting
   _____ Computer Center
   _____ Finance
   _____ Human Resources
   _____ Production
   _____ Purchasing
   _____ Sales
   _____ Shipping and Receiving

3. I favor the idea of a four-day workweek:
   _____ Strongly Agree
   _____ Agree
   _____ Undecided
   _____ Disagree
   _____ Strongly Disagree

4. If a four-day workweek were implemented, which day would
   you want off? Mark that day 1, then mark the next best day off
   for you 2, etc.
   _____ Monday
   _____ Tuesday
   _____ Wednesday
   _____ Thursday
   _____ Friday

5. How do you value the company newsletter as a source of information about company matters? Circle the most appropriate
   number.

Valuable				Not Valuable
1	2	3	4	5

A common use of the observation technique is to gather information on
a worker/machine operation in a factory. The worker's repetitious movements might be timed, production records maintained, and conclusions
drawn about the efficiency of the procedures. Similarly, observers might be
posted in selected areas of cities to count out-of-state cars in order to get a

measure of tourist traffic. Many managers and employers use *informal observation* to obtain information that is helpful to them in performing their jobs. This kind of information, while not scientifically obtained, can be of value in a limited way.

The observation technique must be carefully controlled.

It is important that the observation technique be carefully controlled. All observers must look for exactly the same thing and record their observations in the same way for the information to be of comparative value. Proper control requires that observers and subjects do not interact.

Experiments. The last way to gather primary information for a business study is the experiment. Experiments in business are usually used to compare two ways of doing something to determine the better way. For example, employees in one plant might be placed on a four-day workweek, while employees in another plant would be kept on a five-day workweek. The employees in the two plants would then be observed and surveyed periodically to determine their productivity and their satisfaction with work hours.

Experiments may be conducted to gather primary information.

Another approach would be to have a pre-survey and post-survey of a group of employees that you plan to change from a five-day workweek to a four-day workweek. In this approach, employees who are on a five-day workweek could be asked a series of questions about the effect their work schedule has on their productivity and job satisfaction. Then their five-day workweek would be changed to a four-day workweek. After three months have passed, the employees would be asked the same set of questions they were asked before their work schedule was changed. Then the two sets of answers would be compared.

Experiments are a good way to make comparisons.

Experiments are not as common in business as they are in scientific laboratories, but experiments do have their uses. In an experiment, you can easily compare the old way with the new way, Method A with Method B, or test market a new product. Experiments can be expensive. Carefully designed and controlled experiments, however, have provided businesspersons with much valuable information.

> *A world of facts lies outside and beyond the world of words.*
>
> **Thomas Huxley**

ANALYZE THE INFORMATION

The third major step is to analyze the information.

Once you have planned your study and gathered information, you are ready to begin your analysis. The analysis may take only a few minutes. The information you gathered may speak for itself. It may clearly say yes to adopting a new procedure or product. The information you gathered may clearly say that employees overwhelmingly prefer the four-day to the five-day workweek. On the other hand, you may have gathered a great amount of complex information. It may take you days, weeks, or months to complete the analysis.

Analysis should be objective.

The purpose of the analysis is to make sense, objectively, out of the information you have gathered. You will not want personal bias of any kind to enter into the analysis. Use your brain power—objectively and unemotionally. The word **analysis** means to look at the parts of things separately or in their relationship to the whole. The various parts of your information are compared and contrasted in an effort to try to develop new or better ideas. Separate facts and figures are interpreted by explaining what they mean—what significance they have.

To *analyze* means to look at the parts by comparing and contrasting them.

For example, if you were doing a study to determine which microcomputer to buy for your office, you would collect information on the type of work you are currently doing and the kinds of work you want to do. Then you would gather information on microcomputers, including cost, software compatibility, speed of operation, machine capacity, machine dependability, maintenance availability, potential for upgrading, and other factors. Then you would compare and contrast (analyze) the different machines to determine how well they can do what you want done, what their potential is, how dependable they are, and so on. Once the analysis has been completed, you are ready to determine solutions.

DETERMINE SOLUTIONS

Based on your analysis, you will be ready to offer a solution or solutions to the problem you have been studying. Depending on your position in the organization and the particular business study, the solution you determine will be either the answer that you will use or a recommendation to someone else who will make a decision on its use.

The fourth major step is to determine solutions.

For formal studies and reports, you may draw conclusions from your analysis and state them separately from the recommendation(s). A **conclusion** is an inference drawn from the facts; it is a reasoned judgment that you make from your analysis. If you were to select the most important ideas suggested by your analysis, these ideas would be your conclusions. Based on your conclusions, you could state the study answer or **recommendation**—the study solution.

Solutions may consist of conclusions and recommendations.

The conclusions and recommendations must be based on the findings and your objective analysis, not your personal opinion of what a good solution would be. Your conclusions and recommendations for a report might look like this:

Conclusions:

1. Procedure B appears significantly more cost-effective than Procedure A in the two installations studied.

2. Dependable equipment for implementing Procedure B on a wide-scale basis is not currently available.

3. The XYZ Manufacturing Company currently has in stock 20 Model 3CA machines that can be used to implement Procedure B.

4. The XYZ Manufacturing Company projects that it will have 500 Model 3CAs available within six months.

---

and

Recommendations:

1. Immediately lease the 20 Model 3CAs from XYZ and continue the comparison study of Procedure A and Procedure B for three more months.

2. Enter an option to purchase 500 Model 3CAs from the XYZ Manufacturing Company.

3. If the additional study continues to show that Procedure B is significantly more cost-effective than Procedure A, exercise the option with XYZ to purchase the 500 Model 3CAs.

WRITE THE REPORT

The fifth major step is to write the report.

The final step in a business study is to write the report. It is an important step; you will want to present your results effectively. How to write a successful report is discussed in detail in Chapter 16, "Report Preparation," and Chapter 17, "Visual Aids."

PROPOSALS

Developing and writing proposals is a way to achieve success.

Recognition, professional gains, millions of dollars, and personal rewards will be won today by successful proposal writers. These writers will persuasively propose a solution to a problem, and the reader will accept the proposal and provide the necessary support to carry out the solution. You, too, can develop successful proposals and benefit from their approval by following the recommendations in the remainder of this chapter.

DEFINITION OF A PROPOSAL

Proposals analyze problems and provide solutions.

A **proposal** is an analysis of a problem and a recommendation for a solution. The problem may be a need for equipment, services, research, a plan of action, or a variety of other needs. The recommended solution may be products or personnel, a business study, a description of work to be performed, or any of several other ways of solving a problem.

THE NATURE OF A PROPOSAL

A proposal is a persuasive message designed to win a reader's approval of the writer's recommendations. Proposals are common in business.

Writing proposals is a common way to create ideas to improve productivity and profitability.

A proposal is a gamble.

Proposals may be:

• External

• Internal

• Solicited

• Unsolicited

Businesspersons look for initiative. They welcome suggestions of ways to change things for the better. Customers and suppliers want to receive proposals that will mutually benefit them and you. Successful organizations depend on the creation of ideas that will improve productivity and profitability.

Proposals are gambles. They take time to develop, and often they are rejected. Some proposal developers believe that they are doing well if they win acceptance of one of every ten proposals. Successful proposal writers are risk takers. They will assess the probability of their being successful, and then decide whether to develop a proposal. If a large organization is considering developing a proposal involving millions of dollars in contracts, that assessment will involve many people and departments.

Another dimension of proposals is the variety of ways to categorize them. Proposals can be external or internal, solicited or unsolicited. Understanding these categories will be helpful to you in writing proposals.

EXTERNAL PROPOSALS

Proposals that go to those outside an organization are external proposals. These messages include proposals to supply products or services at given prices—to construct buildings, to provide equipment, to perform research, to design roads, to provide paper, to perform audits, and on and on. Receiving approval of external proposals is essential to the success of many organizations.

INTERNAL PROPOSALS

Proposals sent to others within an organization are internal proposals. These can be proposals to solve problems or meet needs by improving procedures, changing products, adding personnel, conducting studies, reorganizing departments, increasing facilities, reducing budgets, or making other changes. Ideas for internal improvement, creatively developed and convincingly presented, are the lifeblood of organizations.

SOLICITED PROPOSALS

Proposals initiated by a person or an organization with a specific problem or need are solicited proposals. These are requests to others for a solution to the problem or a recommendation for meeting the need. Such a request is called a **Request for Proposal** or, simply, an **RFP.** The form of the solicitation may be a face-to-face request, a telephone call, or a written 1-page, 50-page, or 500-page RFP. When responding to solicited proposals, it is essential to provide the information requested in the format specified.

UNSOLICITED PROPOSALS

Proposals that are not in response to an RFP are unsolicited proposals. They are initiated by an individual or an organization and represent an independent analysis of another's problems or needs and the creation of proposed solutions.

QUALITIES OF A SUCCESSFUL PROPOSAL

Successful proposals have qualities that separate them from unsuccessful proposals. While success sometimes depends on factors such as luck, politics, timing, and reputation, most proposals must have excellent content and be clearly presented to be accepted. The following qualities usually are required for a successful proposal:

1. The purpose of the proposal is stated clearly.
2. The problem or need is understood and defined clearly.
3. The solution is innovative and presented convincingly.
4. The benefits outweigh the costs.
5. The personnel implementing the solution are qualified.
6. The solution can be achieved on a timely basis.
7. The proposal is honest, factual, realistic, and objective.
8. The presentation is professional and attractive.

To convey these qualities in the proposal, the writer must carefully analyze the situation and the receivers, use the you–viewpoint, and apply the principles of business communication.

The proposal should be a powerful, persuasive message. The receivers are going to be looking for the benefits to them, their department, the company, the community, society, or some other group to which they belong. The proposal should get the receivers' attention, show clearly the benefits of accepting the proposal, give proof of those benefits, and motivate favorable action.

THE ELEMENTS OF A PROPOSAL

A successful proposal contains essential elements or parts. In solicited proposals, the elements are specified in the RFP. Careful and complete responses should be made to all the elements requested in the RFP. If you think elements necessary to the acceptance of your proposal are missing from the RFP, then you should try to work those parts into the specified format.

In unsolicited proposals, you must decide which elements to include. For elaborate, detailed proposals you will likely include all the elements listed in this section. For short proposals you will select those elements that you think are essential for the success of the proposal. The order of presentation of the elements may vary based on the situation.

A comprehensive list of common proposal elements includes the following:

1. Cover Letter or Memo
2. Title Page or Cover
3. Reference to Authorization
4. Table of Contents
5. List of Illustrations
6. Proposal Summary
7. Purpose
8. Problem or Need
9. Background

10. Benefits of the Proposal
11. Description of the Solution
12. Evaluation Plan
13. Qualifications of Personnel
14. Time Schedule
15. Cost
16. Glossary
17. Appendixes
18. Bibliography

While all these elements are important for many large proposals, the key elements are the Purpose, Problem or Need, Benefits of the Proposal, Description of the Solution, Qualifications of Personnel, Time Schedule, and Cost. All the proposal elements are described in the following sections.

COVER LETTER OR MEMO

The cover letter or memo highlights the contents and encourages action.

The **cover letter** or **memo,** also referred to as a transmittal message, introduces the proposal to the reader. A letter is used for an external proposal and a memo for an internal proposal. The cover letter or memo should include content that provides coherence for the reader, reviews the highlights of the proposal, and encourages action.

TITLE PAGE OR COVER

The title page or cover includes essential information.

The information contained on the **title page** or **cover** of a proposal can include: title of proposal, name and location of receiver, name and location of submitter, date of submission, principal investigator, proposed cost, and proposed duration of project. The title should be concise. Consider which of the six "W and H" questions—What? Where? Who? When? Why? How?—must be answered by the title. The title of the proposal should attract the reader's attention and, because it will be used to identify the proposal, it should be easy to remember.

REFERENCE TO AUTHORIZATION

If the proposal is solicited, its authorization should be noted.

If the proposal is solicited, the request should be noted in a **reference to authorization**—the permission or request for the proposal. The information contained in the reference to authorization depends on the RFP. For an informal or short RFP, it could be as simple as listing the RFP number on the cover, or including a line in the cover letter or memo that says "This proposal is in response to your telephone call of May 5, 199-." For a formal RFP, it should include a separate page or a number of pages following the title page or cover. A lengthy RFP may require an abstract as a reference to authorization.

TABLE OF CONTENTS

The table of contents orients the reader and serves as a reference.

The **table of contents** lists the titles and page numbers of all the major sections of the proposal. It will assist in orienting readers and will serve as a reference to aid them in quickly locating specific information. The names and page numbers of the appendixes are also included in the table of contents.

LIST OF ILLUSTRATIONS

The titles and page numbers of any tables, figures, graphs, or other illustrations are placed in a **list of illustrations** immediately following the table of contents.

PROPOSAL SUMMARY

The **proposal summary** is the proposal in capsule form. This section must be written after the proposal is complete. It contains the most vital information in each of the major sections of the proposal. It should be short. The summary is designed to give busy people a quick but complete overview of the proposal. For short proposals the summary may be just a paragraph. For a long proposal of 100 to 500 pages, the summary might be 1 to 10 pages long. If the RFP specifies a length, be sure to make the summary that length and no longer.

PURPOSE

Following the summary, the actual proposal begins. The proposal's purpose should be stated first. The **purpose statement** helps the reader understand clearly (1) the reason you are making the proposal, and (2) the nature of the proposal—how it will accomplish the purpose. Example purpose statements are:

> This is a proposal to reduce manufacturing costs 10 percent by replacing Assembly Line A's conveyor system.

> The purpose of this proposal is to increase sales by adding commission sales personnel.

These purpose statements may stand alone or they may be followed with brief explanations. The amount of explanation given depends on the reader's knowledge and his or her need for information.

PROBLEM OR NEED

The next section should describe the problem being solved or the need being met. This section should use coherence techniques so it relates to the section in which the purpose of the proposal was given. For example, the first purpose statement given in the previous section might be followed by a problem statement such as this:

> Manufacturing costs for the second quarter are up five percent over the first quarter. Most of this cost increase can be attributed to the new labor agreement that became effective March 1. To meet competition, we must find new ways to reduce manufacturing costs.

BACKGROUND

If necessary for your reader's complete understanding, you should provide background data on the problem. The background section may be combined with the section on Problem or Need; or if both sections are long it may be a separate section. In the **background** section, you may explain the problem—how it developed, its magnitude, and the consequences if nothing is done.

A proposal writer explains the benefits to be gained if the proposal is implemented.

BENEFITS OF THE PROPOSAL

Benefits, the outcomes of implementing the solution, must outweigh costs.

The benefits of the proposal are important. **Benefits of the proposal** represent the outcomes of the implementation of the proposed solution. The benefits must be in the you–viewpoint; they must clearly serve the interests of the reader and/or his or her organization. The benefits must outweigh their cost. (The cost data will be given later in the proposal.) If your proposal is competing with other proposals, the benefits you cite must be more cost-effective than your competitors' benefits for your proposal to be the winning one.

Emphasize the benefits.

When presenting the benefits of the proposal, use the emphasis techniques given in Chapter 2; but be careful not to overstate the benefits. Make them concrete, realistic, and honest.

DESCRIPTION OF THE SOLUTION

The description contains the solution to the problem.

The description of the solution is the most important section in the proposal. It will likely be the largest section. It contains the solution to the problem or the way you recommend meeting the need.

Depending on the proposal, the description may consist of subject matter similar to the following:

- New information system design
- Products to meet a need
- Complex business study plan
- New job descriptions
- New organizational arrangement
- Personnel qualifications for new employees
- Budget reduction plan

- Building construction plans
- Revised fringe benefits program
- Road design project
- Corporation expansion plan
- Equipment acquisition plan
- Product development plan

Be sure the description is realistic and persuasive.

The description of the solution section must tie coherently to the information given previously in the proposal. References must be made in this section to the proposal purpose, the problem or need, and the benefits of the proposal. From the description of the proposal section, your readers must understand your solution clearly and be convinced that it achieves the purpose, solves the problem, and provides the benefits cited earlier.

The description of the solution should include specifically what you are proposing be done, who will do it, when it will be done, where it is to be done, how it will be done, and why it should be done. If you are responding to an RFP, your response must carefully provide the information called for in each item of the description section.

You will want to stress the innovative aspects of your proposal, the special nature of the resources you are recommending, and the strength of your solution's rationale. Show how these features of your proposal fit your reader's needs. A good way to do this is to relate your solutions directly to each of the benefits given earlier. Those benefits might be listed individually, with each followed by an appropriate part of the description of the solution. The intent is to show clearly that you have carefully thought through all aspects of the proposed solution and that it represents a realistic, feasible, and desirable way of solving the problem or meeting the need.

EVALUATION PLAN

An evaluation plan provides a way to judge success of proposal implementation.

If appropriate for your proposal, you will want to include an evaluation plan. The **evaluation plan** is a way to judge the degree of success achieved if your proposal were implemented. The evaluation plan could consist of a record-keeping system; a review by a panel of experts; statistical analysis procedures; a reporting system; or any number of control, analysis, measurement, or judgment techniques.

An evaluation plan is a major element in proposals for research studies. In other proposals, such as increased staffing proposals, the evaluation system might be an employee performance review procedure already in place. In this case, only a brief reference to the existing plan would be needed.

QUALIFICATIONS OF PERSONNEL

The personnel qualifications section shows ability to provide proposed services.

In the qualifications of personnel section you provide biographical information about each key participant involved in implementing the proposal. You show his or her qualifications to provide the services proposed.

The information should include the education, experience, accomplishments, successes, and evidences of achievement that directly relate to each participant's involvement in the proposed solution. You are, in this section, justifying to the reader that these persons are fully qualified to serve in their assigned roles. The types of data that are appropriate are discussed in detail in Chapter 21, "The Job Search and Resume."

Depending on the nature of the proposal, the length of the data presented for each individual will vary from a few lines to several pages. In some proposals, brief summaries are presented in the qualifications of personnel section and full resumes are provided in an appendix. If you are responding to an RFP, provide exactly the amount and type of personnel information specified.

TIME SCHEDULE

The time schedule shows when activities begin and end.

The time schedule shows when activity is to start and when it is to be completed. For simple proposals, the time schedule may consist of a listing of activities and their beginning and ending dates. For elaborate proposals, it may be necessary to use more complex task-time analysis charts such as Gantt (see page 411), PERT (Program Evaluation Review Technique), Milestone, or other scheduling techniques.

If you need assistance in selecting a time-schedule format, most libraries have good reference materials you can use. Your responsibility in this section is to clearly show the reader a realistic time schedule.

COST

The cost section shows cost of proposed solution.

The cost or the price of the proposed solution is shown next. This section may be labeled Cost, Prices, Budget, or another appropriate title. The cost may be presented in logical parts, such as personnel, supplies, equipment, facilities, etc.; or it may be organized using the benefits, parts of the description of the solution, time phases, or other appropriate categories.

The cost of the proposed solution must cover your expenses and desired profit. It also must be reasonable in relation to the benefits and the products or services to be provided. If you are following the guidelines in an RFP, the format for the cost section will likely be specified and should be used.

GLOSSARY

The glossary defines unfamiliar terms.

Based on a careful analysis of your readers, you may decide to include a glossary in your proposal. A **glossary** lists alphabetically the unfamiliar terms used in the proposal and gives their definitions. A glossary is included only when many unfamiliar, specialized, or technical terms have to be used. When there are only a few such terms, they should be defined the first time they are used.

APPENDIXES

Complex supporting information is shown in the appendixes.

To keep the body of the proposal as short and readable as possible, it is sometimes appropriate to place complex supporting information in an appendix. An **appendix** contains items that are indirectly related to the proposal but are excluded from the body to improve readability.

It was suggested earlier that resumes of key personnel might appropriately be placed in an appendix. Other information that might be placed in appendixes includes your organization's history, product specifications, records of past successes with similar projects, letters of support, details of further supporting information in the description section, questionnaire to be used for the proposed research, or other supporting and reference materials.

An RFP may specify what appendixes are to be included. Be sure to include only those appendixes essential to the reader's understanding and decision making. If the proposal becomes too bulky, it will be less acceptable to a potential approver, funder, or purchaser.

BIBLIOGRAPHY

If you think it strengthens your case to indicate your knowledge of important reference materials, include a bibliography in the proposal. A **bibliography** is an alphabetical listing of all references used as sources of information in the proposal. If you have footnoted material in the proposal, you must include those sources in a bibliography.

WRITING A PROPOSAL

For a long, complex proposal, a writing team may be formed. Sections of the proposal may be assigned to different individuals for writing. In this case, it is important to have one chief writer to assure consistency throughout the proposal and to tie all the parts together coherently. Collaborative writing is discussed in Chapter 3 on pages 77–79.

Normally for short proposals one person is responsible for the writing. It may or may not be appropriate for that writer to ask others to read his or her proposal before it is finalized and submitted.

Figure 15•3 is an example of a **poor** short proposal in which a human resources manager is recommending to the president that the company change its medical insurance carrier. The suggestions in this chapter for writing successful proposals are not implemented in this memo.

An improved proposal for the same situation is shown in Figure 15•4. This example of a **good** short proposal follows the guidelines for developing and writing successful proposals.

Figure 15•5 is an adaptation of an actual proposal from Opryland, U.S.A., for a pilot study designed to test an expanded employee screening system. It is a **good** example of a long proposal and shows most of the proposal elements commonly used in long proposals.

A CONCLUDING COMMENT ON PROPOSALS

Proposals are the ways that new ideas are conveyed to decision makers. Most of the recommendations in this section on proposals apply to both written and oral proposals. Some proposals will be accepted, but many will be rejected. Successful businesspersons develop and submit many proposals in their careers. They are not deterred by rejections. They keep developing and submitting proposals and realize the professional and personal gains when their proposals are accepted.

Limit appendixes to information that is essential to reader's needs.

The bibliography contains appropriate reference sources.

A proposal may be written by a team or by an individual.

Write proposals; they are an important way to succeed in your career.

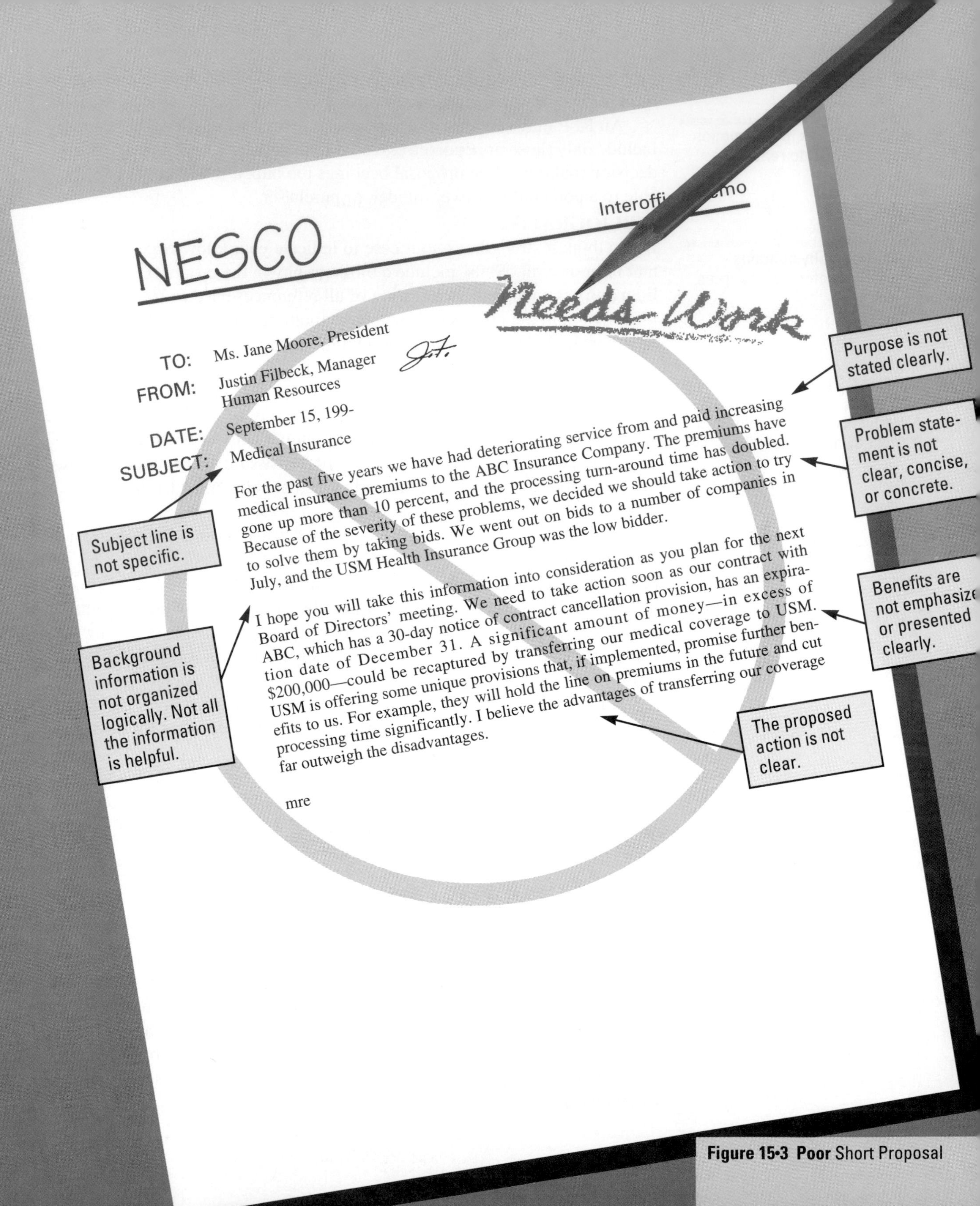

NESCO

Needs Work

TO: Ms. Jane Moore, President

FROM: Justin Filbeck, Manager
Human Resources

DATE: September 15, 199-

SUBJECT: Medical Insurance

For the past five years we have had deteriorating service from and paid increasing medical insurance premiums to the ABC Insurance Company. The premiums have gone up more than 10 percent, and the processing turn-around time has doubled. Because of the severity of these problems, we decided we should take action to try to solve them by taking bids. We went out on bids to a number of companies in July, and the USM Health Insurance Group was the low bidder.

I hope you will take this information into consideration as you plan for the next Board of Directors' meeting. We need to take action soon as our contract with ABC, which has a 30-day notice of contract cancellation provision, has an expiration date of December 31. A significant amount of money—in excess of $200,000—could be recaptured by transferring our medical coverage to USM. USM is offering some unique provisions that, if implemented, promise further benefits to us. For example, they will hold the line on premiums in the future and cut processing time significantly. I believe the advantages of transferring our coverage far outweigh the disadvantages.

mre

Purpose is not stated clearly.

Problem statement is not clear, concise, or concrete.

Subject line is not specific.

Benefits are not emphasized or presented clearly.

Background information is not organized logically. Not all the information is helpful.

The proposed action is not clear.

Figure 15·3 Poor Short Proposal

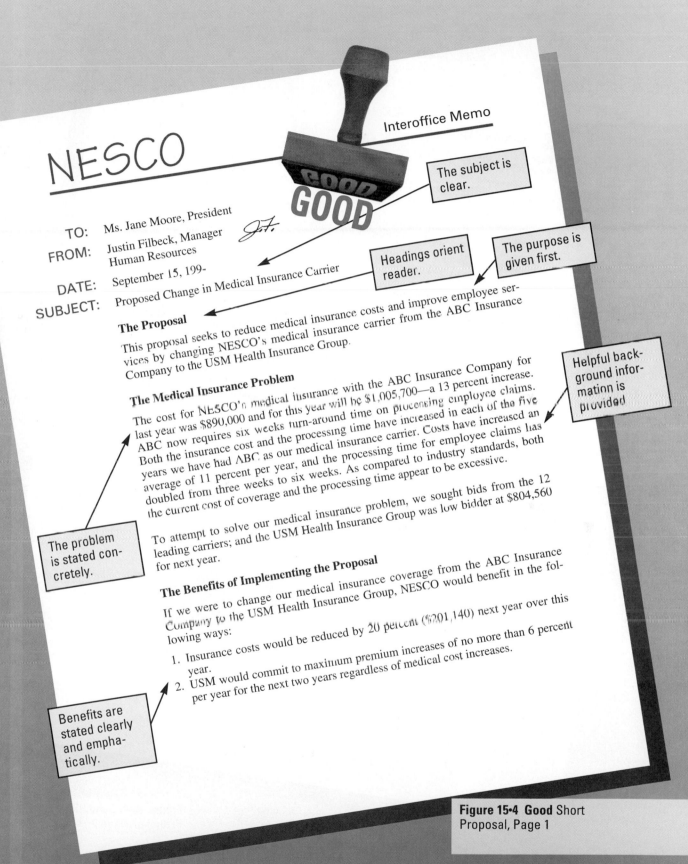

Interoffice Memo

NESCO

The subject is clear.

TO: Ms. Jane Moore, President

FROM: Justin Filbeck, Manager
Human Resources

DATE: September 15, 199-

SUBJECT: Proposed Change in Medical Insurance Carrier

Headings orient reader.

The purpose is given first.

The Proposal

This proposal seeks to reduce medical insurance costs and improve employee services by changing NESCO's medical insurance carrier from the ABC Insurance Company to the USM Health Insurance Group.

The Medical Insurance Problem

The cost for NESCO's medical insurance with the ABC Insurance Company for last year was $890,000 and for this year will be $1,005,700—a 13 percent increase. ABC now requires six weeks turn-around time on processing employee claims. Both the insurance cost and the processing time have increased in each of the five years we have had ABC as our medical insurance carrier. Costs have increased an average of 11 percent per year, and the processing time for employee claims has doubled from three weeks to six weeks. As compared to industry standards, both the current cost of coverage and the processing time appear to be excessive.

To attempt to solve our medical insurance problem, we sought bids from the 12 leading carriers; and the USM Health Insurance Group was low bidder at $804,560 for next year.

Helpful background information is provided

The problem is stated concretely.

The Benefits of Implementing the Proposal

If we were to change our medical insurance coverage from the ABC Insurance Company to the USM Health Insurance Group, NESCO would benefit in the following ways:

1. Insurance costs would be reduced by 20 percent ($201,140) next year over this year.
2. USM would commit to maximum premium increases of no more than 6 percent per year for the next two years regardless of medical cost increases.

Benefits are stated clearly and emphatically.

Ms. Jane Moore, President
Page 2
September 15, 199-

3. If medical cost increases are less than 6 percent in each of the next two years, our premium increases will be limited to the actual percent of the medical cost increases.
4. USM would commit, for the three-year term of the contract, to a maximum employee claim processing time of four weeks.
5. Medical Insurance Rating, Inc., an independent medical insurance carrier rating service, rates USM more highly than ABC—98.7 to 96.3, a significant rating difference.
6. Our medical insurance coverage with USM would be identical to the coverage we currently have with ABC.

Recommended Action

To change NESCO's medical insurance carrier from ABC to USM, we must give ABC notice of our cancellation by December 1. This gives us adequate time to negotiate a contract with USM prior to canceling our current coverage.

I propose that you recommend to the Board of Directors at its September 30 meeting that NESCO's medical insurance carrier be changed from the ABC Insurance Company to the USM Health Insurance Group, Inc.

mre

The proposed action is presented clearly and concretely.

RESEARCH SERVICES, INC.

120 Kings Pike   Seattle, WA 98100-0000   (206) 753-7700

October 15, 199-

Mr. Joe Baron
Director of General Services
Opryland, U.S.A., Inc.
2802 Opryland Drive
Nashville, TN 37314-1234

Dear Mr. Baron:

As you requested, here is a "Proposal for a Pilot Study to Test
an Expanded Employee Screening System."

The proposed study supports the development of an expanded
employee screening system that could reduce turnover and improve
job placement. The proposal is comprehensive. It includes
Opryland and the various Six Flags Parks. Basically the pilot
study will evaluate the current system with two major expansions:
(1) valid bases for interviewer judgments, and (2) appropriate
placement tests. While the full development of the screening system is expected to take three years, this proposal covers the
steps to be taken in the initial study to be conducted during the
first 14 months.

Your approval of this proposed pilot study is requested. It has,
I believe, considerable promise for improving employee productivity at Opryland and the Six Flags Parks.

Sincerely

Ginny Hendon

Ginny Hendon
Consultant

rs

enclosure

Figure 15·5 Good Long Proposal
(Source: Adapted with permission from an actual,
more detailed proposal provided by Opryland, U.S.A.,
Nashville, Tennessee.)

PROPOSAL FOR A PILOT STUDY TO TEST AN EXPANDED EMPLOYEE SCREENING SYSTEM

Submitted to
Joe Baron, Director of Human Resources
Opryland, U.S.A.
Nashville, Tennessee

Submitted by
Ginny Hendon, Consultant
Research Services, Inc.
Seattle, Washington

Pilot Study Cost: $30,000
Project Duration: December 199- to January 199-

TABLE OF CONTENTS

SECTIONS   **PAGE**

PROPOSAL FOR A PILOT STUDY TO TEST AN EXPANDED EMPLOYEE SCREENING SYSTEM

SUMMARY

The purpose of this proposal is to reduce employee turnover through the development and testing of an expanded employee screening system. To expand the system, valid bases for interview judgments and appropriate placement tests would be added. The design of a pilot study to test the expanded system would include selecting a random sample of applicants, screening the applicants, and tracking them on the job. The pilot study would begin December 199- and conclude January 199-. The cost for this study is projected at $30,000.

PURPOSE

The purpose of this proposal is to develop an expanded employee screening system designed to (1) reduce turnover, and (2) improve job placement of seasonal employees at Opryland and various Six Flags Parks. The proposal is that a pilot study be conducted during 199- to test such an expanded employee screening system.

PROBLEM

The turnover rate for seasonal employees at Opryland and the Six Flags Parks over the past two years has averaged 14.7 percent per year. Training costs could be reduced and services improved if this turnover rate could be lowered and job placement strengthened.

BACKGROUND

The current seasonal employee screening system has been effective in reducing turnover at Opryland and various Six Flags Parks. The current screening system basically includes the application form, the ideal leader behavior questionnaire, the management flexibility inventory, and information gained during interviews. An important part of the current screening system is that the interviewers are permitted to hire seasonal employees who do not meet cutoff test scores if, in the interviewer's judgment, the information gained in the interview indicates a promising employee. The turnover rate continues to be too high and initial job placement results inconsistent.

BENEFITS OF THE PROPOSAL

It is believed that the current screening system could be improved significantly by adding to it (1) the valid bases for interviewer judgments, and (2) appropriate placement tests. An example of an appropriate placement test would be a short math test to help decide who should be placed in positions that require handling money.

If, at its completion, the proposed study reduced the seasonal employee turnover rate and misplacements by 50 percent, training cost savings of over $87,000 each year could be realized. In addition, the quality of employee services to park guests would be improved resulting in enhanced goodwill.

DESCRIPTION OF THE STUDY

The proposed pilot study would use an expanded screening system that includes the interviewer judgment items and standard tests. The study will:

1. Compare those hired who quit and those hired who did not quit.
2. Provide profiles of high, average, and low performers.
3. Guide job placement of seasonal employees.
4. Provide improved bases for employee selection.
5. Strengthen our ability to counsel and/or reassign employees.

The full development of the expanded screening system is expected to take three years. During the first year, several employee screening items will be developed and tested in the pilot study. The second year will be devoted to refining the system, and the third year to field testing the final expanded screening system.

This proposal describes the design and procedures for the initial pilot study.

DESIGN OF THE PILOT STUDY AND EVALUATION PLAN

The following steps would be taken at each participating park:

1. Specify a date on which the pilot study would begin after the first 1,000 hirings are completed.
2. Randomly select 300 applicants from the first 1,000 hired after the date specified in Step 1.

2

3. Have each randomly selected applicant complete the screening items in the expanded system on a computerized answer sheet. The expanded system will include the following:

   a. Rational behavior inventory
   b. A short math test
   c. Judgment items suggested by interviewers
   d. Items related to human relations skills
   e. Leadership opinion questionnaire
   f. Ideal leader behavior questionnaire
   g. Opryland management flexibility inventory
   h. Other items from current screening system

4. Track the following information for each interpretation in the study:

   a. Performance appraisal results
   b. Absenteeism
   c. Date of termination
   d. Reason for termination
   e. Rehire status
   f. Employee attitudes (employee perceptions questionnaire)

5. Randomly divide the participants at each park into two groups.

6. Use appropriate statistical techniques to identify the best predictors of each of the variables listed in Step 4 for one of the groups.

7. Use the second group to cross-check the statistical techniques used in Step 6.

8. Divide the participants, based on all the variables listed in Step 4, into three groups:

   a. High performers
   b. Average performers
   c. Low performers

9. Use appropriate statistical techniques to determine how well each of the items in the expanded screening system predicted employee performance.

3

QUALIFICATIONS OF KEY PROJECT PERSONNEL

Project Manager

Dr. Douglas Williams
Degree: Ph.D., University of Pennsylvania, 199-
Major: Business Statistics
Minors: Management and Personnel
Experience: Assistant Human Resources Manager, Opryland;
                Directed several successful research projects

Senior Research Assistant

Dr. Norma Smith
Degree: Ph.D., Indiana University, 199-
Major: Probability Statistics
Minors: Mathematics and Computer Science
Experience: Research Associate, Vanderbilt University; Conducted a
                variety of successful research projects

TIME LINE

December 199-	Meet with interviewers from each participating park to obtain suggested interviewer judgment items. One interviewer from each participating park will meet at Opryland in mid-December.
January 199-	Develop actual items to be used on expanded screening system.
January– November 15, 199-	Start study (date depends on February 199- local park hiring patterns) and gather specific data.
November 15– December 15, 199-	Analyze data.
December 15, 199- January 15, 199-	Revise system for 199- season.

4

PROJECTED COSTS

Salaries

Project Manager (10 percent time)	$ 9,000
Senior Research Assistant (20 percent time)	10,000
Research Assistant (25 percent time)	5,000
Temporary Keyboarder (75 hours)	500

Travel*

Project Manager
Senior Research Assistant
Trips to meet with Six Flags interviewers

Materials   5,500

Computerized answer sheets
Leadership opinion questionnaires
Opryland management flexibility inventories
Ideal leader behavior questionnaires
Rational behavior inventory
Employee perceptions questionnaires
Computer paper
Duplicating

Total $ 30,000

---

*Note: Each park will be responsible for its own travel (except that requests for Opryland consultation from Six Flags Parks would be paid for by the requesting park).

5

DISCUSSION QUESTIONS

1. Describe the reasons why business studies are conducted and reports written.

2. List the five steps in conducting a business study.

3. Explain how you define the problem of a study; indicate two ways of stating the problem.

4. Describe what is involved in setting the boundaries of a study.

5. How can the scope of the study be defined?

6. Explain how to schedule a study.

7. Why is it important during the planning step to determine who will read the final report?

8. Explain the two basic kinds of information sources—secondary and primary.

9. Name the three major ways to obtain primary information and describe each one briefly.

10. How do you analyze information?

11. Describe the conclusions and recommendations in a report.

12. Define a proposal. Give examples to support your definition.

13. Discuss the statement, "Proposals are gambles."

14. Discuss the qualities of successful proposals.

15. What are the two most important parts of the purpose statement of the proposal?

16. Discuss what is meant by the benefits of the proposal.

17. Describe the content that should be included in the description of the solution section of a proposal. Give examples of the types of subject matter that might appear in this section.

18. Give three examples of evaluation plans that might be a part of a proposal.

19. Describe the content of the cost section of a proposal.

20. Discuss the purpose of including appendixes in proposals and give three examples of content for appendixes.

APPLICATION EXERCISES

1. Form teams to do a study to determine students' attitudes toward an important current student issue on your campus. In the study, implement all the major steps in conducting a business study except writing the report. In a group meeting of all teams, fairly assign a portion of the study to each team.

2. Indicate what would be (a) an appropriate statement of the problem, and (b) an appropriate list of factors for a comparative business study of the relative cost-effectiveness of two procedures for processing employment application forms in a personnel office.

3. You plan to determine why students prefer the "fast food" option over the "balanced meal" option in the college cafeteria. State the problem, list the study factors, and indicate the way you would gather data for such a study.

4. Form teams to develop a questionnaire that could be used to survey student opinion on one of the following topics:

    a. Employment opportunities upon graduation.

    b. Cost of school athletic events.

    c. Quality of the school newspaper.

    d. Desirability of implementing an honor system.

    e. Elimination of mid-term grades.

5. Form teams and administer a questionnaire developed in Application Exercise 4 to the students in business classes. Tabulate the students' responses and analyze the information secured.

6. Contact a local businessperson and obtain permission to survey the organization's employees on a mutually agreeable topic. Once the topic is chosen, complete all five steps in conducting a study. Possible topics for your study could be:

    a. The importance of communication in a business organization.

    b. Whether or not continuing education is desirable for full-time employees.

    c. The advantages and disadvantages of flex-time work schedules.

    d. The most important motivators of employee performance.

    e. A topic suggested by the businessperson.

7. Seek the cooperation of a local restaurant to perform a study that will evaluate customer reaction to the food, service, environment, and other appropriate factors. As a class project, develop a questionnaire that can be left in quantity on the tables, completed by customers, collected by restaurant personnel, and returned to the class for tabulation and analysis. Report the findings and appropriate recommendations to the restaurant manager.

8. Develop a proposal on one of the following topics. The proposal is to be sent to the dean or president of your college, as appropriate for the topic.

   a. Coeducational housing.
   b. Establishment of a pass/fail system.
   c. Required class attendance.
   d. Year-round school.
   e. Four-day school week.
   f. Elimination of final examinations.
   g. Development of an honors system for examinations.
   h. Optional class attendance for all classes.
   i. Increased summer school offerings.
   j. Advanced course in business communication.

9. Write a proposal to your instructor in which you recommend ways to strengthen one of the following aspects of your business communication course:

   a. Testing.
   b. Outside assignments.
   c. In-class writing activities.
   d. In-class oral communication exercises.
   e. Student involvement in class discussions.
   f. Student attendance.

10. Write a complete proposal using all 18 proposal elements discussed in this chapter. The subject of your proposal is to suggest that a required report writing course be offered. The receiver of your proposal will be the academic officer of your college. Keep in mind that your receiver will likely ask several other individuals and groups to review your proposal.

11. Write a short proposal on subject matter appropriate to your major. For example, if your major is accounting, write a proposal to your manager recommending that your company change auditing firms, fiscal year, reporting system, banks, inventory accounting, or some other such topic. Select a topic with which you are familiar, and limit the length of your proposal to two pages. Include the following sections in your proposal: purpose, problem, benefits, description of solution, time schedule, and cost.

12. You are the new assistant human resources manager for the Sonta Corporation. Your manager has asked you to propose an extensive seminar that she is calling "Communication Skills for Managers." Using all the proposal elements you think are appropriate, write a long proposal that solves the problem that your manager has specified as "poor communication in the corporate headquarters that interferes with effective operations." You can

draw on the table of contents in this textbook to assist you in the design of the proposed program.

MESSAGE ANALYSIS

Rewrite and improve the quality of the following proposal for a new club for business students. Implement the guidelines given in Chapter 15 for the appropriate elements for this proposal.

The real business world is foreign to most students, and clubs on campus do not solve the problem. For example, only Beta Gamma Sigma has meetings at which businesspersons speak to students. Beta Gamma Sigma devotes less than one-half of its yearly meetings to such programming. Most fraternities, sororities, and other organizations on campus just provide for social interactions among students. Students need more contact with businesspersons, and a new club for business students could provide the kind of interaction needed: increased transfer of real business world knowledge, contacts for future employment, and student leadership opportunities.

I suggest that the club be open to anyone and that the dues be reasonable and that the head of the business department be the faculty adviser and that the meetings—with businesspersons present at each one—be held both on and off campus. What do you think, Dr. Grant?

Report Preparation

Learning Objectives

Your learning objectives for this chapter include the following:

- To list the advantages of correct report formatting
- To distinguish between formal and informal reports
- To describe mechanical methods of report preparation
- To write an informal report
- To report proceedings of a meeting effectively through the use of minutes
- To develop clear policy statements
- To write an effective news release
- To write a formal report

The first step in writing a report is to conduct a business study, as described in Chapter 15. After this research is completed, the writer must present the resulting information in an accurate, objective manner and in a usable, readable format.

The time and effort spent in researching and writing a report are wasted unless the report is read and understood. The probability that a report will be read and understood is increased when certain principles of formatting are followed. These principles should be applied regardless of the length or formality of the report. This chapter discusses the formatting principles for effective report preparation.

Communication Quotes

Report preparation—most important for making good decisions. Decision makers need clear, concise, accurate, and readable reports. Good reports make for good decisions.

Mr. Howard W. Kruse, president of Blue Bell Creameries, Inc., stresses the need for effective reports.

ADVANTAGES OF CORRECT REPORT FORMATTING

Selecting the proper format for reports is as important as selecting the proper format for letters and memos. The reader's first impression of the report will be based on its appearance. A negative first impression may increase the time it takes for a reader to gain confidence in the report writer's credibility.

Formatting a written report properly will improve its readability. Paragraphs averaging six to seven lines make it easy for the reader to concentrate on the written material. Proper spacing between paragraphs and correct margins make it easy for the reader to follow the material.

Properly formatted reports help the reader follow the organization of the material by using appropriate headings. Headings lead the reader from one section to the next by announcing the next topic.

TYPES OF WRITTEN REPORTS

Written reports vary from short, informal reports to long, formal reports. An **informal report** may consist of a body and a title page or of a body only. A **formal report** may consist of all or some of the following parts: title page, title fly, letter or memo of authorization, letter or memo of transmittal, table of contents, list of illustrations, abstract, body, glossary, appendix, and bibliography.

Informal reports are usually written in the first person (I recommend that . . .); formal reports are usually in the third person (It is recommended that . . .). Recent trends, however, lean toward informality in both formats; many formal reports are now written in the first person. The degree of formality is determined after the report originator completes an analysis of the report receiver.

MECHANICS OF WRITTEN REPORTS

The mechanics of a written report—format, spacing, footnotes, etc.—are as important as the mechanics of a letter or memo in that they make the first impression on the reader. The writer must consider general guidelines of report mechanics, as well as the guidelines and policies of the organization for which the report is being prepared. The primary consideration in the physical presentation of a written report is that the mechanics improve the readability of the report.

COVER

The **cover** of a written report is normally a lightweight card-stock material that protects the contents of the report. It should contain the title of the report and the author's name or have a cutout section (window) through which the title and author's name on the title page may be seen. Many organizations use preprinted covers on which the author can place the title and his or her name. Normally the title is in uppercase letters, and the author's name has initial capital letters. The cover should be attractive and may contain an appropriate picture or drawing that will add to its attractiveness. Covers usually are used only on long, formal reports.

MARGINS

Proper **margins** in a report are important because they create the white space that makes the report visually appealing to the reader. As a general rule, report margins should be 1 inch on each side and the bottom, and $1^1/2$ inches on top. However, reports that are bound at the left should have a $1^1/2$-inch left margin, and reports that are bound at the top should have a 2-inch top margin.

SPACING

Reports may be **single-spaced** or **double-spaced.** The trend in business organizations is toward single spacing to reduce the number of sheets of paper that have to be handled. In reports using double spacing, paragraph indentions should be one-half inch from the left margin; no space is added between paragraphs. Single-spaced reports should be doubled-spaced between paragraphs; indenting the first word of the paragraph is optional.

HEADINGS

Appropriate headings help the reader follow the report organization and enable him or her to refer quickly to specific sections within the report. Sections that are of little interest can be skipped or scanned quickly.

Headings may be either informative or structural. An **informative heading** indicates the content of a forthcoming section and orients readers so that they can more easily understand the material. A **structural heading** emphasizes the functional sections within the report. Once the type of heading is selected, it should be used consistently throughout the report. An example of each follows:

Informative Heading:

CUSTOMERS' ATTITUDES TOWARD TELEVISION AS
AN ADVERTISING MEDIA

Structural Heading:

FINDINGS

The ways headings are presented vary according to the style manual used by the organization. Regardless of the method selected, consistency of presentation is vital. An explanation of one widely accepted method follows:

First-level headings (main headings) are centered on the page in uppercase letters. Main headings may be printed in bold-faced uppercase letters, but preferably not in uppercase letters and underscored. Second-level headings (side headings) begin at the left margin, and the first letter of each important word is capitalized. Side headings are often underlined for emphasis. The third-level heading (paragraph heading) begins one-half inch from the left margin, is underlined, and has the first letter of important words capitalized. An example of this method is shown in Figure 16•1.

The headings at each level must be constructed so that they are grammatically parallel. For example, all first-level headings must be parallel; however, first-level headings do not have to be parallel with second-level headings. In the following example, the second-level headings are parallel, but the first-level headings are not.

INCOME FOR FIRST QUARTER

Rent
Dividends

WAYS THAT FIRST QUARTER INCOME IS SPENT

Wages
Insurance
Travel

This example could be corrected by changing "WAYS THAT FIRST QUARTER INCOME IS SPENT" to "EXPENSES FOR FIRST QUARTER."

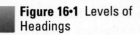
Figure 16•1 Levels of Headings

FIRST-LEVEL HEADING

xxxxxxxxxxxxxxxxxxxxxxxxxxxxxxxxxxxxxxxxxxxxxxx
xxxxxxxxxxxxxxxxxxxxxxxxxxxxxxxxxxxxxxxxxxxxxxxxxxx
xxxxxxxxxxxxxxxxxxxxxxxxxxxxxxxxxxxxxxxxxxxxxxxxxxx
xxxxxxxxxxxxxxxxxxxxxxxxxxxxxxxxxxxxxxxxxxxxxxxxxxx
xxxxxxxxxxxxxxxxxxxxxxxxxxxxxxxxxxxxxxxxxxxxxxxxxxx
xxxxxxxxxxxxxxxxxxx xxxxxxxxxxxxxxxxxxxxxxxxxxxxxxxxx

Second-Level Heading

xxxxxxxxxxxxxxxxxxxxxxxxxxxxxxxxxxxxxxxxxxxxxxx
xxxxxxxxxxxxxxxxxxxxxxxxxxxxxxxxxxxxxxxxxxxxxxxxxxx
xxxxxxxxxxxxxxxxxxxxxxxxxxxxxxxxxxxxxxxxxxxxxxxxxxx
xxxxxxxxxxxxxxxxxxxxxxxxxxxxxxxxxxxxxxxxxxxxxxxxxxx
xxxxxxxxxxxxx

   Third Level Heading. xxxxxxxxxxxxxxxxxxxxxxxxxxxxx
xxxxxxxxxxxxxxxxxxxxxxxxxxxxxxxxxxxxxxxxxxxxxxxxxxx
xxxxxxxxxxxxxxxxxxxxxxxxxxxxxxxxxxxxxxxxxxxxxxxxxxx
xxxxxxxxxxxxxxxxxxxxxxxxxxxxxxxxxxx

   Third Level Heading. xxxxxxxxxxxxxxxxxxxxxxxxxxxxx
xxxxxxxxxxxxxxxxxxxxxxxxxxxxxxx

   Third Level Heading. xxxxxxxxxxxxxxxxxxxxxxxxxxxxx
xxxxxxxxxxxxxxxxxxxxxxxxxxxxxxxxxxxxxxxxxxxxxxxxxxx
xxxxxxxxxxxxxxxxxxxxxxxxxxxxxxxxxxxxx

   Third Level Heading. xxxxxxxxxxxxxxxxxxxxxxxxxxxxx
xxxxxxxxxxxxxxxxxxxxxxxxxxxxxxxxxxxxxxxxxxxxxxxxxxx
xxxxxxxxxxxxxxxxxxxxxxxxxxxxxxxx

Second-Level Heading

xxxxxxxxxxxxxxxxxxxxxxxxxxxxxxxxxxxxxxxxxxxxxxx
xxxxxxxxxxxxxxxxxxxxxxxxxxxxxxxxxxxxxxxxxxxxxxxxxxx
xxxxxxxxxxxxxxxxxxxx

FIRST-LEVEL HEADING

xxxxxxxxxxxxxxxxxxxxxxxxxxxxxxxxxxxxxxxxxxxxxxx
xxxxxxxxxxxxxxxxxxxxxxxxxxxxxxxxxxxxxxxxxxxxxxxxxxx
xxxxxxxxxxxxxxxxxxxxxxxxxxxxxxxx

The rules of outlining should be followed when preparing headings in a written report. That is, when second- or third-level headings are used, each level must have at least two headings.

All headings within a report should be typed or printed a double space following the last line of the text in the preceding section. Text for sections with first- or second-level headings begin a double space below the heading. Text for sections with third-level headings begins two spaces after the period in the heading. This method of organizing headings is shown in Figure 16•1 and in the sample report in Figure 16•9.

> Headings are placed on the second line below the preceding section.

FOOTNOTES

Footnotes must be used to give credit to the source of quoted or paraphrased material. Reports in the business community do not contain as

Information obtained from secondary sources must be footnoted.

Commonly used footnoting methods are:

many footnotes as reports in other fields, because business reports usually contain only information that is based on data gathered through primary research. Two commonly used methods for citing sources follow.

The traditional method of footnoting is convenient for the reader when a report contains information gathered from a number of sources. Material to be footnoted is noted by an Arabic numeral that is placed at the end of the quoted material and raised one-half line (superscripted). The footnote numbers begin with 1 and are consecutive throughout the report. The footnote is separated from the text by a 1fi-inch long rule beginning at the left margin one line below the last line of the text material. The footnote is typed or printed on the second line under the rule; it is single spaced, with the first line indented one-half inch from the left margin. The superscripted number identification precedes the reference material.

Information contained in traditional footnotes varies depending on the source—book, periodical, encyclopedia, government publication, newspaper, or unpublished material. For a book, the footnote contains the author's complete name, the title, the city (and sometimes the state) in which published, the publishing company, the year published, and the page number. An example of a traditional footnote for information taken from a periodical follows. Footnotes for material from other sources vary slightly.

• Traditional

```
The number of new oil wells being drilled has
decreased by 10 percent from the number drilled
last year.¹ There will be a shortage of oil
products if the trend of drilling fewer wells con-
tinues for the rest of this decade.
```

```
¹A. W. Hodde, "Oil Production in 1993," Petroleum
Quarterly (March 1994), 8.
```

A contemporary method of footnoting information is more appropriate for reports that contain information from only a few sources. These sources can be easily documented by placing the information (name of author, date of publication, and page number) in parentheses at the end of the sentence relating to the citation. For information about the source, a reader would refer to the bibliography. An example of this method is:

• Contemporary

```
The number of new oil wells being drilled has
decreased by 10 percent from the number drilled
last year (Hodde, 1994, p. 8). There will be a
shortage of oil products if the trend of drilling
fewer wells continues for the rest of this decade.
```

An authoritative reference manual should be consulted before constructing footnotes or other citations.

PAGE NUMBERS

Reports containing more than two pages should be numbered.

Pages in short reports of only one or two pages do not have to be numbered. Pages in long reports should be numbered consecutively. Preliminary pages (pages prior to the body of a report) should be numbered by placing small Roman numerals (ii, iii, iv, etc.) at the center of the page, one inch from the bottom, beginning with the second page. The title page is considered page i, even though no page number is given.

The body of the report should begin as page one, identified with Arabic numerals (1, 2, 3, 4, etc.). For each section or chapter that is started on a separate page, the page number should be centered and one inch from the bottom edge. On the remaining pages of unbound or left-bound reports, the number should be placed on the fourth line from the top of the page at the right margin; on top-bound reports the page number should be centered and one inch from the bottom edge of the page.

INFORMAL REPORTS

Informal reports do not contain all the parts of formal reports.

An informal report does not contain all the parts of a formal report. As the name indicates, informal reports may be written informally using first person. Most of the time this type of report will not contain graphic aids or material from secondary sources.

In business, the informal report is used much more frequently than the formal report. There are many different types of informal reports; five of the most common—letter, memo, progress, periodic, and technical—are discussed in the following sections.

LETTER REPORTS

A letter report is used to communicate with people outside an organization.

A **letter report** uses a letter format to communicate to individuals outside an organization. A letter report uses a subject line and has headings for sections within the report. The personal style, using first and second person pronouns (*I*, *we*, and *you*), is common in letter reports. Letter reports often are used for submitting annual reports, giving recommendations, and presenting information. A letter report giving a recommendation is shown in Figure 16•2.

MEMO REPORTS

A memo report is used for informal communication within an organization.

A **memo report** is used to communicate information to individuals within an organization. It is used primarily for reporting routine information concerning day-to-day operations. Memo reports may be used to provide a written record; they are less formal than letter reports.

A memo report uses standard memo headings and no salutation, complimentary close, or signature. The originator should initial the memo report next to his or her typed name in the heading. Topic headings frequently are used for easy reading. The progress report in Figure 16•3 is written as a memo report.

Figure 16•2 Letter Report

GREEN VALLEY CABLE, INC.

2168 Conway Road • Dayton, OH 45401-3264
Telephone (515) 555-1798 • Fax (513) 555-4285

April 14, 199-

Dear Stockholder:

PROPOSED MERGER OF GREEN VALLEY CABLE
AND HI-TECH CABLE

You are being asked to consider and vote on a proposal to adopt and approve a merger agreement. If the merger is approved, all the outstanding shares of the company's common stock will be canceled and all stockholders will receive $24 cash for each share of common stock.

In making a determination to recommend the offer of the merger, the board of directors considered, among other things, the marketplace's acceptance of the new company on the New York Stock Exchange. During the past ten years, the price of our common stock has not reached $30, and our stock generally has shown little activity and low volume.

The nature of our company's business is such that predicting the degree of profitability of the company is extremely difficult. Its profits are impacted significantly by factors beyond the control of our company.

As a result of these factors, Green Valley's board of directors believes it would be in the best interests of all stockholders to vote for the merger. We recommend that you sign and return the enclosed computer card voting for the merger by May 6, 199-.

Sincerely,

Moira Haley

Moira Haley
Chief Executive Officer

wn

Enclosure

PROGRESS REPORTS

Significant events and changes in a project are reported in a progress report.

A **progress report** (also called a *status report*) is used to inform readers about the status of a particular project. It assists managers in monitoring and making decisions about the project. The report should inform the reader about the work that has been accomplished, the work that is being done currently, and the work that is scheduled to be done in the upcoming reporting period. Any significant progress or problems should be discussed in the report.

Progress reports may be written daily, weekly, monthly, or quarterly. The frequency of the reports will depend on the type or nature of the project being discussed. An example of a progress report is shown in Figure 16•3.

Figure 16•3 Progress Report in Memo Format

POLAR TELEMARKETING
Interoffice Memorandum

TO: Nicole Albro, Manager
FROM: Morris Batts, Network Administrator *MB.*
DATE: July 9, 199-
SUBJECT: Quarterly Progress Report on Microcomputers

All employees will have microcomputers on their desks at the completion of this project. The employees will also receive forty hours of instruction on the use of word processing, data management, and spreadsheet software.

Work Completed

This project was started on November 15, 199-. During the first quarter, we purchased 60 microcomputers and 25 printers. We trained 10 managers, 25 middle managers, and 25 supervisors during the first three months.

During the past quarter, we purchased 110 microcomputers and 40 printers. Since April 1, 11 managers, 14 middle managers, 21 supervisors, and 64 secretaries have completed training.

Work Remaining

We need to purchase 95 microcomputers and 25 printers to complete this project. During the current quarter we will purchase 50 microcomputers and 10 printers; the rest of the equipment will be purchased during the last quarter of the year.

Only three managers and six supervisors yet need to be trained. All nine will receive their instruction this quarter. We have 30 secretaries who currently need an additional 15 hours of training to complete their education. The remaining 95 secretaries needing instruction will receive training in the next two quarters.

Conclusions

This project of purchasing 265 microcomputers and 90 printers is on schedule with no foreseeable problems. We should have all 304 employees trained on applications software by the end of the year.

qk

PERIODIC REPORTS

A **periodic report** provides managers with statistical information at regularly scheduled intervals. These intervals may be daily, weekly, monthly, quarterly, or annually. Periodic reports follow no set formats, and many organizations use preprinted forms. A form used to report the number of hours that a part-time employee worked in a month is shown in Figure 16•4.

TECHNICAL REPORTS

A **technical report,** as the name implies, conveys specialized or scientific information. There are no standard formats or organizational plans for technical reports. However, organizations will often specify particular formats and plans to be used for reports within their business. Standardization of

Figure 16•4
Periodic Report

MONTHLY TIME REPORT
HAWKINS CARPET

Month of _____ , 199_____

Name of Employee _____

Soc. Sec. # _____

Week	Daily Number of Hours Worked							Weekly Totals
	Mon	Tues	Wed	Thur	Fri	Sat	Sun	
1								
2								
3								
4								
5								
							TOTAL HOURS	

I hereby certify that the above reported hours are the correct number I have worked during the month herein reported.

_____
Signature of Employee

_____
Date

I hereby certify that the above is a true statement of the hours worked by this employee and that the work was performed in a satisfactory manner.

_____
Signature of Supervisor

_____
Department

formats makes it easy for readers to scan reports for information of particular interest to them. Some companies limit the number of pages that a report may contain. An example of a technical report is shown in Figure 16•5.

Technical terms need not be defined when a technical report is prepared for someone familiar with the terminology. If the reader of the report does not have the technical expertise, words used in the report must be clarified. A good rule to follow is to remember the principles of business communication discussed in Chapter 2.

Technical terms must be defined if they are likely to be misunderstood by the reader.

Figure 16·5 Technical
Report

Molded BMC Plastics

Interoffice Memorandum

TO: Stanley Raymer

FROM: Dede Pinion

DATE: February 3, 199-

SUBJECT: Temporary Steam Valve Substitution for Ethylene Plant
Equipment

As you requested, a check has been made to determine
whether a spare TLE shell steam relief valve (SV-906S)
may be used temporarily on the steam drum (TK-101C)
that serves the two large vertical ethylene furnaces. This
substitution would prevent a shutdown of the steam drum
due to a broken spring in its relief valve. A new valve
spring will not be available for at least eight weeks.

Our records and visual examination of the spare relief valve
and the relief valve (SV-1204C) presently serving the
steam drum indicate that the valves are identical with
respect to inlet, outlet, and orifice size. Our findings show
that the only differences between the valves are manufacturer and inset pressure, which is slight.

Based on this investigation, I believe the spare TLE steam
relief valve may be substituted for the relief valve serving
steam drum TK-101C. Resetting of the set pressure on the
spare valve may be done since it falls well within the 10
percent range allowable for the valve spring.

lr

c   A. Phillips
J. Noles
T. Gillies
R. Sweeney

SPECIAL REPORTS

Some business reports require special content or format considerations.
Three common special reports are minutes, policies, and news releases.

MINUTES

Minutes are an official report of the proceedings of a meeting. They should
be concise, accurate, and well organized. Minutes serve as an official
record, assist in refreshing memories of participants, provide information to
individuals who were not present, and assist in preparing members for
upcoming meetings.

Minutes should be brief and should include only pertinent information
that accurately summarizes the meeting. All motions and resolutions should

**Minutes serve as the official
report of a meeting.**

**Only pertinent information
should be included in minutes.**

> *A committee is a group that keeps minutes and loses hours.*
>
> **Milton Berle**

be recorded word-for-word as presented. Individuals presenting motions and resolutions should be identified by name in the minutes. It is important to indicate that a motion was seconded, but the name of the individual who seconds a motion need not be recorded. The outcome—approval or defeat—should be included also.

The parts that normally are included in minutes are: name of the committee or organization conducting the meeting; date, time, and location of the meeting; listing of members present and absent; approval of the minutes of the previous meeting; record of the meeting in chronological order; time of adjournment; and signatures of the secretary and/or chairperson. These parts will vary depending on the purpose and formality of the meeting. Figure 16•6 shows an example of minutes for a committee planning a company-sponsored Labor Day picnic.

Not all minutes will contain the same parts.

POLICIES

Policy statements serve as guidelines for operation of a business.

A **policy statement** in a business organization serves as a guideline that employees must follow. Policy statements normally will be assembled into a policy manual. This manual can be used to orient new employees and can serve as a reference for long-time employees.

Policies should be broad for managerial personnel and specific for nonmanagerial personnel.

Policy statements should be written in the third person and should be clear, concise, and complete. Policies written for managerial personnel are broad guides that allow flexibility, while policies for nonmanagerial personnel are narrower and more restrictive. An example of a policy statement is shown in Figure 16•7.

NEWS RELEASES

News releases build good public relations.

A **news release** is a special business report containing information that will be of interest to the public. News releases need to be newsworthy, accurate, timely, concise, and positive. Common subjects for news releases include promotions, business expansion, employee layoffs, and introduction of new products.

News releases should be written in the inverted pyramid format.

The inverted pyramid format should be used for news releases. The **inverted pyramid format** begins with a summary lead that tells who, what, where, when, and sometimes why or how. The body of the release should be developed by giving details in descending order of importance—most important facts first and least important facts last. A news release should not contain a conclusion. The advantages of using the inverted pyramid format are (1) the release can be shortened easily by cutting from the end without

Figure 16•6 Minutes

MINUTES
Memorial Day Picnic Committee

The meeting was held in the conference room on May 22, 199-, at 1:30 p.m.

Members Present: Allcock, Dempsey, Fultz (Chairperson), Martin, Peyton (Secretary), and Rehmus

Member Absent: Fuqua

The minutes of the previous meeting (May 3, 199-) were approved as distributed.

Selection of Caterer

Ms. Dempsey reported that Stan's Barbecue would cater the event for $5.10 per person and Rita's Catering would charge $4.90 per person. Each firm would furnish meat, beans, potatoes, and soft drinks for these prices. Ms. Dempsey moved and it was seconded that Rita's Catering be hired for the picnic. Motion passed.

Picnic Announcement and Reservations

Mr. Allcock reported that announcements of the picnic had been sent to all employees with instructions to respond by May 23 and to state how many people from their families would be attending the picnic. By noon today, responses indicated that 220 individuals would be attending. Ten employees had not yet responded. On May 23 the number of attendees will be forwarded to Ms. Martin so she can notify Rita's as to the number of people who will be at the picnic.

Softball Equipment

Mr. Rehmus reported that softball equipment had been obtained from the local American Legion post. He would draft a letter for Ms. Fultz' signature thanking the post for the use of its equipment. This letter should be sent within a couple of days after the picnic.

Pony Rides for Children

Ms. Martin reported that she had checked with Jesse's Riding Stables, and the cost of having two ponies at the picnic for children's rides would be $80. Children's safety was discussed. Ms. Martin moved and it was seconded that $80 be allocated to Jesse's Riding Stables for furnishing free pony rides to children. The motion carried.

The meeting was adjourned at 2:10 p.m.

Respectfully submitted,

Tom Peyton

Tom Peyton
Secretary

---

rewriting, and (2) the release satisfies reader curiosity by getting to the main idea quickly.

The news release should be double spaced with the company's name and address typed or printed at the top. The contact person's name and telephone number should be shown on the news release. Special instructions to the newspaper staff (FOR IMMEDIATE RELEASE, FOR RELEASE ON JANUARY 12) should be typed in all capital letters at the top of the news release. The release text is immediately preceded by city, state, and date. A news release should end with a "-30-" or a "###" under the last line to inform the news agency that the news release is complete; if it is longer than one page, "more" should be printed on the bottom of each page that is to be continued. Figure 16•8 on page 457 shows a sample news release about an employee promotion.

News releases should end with -30- or ###.

Figure 16•7 Policy
Statement

POSTAL SERVICES POLICY

The following policies have been established for the operation of the company postal service:

1. The Company Post Office, located in room 2104, provides mail service from 8:00 a.m. to 4:30 p.m. weekdays. It is closed on Saturdays and Sundays. The service window is closed each day from 9:00 a.m. to 10:00 a.m. and from 2:30 p.m. to 3:15 p.m. for mail sorting prior to delivery.

2. The Charter Hospital postmaster will be the source of approvals and advice for all on-site and off-site mailing services. The vice president for administrative services has the responsibility for implementing company mailing policies and the authority to approve any exceptions to these policies. Any request for deviation from the stated policies and procedures should be submitted in writing. The vice president for administrative services will function as the liaison between the U.S. Postal Service and Charter Hospital.

3. All company budget units are eligible to use the company mail service for official mail pertinent to the function and operation of Charter Hospital.

4. Charter Hospital mail carriers deliver and pick up mail from designated mail stops. Company mail carriers are not authorized to change the location of the mail stop within an office, to delete a mail stop, or to add a new mail stop on their route. Written requests for changes or additions to mail delivery routes should be submitted to Charter Hospital's postmaster.

    It is the responsibility of each office or department to distribute mail to the employees served by each mail stop. Each office or department should notify the Charter Hospital postmaster of all changes in both personnel and personnel location.

5. Charter Hospital postmaster is charged with the responsibility for coordinating all mass mailings. Offices and departments should contact the postmaster for technical assistance and scheduling information.

FORMAL REPORTS

A formal report normally contains many pages, is written in third person, contains several sections or chapters, utilizes graphic aids, and is read by individuals in top levels of management and possibly by individuals outside the writer's organization. It may take from several weeks to several months to research and write the report. This research and writing may be accomplished by one person or by a team of several individuals.

A formal report normally is written for upper management.

A formal report may be divided into three major divisions: the preliminary section, the body, and the supplementary section. A formal report may contain all or some of the following parts. Each part is shown in Figure 16•9 (pages 463–482).

A formal report generally contains three main sections.

Figure 16•8 News Release

Edwards Chemical
3251 Ironridge Drive
Cartersville, GA 30120-2134

NEWS RELEASE

CONTACT: FOR IMMEDIATE RELEASE
Gina Hancock
(404) 555-1839

Cartersville, GA, August 3, 199- — Ms. Angela
Mendez has been promoted to Southern Regional
Sales Manager for Edwards Chemical. She will
now have responsibility for 18 sales representatives in nine states.

Ms. Mendez joined Edwards Chemical as a sales
representative in 1985 after graduating Summa
Cum Laude from Jacksonville State University.
Since her employment with Edwards, she has
twice been named the Outstanding Salesperson
for the company.

Ms. Mendez, her husband, Sergio, and their
three children, Ruben, Lidia, and Mario
reside in Scenic Hills.

-30-

1. Preliminary Section
   a. Title Page
   b. Title Fly
   c. Letter or Memo of Authorization
   d. Letter or Memo of Transmittal
   e. Table of Contents
   f. List of Illustrations
   g. Executive Summary

2. Body
   a. Introduction
   b. Procedures
   c. Findings
   d. Analysis
   e. Conclusions
   f. Recommendations

3. Supplementary Section
   a. Glossary
   b. Appendix
   c. Bibliography

PRELIMINARY SECTION

The preliminary section contains all the parts of a report that precede the body. The preliminary pages will vary from report to report according to the formality of the report. A discussion of the individual parts follows.

TITLE PAGE

A **title page** normally contains the following information: the title of the report; the name of the person or organization receiving the report; the writer's name, title, and department; and the date of submission. The title should indicate the purpose and content of the report. *See* page 463.

Many organizations have specific guidelines for the preparation of title pages. When they exist, the company guidelines should be followed. If specific guidelines do not exist, each line on the title page should be centered, and there should be equal vertical spacing between items. The title should be all capitals; other lines may be either all capitals or initial capitals. A courtesy title should be placed before the name of the person to whom the report is addressed, but not before the name of the report writer. *See* page 463.

TITLE FLY

The **title fly** may be either a blank sheet of paper or a sheet of paper with the report title centered horizontally and vertically. It is used to make the report more formal. The title fly may be placed immediately before or immediately after the title page. *See* page 464.

LETTER OR MEMO OF AUTHORIZATION

This message is written before the study begins by the person giving permission for the study. It is included in the final report by the writer of the report. The document will be a letter if the authorization is from an agency outside the organization and a memo if from within the organization. The document gives any relevant information necessary to accomplish the study, such as statement of the problem, amount of money available to support the study, personnel to assist in the study, and due date. *See* page 465.

LETTER OR MEMO OF TRANSMITTAL

The **letter or memo of transmittal** is written by the report writer and is used to introduce the report to the reader. A report to readers outside the organization would contain a letter, while reports for internal use would contain a memo. In more formal reports, a preface or foreword may be used.

All formal reports should contain a title page.

A title fly makes a report more formal.

A letter or memo of authorization gives the researcher permission to do the study.

A letter or memo of transmittal contains items you would tell the reader if you were to hand deliver the report.

The letter or memo of transmittal may be subjective—that is, the writer may offer a suggestion or opinion not supported by data. It may contain personal comments. The letter or memo may also refer readers to parts of the report of special interest or suggest special uses of the information. In general, any item worthy of discussion may be included in the letter or memo of transmittal. A letter of transmittal is included in the proposal in Figure 15•5 (*see* page 431) and in the long report shown in Figure 16•9 (*see* page 466).

TABLE OF CONTENTS

A **table of contents** should follow the letter of transmittal and should list all major sections that follow it. Its purpose is to aid the reader in quickly locating specific information in the report. A table of contents normally is not used in reports of fewer than five pages.

The table of contents is double-spaced between major sections; subsections are single-spaced. Section heads should be listed exactly as they appear in the body and should be connected to the page number by dot leaders (horizontally spaced periods). Page numbers are optional for subheadings. The table of contents normally is prepared after the report is typed or printed in final form. A combined table of contents and list of illustrations is shown in Figure 16•9 on pages 467–468.

LIST OF ILLUSTRATIONS

Graphic aids are identified in a **list of illustrations.** The list may be on the same page as the table of contents, or it may begin on the page following the table of contents if the report contains more than four illustrations. The list of illustrations uses the same format as the table of contents, with illustration captions instead of section heads. A report may group all graphic aids into one list of illustrations, or it may group each type of graphic aid (chart, graph, etc.) separately. This section is normally prepared after the report is typed or printed in final form. *See* pages 467–468.

EXECUTIVE SUMMARY

An **executive summary** is a brief version of the formal report; it restates each section of the report in abbreviated form with an emphasis on findings, conclusions, and recommendations. Other common names for an executive summary are *summary, abstract, overview,* and *synopsis.* Busy executives who do not need to read an entire report are provided with vital information in capsule form. An executive summary also provides an overview for other readers of the report, so that they will have a general idea of what the study is about prior to reading the entire report. *See* page 469.

The maximum allowable length of an executive summary will vary among business organizations. A general rule is that it should be approximately ten percent of the length of the full report, but should not exceed one or two single-spaced pages.

BODY

Most formal reports will contain all the information presented in the sections discussed in this part of the chapter; however, some of the sections

---

The table of contents lists all major items of the report.

A table of contents should be used only when a report exceeds four pages.

A list of illustrations summarizes the graphic aids in the report.

An executive summary is a capsule form of the report.

may be combined. The material in the body may be presented using the direct or the indirect approach. In the direct approach the conclusions, recommendations, or both come at the beginning of the body. They come at the end of the body in the indirect approach. The sample report in Figure 16•9 on pages 470–477 presents the material using the indirect approach.

The body of a report may use the direct or indirect approach.

INTRODUCTION

The **introduction** provides adequate background concerning the study so that the reader can understand the remaining parts of the report body. Material for this section will be similar to what is included in a proposal. (Proposals are discussed in Chapter 15.) The specific parts to be included in this section depend on what is necessary to assist the reader in understanding the scope and sequence of the report. *See* page 470.

The introduction assists the reader in understanding the rest of the report.

Background. The introduction often begins with the **background,** which is a general description of the problem that was studied and the main issues involved in it. The background leads to more specific details that develop into the statement of the problem.

Statement of the Problem. The **statement of the problem** clearly identifies the specific problem that was researched. The statement of the problem should be brief but informative.

The specific topic of the study is given in the statement of the problem.

Purpose of the Study. The **purpose of the study** indicates why the study was conducted. The purpose should help convince the reader of the worthiness of the report. The purpose may be stated as a question (*Which insurance company will best serve our needs?*) or as a statement (*The purpose of this study is to provide information so that the insurance company with the most effective plan will be selected.*).

The purpose provides the reason for the study.

Scope. The **scope** of the study is defined by the main factors that were studied and generally appears next in the introductory section. It lets the reader know the extent of the study. Limitations over which the researcher had no control are listed in this section of the introduction. These limitations may include lack of resources, lack of time, or geographic boundaries.

The scope lets the reader know the extent of the study.

Related Literature. **Related literature** is material collected while doing research on a topic being studied. A review of related literature may be included in the introduction if only a limited amount of literature is available about the topic. A separate section should be used when extensive amounts of related literature are reviewed. *See* page 470.

Unfamiliar Terms. Definitions of terms unfamiliar to the reader may be included in the introductory section. When many terms need to be defined, however, a glossary should be included in the supplementary section.

PROCEDURES

The **procedures,** or methodology, section describes the steps taken in conducting the study. One purpose of this section is to allow readers to determine whether all aspects of the problem were adequately investigated. This section can also be used by another researcher to conduct a similar study that could validate or disprove the results of the original study. *See* page 471.

The steps used in conducting the study are described in the procedures section.

FINDINGS

Findings are results discovered during research on a topic. This section should be presented in a factual and objective manner without personal opinions or interpretations. All findings—positive and negative—are presented in this section. Graphic aids such as those shown on pages 471–476 may be used to assist the writer in communicating the findings of the study.

The results of the study are presented in the findings section.

ANALYSIS

An **analysis** is conducted using the findings presented in the previous section. Findings in related studies should be compared with the findings of the current study. This analysis permits the reader to determine which relationships are significant. *See* page 476.

Significant outcomes and relationships are discussed in the analysis section.

CONCLUSIONS

A **conclusion** is a statement of reasoning that a researcher makes after a thorough investigation. All conclusions should be made using the findings of the study and should be based on the analysis section of the report. In many studies, conclusions are summary statements of the content of the analysis section. No new data should be presented in this section. A study may have one or several conclusions. The conclusions are the bases for the writer's recommendations. *See* page 477.

Conclusions are drawn from the findings of the study.

RECOMMENDATIONS

This section may be combined with the conclusions section. A **recommendation** is the writer's suggestion to the reader as to the action(s) that should be taken to solve the problem that was studied. Recommendations should develop logically from the findings, analysis, and conclusions of the study. A single recommendation or several recommendations may be presented in one study. If more than two recommendations are presented, they may be listed and numbered. This section may contain only the recommendations, or it may contain both the recommendations and the supportive reasoning for their development. *See* page 477.

Recommendations are based on conclusions.

SUPPLEMENTARY SECTION

The final section of a written report contains material that is related indirectly to the main topic of the study. This section may consist of one or more subsections, such as a glossary, an appendix, and a bibliography.

GLOSSARY

A **glossary** is an alphabetic list of terms used in the report. It is used to define terms with which the reader may be unfamiliar. It is used only when numerous unfamiliar terms are included in the text. When there are only a few specialized terms, they should be defined in the introduction or where they are first used in the text.

Unfamiliar terms are defined in the glossary.

APPENDIX

An **appendix** contains information that is related indirectly to the study but that has been excluded from the body to improve readability. When there is

Indirectly related material is placed in an appendix.

more than one item of information, each should be labeled as a separate appendix. Each appendix is identified with a capital letter:

Appendix A: Computer Printout of Daily Sales

Appendix B: Sample Follow-Up Letter

All appendixes should be referred to in the body of the report. If the material is not referred to in the body, it is not relevant enough to be included as an appendix. Some items commonly included as appendixes include:

- Questionnaires
- Computer printouts
- Follow-up letters
- Reports of similar studies
- Working papers
- Intricate tables
- Supporting material

BIBLIOGRAPHY

All references are listed in a bibliography.

A **bibliography** is an alphabetic list of all references used as sources of information in the study. All footnoted sources must be included in the bibliography; however, it may also contain a source not footnoted in the body. A bibliography section may also be called "references" or "sources." A bibliographical reference for a magazine article includes the author's name (with last name first), title of the article, name of the publication, date of publication, and page number(s):

Maddox, Lynda. "Computerized Procedure for Evaluating Employees." *Personnel Quarterly* 31 (February 1993): 37–42.

Different types of sources are arranged differently in bibliographical entries. Reference manuals should be used to ensure proper construction of bibliographical entries.

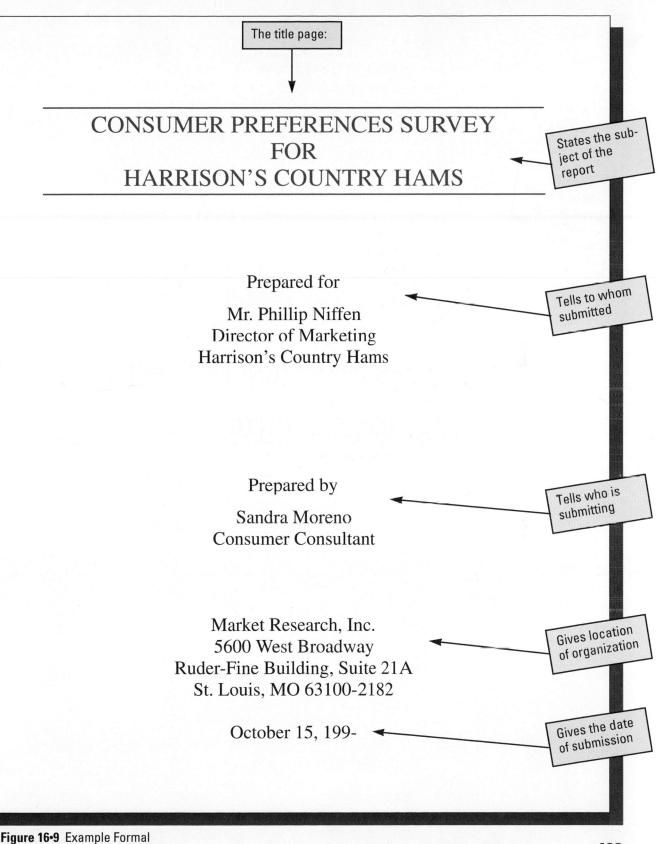

The title page:

CONSUMER PREFERENCES SURVEY
FOR
HARRISON'S COUNTRY HAMS

States the subject of the report

Prepared for

Mr. Phillip Niffen
Director of Marketing
Harrison's Country Hams

Tells to whom submitted

Prepared by

Sandra Moreno
Consumer Consultant

Tells who is submitting

Market Research, Inc.
5600 West Broadway
Ruder-Fine Building, Suite 21A
St. Louis, MO 63100-2182

Gives location of organization

October 15, 199-

Gives the date of submission

Figure 16•9 Example Formal Report.

CONSUMER PREFERENCES SURVEY
FOR
HARRISON'S COUNTRY HAMS

Figure 16•9 Example Formal Report. Cont.

Harrison's Country Hams

1000 Pork Lane • Kansas City, MO 64100-8462 • Tel. (816) 555-1000 • Fax (816) 555-2300

The letter of authorization:

June 20, 199-

Ms. Sandra Moreno, Consumer Consultant
Market Research, Inc.
5600 West Broadway
Ruder-Fine Building, Suite 21A
St. Louis, MO 63100-2182

Gives authority for the study

Dear Ms. Moreno:

Subject: Authorization for Consumer Preferences Study

You are authorized to study consumer preferences for country hams in the Kansas City, Missouri, area. The purposes of your study are:

Gives relevant information, such as purposes and procedures

1. To provide a description of country ham consumers.
2. To analyze consumer perceptions of Harrison's country hams as compared to the competition.
3. To determine if the present Harrison's packaging is adequate for consumers.
4. To help Harrison's increase its market share of ham sales by recommending media vehicles and advertising strategy.

I recommend that you survey shoppers who are entering large supermarket chain stores in Kansas City and its suburbs. Your sample should be randomly drawn.

Describes available funding

As we have agreed, a consulting fee of $7,500 will be paid to Market Research, Inc., upon the successful completion of this study and the submission of an acceptable report. Harrison's may authorize additional consumer preferences surveys in other geographical areas if the results of this study seem worthwhile.

Gives the date the report is due

Your report should be submitted to me by October 30, 199-. Please contact me if you need any further information or guidance from Harrison's.

Sincerely,

Phillip Niffen
Director of Marketing

cr

Figure 16•9 Example Formal
Report. Cont.

❖ *Market Research, Inc.* ❖

5600 West Broadway, Ruder-Fine Building, Suite 21A,
St. Louis, MO 63100-2182, Tel. (314) 555-5000, Fax (314) 555-7933

October 15, 199-

Mr. Phillip Niffen
Director of Marketing
Harrison's Country Hams
1000 Pork Lane
Kansas City, MO 64100-8462

Dear Mr. Niffen:

The letter of transmittal:

Here is the report you requested on consumer preferences for country hams in the Kansas City, Missouri, area.

Transmits the report

We surveyed 100 randomly selected grocery shoppers to determine who buys country hams, how consumers perceive Harrison's hams as compared to the competition, what opinions consumers have on Harrison's packaging, and how Harrison's could increase its market share.

Describes the procedures and purposes

The survey results show that Harrison's country hams are purchased predominantly by high school graduates with less than $30,000 in income and who have a preference for country music. Consumers who have tried and liked Harrison's think it is a high-quality ham and a good value. Consumers who disliked Harrison's country ham said that its price was too high. Consumers prefer clear packaging to the present white paper packaging.

Gives the high-lights of the findings

Based on these survey findings, we recommend a strengthened marketing strategy directed at a more affluent consumer, increased television and radio advertising with a country music orientation, and a change to clear plastic shrink packaging.

Summarizes the recommenda-tions

Thank you for the opportunity to complete this market research for Harrison's. I hope that you find the results valuable and that you will authorize additional, similar studies in other market areas. I am convinced that by doing so you will increase your market share.

Closes the letter

Cordially,

Sandra Morena

Sandra Moreno
Consumer Consultant

kah

Figure 16•9 Example Formal Report. Cont.

TABLE OF CONTENTS

> The table of contents lists names and page numbers of all major sections.

v

Figure 16•9 Example Formal Report. Cont.

LIST OF ILLUSTRATIONS

FIGURES

TABLES

vi

> The list of illustrations lists the titles and page numbers of all illustrations—figures, charts and graphs, tables, etc.

Figure 16•9 Example Formal Report. Cont.

EXECUTIVE SUMMARY

To increase its market share, Harrison's Country Hams requested that Market Research, Inc., conduct a consumer preferences survey in the Kansas City, Missouri, area. The study was designed to describe the country ham consumer, analyze country ham consumer preferences, determine the adequacy of Harrison's packaging, and recommend improvements in Harrison's media vehicles and advertising strategy. One hundred consumers entering supermarkets were randomly selected and interviewed.

A related literature review showed that household incomes of country ham consumers increased 54 percent between 1983 and 1993, indicating the development of an upscale market. Further, research on packaging found that meat consumers prefer to see meat prior to its purchase.

The survey revealed that country ham consumers predominantly were married high school graduates between 25 and 44 years of age. They had one to two children in a family of three to four. They lived in the suburbs and one-half preferred country music. Approximately one-third of the consumers usually buy Harrison's country hams, and about one-half had eaten Harrison's. Of the consumers who had eaten Harrison's, those who liked it thought it had good taste and was a good value. Those who disliked it thought its price was too high and it had too much salt.

In addition, the survey found that Harrison's consumers preferred clear plastic packaging, but a significant number did not like the current pig logo. Only one-third of Harrison's consumers earn more than $30,000, suggesting an untapped upscale market. Most had seen or heard Harrison's advertisements on television or radio. City dwellers were more likely to have seen the ads on television, while suburbanites heard them on radio.

The analysis of the findings revealed (1) that Harrison's current consumers were from predominantly low-income households, (2) its hams had good taste and value, (3) advertising should target the upscale market, (4) and television and radio were the most successful media.

Based on the conclusions, it is recommended that Harrison's marketing strategy should focus on the superior taste and quality of its country hams, Harrison's advertising should be directed at the upscale market, the advertising should be primarily on television and radio with a country music orientation, and Harrison's packaging should be clear plastic shrink wrapping with a modified pig logo.

The executive summary (abstract, synopsis, etc.) summarizes the important parts of the report:

Introductory material

Procedures

Related literature

Findings

Analysis and Conclusions

Recommendations

vii

Figure 16·9 Example Formal Report. Cont.

I. INTRODUCTION

This introductory section includes the background of the problem, statement of the problem, purposes of the study, and scope of the study.

Background

Harrison's Country Hams was interested in increasing its market share. In consultation with Market Research, Inc., Harrison's decided to have a consumer preferences survey conducted in the Kansas City, Missouri, area. Other similar studies will be conducted if this study is deemed helpful.

Statement of the Problem

The focus of this study was to determine (1) selected attributes and preferences of country ham consumers, and (2) improvements that could be made in Harrison's product packaging and promotion.

Purposes of the Study

The purposes of this study were as follows:

• To provide a description of country ham consumers.
• To analyze consumer perceptions of Harrison's country hams as compared to the competition.
• To determine if the present Harrison's packaging is adequate for consumers.
• To help Harrison's increase its market share of ham sales by recommending media vehicles and advertising strategy.

Scope

The scope of this study included analyses of country ham consumers, consumer country ham eating habits and preferences, and Harrison's competition. The study was limited to the Kansas City, Missouri, market area.

II. RELATED LITERATURE

The literature on studies of consumer product preferences is extensive. While this broad expanse of research was generally helpful, two recent studies of consumers were found to be especially valuable for this study.

In a 1993 study by Paula Brockway, it was found that, in constant dollars, the average household income of country ham consumers had increased significantly over the past 10 years. In 1983, the average household income of country ham consumers was $15,543. In 1993, that income level had risen to $26,939, a 54 percent increase over the 1983 level. Brockway's conclusion was that country ham merchandisers should target more of their advertising to the upscale market levels.

In 1992, William Seale surveyed consumers' preferences on the packaging of fresh meat and found that consumers wanted to be able to see the meat prior to purchase. Clear plastic shrink wrapping was preferred to unwrapped meat or opaque packaging.

1

Figure 16•9 Example Formal Report. Cont.

III. PROCEDURES

The procedures section describes the steps taken in conducting the study.

A survey was conducted using a sampling technique to ensure randomization in the respondents. It was determined statistically that a sample of 100 grocery shoppers would provide a .05 precision and 95 percent confidence level. The procedures followed included:

1. A questionnaire was developed that contained simple dichotomous questions, check list questions, open-ended questions, and a semantic differential scale. (See Appendix.)
2. Teams of interviewers were stationed at five large supermarket chain stores located in the Kansas City area.
3. Interviews were conducted over a three-day period—Friday through Sunday—beginning on August 25, 199-.
4. Every 25th adult consumer entering the store was approached for an interview. If the interview was rejected, then the request was repeated of the next available consumer until one was willing to be interviewed.
5. The data were tabulated using a computerized statistical package, SPSS-X.
6. The results were analyzed by a team of Market Research consumer consultants and this report prepared.

IV. FINDINGS

The findings section presents the results of the study in an objective manner.

These findings are presented using the study objectives as a framework. The sections following include: demographic information describing country ham consumers, consumer perceptions of Harrison's compared to the competition, consumer perceptions of packaging, and information on the market and media.

Country Ham Consumers

The demographic information collected for the study—from musical preference to household income—provides a detailed description of country ham consumers. The presentation of these findings are shown in Figures 1 through 8 that follow.

As indicated in Figure 1, 73 percent of the respondents were married. Figure 2 shows that 12 percent of country ham consumers have some high school education, and 40 percent

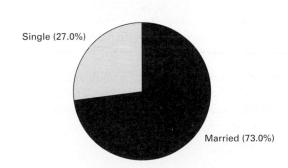

Figure 1. MARITAL STATUS

Single (27.0%)

Married (73.0%)

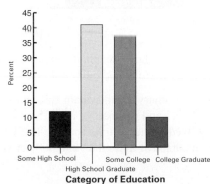

Figure 2. EDUCATION

2

are high school graduates. The remaining respondents reported that they had some college (38 percent), or were college graduates (10 percent). A total of 88 percent have at least a high school education.

Seventy-six percent were 25 years of age or older, with 56 percent 25 to 44, and 22 percent 45 and over. (See Figure 3.) As shown in Figure 4, most of the respondents (69 percent) had one to two children under the age of 18.

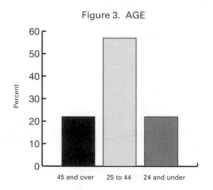

Figure 3. AGE

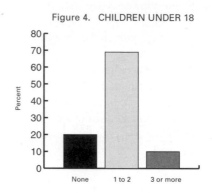

Figure 4. CHILDREN UNDER 18

Figure 5 shows that 65 percent of the respondents' family size was three to four persons. As indicated in Figure 6, most (54 percent) lived in the suburbs.

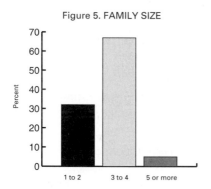

Figure 5. FAMILY SIZE

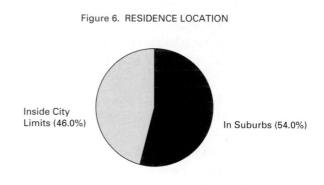

Figure 6. RESIDENCE LOCATION

Figure 7 shows that half (50 percent) preferred country music. Seventy-five percent, as shown in Figure 8, had household incomes of less than $30,000.

In summary, country ham consumers predominantly were married high school graduates between 25 and 44 years of age. They had one to two children in a family of three to four. They lived in the suburbs and one-half preferred country music. Only one-fourth had household incomes of more than $30,000 per year.

3

Figure 16•9 Example Formal Report. Cont.

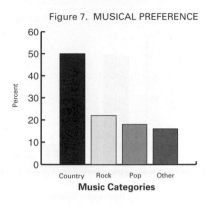

Figure 7. MUSICAL PREFERENCE

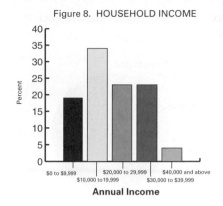

Figure 8. HOUSEHOLD INCOME

Harrison's and the Competition

As shown in Figure 9, almost one-third (32 percent) of the respondents usually choose Harrison's country hams over the competitors' hams, while Figure 10 shows that almost half (49 percent) have eaten Harrison's ham.

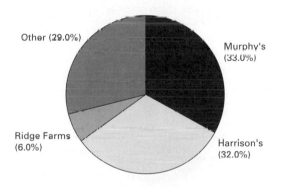

Figure 9. BRAND USUALLY PURCHASED

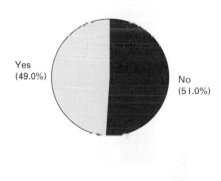

Figure 10. EATEN HARRISON'S HAM

Of the consumers who had eaten Harrison's country hams, we asked what they liked and disliked about the product. As shown in Figure 11, the responses of those who liked it reveal that almost two-thirds (63 percent) thought it had good taste and about one-third (32 percent) thought it was a good value. Figure 12 shows that one-half of the respondents (50 percent) who disliked Harrison's country ham said it was because of high price. Most remaining respondents either thought Harrison's had too much salt (35 percent) or not enough salt (11 percent).

Packaging Preferences

As indicated in Figure 13, 51 percent of the consumers preferred clear plastic packaging. Only 39 percent liked the present Harrison's white paper packaging. Figure 14 shows that over one-third of the respondents (35 percent) did not like Harrison's pig logo.

4

Figure 11. LIKE HARRISON'S HAM

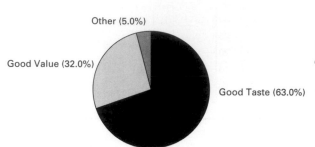

Other (5.0%)

Good Value (32.0%)

Good Taste (63.0%)

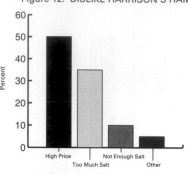

Figure 12. DISLIKE HARRISON'S HAM

Reasons for Dissatisfaction

Some of the specific responses of those who said they liked the Harrison pig logo were "OK," "Cute," and "Gets good attention." Those who disliked the logo, however, commented "Could be better," "Offensive," and "Unfavorable association of the food with a pig's rear end."

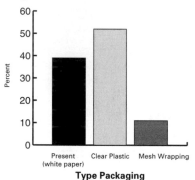

Figure 13. PACKAGING PREFERRED

Type Packaging

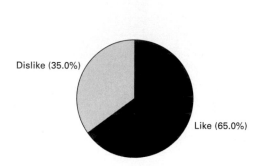

Figure 14. LOGO OPINION

Dislike (35.0%)

Like (65.0%)

Market and Media

Cross tabulations were run to provide additional market and media information for determining media vehicles and marketing strategy for Harrison's Country Ham.

<u>Market.</u> Table 1 shows a statistically significant difference in the number of consumers who had eaten Harrison's by level of household income.

Of those who had eaten Harrison's country hams, only 33 percent had household incomes of more than $30,000. The less-affluent consumers appeared to constitute the larger current market segment for Harrison's.

<u>Media.</u> A second set of significantly different responses were found in the cross tabulations for advertising media. Table 2 shows that 77 percent of the respondents who had seen or

5

Figure 16•9 Example Formal Report. Cont.

TABLE 1. THE NUMBER AND PERCENTAGE OF RESPONDENTS WHO HAD
EATEN HARRISON'S COUNTRY HAM, BY LEVEL OF INCOME

| Level of Household Income | Had Eaten Harrison's Ham | |
	No.	Percent
$0 to $29,999	33	67
$30,000 and above	16	33
TOTAL	49	100

TABLE 2. THE NUMBER AND PERCENTAGE OF RESPONDENTS WHO HAD SEEN
OR HEARD HARRISON'S ADVERTISEMENTS, BY TYPE OF ADVERTISE-
MENT.

| Type of Advertisement | Had Seen or Heard Harrison's Ads | |
	No.	Percent
Television	21	38
Radio	22	39
Billboard	6	11
Other	7	12
TOTAL	56	100

TABLE 3. THE NUMBER AND PERCENTAGE OF RESPONDENTS WHO HAD SEEN
HARRISON'S ADVERTISEMENTS ON TELEVISION, BY RESIDENCE
LOCATION

| Residence Location | Saw Harrison's Ads on Television | |
	No.	Percent
Inside city limits	13	62
In suburbs	8	38
TOTAL	21	100

heard a Harrison's advertisement had seen it on television (38 percent) or heard it on radio
(39 percent). Billboard advertisements were seen by only 11 percent and other advertisements accounted for only 12 percent. Table 3 shows that 62 percent of those who had seen
Harrison's Country Ham advertisements on television lived within the city limits. As shown
in Table 4, however, 77 percent of those who had heard Harrison's advertisements on radio
lived in suburbs.

6

TABLE 4. THE NUMBER AND PERCENTAGE OF RESPONDENTS WHO HAD
HEARD HARRISON'S ADVERTISEMENTS ON RADIO, BY RESIDENCE
LOCATION

Residence Location	Heard Harrison's Ads on Radio	
	No.	Percent
Inside city limits	5	23
In suburbs	17	77
TOTAL	22	100

Obviously, television was more effective in reaching city dwellers, while radio was superior in reaching residents of the suburbs.

V. ANALYSIS

> The analysis presents relationships that are significant.

Country ham consumers in the Kansas City area tended to be educated and married with established family units. These consumers, however, also tended to have relatively low household incomes—only 25 percent had incomes of $30,000 or more. Brockway, reporting a 54 percent increase in average income of country ham consumers between 1983 and 1993, concluded in her April 1994 article in The Grocery Retailer that country ham merchandisers should target more of their advertising at the upscale market levels. Harrison's current market mix (33 percent with over $30,000 incomes) does not now include its potential share of the upscale market segment.

This study found that most consumers who had eaten Harrison's country ham and liked it, thought it had good taste and was a good value. Those who disliked Harrison's, however, did so primarily because of its high price.

Since this study found that most of Harrison's consumers are from the less-affluent segment of the country ham market, a greater effort to reach the untapped higher-income households should be profitable. With Harrison's high-quality product, price should not be a sales barrier in this upscale market.

In addition, this study shows clearly that most consumers had seen or heard a Harrison's advertisement on television or radio versus other media. Consumers who live in Kansas City were more likely to have seen Harrison's advertisements on television, and those who lived in the suburbs heard them on radio. Television and radio are obviously the most successful media for Harrison's. A further media consideration is that one-half of the country ham consumers preferred country music over other types of music.

Finally, both this study and Seale's study (as reported in his May 1993 article in Retail Merchandising) found that most meat purchasers do not like opaque packaging. The

7

Figure 16•9 Example Formal Report. Cont.

consumers preferred clear plastic packaging of meats, including country ham. Further, a significant number of consumers surveyed for this study—35 percent—disliked the pig logo Harrison's uses on its packaging.

VI. CONCLUSIONS AND RECOMMENDATIONS

Conclusions

1. Harrison's current consumers in the Kansas City area tend to come predominantly from low-income households.
2. Harrison's country ham is considered to have good taste and to be a good value. Its price is considered high.
3. Harrison's is not reaching its potential share of the upscale marketing segment.
4. Television and radio are the most successful advertising media for Harrison's.
5. Country ham consumers tend to prefer country music.
6. Harrison's packaging and logo should be changed.

Recommendations

1. Harrison's marketing strategy should advertise its product as superior in both taste and quality in comparison to its competition. Harrisons should promote its product as the "Cadillac" of country hams and aim for a more prestigious image.
2. An increased share of Harrison's advertising content should be directed at appealing to the affluent consumer who is willing and able to pay a higher price for a high quality product.
3. A greater proportion of Harrison's advertising budget should be spent on television and radio programming with a country music orientation so as to reach more country ham consumers.
4. Harrison's should go to clear plastic shrink packaging as soon as feasible to make its hams more visible. To help reduce consumer dissatisfaction, the pig logo should gradually be changed in appearance to show more of a side view of the pig instead of the straight rear view.

Conclusions are drawn from the analysis of the study.

Recommendations are developed from the study's conclusions.

8

Figure 16•9 Example Formal Report. Cont.

APPENDIX

STUDY QUESTIONNAIRE

An appendix contains material that is indirectly related to the study.

Figure 16•9 Example Formal Report. Cont.

HARRISON'S CONSUMER PREFERENCES SURVEY

Hello, I am _____ with Market Research, Inc., and I am doing a survey for Harrison's Country Hams. May I ask you a few questions?

1. Are you responsible for most of the grocery shopping for your household?

    ( ) yes   ( ) no [if no, terminate]

2. For each of the following characteristics, how would you rate country ham? (Check the space describing how you feel.)

    Characteristic
    A. Taste   ____ Tasty   ____ Not tasty
    B. Nutritional value: ____ Healthy   ____ Not healthy
    C. Price   ____ Inexpensive   ____ Expensive
    D. Packaging   ____ Important   ____ Not important

3. What brand of country ham do you usually buy? (Specify)

    _____

4. Have you ever eaten Harrison's country ham?

    ( ) yes   ( ) no

5. If your answer to question 4 is yes, please state what you liked or disliked about Harrison's country ham. _____

    _____

6. Harrison's country ham is currently sold in a white paper package like this one (show wrapping to consumer). It could also be sold with a clear plastic cover, or a cloth mesh cover. Which would you most prefer?

    ( ) present white paper   ( ) clear plastic cover
    ( ) cloth mesh cover   ( ) other _____

7   Have you ever seen or heard a Harrison's advertisement?

    ( ) yes   ( ) no

8. If your answer to question 7 is yes, where?

    ( ) TV   ( ) radio   ( ) billboard   ( ) other _____

9. What do you like or dislike about the Harrison's Country Ham logo? (Show them the logo of the pig—a direct rear view of a pig who is looking back and smiling at the viewer.)_____

10

10. What type of music do you prefer?

( ) country   ( ) rock   ( ) pop

( ) blues   ( ) other _____

11. Which age category best fits you?

( ) 24 and under   ( ) 25–44

( ) 45–64   ( ) 65 and over

12. Which family size category best fits you?

( ) 1 to 2   ( ) 3 to 4   ( ) 5 or more

13. Are you married?

( ) yes   ( ) no

14. How many of the children in your household are under 18?

( ) 0   ( ) 1 to 2   ( ) 3 or more

15. What is the highest level of education you have achieved?

( ) attended grade school   ( ) attended some high school

( ) high school graduate   ( ) attended some college

( ) college graduate

16. Which household total income category best fits your household?

( ) Under $10,000   ( ) $10,000–$19,999

( ) $20,000–$29,999   ( ) $30,000–$39,999

( ) $40,000 and above

11

Figure 16•9 Example Formal Report. Cont.

BIBLIOGRAPHY

The bibliography is a list of all the references that were used as sources of information in the study.

BIBLIOGRAPHY

Brockway, Paula G., "The Buying Power of Grocery Shoppers," *The Grocery Retailer* 32 (April 1994): 26–32.

Seale, William S., "Meat Packaging: What Does the Consumer Prefer?" *Retail Merchandising* 26 (May 1993): 44–51.

13

Figure 16•9 Example Formal Report. Cont.

DISCUSSION QUESTIONS

1. What are the advantages of correctly formatting a report?

2. How do formal and informal reports differ?

3. Describe how the first three levels of headings are formatted in written reports.

4. Describe two methods of footnoting sources of information in reports and give reasons for the use of each.

5. List the purposes of meeting minutes.

6. Briefly describe four types of informal reports.

7. How do policy statements written for managerial personnel differ from those written for nonmanagerial personnel?

8. Describe the inverted pyramid format for composing news releases.

9. Compare a title fly to a title page.

10. What is the general purpose of placing an executive summary at the start of a report?

11. How do conclusions and recommendations differ?

12. What is a bibliography? List the items that may be included in a bibliographical entry.

APPLICATION EXERCISES

1. You think that students often do well on all but one exam in a course. This poor performance on one exam may lower the student's final course grade a letter or more and not be representative of the student's ability. Write a report to your school's top academic officer that will convince him or her that students should be permitted to substitute the grade from a make-up project for one low exam grade.

2. Assume that your aunt is willing to loan you money to open a restaurant in the town where you go to school. Using the information you learned in Chapter 15, devise a questionnaire to survey students and faculty to determine the type of facility that would be most successful. Using the results gathered in the survey write a formal report that can be presented to your aunt to convince her that she will be making a sound investment.

3. You are the secretary for a student organization in your business department. Your organization is planning to send eight members to a national conference in Houston, Texas. Your organization needs its faculty adviser to attend this conference but has insufficient funds for travel expenses. Gather facts and write a report to the appropriate administrator requesting that the institution pay for your adviser's travel expenses.

4. You have learned that a local civic organization has decided to give grants to students with financial need who make above-average grades. Demonstrate your need by preparing a report describing your past year's income, expenses, and academic achievements. Be sure to include in your report justification for why you deserve the grant.

5. The relationship between students in your school and the local area residents could be improved. Specific concerns of both groups need to be determined so that progress can be made toward improving the relationship. Divide into teams of three or four and develop questionnaires for the students and for the local area residents. Administer the questionnaires to each group. Using the data obtained in the surveys, write a formal report that can be presented to the student government organization convincing them to carry out your team's recommendations.

6. Your school has received a large monetary gift that can be used for whatever purpose the administration wishes. The Student Government Association has been assigned the task of determining how students would like to spend the money. Some ideas that have been suggested are: purchasing classroom equipment, creating student scholarships, building additional recreational facilities, and providing for faculty development. Develop a questionnaire to determine what the students want. After completing the secondary research and the survey, write a formal report that will inform the administration of the desires of the students.

7. A copy of the minutes of the Butler Insurance Company Fringe Benefits Committee meeting is shown below. List the items that have been omitted from the minutes.

MINUTES
FRINGE BENEFITS COMMITTEE
BUTLER INSURANCE

The meeting was called to order at 10:30 a.m. on April 18, 199-.

Copies of the last meeting's minutes were distributed.

Ms. Carson presented a proposal on the new procedures for vacations. Mr. Wilson moved that the proposal be approved.

The committee unanimously approved the motion.

The proposal for adding dental insurance to the family policy was defeated by a 5 to 2 vote.

The president appointed Mr. Thomas to gather information on eye care insurance. He was directed to report his findings at the next committee meeting.

The meeting was adjourned at 11:15 a.m.

CASE PROBLEMS

1. The employees of Jefferson Lumber have asked about the possibility of classes being offered on-site. Upon inquiring at Tremont College, it was learned that up to three classes could be taught if enough students would enroll to make the classes cost effective. A survey was taken; 111 employees responded. The results are given below. Write a memo report to the human resources director, Eric Cruz, giving the results of the investigation and your recommendations.

    1. What courses would you be interested in taking? (Give your top 3 choices as 1,2,3.)

	1	**2**	**3**
Business Communication	18	28	21
Human Relations	9	3	9
Spreadsheets	28	21	13
Word Processing	23	17	23
Database Management	16	15	13
Desktop Publishing	8	14	22
Programming	0	2	1
Time Management	9	11	9

    2. What would be the best day for the class?

Monday	11
Tuesday	45
Wednesday	21
Thursday	33
Friday	1

    3. What would be the most convenient time for the class?

4–7 p.m.	26
5–8 p.m.	56
6–9 p.m.	29

2. You are an instructor at Valley View Business College. Ms. Fusako Wilson, the vice president for academic programs, asked you to survey businesses in the area to determine to what extent dictation is used. You developed a questionnaire and mailed it to 75 managers of area businesses. Usable responses were received from 47 managers. The number of responses for each question is as follows:

1. Age:

Less than 25	5
25–34	8
35–44	17
45–54	6
55–64	10
65 and over	1

2. Number of employees under your direct or indirect supervision:

Less than 5	13
5–24	24
25–99	8
100–499	1
500 or more	1

3. Classification that best describes the business or organization in which you are presently employed (check only one):

Banking	2
Construction/Engineering	1
Consulting	6
Education	8
Insurance	6
Government	2
Manufacturing	8
Sales	11
Utilities/Energy Diversified	2
Other	1

4. Show the amount of time that you spend each day originating written messages by each method:

	None	Less than 10%	10–25%	26–50%	51–75%	76–100%
Dictation	15	10	13	2	3	4
Handwriting	1	4	14	11	7	10
Keyboarding	4	7	12	6	4	14
Other	38	3	4	0	1	1

If your answer does *not* include dictation as a method of originating messages, go to Question 8.

5. Show the division of time that you spend dictating to a secretary and/or a machine:

	Less than 10%	10–25%	26–50%	51–75%	76–100%
Secretary	1	3	4	3	18
Dictation Machine	4	6	5	7	9

6. Types of messages you dictate (check all that apply):

Memos	34
Reports	3
Letters	30
Other	1

7. For each of the following types of messages, indicate the average number you *dictate* per day:

	Less than 4	4–6	7–10	More than 10
Memos	20	9	2	3
Letters	14	9	3	4
Reports	3	0	0	0

8. Is it important that students in a business communication class be taught how to dictate?

Yes	34
No	5
Don't Know	8

Write a report to Ms. Wilson giving your recommendations on the inclusion of dictation in the business communication course. Your report should include appropriate report sections and appropriate graphic aids to complement the text of your findings.

3. Northeastern Savings and Loan's contract with an insurance company elapses in four months. It is trying to determine its employees' attitudes toward medical coverage. Listed below are the results of a survey to which 78 of the 90 employees responded. The responses have been organized into three groups—single persons, individuals with one dependent, and individuals with two or more dependents. Use these data to prepare a report that could be sent to the company's president.

	Single	1 Dependent	2+ Dependents
1. Which type of coverage is best?			
a. Employee only	20	3	2
b. Family plan	6	14	33
2. What coverage should be available?			
a. Basic medical	26	17	35
b. Major medical	25	17	35
c. Hospitalization	25	17	35
d. Dental	12	9	27
e. Optical	12	4	29
f. Prescriptions	18	10	24
3. What limit should policy place on out-of-pocket expenses?			
a. $500	20	11	28
b. $1,000	4	4	4
c. $2,500	1	2	2
d. $5,000	1	0	1
4. Should the company offer a menu insurance program where employee can choose type of coverage desired?			
a. Yes	23	16	33
b. No	3	1	2

	Single	1 Dependent	2+ Dependents
5. Which would you prefer?			
a. Minimum coverage— company pays premium	17	9	25
b. Increased coverage— employee shares in paying premium	9	8	10
6. What should be the maximum premium that the employee must pay each month?			
a. $ 0	21	10	28
b. $ 25	4	3	5
c. $ 50	1	2	0
d. $100	0	2	2

4. You are the human resources manager at Allen, Holland, and Elam, a corporate law firm with more than 150 attorneys. The firm's volume of work has increased 10 percent each year for the past three years. The number of attorneys has increased 20 percent; however, the administrative staff has not been increased. The administrative staff includes 18 word processing specialists, 130 legal secretaries, and 35 paralegals.

Write a memo report using the data below to convince the senior partners that 25 new administrative personnel (word processing specialists, legal secretaries, and paralegals) must be hired. Hiring these additional individuals would reduce overtime pay and improve the quality of work. Your report should recommend the number of administrative personnel that would be hired in each category (word processing specialists, legal secretary, paralegal).

Hours Worked for First Quarter of 199-

Divisions	Word Processing Specialists			Legal Secretaries			Paralegals		
	Jan	**Feb**	**Mar**	**Jan**	**Feb**	**Mar**	**Jan**	**Feb**	**Mar**
Bankruptcy	607	543	541	4,487	3,874	4,738	979	936	963
Corporate	146	197	329	2,613	2,189	2,267	648	578	647
Criminal	403	348	395	2,933	2,568	2,889	743	744	783
Litigation	426	369	272	2,842	1,852	1,970	749	471	479
Probate	174	194	216	1,264	1,458	1,703	351	379	337
Real Estate	252	324	326	1,179	2,316	2,315	504	587	645
Tax	201	422	628	2,201	3,070	3,386	639	937	841

5. A consulting company is interested in providing training to accountants. They have asked you to research the type of training that accountants have received. You send out 450 questionnaires of which 294 are returned. The results are given below; use the data that is helpful in explaining your recommendations. Write a letter report to Paul Sagar giving the results of the investigation and your recommendations.

	Public Accounting	Industry
1. Gender:		
Male	47	104
Female	94	49

	Public Accounting	Industry
2. Age:		
Less than 25	6	2
25–34	70	64
35–44	62	71
45–54	2	15
55 and over	1	1

	Public Accounting	Industry
3. Type of Training Received in Past Year:		
In-house	42	80
Workshops	15	64
No formal	81	8
Other	3	1

	Male	Female
4. Respondents' Position within Company:		
Staff Accountant	70	97
Senior Accountant	31	36
Manager	33	7
Partner	17	3

	Public Accounting	Industry
5. Type of Training Desired (check all that apply):		
Accounting Information Systems	43	62
Individualized Income Tax	83	21
Partnership Taxation	56	33
Budgeting	8	46
Auditing Procedures	61	79
Financial Planning	34	40
Government Fund Planning	7	3
Corporate Income Tax	12	84
Accounting Principles	67	25

6. While working in the Human Resources Department, you have become concerned about the effects that computers may be having on your company's employees. The tabulations of the 147 responses that you received from the company's 163 employees is shown below. Write a memo report to the company's general manager explaining the results of your survey and make any recommendations that you deem necessary.

1. Average number of hours you spend in front of your computer each workday.

	Number of Respondents
More than 6	14
5 or 6	42
3 or 4	68
1 or 2	18
Fewer than 1	5

2. The computer:

	Strongly Agree	Agree	Disagree	Strongly Disagree
a. Increases my productivity	78	43	18	8
b. Forces me to work alone	31	66	39	11
c. Gives me job security	40	48	42	17
d. Makes my job frustrating	14	52	43	38
e. Helps me solve problems	32	74	29	12
f. Requires me to get training	61	27	31	28
g. Requires me to think	18	81	35	13

3. What impact has the computer had on you?

	Strongly Agree	Agree	Disagree	Strongly Disagree
a. Helps me get pay raises	43	68	22	14
b. Makes my job more challenging	15	92	30	10
c. Gives me more career options	37	88	17	5
d. Weakens my job security	16	43	46	42
e. Makes me wish I had selected another field	11	16	92	28

7. Barnard's Industrial Supply is attempting to improve its image. It is conducting a workshop on Ethical Business Practices. A questionnaire sent to employees asking them to rate selected aspects of their behavior as *Never, Rarely, Sometimes,* and *Often* was returned by 243 of Barnard's 287 employees. Use the results given below to write a memo report that could be distributed to the employees at the workshop.

In the past 5 years I have

	Never	Rarely	Sometimes	Often
1. Taken money from the company	225	16	1	1
2. Withheld truth to cover my mistakes	76	87	59	21
3. Withheld truth to cover others' mistakes	54	63	103	23
4. Reported hours that weren't worked	198	12	24	9
5. Made long-distance calls on business phones	17	53	97	76
6. Taken supplies for personal use	51	17	42	133
7. Given false reasons for missing work	36	69	107	31
8. Used unethical behavior to make a sale	202	21	9	11
9. Submitted false expenses for travel	164	33	28	18

	Never	Rarely	Sometimes	Often
10. Stayed past break/lunch periods	8	14	168	53
11. Used equipment for personal projects	21	37	149	36
12. Made illegal copies of software	104	52	71	16

8. Peoples Bank plans to build a Wellness Center for its employees. Harold Shen, bank president, has asked the human resources department to survey the bank's employees to learn what facilities they would most likely use. Seventy-four of Peoples' 81 employees responded. The results of the survey are shown below. Write a memo report to Mr. Darnell explaining the results of the survey and your recommendations.

1. How often would you use the facility?

	Male	Female
Daily	19	14
2–3 times a week	4	10
Once a week	2	4
Once or twice a month	1	0
Never	4	16

2. When would you use the center? (Check all that apply)

Before work	7	4
Lunch hour	13	17
After work	9	5
Evening	4	0
Would not use	4	22

3. Would you like the center to open on weekends?

Yes	21	10
No	9	34

4. Check all the activities in which you would participate.

Weights	19	9
Jogging/Walking	15	24
Basketball	12	1
Racquetball	14	11

5. How often would you like to meet with medical staff for consultation?

Weekly	1	2
Monthly	0	6
Quarterly	4	24
Semi-Annually	8	5
Annually	15	3
Never	2	4

Text 16C

Rewrite and improve the quality of the following news release for Smoky Tobacco.

Hopkinsville, KY, June 12, 199- — Smoky Tobacco has been having a difficult time making a profit. Tobacco sales are down because of the negative campaigns against smoking. In addition to the health hazard, Smoky is losing ground on its premium-price cigarettes to lower-price generics.

Smoky was formed in 1922 and has grown steadily until the past three years. Today it is one of the largest income-producing companies in Christian County. Smoky has hired a new president to try and get the company back to making a profit.

Mr. Billy Ray White will become the new president on July 1. White has been CEO of Tobacco Conglomerates since 1985. At Conglomerates he increased its income by diversifying its products. Last year Conglomerates had sales of $75 million.

White and his wife, Connie, have three children—Mary Jo, Bennie, and Jetta. They will relocate to Hopkinsville in June.

Graphic Aids

Learning Objectives

Your learning objectives for this chapter include the following:

- To describe the purposes of graphic aids in written reports
- To explain where to place a graphic aid within a report
- To label graphic aids properly
- To select the appropriate type of graphic aid to present data most effectively
- To construct tables that present statistical information
- To construct the three types of charts that commonly appear in business reports
- To describe how miscellaneous graphic aids are used in reports
- To explain how readers can avoid being deceived by graphic aids

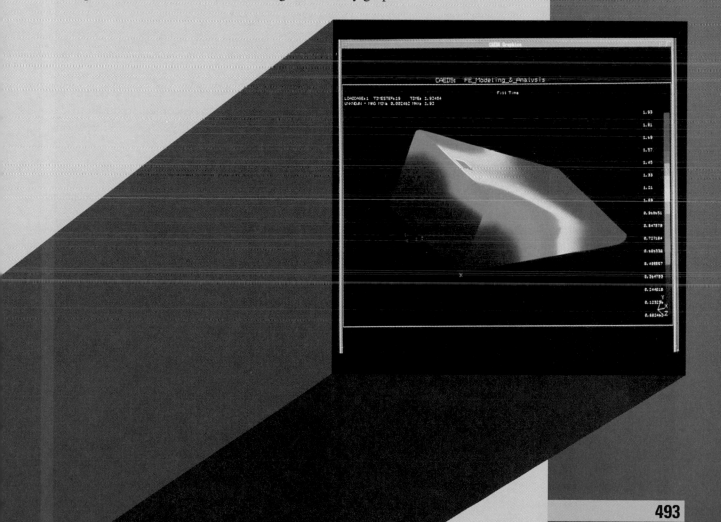

A **graphic aid** is an illustration used to assist a reader in understanding the text material in a report. Graphic aids may be in the form of tables, graphs, charts, drawings, photographs, diagrams, or maps. These illustrations are used to complement the communication. Graphic aids may reduce the volume of text, but they do not eliminate the written material completely.

USE OF GRAPHIC AIDS

When used properly, graphic aids can be helpful in effectively communicating ideas in written reports. Indiscriminate use of graphic aids may impede rather than promote communication. The selection of effective visuals requires a basic knowledge of the purposes of graphic aids and the design elements of these visuals, as well as careful consideration of how they will be used to complement the written or spoken word.

PURPOSES OF GRAPHIC AIDS

Graphic aids can complement your communication by summarizing complex figures in charts and graphs, by identifying your company through the use of a drawing or photograph for a logo, by showing relationships in a chart, by indicating trends in a graph, or by abstracting in a table details that are too cumbersome for written text. Appropriate placement and identification of graphic aids will enhance the effectiveness of your communication.

> *One picture is worth more than ten thousand words.*
>
> **Chinese Proverb**

PLACEMENT OF GRAPHIC AIDS

Graphic aids (also referred to as *illustrations*) must be placed in appropriate locations to enhance the written message of the report. Illustrations that directly relate to the topic should be placed within the written text. A small illustration, less than one-half page, should be placed after the first reference to the aid, preferably on the same page. A large illustration, one-half to one page, should be placed on the page following the first mention of the illustration. Avoid dividing a graphic aid between two pages. It is more desirable to place the entire illustration on one page, separate from the copy, than to divide it.

Illustrations that indirectly relate to the copy may be of interest to only a few readers. These illustrations will add unnecessary bulk to the main body of the report and should be placed in an appendix.

You should refer to a graphic aid within the written text of the report *prior* to its appearance. This reference is a powerful tool—it guides the reader to the items you want to stress. The reference may be nothing more than telling the reader, "as shown in Graph 2," or "(see Table 3, page 12)". A reference to a graphic aid should be casual and not distract the reader's attention from the material being read.

IDENTIFICATION OF GRAPHIC AIDS

All formal graphic aids within a written report should be identified by appropriate titles. The title of a graphic aid should describe its contents. The title should contain enough detail so that the reader can understand the graphic aid without reading the text of the report, but it should not be extremely lengthy. You should consider the five W's (Who, What, When, Where, and Why), and use those that will make the title most clear.

Methods of numbering graphic aids vary. One method is to call all graphic aids *Illustrations* and number them with either Arabic or Roman numerals. A second method is to divide the graphic aids into two categories and use Roman numerals for *Tables* and Arabic numerals for *Figures* (all illustrations other than tables grouped together). A variation of the second method is to categorize and number each type of figure separately (*Chart, Diagram, Graph,* etc.) but still using Arabic numerals for identification.

Graphic aids should be numbered consecutively. However, if there is only one graphic aid in a report, it need not be numbered. If the report contains more than one section or chapter, the illustrations may be numbered consecutively throughout the report (Figure 1, Figure 2, etc.); or they may be numbered consecutively by sections or chapters (Figure 1-1, Figure 1-2,

Figure 2-1, etc.). The most important consideration in numbering illustrations is consistency.

Illustrations must be numbered in a consistent manner.

Illustration titles may be printed either in uppercase or in uppercase and lowercase letters. Traditionally, titles are placed above tables and below all other illustrations. Today, businesses use either location. As in the numbering of illustrations, consistency is the important guideline in title placement.

Titles may be placed above or below illustrations.

IDENTIFICATION OF GRAPHIC AIDS SOURCES

The same consideration for acknowledging sources of text material should be used in acknowledging sources of graphic aids. If the content of an illustration is originated by the writer, no source note is required. A **source note** is used whenever content is obtained from another source. The source note normally consists of the word *source* in uppercase letters followed by a colon and the source. An example of an illustration using material from a report written by Toshi Okano is:

Source notes have to be used for illustrations obtained from others.

SOURCE: *Toshi Okano Report,* January 11, 1994, p. 17.

Although a source note usually is placed a double space below the illustration, it may be placed under the title of the illustration.

DEVELOPMENT OF GRAPHIC AIDS

Effective communication may depend on the selection of the most appropriate graphic aid for a specific situation. You must be knowledgeable about the various illustrations so you can select the one that will most effectively convey information under specific conditions. The most frequently used graphic aids in business reports are tables, charts, and graphs.

Selecting the right graphic aid improves communication.

TABLES

A **table** is a typed or printed display of words and numbers arranged in columns and rows. The data in tables should be presented in an orderly arrangement for easy and clear reference. In addition to the title, a table includes headings for the columns and entries in the first column that classify the categories of data in each row. These headings and columnar entries need to identify the data clearly, but should be short so they do not detract from the data.

Tables show data arranged in rows and columns.

Statistical information can be presented more effectively in a table than in text material. To illustrate this point, consider the following information:

Travelers from around the world visit Washington, D.C. Many of these individuals travel great distances to the capital of the United States. Air distances from some major world cities to Washington are: Hong Kong—8,155; Madrid—3,792; Rome—4,497; Melbourne—10,180; Montreal—489; and Paris—3,840. These mileages were obtained from the 1994 *World Almanac.*

This statistical information would be communicated more effectively if presented in a table, as shown in Figure 17•1.

Figure 17•1 Table

People from around the world visit Washington, D.C., every day. Many of these visitors travel long distances to view the capital of the United States. The table below shows distances from other world cities to Washington, D.C.

TABLE 1. AIR DISTANCES FROM WORLD CITIES TO WASHINGTON, D.C.

City	Miles
Hong Kong	8,155
Madrid	3,792
Rome	4,497
Melbourne	10,180
Montreal	489
Paris	3,840

SOURCE: The 1993 *World Almanac*

When information to be presented in a table requires numerous columns, the table may be constructed horizontally on the page rather than vertically. Figure 17•2 is a table constructed horizontally.

CHARTS

The three types of charts commonly used in business reports are organization charts, flowcharts, and pie charts. None of these charts needs lengthy text interpretation. The first two types, organization charts and flowcharts, clearly present relationships and procedures. The pie chart is used to illustrate the proportion of a part to the whole.

ORGANIZATION CHARTS

An **organization chart** shows lines of authority among the various positions within an organization. This type of chart illustrates the relationships among departments and of personnel within the departments. The chart may depict the entire organization or a selected portion of it. The senior position is placed at the top of the chart. Other positions are placed on the chart in descending order of authority. These positions are connected by solid lines if they are line positions with authority over other positions, and by broken or dotted lines if they are advisory or staff positions. An example of an organization chart is shown in Figure 17•3.

FLOWCHARTS

A **flowchart** may be used to illustrate step-by-step progression through complicated procedures. Such procedures could include the steps needed to manufacture a product, the route that a form follows when processed in an office, or the steps in a computer program.

Complicated written instructions are more easily understood when accompanied by a flowchart. Each step of the procedure needs to be

Pie charts, flowcharts, and organization charts are commonly used in business reports.

An organization chart shows lines of authority and relationships within an organization.

Flowcharts simplify the interpretation of complicated procedures.

Figure 17·2 Lengthwise Table

EMPLOYEE ABSENTEE REPORT—DAYS ABSENT FOR 1993

Employee	Jan.	Feb.	Mar.	Apr.	May	June	July	Aug.	Sep.	Oct.	Nov.	Dec.	Total
Rick Adkins	1	0	0	0	2	0	0	0	1	0	0	0	4
Kris Bell	3	4	2	1	0	4	2	1	1	3	2	1	24
Lea Davis	2	0	0	0	1	0	0	0	0	1	0	0	4
Benito Espino	0	0	0	0	0	0	0	0	0	0	0	0	0
Rosa Flisowski	3	2	2	3	2	1	3	2	2	3	1	1	25
Dan Griffin	0	2	0	0	0	2	0	0	0	0	1	0	5
Gene Higgs	0	0	0	0	1	0	0	0	0	0	7	0	8
Rita Kelm	4	0	2	0	1	1	1	0	3	2	0	0	14
Jean Miranda	5	0	0	2	0	1	0	0	0	2	0	0	10
Bill O'Shea	0	1	0	0	0	0	2	0	0	0	0	1	4
Tina Phillips	0	0	0	0	0	0	0	0	0	0	3	0	3
Lydia Supak	7	3	1	0	0	2	0	0	0	0	0	1	14
Cecil Watson	2	0	1	0	0	0	1	0	0	0	2	0	6
TOTALS	27	12	8	6	7	11	9	3	7	11	16	4	121

Figure 17•3 Organization Chart

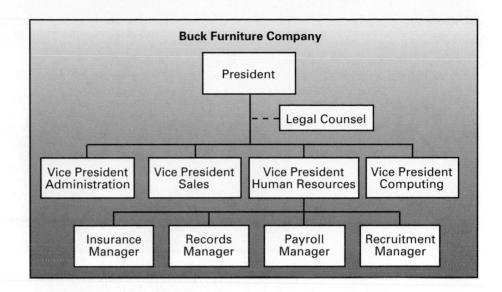

included, but the chart should not be so detailed that it becomes difficult to understand. Boxes of various shapes are connected by arrows to illustrate the direction that the action follows during the procedure. The size of a box is determined by the number of words in the label and does not indicate the importance of that particular portion of the procedure. A flowchart displaying the procedure used to take blood pressure is shown in Figure 17•4.

PIE CHARTS

A pie chart is a circle; its slices show the relationships of the parts to a whole.

A **pie chart** can be used to show how the parts of a whole are distributed and how the parts relate to each other. To make the chart easy to read, you should begin slicing the pie at the twelve o'clock position and continue in a clockwise direction. The pieces should be arranged in descending order of size. If several smaller pieces are combined into an "Other" category, this piece should be placed last. "Other" should never be the largest segment. Individual pieces should be labeled by showing the quantity, or percentage,

Figure 17•4 Flowchart

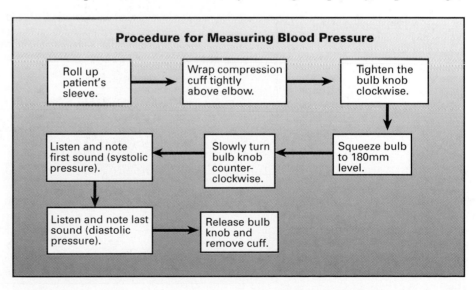

Figure 17·5 Pie Chart

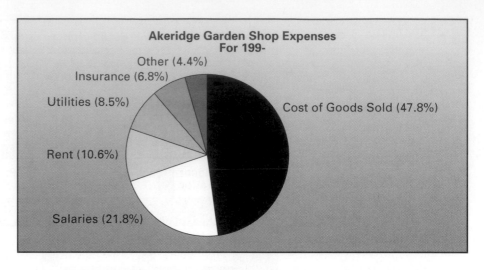

of each piece. A company's expenses are broken down in the pie chart shown in Figure 17•5.

Pie charts are easy for most readers to understand, but there are certain considerations to remember when constructing them. All the pie charts within a report should be the same size. A pie chart should contain from two to eight pieces. If more than eight pieces are used, a pie chart becomes unclear. The percentages shown in a pie chart need to total to 100 percent.

When a writer wants to emphasize a specific segment, an exploded pie chart may be used. In an exploded pie chart, one segment is separated from the rest of the chart for emphasis. Figure 17•6 shows the same data as Figure 17•5, with the category "Salaries" being emphasized.

GRAPHS

A **graph** is a drawing that represents the relationships of quantities or qualities to each other. A graph provides a convenient medium through which data can be compared. Graphs should use a simple design so that the reader can

Certain design principles should be followed when constructing pie charts.

An exploded pie chart is used to emphasize one segment.

Graphs show relationships among variables and should not have a complex design.

Figure 17·6 Exploded Pie Chart

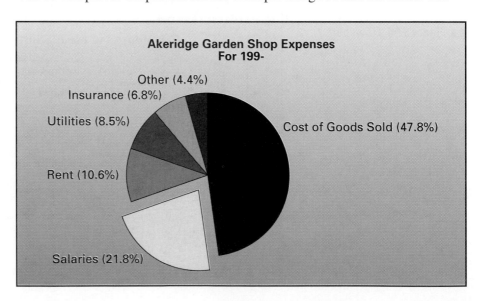

easily interpret the information. Using complex graphs to impress readers will only confuse them. The most frequently used graphs in business organizations are bar and line graphs. These types of graphs have several variations.

BAR GRAPHS

A **bar graph** can be effective in comparing differences in quantities. These differences are illustrated graphically by changes in the lengths of the bars. Bar graphs may be constructed either horizontally or vertically. The most widely used bar graphs include simple, broken, multiple, stacked, and positive–negative. All bar graphs except a positive–negative one should begin with zero at the bottom or extreme left.

In a **simple bar graph,** the length or height of a bar indicates quantity. You should use a bar width that makes a good visual impression. The width of individual bars should be the same throughout a graph. A simple vertical bar graph is shown in Figure 17•7, and a simple horizontal bar graph is shown in Figure 17•8 on page 502.

Comparisons of quantitative differences can be shown in bar graphs.

The length or height of a bar indicates quantity in a simple bar graph.

Figure 17•7 Simple Vertical Bar Graph

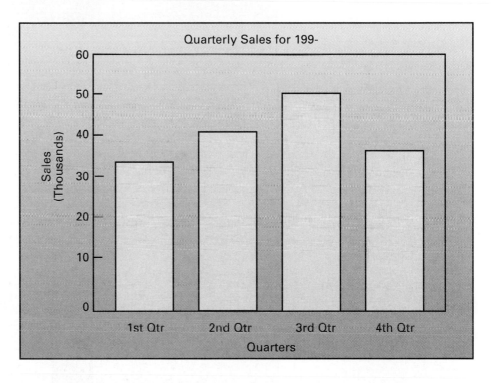

Graphs depicting very large amounts may make it impractical to include the entire amounts. In such cases a **broken bar graph**, as shown in Figure 17•9, on page 502, may be used.

A **multiple bar graph** is used to compare several quantitative areas at one time on a single graph. Cross-hatching, shading, or color variation can be used to distinguish among bars representing different areas. Bars should be labeled, or a legend should be included on the graph to identify the different cross-hatching, shading, or color variations. The graph will become cluttered and difficult to read if more than four areas are compared on one graph. Figure 17•10, on page 503, shows a multiple bar graph.

Several quantitative variables can be compared on one multiple bar graph.

Figure 17•8 Simple
Horizontal Bar Graph

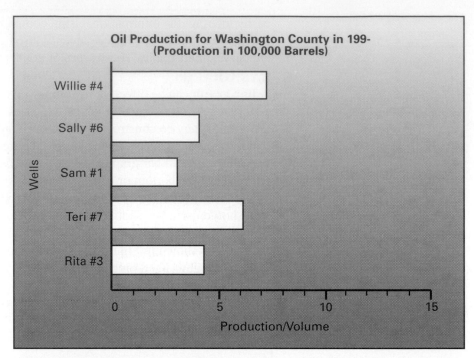

Figure 17•9 Broken-Bar
Graph

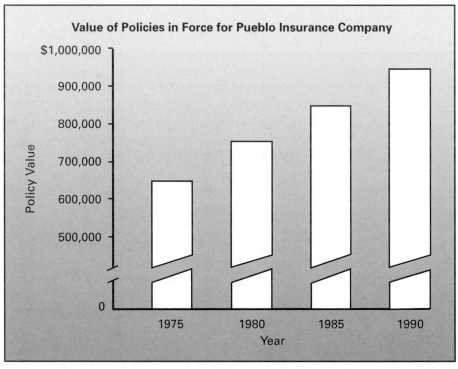

A stacked-bar graph shows differences in values within variables.

Elements within a variable may be illustrated in a **stacked-bar graph.**
This type of graph is useful in demonstrating differences in values within
variables by dividing each bar into its parts. Values should be included for
each part, and the parts should be differentiated and identified as in multiple-bar graphs. A stacked-bar graph is shown in Figure 17•11.

Figure 17·10 Multiple-Bar Graph

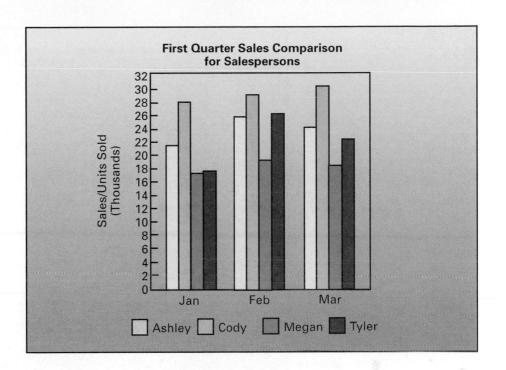

Figure 17·11 Stacked Bar Graph

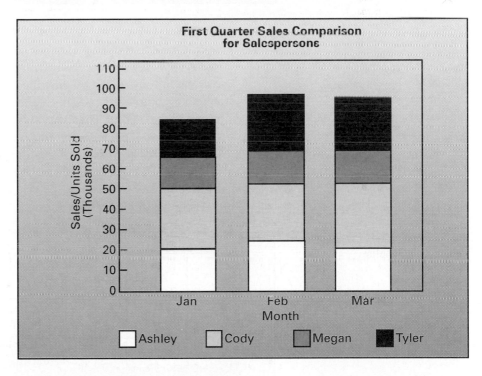

A comparison of variable values that fall above or below a reference point can be shown on a positive–negative bar graph.

A **positive–negative bar graph** shows plus or minus deviations from a fixed reference point. The bars go up or down from this fixed reference point. Relationships between positive and negative values can be illustrated clearly using a positive–negative bar graph as shown in Figure 17·12.

Figure 17•12
Positive–Negative Bar
Graph

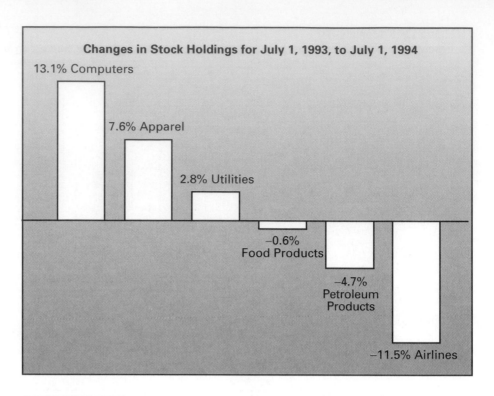

Changes in Stock Holdings for July 1, 1993, to July 1, 1994

13.1% Computers

7.6% Apparel

2.8% Utilities

−0.6%
Food Products

−4.7%
Petroleum
Products

−11.5% Airlines

LINE GRAPHS

Line graphs show changes over time.

A **line graph** is used to illustrate changes over time. Trends can be effectively portrayed by showing variations within each time period.

A line graph is constructed by drawing a line on an equally divided grid, with the horizontal reference line called the X-axis and the vertical reference line called the Y-axis. The interval between each vertical and horizontal line depends on the data being illustrated. The grid lines may or may not appear on the finished version of the line graph. All the data needs to be included to give an accurate and informative illustration. If the data is so excessive that it becomes unwieldy, the grid may be broken by a slash or by wavy lines as shown in Figure 17•13.

Figure 17•13 Broken Scales on Line Graphs

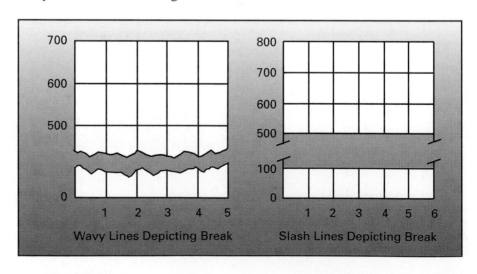

Wavy Lines Depicting Break

Slash Lines Depicting Break

A line graph can include either a single line or multiple lines. A **single-line graph,** which is shown in Figure 17•14, depicts movement of one variable. Shading or color may be used in a single-line graph to add emphasis.

Figure 17•14 Single-Line Graph

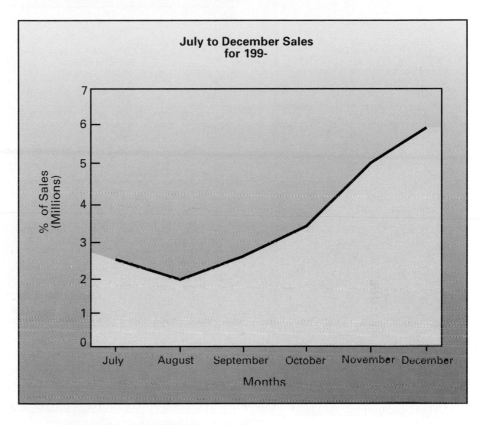

A **multiple-line graph** is used to illustrate changes in more than one value. The lines can be differentiated easily by using dotted, broken, and solid lines. Some writers prefer using different colors for each line; however, this technique requires that the report be printed using several colors, which increases the printing costs. Regardless of the method used to differentiate the lines, a legend should be used to identify lines that are ambiguous or difficult to interpret. A multiple-line graph is shown in Figure 17•15.

Changes in several values can be shown at one time on a multiple-line graph.

> *Originality is simply a pair of fresh eyes.*
>
> **Thomas Wentworth Higginson**

MISCELLANEOUS GRAPHIC AIDS

Any illustration that complements the written text should be considered for use.

Although the most commonly used graphic aids are tables, charts, and graphs, these are not the only effective graphic aids that can be used in reports. Graphic aids such as maps, photographs, pictographs, and drawings are used infrequently, but can be extremely effective in conveying

Figure 17•15 Multiple-Line Graph

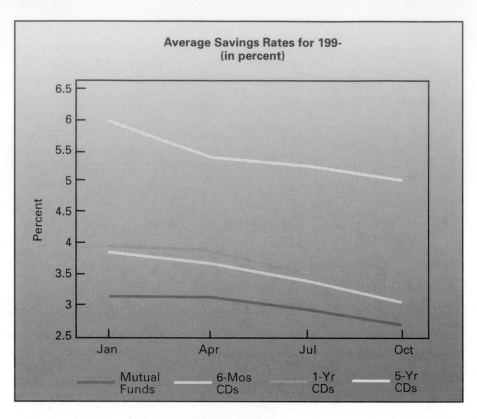

specific messages at appropriate times. Any relevant graphic aid that clarifies and strengthens the written text should be considered for use in a report.

A **map** can be effective in helping a reader visualize geographic relationships. The complexity of maps ranges from simple sketches to detailed, multicolored presentations. The content of the map determines the size of the graphic aid. Notice how the states containing a larger number of Omicron Delta Kappa circles are differentiated from the states with only a few circles on the map in Figure 17•16.

A personal touch can be added to a business report by including a **photograph** of a facility, product, or employee. In order to enhance communication, the photograph must be clear and well planned. A mistake often made in the use of photographs is including too much material. If a photograph shows something extremely large or extremely small, a reference point should be included. A coin or a pin can be a useful reference point for small items, and a person can be a good reference point in a photograph of a large item. A photograph can be used to stimulate interest in vacationing at a resort. *See* page 508.

A **pictograph** is similar to a bar graph in that it emphasizes differences in statistical data, but it differs in that it uses images of items or symbols instead of bars. All the images or symbols should be the same size to avoid distorting their values. The pictograph in Figure 17•17 graphically accentuates the increase in microcomputer sales over a period of time.

A **drawing** may be the most effective means of communicating a complicated idea or procedure. A photograph may not be desirable because it would contain clutter that would distract from the idea to be communicated.

Maps can help the reader understand geographic details.

Photos used as graphic aids should not contain too much material.

Pictographs use images to emphasize differences in quantitative data.

Drawings can be used to emphasize one point within a procedure.

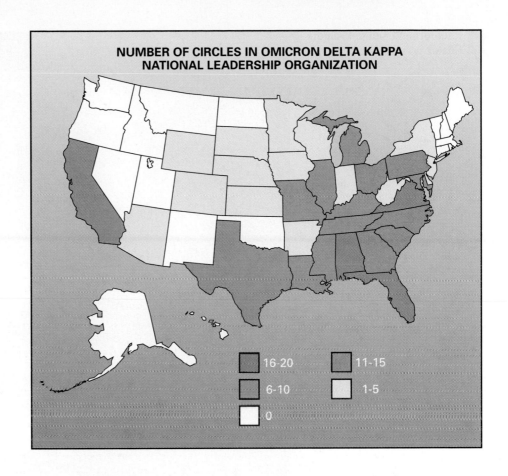

Figure 17·16 Map

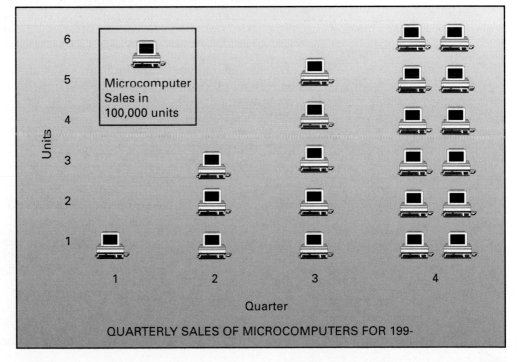

Figure 17·17 Pictograph Showing Microcomputer Sales

A drawing can omit the clutter and emphasize the desired details in an idea or procedure. Furthermore, a drawing can reflect parts or components not visible when viewing the "finished" product. A drawing of part of an automobile is shown in Figure 17•18.

Figure 17•18 Drawing of Part of an Automobile

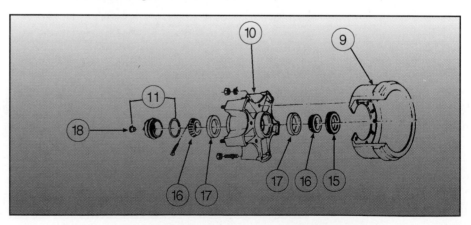

The keyboard and mouse are used to input data. The software uses the data to produce pie charts or other types of graphic aids.

COMPUTER-GENERATED GRAPHIC AIDS

Graphic aids are extremely powerful tools for supplementing written text. They have become more popular because technology makes them easier to construct. Many computer programs are available that can integrate graphics software with word processing software to develop an easy-to-read and informative written report.

Computers have simplified the creation of graphic aids.

Graphics software programs are easy to use. The report writer needs only to enter the raw data and select the type of graphic aid desired. The computer will create the chart or graph selected. These graphic aids may be printed using several colors, depending on the type of software and printer.

Many types of graphic aids may be generated using computer software.

Using graphics software the report writer can produce graphic aids from the simple to the sophisticated. A spreadsheet may be used to display raw data. Current spreadsheet software permits the writer to change fonts and to bold or shade data to emphasize selected figures in the spreadsheet. Graphs and tables that are produced using spreadsheet programs can also be imported into word processing or desktop publishing programs. Figure 17•19 shows a spreadsheet prepared using Excel®.[1]

Clip art can make reports more attractive.

The appearance of reports can be improved by the use of **clip art,** prepackaged art images designed to be imported into word processing, presentation graphics, or desktop publishing programs. Clip-art program files normally are grouped into categories, such as business, travel, history, automobiles, airplanes, or holidays. Clip art is included in most word processing, presentation graphics, and desktop publishing programs; additional clip art may be purchased from third-party clip art vendors. Examples of clip-art are shown in Figure 17•20.

Numerous software packages that can produce graphic aids are available.

Graphics software packages such as Harvard Graphics®[2], Freelance Graphics®[3], Aldus Persuasion®[4], Corel Draw!®[5], Claris's McDraw®[6], Charisma®[7], and GraphShow®[8] can easily produce bar graphs, line graphs, pie charts, area charts, and combination charts. Most software programs permit the creation of several variations of each type of graphic aid, such as stacked-bar graphs or exploded pie charts.

---

[1]Excel is a registered trademark of Microsoft Corporation.
[2]Harvard Graphics is a registered trademark of Software Publishing Corporation.
[3]Freelance Graphics is a registered trademark of Lotus Development Corporation.
[4]Aldus Persuasion is a registered trademark of Aldus Corporation.
[5]Corel Draw! is a registered trademark of Corel Corporation.
[6]Claris's McDraw is a registered trademark of Claris Corporation.
[7]Charisma is a registered trademark of Micrografx, Inc.
[8]GraphShow is a registered trademark of Chartersoft Corporation.

B & PA
SUMMARY OF SUMMER ENROLLMENTS

1991

DEPT.	# SECTIONS	HEAD-COUNT	AVERAGE
ACC	6	88	15
CS & IS	4	93	23
E&F	11	225	20
M&M	11	310	28
BA & OSY	4	86	22
PCL	7	129	18
	43	931	22

1992

DEPT.	# SECTIONS	HEAD-COUNT	AVERAGE
ACC	5	100	20
CS & IS	3	56	19
E&F	11	254	23
M&M	13	303	23
BA & OSY	4	61	15
PCL	8	189	24
	44	963	22

1993

DEPT.	# SECTIONS	HEAD-COUNT	AVERAGE
ACC	5	121	24
CS & IS	4	95	24
E&F	10	191	19
M&M	11	302	27
BA & OSY	4	79	20
PCL	10	219	22
	44	1,007	23

1994

DEPT.	# SECTIONS	HEAD-COUNT	AVERAGE
ACC	4	60	15
CS & IS	3	65	22
E&F	7	144	21
M&M	13	285	22
BA & OSY	3	71	24
PCL	9	189	21
	39	814	21

NOTE: Headcount data has not necessarily been taken from the summer schedules at the same point in time each year. However, the conclusions reached will be the same----ENROLLMENT FOR 1994 IS DOWN AND EACH DEPT., IF PRUDENT, SHOULD ASK WHY !!!

Figure 17•19 Excel Spreadsheet

A variety of visuals can be produced with different software packages.

More sophisticated software programs have additional options: photographs may be printed in a report; the size of graphic aids may vary; lines, curves, and geometric shapes may be created instantly; main headings and captions with special fonts may be inserted; and color and patterns may be added. The software programs allow the user to size, rotate, flip, recolor, and distort digitally stored drawings or photographs to enhance the report.

Once data is entered into a software program, different graphs and charts can easily be generated. A spreadsheet is used to generate a line

Figure 17•20 Examples of Clip Art

Different graphs and charts can be created without rekeying data.

Consideration should be given to the advantages and disadvantages of each program when selecting computer graphic software.

graph for the data in Figure 17•21. A report writer using the same data can press a couple of keys to generate a bar graph instead.

An advantage of using a simple graphics software program is that little training is required to produce a graphic aid. A disadvantage of using a simple program is that the graphic aid produced may not be exactly what is desired. For instance, some elementary graphics software programs do not begin pie charts with the largest piece at the 12 o'clock position. Also, a simple program may limit the number of characters that may be included in the titles or captions of the graphic aids. Care should be taken in selecting a graphics software program so that it will meet the report writer's needs.

SELECTION OF APPROPRIATE GRAPHIC AIDS

The purpose of a graphic aid is to complement the written text by communicating information quickly. Presenting accurate data in a clear and

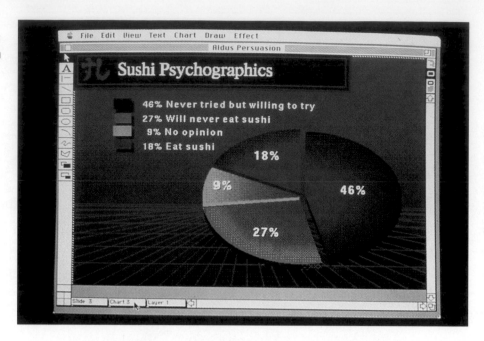

Computers can be used to make realistic estimates and to present these estimates in attractive illustrations.

Selecting appropriate illustrations is critical for effective communication in a report.

Compare quantities in bar graphs.

Illustrate trends in line graphs.

Key points may be projected for emphasis.

organized manner is important. The reader will have little difficulty in interpreting the data when the appropriate graphic aid is selected.

Comparisons of quantities in data are best illustrated by bar graphs. For instance, a report comparing the various fixed costs with the assorted variable costs can be complemented by the use of bar graphs.

If a report discusses trends in quantitative data over a period of time, a line graph would be the most appropriate graphic aid. A multiple-line graph is also an effective device for showing changes in two or more related

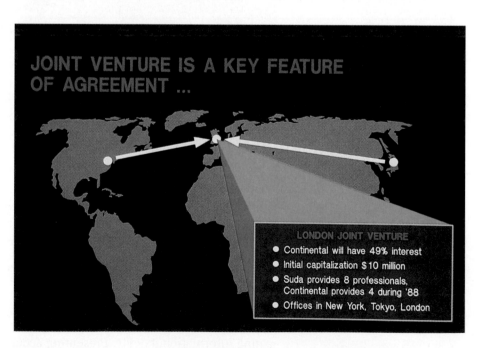

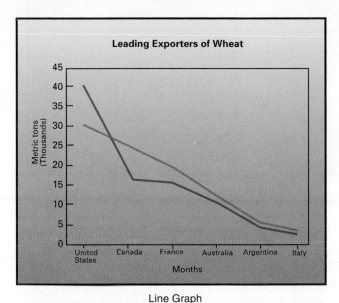

Line Graph

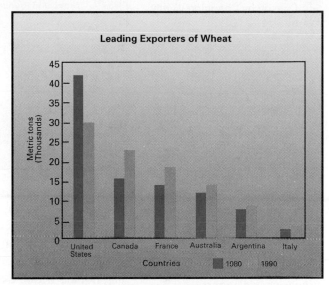

Bar Graph

Figure 17•21 Line and Bar Graphs Using Identical Data

Show relationships with pie charts.

Illustrate steps with flowcharts.

variables. A company comparing the sales trends for its four salespersons can effectively utilize a line graph.

Pie charts are used to show the relationships between the parts and the whole. Budgets are commonly displayed in pie charts in order to illustrate the proportion each item is to the entire budget.

Flowcharts illustrate steps within a procedure. A new employee can easily learn the flow of a work order within an organization by carefully studying a well-designed flowchart.

Careful selection of the appropriate graphic aid may enhance the effectiveness of a written report. The length of the written text can be reduced by the use of a well-chosen graphic aid. Many times it is easier to interpret a graphic aid than to struggle through pages of written text.

POSSIBLE DECEPTION IN GRAPHIC REPRESENTATION

Graphic aids can mislead a reader.

Not only should the reader of a report be aware that graphic aids can be misleading, but the report writer should also be careful not to use graphics to mislead readers. This misrepresentation may occur if certain principles of construction are violated—intentionally or unintentionally.

Bars should be of the same width.

Unproportionate sizes of images in a pictograph or inconsistent widths of bars in a bar graph can deceive the readers of a report. A reader scanning a report containing the pictograph in Figure 17•22 may interpret more wells producing oil in 1994 than in 1993; in fact, there was more production in 1993. Individuals only glancing at the bar graph in Figure 17•22 may perceive the test scores for the 12th grade as being higher than the 11th grade

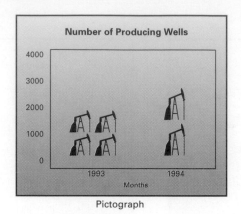

Number of Producing Wells

Pictograph

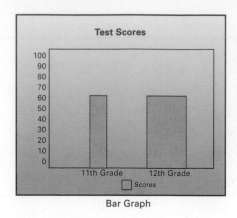

Test Scores

Bar Graph

Figure 17·22 Deception Caused by Changing Width or Size

Pieces of pie charts need to be drawn to correct proportions.

The reference point of all bar graphs should be zero.

Grid increments should be of consistent value throughout a line graph.

test scores; however, the test scores represented by the two bars are of equal value. Specific principles must be followed in creating and interpreting pictographs and bar graphs. In a pictograph, the number of images, not their size, determines the value; and in a bar graph, the height or length of the bar, not the width, determines the value.

A report writer could deceive a reader into thinking the administrative costs in Pie Chart A of Figure 17·23 is one-fifth of the whole; it is actually one-third. Pie Chart B in Figure 17·23 displays the expenses correctly. The size of each piece of a pie chart must be in the same proportion to the whole pie as is the value of the part to the total value.

Another method of deceptive illustration is beginning the bottom of the bars in a bar graph at a point other than zero. This method exaggerates the differences between the individual bars. A company can lead its stockholders to believe that the company has experienced significant growth in sales during the three quarters shown in Graph A of Figure 17·24; Graph B better represents the true sales of the company.

Improper construction of a line graph can also deceive the reader of a report. Inconsistent intervals on the Y-axis can make changes appear greater or lesser than they actually are. Notice that in Figure 17·25 the $30,000 increase from 1990 to 1994 appears greater than the $100,000 decrease from 1988 to 1989.

Figure 17·23 Pie Charts Showing Disproportionate and Correct Division

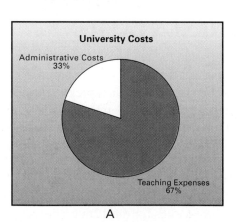

University Costs

Administrative Costs 33%

Teaching Expenses 67%

A

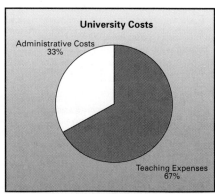

University Costs

Administrative Costs 33%

Teaching Expenses 67%

B

Figure 17•24 Deception
Caused by Not Starting
Baseline at Zero

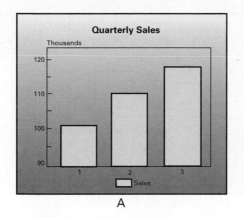
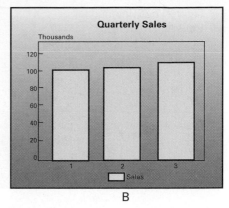

The labels of a graphic aid should also be critically evaluated. A reader looking at the bar graphs in Figure 17•26 should question why the even years have been omitted in Graph A. Is the report writer attempting to make the reader believe that there has been a steady increase in the values throughout the period? What happened in 1988 and 1990?

Text references to graphic aids should be considered, too. Suppose a report reads, "Student enrollments, as shown in Figure 17•27, have grown steadily during the four years." Would the reader assume that all three types

Figure 17•25 Inconsistent
Increments on a Line Graph

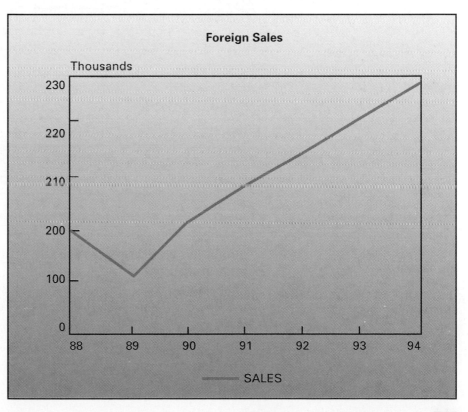

Figure 17·26 Intentional
Omission of Data

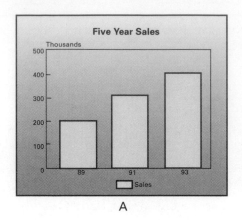

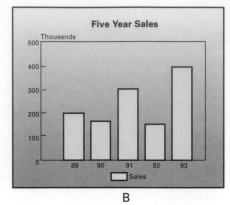

Figure 17·27 Stacked-Bar
Graph Showing Student
Enrollments

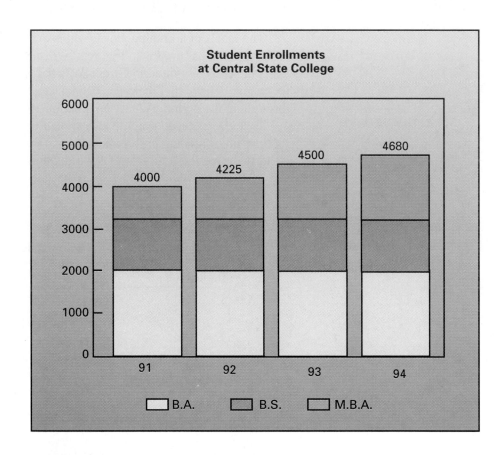

of enrollments have grown or would the reader assume that only MBA
enrollments have grown?

The selection of appropriate graphic aids and accurate descriptions of
them are of equal importance to successful communication when preparing
a report.

The written text must accurately
describe the graphic aid.

DISCUSSION QUESTIONS

1. List five purposes for which graphic aids are used in business reports.

2. Discuss the use of graphic aids in reports. Include in your discussion improper uses of graphic aids.

3. Explain the criteria for selecting the placement of graphic aids in a report.

4. Discuss the proper method of identifying graphic aids.

5. Describe the three types of charts commonly used in business reports.

6. Compare a simple bar graph with a multiple-bar graph.

7. Distinguish between a single-line graph and a multiple-line graph.

8. Describe how pictographs differ from photographs in written reports.

9. Describe how graphics software programs can be used to improve a written report.

10. Give four examples of how graphic aids can be deceptive.

APPLICATION EXERCISES

1. Collect five magazine or newspaper articles that contain illustrations. Analyze the graphic aids. Include in your analysis the placement of the aids, their labels, references to them in the text, and how they can be improved.

2. Prepare a graphic aid that will illustrate each step of the procedure you follow in preparing yourself for an examination in one of your classes.

3. Construct a graphic aid that illustrates the grades you have made in this course.

4. Select the most appropriate graphic aid to illustrate each of the following. Give justification for each of your selections.

   a. The average weekly temperature for a three-month period.
   b. Damage to a house from a tree blown down during a tornado.
   c. The number of freshmen, sophomores, juniors, and seniors attending a college.

d. Monday gold, silver, and platinum prices (individually shown) in relation to interest rates for a one-year period.

e. Procedure that students must follow to register for classes.

f. The dollar amount of loans that specific bank branch offices have made each month for a year.

g. Monthly change in fish population for a lake after an antipollution plan is put into effect.

h. Comparison of weekly absences of company personnel during the first quarter of 1993 and the first quarter of 1994.

i. Correct placement of fingers on home-row keys of a microcomputer.

j. Low temperatures of major cities in the United States.

5. Construct the graphic aid that best illustrates the data for each of the following situations. Create your own titles and labels. Write the introduction to the aid. Be sure to direct your reader to some aspect of the data and refer to the illustration by number.

a. Grocery list: eggs, 75 cents; bacon, $2.19; beans, 32 cents; crackers, 79 cents; liver, $1.54; apples, 75 cents; macaroni, 42 cents

b. Number of employees:

1990: laborers, 32, supervisors, 5; managers, 2
1991: laborers, 34; supervisors, 6, managers, 4
1992: laborers, 36; supervisors, 8, managers, 6
1993: laborers, 40; supervisors, 11, managers, 8
1994: laborers, 41; supervisors, 12, managers, 8

c. Times for three-mile jog:

April 2:	Ann, 18 min 37 sec	April 21:	Ann, 18 min 17 sec
	Bob, 19 min 43 sec		Bob, 18 min 57 sec
	Tom, 23 min 12 sec		Tom, 21 min 49 sec
April 9:	Ann, 18 min 21 sec	April 25:	Ann, 18 min 20 sec
	Bob, 19 min 30 sec		Bob, 18 min 59 sec
	Tom, 22 min 37 sec		Tom, 21 min 33 sec
April 15:	Ann, 18 min 28 sec	April 29:	Ann, 18 min 15 sec
	Bob, 19 min 18 sec		Bob, 18 min 55 sec
	Tom, 22 min 03 sec		Tom, 20 min 58 sec

d. Composition of 24-hour viewing day:

1993:	news, 3 hr 30 min	1994:	news, 5 hr
	sports, 4 hr 15 min		sports, 2 hr 30 min
	movies, 4 hr		movies, 6 hr
	weekly series, 8 hr		weekly series, 9 hr
	other, 4 hr 15 min		other, 1 hr 30 min

e. Number of customers for each day of the week:

Monday, 321
Tuesday, 290
Wednesday, 354
Thursday, 311
Friday, 298
Saturday, 391
Sunday, 277

Text 17A

6. Construct a graphic aid that most effectively illustrates how each expense compares with the other expenses. A student's expenses for a semester may consist of the following:

Tuition	$2,100
Room and Board	1,900
Clothing	625
Entertainment	1,375
Other	950

Text 17B

7. Construct the most appropriate graphic aid to compare the monthly rainfall in inches for the past three years.

	1991	**1992**	**1993**
January	1.9	2.9	0.9
February	2.1	1.8	1.4
March	2.8	3.7	1.1
April	1.9	2.4	1.8
May	2.5	2.2	0.6
June	1.3	1.5	0.8
July	0.3	1.0	0.2
August	0.9	0.9	0.5
September	3.1	2.1	1.9
October	2.1	2.3	3.4
November	3.8	1.8	4.9
December	2.4	2.3	2.4

8. Divide into groups of three and perform a library search to determine the five leading wheat exporting countries for the past year and for ten years ago. Ascertain the principal language that is spoken in each of the ten countries. Construct a graphic aid(s) that could be used in a report discussing languages used in leading agricultural nations.

Text 17C

Rewrite and improve the quality of the following report. Use a graphic aid that would be appropriate for the report.

Individuals have been going to movies at a fast pace this summer. Many movies have been released this summer. The six newest movies with their gross income are: *Cream Puff Express*, $270,000; *Metroman,* $61,800,000; *Murder After 12*, $51,600,000; *The Perfect Vacation,* $12,325,000; *The Mad Musician,* $70,000,000; *Hounds and Kittens,* $62,500,000. It looks as if *The Mad Musician* will outperform all the rest of the movies this summer.

PART 5

Oral and Nonverbal Communication Applications

COMMUNICATION NEWS

Steps to Making an Effective Oral Presentation

Making an effective oral presentation can help you get promoted, make a sale, or even get a bank loan. Use the following techniques, recommended by media trainers/speech coaches Midge Costanza and Kathleen Martin, to help you.

Let fear work for you. Fear produces energy. Use the energy to project your voice more or to let gestures flow more freely. Relax by taking deep breaths and by visualizing yourself as a confident speaker. The more you speak in public, the less fearful you will be.

Respect your audience. Learn as much as you can about your audience and treat its members as a special group with whom you will share information. Making and briefly holding eye contact with people in various parts of the room will make you feel like you are speaking to individuals rather than to a group. Doing so will also make your audience feel more involved in the presentation.

Be prepared. Decide what you want to say, make some notes, study the notes, and practice—preferably before a live audience of family or friends. When you are hired to make a presentation, be sure to ask your client exactly what she or he wants the audience to know.

Eliminate annoying speech habits. Audiotape a practice session and listen for "ums," "uhs," "you knows," and other unconscious speech patterns.

> The more you speak in public, the less fearful you will be.

People who are afraid of silence often use sounds or phrases as filler. Remember, though, that silence can be useful. A pause will be more emphatic and will give you time to think of what you want to say next.

Be conscious of your appearance. Dress slightly better than your audience will be dressed. Good posture will make you look confident.

Pay attention to how you sound. Modulation, inflection, and pace are all important. To help project your voice, breathe deeply from the diaphragm.

Become comfortable with the surroundings. Get as much information as possible about the setting in which you will speak. Better yet, check the room ahead of time so that you are not surprised. Test all equipment to ensure that it is working properly.

Treat yourself well. Dress comfortably. Avoid eating heavy meals. Drink enough liquids to quench your thirst, but not so much that you need a restroom break during your presentation.

Public speaking skills can be improved with practice and experience!

As reported in Sharon Nelton, "Address for Success," *Nation's Business* (February 1991), pp 43–44.

It's Your Turn

What words or sounds do you, your classmates, or instructor use to fill silence?

If someone scheduled to speak to your class about careers in business were to ask you for information about the group, what would you say?

What happens to your voice when you become nervous?

CHAPTER 18 | Listening and Nonverbal Messages

Learning Objectives

Your learning objectives for this chapter include the following:

- To describe the four elements of the listening process
- To list the guidelines for effective listening
- To describe barriers to effective listening
- To describe the advantages of effective listening
- To explain the importance of nonverbal messages
- To identify different types of nonverbal messages and their impact on the communication process

The significant roles of written communication have been stressed in the preceding chapters of this book. The importance of listening, nonverbal communication, and oral communication in the business environment should not be overlooked. This chapter will discuss listening and nonverbal communication. Chapters 19 and 20 discuss oral communication.

LISTENING

There are various reasons for listening. Some common ones are to enjoy entertainment, to gain information, to receive instructions, to hear complaints, and to show respect. For each reason for listening, there are various situations in which listening takes place. For example, information may be acquired in several types of situations: listening one-on-one over the telephone or in face-to-face conversation; listening in a small group, such as a few supervisors receiving instructions from their manager; and listening in a large group, such as hearing a keynote speaker at a conference.

HEARING VERSUS LISTENING

You may have attended a class and heard the teacher give instructions for completing a report or project. Later, as you began preparing the assignment, you realized that you could not recall the details needed to complete the work. Consider another situation where George, an office manager, is told to develop his office's budget for the next year using a three percent decrease in his calculations. After submitting the budget to his manager, George is informed that he used a three percent increase instead of a decrease in his calculations. These are two examples in which hearing occurred, but the entire listening process was not utilized.

THE LISTENING PROCESS

The listening process consists of four elements. Hearing is only one of these elements; the other three are filtering, interpreting, and recalling. Figure 18•1 shows the four elements of the listening process.

HEARING

The first element in the listening process, **hearing,** involves the physiological process of the auditory nerves being stimulated by sound waves. Everyone hears sounds unless he or she has a hearing impairment.

Figure 18•1 The Listening Process

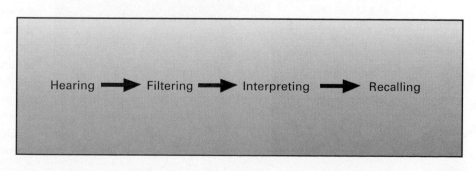

Hearing → Filtering → Interpreting → Recalling

FILTERING

The second element in the listening process, **filtering,** is the elimination of unwanted stimuli. Filtering allows a listener to focus on stimuli that are of specific interest. Consider an example illustrating both unwanted and wanted stimuli: Suppose someone attending a meeting on insurance benefits is seated near an open window through which the aroma from a nearby fast-food restaurant is wafting, making the listener hungry. The unwanted stimulus is the food aroma, and the wanted stimulus is the speaker's information about the insurance. An individual has difficulty concentrating on an oral message when his or her filtering process is unable to eliminate or at least minimize distracting stimuli.

INTERPRETING

The third element of the listening process is interpreting. When **interpreting** stimuli, the listener's mind assigns meaning to the stimuli. This assignment of meaning is done through the use of the person's mental filters. As pointed out in Chapter 1, it is important for the receiver to interpret the stimuli in the way the sender intended.

RECALLING

The fourth element, **recalling,** involves remembering at a later time the information that was interpreted earlier. The success of this element depends heavily on the association (relationship) placed on the stimuli during the interpretation phase.

SUCCESSFUL LISTENING

The success of the listening process depends upon all four elements. If one of the elements is omitted or fails to function properly, the entire listening process is jeopardized. To ensure that the listening process is carried out properly, certain guidelines need to be followed.

GUIDELINES FOR LISTENING

Listening is an active process that can be improved if the receiver takes an active role. The following guidelines can help you to improve your listening skills.

CONCENTRATE ON THE MESSAGE

People normally speak at a rate of 100 to 200 words a minute. Listeners, however, are capable of hearing at rates up to 500 words a minute. This discrepancy makes it necessary for people to concentrate diligently in order to listen effectively. If you do not concentrate intensely, your mind may wander to another topic.

One concentration technique is to mentally summarize the message.

Filtering eliminates unwanted stimuli.

Stimuli are interpreted and assigned meanings by the receiver.

Proper association improves recall ability.

Listening is an active process and can be improved.

To be a successful listener you need to take an active role in the listening process.

You can hear at a faster rate than you can speak.

This technique is especially important when the speech is not well organized. Also, you should concentrate on the main points the speaker is trying to convey, look for hidden messages, and determine if the speaker is using facts, opinions, or inferences. Do not allow the speaker's physical appearance, manner of speaking, or manner of dress to distract you from concentrating on what is said. Concentrating on the message will assist you in overcoming barriers that may interfere with your hearing the entire message.

> ### *A patient hearer is a sure speaker.*
>
> **George Savile**

DETERMINE THE PURPOSE OF THE MESSAGE

Messages presented orally have purposes, as do written messages. You, as a listener, need to determine the purpose of the oral message so that you can decide on the mode that you will use to listen to the message. The three modes commonly used to listen to messages are cautious listening, skimming, and scanning.

Cautious Listening. This mode, **cautious listening,** is used when you need to understand and remember both the general concept and all the details of the message. This mode requires more energy than the other modes because of the amount of spoken material on which you must concentrate. When listening in this mode, your mind does not have any time to relax.

Skimming. **Skimming** is used when you need to understand only the general concept of the message. When using this mode for listening, your mind has time to relax because you do not need to remember all the details being presented. Think of your mind as a computer. The amount of storage is vast but not limitless. Cluttering your mind with insignificant matter causes it to tire, which could cause you to forget the important facts.

Scanning. When **scanning,** you concentrate only on the details that are of specific interest to you, instead of on the message's general concept. No energy is wasted trying to retain information that is not of specific interest. One shortcoming in using this mode is that your mind may wander, and you may miss material that is important.

KEEP AN OPEN MIND

The speaker is presenting the message from his or her viewpoint. Respect this viewpoint by not allowing your own biases to block out what is being said. Your listening ability may be impaired when you are not receptive to the message being presented. When you listen with an open mind, both you and the speaker will benefit. The speaker will believe that what he or she is saying is worthwhile, and you may acquire valuable information.

Concentrate on the main concepts, but be aware of hidden meanings.

Block distractions and concentrate on the message.

The three modes of listening are cautious listening, skimming, and scanning.

Cautious listening is when you attempt to remember concepts and details.

You can skim the spoken material when you only need to remember the general concept.

Scanning is the least careful type of listening.

Don't allow biases to influence listening.

Evaluations of a speaker's message should be made after the entire message is heard. **Frozen evaluations**—judgments made early on and often rigidly set—benefit no one.

USE FEEDBACK

Feedback is important. It is your response to the speaker. The speaker may volunteer more information if positive feedback is received. For instance, a worker describing a problem in the office may expand on his or her comments when you offer feedback, such as "Tell me more about . . ." or "Yes, but . . ." or even "Uh-huh." Some listening situations are not conducive to giving any type of feedback to the speaker. These situations include radio, television, and video presentations. Small group presentations lend themselves best to oral feedback. Each situation should be analyzed as to its appropriateness for providing feedback.

MINIMIZE TAKING NOTES

It may be wise to record complicated presentations for later review; however, the amount of recording should be kept to a minimum so that you are not distracted from listening. You will not be able to concentrate on listening if you attempt to record everything that is said. In oral communication situations that are not complex, just the major points should be recorded; notes should only be used to refresh your memory. Try to remember what is said without using notes.

ANALYZE THE TOTAL MESSAGE

Watch the speaker's actions and facial expressions, and also listen to his or her tone of voice. A speaker can change the entire meaning of a message by raising an eyebrow or by changing the inflection of his or her voice. Such cues as these enable the listener to understand hidden messages.

DO NOT TALK OR INTERRUPT

An individual cannot talk and listen effectively at the same time. When you are talking, you cannot use all the elements of effective listening. Interrupting a speaker at inappropriate times or talking to others while the speaker is speaking is rude and reduces the effectiveness of the communication.

BARRIERS TO LISTENING

A **listening barrier** is any obstacle that interferes with the listening process. You should be aware of barriers so that you can avoid letting them interfere with your listening. Some of the more important barriers to listening are discussed here.

PHYSICAL DISTRACTIONS

The individual responsible for setting up the meeting place in which the listening will occur has primary responsibility for minimizing physical distractions. However, you can take actions to limit this barrier, such as sitting at the front of the room if you have a hearing impairment, not sitting near a corridor or an open window, or not sitting next to an individual who will talk or whisper during the presentation.

MENTAL DISTRACTIONS

You have a responsibility as a listener to give your undivided attention to a speaker. You should avoid daydreaming or allowing your mind to wander. You can think about four times faster than the speaker can talk, so it is easy to begin thinking about other business or personal interests instead of paying attention to the speaker.

A very common distraction is mentally constructing a comment to make or a question to ask rather than concentrating on what is being said. A related mental distraction is forming an opinion or rebuttal during a presentation. To listen effectively, keep an open mind—that is, hear what is said before making judgments.

HEALTH CONCERNS

Good health and well-being play a definite role in effective listening. When a listener is hungry, nauseous, or tired, he or she will find it difficult to listen. To ensure that a verbal message is communicated properly, the speaker may wish to repeat later a message that was transmitted to an individual who was not in good health at the time of the original communication.

NONVERBAL DISTRACTIONS

A listener may give a speaker negative nonverbal feedback. Facial expressions—frowning, yawning, raising an eyebrow, or closing the eyes—can convey a message of disinterest or disapproval. Glancing at a watch or a clock may tell the speaker that you are ready for the presentation to be terminated. The lines of communication will remain open when these nonverbal distractions are avoided.

INAPPROPRIATE TIMING

A listener should ensure that a speaker can present his or her message at an appropriate time. A listener often knows if the time is appropriate. For

Don't let your mind wander when listening.

Be sensitive to a listener's health.

Give the speaker positive feedback by avoiding negative nonverbal actions.

The timing of the communication is important.

A nonverbal distraction, such as gesturing, can give a speaker negative feedback and interfere with the listening process.

example, a manager going through a plant may casually ask a worker, "Any problems?" It may seem to the worker that the manager does not really want to listen to him or her if a supervisor is standing nearby and the manager is aware that the worker would be reluctant to complain in front of the supervisor. A more appropriate comment from the manager would be, "If you have any problems, I have an open-door policy and have reserved Wednesday afternoons to listen to employees." This would allow the speaker (the worker) to present his or her message at an appropriate time.

A listener should give a speaker adequate time to present a message.

An individual presenting a message should be given adequate time so that he or she does not have to rush. It is the listener's responsibility to ensure that the speaker will have enough time to present the entire message. For example, if a manager has to leave for a meeting in 5 minutes and a supervisor enters the office to discuss a problem that will take 15 minutes, the manager should make an appointment to hear the supervisor at a later time. The manager should not expect the supervisor to condense the presentation into 5 minutes.

PARALANGUAGE OR INEFFECTIVE SPEECH CHARACTERISTICS

A listener must be able to hear and understand a speaker in order to interpret the message. If the words are spoken at insufficient volume or at such a high pitch that the listener has trouble hearing the words, listening will be difficult, if not impossible. Other characteristic speech barriers include articulation, dialects, unusual pronunciations, jargon, regional speech patterns (accents), vocalization (tongue clicking, *um*s) and speech impairments. These barriers are difficult to overcome because a listener cannot review a spoken message in the same way as a written message. Careful concentration may help a listener deal effectively with speech characteristic barriers.

Speech barriers are difficult to overcome.

ADVANTAGES OF EFFECTIVE LISTENING

One of the best ways to acquire information is through effective listening. Effective listening will help you develop better attitudes. Also, it can improve your relationships with others because they will realize that you are interested in them. Interested individuals will work diligently to communicate with you. This, in turn, will allow you to do a better job because you will have the support of the people around you. Effective listening will encourage individuals to relate minor problems to you before they become major problems.

Effective listening will enable you to be more successful.

NONVERBAL COMMUNICATION

A **nonverbal message** is a communication that is not written or spoken. We are constantly communicating, either consciously or unconsciously, through nonverbal messages. These messages are an important part of the communication process. Nonverbal messages can add to, or detract from, communication. Nonverbal messages may be delivered in various ways.

Nonverbal communication is a message without words.

Nonverbal messages are important.

As an example, suppose that every day on your way to work you meet the same person at the same place. Each morning as you pass each other you exchange greetings. Suddenly, one morning your greeting is met with indifference; the person does not acknowledge your presence. Later in the day someone asks you if you had seen the passerby that morning and you recall your encounter. Would you be so aware of the encounter if the passerby had spoken to you as usual? Was the passerby's nonverbal message stronger than a verbal communication would have been?

Here is another example of how nonverbal messages affect other forms of communication: A prospective customer receives a poorly printed sales letter announcing a clothing sale. The poor printing is a nonverbal message suggesting carelessness. How quickly will the customer rush to the store for the sale? Which message is more effective—the written or the nonverbal?

Silence is one great art of conversation.

William Hazlitt

THE IMPORTANCE OF NONVERBAL COMMUNICATION

A person should be aware of the impact of nonverbal communication. Nonverbal messages may not always be intended; nevertheless, they clearly communicate with and influence people. Nonverbal messages may aid or hinder communication. The following summarizes the more important characteristics of nonverbal communication:

1. The nonverbal communication can be unintentional. The sender may be unaware that he or she is sending a nonverbal message and, consequently, may not be aware of the impact that message may have.

2. A nonverbal communication may be more honest than a verbal one. Since the message may be unconsciously transmitted, the sender will not have planned it. Therefore, a nonverbal message can be more reliable than a verbal or a written one that had been thought out ahead of time.

3. Nonverbal communication makes, or helps to make, a first impression. At times, this first impression can result in the recipient of the message forming a frozen evaluation of the sender, and this frozen image may be very difficult for the sender to alter.

4. Nonverbal communication is always present. Neither verbal nor written communication exists without nonverbal communication being present.

TYPES OF NONVERBAL COMMUNICATION

Nonverbal messages come in various forms. Some of the common types of nonverbal communication will now be considered.

PHYSICAL APPEARANCE

The physical appearance of a written message influences its first impression.

Physical appearance is an important type of nonverbal communication. It may cause the receiver of a written message to form a frozen evaluation about the subject. An individual will form a first impression from a letter's envelope, stationery, letterhead, format, and neatness. This first impression will definitely influence the reaction of the receiver to the letter.

The physical appearance of a speaker influences an oral message as much as the appearance of a letter influences a written message. A sloppily dressed salesperson will find it difficult, if not impossible, to sell expensive clothes.

Manner of dress communicates a nonverbal message.

People often judge the status of others by the appearance of their possessions. For instance, an individual who wears designer clothes, custom-made shoes, and expensive jewelry will transmit a nonverbal message. This nonverbal message will be perceived differently by receivers depending on the occasion for which the individual is dressed. If the individual is going to lunch or dinner at an elegant restaurant, most people would perceive the person to be wealthy and successful. If the individual is washing a car or mowing a lawn, many people would perceive the person to be a show-off or to be lacking in common sense.

BODY LANGUAGE

The meaning of verbal messages may be changed by body language.

Nonverbal messages are being transmitted constantly through the actions of our bodies. These messages may be intentional or unintentional. Body language may change the meaning of a verbal message. The same gesture may be interpreted differently in different cultures. For instance, in the United States crossing the arms over the chest usually means that one's mind is made up and is not open to change. However, in Finland folded arms are a sign of arrogance. Researchers have studied body language extensively in

People transmit nonverbal messages through the actions of their bodies.

A person's posture while sitting is another form of body language that communicates a nonverbal message. By sitting erect, a person conveys confidence and pride; by slumping, a person conveys tiredness and depression.

Body language may give instant feedback.

Nonverbal messages are communicated through a person's posture.

Handshakes communicate messages.

Gestures are an integral part of nonverbal communication.

recent years and have developed body language dictionaries such as Bäuml and Bäuml's, *A Dictionary of Gestures.*

An advantage of using body language to respond with nonverbal messages is that it conveys instant feedback to the sender of a message. A smile indicates satisfaction, a frown shows disagreement, and a raised eyebrow communicates uncertainty on the part of a receiver of a message. An instant message is communicated by an individual's eye contact during a conversation. Failure to look a person in the eye when speaking may indicate shyness, dishonesty, or embarrassment. Eye contact may indicate confidence, agreement, or interest in the subject of a conversation. An individual who glances around while speaking is exhibiting nervousness or lack of interest.

Other forms of body language include postures and gestures. The way a person sits or stands communicates a nonverbal message. An individual standing or sitting erectly conveys confidence and pride, while a person slumping over may be perceived as being tired or depressed. If an individual leans toward another person during a conversation, body language indicates that the person likes or is interested in the other communicator. If the person leans away from the other person, the posture shows a dislike or disinterest in the other individual.

A handshake also communicates a nonverbal message. A person who firmly grips your hand demonstrates confidence, while an individual who squeezes your hand so tightly that it causes pain gives the impression of being overly aggressive or inconsiderate.

It is practically impossible to communicate without some use of gestures. A gesture may be as simple as a thumbs-up to signify approval or a thumbs-down for disapproval. A gesture may be used to emphasize a critical point in an oral presentation. How interesting would a speech be if the only communicative motion was the opening and closing of the speaker's mouth? Care should be taken in using gestures because, as pointed out in

A nonverbal message can be communicated by the way a person shakes hands. Confidence, aggression, or insecurity may be conveyed.

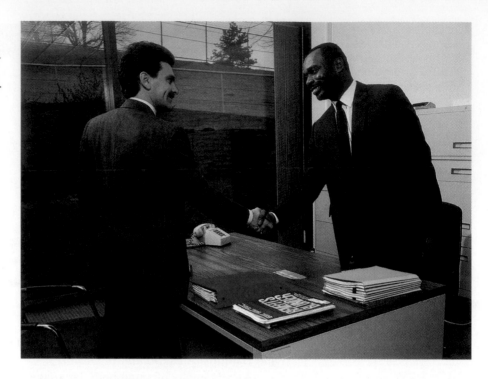

A nonverbal message can be communicated by the way a person shakes hands. Confidence, aggression, or insecurity may be conveyed.

Chapter 5, different cultures interpret gestures in different ways. For instance, if a woman in southern Germany tilts her head to the side and leans forward to listen, she is considered attentive; but in northern Germany, she would be perceived as cringing and timid. To be considered attentive in northern Germany, she would sit up straight and look the speaker directly in the eye (which, in southern Germany would indicate that she is angry). Similar cultural differences apply to other nonverbal messages.

SPACE

Communication is influenced by space. **Space,** as used in nonverbal communication, includes the size of a physical area, proximity to another person, and obstacles between you and the person with whom you are speaking.

The amount of space in an office or home indicates the status of the occupant.

The size of a person's office is an indication of importance within the hierarchy of an organization. The larger the office, the higher the position. People in our society are influenced by sizes and locations of homes. The amount of space people possess influences our attitudes and, therefore, inadvertently is a form of nonverbal communication.

Space transmits a nonverbal message.

A person in charge wants to keep his or her most trusted aide nearby. Therefore the proximity of an employee to a supervisor communicates nonverbally the importance of the employee within the organization. The employee's importance also may be indicated nonverbally by location of parking space, by location and size of office, or by seating location at meetings.

Research has shown that eliminating obstacles such as desks, chairs, and tables will improve oral communication between individuals. The communication will improve if both communicators are on the same level—

sitting or standing. The distance between the communicators will also affect the communication. This distance will vary with individuals from different cultures.

TIME

Emphasis on time transmits a message.

As communicators, we must be aware that the amount of time devoted to a subject transmits a nonverbal message. If the president of a company, for instance, meets with one manager for ten minutes and another manager for two hours, a nonverbal message is being transmitted.

Punctuality relays a nonverbal message. A person who is always on time is perceived as being well organized. A person who is always late transmits a message that he or she is unorganized or that the appointment is unimportant. For instance, if two people of equal credentials were interviewing for a job and one arrived 15 minutes late for the interview, it is more likely that the punctual applicant would be hired.

The importance of time will vary among cultures. Punctuality is very important with individuals from most European countries; however, a 30-minute delay is customary in most Latin American countries. Asians expect others to be punctual, but they often will be late.

DISCUSSION QUESTIONS

1. Describe the four elements of the listening process.

2. How do hearing and speaking rates affect listening concentration?

3. List seven guidelines for listening.

4. How can a listener keep an open mind about the topic?

5. Describe six barriers to listening.

6. What can be gained from effective listening?

7. Explain how nonverbal messages may aid or hinder communication.

8. Describe several forms of body language, and explain how they transmit nonverbal messages.

9. Give three examples of nonverbal communication and discuss how each is interpreted differently by different cultures.

10. How do time and space communicate messages?

APPLICATION EXERCISES

1. Watch the governor of your state give a speech or conduct a press conference. Record nonverbal messages that are transmitted. Be prepared to discuss the effects of the nonverbal messages on the presentation.

2. After the class has been divided into at least two teams, take turns acting out, without speaking, roles presented by the teacher.

3. Interview a foreign student or faculty member and ask him or her to indicate differences in interpretations of nonverbal messages that he or she has observed between Americans and people of his or her culture. Report your findings to the class.

4. Visit offices of different levels of managers in a business and write a short report on how the use of space communicates a message in the organization.

5. Observe students' and instructors' body language on Monday and Friday. Record the differences in the communication for the two days. Are the differences easily apparent?

Text 18A

Rewrite the following guide, "Avoiding Obstacles in Listening to Subordinates," correcting the errors in content. Refer to the Chapter 18 section on "Barriers to Listening" as a resource.

1. *Nonverbal Distractions.* A manager should not give a subordinate any nonverbal feedback. The lines of communication will close when the subordinate notices the manager giving him or her positive nonverbal messages.
2. *Mental Distractions.* A manager should be forming a rebuttal to the problem while the subordinate is explaining it so that a quick response or solution can be given to the problem. When the subordinate takes too long in stating the problem, the manager should not hurry the subordinate but should mentally organize his or her schedule for the remainder of the day to avoid wasting valuable time.
3. *Ineffective Speech Characteristics.* When addressing subordinates, a manager should whisper or speak very softly to avoid intimidating a subordinate. Also, pronouncing words differently will force the subordinate to concentrate on what is being said.
4. *Physical Distractions.* A manager does not have to worry about selection of a proper room for holding a meeting because it is the responsibility of the subordinate to hear what is discussed.
5. *Inappropriate Timing.* A subordinate should carefully select the best time for presenting a problem to the manager. Any time will be appropriate for the manager since it is his or her responsibility to listen to concerns of all employees.

CHAPTER 19

Oral Communication Essentials

Learning Objectives

Your learning objectives for this chapter include the following:

• To describe the role and the importance of oral communication in business
• To improve the basic quality of your voice
• To use your voice effectively
• To strengthen your personal presence

Most of your communication in business will be oral. Your personal success and achievement, therefore, will depend primarily on the effectiveness of your oral communication. The effectiveness of your oral communication relates directly to your understanding of the principles, processes, and goals of business communication. All that you have learned about written communication—grammar, direct and indirect approaches, message development, and visual aids—can be of value to you in oral communication.

If you want to provide leadership to others, your degree of success will relate directly to your ability to speak clearly, intelligently, and persuasively in a confident, convincing manner. Your effectiveness will depend on the quality of your voice and the strength of your presence.

In this chapter, the role of oral communication in business, the improvement of your voice qualities, the effective use of your voice, and the strengthening of your presence are the major topics.

Most business communication is oral.

Leadership depends on oral communication ability.

COMMUNICATING ORALLY IN BUSINESS

A business that provides products or services needed by customers possesses the basic requirement for success. How successful the business is, however, depends on the quality of its internal and external communication. Unsuccessful communication results in lost orders, lost customers, and even failed businesses. In other parts of this textbook, you have studied the general foundations and principles of written business communication. This part of the text concentrates on oral business communication. Both forms of communication—written and oral—are vital to success. Oral communication is critical to the success of a business because it is used so extensively.

Business success depends on communication.

USES OF ORAL COMMUNICATION IN BUSINESS

Depending on your position and level of responsibility in an organization, the amount of time spent in oral communication can vary from 10 to 95 percent of your day. Generally speaking, the higher the level to which you are promoted in an organization, the greater the amount of time you will spend in oral communication. Also, there are certain jobs that require an especially high level of oral communication.

Businesspersons may spend up to 95 percent of their time in oral communication.

MANAGERIAL USES OF ORAL COMMUNICATION

Supervisors, managers, and executives spend most of their time communicating orally. They must be skilled in receiving oral communication—hearing and listening effectively—and sending oral communication—speaking effectively. They must be able to instruct, inform, persuade, inspire, convince, and correct others. They are required by their positions to give leadership to others through the strength and forcefulness of their oral communication.

Managers lead through oral communications.

Supervisors, managers, and executives must communicate orally downward. They are responsible for the morale, productivity, and quality of performance of their subordinates.

Communication Quotes

Business success is dependent on the ability to communicate orally. It's the way we share and build ideas, the way products are sold, and the way leadership is exercised. Effective oral communication is more than a necessary business skill; it's a competitive advantage.
Brenda Barnes, Chief Operating Officer, PepsiCo

Supervisors, managers, and executives also communicate orally upward, horizontally, and diagonally. They are responsible for making effective oral proposals, recommendations, and reports to their peers, superiors, boards, and stockholders, as well as to the public.

EMPLOYEE USES OF ORAL COMMUNICATION

Some jobs require extensive oral communication.

Certain jobs in business require extensive oral communication. The most extensive oral communication is required of people in marketing. The primary requirement for any salesperson is skill in the effective use of oral communication—the ability to convince customers to buy a business' products or services.

Many other positions in business firms require extensive oral communication. These positions include receptionist, purchasing agent, union negotiator, customer relations agent, auditor, bank teller, budget director, union official, public relations specialist, office manager, secretary, and loan officer. The list could go on at great length. Because the use of oral communication in business is extensive, the importance of oral communication to the success and achievement of individuals and business firms is paramount.

Supervisors, managers, and executives spend most of their time communicating orally.

TYPES OF ORAL COMMUNICATION IN BUSINESS

There are three categories of oral communication.

There are many different types of oral communication in business. Three basic categories of these types are one-to-one, one-to-small-group, and one-to-large-group. Within each type, there can be different forms and methods of oral communication.

ONE-TO-ONE ORAL COMMUNICATION

One-to-one: Talking to one other person.

One-to-one oral communication can be a face-to-face conversation, dictation to a secretary or a machine, a telephone conversation, a video conversation, or communication through other electronic devices for voice transmission. Face-to-face conversation can include conferring with a subordinate about work plans, performance evaluation, or non-work-related topics. Businesspersons also frequently talk on the telephone with each other, customers, and members of the public.

To be effective, one-to-one oral communication requires intelligent word choice, clarity of enunciation, variety in voice inflection, and conveyance of positive personal feelings.

ONE-TO-SMALL-GROUP ORAL COMMUNICATION

One-to-small-group: Speaking to fewer than 20 persons.

It is common in business for three or more persons to meet and talk. Small groups—usually fewer than 20 persons—meet to solve problems, to develop policy, to develop new products, to hear progress reports, and for many other reasons. For example, a committee (or a team, a task force, etc.) may be formed to consider an employee tardiness problem, to determine a pricing policy, to decide on a new product line, or to hear a report on the past quarter's sales.

The most extensive oral communication in business is required of people in marketing.

In addition to the requirements for effective one-to-one oral communication, effective one-to-small-group communication requires understanding group dynamics, increased voice volume, and the use of special techniques to facilitate group effort.

ONE-TO-LARGE-GROUP ORAL COMMUNICATION

One-to-large-group: Speaking to 20 or more persons.

One-to-large-group oral communication is commonly referred to as giving a speech. For most purposes, a large group can be defined as 20 or more people. Large groups can be huge. Businesspersons may find themselves speaking to as many as 100 or more employees or attendees at a professional conference. The main speaker at a general session of a meeting may speak to 500, 5,000, or more people at one time. Of course, television and radio enable some individuals to speak to millions of people at one time.

Specific examples of types of speeches can be quite varied. You may be called on to give a speech to your company's employees in which you report last year's financial activities. You may speak to a college class on your profession, or you may speak to a community service club on the need for support of a community activity.

You may be a member of a small group—a committee, task force, panel, or team—that is responsible for giving a presentation to an audience. In most cases, the group would have worked cooperatively in determining and developing the presentation. Then each group member would be responsible for a portion of the presentation. Effective group collaborative work is discussed in Chapter 3, Developing Business Messages, pages 77–79. While some feel there is "safety in numbers," most speakers experience the same emotions in small-group-to-large-group communication as they do in one-to-large-group communication.

Having to give any speech makes most people somewhat anxious. It is, however, a unique opportunity to inform or persuade a group of people. It is an opportunity for you to be in the spotlight and on center stage for a time. It can be an extremely rewarding experience. Later in this chapter, we will discuss methods that you can use to overcome the anxiety you may feel in one-to-large-group oral communication.

In addition to the requirements for effective one-to-one and one-to-small-group oral communication, one-to-large-group oral communication requires particular considerations of body movements, voice volume, audience analysis, and visual aids.

Improving your oral communication—whether to one person or to several persons—involves improving the quality and effectiveness of your voice and strengthening your personal presence. These topics are covered in the remaining sections of this chapter. Chapter 20 discusses successful techniques for planning and presenting oral communications.

Improving your voice quality and personal presence will improve your oral communication.

IMPROVING YOUR VOICE QUALITIES

Because the use of oral communication is extensive and its effective use is so important to you and your organization, it is vital that you do all you can to improve the quality of your voice. The starting point for improving your oral communication, then, is to improve the physiological aspects of your speaking voice.

PROPER CONTROL OF BREATHING

Quality sound depends on proper use of air.

High-quality sound with adequate volume depends on the proper use of the raw material, air. You use air for speaking in two basic ways. First, with two or three deep breaths you can relax your sound-producing organs and prepare them for speaking. Second, with sufficient inhalation of air and proper control of exhalation of air while speaking, you can improve the quality of the sounds you make.

Inhale deeply to fill the lungs with ample air for speaking.

Controlled deep inhalation of air—called abdominal or diaphragmatic breathing—fills your lungs and provides ample air for speaking. When you inhale deeply, you should not raise your shoulders; you should expand your abdomen, lower back, and sides. The air should go all the way to the diaphragm—a muscle between the chest and the abdomen (see Figure 19•1). When you are nervous, you tend to breathe shallowly and not fill your lungs, and, as a result, you do not provide enough air for rich and full sounds.

Exhale air past vocal cords to fill the head cavities for full, rich sounds.

The exhalation of air as you make sounds should come from your diaphragm. With a sufficient amount of air in the lungs, you can bring the air up from the diaphragm, past your vocal cords, and fill the orifices in your head with enough force to cause the sound to be rich and full. The orifices in your head—mouth, nose, and sinuses—are like echo chambers and enrich the sound of your voice.

Figure 19•1 Deep inhalation of air should be controlled by the diaphragm—a muscular partition between the chest and the abdomen.

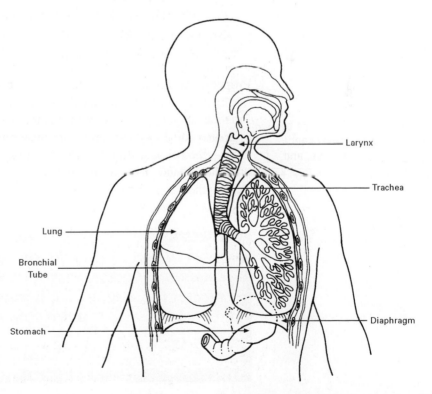

PROPER CONTROL OF JAW, TONGUE, AND LIPS

Avoid the troublesome *T*'s.

The "troublesome *t*'s" of tight jaw, tight tongue, and tight lips cause mumbled, muffled speech sounds that are hard to hear and understand. Pronunciation, enunciation, and clarity of sound depend on your jaw being flexible and your tongue and lips being loose and alive.

Keep a flexible jaw for clear sounds.

Practice freely flexing your jaw by saying *idea, up and down,* and *the sky is blue.* Now say those same expressions with a tightly clenched jaw. Notice how clenching your jaw muffles the sounds. For more jaw-flexing practice, count from 91 to 99, and say *fine, yes, no, pay, buy,* and *like* over and over.

Keep your tongue free and alive for good enunciation.

For practice in freeing your tongue and making it come alive, say *either, left,* and *wealth.* Try to say the same words holding your tongue still. This exercise shows the importance of your tongue being loose and alive for good enunciation. Now count from 21 to 29 and let your tongue move freely and loosely. Say *health, thin, think, alive,* and *luck.* Practicing these and similar words will increase the flexibility and mobility of your tongue.

Good enunciation also depends on freely moving lips.

To free your lips—important controllers of voice quality—say *when, where, be,* and *back.* See what happens to your enunciation when you try to say these words without moving your lips. Other words that are good to practice to free your lips are *west, window, puff, lisp,* and *lips.*

Here are some sentences you can use to practice keeping your jaw, tongue, and lips flexible:

> Loose lips sink ships.
>
> Shave a single shingle thin.
>
> Peter Piper picked a peck of pickled peppers.
>
> Hickory dickory dock, the mouse ran up the clock.
>
> She sells seashells by the seashore.

You can improve your voice by practicing breath control and keeping your jaw, tongue, and lips flexible.

Proper control of the physical aspects of speaking is basic to high-quality oral communication. Practice deep breathing until it comes naturally to you. Practice keeping your jaw, tongue, and lips flexible. This practice will result in greater capability in using your voice effectively and achieving full, round tones—the voice quality that you hear major announcers and broadcasters on radio and television using. The next section builds on these basic skill-development exercises with suggestions for refining the use of your voice.

> *With the sense of sight, the idea communicates the emotion, whereas, with sound, the emotion communicates the idea, which is more direct and therefore more powerful.*
>
> **Alfred North Whitehead**

USING YOUR VOICE EFFECTIVELY

Once you have control of the basic sound-making mechanisms, you are ready to improve the use of your voice. The important considerations in this improvement are pitch, volume, speed, emphasis, tone, enunciation, and pronunciation. These aspects of using your voice effectively can each be improved by using a tape or video recorder for self-analysis, or by obtaining feedback from a family member, a friend, or others.

PITCH

Pitch refers to the highness or lowness of your voice. A voice that is too high or too low will be distracting to your listener or audience. There are two important aspects of pitch. One is to find your natural pitch and, assuming it is not too shrill or too deep, to use it. The second is to vary your pitch while speaking to provide interest and emphasis.

FIND YOUR PITCH AND USE IT

To determine your natural pitch, yawn deeply three times. Then say aloud, "My natural pitch is. . . ." Yawn deeply, and say these words again. Note that your pitch (your voice sound) became lower—deeper, richer, and fuller. Yawn and repeat the words one more time for a total of three times. Let your voice rest for at least one minute. Now, once again say, "My natural pitch is. . . ." With this exercise you will have found your natural pitch.

To avoid damage to your vocal cords, it is important to find your natural pitch and use it. If, because of nervousness or stage fright, you speak in a pitch higher than your natural one, you will strain your vocal cords. If you force yourself to speak in a pitch that is artificially lower than your natural one, you will also strain your vocal cords. Strained vocal cords can result in a hoarse, raspy voice; or you may even lose your voice for a time.

If you think your pitch is too high or too low, consult a speech correction specialist. Most colleges have one or more speech correction specialists. With exercises prescribed by a professional, your natural pitch can be changed to a more attractive, pleasant level.

VARY YOUR PITCH WHILE SPEAKING

The second aspect of improving the use of your voice is to learn to vary your pitch while speaking. The sparkling, interesting, enthusiastic speaker varies the pitch of his or her voice while speaking. Variation in the use of high and low sounds avoids the dullness of a monotone voice—a voice with a sameness in pitch level. Nothing will lose an audience faster than a monotonous voice, regardless of the quality of the content of the message.

You can make your presentation style interesting and even exciting by using variations in pitch effectively. As you speak, think of your voice soaring up mountains and gliding down through valleys. Emphasize the ending of a declarative sentence with a definite drop in pitch. Make a question clear and forceful by raising your pitch at the end of the question.

There are other, more sophisticated uses of pitch variation that you can adopt. Comparisons can be indicated by using the same pitch level, while contrasts can be indicated with differing pitch levels. For example, equal

---

Sidebar notes:

Pitch is the highness or lowness of a voice.

Determine your natural pitch.

Use your natural pitch to avoid damaging your voice.

With proper exercises you can lower or raise your natural pitch.

Avoid being monotonous by varying your pitch.

Varying your pitch adds life to your voice.

Pitch can be used to give meaning to what you are saying.

comparisons can be shown as follows: "The market is *up* (moderate pitch), and its gains are *solid* (moderate pitch)." On the other hand, differing pitch levels can emphasize contrasts as follows: "While the market is *up* (high pitch), its gains are *not solid* (low pitch)." You can show finality by dropping the pitch. Doubt or hesitation is shown by raising the pitch.

Giving attention to varying your pitch while speaking is one of the most important ways to improve the effectiveness of your voice. Variation of pitch holds your listeners' attention and helps them understand the meaning of your messages.

VOLUME

A major aspect of using your voice effectively is **volume control.** Proper volume control enables you to be heard appropriately by your listeners—essential for effective oral communication. Volume control also enables you to vary your emphasis—essential for dynamic, forceful oral communication.

USE THE APPROPRIATE VOLUME LEVEL

The first goal of volume control is to be heard by every member of the audience—whether the audience is one person or 500 persons. Although you want to speak with sufficient force to be heard, you do not want to speak too loudly. If your audience thinks you are shouting, you will have created a communication barrier.

An important responsibility of a sender in the communication process is to obtain feedback. You can obtain feedback on the adequacy of your volume level by asking if you are being heard clearly or if you are too loud. Another source of feedback is the nonverbal signals you get from your listeners. Does your audience seem to be getting restless? Are people straining to hear you? Is anyone cupping a hand behind an ear or covering both ears? If any of the feedback indicates your volume level needs to be adjusted, do so immediately.

VARY YOUR VOLUME FOR EMPHASIS

The second goal of voice volume control is to vary your volume level for emphasis. You can communicate strength, power, forcefulness, and excitement through louder speech. You can create a mood of sorrow, seriousness, respect, and sympathy by lowering the volume of your voice. Both ways can be used to attach importance and emphasis to what you are saying.

You can maintain the attention of an audience, regardless of its size, through variation in the volume of your voice. In a one-to-one situation, your volume variation should be subdued; with a larger group, the volume variation can range from simply being heard clearly to a moving, high-volume level.

SPEED

Variation in the speed of your oral communication provides interest and emphasis. The monotone voice we all try to avoid is not only at the same pitch and volume level, it is also at the same speed. It is recommended that, for large audiences, you vary your rate of speaking from 75 to 150 words a minute. For one-to-one conversations and small groups, your rate should range from 75 to 250 words a minute.

Vary your rate of speaking for emphasis.

If you want to stress selected parts of your messages, slow your speed at those points. For less-important material, speak at a faster rate. Excitement can be conveyed with a high rate of speed, while seriousness can be communicated with a slow rate. The important point in regard to speed is to vary your rate as you speak.

TONE

Tone is possibly your most important voice quality. Tone is the way the message sounds to a receiver. Using the same word and phrases, your tone can convey concern, irritation, confidence, tentativeness, excitement, calmness, disrespect, courtesy, detachment, etc. The words, *I know what you mean,* can be said with a concerned tone, conveying understanding, or with an irritated tone, conveying mistrust.

Tone is such a critical voice quality that special attention must be given to analysis of your receivers in oral communication situations. What is the relationship you want to establish with your listeners. Do you want them to listen to you? Be persuaded by your words? Know that you respect them? Be friends with you? Whatever you want the relationship to be, you will have to convey its true meaning with the tone of your voice.

Most business communication situations call for a friendly, objective, businesslike tone that conveys warmth, strength, and respect. You will not want to sound negative, overly formal, insincere, condescending, prejudiced, weak, or disrespectful. You should consciously determine how you want your tone quality to sound in any given communication situation.

EMPHASIS PRACTICE

Practice giving emphasis.

You can give emphasis to your oral communication by varying your pitch, volume, speed, and tone. The following exercise will help you vary your emphasis and give different meanings to the same words. Say each of the following sentences out loud giving emphasis to the italicized word:

You can change your life.	(You have the power.)
You *can* change your life.	(It is possible.)
You can *change* your life.	(It can be different.)
You can change *your* life.	(The life you own.)
You can change your *life.*	(The life you are living.)

Did you vary the emphasis in each sentence by using different pitches? volumes? speeds? Probably you used a combination of these techniques. Now repeat each sentence in the exercise and emphasize the italicized words by varying your pitch. Next, say the sentences and vary your volume by saying the italicized words more loudly. Then, repeat the sentences and vary your rate by saying the italicized word slowly and the rest of the words quickly.

Finally, say the sentences and vary your tone from a disinterested to a caring quality.

From your use of the different emphasis techniques, you can easily see the powers you have in the variation of your voice. You can generate interest and communicate different meanings. You can strengthen the forcefulness, powerfulness, and effectiveness of your oral communication by using variations in your voice.

ENUNCIATION

Sound each part of each word clearly and accurately.

For effective use of your voice, sound each part of a word clearly and accurately. The manner in which you sound the parts is called *enunciation*. An example of correct enunciation is sounding clearly the *g*'s in words ending in *ing*. Say "talk*ing*" instead of "talk*in*," "go*ing to*" instead of "go*nna*," and "study*ing*" instead of "study*in*."

To improve your enunciation, examine your own sound-making patterns by recording your voice (or ask others to assist you) and correct any errors detected. One way to correct errors in enunciation is to slow down your rate of saying individual words. Give each word its fair share of time so that each part of it can be sounded properly. High-quality enunciation reflects favorably on your intelligence and credibility.

PRONUNCIATION

Join sounds together correctly for proper pronunciation.

The way in which you join sounds to say a word is called *pronunciation*. You can make sounds distinctly (enunciate clearly) but still not pronounce a word correctly. The dictionary is your best source of information for correct pronunciation of individual words. Generally speaking, the first pronunciation definition given in a dictionary is the preferred one. The second pronunciation also is considered acceptable but is used less frequently.

As in the case of high-quality enunciation, the correctness of your pronunciation reflects on your intelligence and credibility. Good oral communicators pronounce words correctly. They say *library* instead of *libary*, *was* instead of *wuz*, *again* instead of *agin*, *just* instead of *jist*, and *our* instead of *ar*. If you are not sure how to pronounce a word, do not use it until you check a dictionary or find out from another person how to pronounce it correctly.

ANALYSIS

Analyze your voice to improve its effectiveness.

You can improve the effectiveness of your voice by analyzing its qualities and the way in which you use it. There are several ways you can perform this analysis. You can record your voice on a tape recorder for self-analysis. You can ask a family member who speaks effectively and correctly to analyze your oral communication. You can ask an instructor at school for feedback, or you can seek a professional speech correction service.

Because most of your communication will be oral communication, it will serve your personal and career interests well to use your voice effectively. Based on high-quality speaking skills, you can build your ability to relate to others clearly, forcefully, and persuasively.

STRENGTHENING YOUR PRESENCE

Improve your oral communication by strengthening your poise and bearing.

You can further improve your oral communication by strengthening your personal presence. Your presence is your poise and bearing. It includes your tangible and intangible nonverbal communication. Some refer to an effective presence as **charisma**—a personal magnetism and grace that causes others to react positively and favorably toward the person possessing this quality. The important aspects of charisma are confidence, enthusiasm, sincerity, friendliness, eye contact, body actions, and appearance.

CONFIDENCE

Your listeners sense your self-confidence.

Whether you are talking to one person or several, the amount of confidence you possess will be sensed by your receiver(s). For a strong presence in support of your oral communication, you need the right amount of confidence—neither too little nor too much.

TOO LITTLE CONFIDENCE

Too little confidence results in nervousness and poor oral communication.

In one-to-one situations, too little confidence is referred to as nervousness; when speaking to larger groups, it is called *stage fright*.

When communicating orally, too little confidence causes discomfort in both yourself and your audience. Your discomfort may be reflected in a shaking voice, shaking hands, perspiration, inability to think clearly, and other unpleasant mental, emotional, and physical symptoms. With too little confidence in yourself, you are not able to say what you want to say in the way you want to say it. Your effectiveness in achieving your oral communication goals is reduced or eliminated. The oral communication is not a pleasant, productive experience for you or your audience.

TOO MUCH CONFIDENCE

Too much confidence causes a negative, know-it-all attitude and conveys a lack of concern for your audience.

On the other hand, too much confidence can also inhibit oral communication effectiveness. The overconfident speaker projects a know-it-all attitude and a lack of concern for the audience. Your audience will respond negatively to overconfidence by rejecting you personally and by rejecting your message.

AN EFFECTIVE LEVEL OF CONFIDENCE

Achieve the appropriate level of self-confidence by concentrating on the audience and using the you–viewpoint.

What many oral communicators fail to realize is that too little or too much confidence is caused primarily by self-centeredness. If speakers concentrate exclusively on themselves and do not consider their receivers, they will be perceived as having either too little confidence or too much. The principal way to achieve an appropriate, effective amount of confidence is to keep the emphasis on your listeners and to use the you–viewpoint. You won't be too concerned about yourself if you are thinking about the needs, concerns, and interests of others.

Have realistic expectations for your oral communication.

For some individuals, too little confidence is caused by negative thinking and unrealistic expectations for their oral communication. It is important for these persons to accept that they do not necessarily have to be admired or respected by everyone in the audience. In addition, they must realize that it is normal to misspeak occasionally; they must not allow those errors to reduce their confidence level.

In addition to placing your listeners first, there are other ways of developing an effective level of confidence. These include careful preparation of your oral presentation, diligent practice, and attention to your personal appearance. Ways to maintain confidence while communicating orally include maintaining eye contact with your audience; talking in a strong, clear voice with sufficient volume; and observing and reacting to the feedback you receive from your audience.

ENTHUSIASM

Enthusiasm is contagious if it is genuine. If you are enthusiastic about the ideas in your oral communication, your listener or audience will become enthusiastic and positive about those ideas. Dullness can put receivers to sleep. Enthusiasm can excite them, build their interest, and keep them alert.

An enthusiastic speaker holds the listener's attention and gets a positive reaction.

Show enthusiasm by speaking with energy and animation.

You can project your enthusiasm if you speak with energy and animation. Variations in pitch, volume, and speed will assist in showing enthusiasm. Facial expressions—smiles, raised eyebrows, wide open eyes—indicate enthusiasm. Energetic and definite gestures and body movements also help. Eyes that are alive and sparkling show enthusiasm.

You can build a positive, enthusiastic presence by realizing its importance and practicing it every time you have an opportunity—in conversations, oral reports, discussions, and speeches.

> *Enthusiasm is the propelling force necessary for climbing the ladder of success.*
>
> **Anonymous**

SINCERITY

Being sincere strengthens credibility.

An oral communicator will be more effective if the audience perceives that the speaker is sincere. Believability and credibility rest heavily on sincerity. Insincerity is reflected by flippancy, inappropriate nonverbal signals (for example, a smirking facial expression), and an apparent lack of concern for the audience and its reception of the message.

Believe in the importance of what you are saying.

If you want to be able to inform, persuade, and/or convince a person or an audience, you must believe in what you are saying. You must believe it is worthy enough to take your receiver's time and your time to talk about it. Sincerity is closely related to your belief in the importance of the content of the message. Sincerity is rooted in a message with integrity; a message with honest and ethical content.

Your bearing must reflect your sincerity.

Also, sincerity is related to your personal presence: you must appear to be sincere. Your verbal and nonverbal signals should reflect sincerity. This does not mean that you cannot have any humor in your oral communication. It does mean the humor should not detract from your sincerity. You will

The speaker who projects warm friendliness relates more effectively to the audience.

communicate sincerity if the general tone of your oral presentation conveys that your message is important. Your message should be presented in a warm, friendly, and caring manner.

FRIENDLINESS

Friendliness builds positive relationships with listeners.

The speaker who can project a congenial, pleasant, cordial, caring image—a warm friendliness—can relate more effectively to a listener or to an audience. As with other personal aspects of oral communication, the appearance of friendliness must be supported primarily by your true friendly feelings toward other people.

Show friendliness by feeling friendly and exhibiting it.

Knowing that you can increase your effectiveness significantly with friendliness should motivate you to develop your ability to be sincerely friendly and gracious. A smiling face, an unhurried approach, and a concern for feedback exhibit friendliness and an honest caring for your receivers. As with confidence, enthusiasm, and sincerity, concentrating on the needs and interests of your audience will help convey your friendliness.

EYE CONTACT

Good eye contact reflects confidence, interest, honesty, and sincerity.

Eye contact with your receivers is such an important nonverbal signal that it will be discussed separately from other body actions. Appropriate eye contact reflects confidence, interest, honesty, and sincerity. A lack of eye contact reflects a lack of confidence and interest and, therefore, may project an image of weakness, insincerity, fear, and dishonesty.

Try to have eye contact with American listeners about 75 percent of the time.

While the amount of eye contact possible and appropriate in different oral communication situations will vary, a good target is to have eye contact with American receivers about 75 percent of the time. Eye contact with Asian receivers should be less—about 10 percent of the time—because they consider too much eye contact to be offensive. On the other hand, the

French tend to have eye contact with their receivers almost 100 percent of the time. Consider your receiver's culture when making eye contact.

In one-to-one conversations, you should build effective communication bridges with relaxed, comfortable eye contact. In one-to-group situations, you should look into the eyes of every member of the audience, lingering long enough so that each person feels you are talking to him or her individually. The impression you should convey is that you are indeed talking to each one personally, and although you need to talk to others in the audience too, you will return to the individual again.

Good eye contact takes practice and effort. Its benefits are so rewarding to the oral communicator that it is critically important for you to work on it. For example, if you fail to achieve the 75 percent goal for American receivers in your early efforts, do not be discouraged. Keep practicing until you fully realize the benefits of good eye contact with your receivers.

BODY ACTIONS

In addition to eye contact, other important nonverbal signals during oral communication fall under the heading of body actions. These nonverbal signals include facial expressions, posture, gestures, and other body movements. Each of these topics will be reviewed briefly here. They are dealt with in more detail in Chapter 18, "Listening and Nonverbal Messages."

FACIAL EXPRESSIONS

Regardless of the words you are saying to your audience, your eyes and your face appear to convey your true feelings. If you are sincere and feel friendly toward your receivers, show those feelings in your facial expressions. As you practice an oral communication, look in the mirror to see if

Show that you are interested, enthusiastic, and friendly.

you appear to be interested, enthusiastic, and friendly. If not, practice the necessary facial expressions until your nonverbal signals are comparable to your true feelings and your verbal message.

GESTURES

Use gestures to generate interest and convey meaning. Your gestures should be natural.

While communicating orally gestures of the hands, arms, shoulders, and head are important supporting nonverbal signals. Sitting behind a desk like a statue or standing immobile behind a lectern results in a dull, uninteresting appearance. You should use gestures to strengthen your verbal messages.

The gestures should be natural, not contrived. Raising the arms with palms facing upward, for example, can accent a verbal message that asks the rhetorical question, What is the answer? Pointing to an item on an audiovisual aid helps stress the point being made. Gestures should be varied, not repetitious. To develop gestures appropriate for you and the situation, you should practice in front of a mirror until you find movements that are genuine and comfortable for you. The two most important points relative to gestures are that they should be used and they should be natural.

POSTURE

Good posture improves your appearance and gives you confidence.

An upright, correct posture will improve your appearance and give you a feeling of confidence. You do not want to appear pompous or stiff, but rather natural and comfortable. If you are standing during an oral communication, keep your weight evenly distributed on your feet. Do not lean on a lectern, table, or chair. If sitting, sit erectly and comfortably. Do not slouch or hang one leg over a chair arm. Correct posture reflects your confidence and respect for your audience.

Gestures are important supporting nonverbal signals. The ones you choose to use should be natural, not contrived.

OTHER BODY MOVEMENTS

Other important body movements can be useful.

Walking, leaning, turning, and other body movements are nonverbal signals to your receivers. Some body movement is important to hold attention and to relax your muscles. These movements should be graceful, unhurried, and natural. You can draw an audience's attention to a visual aid by turning your body to it or walking to it. You can signal the end of a one-to-one conversation by moving your chair back and standing up. Body movements are important, and their use during oral communication should be considered carefully. As with facial expressions and gestures, you can observe and practice your body movements in front of a mirror until they feel comfortable and convey the nonverbal message you want them to convey.

> *If you want to get across an idea, wrap it up in a person.*
>
> **Ralph Bunche**

APPEARANCE

Strengthen your presence with a good personal appearance.

The final personal aspect to be considered in strengthening your presence during oral communication is your appearance. Your personal appearance can be a barrier to effective oral communication, or it can be an asset. It is an important part of the total communication environment, particularly as a first impression.

Use what you have to best advantage by wearing appropriate clothing and being neatly groomed.

You have to accept and work with the raw material of your own basic appearance. What you do with what you have is what will influence your audience. The clothing and accessories you select should be appropriate for the occasion and the audience, and you should be neatly groomed. Good appearance not only sets a favorable stage for oral communication, but it also serves to increase your confidence.

This chapter has concentrated on improving your oral communication through recommendations for improving your voice qualities, for using your voice effectively, and for strengthening your presence. By following these recommendations, you can become an effective oral communicator. Effective oral communication is rewarding, enjoyable, and well worth your efforts in improving yourself.

DISCUSSION QUESTIONS

1. Describe the importance of oral communication to businesses.

2. List five examples of jobs in business that require an extensive use of oral communication. For each job give an example of oral communication that is commonly required.

3. Describe each of the following types of oral communication in business: (a) one-to-one, (b) one-to-small-group, and (c) one-to-large-group. Include in your descriptions examples of each of these types of oral communication and the requirements for effective communication for each.

4. Describe how to use the raw material of air effectively for speaking.

5. How do you control the jaw, tongue, and lips to avoid the "troublesome *t*'s"?

6. Describe how you can strengthen your oral communication by varying your pitch.

7. Using your voice effectively involves proper volume control. How can you (a) determine appropriate volume level, and (b) vary your volume for emphasis?

8. Discuss how you can use the speed of your oral communication to provide interest and emphasis.

9. Explain ways to analyze your voice to improve its quality.

10. What role does personal presence play in the effectiveness of a person's oral communication?

11. Discuss the causes of too little confidence and too much confidence. How does a speaker maintain an effective level of confidence while speaking?

12. What roles do enthusiasm, sincerity, and friendliness play in effective oral communication?

13. Describe the benefits of appropriate eye contact and the impact of poor eye contact.

14. How can you strengthen your personal presence through appropriate facial expressions?

15. Name a successful leader and describe his or her personal presence and how it affects the message he or she wants to convey.

16. Describe the difference between enunciation and pronunciation.

APPLICATION EXERCISES

1. Reflect on your experiences with oral communication over the past week. Select one example of excellent oral communication and one example of poor oral communication. Share these examples in class. Analyze the importance of effective oral communication in human relationships.

2. Name a prominent world or local figure who frequently and publicly uses oral communication. Analyze his or her pitch, volume, and speed, and indicate the person's strengths and weaknesses in the use of these voice qualities.

3. Record your voice on a cassette tape recorder. Listen carefully to the recording; analyze your voice qualities in regard to pitch, volume, and speed. Write a brief report of your findings including the following: (a) The way your voice sounds to you, (b) the strengths of your voice, (c) the weaknesses of your voice, and (d) a plan for improving your voice.

4. Interview a foreign student or faculty member and ask him or her to indicate the greatest barriers persons of his or her culture face in communicating orally with Americans. Report your findings to the class.

5. Interview a successful manager and ask him or her to tell you the most important qualities in an effective oral communicator. Specifically, ask the following two questions: To be an effective oral communicator, (a) What voice qualities should a person possess?, and (b) What personal presence qualities? Share your findings with the class.

6. Give emphasis to the important points in the following paragraph by varying (a) your pitch, (b) your volume, (c) your speed, and (d) your pitch, volume, and speed in appropriate combinations.

If you want to provide leadership to others, your degree of success will relate directly to your ability to speak clearly, intelligently, and persuasively in a confident, convincing manner. Your effectiveness will depend on the quality of your voice and the strength of your presence.

7. Describe how the meaning changes in the following sentence when the emphasis is moved from word to word.

   a. *Most* of your communication in business will be oral.
   b. Most of *your* communication in business will be oral.
   c. Most of your *communication* in business will be oral.
   d. Most of your communication *in* business will be oral.
   e. Most of your communication in *business* will be oral.
   f. Most of your communication in business *will be* oral.
   g. Most of your communication in business will be *oral.*

8. The purpose of this exercise is to increase effective eye contact. Select a member of your class and talk to him or her for a few minutes. The goal will be to have effective eye contact with your partner at least 75 percent of the time. After the exercise, the whole class will discuss what took place.

9. Observe other students for one week, recording evidences of strong, positive personal presences. Report your findings to class.

10. Form groups of five to seven students each. Have each person in the group speak for one minute about a different section of Chapter 19. The speakers should practice trying to show a strong positive personal presence while speaking.

11. Select a well-known radio or television announcer or broadcaster. Analyze his or her voice qualities and presence, and share your analysis with the class.

MESSAGE ANALYSIS

Rewrite the following SUGGESTIONS FOR SALESPERSONS and correct the errors in content. Refer to the Chapter 19 section on "Strengthening Your Presence" as a resource.

To be effective, Evergreen Company salespersons must give careful consideration to their personal presence in each of the following categories in the manner indicated:

Confidence. Maintain an effective level of confidence by concentrating on yourself and projecting an image of complete knowledge of everything.

Enthusiasm. Project enthusiasm, but be sure not to vary your facial expressions.

Sincerity. Appear sincere by using extensive humor and by indicating that your sales message is not really that important.

Friendliness. Be friendly, but businesslike by avoiding smiling, an unhurried approach, and a concern for feedback.

Eye Contact. Have appropriate eye contact with customers the appropriate percentage of time as follows: Americans, 10 percent; Japanese, 90 percent; and French, 35 percent.

CHAPTER 20

Oral Communication Applications

Learning Objectives

Your learning objectives for this chapter include the following:

- To describe the dynamics of interpersonal oral communication
- To communicate successfully in one-to-one oral communication situations
- To be an effective small-group leader and participant
- To prepare and deliver an effective presentation to a large group

C ommunicating orally is both challenging and rewarding. Because most business communication is oral, your success in business depends primarily on your ability to communicate orally. If you are a powerful oral communicator, you can effectively inform and persuade others—you can become a successful leader.

An understanding of the dynamics of interpersonal oral communication is necessary if you are to be effective. Also, if you are to improve your effectiveness, it is important to follow the keys for planning and presenting oral communication. It will be helpful to you in your study to think in terms of the three basic types of oral communication: one-to-one, one-to-small-group, and one-to-large-group.

The dynamics of interpersonal oral communication are discussed in the next section. This material is followed by keys for successful oral communication.

THE DYNAMICS OF INTERPERSONAL ORAL COMMUNICATION

When people communicate with each other, the communication situation is not static—the communication environment, the sender, and the receiver(s) are continually changing. The communication situation becomes increasingly complex when the communication is oral.

The important *human* variables in oral communication, which are continually changing and adding to the complexity of the situation, include such things as moods, interests, alertness, knowledge, status, trust, respect, power, confidence, honesty, needs, concerns, roles, beliefs, values, and opinions. Other important variables in interpersonal oral communication are the oral communication abilities of the senders and receivers.

The important *environmental* variables, which differ from situation to situation, include the number of people participating, the timing of the communication, the formality or informality of the situation, the nature of the physical location, and the purpose of the communication.

ONE-TO-ONE ORAL COMMUNICATION

One-to-one oral communication is probably the most important form of communication used in business. More critical business decisions are made in conversations between two people than in any other communication format.

Analysis of the receiver for the you–viewpoint (Chapter 1), use of the principles of business communication (Chapter 2), and effective message development (Chapter 3) are essential for effective one-to-one oral communication. As oral communication involves a constantly changing situation, continual analysis of your receiver during the communication is required. In addition, applying the principles of business communication as you carefully develop your next oral message in the exchange will help ensure your effectiveness. The success of an oral communication in this dynamic situation also depends on using care in sending the oral message, obtaining and using feedback, and eliminating any communication barriers that threaten the conversation.

Using several specific keys for successful one-to-one oral communication will further ensure success. Important types of one-to-one oral communication are face-to-face meetings and telephone conversations.

KEYS FOR SUCCESSFUL FACE-TO-FACE COMMUNICATION

The keys for successful face-to-face communication are based on an understanding of the dynamics of interpersonal oral communication. The situation is continually changing and evolving during a meeting with another person. Here are the keys for successful face-to-face oral communication.

> *Brevity is the best recommendation of speech, whether in a senator or an orator.*
>
> **Cicero**

BE CLEAR AND CONCISE

Use the principles of business communication so that your comments will be clear and concise. Think before you speak. Structure your sentences so that the receiver will understand them. Most receivers react favorably to the ideas of a sender who is concise and to the point. They do not want to hear extensive details that are not necessary for their understanding of the message. The strongest, most effective message is short and simple. However, in applying this key, use care not to appear abrupt.

LISTEN CAREFULLY

When people are conversing, they often think about what they are going to say next instead of listening to what the other person has to say. By giving your full attention, you hear what the other person is saying and can participate effectively in the conversation. If you listen carefully, you also make the other person feel that he or she is intelligent and interesting. Another important aspect of effective listening is not interrupting. Wait until you are sure the other person is through speaking before you start to talk.

OBSERVE NONVERBAL BEHAVIOR

Regardless of the verbal responses your receiver makes, his or her nonverbal behavior should be taken as the real message. You may tell an employee that you have decided to give a desirable assignment to a coworker. If the employee becomes teary-eyed while saying "fine, good," you know that it is not really fine and good. React to the nonverbal signals as well as to the verbal signals in face-to-face conversations.

Your conversations will produce more effective results if you give your full attention to those speaking to you.

- Ask questions to encourage effective conversation.

- Maintain eye contact to convey positive feelings.

- Use the receiver's name to show respect.

- Smile to create a favorable environment.

- Be appropriately assertive when handling difficult topics.

ASK QUESTIONS

One of the best ways to encourage another person to communicate is to ask questions. Carefully structured questions can elicit information you both want discussed. For example, if you are trying to help a subordinate improve the quality of his or her work, you can ask, "What can I do to help you do a better job?" This question will bring out the things you and the subordinate can do to improve the work. Receiver-centered questions will encourage involvement in the conversation. While you do not want the entire conversation to be an interrogation, carefully selected questions will stimulate response.

MAINTAIN APPROPRIATE EYE CONTACT

It has been said that the eyes are the mirror of the soul. Among humans, the eyes communicate a great deal. Shifting eyes with limited eye contact can communicate dishonesty, fear, or a lack of interest—all barriers to effective communication. Good eye contact conveys strength and sincerity. It makes people feel that you think they are important. Good eye contact is essential in face-to-face communication. In the American culture, a realistic goal is to maintain eye contact about 75 percent of the time. The desired amount of eye contact varies from culture to culture. The French are comfortable with eye contact almost 100 percent of the time, while most southeast Asians think eye contact in excess of approximately 10 percent of the time is rude. (See Chapter 5, International and Cross-Cultural Communication, for discussions of cultural variations.) Let your receiver and the circumstances determine when you will have eye contact.

USE THE RECEIVER'S NAME

A person's name is his or her most important possession. Find out what name a person likes to be called, and then use that name in conversation. You show care, concern, and respect for others when you use their names. In turn, they will show their appreciation by responding favorably.

SMILE APPROPRIATELY

When you smile at another person, you are saying "I like you." And everyone wants to be liked. A hostile atmosphere in a face-to-face conversation will cause many communication barriers. A warm, friendly environment improves oral communication.

BE APPROPRIATELY ASSERTIVE

It is possible to disagree without being disagreeable. Assertiveness does not mean aggressiveness; assertiveness does not alienate others. Be assertive by stating your views clearly and in a straightforward manner appropriate to the circumstances. For example, if you feel you deserve an above-average increase in salary, start a conversation with your boss by stating your view clearly: "Because of my performance this past year, I think that I deserve an above-average raise. Can we discuss this?"

CONTROL EMOTIONAL REACTIONS

• Control emotional reactions to build good business relations.

In business relationships people are expected to be calm, cool, controlled, and collected. Successful businesspersons do not argue; they discuss. In addition, avoid sarcastic remarks or inappropriate laughter that may embarrass others. Treat others as you would like to be treated, and your face-to-face conversations will be productive.

OTHER KEYS FOR SUCCESSFUL FACE-TO-FACE CONVERSATIONS

• Be honest, objective, sincere, and reasonable.

Other keys for successful face-to-face conversations are honesty, objectivity, sincerity, and reasonableness. Effective human interpersonal relations and communications are dependent on these attributes.

KEYS FOR SUCCESSFUL TELEPHONE CONVERSATIONS

Most of the keys for successful face-to-face conversations apply to telephone conversations as well. Only two do not apply directly—observing nonverbal behavior and maintaining appropriate eye contact. Even the suggestion to smile pleasantly applies to telephone conversations because the tone of your voice is more pleasant when you are smiling.

Telephone messages may be your most important oral communication.

The telephone is important for sending and receiving business messages. For some message receivers, in fact, the entire image of the company rests on their experience with you on the telephone. It is important, therefore, to use telephone equipment and the telephone system efficiently, to be considerate of callers, to plan calls carefully, to be businesslike, to avoid telephone tag, and to use answering machines and voice mail effectively. These keys for successful telephone conversations are fully discussed in the following paragraphs.

Follow these keys for successful telephone conversations:

USE THE TELEPHONE EQUIPMENT AND SYSTEM PROPERLY

• Use the telephone properly for efficiency.

Hold the telephone mouthpiece one to two inches from your mouth and talk directly into it. Keep the earpiece pressed gently against your ear to hear the caller. Of course, you should be careful not to drop the telephone because of the loud sound that would be transmitted to the caller. Remember that both the mouthpiece and the earpiece must be covered if you do not want your caller to hear you talking to a third party.

Be sure to learn how to use the telephone system in your organization. Know how to transfer calls efficiently, arrange conference calls, use a speaker phone, set up call-backs, and use other special features of your system. Employees who are not able to use the company telephone system properly will be perceived as inefficient, as will the organization.

BE CONSIDERATE OF YOUR CALLER

• Be considerate of your caller by being prompt and courteous.

Time passes very slowly while holding a telephone and waiting for an answer, waiting for a call to be transferred, or waiting for someone to return

Learn how to use the company telephone system.

to the phone. Fifteen seconds may seem like one to three minutes. Because the caller's perception of time is distorted, you must try to minimize his or her waiting time. Answer your phone on the first ring if possible. Transfer calls quickly and efficiently.

If you have to leave the telephone for more than 30 seconds during a conversation, return to the phone to let the caller know you are still there and will be back to the conversation as soon as possible.

Keep a pencil and notepad close to the telephone so that you do not waste the caller's time looking for these items if they are needed. Showing consideration for the caller in these ways will improve the effectiveness of your communications. Some companies try to alleviate, to a degree, the problem of customers and other callers being on hold by playing background music and periodically having a recorded message say that someone will be with the caller as soon as possible. These message may also include informational product advertising that would be of interest to the callers.

In addition, it is recommended that you place your own calls. Having an assistant place your calls and then keeping the party called waiting while you get on the line makes it appear that you feel your time is more valuable than the receiver's. Such a procedure is inconsiderate and gets the conversation off to a bad start.

Finally, be sure to use courteous words. Because you cannot be seen, your voice has to carry the whole message and convey its tone. Use cordial terms such as *please, thank you,* and *appreciate.*

PLAN YOUR CALLS CAREFULLY

- Plan your calls as you would plan any important message.

Before placing a telephone call, determine its specific purpose and outline its major points. Know what your opening remarks will be and have in mind any other comments you plan to make. It is often a good idea to do this planning on paper. Remember, a telephone call is a message—it is an oral letter, memo, or report. Planning is needed to make the call successful. Base your planning on both the purpose of the message and an analysis of the individual you are calling.

BE BUSINESSLIKE

- Be businesslike for effective telephone communication.

When answering the telephone, identify yourself immediately by giving the name of your organizational unit and your own name. For example, say, "Information Systems Department, John Sims." When you are placing a call, the telephone will most likely be answered initially by a receptionist, switchboard operator, or secretary. Either ask, "May I speak to Miss Lidia Sanchez, please?" or say, "Lidia Sanchez, please." It may be appropriate to respond to the initial answer to your call with more information such as,

"My name is John Sims, and I am calling Lidia Sanchez about a new tele-conferencing system."

During telephone conversations, take special care to enunciate clearly, use businesslike language, and keep messages short and simple. As is true of all communication, telephone messages will be more effective if they are receiver-centered. Visualize the person on the other end of the line and adapt the message to that person.

AVOID TELEPHONE TAG

- Avoid telephone tag to save time.

Telephone tag—two people calling back and forth and missing each other—is frustrating and unproductive. Avoid telephone tag by asking whoever answers for the best time to call the person you are trying to reach. Then call at that time. If that is not successful, try leaving a message indicating the times you would be available for a return call. Then be sure you are available when you say you will be. When leaving a message, indicate the purpose of your call so that when contact is finally made both persons can be prepared for a productive telephone conversation.

USE ANSWERING MACHINES AND VOICE MAIL EFFECTIVELY

- Use answering machines and voice-mail systems effectively for improving your efficiency.

If someone is not available at all times to answer your phone, consider installing an answering machine or a voice mail system. Answering machines and voice-mail systems have several advantages. They permit your caller to record the purpose of the call, his or her telephone number(s), and the best times to call back. Further, they may eliminate the need for additional calls by allowing the caller to simply record the message. Be prepared to have your calls answered by a machine or a computer. Have clearly in mind the message you will leave on an answering machine or in the voice-mail system.

ONE-TO-SMALL-GROUP ORAL COMMUNICATION

Small groups are formed to share information or solve problems.

Small group meetings in business are quite common. Small groups—usually referred to as committees, teams, or task forces—are formed for one of two basic purposes: to share information or to solve problems. Because of the interactions within small groups, the quality of the thinking that emerges from their meetings is almost always higher than what one person can achieve alone.

The Importance of Meetings

Top executives in the United States spend 17 hours a week in business meetings, and "preparations for the meetings average another six hours," said Ronald E. Gerevas, president of Heidrick & Struggles, a management recruiting firm. Because top executives typically work 61 hours a week, the meetings—and thinking about them—account for almost 38 percent of their time.

Source: As reported in *The Stars and Stripes*, July 1, 1988, p. 16.

TYPES OF SMALL GROUPS

Committees are standing or ad hoc.

Small groups are generally of two types: standing committees or ad hoc (a Latin term pronounced "add hock") committees. A standing committee has a continuing purpose and usually meets at regularly scheduled times. Standing committees in business have titles such as Finance Committee, Personnel Policy Committee, Social Committee, and Board of Directors. An ad hoc committee is a small group formed for a specific short-term purpose. It usually meets over a brief period of time and then is disbanded. Ad hoc committees in businesses have titles such as Task Force on Budget Reduction, Centennial Planning Committee, and Reorganization Committee.

SIZE OF SMALL GROUPS

Small groups have three to twenty members.

Small groups are defined as having three to twenty members. The most cost-effective size for meetings is thought by many to be five to seven members. Because most small-group meetings are operated democratically and votes are taken on issues, it is best to have an odd number of members in order to avoid tie votes.

During your career you will have many opportunities to be a group leader or a group participant. If you follow proven keys for successfully leading and participating in small groups, you can increase your personal effectiveness and the effectiveness of those groups.

KEYS FOR SUCCESSFUL SMALL-GROUP LEADERSHIP

Small group meetings are costly.

Small-group meetings in business are costly both in time and money. It is important that such meetings be conducted efficiently and effectively. Both

A group leader is primarily responsible for the efficiency and effectiveness of a meeting. Following the keys for small group leadership will help a group leader achieve success.

Follow these keys for successful small-group leadership:

• Determine the purpose and communicate it to participants.

• Plan the meeting agenda carefully and logically.

• Prepare the meeting properly and well in advance.

group leaders and participants must prepare themselves for meetings by analyzing the group members and planning for the communication that will take place. As in the case of one-to-one communication, group meetings are dynamic and require continual receiver analysis and message development.

The person primarily responsible for the success of a small-group meeting is the group leader. The keys for successful small-group leadership are presented in the following paragraphs.

DETERMINE THE PURPOSE OF THE GROUP

The purpose for forming the group should be clearly understood and communicated to all members. Is it an information-receiving group or a problem-solving group? What is the scope of its responsibility and authority? While the group will refine its purpose in its early meetings, the group leader is responsible initially for providing as much definition of the group's purpose as possible.

PLAN THE MEETING AGENDA

The group leader must prepare the meeting agenda carefully. The topics to be discussed should be listed in some logical order that will best serve the purpose of the group. For an informal meeting, the leader may simply have mental notes on the agenda that are shared with the participants at the outset of the meeting. For a formal meeting, copies of a written agenda should be distributed to the participants in advance of the meeting so that the members can prepare themselves. A sample agenda for a Personnel Policy Committee meeting is shown in Figure 20•1.

PREPARE THE MEETING FACILITY

The group leader is responsible for arranging for the meeting room and being sure it is properly prepared for the meeting. In preparing a meeting facility, the leader needs to consider the following: an adequate number of

Figure 20·1 Sample Meeting Agenda

❋ ORTEGA PRODUCTS, INC.

Human Resources Policy Committee
Agenda for Meeting
Tuesday, October 16, 199-
Room 207, Corporate Headquarters Building

1. Call to Order
2. Minutes of September 20 Meeting
3. Report of Salary Subcommittee
   a. Cost-of-Living Proposal
   b. Status of Merit Policy Survey
4. Report of Benefits Committee
   a. Increase in Medical Insurance Costs
   b. Recommendation on Group Life Policy
   c. Bids for Dental Health Plan
   d. Bids for Vision Care Plan
5. Old Business
6. New Business
7. Information Items
   a. New Employee Handbooks Availability
   b. Report on Multicultural Celebration
   c. Diversity Management Statistics and Report
8. Announcement of Next Meeting
9. Adjournment

chairs for participants; a table or tables, if needed; comfortable room temperature; lighting and location of light switches; the necessary audiovisual equipment, electrical outlets, cords, etc.; and, if appropriate, pens or pencils, notepads, refreshments, and extra copies of the agenda and related materials. The preparation of the meeting facility should be completed well in advance of the meeting. In addition, it is wise to check on the facility an hour before the meeting starts to be sure all is in order. The leader should arrive a few minutes early for the meeting to make a final check of the meeting facility.

LEAD THE GROUP DISCUSSION

• Lead the group discussion to achieve the group's purpose.

During the meeting the primary role of the leader is to assist the group in achieving its purpose. This means keeping the discussion focused on the group tasks and not allowing the discussion to stray to unrelated topics. It means moving from one item on the agenda to the next after adequate discussion.

When speaking to a small group, the group leader must be prepared to be interrupted with questions or comments. A good group leader actually talks very little during group discussion. Rather he or she encourages participation, controls excessive talkers, and summarizes periodically. A good group leader is a catalyst—one who causes the group participants to work together effectively.

An effective leader secures group decisions after adequate discussion. Group decision-making may be by consensus or by vote, depending on the subject matter and the formality of the group. The formality of the group also determines the procedures that will be followed. Formal groups will likely use parliamentary procedure as described in *Robert's Rules of Order,* or a similar guide. Informal groups will give less attention to procedure and more attention to achieving the group purpose by whatever approach seems most expedient.

RESOLVE GROUP CONFLICTS

Often participants in group meetings take opposing positions. If the group leader does not resolve these conflicts within the group, the meeting's progress may be inhibited. The first task in conflict resolution is to be sure the basic issue in the disagreement is clear. Sometimes clarifying the issue resolves the conflict. If the conflict continues after the issue is clarified, the leader has several options including the following:

1. A group vote can be taken, leaving the decision to majority rule.
2. The discussion can be postponed, giving time for reflection.
3. The conflict can be submitted to an arbitrator, such as a superior officer in the company.
4. A compromise can be sought through group discussion.
5. The leader may simply move on to the next agenda item after deciding the conflict is not worthy of the group's time.

ENCOURAGE APPROPRIATE PARTICIPATION

The group leader is responsible for eliciting the best contributions possible from each participant. If the group is a committee formed of employees from different levels in an organization, there is the possibility that some higher-level people might intimidate some of the lower-level people. This must be avoided if at all possible. While formed into a group with a specific purpose, all employees should be considered equal in order to obtain effective contributions from all participants.

The leader usually faces two challenges in achieving appropriate participation by members of the group. One challenge is to politely curtail those who talk too much, and the other is to encourage those who talk too little.

Ways to control those who talk too much are as follows:

1. At the end of a sentence, thank the excessive talker and then ask other participants for their opinions on the topic.
2. Stress to the whole group that it is important for everyone to have an equal chance to comment.
3. Suggest that the group is beginning to cover the same territory again and that it needs to move on.
4. Remind the whole group (never an individual publicly) that participation should be uniform.

The following are effective ways to encourage those who talk too little:

1. Ask them directly by name for their viewpoints.
2. Accept any comments they make, even if they are not of the highest quality.

- Resolve group conflict by clarifying the issue or using other proven techniques.

- Encourage participation by ensuring equality, curtailing those who talk too much, and motivating those who talk too little.

3. Ask them direct questions, drawing on their particular expertise relative to the topic.

4. Thank them for their contributions.

BE TIME CONSCIOUS

• Be time conscious at the beginning of, during, and at the ending of the meeting.

The group leader should start the meeting on time (not waiting for latecomers) and adjourn the meeting on time. Periodically, the leader may need to remind the group that it has time constraints. Comments on time must be made judiciously, however, or they will curtail desirable discussion. The leader, probably in cooperation with the group, should make judgments on how much time will be devoted to each topic and when the meeting will adjourn. Some of these decisions can be made at the beginning of the meeting; others may be made while the meeting is in progress. The leader should end the meeting positively by summarizing what has been accomplished.

MAINTAIN APPROPRIATE RECORDS

• Maintain appropriate records yourself or elect or appoint a secretary to do it.

The group leader should maintain a record of the group's accomplishments. If a detailed record is desired, the leader should have a secretary elected or appointed for recording and distributing minutes of the meetings. A group may have the secretary keep minutes on newsprint or flip charts during the meeting so that all members can see and agree on the actions being recorded. Suggestions for preparing minutes for group meetings are given in Chapter 16, pages 453–454.

If formal minutes or other records of the group's activity are kept, they should be distributed promptly to members following each meeting. This procedure will enable members to note any corrections for the record while the meeting is still fresh in mind.

KEYS FOR SUCCESSFUL SMALL-GROUP PARTICIPATION

An effective small-group leader will also be an effective small-group participant. There are, however, a few additional considerations for those serving as participants. The following keys for successful small-group participation will increase your effectiveness in meetings.

Follow these keys for successful small-group participation:

PREPARE TO PARTICIPATE

• Prepare to participate by gathering and studying information.

Every member of a small group should learn as much as possible about the group's purpose. If an agenda is provided in advance, information can be gathered on each topic to assure intelligent participation. All available background information should be gathered and studied for the first and succeeding meetings of the group.

PARTICIPATE APPROPRIATELY

• Participate appropriately by giving businesslike input.

The knowledge of all the participants in a group is essential for group success. All group members should talk during group meetings, but not talk too much. The basic principle of business communication—keep it short and simple—should be followed. Also, participants must maintain objectivity in their comments and control their emotions. Meetings are not the place to argue, but rather to discuss.

LISTEN EFFECTIVELY

Committee meetings or other small-group meetings can challenge listening skills. Group members will spend most of their time listening to other participants' comments and must strive to keep their concentration. Members should not have side conversations, gaze into space, or exhibit other behavior that detracts from the effectiveness of their participation as listeners. More than once participants have been surprised when, without warning, a speaker asked them what they thought. Listeners must be ready to become speakers at any time.

BE COURTEOUS

In small-group meetings it is important for all participants to respect the rights and opinions of others. Opinions should be expressed tactfully, avoiding any indication of self-righteousness. By accepting different viewpoints and by being willing to discuss them, participants can help encourage open, free discussion. Members should avoid interrupting speakers or using sarcasm, and should use humor carefully. In successful small-group meetings, members treat each other the way they would like to be treated.

ONE-TO-LARGE-GROUP ORAL COMMUNICATION

Many people in business are required to make oral presentations to large groups—20 or more people—from time to time. The purpose of these oral presentations will be either (1) *to inform* the audience of certain facts, or (2) *to persuade* the audience to accept a point of view or take a certain action. Your career and your organization will benefit if you can achieve these two purposes effectively in your one-to-large-group oral communication.

TYPES OF ORAL PRESENTATIONS

There are several different types of oral presentations in business: briefings, oral reports, talks, and speeches. The length of these presentations can vary from less than a minute to an hour or more. The ideal length for a long presentation is 20 minutes or less.

Depending on your position, you may be asked to brief a group of employees on, for example, the status of union negotiations. Or you may be asked to give an oral report to company officers on the market research your department has been conducting. You might be requested to give a 20-minute talk to a college group on the rewards of your profession. Or you may be asked to give a 30-minute speech to a financial officers association on financing overseas production facilities. Assuming that you have the time, knowledge, and expertise needed, you will want to respond positively to these requests. Making such presentations will generally serve you and your organization well.

Other types of oral presentations that businesspeople are commonly asked to make are introductions, greetings, and recognitions. You may be asked to introduce a speaker, extend a welcome and greetings to a visiting group, or give recognition or an award for outstanding service.

A final way of looking at the different types of oral presentations is by the way they are delivered to the audience. There are four basic types of delivery: manuscript, memorized, impromptu, and extemporaneous.

MANUSCRIPT ORAL PRESENTATION

A **manuscript oral presentation** is written word for word and then read to the audience. This type of presentation is used when precise wording is required, as in a presidential address. Delivering such a presentation is difficult and should be avoided except in very special circumstances.

MEMORIZED ORAL PRESENTATION

A **memorized oral presentation** is one in which the speaker has memorized the content verbatim. While this is a way of avoiding notes, it, too, is a difficult presentation to do well. It is likely to appear canned, and there is the danger of forgetting parts of the presentation. A better method is to memorize parts—for example, the opening and closing remarks—rather than trying to memorize the entire presentation.

IMPROMPTU ORAL PRESENTATION

An **impromptu oral presentation** is one a person is required to give without special preparation. This request to talk comes as a surprise; the speaker is given no preparation time. For example, in a meeting of the company's sales force, you may be asked by your boss, "Owen, would you say a few words to the group about your experience in the Indiana territory?" While you must remain calm and think quickly in this situation, following the suggestions in the remainder of this chapter will help you do a good job.

EXTEMPORANEOUS ORAL PRESENTATION

An **extemporaneous oral presentation** can be defined in one of two ways. It is a briefing, talk, oral report, or speech that is (1) quickly composed and delivered with little preparation time, or (2) carefully prepared and delivered

---

Oral presentations include briefings, oral reports, talks, and speeches.

Other types of oral presentations are introductions, greetings, and recognitions.

A manuscript oral presentation is read to the audience.

A memorized oral presentation is learned verbatim.

An impromptu oral presentation is one that has to be given without preparation.

An extemporaneous oral presentation is prepared and given from notes.

from notes or an outline. The latter type of extemporaneous presentation is the most effective delivery style and the one recommended. This type of extemporaneous presentation does not require reading from a script, memorizing, or speaking without preparation. It is a more spontaneous and a more natural way to relate to an audience, because speaking from brief notes or an outline permits good eye contact, allows free movement, and permits the speaker to respond to audience feedback. This method of extemporaneous oral presentation is the basis for the discussion in the rest of this chapter.

Effective one-to-large-group oral communication depends on careful preparation and good delivery techniques. Keys for successfully preparing and delivering an oral presentation are given in the following paragraphs.

KEYS FOR SUCCESSFULLY PREPARING AN ORAL PRESENTATION

The foundation for a successful oral presentation is adequate preparation. Adequate preparation will give you confidence and will assure your audience of an interesting and informative presentation. What is adequate preparation? Some speakers say they spend 40 hours in preparation for each hour of oral presentation. As an average, that is probably a good guideline.

> *It usually takes more than three weeks to prepare a good impromptu speech.*
>
> **Mark Twain**

As noted in Chapter 19, you may be a member of a small group—a committee, task force, panel, or team—that is responsible for giving a presentation to an audience. If so, you will collaborate with others to some degree in preparing the oral presentation. Effective group collaborative work is discussed in Chapter 3, Developing Business Messages, pages 77–79.

DETERMINE YOUR PURPOSE

The first key is to determine the purpose of the oral presentation. It will fall into one of two categories: *to inform* or *to persuade*. Stating the purpose clearly and simply will assist you in focusing on the remaining part of the preparation. Your statement of the purpose of an oral presentation should be in terms of the expected result. Here are some example purpose statements:

1. To inform the employees of Leigh Acala's contributions during her 20 years of service.
2. To inform the audience of recent market research for a product line.
3. To persuade employees to give to the United Appeal fund.
4. To persuade management to increase the department's budget for salaries.

When the primary purpose of an oral presentation is *to inform,* you want the audience to learn, to understand, or to know more about the topic. That is the expected result. When the primary purpose is *to persuade,* you want the audience either to adopt your viewpoint or take specific action; that is the expected result.

ANALYZE YOUR AUDIENCE

- Analyze your audience for a you–viewpoint presentation.

The second step in preparing an oral report is to decide exactly who will be in the audience. Then, in so far as possible, analyze each member's knowledge, interests, opinions, and emotional state regarding your topic. For extremely large audiences, you may need to think in terms of categories of receivers. Build your oral presentation on this analysis of the audience. Plan to provide information that is not already known. Choose your words to fit your listeners' vocabulary. Consider carefully the audience motivation for listening to the presentation. Why is it important personally to your listeners? Prepare to offset any potential negative emotional reaction to your presentation. Audience analysis should continue during the presentation; for improvement or for record purposes, a formal evaluation of audience reaction should be made after the presentation.

GATHER SUPPORTING INFORMATION

- Gather supporting information for the presentation.

When you have stated your purpose and analyzed the audience, you are ready to gather ideas and materials to support the development of your oral presentation. An oral presentation is researched in the same manner as a written presentation.

The kinds of helpful information to gather include definitions, examples, illustrations, explanations, quotations, statistics, testimonials, comparisons, and analogies. This information can come from your personal knowledge and resources, secondary sources, or primary sources.

ORGANIZE YOUR PRESENTATION

- Organize your presentation using a logical organizational pattern.

As you gather supporting information, you will begin to have an idea of the best way to organize the information for presentation. The overall organizational framework you should use for an oral presentation is as follows:

1. Opening
2. Body
3. Closing

This framework will assist you in following the successful public speaking formula: Tell them what you are going to tell them, tell them, and then tell them what you told them.

In addition to the overall framework of opening, body, and closing, you need to determine a logical organizational pattern or patterns for the body of the presentation. Here are some frequently used patterns:

1. *Time sequence.* Review pertinent material from oldest to newest or from newest to oldest.
2. *Spatial relation.* Describe from top to bottom, bottom to top, left to right, right to left, inside to outside, outside to inside, room to room, desk to desk, or from some other spatial flow pattern.

3. *Problem–solution.* Describe the problem(s) and present the solution(s).
4. *Cause–effect.* Show the relationship between events.
5. *Direct or indirect.* Start or end with the main point.
6. *Comparison or contrast.* Show the similarities and dissimilarities of the subject matter.
7. *Topics–subtopics.* Organize the subject according to its logical parts.

A combination of these organizational patterns may be used within the body of an oral presentation. Use the patterns that you think will best serve your audience.

The supporting information you gather should be arranged following the organizational patterns you have selected. Once the information is organized, you can determine the types of audiovisual aids that will best strengthen the presentation.

PREPARE AUDIOVISUAL AIDS

- Prepare audiovisual aids to strengthen the message.

Audiovisual aids should be clear, simple, and cost-effective.

Audiovisual aids can be used to strengthen the message—make it more interesting, understandable, and comprehensive. The use of these aids can spark audience attention and add desirable variety.

When deciding on audiovisual aids, ask yourself the following questions: Will this aid make my message clearer? Will it be simple enough to be understood? Will it be worth the time it will take to develop it? Will it

> Once your information is organized, you can determine the types of audiovisual aids that will best strengthen your presentation.

enhance my message? If your answer to any of these questions is no, you should not use the aid.

Some speakers hand out copies of their speeches to the audience as a visual aid. This type of handout violates every one of the criteria implied by the preceding questions. Be sure the audiovisual aid you select will enhance your remarks rather that detract from them.

There is a great variety of audiovisual aids from which to choose. Chapter 17 will be helpful to you in preparing visuals. A brief review of some of the best audiovisuals is presented here.

Projected Material. The most common and the most helpful audiovisual aids are those that project information onto a large screen that can be seen by every member of the audience. Probably the simplest, most flexible, least costly technique is to project information using a transparency on an overhead projector.

The most sophisticated projection technique uses computer-generated visuals. Extensive computer software and projection equipment is available for creating a great variety of high-quality projected material. With this software and equipment, you can use a microcomputer to project material from your color monitor. Just key in new assumptions and create a multiplicity of attractive visual aids—changing line charts, pie charts, spreadsheets, organization structures, plant layouts, and on and on. This flexibility permits you to interact with your audience, explore alternatives and answer questions. Some equipment permits you to write on the images to support your explanation. See Chapter 4 for additional communication technology information.

A computer can be used to create any number of slides that can be projected automatically on a timed basis for employee training sessions, for an automated trade-show display, or other similar purposes. If preferred, a presenter can control the rate, timing, and order of the slide projection to coincide with points in a speech. Copies of the computer-generated visuals can be printed for distribution to the audience.

Videodisc technology provides a presenter with almost unlimited flexibility in playing back slides in any order, starting and stopping movies at any point, and displaying a variety of images. Graphics, sounds, animation, photos, and movies can be integrated using videodiscs. Many other types of projection alternatives exist, including opaque, 35-mm slide, video cassette, motion picture film, and filmstrip. Each technique can be an effective complement to an oral presentation.

Flip Charts and Posters. Easels are available for displaying flip charts or posters. These visual aids can be produced easily at a low cost or prepared professionally at a higher cost. They can be effective if they are kept very simple and if they can be read by every member of the audience. Flip charts are good for topical outlines of a presentation. Posters can be used effectively for charts, graphs, tables, drawings, and pictograms.

Whiteboards. Many well-equipped meeting rooms now have whiteboards—easily wipeable marker boards—for speakers' use. Also, you can arrange for portable whiteboards. Markers in varied colors can be used on

> You can project material in a variety of ways.

> You can display material on an easel.

> You can use whiteboards to develop a visual aid while you speak.

the whiteboards, permitting the visual aid to be developed and changed as the presentation is being made.

Use simple handouts before and during your presentation and detailed ones afterwards.

Handouts. Handouts can be used effectively to present an outline of your presentation to an audience. Also, illustrative material can be distributed in this manner. Handouts that are too extensive will detract from a presentation. If you are going to hand out a copy of your talk or speech at the end, let the audience know this in advance. They can concentrate better on your comments if they do not have to worry about taking notes. Pass out any complex supplementary material you think the audience should have at the end of the presentation rather than before or during it.

Models and physical objects can strengthen a presentation.

Models and Physical Objects. In many business presentations you will have a product to display, either in actual or in model form. This kind of visual aid can strengthen a sales presentation to the extent that the sale might be impossible without it. Again, it is important that any physical objects or models used as visual aids be large enough so that every member of the audience can see them.

Audio aids should be used selectively.

Audio Tapes and Recordings. Variety and impact are made possible by supplementing your oral presentation with an audio aid. When speaking on noise reduction in a factory, it could be effective to have recordings of factory sounds in different settings with different sound treatments. Because audio aids are, in a sense, disembodied sounds, limited use of them is appropriate. An audience can tire quickly of simply listening to sound and not having visual stimuli.

PREPARE YOUR PRESENTATION

Prepare your presentation by organizing supporting data.

You know your purpose. You have analyzed your audience. You have gathered and organized supporting data. You have prepared your audiovisual aids. You are now ready to put all this information together in a coherent oral presentation.

> *Speak clearly, if you speak at all; carve every word before you let it fall.*
>
> **Oliver Wendell Holmes**

Plan to use an extemporaneous delivery technique.

Different speakers approach this task differently. You will recall that the carefully prepared, extemporaneous delivery technique has been recommended for business presentations. So you must prepare notes to prompt you and guide you through the presentation. These notes may be on 5″ by 8″ cards, on sheets of paper in large print, or in some other form. Some speakers write out their entire presentation and then make notes from the manuscript. After reading through the manuscript a few times, they put it aside (maybe even throw it away) so that they will not be tempted to read it to the audience. Other speakers simply make an outline and then make notes from the outline, never writing the entire presentation. However you arrive at your fully developed presentation, here are suggestions for each of the major parts.

The audience evaluates the speaker during the opening.

The Opening.   An effective opening to an oral presentation is crucial. The audience evaluates your credibility and capability as a speaker in the first few minutes; and, regardless of what you do later, it is almost impossible to change that evaluation. A good first impression will serve you and your audience well throughout a presentation.

After thanking the person who introduced you, use your opening to get the audience's attention and interest. Effective ways to open a presentation include the use of a surprising statement, a quotation, an anecdote, a humorous story, a question, a statement of a problem, a historical reference, an impressive statistic, a visual aid, a reference to the situation, or an illustration. Whatever way you choose to open a presentation, be sure that you know the opening well and that it relates closely to your topic.

The opening should be brief. Use it to lead into the body of your presentation. Include a preview or overview of the main part of the talk and a transition statement. The opening should set the mood for the presentation and establish rapport between you and the audience. The opening is so crucial to the success of your presentation that you should give it careful attention in your preparation.

The body contains most of the information.

The Body.   Most of the information you present to the audience will be contained in the middle of the presentation—in the body. Using the organized information developed earlier, plan this portion of your oral presentation carefully. Follow the selected organizational pattern and make final decisions on how you will present and use the audiovisual aids.

As you develop the body of an oral presentation consider these guidelines:

Successful oral presentations depend on careful preparation and good delivery techniques.

1. *Hold the listeners' attention.* Maintain the listeners' attention and interest developed in the opening. Continue to keep your presentation audience-centered. Use the you–viewpoint. Use many examples and illustrations to create images in the minds of your listeners.

2. *Emphasize your main points.* Use the emphasis techniques given in Chapter 2—short sentences, repetition, specificity, mechanical means, and pointing out what is important. You might say, "This is my most important point . . . ," "Listen to this . . . ," "This, then, is the critical issue." You can use audiovisual aids to give emphasis. Use statistics and examples to support main points. Make descriptions vivid.

3. *Keep your presentation simple.* Deal with a few main points. Audiences cannot comprehend complex, detailed information. That kind of information should be presented in written form so that it can be studied and reread. Match your vocabulary to that of your audience. Provide a smooth transition from one point to the next. Limit uninterrupted talking (talking without any audience activity) to no more than 20 minutes.

4. *Involve your listeners in the presentation.* One way to involve listeners was mentioned earlier—helping them to form images that support your points. More direct ways of getting audience involvement include asking questions and conducting discussions. Encouraging members of the audience to ask questions is another way. Finally, there are many ways to have the audience participate directly in activities related to the topic, such as small-group discussions, exercises, and demonstrations. Providing for listener involvement in some manner is important to your success.

The Closing. In the closing, definitely let the audience know that you are ending; summarize the main points of your presentation; specify what the audience should do; and part with the audience on a positive, professional note.

Use both verbal and nonverbal signals to let the audience know you are ending the oral presentation. Ways you can do this include saying, "In summary . . . ," "In closing . . . ," "To review . . . ," or "In conclusion . . . ." A more subtle way is to pause and lower the pitch of your voice to show finality. Making a significant change in your stance relative to the lectern is another way.

In summarizing the main points of your presentation, you can repeat them, have a visual aid summary, or ask the audience to review them with you. The summary should be a very simple statement designed to tie together all the main points.

Specifying what the audience is to do is tied closely to the summary. You may tell your listeners how to use the information you have given them or what action to take based on your persuasion.

Your final goal in the closing will be to part from your audience on a positive, professional note. You want your listeners to remember you and your presentation. You can use some of the suggested opening techniques for the closing. The suitable techniques include a surprising statement, a quotation, an anecdote, a humorous story (carefully used), or an illustration. The closing is an important point of emphasis for your presentation. Be positive and optimistic. Be professional. Most important of all, use the you–viewpoint in the closing.

REHEARSE YOUR PRESENTATION

Rehearse your presentation aloud using your notes and audiovisual aids.

Using the notes and audiovisual aids you have developed, rehearse your oral presentation. Some speech authorities recommend that you rehearse a presentation aloud at least six times, on your feet, as though you were in the real-life situation.

Get feedback on your rehearsal.

Feedback on your rehearsal will be important to you. To get feedback, rehearse in front of a mirror or before friends, relatives, or colleagues. You can use an audio or a video recorder for this purpose as well. This practice affords the opportunity for revising content and fine tuning your delivery. It also gives you experience in handling your audiovisual aids efficiently. It is the only way you can be sure of the length of your presentation.

Communication Notes

Speaking in Public

The greatest cause of failure among speeches is not stage fright or delivery technique or the appearance of the speaker. If a speech fails, it is usually because it was written at the last minute and delivered without ever being rehearsed.

The speaker most likely to succeed is the one who has put many long hours into preparation. The public platform should hold no terrors for the person who knows the subject and knows what he or she wants to say.

As reported in *Royal Bank Letter,* Royal Bank of Canada, Vol. 73, No. 6, November/December 1992, p. 1.

Rehearsing your oral presentation is essential to its success. Practice will increase your familiarity with the material and your confidence in delivering it.

KEYS FOR SUCCESSFULLY DELIVERING AN ORAL PRESENTATION

Use all the information in Chapter 19 to strengthen the delivery of presentations.

All the material you studied in Chapter 19, "Oral Communication Essentials," applies to the delivery of an oral presentation. You will want to use your voice effectively and project a strong presence. You will want to vary your pitch, volume, and speed for emphasis while speaking. You will want to enunciate sounds clearly and pronounce words correctly. Your poise and bearing should convey confidence, enthusiasm, sincerity, and friendliness. Have the appropriate eye contact with your audience. You will want to use natural gestures. Your appearance should be appropriate for the audience and the situation.

Follow these keys for successfully delivering your presentation:

You have prepared your oral presentation and now you are ready to deliver it. Here are keys to guide you in successfully delivering your oral presentation.

START POSITIVELY

Several hours before you are to speak, check the speaking location to orient yourself and to determine if everything you need is in place (or will be before your presentation). Check the lectern and make sure it is the right height for you. Learn how to operate the equipment controls and the power supply and locate the room thermostat. Determine who can help if things go wrong.

Arrive five to ten minutes prior to the time you are to speak so you can make a final check of the facilities and the equipment. The lighting, room temperature, public address system, audiovisual equipment, lectern, and seating arrangement should support and strengthen your presentation. Be sure your notes and visual aids are with you and in correct order.

When the program starts and while you are being introduced, look pleasantly and confidently at the audience. After your introduction, walk with authority to the lectern. Arrange your notes and audiovisual aids. Look at the audience, and give the opening of your presentation. It is good to memorize at least the first part, if not all, of the opening. In this way you can concentrate on the audience and your delivery and not have to worry about checking your notes for the content of the opening.

Remember that your delivery is part performance and part content. Both must be well prepared for a successful delivery.

HANDLE STAGE FRIGHT

One way to handle stage fright is to realize that even the most practiced and professional speakers have some "racehorse" nervousness before speaking to an audience. One night while Johnny Carson was standing in the wings ready to go on the "Tonight Show," his pulse rate was taken. This seasoned performer's heart rate was an excited 180 beats a minute! Don't be surprised if your own heart rate is accelerated. Inconspicuously taking a few deep breaths before getting up to speak helps calm many speakers.

Another way of dealing with nervousness that threatens to detract from a successful delivery is to talk to yourself. As you go to the lectern tell yourself that you are glad to be there and glad that the audience is there. Remind yourself that you know more about your presentation than anyone in the audience. You have prepared thoroughly and look forward to this opportunity to share information with your audience or persuade it to some action.

Finally, an important way to handle stage fright is to concentrate on the you–viewpoint. Keep the audience's needs, interests, and concerns at the center of your attention. Keep reminding yourself that you are there to benefit the audience and that you can do it.

USE AUDIOVISUAL AIDS EFFECTIVELY

You have chosen visuals that complement your presentation and have designed them so that the audience can read or hear everything in them. You have practiced handling them efficiently. To use them effectively during your delivery, simply take advantage of your careful preparation.

EVALUATE AUDIENCE FEEDBACK

Maintain good eye contact with the members of the audience so that you can secure feedback on how the presentation is progressing. As you will recall, during interpersonal oral communication the situation is constantly changing.

- Start positively by checking the facility, being prepared, and giving the opening confidently in a clear, strong voice.

- Handle stage fright by thinking positively, talking to yourself, and concentrating on the you–viewpoint.

- Use audiovisual aids effectively based on your preparation.

- Evaluate audience feedback and make necessary adjustments.

Assess your listeners' changing reactions and make necessary adjustments to keep their attention and interest. Are you sure they can all hear you? If not, speak louder. Can they all see the visual aids? If not, make adjustments. Is their interest waning? If so, change your pace, pick up your enthusiasm, and start involving them in some way. Do they seem not to understand a point? If so, ask them questions about it, repeat it in other words, or ask a volunteer to explain his or her understanding of the point. Do members of the audience show signs of discomfort? Do they appear to be too hot or too cold? If so, ask them about it and have the necessary adjustment made. Using the feedback you get from an audience can strengthen the effectiveness of an oral presentation.

END POSITIVELY

- End positively using a clear, strong voice.

Endings, like beginnings, are important. They are points of emphasis. You have prepared the content for the closing of your oral presentation. During your delivery of that closing, use a clear, strong voice. Your poise and bearing should be at their best. Even if the body of your presentation did not meet your highest expectations, you can recoup a great deal with an effective closing. At this point, eye contact with the audience should be 100 percent. You should be focusing exclusively on your audience and using the you–viewpoint.

A question-and-answer session following a presentation can be used to enhance your relationship with the audience.

After the closing there may be a question-and-answer session. This is common in business oral presentations. This is an excellent opportunity to relate positively to the audience. You can clarify your points, you can reemphasize points, and you can directly answer any concerns of the audience. In your preparation, you may have been able to anticipate many of the questions and thus have the answers ready.

Use all your knowledge about interpersonal oral communication during the question-and-answer session. Listen carefully, answer concisely, respect opposing viewpoints, and control your emotions.

A CONCLUDING COMMENT ON ORAL COMMUNICATION

Following the keys for successfully preparing and delivering oral presentations can make your one-to-large-group oral communication a most enjoyable and rewarding experience. With practice and additional opportunities to speak, your ability to make oral presentations will improve. Chances are your business career success will grow as you grow in your ability to make effective oral presentations.

Business career success depends on effective oral communication.

This chapter has dealt with the keys for successfully planning and presenting oral communications. These keys concentrated on improving your effectiveness in one-to-one, one-to-small-group, and one-to-large-group oral communication in business settings. Using the information given in Chapters 19 and 20 can enhance your success as an effective oral business communicator.

DISCUSSION QUESTIONS

1. Describe the dynamics of interpersonal oral communication.

2. Describe each of the following keys for successful face-to-face oral communication and give an example of its implementation: (a) Observe nonverbal behavior, (b) ask questions, (c) be appropriately assertive, and (d) control emotional reactions.

3. What are the six keys for successful telephone conversations?

4. Describe the types of small groups.

5. Discuss the nature of small-group meetings.

6. The keys for successful small-group leadership can be categorized as things to do before meetings, during meetings, and after meetings. Briefly describe the keys for each category.

7. Describe in detail how to resolve group conflicts.

8. What are the responsibilities of a small-group participant?

9. Briefly describe the four basic types of delivery of oral presentations.

10. Discuss the purposes of presentations to large groups.

11. Discuss the keys for successfully preparing an oral presentation.

12. How do you decide on the content and nature of audiovisual aids for use with a presentation to a large group?

13. Discuss the important functions of the opening, the body, and the closing of an oral presentation.

14. Describe how a person who is speaking to a large group can handle stage fright effectively.

APPLICATION EXERCISES

1. Select a national leader and analyze his or her oral communication delivery techniques in (a) news conferences, and (b) speeches.

2. Analyze the last three face-to-face conversations you have had. Write a report indicating the strengths and weaknesses of your oral communication performance in these conversations. Suggest improvements that should be made in your next face-to-face conversations.

3. Prepare a manuscript on a topic of your choice for a one-minute oral presentation to the class. Read the manuscript to the class. The class members will provide brief, anonymously written evaluations of the effectiveness of the presentation.

4. Memorize a one-minute oral presentation on a topic of your choice. Deliver the presentation to the class. The class members will provide brief, anonymously written evaluations of the effectiveness of the presentation.

5. Members of the class will be selected by the instructor to give impromptu oral presentations to the class. Each speaker's topic will be assigned immediately before his or her presentation.

6. Form teams of three to four students. Each team is to interview a manager and ask for his or her opinion on the effectiveness of committees, teams, or task forces in business organizations. Share the findings with the class.

7. Prepare a three-minute (or longer, as specified by your instructor) extemporaneous oral presentation for the class on a topic of your choice. Be sure to use all the keys given in this chapter for successfully preparing an oral presentation.

8. Deliver the oral presentation that you prepared for Exercise 7. Be sure to use all the keys for successfully delivering an oral presentation.

9. In a small group of five or seven students, choose a leader and an observer. Discuss the problems of handling stage fright before and during a presentation to a large group. In this exercise, practice either the keys for successful leadership or the keys for successful participation, depending on your role in the group. After the group discussion, the observer should report to the class on the group's findings and its successes and failures in achieving effective and efficient group discussion.

10. Introduce a member of the class to the class. Use the overall framework of opening, body, and closing for your introduction.

11. In one minute, convince the members of the class that they should study business communication. Have an opening, body, and closing in your remarks.

12. Welcome members of the class (a) to the first class meeting, (b) to the final examination, (c) to the first day of oral presentations, or (d) to some other interesting class meeting.

MESSAGE ANALYSIS

Text 20B

Rewrite the following INSTRUCTIONS FOR COMMITTEE CHAIRS, correcting the errors in content. Refer to the Chapter 20 section on "Keys for Successful Small-Group Leadership" as a resource.

1. *Purpose.* When you meet with your committee, ask it what its purpose is.

2. *Agenda.* At the beginning of each committee meeting, determine from the group the agenda it thinks most important.

3. *Facility.* Upon arriving at the meeting facility, determine that it meets committee needs.

4. *Discussion.* Do not interrupt committee members; let them determine the direction and flow of the discussion.

5. *Conflicts.* If conflict develops, change the subject and later meet with each individual member of the committee to try to reach consensus.

6. *Participation.* Let each member of the committee determine the amount, nature, and content of his or her participation in the group discussion.

7. *Time Factors.* Do not start committee meetings until all members are present. Have committee members vote on the meeting ending time.

8. *Records.* The committee chair's primary responsibility during committee meetings is the recording of a detailed record of the proceedings.

PART 6

Employment Communication

COMMUNICATION NEWS

Learn All You Can About a Potential Employer

An important part of a job search is to learn as much as you can about each potential employer. Learn about the company's goals, products, financial status, managerial philosophy, and employee selection process. A basic marketing principle is that you can be successful in selling a product if you know all about the customer. In a job search, the product is you and the customer is the potential employer. Here is an analysis of a company's recruitment process. If you were to apply for a position with Toyota Motor Manufacturing, U.S.A., Inc., you should know that:

- *Toyota is committed philosophically to the concept of kaizen, or the gradual, ongoing improvement of every employee.*

- *The employee selection process focuses primarily on the job candidate's potential rather than background.*

- *The candidate must show that he or she can accept responsibility and work effectively with others.*

- *Essential employee qualities are flexibility, diligence, perseverance, and a commitment to kaizen.*

- *Effective employee performance depends on abilities to meet with management, identify and solve problems, provide initiative, and communicate orally.*

To determine if job candidates were acceptable for employment in its Georgetown (Kentucky) facility, Toyota followed a multiphase selection system:

Advertising and Recruitment. *Jobs were advertised in all Kentucky state employment offices.*

Orientation and Application. *Job candidates completed application forms, received a Toyota fact sheet, and saw a video on management philosophy. Applicants could opt out at this point.*

Technical Skills Assessment. *Several written tests were administered including the Situational Judgment Inventory (SJI) test.*

> You can be successful in selling a product if you know all about the customer. In a job search, the product is you and the customer is the employer.

Day of Work Simulation. *Job candidates were evaluated using simulations on teamwork, group discussion, problem solving, and work output.*

The Toyota Assessment. *Candidates still under consideration at this point were interviewed by Toyota human resources and line managers using a special targeted selection technique. Preliminary job offers were extended at this stage in compliance with the Americans with Disabilities Act.*

Health Assessment. *Drug and alcohol tests and a physical examination were administered. Confirming job offers were extended to successful candidates.*

As reported in Chuck Consentino, John Allen, and Richard Wellins, "Choosing the Right People," *HRMagazine* (March 1990), pp. 66–70. Updated April 1994 by Toyota Motor Manufacturing, U.S.A., Inc.

It's Your Turn

How would you have obtained the above information about Toyota? Research a company of your choice and list essential information that a job candidate should know.

CHAPTER 21

The Job Search and Resume

Learning Objectives

Your learning objectives for this chapter include the following:

- To describe the sources of information about job opportunities and job requirements
- To analyze your qualifications for employment
- To prepare effective general and personalized resumes

Your most important business communication will be about your employment. During your life, you will spend most of your waking hours at work. Your work should be enjoyable, challenging, and rewarding. When you have completed this chapter and the next one, you should have a plan for successfully obtaining employment—employment that best matches your interests and qualifications.

To obtain employment, you will need to conduct a job campaign. This campaign will include (1) finding positions for which you can apply, (2) determining your qualifications, (3) developing a resume, (4) writing application letters, (5) interviewing for positions, and (6) conducting follow-up communications.

The first three steps in the job campaign are discussed in this chapter, and the last three steps are discussed in Chapter 22.

Employment communication is your most important communication.

The job campaign involves several steps.

OBTAINING EMPLOYMENT OPPORTUNITIES

Finding positions for which you can apply generally requires an organized effort. The first step in your job campaign involves determining which jobs are available and what the job requirements are for those positions.

Many career related positions are solicited. A **solicited position** is a specific job for which employers are seeking applicants—jobs listed with school or college placement offices, advertised in newspapers or journals, or announced through private or government placement agencies.

A job that is available but is unlisted or unadvertised is called an **unsolicited position.** These positions may be an important part of your job campaign. Unsolicited positions, if available, are obtained by direct contact with a company of your choice. You will learn of the availability of many of these positions through your network of friends, relatives, instructors, and acquaintances.

An effective job campaign requires careful, documented research. You will want to use all appropriate sources of information about the availability of jobs and about their requirements. The following sections discuss possible sources.

Determining job availability and requirements is the first step.

Positions are either solicited or unsolicited.

SCHOOL OR COLLEGE PLACEMENT OFFICES

The most valuable source of information about jobs will likely be your school or college placement office. Whether you are an undergraduate student looking for your first career position or a graduate seeking a change in employment, the placement office can provide many services.

Among the placement services offered by most school or college placement offices are job-related publications, listings of job openings, arrangements for on-campus interviews with company representatives, maintenance of a credentials file, advice on the preparation of resumes and application

Your school or college placement office is a valuable source of information and services.

Your college placement office is a valuable source of information about jobs.

letters, and guidance or training for a job interview. These services are free or offered at minimal cost. The placement office should be one of the first places you visit as you start your job campaign.

Of the publications available at the placement office, the *College Placement Annual* is one of the most helpful. This publication contains positions available across the nation. It lists the positions for which employers are seeking applicants and the educational requirements for those jobs. The employers are listed by geographical location, by occupational specialty, and by company name. From this list of employers, you can develop a prospect list of job opportunities in your field. The person to contact within each company is listed; this enables you to develop a mailing list for your job campaign.

Several other job-related publications will be available at the placement office. These will likely include trade association publications, government publications, and individual company publications.

Two major services of placement offices are listings of specific job openings and, in larger schools and colleges, arrangements for on-campus interviews with company representatives. Generally, the listings of job openings are published periodically. Placement offices will post these listings on campus and may mail them to graduates. If you find a position opening that interests you, request that the placement office assist you with contacting the employer by sending your credentials or by arranging an on-campus interview.

Job-related publications aid the job campaign.

Placement offices provide job listings and arrange interviews.

Communication Quotes

When searching for a job that fits your abilities, use all the resources available to you, including placement services, newspaper advertisements, as well as your network of friends and acquaintances.

Michele J. Hooper, Corporate Vice President and President, International Business Group of Caremark International Inc.

Register with the placement office and complete your credentials file.

To take advantage of your school's placement services, register with that office. This registration will involve the careful, accurate, thorough, and neat completion of your credentials file. The credentials file contains information about your education and experience. In addition, it contains the letters of reference that you request be placed there.

Completing your credentials file will serve you in at least two ways. One, it will motivate you to gather and record important data about yourself; these data will be helpful to you in preparing your resume. Two, the credentials file will be duplicated and, with your permission or at your request, provided to potential employers.

Many positions are obtained through the services of a placement office. It should be your first source of information when you initiate a job search.

NEWSPAPER AND JOURNAL ADVERTISEMENTS

Classified ads are sources of jobs.

The classified advertisement sections of newspapers and many trade or professional journals are other sources of information about job openings. You can obtain trade or professional journals for your field at your school library or public library.

Generally, journal ads are national in scope and newspaper ads are local in scope.

While journal job advertisements generally are national in scope, newspaper job advertisements are a good source of information about specific positions in a given geographic area. Most classified advertisements of position openings also carry information about the job requirements and salary levels. By studying advertisements, you can determine what jobs are available in a geographic area, the salaries offered, and whether you can meet the job requirements. Most newspapers have several editions, and the job opening advertisements may vary from edition to edition. If you wish to relocate to Chicago, for example, be aware that the edition of the *Chicago Tribune* distributed within Chicago will likely contain a more comprehensive listing of job openings than the edition distributed elsewhere.

PRIVATE OR GOVERNMENT EMPLOYMENT AGENCIES

Private agencies can be sources of jobs.

Private employment agencies bring together job seekers and employers. Their services will be similar to those offered by your school or college placement office. Private employment agencies are in business both to provide these specialized services and to make a profit. Therefore, either the employee or the employer will have to pay the significant fee charged.

They charge the employee or the employer a fee for their services.

Before using a private employment agency, be sure that you understand clearly what services are provided, how much the fee will be, and who is to pay the fee.

Some professional organizations can assist in your job search.

Another category of private employment agency is the nonprofit service of professional organizations. Some professional organizations publish job opening announcements, provide a hotline with recorded job listings, assist in linking job seekers and employers at professional conferences, and maintain a credentials file service. These services are usually offered at low or no cost to members. To determine what services are available to you from professional organizations, ask a professional in your field.

Government employment agencies can be sources of jobs.

Public employment agencies are also found at all levels of government: federal, state, regional, and local. There is usually no charge for their services.

At the federal government level, the U.S. Office of Personnel Management administers an extensive employment service. There are hundreds of

Federal employment offices provide information on jobs with the federal government.

area federal employment offices throughout the United States that are sources of job opportunities within the U.S. government. You can locate your nearest federal employment office by contacting any federal government agency in your area. Also, at the federal level, there are job opportunities available in the United States Army, Navy, Marines, Coast Guard, and Air Force. These branches of the military service have recruiters in most local communities.

State government employment services list jobs in the private sector and in state government.

State governments also provide employment services. These services are more extensive than the employment services provided by the federal government. They include employment opportunities both in the private sector and in the state government. Most states have regional employment offices throughout the state to serve local geographic areas. Usually, you can locate these services by looking under the name of your state in the telephone book or by contacting any state government office.

Local and regional employment offices provide information on jobs within their agencies.

Local and regional government agencies provide employment services to link potential employees with positions within their agencies. Cities, counties, and regional service units are all sources of jobs. Usually, you can locate their employment or personnel offices by looking in the telephone book under the name of the government unit—city, county, or region.

Many cities and Chambers of Commerce publish directories listing the names, addresses, and phone numbers of businesses in their localities. These directories often contain the names of top executives and departmental managers and are a good source for contacting individual businesses for possible unpublished job openings.

OTHER SOURCES OF JOB INFORMATION

Friends, relatives, instructors, acquaintances, and past or present employers are important sources for job leads.

Other possible sources of information on available jobs and their requirements are friends, relatives, instructors, acquaintances, and past or present employers. In an aggressive, vigorous job campaign, you will want to seek assistance from all sources. You may even want to advertise your job interests and qualifications in a newspaper or journal in order to obtain job leads.

ANALYZING YOUR QUALIFICATIONS

Because the product you are selling in your job campaign is *you,* you need to know yourself well. While you will want to sell yourself honestly and fairly, concentrate on your most positive features—your accomplishments, education, experience, positive attitudes, and potential.

> *Accuracy is the twin brother of honesty; inaccuracy, of dishonesty.*
>
> **Charles Simmons**

Analyzing your qualifications is an important part of your job campaign. It is the step that precedes preparing your resume—a list of your qualifications in their most positive light. Your resume will be your primary tool in securing interviews.

From your examination of the job market, you will know the kinds of jobs available in your field and their requirements. You will know the type of job you want. Your job campaign may be aimed at one particular solicited job—salesperson for ABC Insurance Agency—or it may involve sending unsolicited applications to a large number of potential employers. In either case, you will need to analyze your qualifications in relation to each job and its requirements.

In analyzing your qualifications, start by brainstorming (alone or possibly with friends and relatives) to list facts about yourself. The most important facts are evidences of your accomplishments—achievements, honors, and knowledge. Think of your accomplishments as you list the facts that show the record of your education and experience. Note the items listed in Figure 21-1 on page 595. In addition, you should list personal information about yourself. Finally, list persons who can serve as your references.

Here is an idea to use as you begin to brainstorm. Take four blank sheets of paper and label them at the top as follows: Write "Personal Information" at the top of the first page, "Education" on the next, "Experience" on the third, and "References" on the last. At a good time of the day for you, find a quiet place and start thinking of facts about yourself. Suggestions for the kinds of facts to list are in the following sections.

PERSONAL INFORMATION

Start with personal information because it will be the easiest category. List your personal data in random fashion. Do not try to organize or evaluate the information at this point.

The information on the personal information sheet should include your name, temporary and/or permanent address, telephone number(s), interests and hobbies, community service activities, public-speaking experience, church activities, volunteer work, and organization memberships. As appropriate, include accomplishments, offices held, experience gained, and honors or awards.

In addition, list your special talents or skills (such as ability to keyboard, use software, write computer programs, or speak or write foreign languages), and personal attributes (such as enthusiasm, positiveness, initiative, drive, sincerity, dependability, sense of humor, or adaptability). Include in your personal data listing your salary expectations, job campaign and career objectives, whether you are willing to relocate, and any other personal information that might be of interest to an employer.

Some of this personal information will be used in preparing your resume. Other parts of it will assist you in choosing specific jobs, writing application letters, answering questions during interviews, and completing employment forms.

EDUCATION

List educational information.

On the sheet of paper labeled "Education," list information about the schools you have attended. Even more important, list those facts that show what you have learned, evidences of achievement, honors, and extracurricular activities.

List all your schools, key facts, and achievements.

For each school, list its name, its location, the dates you attended, your major, your minor, your grade-point average in your major and overall, and the diplomas or degrees you received. Indicate any special groupings of courses that especially qualify you for the position or positions in your job campaign, and list any honors or awards received (such as outstanding student, membership in honorary organizations, dean's honor lists, certificates of recognition or appreciation, or scholarships). Specify any special research reports you have prepared. Indicate all extracurricular activities (such as professional organizations, service organizations, fraternity or sorority activities, intramural or intercollegiate athletics, or special service activities). List any other educational information about yourself that might be of interest to an employer.

EXPERIENCE

List all prior job experience.

List all your work experience—part time and full time—on the third sheet. Keep in mind two basic categories as you reflect on each job you have held: (1) responsibilities, and (2) accomplishments, such as achievements, knowledge or skills acquired, and contributions while performing the job. Most persons list only their job responsibilities on their resumes. While employers are interested in the responsibilities you have had, they are more interested in how successfully you fulfilled those responsibilities. You should list all factual evidences of successful job performances (such as supervised ten employees, increased sales by 25 percent, and promoted to assistant manager).

For each job, concentrate on responsibilities and accomplishments.

List each job held, including any military service. For each, list your job title, employer and location, and dates of employment. Indicate responsibilities and give evidence of achievements. Specify what you learned while performing the job, any innovations you developed to improve job performance, sales quotas or other goals met, letters or other commendations received regarding your performance, promotions, or increases in responsibilities. List reasons why you held each job, reasons why you left each job, and salaries received.

Include volunteer work.

Add any other work experience information you think might be helpful in your job campaign. You may include jobs held as a volunteer worker. These jobs will be especially important if you have little paid work experience to list.

REFERENCES

List references who will give you favorable recommendations.

References should be individuals who know you or your work well and who are willing to write letters or talk to potential employers on your behalf. You should have at least three references and may have several more if you have been employed many years. You can select as references those

Resume Content Items In Order of Importance	Percent Ranking Items Important	Resume Content Items In Order of Importance	Percent Ranking Items Important
1. Name	99.8	35. Publications	57.2
2. Degree	99.3	36. Resume Title	57.1
3. Name of College	99.2	37. Community Involvement	53.8
4. Employing Company(s)	98.9	38. Date of Graduation—High School	51.6
5. Jobs Held (Titles)	98.8	39. Salaries Received for Jobs	50.9
6. Telephone No.	98.6	40. Diploma—High School	50.4
7. Dates of Employment	98.3	41. Hobbies/Interests	49.6
8. Address	97.8	42. Health	48.4
9. Duties—Work Experience	97.6	43. Personal References	46.2
10. Major	97.1	44. Yearbook Editor, etc.—College	45.9
11. Special Aptitudes/Skills	93.5	45. Social Organizations—College	43.0
12. Achievements—Work Experience (learning, contributions, accomplishments)	91.1	46. Years Attended—High School	42.4
13. Previous Employers—References	90.4	47. Athletic Involvement—College	41.5
14. Date of Graduation—College	89.4	48. Social Security Number	35.2
15. Job Objective	88.5	49. Band, Choral Groups, etc.—College	34.2
16. Career Objective	86.6	50. Awards, Honors—High School	33.6
17. Years Attended—College	84.0	51. Grade Average—High School	29.1
18. Summary of Qualifications	81.9	52. Professional Organizations—High School	28.2
19. Awards, Honors—College Achievements	81.6	53. List of College Courses Taken	28.1
20. Willingness to Relocate	79.5	54. Marital Status	23.6
21. Combined Job and Career Objective	77.8	55. Student Government Activities—High School	23.1
22. Professional Organizations/College Extra-curricular Activities	77.3	56. Resume Heading Information— Other Suggestions	21.1
23. Grade Point Average	76.6	57. Class Rank—High School	20.2
24. Minor	75.7	58. Church Involvement	20.0
25. References Supplied Only on Request	75.6	59. Yearbook Editor, etc.—High School	17.2
26. Military Experience	70.2	60. Height/Weight	17.2
27. Current Organization Memberships	67.8	61. Athletic Involvement—High School	16.3
28. Professors/Teachers—References	67.5	62. Social Organizations—High School	16.2
29. Reason(s) for Leaving Job(s)	65.2	63. Band, Choral Group, etc.—High School	13.7
30. Scholarships—College Achievements	62.1	64. Gender	11.2
31. Student Government Activities—College	58.8	65. Birthplace	10.3
32. Work Supervisor Names	58.8	66. Transcript of Grades—High School	8.5
33. References—Completeness of Data	58.4	67. Photograph	7.3
34. Name of High School	58.1	68. Race	3.2
		69. Religion	1.9

SOURCE: Adapted from Jules Harcourt and A. C. "Buddy" Krizan, "Resume Content: A Comparison of Personnel Administrators' and Hiring Officials' Preferences," *Southwest Business Review,* School of Business, Southwest Texas State University, Vol. 1, No. 2, Fall 1991, pp. 55–73.

Figure 21·1 Ranking of Importance of Resume Content Items by Managers Who Make Hiring Decisions for Their Companies

persons who know your character or who are former employers, current employers, professors, and coworkers. Potential employers consider former or current employers the best types of references. At this point simply list those potential references who will give you a favorable recommendation. Depending on the job you are seeking, you may use all or part of this list.

Before using anyone as a reference, verify that person's willingness to write a letter of recommendation or speak with a potential employer. While you will need to deal honestly with any unfavorable information in your background, you are not required to list references who will hurt your chances for employment.

For each potential reference, list the person's title, name, position, organization, business (or home) address, and business (or home) telephone number. Be sure to ask your references where they would like to be contacted—at their business, home, or other location.

When you have completed the thorough analysis of your qualifications, you will be ready to prepare your resume—the key written document in your job campaign.

PREPARING YOUR RESUME

A **resume** is a summary of your qualifications. It should be a clear, concise, positive review of who you are and what you have to offer an employer.

While most job applicants use a standard written resume, some use a videotape, portfolio, or computer database resume. Assistance in doing a videotape resume for some sales, acting, and other selected job applications is available from some college placement offices and private employment services. Assistance in developing an attractive portfolio containing draw-

Communication Quotes

Preparing a resume is not an easy task. It takes considerable thought and prior organization, as well as careful choice of language. It is a selling document, designed to get an individual in the door and must be written so as to command the attention of the person to whom it is directed.

James E. Challenger, President of Challenger, Gray & Christmas, Inc., international outplacement consultant and a nationally recognized job search authority.

ings, designs, writing samples, etc., for advertising, sales promotion, graphic arts, and other similar positions is available from individual faculty members and other professionals in your field. Some applicants place their credentials on file with a resume database service. Employers seeking to fill positions can have direct online access to the database to search for candidates, or the service agency will do it for them. Both the candidate and the employer pay fees for this service.

Practically all applicants, however, must use standard written resumes if

Former and current employers are the most important references.

Request permission from references to list them.

List complete information for each reference.

Resume: A summary of your qualifications.

Some job applicants use videotape, portfolio, or computer database resumes.

they are to be successful in securing job interviews. The rest of this chapter is about how to develop an effective written resume.

You will be judged on the appearance of your resume; it is a potential employer's first impression of you. Your resume should be typed or printed—use a laser printer if possible—on white, buff, or some other light-color paper. Use high-quality, clean, 8 1/2 - by 11-inch bond paper. Be sure your resume is neat, unwrinkled, and error free. The quality and clarity of its content will be a potential employer's second impression of you.

The primary purpose of a resume, along with an application letter, is to obtain a job interview. Fewer than one in ten applications for employment result in an interview. To get an interview, your resume must be better than your competitors' resumes in both appearance and content. If you do not get an interview, you will not be hired.

The primary purpose of your resume is to obtain a job interview.

There are two basic types of resumes: personalized and general. Some applicants use a combination of the two basic types. A **personalized resume** is prepared for a specific job application. It is individually key-boarded and printed, and it contains information to show specifically how you qualify for that one job. For example, it may list the courses you had in college that particularly apply to the responsibilities of the specific job.

Resumes can be personalized or general.

A **general resume** is a description of your qualifications that can be used for any job and sent to any employer. It is appropriate for use in applying for unsolicited jobs. For example, if you are applying for management trainee positions in several different companies representing different industries, you can use a general resume that is printed in quantity and sent to all the prospective employers.

Use general resumes for unsolicited jobs.

While it is possible you will prepare and use a general resume for your first career job, a personalized resume is more powerful and should be used for solicited job applications. If you use word processing to prepare your resume, it is easier to personalize and update it.

Use personalized resumes for specific jobs.

There are two basic formats of resumes: reverse chronological and functional. A **reverse chronological resume** presents the most recent information first within each section. For example, in the section containing your experience, your current or most recent position is described first. The listing then describes each previous position with the first position you held listed last. The same reverse chronological approach is used in the sections for education, publications, community service, or any other section containing information accumulated over time. The reverse chronological resume is more traditional than is the functional resume. (Examples of reverse chronological resumes are shown in Figure 21•2 on page 608 and Figure 21•3 on pages 609 and 610.)

The basic resume formats are reverse chronological and functional.

A functional resume does not indicate your qualifications chronologically. Instead, a **functional resume** provides information showing qualifications categorized by skills and knowledge and related accomplishments; in other words, by functions. The headings used for functions may include Capable Manager, Effective Communicator, Profit Producer, and Quality Controller. More conservative headings for functions may include Management, Production, Marketing (or Sales), Advertising, Operations, or

Systems. (An example of a resume in functional format is shown in Figure 21•4 on page 611.)

An example of a resume in functional format is shown in Figure 21•4 on page 611.

Research indicates that managers who review resumes and make decisions on who will be granted an interview prefer reverse chronological resumes; therefore, they are more appropriate for most job campaigns.

The format you choose depends on the job you are seeking. If you are applying for a position in a conservative industry, such as banking, public accounting, or manufacturing, you should use the traditional reverse chronological resume. If you are applying for a position in advertising, sales promotion, or entertainment, you may want to choose the nontraditional functional format. The functional format for a resume works well for an individual who has held several jobs and needs to combine them to make the presentation more concise or more favorable. As mentioned previously, some applicants use a combination of the reverse chronological and functional formats. In addition, several computer software programs for developing and formatting resumes are available.

Regardless of the type or format of resume you use, your resume should be a carefully prepared, attractive, high-quality representation of you. As has been indicated, it is the primary sales tool you will use to obtain an interview. Through the wording of the content of your resume, convey to employers information about yourself that reveals the four qualities in the following box.

A few large companies are using scanners and computers to analyze content and screen resumes initially. The computers are programmed to seek out key phrases and words and rate the resumes on the findings. To have your resume selected for human review in this computerized process, you must learn how the

Communication Notes

What Employers Want to Know About You
The four qualities that employers want and that should be revealed in an applicant's resume are:
1. Industriousness and ambition
2. Cooperative attitude
3. Interest in the work and enthusiasm for the employer's product or service
4. An orderly and businesslike mind

John L. Munschauer, "The Resume: How to Speak to Employers' Needs," CPC Annual, College Placement Council, Inc., 36 ed., 1992–93, p. 27.

computer programming works. If you know your resume will be scanned by a computer, find out—from the company or another source—the nature of the computer program so you know what content to include.

Specific content selected for a resume that will be reviewed by humans—by managers—should include the items they prefer. The resume content items desired by those managers who make most of the final hiring decisions are shown in Figure 21•1. While each job application and each individual's situation will be somewhat different, you will want to include in your resume most of those items that a majority of managers want. For some applications you may even want to include resume content that less than 50 percent of the managers say they want. Your objective will be to construct the most powerful resume that you possibly can for each job application.

With the information you developed when you analyzed the job market and your qualifications, you are now ready to prepare your resume. While following the principles of business communication, exercise creativity in presenting the best possible picture of yourself. The following are the major sections commonly included in a resume:

1. Opening
2. Education
3. Experience
4. Activities, Honors, Special Skills (and/or some other appropriate title)
5. References

Resumes have commonly used sections.

You may not need or want all these sections in your resume. Also, you may want to arrange them in some other order. For example, if your experience is your strong point, it should be presented immediately following the opening. If you are a recent college graduate and have limited experience, have the education section follow the opening.

Include the sections that fit your background.

OPENING

The opening of your resume should include a heading with your name, address, and telephone number; your job and/or career objective; and a summary of your qualifications. A resume title may be used. The purposes of the opening are to get potential employers to read the remainder of the resume, to inform them briefly of your interests and qualifications, and to make it easy for them to contact you.

The opening includes a heading, an objective, and a summary of qualifications.

HEADING

A resume heading with your name, address, and telephone number is essential. Be sure that your name is in the largest and darkest type. Include both your permanent and temporary school addresses and telephone numbers. You may or may not include a title for your resume. You can be conservative or quite creative in the development of the heading, but remember that the majority of potential employers prefer a conservative and traditional resume.

The heading must include your name, address, and telephone number.

It is possible to use a general or a personalized heading for your resume. A variety of headings are shown here:

1.

MARY JO BOGGS

1910 Ginnway Drive
New Castle, DE 19720-2810
(302) 555-1933

2.

MARY J. WHITHALL

Address: 1223 Parker Street
          Riverside, CA 92500-1703
Phone: (714) 555-2743

3.

Qualifications of Manuel P. Mercado
for the
Position of Accountant
with the
Ranage Retail Stores

Current Address:
P.O. Box 826
Bridgeport, CN 06600-2361
(203) 555-9173

Permanent Address:
9917 Wellman Drive
Bridgeport, CN 06600-9845
(203) 555-7845

4.

ICHIRO SUMIDA
Applicant for
Information Processing Manager
Hale and Oates Company, Inc.

Address: 14165 Woodward Avenue
Tampa, FL 33600-3316

Telephone No: (813) 555-1731

CAREER AND/OR JOB OBJECTIVE

A career or job objective can gain favorable attention.

Most employers like to see a career and/or job objective in the opening of a resume so they can tell if their interests match yours. While this is an optional part of a resume, it is another opportunity in your job campaign to get the favorable attention of your receiver. Here are examples of career and job objectives:

1.

`                    Career Objective`

`   Entry-level position in sales leading to sales management.`

2.

Job Objective

To obtain a summer internship in accounting to better prepare myself for a professional career.

3.

Objective

Management position that will afford opportunities for advancement.

4.

<u>OBJECTIVE</u> President of the Salem Valley Savings and Loan Association.

SUMMARY OF QUALIFICATIONS

Convey a sense of accomplishment in your qualifications summary.

This section provides a very brief abstract of your qualifications. It is a recent addition to resumes and is gaining the support of busy managers. You may find it advantageous. From this information managers can quickly tell if you seem to offer the qualities they are seeking. Prepare your Summary of Qualifications after you have completed the remainder of the resume, so that it is comprehensive and high quality. The summary should convey a sense of accomplishment. Some examples of summaries of qualifications follow:

1.
Summary of Qualifications

Bachelor of Science in Business Administration with emphasis on computer information systems. Seven years of part-time work in a variety of jobs from janitor to motel night manager-bookkeeper. Work effectively with people and have productive work habits.

2.
General Qualifications

- **Successful experience in retail sales**
- **Promotions for consistently exceeding quotas**
- **Associate of Arts degree in retail sales management**
- **Dean's Honor Roll last four quarters.**

EDUCATION

Education is the next major section for recent graduates.

Following your resume opening, present your strongest qualifications. If you are, or will soon be, a recent college graduate and have limited experience, your education and related activities will be your strongest qualifications. That information should follow the opening. If you have been employed for many years and can relate that employment to the job you are seeking, your Experience section should follow the opening.

If you have or will soon be graduated from a postsecondary institution, you may want to review your high school record in the Education section. If your high school record is fairly recent and shows considerable accomplishment, include it. If not, omit it. List your major and overall grade-point averages if they are B level or higher. Be sure to emphasize your educational achievements.

Titles that you might use for the education section are "Education," "Educational Qualifications," "Training for . . . ," "Specialized Education," "Academic Preparation," "Professional Education," "Educational Data," and "Educational Preparation." Remember that all headings at the same level should have parallel construction.

Use reverse chronological order for presenting your education.

Use reverse chronological order to list the name and location of each school attended and the dates of attendance. Also, for each school show your degrees, major, and other selected information to reflect your achievements and extent of learning. Here are examples:

1.
                                    EDUCATION

1990-1994   University of Wyoming, Laramie, Wyoming
                Degree: Bachelor of Science
                Major: Business Administration (AACSB Program)
                GPA: 3.3 (4.0 = A)
                Honors: Dean's Honor Roll last five semesters

Dade County Community College, Miami, Florida (1992–94)

Degree: Associate of Arts in Office Administration

Courses that especially prepared me for your executive secretary position:

Word Processing	Information Systems
Keyboarding	Administrative Supervision
Records Management	Office Administration

Marshall High School, Marshall, Florida (1990–92)

Diploma: College Preparatory

Class Rank: Tenth in class of 100

Activities: Business Club (President), Hi-Y (Treasurer), Student Council (Secretary), Senior Yearbook Editor, Band, Basketball

3.　　**EDUCATION:**　<u>**Brown College, Cedar Rapids, Iowa (1990–94)**</u>

Degree: Associate of Science in Business

Major: Retail Sales Management

Grade Point Average Overall: 3.21 (4.0 = A)

Grade Point Average in Major: 3.57

Financed 80 percent of college undergraduate education through part-time employment and student loans.

EXPERIENCE

Experience is rated highly by employers.

For applicants other than new graduates, employers rate work experience as the most important information in a resume. More decisions to grant or not to grant interviews are based on the quality of work experience than on any other basis.

Although all your work experience is important, the work experience that prepared you for the position or positions you are seeking is especially important and should be highlighted. Your experience indicates your record of responsibility and accomplishments, provides the primary sources for references, and reflects your personality and personal preferences. When analyzing your qualifications, you developed the information needed for the experience section of your resume. Now you must decide how to present it most effectively.

Focus on your accomplishments.

Your accomplishments should be the focal point of your experience presentation, including what you learned from the experience, your achievements, and your contributions to each position. Your responsibilities for each position may also be listed briefly. Note in the examples that follow how the use of bullets makes the items easy to read. Use appropriate action verbs in your listings of accomplishments and responsibilities. For each position you should include dates of employment, job title, employer, and employer's address.

Titles you might use for this section include "Experience," "Work Experience," "Qualifications," "Career-Related Experience," "Experience

USE ACTION VERBS

Accomplished	Achieved	Acted	Adapted
Administered	Advised	Analyzed	Applied
Approved	Arranged	Assessed	Assigned
Assisted	Attained	Budgeted	Collaborated
Communicated	Conceived	Conducted	Cooperated
Coordinated	Created	Delegated	Demonstrated
Determined	Developed	Directed	Drafted
Edited	Established	Evaluated	Expanded
Guided	Handled	Hired	Identified
Illustrated	Implemented	Improved	Increased
Initiated	Installed	Instructed	Integrated
Interpreted	Interviewed	Investigated	Invented
Lead	Listened	Maintained	Managed
Marketed	Mediated	Merchandised	Moderated
Modified	Monitored	Motivated	Negotiated
Obtained	Operated	Ordered	Organized
Originated	Participated	Performed	Persuaded
Planned	Presented	Presided	Processed
Produced	Provided	Publicized	Published
Recommended	Recorded	Recruited	Redesigned
Renewed	Reported	Represented	Researched
Resolved	Reviewed	Revised	Scheduled
Screened	Selected	Served	Solved
Spoke	Stimulated	Summarized	Supervised
Surveyed	Taught	Trained	Transmitted
Updated	Used	Worked	Wrote

That Has Prepared Me for . . . ," "Experience in Sales Promotion," "Business Experience," "Skills Developed Through Experience," and others.

Examples of how the same information might be presented in both the reverse chronological and the functional formats are as follows:

Present your experience using the reverse chronological or the functional format.

1.   **EXPERIENCE**

<u>**Night Manager**</u> Holiday Motel, De Kalb, Illinois (1991-94)
Responsibilities   • Supervised four employees
                            • Greeted and registered guests
                            • Maintained accounting and guest records

Achievements	• Learned to work effectively with people
	• Gained skill in meeting difficult customer needs
	• Developed new guest accounting records that saved an average of two hours of clerical time each night

Part-time Work Various employers in the De Kalb area (1987-91)

Responsibilities	• Motel desk clerk, research assistant, appliance salesperson, and janitor
Achievements	• Promoted from motel desk clerk to night manager
	• Learned research techniques while assisting professor in business communication study
	• Led appliance sales force of four in sales during three of six months of employment
	• Learned to work with a variety of people

2.   **SKILLS DEVELOPED THROUGH EXPERIENCE**

MANAGERIAL SKILLS

As a motel night manager, developed skill in motivating employees and performing a variety of jobs. Assumed additional responsibilities readily. Improved employee productivity. Observed other managers and practiced their effective behavior.

COMMUNICATION SKILLS

Learned to communicate clearly and concisely with employees and customers in many different situations. Developed ability to provide written and oral reports for financial and customer accounting data.

ACCOUNTING SKILLS

Developed thorough knowledge of double-entry bookkeeping system. Became proficient in completing trial balances, balance sheets, profit and loss statements, and other statements.

ACTIVITIES, HONORS, SPECIAL SKILLS, OR OTHER APPROPRIATE TITLES

Special sections may be included if your qualifications and the job justify them.

Include additional sections in your resume if your background justifies them. Any additional section included should be one that employers would consider positively. For example, if you were involved extensively in extracurricular activities during college, include a separate section on these activities immediately following the education section. Your background may justify a separate section on honors, special skills, community services, published works, public presentations, military service, organization memberships, special interests, or any number of other possible categories. If you have a variety of activities, you may combine them into one section labeled simply "Activities." The important point is that you should not leave out any vital information that would enhance your resume.

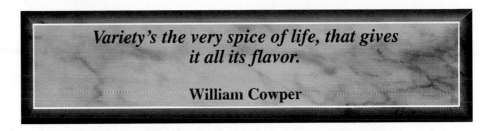

Variety's the very spice of life, that gives it all its flavor.

William Cowper

Place special sections in appropriate locations in your resume.

Special sections should be placed near related information or at an appropriate point of emphasis. For example, a special section on academic honors should follow the education section. A special interests section, because it is likely less important, should be placed just before the section on references. References are traditionally listed in the last section of a resume. Examples of special sections in resumes are:

1.   HONORS

```
Outstanding Employee, Bowling (Idaho) Steel Company, 1994
Citizens' Sparkplug Award, Bowling Green Club, 1993
Outstanding Young Woman in Idaho, 1993
Dean's Honor List, Fredricksburg State College, 1993–94
State Academic Scholarship to Fredricksburg College, 1990–94
```

2.   **EXTRACURRICULAR ACTIVITIES**

President, Phi Sigma Omicron Social Fraternity	1992–93
Treasurer, Phi Sigma Omicron Social Fraternity	1991–92
Manager, Phi Sigma Omicron House	1991–93
Coach, Chugger's Basketball Team	1991–93
Business Manager, <u>State College News</u>	1990–92
Photographer, <u>State College News</u>	1988-90

3.   <u>ORGANIZATION MEMBERSHIPS</u>

Administrative Management Association (Chapter Secretary, 1992–94)
Information Processing Association
Association for Data Processing Management
Civitan Club (Club President 1991–92, Area Governor 1992–93)

4.　SPECIAL SKILLS

Know microcomputer software including LOTUS 1-2-3,
WordPerfect, and dBase III. Speak and write Spanish.
Speak and understand limited German and French. Keyboard
at 75 words per minute. Know how to use most electronic
office equipment.

5.　SPECIAL INTERESTS

Camping, Basketball, Photography, and Cooking

6.　INTERESTS

Enjoy outdoor activities, including camping, basketball,
and photography. Am considered a gourmet cook.
Energetic. Have sense of humor. Enjoy life. Willing to
relocate.

Employment laws prohibit employers from discriminating among applicants on the basis of race, color, religion, age, gender, marital status, or national origin. Employers cannot ask for this information, and supplying such information is not recommended.

Present only the information that will strengthen your application.

In some job situations, however, your job application can be strengthened if you let a potential employer know your religious affiliation, race, national origin, sexual orientation, marital status, handicap status, or other special qualification. For example, if you were applying for an administrative position with a Baptist Church headquarters office, letting the employer know that you are a member of the Baptist Church could be helpful. As a way to provide this type of information in your resume, you could list the church as one of your organization memberships, citing accomplishments related to your special qualification. Or, you could include the information in a special section devoted to your status. Another way is to mention the unique qualification in your application letter.

Many employers want to know if you are willing to relocate. You can place that information in a special section, or as the last item in the Summary of Qualifications section.

Do not include information an employer might prefer not to have.

Omit from your resume any information you think a given employer would prefer not to have. Do not include a photograph of yourself unless you feel certain it would strengthen your job application. Today, very few applications include photographs; and, because reactions to personal appearances are so varied, it is better not to take a chance on getting a negative reaction.

REFERENCES

A vital part of your resume is a listing of carefully chosen references. Though you want to list only those references who will give you positive

References are vital.

recommendations, you should list your most important previous employers. You may also want to list college instructors, possibly high school teachers, and—in special circumstances—coworkers. You may list different references for different job applications. Let the nature of the job and its requirements determine the references you think would be the most helpful to the potential employer. Then use those persons for that application.

Provide full information, including a telephone number.

You are encouraged to provide full information on your references in this section of your resume. Including the telephone numbers of your references for the potential employer's convenience, for example, may make the difference in whether you get an interview. If a potential employer finds your qualifications of interest and can easily pick up the phone, call, and receive a favorable recommendation from one or more of your references, you are likely to get an interview. For each reference—unless a reference directs you otherwise—list courtesy title, name, position, organization, business address, and business telephone number. Here is the way a reference section might appear:

REFERENCES

```
Mr. A. D. Ortiz, Instructor        Mr. Charles Davenport, Manager
Department of Accounting           Steak Stockade
Middle State College               1700 Main Street
Las Cruces, NM 88001-7263          Las Cruces, NM 88001-3461
(505) 555-9322                     (505) 555-1212

Ms. Rowena Kelsey                  Miss Rita Sandoval, Manager
Communications Consultant          Albuquerque Office
Avery Corporation                  Randolph and Sandoval, CPAs
2387 Seboyeta Avenue               1234 Crownpoint Street
Albuquerque, NM 87100-9922         Albuquerque, NM 87100-7749
(505) 555-7817                     (505) 555-7835
```

In certain unusual circumstances you may want to replace the names of references with "References Available Upon Request." For example, you may have to keep your job search confidential for some reason. Such omission of references is not recommended as a regular practice because it will likely decrease your chances for getting an interview. Most employers like to make at least a preliminary telephone check with one or more references prior to offering an interview.

SAMPLE RESUMES

Three complete resumes are shown as samples. Two are in the traditional, reverse chronological format; the other is in the functional format.

Most employers prefer the reverse chronological resume.

In Figure 21•2, the traditional reverse chronological format for a one-page general resume is shown. As you have learned, most employers prefer this format. It gives the information they need in a familiar sequence. It helps them compare resumes. If they have to search too hard to find a vital

Figure 21•2 A One-Page General Resume in Reverse Chronological Format

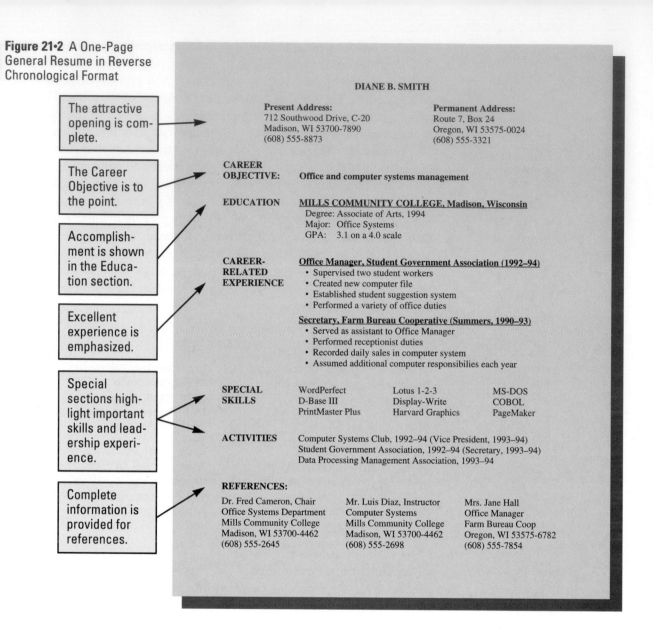

The attractive opening is complete.

The Career Objective is to the point.

Accomplishment is shown in the Education section.

Excellent experience is emphasized.

Special sections highlight important skills and leadership experience.

Complete information is provided for references.

DIANE B. SMITH

Present Address:
712 Southwood Drive, C-20
Madison, WI 53700-7890
(608) 555-8873

Permanent Address:
Route 7, Box 24
Oregon, WI 53575-0024
(608) 555-3321

CAREER OBJECTIVE: Office and computer systems management

EDUCATION   <u>MILLS COMMUNITY COLLEGE, Madison, Wisconsin</u>
Degree: Associate of Arts, 1994
Major: Office Systems
GPA: 3.1 on a 4.0 scale

CAREER-RELATED EXPERIENCE

<u>Office Manager, Student Government Association (1992–94)</u>
• Supervised two student workers
• Created new computer file
• Established student suggestion system
• Performed a variety of office duties

<u>Secretary, Farm Bureau Cooperative (Summers, 1990–93)</u>
• Served as assistant to Office Manager
• Performed receptionist duties
• Recorded daily sales in computer system
• Assumed additional computer responsibilies each year

SPECIAL SKILLS
WordPerfect	Lotus 1-2-3	MS-DOS
D-Base III	Display-Write	COBOL
PrintMaster Plus	Harvard Graphics	PageMaker

ACTIVITIES   Computer Systems Club, 1992–94 (Vice President, 1993–94)
Student Government Association, 1992–94 (Secretary, 1993–94)
Data Processing Management Association, 1993–94

REFERENCES:

Dr. Fred Cameron, Chair	Mr. Luis Diaz, Instructor	Mrs. Jane Hall
Office Systems Department	Computer Systems	Office Manager
Mills Community College	Mills Community College	Farm Bureau Coop
Madison, WI 53700-4462	Madison, WI 53700-4462	Oregon, WI 53575-6782
(608) 555-2645	(608) 555-2698	(608) 555-7854

bit of information about you, your application may go into the "reject" pile. Figure 21•3 is another version of this traditional format.

In Figure 21•4, the functional format is shown for a personalized resume. This format is more creative in a sense. It is appropriate if you have already provided all the standard information to the employer in an application form. It can be used to apply for positions that require more creativity, such as advertising, design, or copywriting. Also, applicants who have held many jobs can use the functional resume format to combine jobs and make the presentation more concise or more favorable.

Figure 21•5 is an example of a resume that combines the reverse chronological and functional formats. The work experience is in reverse

The functional format can fit some application situations.

The opening is complete and balanced.

The Career Objective reflects short- and long-range goals.

The Summary of Qualifications emphasizes accomplishments.

Education is this applicant's strongest qualification and is presented first. Both vital data and achievements are included.

JOHN V. BROWN

Address:	15200 Crestwood Lane	Telephone:	(303) 555-6172 (Office)
	Fort Collins,		(303) 555-1259 (Home)
	CO 80521-6633		

CAREER OBJECTIVE

Accounting position leading to increased responsibility and advancement.

SUMMARY OF QUALIFICATIONS

Bachelor of Science in Business degree from AACSB accredited school with major in accounting. A variety of part-time and summer employment positions, including two summer accounting internships and other work experience. Willing to relocate.

EDUCATION

1990–94   **Colorado State University, Fort Collins, Colorado**
Degree: Bachelor of Science in Business
Major: Accounting (AACSB accredited program)
Grade Point Average: 3.3 (Based on 4.0 = A)
Extracurricular Activities: Accounting Club (Vice President, 1993–94),
     Phi Beta Lambda, Beta Sigma Gamma, intramural athletics.
Self-supporting through college with scholarships, part-time work,
     and student loans.

1986–90   **Wellington High School, Wellington, Texas**
Diploma: General College Preparatory
Rank in Graduating Class: 15th of 194
Extracurricular Activities: Yearbook staff, basketball (four years), Hi-Y
     Club, Future Business Leaders of America (President, 1989-90).

EXPERIENCE

Accounting Intern, Howe & McBride, CPAs, Denver, Colorado
(Summers 1992, 1993)

Duties:	Assisted CPAs with bookkeeping records for small businesses, audits of public and private organizations, and clients' State and Federal income tax returns.
Achievements:	Learned to apply accounting theory. Became effective team member. Developed human relations skills. Created and implemented bookkeeping services on microcomputer.

There is no magic number of pages for a resume.

chronological order and is categorized by functions. The combined format has the advantages of both formats. It has the disadvantage of not being a pure reverse chronological format—the format that most businesspeople favor, particularly those in the more conservative business fields and companies.

A resume may be one page or longer, depending on the amount of education, experience, and other activities. While there is no magic number of pages for resumes, many businesspersons prefer that they be two pages or less for new college graduates with limited experience. Resumes should be long enough to include all vital information and provide attractive open space for easy readability. In addition, they should be written as concisely

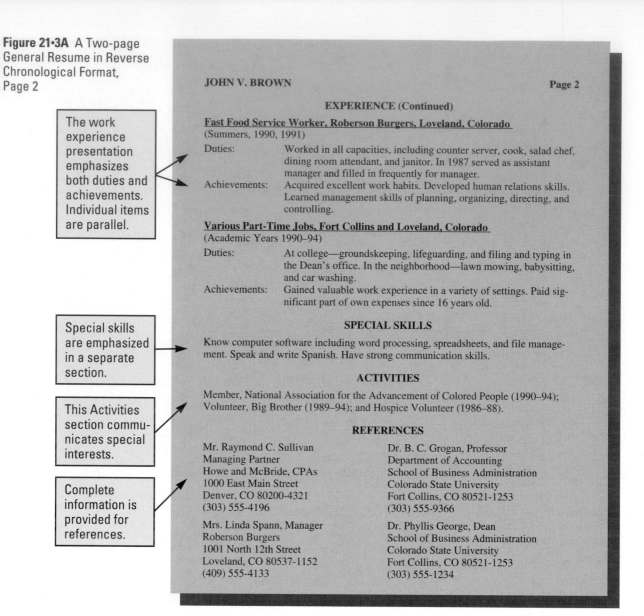

The work experience presentation emphasizes both duties and achievements. Individual items are parallel.

Special skills are emphasized in a separate section.

This Activities section communicates special interests.

Complete information is provided for references.

JOHN V. BROWN   Page 2

EXPERIENCE (Continued)

Fast Food Service Worker, Roberson Burgers, Loveland, Colorado
(Summers, 1990, 1991)

Duties: Worked in all capacities, including counter server, cook, salad chef, dining room attendant, and janitor. In 1987 served as assistant manager and filled in frequently for manager.

Achievements: Acquired excellent work habits. Developed human relations skills. Learned management skills of planning, organizing, directing, and controlling.

Various Part-Time Jobs, Fort Collins and Loveland, Colorado
(Academic Years 1990–94)

Duties: At college—groundskeeping, lifeguarding, and filing and typing in the Dean's office. In the neighborhood—lawn mowing, babysitting, and car washing.

Achievements: Gained valuable work experience in a variety of settings. Paid significant part of own expenses since 16 years old.

SPECIAL SKILLS

Know computer software including word processing, spreadsheets, and file management. Speak and write Spanish. Have strong communication skills.

ACTIVITIES

Member, National Association for the Advancement of Colored People (1990–94); Volunteer, Big Brother (1989–94); and Hospice Volunteer (1986–88).

REFERENCES

Mr. Raymond C. Sullivan
Managing Partner
Howe and McBride, CPAs
1000 East Main Street
Denver, CO 80200-4321
(303) 555-4196

Dr. B. C. Grogan, Professor
Department of Accounting
School of Business Administration
Colorado State University
Fort Collins, CO 80521-1253
(303) 555-9366

Mrs. Linda Spann, Manager
Roberson Burgers
1001 North 12th Street
Loveland, CO 80537-1152
(409) 555-4133

Dr. Phyllis George, Dean
School of Business Administration
Colorado State University
Fort Collins, CO 80521-1253
(303) 555-1234

and clearly as possible because it is estimated that employers spend only about 30 seconds per resume in their first screenings. If you know that an employer specifies the number of pages in applicants' resumes (such as, "Applicant resumes shall not exceed one page"), be sure to limit your resume length accordingly. If your resume is two pages or longer, be sure to include your name and the page number on the second and succeeding pages.

You should make effective use of blank space (sometimes called *white space*) and other techniques for emphasis in your resume. Some of these techniques include the use of capital letters, boldfacing, underscoring, italics, lines, and different type sizes. Be sure that the information is not

Use emphasis techniques, including blank space, effectively.

Figure 21•4 A One-Page Personalized Resume in Functional Format

The creative opening includes essential data.

The functional format combines education and experience information and presents it concisely by functions. Selected items are emphasized by underlining.

Using quotes of recommendations is creative.

References may not be listed if there is a good reason. For example, you do not want your current employer to know that you have applied for another job.

Avoid personal pronouns.

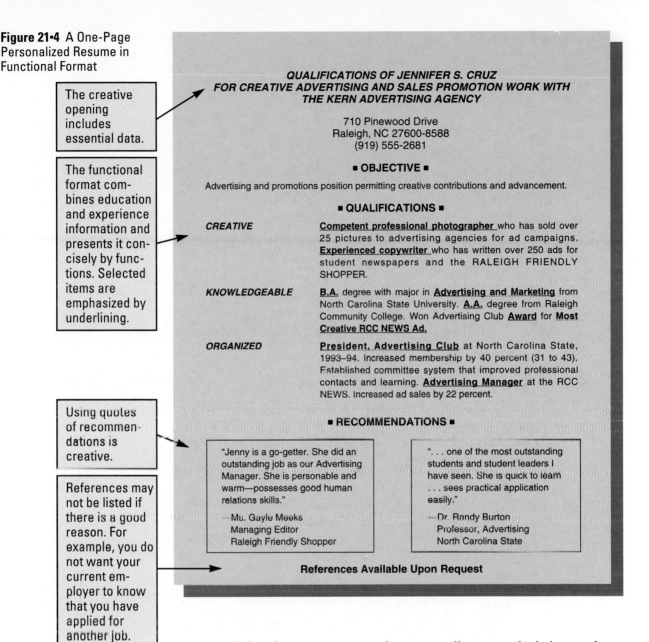

QUALIFICATIONS OF JENNIFER S. CRUZ
FOR CREATIVE ADVERTISING AND SALES PROMOTION WORK WITH
THE KERN ADVERTISING AGENCY

710 Pinewood Drive
Raleigh, NC 27600-8588
(919) 555-2681

■ OBJECTIVE ■

Advertising and promotions position permitting creative contributions and advancement.

■ QUALIFICATIONS ■

CREATIVE
Competent professional photographer who has sold over 25 pictures to advertising agencies for ad campaigns. **Experienced copywriter** who has written over 250 ads for student newspapers and the RALEIGH FRIENDLY SHOPPER.

KNOWLEDGEABLE
B.A. degree with major in **Advertising and Marketing** from North Carolina State University. **A.A.** degree from Raleigh Community College. Won Advertising Club **Award** for **Most Creative RCC NEWS Ad.**

ORGANIZED
President, Advertising Club at North Carolina State, 1993–94. Increased membership by 40 percent (31 to 43). Established committee system that improved professional contacts and learning. **Advertising Manager** at the RCC NEWS. Increased ad sales by 22 percent.

■ RECOMMENDATIONS ■

"Jenny is a go-getter. She did an outstanding job as our Advertising Manager. She is personable and warm—possesses good human relations skills."

—Ms. Gayle Meeks
Managing Editor
Raleigh Friendly Shopper

". . . one of the most outstanding students and student leaders I have seen. She is quick to learn . . . sees practical application easily."

—Dr. Randy Burton
Professor, Advertising
North Carolina State

References Available Upon Request

overcrowded or does not appear so dense as to discourage its being read. Complete sentences are not required; phrases are appropriate to save space. A note of caution: Avoid the use of personal pronouns.

Though there are many helpful examples available, you should never simply try to make your information fit another resume format. Following the guidelines given in this chapter should enable you to create your own distinctive resume that will serve you well in your job search.

Figure 21-5 A One-Page Combined Reverse Chronological and Functional Resume For a College Graduate with Experience

Complete information is provided in attractive opening.

Career Objective is action oriented.

College education data is presented concisely.

Applicant's experience is presented in combined reverse chronological and functional formats.

Some placement centers provide graduates' reference letters to employers upon request.

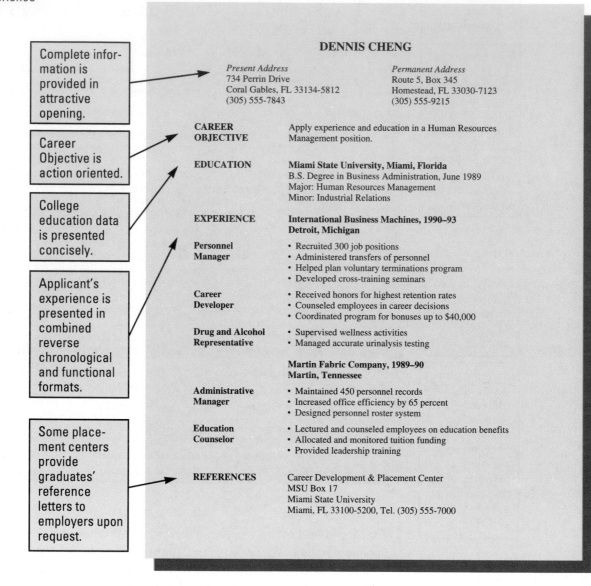

DENNIS CHENG

Present Address
734 Perrin Drive
Coral Gables, FL 33134-5812
(305) 555-7843

Permanent Address
Route 5, Box 345
Homestead, FL 33030-7123
(305) 555-9215

CAREER OBJECTIVE
Apply experience and education in a Human Resources Management position.

EDUCATION
Miami State University, Miami, Florida
B.S. Degree in Business Administration, June 1989
Major: Human Resources Management
Minor: Industrial Relations

EXPERIENCE
International Business Machines, 1990–93
Detroit, Michigan

Personnel Manager
• Recruited 300 job positions
• Administered transfers of personnel
• Helped plan voluntary terminations program
• Developed cross-training seminars

Career Developer
• Received honors for highest retention rates
• Counseled employees in career decisions
• Coordinated program for bonuses up to $40,000

Drug and Alcohol Representative
• Supervised wellness activities
• Managed accurate urinalysis testing

Martin Fabric Company, 1989–90
Martin, Tennessee

Administrative Manager
• Maintained 450 personnel records
• Increased office efficiency by 65 percent
• Designed personnel roster system

Education Counselor
• Lectured and counseled employees on education benefits
• Allocated and monitored tuition funding
• Provided leadership training

REFERENCES
Career Development & Placement Center
MSU Box 17
Miami State University
Miami, FL 33100-5200, Tel. (305) 555-7000

DISCUSSION QUESTIONS

1. List the six steps involved in conducting a job campaign.

2. Describe the information and services offered by school or college placement offices.

3. Describe the private employment agencies that are available for job applicants.

4. Describe the public employment agencies found at various levels of government.

5. Discuss the approach that a person should take in analyzing his or her qualifications.

6. What are the most important facts about you that you should list when you are analyzing your qualifications?

7. What are examples of personal information you should list when analyzing your qualifications? How will you use personal information about yourself in a job search?

8. When analyzing your qualifications, what educational data should you list for each school you have attended?

9. To prepare yourself to write the Experience section of a resume, what information will you need about your past employment?

10. Whom should you choose to list as your references, and what information do you need for each?

11. What forms of resumes are there other than the standard written resume? When might one of these forms be used?

12. How can you ensure that your resume has a professional appearance?

13. Discuss the relative merits of (a) personalized resumes, and (b) general resumes.

14. When should you use (a) the reverse chronological resume format, and (b) the functional resume format?

15. Employment laws prohibit employers from asking you to supply certain information about yourself. How can you strengthen a job application by providing some of this information to employers on your resume?

APPLICATION EXERCISES

1. Assume that you will graduate soon. Using actual information and assuming the course work, activities, and experience you will have between now and then, analyze your qualifications following the recommendations given in this chapter.

2. Using the information gathered in Application Exercise 1, prepare a general resume in reverse chronological format.

3. Prepare a personalized resume in reverse chronological format to apply for a job in your field based on an analysis of the job and its requirements and on the information obtained in Application Exercise 1.

4. Prepare a general resume in functional format based on the information obtained in Application Exercise 1.

5. Prepare a personalized resume in functional format to apply for a job in your field based on an analysis of the job and its requirements and on the information obtained in Application Exercise 1.

6. Visit a school or college placement office and gather data on the information and services available to assist you in a job campaign.

7. Gather information from a local, regional, state, or federal employment office on its services and job availability.

8. Determine the services available from a private employment agency in your local area. What is the cost of these services? Who pays the cost?

9. Review the employment section of a local or regional newspaper and assess the employment opportunities and salaries in your field.

10. Interview two executives to learn what qualities they would look for in an applicant who (a) is a new college graduate and (b) has a college education and ten years' experience. Share your findings with the class.

11. Contact three individuals who might be willing to serve as references for you. Ask their permission to use their names and secure the addresses and telephone numbers they prefer to have you use. Write a brief report summarizing your conversations with these individuals.

12. Discuss employment law requirements of employers with a manager. Ask whether providing selected information about your special qualifications would hurt or help a job application with the manager's company. Share your findings with the class.

13. Analyze the professional organizations in your field of study. List those organizations in which you feel membership would strengthen your job candidacies.

14. List the names of individuals in your personal network of friends, relatives, instructors, and acquaintances who you think could be valuable to you in a job search.

MESSAGE ANALYSIS

Revise and improve the following Education section for a resume of an individual applying for a retail sales position.

MY EDUCATIONAL RECORD

GPA: 2.1 on a 4.0 scale; Rend Lake Community College, Rend Lake, Michigan; Dates of attendance: 1992–1994; Member of Student Chapter of the American Marketing Association, Retail Sales Management Club, basketball team, Tutors for Tots; Received the "Most Effective Sales Presentation" award in the Principles of Selling class (1994); at graduation will have completed 20 hours of general education, 20 hours of business administration courses, and 20 hours of retail sales management courses; Major: Retail Sales Management; and, upon graduation, will receive an Associate of Arts degree.

CHAPTER 22

Employment Communication and Interviewing

Learning Objectives

Your learning objectives for this chapter include the following:

- To write effective letters of application for solicited and unsolicited positions
- To prepare for a successful job interview
- To compose a variety of other messages related to employment

After completing the first three steps in your job campaign covered in Chapter 21—locating positions for which you can apply, determining your qualifications, and developing a resume—you are now ready for the next three steps. You are ready for writing application letters, interviewing for positions, and conducting follow-up communications. These steps are covered in this chapter.

WRITING APPLICATION LETTERS

Sell yourself in an application letter.

Once your resume is completed, you are ready to write a more personal selling tool—an application letter. An **application letter** is a sales letter—with *you* as the product. Follow the guidelines for persuasive messages given in Chapter 13 for developing application letters. An application letter and your resume make up the application package for your job campaign.

Application letters may be either general or personalized.

Application letters can be either general or personalized, as are resumes. Again, the choice depends on whether you are seeking a solicited or an unsolicited position. In some situations you may be able to combine a general resume and a personalized application letter into an effective application package.

The major parts of an application letter are: opening, summary of qualifications, and request for interview.

There are three major parts in a well-designed application letter—an opening that gets favorable attention, a summary of qualifications that is related to job requirements, and a request for an interview. The primary purpose of an application letter is to motivate a potential employer to read your resume. Then, you hope the employer's reading of your letter and resume will result in your getting an interview. The three major parts of an application letter are discussed in the following sections.

GAINING ATTENTION IN THE OPENING

In the opening, you want to gain the favorable attention of your reader—get him or her to read the remainder of the application letter. Also, you want to provide information on why you are writing—provide orientation and transition for the reader.

The opening should gain favorable attention and provide transition.

You can indicate, for example, that you are applying for a position that is listed with your placement bureau, is advertised in the newspaper, is recommended by a current employee of the employer, or is unsolicited. Provide for this transition in the first sentence or no later than the second sentence.

There are creative and traditional attention-getting openings for application letters. Your analysis of your reader and the position you are seeking will guide you in determining what kind of opening you should use. Here are examples of openings:

Example openings for:

• An unsolicited position

1. Are you interested in a hard worker with a solid record of accomplishment for your management trainee program?

• A solicited position

2. Please compare my qualifications with the job requirements for the auditor's position that you advertised in the May issue of the AAA JOURNAL. I believe we will both be glad you did.

3. Creative! Knowledgeable! Organized! Just what you want and need in a new copywriter for Brun's Advertising Agency.

4. Mrs. Sonya Rodreguis, Manager of your Purchasing Office, recommended that I apply for the systems position you have open in the Division of Operations Research. Please note how well my qualifications, as described in the enclosed resume, match the job requirements of your opening.

CONVINCING AN EMPLOYER THAT YOU FIT THE JOB

Show the employer how you fit the job.

The purpose of the second major part of an application letter is to convince a potential employer that you fit the job requirements of the position you are seeking. This is the most important part of your letter. In it, you should

> *When you hire people that are smarter than you are, you prove you are smarter than they are.*
>
> **R. H. Grant**

show how employing you will benefit the employer. As in a resume, you will want to emphasize your accomplishments.

Specify job requirements, review qualifications, and refer to resume.

In this section of an application letter: (1) specify the job requirements; (2) review your education, experience, and other qualifications relative to the job requirements; and (3) refer to your enclosed resume (this reference may be elsewhere in the letter). The order of content may vary in different application letters. The intent, however, is to compose a clear, concise, concrete, and convincing paragraph or two that will motivate the employer to look closely at your resume. Here are examples of the second part of an application letter:

1. Your Director of Employment position requires someone who knows human resources management theory and how to practice it. Mr. Grayson, I am that person. My education, experience, and personal qualities, as shown on the enclosed resume, qualify me for your opening.

Upon graduating from Sagamon Community College with a major in human resources administration, I was employed as Assistant Human Resources Manager by the Dayton Manufacturing Corporation. Four years of experience with Dayton gave me the opportunity to apply the theories I had learned, to become thoroughly acquainted with state and federal laws governing employee relations, and to make innovative changes in the operation of the office. While at Dayton, I designed and administered a comprehensive skills training program for all nonexempt personnel. The program was credited with increasing production 27 percent this past quarter.

2. McLaren salespersons are known throughout the industry for their integrity and productivity. My education and work experience, as detailed on the enclosed resume, have all been directed at preparing me to join McLaren's sales force.

My education consists primarily of four years of marketing, general business administration, and general education courses at Western State University. The Bachelor of Science in Business Administration degree I will receive in May will assure you that I have both a broad business education and a specialized knowledge of sales.

Mrs. Mendoza, the experience I offer McLaren complements my education and has prepared me further for sales work. During the summers 1992 through 1994, I sold encyclopedias door to door. My ranking of first in sales in the Northeastern District (a seven-state area) and fifth in the nation during the summer of 1993 indicates my productivity level. During the academic year, I sold furniture part time, earning a major share of my educational expenses.

In addition, I believe I have the personal qualities that would fit your organization. I am an energetic, goal-oriented individual who can work effectively with others in team efforts or alone in sales situations.

PROMOTING ACTION IN THE CLOSE

Motivate the employer to read your resume.

Ask directly for the interview in the close.

Make it easy to call or write you.

Be flexible about your availability.

Now you are ready to try to motivate the employer to take action—to read your resume and grant you an interview. In practically every application letter, you will be trying to get an interview. The way to get an interview is to ask directly for it. This request should be made in a positive, pleasant manner; do not push or beg.

In the close of your application letter you should make it easy for an employer to grant you an interview by providing your telephone number and by offering to be at the employer's office at his or her convenience. Even if you do have some limitations on your flexibility—such as another interview scheduled for one day next week—you can usually work those things out if the employer calls you. Here are examples of appropriate closings for application letters:

1. I can contribute to the continuing success of Rushton's Implement Sales; please call me at (601) 555-1300 so that we can arrange an interview. I would enjoy meeting with you to discuss the possibility of joining your staff.

2. If this brief description of my qualifications and the additional information on the accompanying resume indicate that I meet your requirements, may I have an interview. My school day ends at 3 p.m. After that time you can reach me at (601) 555-1300. I could arrange a visit to your office at any time convenient for you.

3. May I have an interview to discuss this opportunity with you, Mr. Watanabe. The possibility of joining the Asano Agency is exciting to me. Please write me or call me at (417) 555-7192 to set up an appointment.

SAMPLE APPLICATION LETTERS

The application letters you use in your job campaign must meet the same high standards as resumes for neatness, clarity, and conciseness. Application letters should be brief, generally no more than one page. Analyze your reader, use the you–viewpoint, use the principles of business communication, and follow the guidelines given in Chapter 13 for persuasive messages.

Use 8½ by 11″ bond paper for application letters. The paper should be the same color and quality as was used for your resume. Many applicants use a 9″ by 12″ mailing envelope to avoid folding the letter and resume. An application letter should be addressed to a specific person and individually prepared. Never photocopy a general application letter for distribution to prospective employers. If responding to a blind ad, use the AMS Simplified Letter format (see Figure 10•3d, page 267); do not address an application letter to, To Whom It May Concern.

If you are sending out several letters, word processing equipment can be helpful in preparing them so that variable information may be inserted. Be sure to keep copies of the letters and resumes sent to each potential employer.

Figure 22•1 shows a general letter that could be addressed to human resources managers at several companies. It is directed at obtaining an unsolicited job.

Figure 22•2 is an example of a personalized letter sent in response to a solicited job announcement. Personalized letters usually are more powerful than general letters; in a personalized letter you can show specifically how you will benefit the employer.

INTERVIEWING FOR A JOB

The goal of sending your application letter and resume was to obtain a job interview. The interview can be one of the most important experiences in your life because it can determine the course of your career.

The decision as to whether you will be offered the job will be made as a result of the interview. Your decision as to whether you will accept an offer may be made at this time also. A job interview is obviously a critical

Figure 22·1 General Application Letter for Management Trainee Position. Applicant has limited work experience.

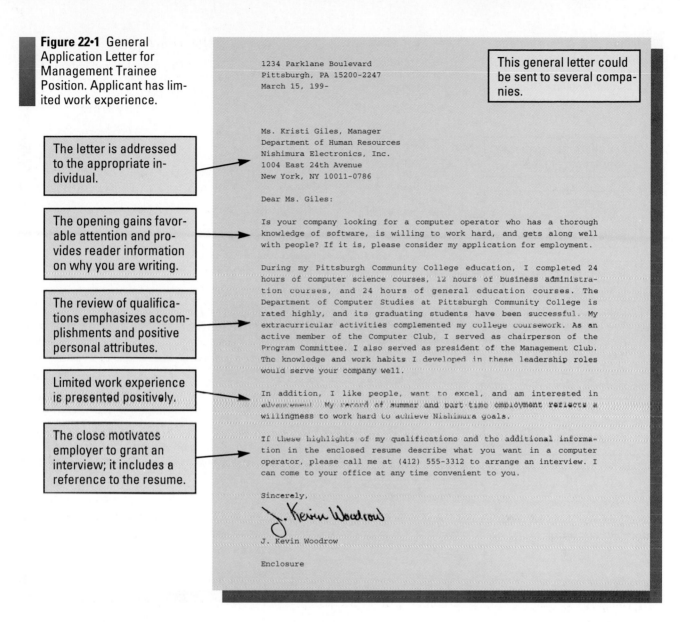

The letter is addressed to the appropriate individual.

The opening gains favorable attention and provides reader information on why you are writing.

The review of qualifications emphasizes accomplishments and positive personal attributes.

Limited work experience is presented positively.

The close motivates employer to grant an interview; it includes a reference to the resume.

1234 Parklane Boulevard
Pittsburgh, PA 15200-2247
March 15, 199-

This general letter could be sent to several companies.

Ms. Kristi Giles, Manager
Department of Human Resources
Nishimura Electronics, Inc.
1004 East 24th Avenue
New York, NY 10011-0786

Dear Ms. Giles:

Is your company looking for a computer operator who has a thorough knowledge of software, is willing to work hard, and gets along well with people? If it is, please consider my application for employment.

During my Pittsburgh Community College education, I completed 24 hours of computer science courses, 12 hours of business administration courses, and 24 hours of general education courses. The Department of Computer Studies at Pittsburgh Community College is rated highly, and its graduating students have been successful. My extracurricular activities complemented my college coursework. As an active member of the Computer Club, I served as chairperson of the Program Committee. I also served as president of the Management Club. The knowledge and work habits I developed in these leadership roles would serve your company well.

In addition, I like people, want to excel, and am interested in advancement. My record of summer and part time employment reflects a willingness to work hard to achieve Nishimura goals.

If these highlights of my qualifications and the additional information in the enclosed resume describe what you want in a computer operator, please call me at (412) 555-3312 to arrange an interview. I can come to your office at any time convenient to you.

Sincerely,

J. Kevin Woodrow

J. Kevin Woodrow

Enclosure

The interview is the critical step in your job campaign.

juncture in your job campaign. You will want the interview to go as well as possible. When you find out you are going to have an interview, start your final preparation for it.

PREPARING FOR A JOB INTERVIEW

Preparing for an interview includes:

• Reviewing information gathered to this point

You have already done a great deal of preparation for your job interviews. You have examined the job market and job requirements, analyzed your qualifications, prepared your resume, and written application letters. Through this process you have learned more about yourself. In addition, you have organized this information so that you can talk about it efficiently and logically. All this is important preparation for representing yourself in an interview. There are additional things you need to do in preparation for job interviews.

Chapter 22 • Employment Communication and Interviewing   **621**

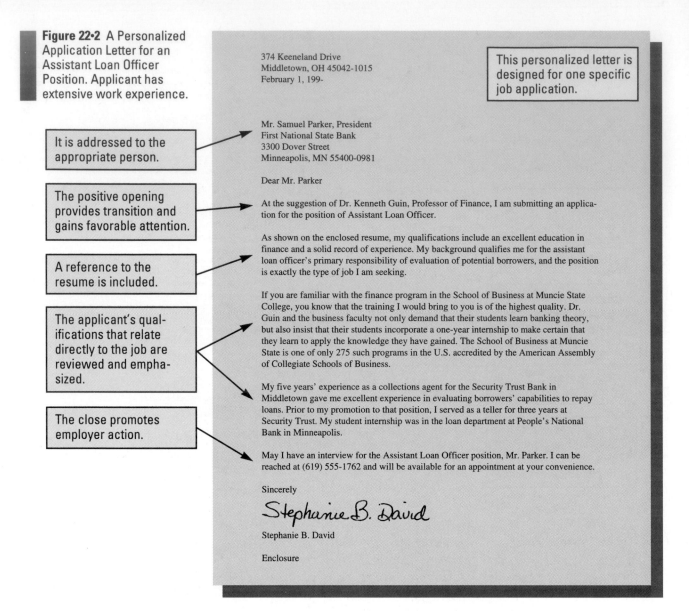

Figure 22•2 A Personalized Application Letter for an Assistant Loan Officer Position. Applicant has extensive work experience.

This personalized letter is designed for one specific job application.

It is addressed to the appropriate person.

The positive opening provides transition and gains favorable attention.

A reference to the resume is included.

The applicant's qualifications that relate directly to the job are reviewed and emphasized.

The close promotes employer action.

374 Keeneland Drive
Middletown, OH 45042-1015
February 1, 199-

Mr. Samuel Parker, President
First National State Bank
3300 Dover Street
Minneapolis, MN 55400-0981

Dear Mr. Parker

At the suggestion of Dr. Kenneth Guin, Professor of Finance, I am submitting an application for the position of Assistant Loan Officer.

As shown on the enclosed resume, my qualifications include an excellent education in finance and a solid record of experience. My background qualifies me for the assistant loan officer's primary responsibility of evaluation of potential borrowers, and the position is exactly the type of job I am seeking.

If you are familiar with the finance program in the School of Business at Muncie State College, you know that the training I would bring to you is of the highest quality. Dr. Guin and the business faculty not only demand that their students learn banking theory, but also insist that their students incorporate a one-year internship to make certain that they learn to apply the knowledge they have gained. The School of Business at Muncie State is one of only 275 such programs in the U.S. accredited by the American Assembly of Collegiate Schools of Business.

My five years' experience as a collections agent for the Security Trust Bank in Middletown gave me excellent experience in evaluating borrowers' capabilities to repay loans. Prior to my promotion to that position, I served as a teller for three years at Security Trust. My student internship was in the loan department at People's National Bank in Minneapolis.

May I have an interview for the Assistant Loan Officer position, Mr. Parker. I can be reached at (619) 555-1762 and will be available for an appointment at your convenience.

Sincerely

Stephanie B. David

Stephanie B. David

Enclosure

BE READY TO ANSWER QUESTIONS

• Anticipating questions

The next step in your preparation is to anticipate all the questions that might be asked in an interview and prepare generally the answers you will give. Have a friend or relative ask you the questions to give you practice answering. Examples of the questions you may be asked are as follows:

1. Why do you want to work for our company?
2. Tell me about yourself.
3. I see you took a course in information processing. What was that course about?
4. What do you consider your strengths?
5. What do you consider your weaknesses?
6. What kind of work do you like best?

7. What work do you like to do least?
8. What did you do on your job at . . . ?
9. What do you want to be doing five years from now?
10. Do you like to work alone or with other people?
11. Why did you choose this field of work?
12. For what kind of supervisor do you like to work?
13. Tell me about your education at . . . .
14. What courses did you like best? Why?
15. What courses did you like least? Why?
16. Do you consider yourself ambitious?
17. Why should we hire you for this position?
18. What do you think should determine the progress a person makes in a company?
19. What does *teamwork* mean to you?
20. Do you have plans to get additional education?
21. What are the main things you have learned from your work experience?
22. How important is money to you?
23. Are you willing to relocate?
24. Tell me about your extracurricular activities while you were in school.
25. What salary do you expect to receive in this job?

These are questions that have been asked in many interviews. Have your answers ready for these questions and any others that you can anticipate.

Be honest, sincere, positive, and enthusiastic when answering. Be yourself, be polite, and be attentive. Relate your answers to the job for which

Mention your strengths in the interview. If computer capabilities are your strengths, stress these.

you are applying. Take advantage of the opportunity to show your knowledge of the company and the position. Your answers should be brief, but not just Yes or No. For example, in answering the question, "Do you have plans to get additional education?" you might say, "Yes, I think it is important to keep up-to-date. I am interested in taking short continuing education courses and, in a few years, working on an MBA degree." In response to, "What do you consider to be your weaknesses?" you might say after reflecting for a moment, "Well, some people may think I am reserved, but thinking before acting has helped me relate effectively to others."

BE PREPARED TO DISCUSS SALARY

- Discussing salary, if appropriate

The salary question—the last one in the list of example questions—is an important one. Be sure to be ready to answer it. The employer may have set a salary or a salary range for the position. You should try to get that information before the interview if you can. Also, you should try to learn before the interview what salaries are being paid for similar jobs. Newspaper employment ads sometimes carry this information. Your school or college placement office is another good source of salary information. If pinned down to a specific answer, respond in a straightforward objective manner. You might say, "Apparently the starting salaries for this kind of position range from $_____ to $_____. In comparing my qualifications with others in the job market, I would hope to start at $_____." If you do not feel pinned down to a specific answer, you might say, "I would want a salary that is appropriate for my education and experience."

DEVELOP QUESTIONS TO ASK

- Asking questions

You should have some key questions of your own for the interviewer. Do not just concentrate on questions of personal benefit to you, such as ones about fringe benefits, retirement programs, vacation policies, and salary. Probably all that information will be given to you without your asking. Your questions might be about such subjects as job duties, employee evaluation system, management philosophy, company progress and plans, promotion policies, and employee development programs.

RESEARCH THE COMPANY

- Learning all you can about the company

Learn as much as you can about the company prior to the interview. Secure descriptive materials on the company and its industry from the company, your placement bureau, the library, the Chamber of Commerce, the Better Business Bureau, a trade association, or some other source. Study these materials carefully. A thorough preparation of this kind will help you in the interview in two basic ways: it will aid your communication with the interviewer, and it will set you apart from the other interviewees who learn nothing about the company prior to an interview.

PREPARE YOURSELF PERSONALLY

- Organizing yourself personally; building your confidence

Choose your clothes carefully, and give attention to personal grooming. Choose clothes that are similar to the ones worn by those who hold the type of job you are seeking. Plan your schedule so that you arrive early. Allow time for heavy traffic, a flat tire, or other delay. Plan to take two additional copies of your resume with you in case they are needed. Take a copy of your transcript and any appropriate examples of your work. Take a pen and a small notebook for use immediately after the interview. Write the names of the people you meet and record notes about the position.

Talk (mentally) to yourself. Build your confidence by telling yourself that you have done all you can to prepare for the interview. You have anticipated questions and have prepared answers, you have learned about the company, and you have prepared yourself personally. You are ready for the interview.

PARTICIPATING IN AN INTERVIEW

An interview should be viewed as an opportunity to share your qualifications with someone who is interested. View the interview as important, but not so important that you become overly nervous. Some "racehorse" nervousness is natural and helpful to you; but too much nervousness will make a poor impression.

Greet your interviewer warmly and call him or her by name, pronouncing it correctly. Let the interviewer take the lead. If an offer is made to shake hands, do so with a firm grip and a smile. Sit when asked to do so. See your role as primarily responding to questions in a businesslike fashion. Keep appropriate eye contact with the interviewer; 75 percent of the time is a good goal for interviews with Americans. The amount of appropriate eye contact with interviewers will vary depending on their cultural backgrounds. Other cultural variations that are important in interviews include many verbal and nonverbal communication considerations (see Chapter 5 for further information).

The interviewer may intentionally challenge you by asking difficult questions or by appearing disinterested or even irritated. Be knowledgeable, calm, positive, gracious, and friendly.

Some nervousness is natural and helpful.

Greet interviewer warmly; let the interviewer take the lead.

Show your knowledge and interest.

An effective exchange of information takes place in a successful job interview.

During the interview avoid appearing overly aggressive or conceited, meek and mild, negative about past employers or other topics, unenthusiastic, too interested in money, too ambitious, humorless, too vague with answers, or unappreciative of the interviewer's time. Don't smoke, act immature, or laugh nervously.

Be alert for signals that the interview is ending. The interviewer may slide her or his chair back, stand up, or send you verbal signals. When the interview is over, express appreciation for the time and information given you. Indicate that you look forward to hearing from the interviewer. Shake hands, and warmly tell the interviewer goodbye.

After the interview, evaluate how you did. Make written notes of those things that went well and those that you will change the next time you interview. Make a record of the information you learned about the job for comparison with other job opportunities. Record the correct spellings of the names and titles of those who interviewed you, and note what you will want to say in your follow-up communication.

PREPARING OTHER EMPLOYMENT COMMUNICATION

Employment communication is not limited to resumes, application letters, and interviews. Other employment communication can include telephone calls, letters, and in-person contacts. You may need to follow up on a pending application or communicate your acceptance of an invitation for an interview. You may want some kind of follow-up contact after an interview. It will be necessary to communicate your rejection or acceptance of a job offer. If you accept a job, you may need to resign from another job. Finally, you should express appreciation to all those who assisted you in your job campaign. Suggestions for composing these communications are given in the following sections.

FOLLOWING UP AN APPLICATION

If you think it has been too long since you heard about your application with an employer, you may want to initiate a follow-up contact. Remember, many unsolicited applications are not acknowledged. Your follow-up contact, depending on the circumstances, can be by letter, in person, or by telephone (be prepared to leave your message on an answering machine or in voice mail). Such a message would be neutral news for the employer; and, consequently, the direct plan should be used. Here is an example of such a follow-up message:

> In February I sent you an application for a position in your marketing department. As I am very much interested in employment with B. J. Harold and Company, I am wondering if I could furnish any additional information that would be helpful to my application.
>
> I want you to know that I remain an active candidate and will appreciate your giving me an interview.

ACCEPTING AN INTERVIEW INVITATION

Be prepared to accept an interview invitation.

Most of the time interview invitations will be by telephone. Be prepared to receive this kind of call any time during your job campaign. Your communication accepting an interview should use the direct plan (for positive news) and should (1) express appreciation, (2) indicate availability, and (3) convey a positive and optimistic attitude. Here is an example of the content for either a written or an oral message:

> Thank you for the opportunity to interview for the position in the Accounting Department. I am very much interested in meeting with you to discuss the position and my qualifications.
>
> Because of my work and class schedules, the best dates for me for the interview are March 7, 9, or 10. I appreciate your offer that I give you three alternative dates. Any one of them will be fine with me.
>
> I am looking forward to visiting your offices and learning more about the auditing position.

FOLLOWING UP AN INTERVIEW

Following up an interview is appropriate.

A letter of appreciation is appropriate after an interview. This letter should be sent within one or two days following the interview. If you think you are still interested in the position, you should express that interest in the letter. If you are definitely not interested in the position, a letter of appreciation for the interview is still appropriate. In the latter case, in fairness to the employer, you should withdraw your candidacy. The letter in which you express your continuing interest should use the direct plan, and the letter in which you withdraw your candidacy should use the indirect plan. Both of these letters should be brief, cordial, businesslike, and typewritten. Examples of each follow:

Example expressing continuing interest

1. Thank you for talking with me last Tuesday about the operations management position. The interview was enjoyable and informative. Your explanation of the job responsibilities and the plant tour made me even more interested in the position. I am confident that, as operations manager, I could make major contributions to Diaz-Zapato Manufacturing Corporation.

   I look forward to hearing from you soon.

Example withdrawing a candidacy.

2. Thank you for the informative interview yesterday and all the courtesies you extended me. My visit to the Abrams Publishing Company offices was most pleasant, and the meeting you arranged with members of the office staff was informative.

   The position of assistant office manager would be challenging. However, because its emphasis is on computer systems analysis while my primary interest is in accounting work, I believe it is best to withdraw my candidacy. I am sure that working with the people I met at Abrams would have been enjoyable.

I appreciate the time you have given me. I hope to see you at the next DPMA Seminar.

> *The employer generally gets the employees he deserves.*
>
> **Walter Gilbey**

ACCEPTING EMPLOYMENT

Use the direct plan when accepting employment.

The communications offering employment and accepting employment most likely will be by telephone, followed by confirming letters. A letter accepting employment is a positive communication and should use the direct plan: (1) the offer should be accepted, (2) any essential information about assuming the position should come next, and (3) an expression of appreciation should close the letter. A confirming acceptance letter might look like this:

> I am pleased to confirm my acceptance of the sales position with Moser Corporation.
>
> It is my understanding that this position pays a salary of $450 a week and a 10 percent commission on sales. I am to assume the position August 1.
>
> Thank you for this opportunity. I am eager to begin work with you.

REJECTING EMPLOYMENT

Employment rejection messages should use the indirect plan.

As is the case with accepting employment, the first communications offering employment and rejecting employment most likely will be by telephone. An indirect message following up an oral employment rejection may be appropriate. If so, it would be very similar to the letter withdrawing a candidacy shown previously.

EXPRESSING APPRECIATION TO REFERENCES AND OTHERS

Thank those who helped in your job campaign.

When you have accepted an employment offer and completed a successful job campaign, share the good news with your references. Also, it will be important to notify any placement service and others who assisted you. These expressions of appreciation for assistance may be by telephone, by letter, or in person.

RESIGNING FROM A JOB

Once your job campaign is completed, it may be necessary to resign from your present position. It is best that your resignation not be a surprise for your employer. If you can, let your employer know that you have applied for another position while you are searching. If you think your employer would react negatively to your search for another position, you will want to keep your job search confidential.

Most resignations will use the indirect plan.

Most resignations will be oral and in person. The employer may then request that you put your resignation in writing. Be sure to give your employer the amount of notice required in company policy. In most cases a resignation would be a negative message that should be written using the indirect plan. Here is an example:

Thank you for the support and the opportunities you have provided me.

I have developed professionally over the past three years as assistant human resources manager. Although my tenure has been enjoyable, I now must resign effective June 30 and accept another challenge.

In my new position as human resources manager for Bayshore Communications, I am sure we will have continuing contact. I look forward to that. Best wishes for continued success with your work.

A CONCLUDING COMMENT

Following the suggestions in Chapters 21 and 22 has enabled many to secure rewarding positions that match well with their aptitudes and interests. Best wishes for success in all of your job campaigns.

DISCUSSION QUESTIONS

1. Discuss the nature of application letters.

2. Describe briefly the purposes of each of the three major parts of an application letter.

3. Describe how to answer questions during an interview.

4. How would you answer the question, "What do you consider your strengths?"

5. How should you answer the question, "What salary do you expect for this job?"

6. What questions should you be prepared to ask?

7. List four sources of information about a company to which you are applying for a position.

8. How should you prepare yourself personally for an interview?

9. What are the major types of follow-up employment communication?

10. To whom should you express appreciation when you have accepted an employment offer?

APPLICATION EXERCISES

1. Prepare a personalized application letter to accompany the resume you prepared for Chapter 21. The reader of your letter will be a hiring official in your field at a company of your choice.

2. Prepare a general application letter to accompany your general resume. Your readers will be human resources managers in companies with positions in your field.

3. List your answers to the 25 example interview questions given on pages 622–623 in this chapter.

4. Assume that you submitted an application for a job opening in your field six weeks ago. You are interested in the position and have not heard from the employer since they acknowledged receipt of your application letter and resume. Write a letter following up on this application. Assume that you are able to add some additional information that developed in the past six weeks that might help your candidacy.

5. Assume that you graduated from college five years ago and have

been employed as an assistant cashier in a bank since graduation. Your experience in this position has been excellent. The cashier, your immediate supervisor, gave you increasing amounts of responsibility, and you grew professionally. In fact, you did so well that you were the successful candidate for a cashier's position in a bank that is a major competitor of your current employer. Your supervisor is aware that you have accepted the new position and has asked that you put your resignation in writing. Write two letters: (a) a letter accepting the new position, and (b) a letter resigning from your present position. Create any facts necessary for complete letters.

6. Write a letter following up an interview you have had for a job in your field. Assume that you want the position.

7. Write a letter following up an interview you have had for a job in your field. Assume that you definitely are not interested in the position.

8. Write a letter to a reference of your choice expressing your appreciation for his or her assistance in your recent successful job campaign. Assume that your new position is appropriate for your field of study.

MESSAGE ANALYSIS

Text 22B

Rewrite the following letter accepting an interview invitation. Strengthen the letter's effectiveness.

I have to go to school Monday through Friday from 8 a.m. to 3 p.m. and, therefore, cannot get to your office for an interview until about 3:30 p.m. The only days I will be available in April are the 2, 3, 4, 5, 6, 22, 23, 24, 25, and 27. As you suggested that I come on the 6th if possible, I will plan to be there at 3:30 p.m. that day. Thanks for letting me talk with you about the radio advertising sales position you have at the station.

APPENDICES

WORD USAGE

The words listed in this Appendix are many of those that can pose problems for writers. Some words are included because they are misused; some are included because they are often confused with other words. The words are listed alphabetically according to the first word in each pair.

ABOVE	Avoid using these words in business writing.
BELOW	Instead, use *preceding* to indicate what came before and *following* to indicate what will come after.
ADVICE	*Advice* is a noun; *advise* is a verb. When you advise, you give
ADVISE	advice.
AFFECT	Although both words may be either a verb or a noun, *affect* is
EFFECT	most often used as a verb showing change or influence; *effect* is most often used as a noun denoting a result or an outcome.
ALL READY	Refers to a state of complete readiness.
ALREADY	Refers to time.
ALL RIGHT	The word *alright* is considered inappropriate for business writ-
ALRIGHT	ing; use *all right*.
ALL TOGETHER	Refers to physical or figurative unity or closeness.
ALTOGETHER	Means entirely or wholly.
AMONG	When referring to three or more, use *among*; when referring to
BETWEEN	two, use *between*. The appropriate conjunction to use with *between* is "and."
AMOUNT	*Amount* is used with "mass" nouns—things that can be mea-
NUMBER	sured but cannot be counted; *number* is used with "count" nouns.
ANXIOUS	Use *anxious* when you wish to show anxiety or great concern.
EAGER	*Eager*, which has a positive connotation, is usually a better choice.
ANY ONE	Stresses *one* of a group of persons or things.
ANYONE	Stresses *any* and refers only to persons.
ANY WAY	Empahsizes *any*; no preference for method.
ANYWAY	Means in any case.
ARBITRATE	To decide between two disagreeing people or groups, such as an employer and a union.
MEDIATE	To work to gain agreement between two disagreeing people or groups.

ASSURE **ENSURE** **INSURE**	All three refer to making something certain. Use *assure* when indicating you are placing a person's mind at rest; use *ensure* when indicating you are making safe from harm; and use *insure* when indicating you are guaranteeing the safety of life or property.
BAD **BADLY**	*Bad* is used with "sense" verbs (feel, hear, see, smell, taste, touch, etc.) and is an adjective—it modifies a noun. *Badly* is an adverb; it modifies a verb, adjective, or another adverb.
BIANNUAL **BIENNIAL**	Twice a year. Every two years.
BI-MONTHLY **SEMI-MONTHLY**	Every two months. Twice a month.
BRIEF **SHORT**	Used only when referring to time. Used when referring to time or to measurement.
BRING **TAKE** **GET**	*Bring* denotes movement toward the speaker or writer or the place she or he occupies; *take* denotes movement away from the person or place; and *get* refers to gaining possession.
CAN **MAY**	Refers to ability to do something. Refers to permission to do something.
CANNOT **CAN NOT**	Unable to do otherwise. Unacceptable in business writing.
CAPITAL **CAPITOL**	Use the *al* ending when referring to assets or uppercase letters; use the *ol* ending when referring to a state or national government building.
CITE **SIGHT** **SITE**	Means to refer to or quote; is root of the word citation. As a noun, *sight* relates to vision; it is also used to refer to a spectacle or view. As a verb, *sight* means to see, observe, or perceive. Refers to a place, an area, or a location.
COMPARE **CONTRAST**	Refers to an examination of similarities *and* differences. Refers to an examination of differences.
COMPLEMENT **COMPLIMENT**	Means to complete or to enhance. Means to praise.
COMPOSED **COMPRISED**	Is used when referring to the parts or components of something. Is used when referring to things included within something.
CONSUL **COUNCIL** **COUNSEL**	Refers to a government official who resides in a foreign country for the purpose of representing the citizens of his or her home country. Refers to an advisory group. Refers to advice or one who gives it.

CALL/WRITE **CONTACT**	*Contact* is very abstract and should be avoided in business communication. Writers should use specific words, such as *call,* and *write,* or the more general "let us know."
CONTINUAL **CONTINUOUS**	Means recurring activity with pauses or breaks. Means uninterrupted activity.
DATA **DATUM**	*Data* is the plural form of *datum,* a noun meaning fact. In business writing, *data* may be followed by either a singular or a plural verb form.
DECENT **DESCENT** **DISSENT**	Means in good taste. Means a movement downward. Means to disagree or to hold a different opinion.
DISBURSE **DISPERSE**	Means to pay. Means to break up or spread.
ELICIT **ILLICIT**	Means to bring out. Refers to something unlawful or not permitted.
EMINENT **IMMINENT**	*Eminent* is used when referring to someone or something that stands out about others in quality or in position. *Imminent* refers to something that is threatening, such as a storm.
FARTHER **FURTHER**	Refers to distance—*far*ther. Means additional or advanced.
FEWER **LESS**	*Fewer* applies to things that can be counted; it is used with references to people and to modify other plural nouns. *Less* is most often used to modify plural nouns involving time, distance, weight, and money.
IF **WHETHER**	Used to establish or describe a condition. Used with implicit or explicit alternatives.
INVALUABLE **VALUABLE**	Things that are *invaluable* are priceless. Things that are *valuable* have a desirable monetary value.
IT'S **ITS**	Is the contraction for *it is.* Is the possessive form of the pronoun *it.*
LAST **LATEST**	*Last* refers to something final, something at the end. *Latest* refers to something recent, the most current of a series.
LAY **LIE**	Means to put or to place. Means to recline or to rest.
LOSE **LOOSE**	Is a verb; it is the opposite of find. Is an adjective used to describe fit; it is the opposite of tight.
ME **MYSELF**	*Me* is the objective case of the personal pronoun *I.* *Myself* is a reflexive pronoun. It should be used in business writing only when you have been identified earlier in the sentence.

MEDIA **MEDIUM**	*Media* is the plural; it refers to several mass communication methods. Each mass communication method (TV, radio, etc.) is a *medium*.
PERPETRATE **PERPETUATE**	Means to bring about or commit an act, such as a crime. Means to continue something indefinitely.
PERSONAL **PERSONNEL**	Means private or relating to a person. Refers to a group of workers or employees.
PRECEDE **PROCEED**	Means to go or to come before. Means to go forward with or continue some action.
PRINCIPAL **PRINCIPLE**	Refers to a leader or to something *chief* or *primary*. Refers to a rule or a basic truth.
SET **SIT**	Means to place or to put. Means to lie or to rest.
SOME TIME **SOMETIME**	Refers to a specific time. Refers to an indefinite time.
STATIONARY **STATIONERY**	Means in a fixed position. Means writing paper.
STATUE **STATUTE**	Refers to a three-dimensional figure. Refers to a law or permanent rule.
THAN **THEN**	Used as part of a comparison. Used with reference to time.
THAT **WHICH** **WHO**	*That* is used to refer to persons, animals, or things; it introduces restrictive clauses. *Which* is used to refer to animals or things; it introduces nonrestrictive clauses. *Who* is used to refer only to persons; it may be used to introduce either a restrictive or a nonrestrictive clause.
THOROUGH **THROUGH** **THRU**	*Thorough* refers to the fullest level of detail. *Through* is used to show movement into and out of, to specify methods, or to show completion. *Thru* is informal and should not be used in business writing.
TO **TOO**	Indicates movement or direction. Means also or to an excessive degree.
TRACK **TRACT**	Means a path. Refers to a defined piece of land.
WHO **WHOM**	*Who* is a pronoun used in questions to indicate what or which person or persons. *Whom* is an objective case pronoun; it is used as an object of a verb or a preposition.

APPENDIX B

Editing Symbols

DEFINED		EXAMPLES
Paragraph	¶	¶ Begin a new paragraph at this point.
Insert a character	∧	Insrt a letter here.
Delete	e	Delete these words. Disregard
Do not change	stet or	the previous correction.
Transpose	tr	To transpose is to around turn
Move to the left	[	[Move this copy to the left.
Move to the right	]	Move this copy to the right.
No paragraph	No ¶	No ¶ Do not begin a new paragraph
Delete and close up.	℈	here. Delete the hyphen from pre-empt and close the space.
Set in caps	Caps or ≡	a sentence begins with a capital letter.
Set in lower case	lc	This Word should not be capitalized.
Insert a period	⊙	Insert a period⊙
Quotation marks	⌄ ⌄	Quotation marks and
Comma	∧	a comma should be placed here he said.
Insert space	#	Space between these words.
Apostrophe	⌄	An apostrophe is whats needed here.
Hyphen	=	Add a hyphen to Afro American.
Close up	⌢	Close the extra spa ce.
Use superior figure	⌄	Footnote this sentence.
Set in italic	Italic or ___	Set the words, sine qua non, in italics.
Move up	⌐	This word is too low.
Move down	⌎	That word is too high.

Proofreading Procedures

EVERYONE'S A PROOFREADER: HOW TO CHECK YOUR DOCUMENTS

by Carolyn Boccella Bagin and Jo Van Doren

The man who makes no mistakes does not usually make anything.—E. J. Phelps

For most people in our profession, proofreading is drudgery. Hardly anyone notices the perfect proofreading job, but everyone spots the lone, unsightly error after you've gone to press. Uncaught, proofreading mistakes can be embarrassing and sometimes costly. That's why you should make everyone responsible for proofreading the documents you produce. As Phelps implies, if you write documents, you make mistakes. The key is catching them before they cost you money.

Over the years, we've gathered many proofreading hints to help make the job go more smoothly. Since this topic has been popular with our readers, we've updated the article from *Simply Stated No. 65* to give you techniques that you can use every day.

GET SOME HELP WITH THE JOB

1. Never proofread your own copy, if you can help it. You'll tire of looking at the document in its different stages of development, and you'll miss new errors.

2. Keep the nature of the document in mind. Interoffice memos need a different level of attention than contracts, books, or clients' publications. Typeset mistakes are more expensive to fix than word-processed ones.

3. If you work with several proofreaders, consider having them initial the copy they check. You might find that your documents have fewer errors because your proofers feel accountable for the ones they miss.

4. Learn from your staff's mistakes. Take notes on what you've missed before—especially those mistakes that have cost time and money to fix. Make sure no one makes the same mistake twice.

5. Use a partner to proof numbers that are in columns. Read the figures aloud and have your partner mark the corrections and changes on the copy being proofread.

6. Not everyone knows and uses traditional proofreading marks. If your staff doesn't know them, create a simple marking system that all of your people can understand. Make a style sheet as a desk reference to avoid confusion.

7. Keep a notebook of unusual spellings, changes in usage, clients' preferences and quirks, common acronyms of your trade, and abbreviations. Before you know it, you'll have a handy reference guide to pass along to new staff members.

SOURCE: Document Design Center, 3333 K Street NW, Washington, DC 20007, (202) 342-5000

What if You Do It Yourself?

8. The hardest thing in proofing your own copy is concentrating on your goal—and not reading for content. If you proofread your own copy, make a line screen for yourself or roll the paper so that you view only one line at a time. This will stop you from skimming the material for content and will help you focus on the proofing task.

9. First read everything in the copy straight through from beginning to end. Then read your document again several times, looking for different types of errors each time. For instance, read all of the headings, then check them against the table of contents. Next, read through again for punctuation. Try another round to check if the spacing is consistent. Continue the process until you've covered everything.

10. Read your copy backwards to catch spelling errors. Reading sentences out of sequence will let you concentrate on individual words.

Timing Is Everything

11. If you can, alter your routine. Don't proofread at the same time every day. Varying your schedule will help you approach the task with a keener eye.

12. If time allows, put your material aside for awhile. After a break, reread the last few lines to refresh your memory.

Techniques That Work

13. Read the pages of a document out of order. Changing the sequence helps you review each page as a unit.

14. Look at copy upside down to help check spacing and placement inconsistencies.

15. If you are interrupted in the middle of a proofing task, mark your place with a pencil, paper clip, or colored sheet.

16. If you don't have a style sheet for the format, make notes before you check a lengthy document. You'll need to rely on more than just your memory to check for consistency.

Errors Tend to Hide in Particular Places

17. Mistakes cluster. If you find one typo, look carefully nearby for others.

18. Inspect the beginnings of pages, paragraphs, and sections. Some people skim these spots and miss hidden typos. Double-check page and line breaks.

19. Beware of changes in typeface—especially in headings and titles. If you change to italics, boldface, or underlined copy, read those sections several times.

20. Copy printed in all uppercase letters is particularly difficult to proof because the letters have a uniform outline.

21. Check all titles, subtitles, and page numbers against your table of contents and index. Mistakes with numbers are easy to make and difficult to catch.

22. Read sequential material carefully. Check that all numbers or letters are in order. Look for duplications in lists, outlines, or tables.

23. Double-check references such as, "see the chart below," or "go to page 10." After several drafts, referenced material may have moved several pages away.

24. Bibliographies are especially troublesome for some proofers. Make sure your entries are in alphabetical order. Then check the authors' names and titles to verify spelling. Next, match each citation against your style sheet to ensure that the order of items listed is correct. Then examine the punctuation in each citation; skim to make sure quotation marks are paired and commas and periods are in place.

25. Examine numbers and totals. Refigure all calculations and look for misplaced commas and decimal points. If numbers are displayed in columns, make sure that they are properly aligned.

26. Scrutinize features that come in sets—brackets, parentheses, quotation marks, and dashes. It's easy to miss the second half of the pair.

APPENDIX D

Two-Letter Postal Abbreviations

U.S. STATE, DISTRICT, AND TERRITORY NAMES

Name	Two-Letter Abbreviation	Name	Two-Letter Abbreviation
Alabama	AL	Montana	MT
Alaska	AK	Nebraska	NE
Arizona	AZ	Nevada	NV
Arkansas	AR	New Hampshire	NH
California	CA	New Jersey	NJ
Colorado	CO	New Mexico	NM
Connecticut	CT	New York	NY
Delaware	DE	North Carolina	NC
District of Columbia	DC	North Dakota	ND
Florida	FL	Ohio	OH
Georgia	GA	Oklahoma	OK
Guam	GU	Oregon	OR
Hawaii	HI	Pennsylvania	PA
Idaho	ID	Puerto Rico	PR
Illinois	IL	Rhode Island	RI
Indiana	IN	South Carolina	SC
Iowa	IA	South Dakota	SD
Kansas	KS	Tennessee	TN
Kentucky	KY	Texas	TX
Louisiana	LA	Utah	UT
Maine	ME	Vermont	VT
Maryland	MD	Virgin Islands	VI
Massachusetts	MA	Virginia	VA
Michigan	MI	Washington	WA
Minnesota	MN	West Virginia	WV
Mississippi	MS	Wisconsin	WI
Missouri	MO	Wyoming	WY

CANADIAN PROVINCES

Name	Two-Letter Abbreviation	Name	Two-Letter Abbreviation
Alberta	AB	Nova Scotia	NS
British Columbia	BC	Ontario	ON
Manitoba	MB	Prince Edward Island	PE
New Brunswick	NB	Quebec	PQ
Newfoundland	NF	Saskatchewan	SK
Northwest Territories	NT	Yukon Territory	YT

INDEX

Note: The letter *f* following a page number indicates that the item is found in a figure.

PHOTO ACKNOWLEDGMENTS

For permission to reproduce the photographs on the pages indicated, acknowledgment is made to the following.

page iii (center):   Spectralink Corporation, Boulder, Colorado
page iii (bottom):   Photography by Alan Brown/Photonics
page iv (top left):   Photography by Erik Von Fischer/Photonics
page iv (top right):   Photo Courtesy of General Parametrics
page iv (bottom):   Courtesy of International Business Machines
page v (top left):   Unisys Corporation
page v (bottom left):   Courtesy of International Business Machines Corporation
page vi (bottom):   Hewlett-Packard Co.
page vii (top right):   Xerox Corporation
page vii (bottom left):   Hewlett-Packard Co.
page viii (top left):   Photography by Alan Brown/Photonics
page xiv–xvii: Photography by Alan Brown/Photonics

PART 1 OPENER: Nick B. Wood
page 18:   © Jose L. Pelaez/The Stock Market
page 33:   © Frank Herholdt/Tony Stone Images
page 39:   Hewlett-Packard Co.
page 100:   Dolch Computer Systems
page 103 (top left):   a. Courtesy of Toshiba
page 103 (top right):   b. Courtesy of International Business Machines Corporation
page 103 (bottom right):   Typist Plus Graphics—Caere Corporation
page 109:   Pitney Bowes Facsimile System
page 113:   Courtesy of Sayett Technology
page 125:   Courtesy of International Business Machines Corporation
page 133:   Hewlett-Packard Co.
page 136:   G.L. French/H. Armstrong Roberts
page 141:   © Loren Santow/Tony Stone Images

PART 3 OPENER: Courtesy of International Business Machines Corporation
page 286:   © 1990 Jeff Zaruba/The Stock Market
page 299:   Hewlett-Packard Co.
page 324:   © Brett Froomer/The Image Bank
page 329:   © John Colette/Stock, Boston, Inc.
page 392:   © 1992 John Feingersh/The Stock Market

PART 4 OPENER: Created by Hyperwriter, NTERGAID Inc.
page 408:   Courtesy of International Business Machines Corporation
page 410:   Hewlett-Packard Co.
page 413:   © 1989 Gregory Heisler/The Image Bank
page 424:   Courtesy of International Business Machines Corporation
page 493:   Courtesy of International Business Machines Corporation
page 494:   Courtesy of International Business Machines Corporation
page 507:   Florida Department of Commerce/Division of Tourism
page 509:   Photo courtesy of Kelly Services, Inc.
page 512 (top):   Aldus Corporation
page 512 (bottom):   Photo Courtesy of PRESENTATIC GRAPHICS, INC.

PART 5 OPENER: Courtesy of International Business Machines Corporation

page 526:   Courtesy of International Business Machines Corporation

page 532:   © Michael Newman/Photo Edit

page 533:   TANDY CORPORATION

page 538:   Photo by Mimi Ostendorf-Smith/Photonics

page 540:   Courtesy of International Business Machines Corporation

page 541:   © 1984 Richard Gross/The Stock Market

page 551:   © Walter Hodges/Allstock

page 552:   Hewlett-Packard Co.

page 553:   Courtesy of nView Corporation

page 561:   Courtesy Long Beach Area Convention and Visitors Council

page 563:   Photo courtesy of Kelly Services, Inc.

page 566:   Courtesy of Sperry Corporation

page 570:   Hewlett-Packard Co.

page 574:   Telex Communications, Inc.

PART 6 OPENER: Toyota Motor Manufacturing, U.S.A., Inc.

page 623:   Apple Computer Corporation

page 625:   © Jim Pickerell/West Light